DANGEROUS KITCHEN
The Subversive World of Zappa

KEVIN COURRIER

ECW PRESS

Copyright © Kevin Courrier and ECW PRESS 2002

Published by ECW PRESS
2120 Queen Street East, Suite 200, Toronto, Ontario, Canada M4E 1E2

All rights reserved. No part of this publication may be reproduced, stored in a retrieval system, or transmitted in any form by any process — electronic, mechanical, photocopying, recording, or otherwise — without the prior written permission of the copyright owners and ECW press.

NATIONAL LIBRARY OF CANADA CATALOGUING IN PUBLICATION DATA

Courrier, Kevin, 1954–
Dangerous Kitchen: the subversive world of Zappa
ISBN 1-55022-447-6
1. Frank Zappa. 2. Rock musicians — United States — Biography. I. Title.
ML410.Z35C86 2001   782.42166'092   C2001-900806-6

Cover and Text Design: Tania Craan
Typesetting: Wiesia Kolasinska
Cover artwork: Pierre-Paul Pariseau
Production: Mary Bowness
Printing: UTP
Photo research: Jane Affleck
Index: Dana Cook
Front cover photo of Zappa: Steve Schapiro

This book is set in Minion and Rosewood

The publication of *Dangerous Kitchen: The Subversive World of Zappa* has been generously supported by the Canada Council, the Ontario Arts Council, and the Government of Canada through the Book Publishing Industry Development Program.

DISTRIBUTION

CANADA: Stewart House, 195 Allstate Parkway, Markham, ON L3R 4T8

UNITED STATES: Independent Publishers Group, 814 North Franklin Street, Chicago, Illinois 60610

EUROPE: Turnaround Publisher Services, Unit 3, Olympia Trading Estate, Coburg Road, Wood Green, London N2Z 6T2

AUSTRALIA AND NEW ZEALAND: Wakefield Press, 17 Rundle Street (Box 2066), Kent Town, South Australia 5071

PRINTED AND BOUND IN CANADA

ECW PRESS
ecwpress.com

TABLE OF CONTENTS

ACKNOWLEDGMENTS IV

PREFACE
THE PERFECT STRANGER 1

CHAPTER ONE
NO NOT NOW 5

CHAPTER TWO
YOU'RE PROBABLY WONDERING WHY I'M HERE
(1940-1964) 21

CHAPTER THREE
WHO NEEDS THE PEACE CORPS?
(1965-1969) 65

CHAPTER FOUR
I'M THE SLIME
(1969-1980) 193

CHAPTER FIVE
THE MEEK SHALL INHERIT NOTHING
(1980-1988) 343

CHAPTER SIX
YOU CAN'T DO THAT ON STAGE ANYMORE
(1988-1993) 433

EPILOGUE
BEAT THE REAPER
(1993-2000) 499

DISCOGRAPHY 505

BIBLIOGRAPHY AND SOURCES 517

ACKNOWLEDGMENTS

This project was a labor of love that was started at the end of a rather unforgiving decade. Mimi Gellman summed it up perfectly when she remarked, "When you stick your foot in the river, you gotta take whatever comes down the stream." Putting my foot in this river certainly got the current decade off to a promising start. As a result, I have many people to thank for contributing to this welcome turn of events.

First of all, deep gratitude to Nick Power, for introducing me to ECW Press. My publishers turned out to be a highly professional group of people who also happened to be a lot of fun to be around. Thanks to Jack David, who not only enthusiastically backed the project, but also created the ideal conditions a writer needs to be creative. My editor, Jen Hale, guided me as nimbly through this unwieldy manuscript as she did episodes of *Buffy the Vampire Slayer*. Deep appreciation goes to my copy editor, Stuart Ross, whose sharp attention to detail made every page that much better. I'm also grateful to the Writer's Reserve Program of the Ontario Arts Council for their generous assistance.

A few readers helped during the early drafts of this book, making invaluable suggestions that a writer can only cherish. First of all, Donald Brackett, who became something of a secret collaborator on this project. Our weekly Zappa chats (which usually concluded with me carting off tons of research material) deepened our friendship as much as they helped me deepen the narrative. Brian Quinn, my valued colleague at the Royal Conservatory of Music, raised penetrating questions and provided some quick-witted insights. His positive impact on this book can't be stressed enough. David Churchill, my good friend for many years, was the first

ACKNOWLEDGMENTS

person to finish reading the rough draft — and his rewarding remarks brought me deep satisfaction. Suzie Chong came late to the process, but she — as much as anyone — understood exactly why I had to write this book. I'm eternally grateful for the time she spent, and her kind and thoughtful comments.

Many people contributed something special to the book. Michael Pinsonneault was in on the early discussions of the project before I found a publisher. Our penetrating talks helped me quickly find my focus. My brother, Scott Courrier, eagerly sought out interview material that I didn't have time to hunt down. Joanne Setterington, at Rykodisc, was kind enough to provide me with some of Zappa's remastered catalogue. Andrew and Eric, of Urban Sound Exchange, always showed great generosity in helping me find any related music I needed. Al Kelso, of the late, lamented Driftwood Music, came up with the GTO's album. My good buddy Chris Bennett, who enjoys sitting around listening to music as much as I do, dug up the Wild Man Fischer disc. Brad Gordon, an ardent fan, supplied a variety of invaluable Zappa concert and interview tapes. Thanks to Debbie Lindsey and her crew at CBC Radio archives, for their diligence and support in getting me interview material (especially Mark Kilpatrick, who went beyond the call of duty repairing a rapidly decaying tape). Kelly Falls, of Chapters, provided the information on Salman Rushdie. Dave Field, from CBC Ideas, who got me the dub of their special on Igor Stravinsky. Dianne Collins, of Galaxie, gave up her only Johnny "Guitar" Watson CD at a crucial moment. I'm also grateful to Chris Trebilcock for making numerous dubs of research videotapes. Those particular videos were provided by Steve Carmichael, whose periodic phone calls to check up on my progress were the gentle proddings of a benign conscience. My gratitude also to the dedicated Zappologists on the Internet.

Thanks to Bob Douglas for a rich and rewarding friendship that extends back to my years in high school when he was my teacher — which, in many important ways, he still is. Mi-Kyong Shim for a love and support that has greatly enriched my life. Shlomo Schwartzberg, who over the years has become my most supportive friend and colleague. His integrity and assistance — quite literally — helped me keep the faith in this fickle profession. Avril Orloff, my closest friend and ally, is the critic's critic — and I appreciate her more than I can say. Susan Green, my dear friend and occasional writing partner, was always there with her firm and kind heart. Special thanks to Steve Vineberg, who provides the kind of deeply treasured friendship that's all too rare in the world.

ACKNOWLEDGMENTS

Finally, there are many other old friends and colleagues who have provided another kind of help — the kind that gets you through life. Thanks to Larry Rooney, Tom Fulton, Annie Bryant, Gayle Burns, Mary Frances Ellison and Paul Carney, Mary Hynes and Randy Starkman, Evan Orloff, Lori Walker, Susan Clark, Tim Keele, Lorraine Speer, John Corcelli, Michele Bullock, Alex Patterson, Jean Jinnah, Irene Luxbacher, Ellie Skrow, Anne and Al, Mirjana Banicevic, Catherine Ferguson, Peggy Vidya, Al Clouter, Louise Yearwood, Dave King and Lynn Godfrey, Emily Larimer, Susan Clark, Cathy Heard, Clark Campbell and John Jones (who both introduced me to Zappa's music), Brandy Brass, Alan Guettel, Sheila Courrier and Albert Vezeau, Shawn Courrier, and, of course, Dave Downey and Anton Leo, without whom none of this could have been written.

Kevin Courrier
March 2002

PREFACE

THE PERFECT STRANGER

Whenever you shut a human being out of the world, he will, for better or worse, build one of his own.... With us ugliness and beauty, the grotesque and the tragic, and even good and evil, go their separate ways: Americans do not like to think that such extremes can mingle.

NELSON ALGREN

To make true political music, you have to say what decent people don't want to hear.

GREIL MARCUS, *Ranters & Crowd Pleasers: Punk in Pop Music, 1977–92*

An unusual, unpublicized event took place at *Billboard* magazine's First International Talent Forum in June 1975 in Los Angeles. One of the featured guests, pop musician Richard Carpenter, had been invited to speak at a seminar. The MC for the evening introduced Carpenter as a "straitlaced piano player." Carpenter made his way to the podium bristling with indignation. Carpenter was half of the brother/sister middle-of-the-road group the Carpenters. Richard and his sister Karen had, during the early '70s, built a successful career performing smoothly constructed romantic tunes that many considered the epitome of squareness. Those melodies poured from the nation's radios following one of the most turbulent social periods in American history.

DANGEROUS KITCHEN

The Carpenters created one hit after another. Their songs de-emphasized the driving pulse of rock, instead embracing four-part harmonies laid over gentle arrangements. The mood of the United States by the '70s, however, was anything but harmonious or gentle. There was the prolonged war in Vietnam, student killings at Kent State, the bombing of Cambodia, and the Watergate scandal. In the face of that tumult, the Carpenters became the kind of cuddly toys that made Richard Nixon's beleaguered White House sleep better at night. But whatever one thought of the music Richard Carpenter arranged and performed, he was a piano prodigy and a supremely sophisticated musician.

When Carpenter took the stage at the *Billboard* event, he immediately tore into the host. First, he informed everyone that he was personally responsible for almost every aspect of the Carpenters' song arrangements and repertoire. Then he paused. Looking down toward the table where he'd been sitting, he asked the crowd how he could be considered so "straitlaced" when he and his sister owned every record by the Mothers of Invention.

The Mothers of Invention! Sitting at the table, right beside Carpenter's empty seat, was Frank Zappa, the founder of one of America's most reviled and controversial bands. If the Carpenters were the sentimental darlings of AM pop radio in the '70s, the Mothers of Invention were the ugly, sneering antithesis of everything the Carpenters represented. Yet for one incongruous moment, Richard Carpenter was now feeling every bit the outsider, totally misunderstood, and unfairly labeled as a square by a magazine that lauded his hit records year after year. For one peculiar instant, Richard Carpenter *needed* Frank Zappa so he could feel validated among his peers.

Despite his enormous success and popularity, Carpenter suddenly felt like the freak. Certainly, Frank Zappa had understood that sensation for most of his career. Zappa, the man who composed such crude and comical numbers as "Bwana Dik" and "Titties 'n Beer," had little in common artistically with Carpenter. Yet on this night, they became as one, railing against the music industry's need to pigeonhole its performers. Carpenter would use this opportunity to inform the audience of one thing. Even if he was responsible for the sweet, accessible "We've Only Just Begun," he actually owned and listened to *We're Only in It for the Money*. The perfect irony of that evening probably wasn't lost on Zappa. Having long been considered too weird and obscene to be heard on American radio, and too lethal to be in the homes of American teenagers, Zappa was now being legitimized by Richard Carpenter.

THE PERFECT STRANGER

For many people, the name Frank Zappa conjured up the image of a deranged, cynical, and obscene satirist. Between 1966 and his death in 1993 from prostate cancer, Zappa became one of the most influential, innovative — and, yes, castigated — musicians in contemporary popular music, despite little airplay on the radio. He built a formidable career in rock 'n' roll by pushing the music into alternative territories.

By combining serious contemporary music with rock, jazz, and social and political satire, Zappa became one of North America's most ambitious artists. No musical ghetto could contain or define him, and no sacred cow or social group was beyond his reach. Zappa created a unique and sophisticated form of musical comedy by integrating the canon of 20th-century music with the scabrous wit of comedian Lenny Bruce and the irreverent clowning of Spike Jones. He poked fun at middle-class conformity (*Freak Out!*), the '60s counterculture (*We're Only in It for the Money*), disco (*Sheik Yerbouti*), the rock industry (*Tinsel Town Rebellion*), and the Reagan era (*You Are What You Is*). Zappa was just as content writing inspired orchestral compositions — performed by the London Symphony and the Ensemble Modern — as he was writing seemingly dumb little ditties like "Dinah-Moe Humm" or "Valley Girl." He could just as readily quote contemporary classical giants like Igor Stravinsky, Charles Ives, Edgard Varèse, and Anton Webern, blues greats like Johnny "Guitar" Watson and Clarence "Gatemouth" Brown, or doo-wop groups like the Channels and Jackie & the Starlites.

I first discovered Frank Zappa during the summer of 1970. His second solo album, *Hot Rats*, had opened a world of fascinating new sounds for me. What I enjoyed most were the vastly diverse styles he incorporated into his compositions. I wasn't just hearing jazz in one piece, hard rock in another, chamber music in the next — these elements were happening all at once, and often in the same tune. Never had I encountered a composer who combined so many musical genres so freely. Zappa created — for me — the possibility that all forms of music could coexist without judgment, as long as they were played with great skill and imagination. When I was fifteen, Frank Zappa liberated my musical tastes and sent me fleeing to the library to enthusiastically seek out new types of music.

Dangerous Kitchen: The Subversive World of Zappa is most importantly a book about music, and about a composer who had an unbridled love affair with it. "Music is the best," Zappa once proclaimed, and, speaking as someone with an active ear for music since age five, I fully understand the sentiment. A word of warning, though: I don't expect everyone who reads this book to end up loving Frank Zappa, or his work. Some will disagree with my tastes and sentiments. After all, my argument for Zappa cuts close to the core of deep divisions in opinion about the function of art in social, political, and cultural life. But I do hope that my views persuade readers to come to their own conclusions. What I have tried to capture — beyond reproach — is the larger cultural context to which Zappa irrefutably belongs. For those open and willing enough to submerge themselves into Frank Zappa's vast repertoire, *Dangerous Kitchen* should be a suitable companion, making that leap — right out on the fringe — a worthwhile journey.

CHAPTER ONE

NO NOT NOW

You can't have progress without deviation from the norm, because if you don't go beyond the norm you can't have any progress. How do you invent something new, if you're only doing normal stuff? You can't. You can only recycle the norms. So somebody has to take the chance and go outside the norms, and build the next thing.

FRANK ZAPPA

1

It started as a rumor. And rumors were always synonymous with Frank Zappa. Many of his interviews, in fact, were devoted to dispelling each and every one of them. Whether it was the long-standing myth that he once ate shit onstage or the assertion that his father played Mr. Green Jeans on the children's TV show *Captain Kangaroo* (Zappa had written a song called "Son of Mr. Green Genes"), Zappa always needed to prove that he wasn't weird.

This latest bit of hearsay, however, was far more lethal than any accusation of weirdness. It didn't carry the ludicrous associations that the other more outrageous falsehoods had, either. It was 1991. The word was out that Frank Zappa was dying of cancer. And unlike all the other scandalous untruths that Zappa refuted, this one had yet to be dismissed.

2

New York City had always been a favorite place for Frank Zappa. His fondness for the Big Apple began when, as a teenager, he discovered that his musical mentor, the French composer Edgard Varèse, had lived in Greenwich Village. When Zappa's group, the Mothers of Invention, played a small venue called the Garrick Theatre in the late '60s, he pioneered a preposterous form of rock theater that has yet to be paralleled. Throughout the '70s and '80s, on Halloween night, Zappa would also play for delirious fans — all decked out in their witch and goblin costumes — at the Palladium. "By the time a scene did finally erupt in New York City, it was much more interesting because it had ethnic diversity," Zappa told Nigel Leigh of the BBC. "It had cultural diversity because of all the different parts of the city where there were concrete artistic things going on." In November 1991, Zappa's music was being performed and celebrated again in New York City, at the Ritz Theatre, for four evenings. The show, aptly titled *Zappa's Universe*, featured a number of familiar figures from his vast and storied history.

Onstage for those special evenings would be a variety of performers — two *a cappella* groups, a rock band, an orchestra, opera singers, plus assorted guests from outside the world of music, like comedian Penn Gillette (of Penn & Teller) and Eric Buxton, a devoted fan who turned up at every Zappa concert. The evening was organized by Joel Thome, conductor of the Orchestra of Our Time. Thome had first encountered Zappa during a Varèse tribute in 1981, and later became an enthusiast of his music. The "house band" consisted of Mike Keneally, who played guitar in Zappa's last touring band in 1988; Scott Thunes, bass player in Zappa's groups since 1981 (and held responsible, by some, for the demise of the 1988 ensemble); keyboardists Mats Oberg and Marc Ziegenhagen, and drummer Morgan Agren, all from Sweden; and percussionist Jonathan Haas.

Throughout the evenings, various guests would join the band onstage. They included guitar virtuoso Steve Vai, who got his professional start with Zappa in the early '80s; guitarist and vocalist Denny Walley, who also played in the early-'80s outfit; and Dale Bozzio, wife of drummer Terry Bozzio, reprising the pivotal role of Mary from Zappa's rock opera *Joe's Garage*. Other guests included the Persuasions, a black vocal group from Brooklyn who got their start in the music business, in 1969, because of Zappa. Rockapella were a white doo-wop group who embraced Zappa's unabashed love for '50s R&B. Finally, there was the Zappa family. Frank's children, Dweezil, Moon Unit, and Diva, were all set to appear. It was shaping up to be quite a homecoming; there was even a plan afoot for Frank Zappa to attend.

The repertoire for the concerts was varied, and, in typical Zappa fashion, the tone and genre would constantly shift throughout the evening. Many of his classic numbers were included: "Brown Shoes Don't Make It," his hilarious mini-opera attacking sexual and political hypocrisy; the beautifully lyrical "folk" song "The Idiot Bastard Son"; and his two broadsides against organized religion, "The Meek Shall Inherit Nothing" and "Heavenly Bank Account." But these genuinely imaginative rock songs were mixed in with Zappa's more rhythmically complex orchestral work like "The Black Page," the big-band extravaganza "Waka/Jawaka," and soprano Maureen McNally's piquant reading of Zappa's speech-song tribute to Arnold Schoenberg, "The Dangerous Kitchen."

With the first show scheduled for November 7, everyone was anticipating the arrival of Frank Zappa. That expectation was dashed, however, by a sudden press conference scheduled by the Zappa family that afternoon. First, it was announced that his plane from Los Angeles had mechanical problems, so he couldn't attend. The gathered throng was then informed that a case of the flu had grounded him. Within a few moments, there was the news that most suspected.

Moon Unit and Dweezil took the podium. "We're here to make a statement on behalf of our family," Moon read. "Although Frank was looking forward to being here and really intended to be here, unfortunately he's not here. As many of you know, he's been diagnosed by journalists as having cancer. We'd like you to know his doctors have diagnosed prostate cancer, which he's been fighting successfully and he has been feeling well and working too hard and planned to attend. Up until the last minute, we were still hoping he'd feel well enough to get on a plane and come here. There are occasional periods where he's not feeling as well and it's really unfortunate it happened to coincide with this event."

After years of the many specious Zappa rumors being discredited, one of them finally turned out to be true. This particular hearsay, unlike the others, turned out to have no cure.

3

Despite the absence of Frank Zappa from the opening night of *Zappa's Universe*, the show went on as planned. Yet, who knows if it was just mere coincidence, or whether it was a form of cosmic convergence, but before each concert, conductor Joel Thome and the Orchestra of Our Time began with a piece of music not associated with Frank Zappa — Erik Satie's *Socrate*, a "symphonic drama" drawn from Plato's dialogues with Socrates in *Symposium*, *Phaedrus*, and *Phaedo*. For many in the audience, it was a puzzling inclusion. Here was a score that Satie described, in a letter to a friend, as something he wanted "to be as white and pure as antiquity." Why choose this as a concert opener for a man who once warned us not to eat the yellow snow? You wouldn't hear any resemblance between the works of Erik Satie and Frank Zappa.

Where Satie was sparse and minimal, Zappa combined vast musical colors with a sardonic fervor. While Satie bled the sensuality out of his music, Zappa embroidered his with a satyr's grin. As for their personal lives, Zappa had a healthy appetite for sex, while the nearest Satie got to promiscuity was a torrid and traumatic affair with the painter Suzanne Valadon in 1893. Yet Zappa and Satie *were* kindred spirits of a sort. Their outrageous wit, and the methods by which they employed it, bonded them. According to Thome, it was also their adventurous spirit that tied them together.

"In Satie . . . you have the Dadaist sense of leaping off the cliff," Thome told journalist Richard Gehr, "letting anything happen, combined with tremendous craft and imagination. In Satie, all the works add up to a single, powerful, evolving idea. A similar thing happens with Zappa. Taken together, Frank's works add up to one extraordinary opera." As recently as 1991, in the cultural commentary magazine *Telos*, one journalist even wrote that Zappa had "pushed the boundaries of what is musically acceptable." And although he acknowledged that Zappa's music was obviously more an extension of the work of Varèse and Stravinsky, "his disdain for the way music is accommodated in contemporary culture and his desire to address it with satire, humor, parody, and a sardonic wit is reminiscent of Satie." Both Satie and Zappa saw their work as part of a larger evolving project. "Satie's music [is] designed to engage the performer's mental processes in an entirely different way from that assumed by the 19th-century cult of the performer as interpreter," writes musicologist Stephen Whittington. "Satie is not interested in music for the purpose of 'expression' but rather for its psychological effect on both performer and audience."

Satie had led a whole movement of French composers, including Claude Debussy and Darius Milhaud, away from the excesses of the German romantic school into something leaner and more epigrammatic. He did this with an eccentric brand of buffoonery that took the pomposity out of the picturesque aspects of romanticism. Like Zappa, Satie wrote absurdly titled pieces, such as *Genuine Floppy Preludes (for a Dog)* and *Shriveled Embryos*, that shunned academic rules and regulations. In his later ballets, he mixed musical genres, and in *Parade* (1917) he included the sounds of a typewriter, a gunshot, and sirens. Satie was also a progenitor of Dadaism and surrealism, movements that created an absurdist response to political expedience and hypocrisy.

During Satie's time, the importance of the 18th-century classical model in European music had slipped into a sharp decline. Composers who were once concerned about form and symmetry, which made the work analogous to the ideals of classical Greek and Roman art and philosophy, were now exalted for becoming cult virtuosos. This radical departure started taking form in the 18th century, beginning with the heroic figure of Mozart's opera *Don Giovanni* in 1787, and Haydn's *Sturm und Drang* realization of *The Creation* in 1798. It reached its zenith in the heroic operatic myths of Giuseppe Verdi and Richard Wagner, and was soon embodied in the flesh by the flamboyant violinist Paganini and the spellbinding Hungarian pianist Franz Liszt. The most celebrated music — as great as some of it was — was also filled with what critic Frank Rossiter calls "bombastic self-assertion, sentimentality, intense emotional subjectivity, and self-revelation."

Some of the pop music of the '60s also suffered from many of these qualities. Reacting to this, Frank Zappa developed a satirical style that patently rejected sentimentality, or genuine romantic longing. "The part of me that people should be most interested in, if they have any interest in me at all, is what I do," Zappa told Canadian journalist Bob Marshall. "Not how I do it, or who I am, or whatever . . . there is quite a bit of me in the music, but. . . nobody wants to know about my toothache. They don't want to know about my personal traumas and tragedies. Who gives a shit about that stuff? You want that kind of stuff? Go listen to a sensitive singer-songwriter with an acoustical guitar in his hand."

Both Satie and Zappa sought to create "an art in which sense and nonsense, seriousness and humor, mystery and mystification co-exist," writes Whittington. Though both artists composed their work in vastly different times, they still managed to "transcend such dualities, going 'beyond sense and nonsense' as Nietzsche and the Zen Masters sought to go 'beyond good and evil.'"

4

What those evening concerts in New York illustrated was that Zappa was as much a product of the discontent growing in the late 19th century as he was an expression of that discontent in the late 20th century. If you consider his antecedents, and the events that made him possible, you can start to make sense out of the diversity of his albums. If Satie's minimalist compositions, like *Les Trois Gymnopédies* (1888), bore little resemblance in form to Zappa's music, it was the impure essence of Satie's spirit that Zappa absorbed. But the inclusion of Satie on the program of *Zappa's Universe* also indicated the scope of Zappa's art. For instance, Pierre Boulez, the classical composer and conductor who worked with Zappa on *The Perfect Stranger: Boulez Conducts Zappa* (1984), knew just how daring Zappa's grasp of music actually was. "As a musician, he was an exceptional figure because he was of two worlds: the pop world and the classical world," Boulez remarked. "That's not a very easy position, because you are regarded by both camps as a traitor."

Frank Zappa brought to popular music a desire to break down the boundaries between high and low culture. He presented musical history through the kaleidoscopic lens of social satire, then turned it into farce. This potent mixture upset many listeners who wanted to cling to a safer, more romantic view of art as something morally and spiritually edifying. "One of the things that always impressed me about Zappa, besides just the delight with his rhythmic invention, was that he didn't allow anything to be beyond him — high culture, low culture," recalls Matt Groening, creator of *The Simpsons* and a longtime fan and friend of Zappa. "I mean, who other than Frank Zappa would have thought of combining Varèse with doo-wop?" That's just it. No one else did think of it, and ultimately that inspired Groening. "It didn't matter how high or low it was, I was going to see what was going on," Groening continues. "Most people say, 'Oh, that area of culture over there is too grubby for me,' or, 'That area of culture is for rich fops,' and I tried not to let that get in the way."

Jill Christiansen, catalog development manager for Rykodisc, the independent label that first released Zappa's work on CD, believes that it was that very versatility that left North American culture either scratching its head or dismissing Zappa altogether. "Frank persisted in discussing all of those subjects that make people squirm — politics, sex, religion, whatever," Christiansen remarks. "He demanded that you think. There are so many paradoxical elements to him, [that] I think it confuses people." Yet it was those paradoxical qualities Christiansen refers to that North American audiences rarely engaged. People preferred, usually out of ignorance (and often contempt), to portray Zappa as a freak who imbibed copious chemicals, even when he consistently denounced drugs. He was scorned as a fetishist with a predilection for adolescent humor ("Don't Eat the Yellow Snow"), who possessed a leering smugness ("Broken Hearts Are for Assholes"), while in truth he led a relatively normal married life, with kids who loved their parents.

Indulging in these specious myths, however, was consolation for those who didn't want to tackle what the music — or the man — was actually about. "A lot of people couldn't get past the way he looked," said former band member Warren Cucurullo, referring to Zappa's scruffy hair and trademark imperial goatee. "He did come out of the '60s. It would be hard in the '90s to come out with avant-garde, classical-tinged rock music." Zappa embarked on a career that traced a fascinating but turbulent period in popular music when the possibilities for great change were up for grabs. The counterculture audience, though, despite their political savvy, turned out to desire as much romance in their music as their parents' generation did. Zappa, with his preposterous wit, instigated and offended this crowd rather than broadening their tastes or enlarging their expectations.

The ambiguity in Zappa's work at times became a difficult pill for audiences to swallow. For instance, reviewer Richard Williams, writing in the *Times* of London, after one of Zappa's mid-'80s concerts, caught the tensions at work in his music that likely distanced him from the counterculture. "Frank Zappa was the first rock musician to saturate his work with irony, setting a fashion so widely copied that the music has practically drowned in self-awareness," Williams wrote. "It also makes his music interesting to deal with in critical terms, since it is often difficult to guess his intention and thereby assess his achievement. . . . To maintain such ambiguity is an achievement on its own, although some may feel that it closes off the opportunity for emotional expression. Perhaps that was never his aim."

The radical climate of the '60s practically demanded a speaking out against the status quo. But the counterculture audience was rarely self-critical, could barely grasp irony, and definitely did not laugh at itself. Rock 'n' roll was also the music of the battle charge against the establishment. Zappa, on the other hand, was an unaffected utopian who saw no difference between a string quartet and a rock combo except the form itself. As early as his adolescent years in high school, Zappa just listened to — and accepted — what he thought was good music. "Since I didn't have any formal training, it didn't make any difference to me if I was listening to Lightnin' Slim, or a vocal group called the Jewels (who had a song out then called

'Angel in My Life'), or Webern, or Varèse, or Stravinsky," Zappa wrote in his memoir, *The Real Frank Zappa Book*.

Zappa eventually did find an audience, however, among disenfranchised outsiders who felt no sentimental attachment to their culture. "I did it at a time in American musical history when you could get *away* with it," he told Matt Resnicoff in *Musician*. "And I established a franchise for a certain clientele that happened to enjoy that particular service provided by me. I don't think in a world of MTV, fake award shows, and massive beverage sponsorship for mega-tours which rely more on stage lighting than musical artistry . . . that anyone could manage to do what I did and survive. . . . Because when I started, *nobody* knew what the fuck they were doing — there were no rules. You made it up as you went along and [did] whatever worked. . . . I refused to stop doing it and that's the reason I'm still here."

Yet one of the problems in music, whether it is avant-garde, modernist, or conventional, is that the people who play it always end up operating only within the rules of that genre. Modern jazz trumpeter Dizzy Gillespie, for instance, might seem a radical departure from a traditionalist like Louis Armstrong, but both became defined only by the styles they heralded. Neither would be caught dead playing the music of the other. This was true of almost all musicians and composers in every field. Zappa reacted against this. "I asked myself the basic question: if the intrinsic value of the music depends on your serial pedigree, then who in the fuck is going to know whether it's any good or not?" Zappa asked Don Menn in 1992. "I started moving in the direction of what you might call a haphazard style. That's whatever sounded good to me for whatever reason, whether it was some crashing dissonance or a nice tune with chord changes and a steady beat in the background."

Matt Groening once remarked, "Frank was *my* Elvis." For Groening, this wasn't meant as a flippant remark designed to outrage people. He and many other fans genuinely felt that Zappa accomplished what had already been claimed for Elvis Presley. Presley may have fused gospel, country, and the blues into a form that became rock 'n' roll, but it was still only within the realm of popular music. Zappa's leap was much bolder. He set out to blur the boundaries between the classical and popular schools of music. He brought the sophistication of modern orchestral forms into the rambunctious world of rock with the same enthusiasm he used to blow the earnest cobwebs right out of the sacred halls of high culture. Unlike Presley, he didn't just interpret, redefine, or pay homage to black music, either — Zappa played in bands that included blacks. Where Presley's music was torn between kitschy nostalgia ("An American Trilogy") and an ingenuous embrace of his American roots ("That's All Right, Mama"), Zappa treated the source music of American culture with a candid irreverence. He tore into the cultural fabric with ridicule and sharp criticism, using every musical ingredient he could find to undermine nostalgia.

Nostalgia is the utopian's nightmare. The curse of yearning is that it can deny the present and foreclose the future. Only romantic historians prefer to dwell longingly on the past, where they can then fix it in time and honor it from a safe distance. This may be why our most obstreperous artists get accepted and considered great only *after* they are dead. True historians, however, draw upon the past in order to forge a certain timelessness. They seek to find a context for the past and future in the content of current events. The past illuminates the present and throws a shadow on the future.

Zappa set out to synthesize various musical forms to make history fold in on itself. Only then could everything that came before be experienced simultaneously. "None of the people who have reviewed my albums, with maybe two or three exceptions in the last twenty years, had a broad enough knowledge to know that what they were listening to was more outrageous, in terms of how it was flying in the face of music history, than any lyric or any individual story idea in the song could ever be," Zappa once told *Keyboard*. "They weren't historically equipped to understand what the references were and to see why the music that was being done based on those references was either utterly hilarious or completely outrageous. You've got to know a certain amount of stuff in order to derive the maximum impact from those albums. That's the way it works. I hate to be a guy sitting around saying, 'I'm misunderstood,' but it's not even a matter of being misunderstood. It's a matter of being uncomprehended."

To call yourself "uncomprehended" might appear wildly arrogant, but Zappa was pointing out something that for him was essential. Without the knowledge, or at least a grasp, of the vehement changes that occurred in music during the last hundred years, one might not fully appreciate what was at work in his compositions. "Before you judge, you really should ask yourself whether you have enough data to make that judgment," Zappa continued. "For a guy who has never heard Anton Webern or Igor Stravinsky . . . if you don't even know what that stuff is, where it comes from, what it sounds like, and what the intention of it is, how can you even make a guess at what extrapolations you may be hearing?"

Inspired by Satie's initial barbs at feigned respectability, Zappa decided to draw on an American equivalent. There was probably no better place to start than with composer Charles Ives. Born in 1874, in the small town of Danbury, Connecticut, Ives created an original, discordant, and distinctly American form of music. In essence, he brought to life the contradictions and schisms that existed in the American spirit.

Zappa also adopted the attitude of Edgard Varèse, an expatriate French composer who settled in New York in 1915. Varèse went so far as to question the very principles of Western music itself. He abandoned the idea of pitch and reached out to elements of pure sound. His aggressive percussive rhythms led other composers (including Zappa) into the uncharted territory of electronic music. Varèse's famous quote, "The present-day composer refuses to die," became a Zappa motto that was boldly featured on the inside cover of his first three albums.

The Russian composer Igor Stravinsky offered Zappa a map to explore the musical past without necessarily having to repeat it. Through neoclassicism, a break with 19th-century tonality, Stravinsky's jabbing polyrhythms and unorthodox orchestral color (which reached its apogee in 1913 with the infamous premiere of his ballet *The Rite of Spring* in Paris) provided a balanced harmonic framework for Zappa's dissonant elements.

The final ingredient of Zappa's disparate brew was the rock 'n' roll music he grew up on, and the experiences of being a teenager in America in the '50s. Although he had a particular disdain for love lyrics in songs, he did acknowledge the romantic yearnings in doo-wop and the harshly defined sexual attitudes of the blues. Zappa recognized that this demeanor had its basis in the desire for, and the pursuit of, sex. By drawing on adolescent longings, Zappa set out to overturn the hypocrisy of America's moral prerogatives.

Guitarist Nigey Lennon, in her memoir, *Being Frank*, details her brief period sitting in with the Mothers of Invention in 1971 (including an affair she says she had with Frank). She sees clearly how Zappa connected the world of his antecedents to the modern era:

> The battles, sexual and musical, Frank was fighting were Victorian: his musical heroes . . . had all been born in the 19th century and had struggled to throw off the shackles of 19th-century musical convention, albeit each in a different way. Even Frank's obsession with technology was Victorian, as was his droll, largely verbal sense of humor. He claimed not to be much of a reader, but his vocabulary was so flexible, and precise, not

to mention picturesque, that it gave him away as an autodidact, whether he liked it or not. I imagine that, growing up as the first-generation child of immigrant parents, he had absorbed their 19th-century European attitudes. In fact, he was scornful of everything American — beer, sports, Manifest Destiny, you name it. . . . He had been condemned to, whether he really knew it or not, *Life in the Wrong Era* — he belonged in *belle epoque* Paris, or Berlin of the '20s, not "I Like Ike" America.

Nonetheless, Zappa *was* a consumer of American culture. He was shaped by the cheapness of Cold War monster movies during the Eisenhower '50s, as well as the fierce authenticity of black R&B, doo-wop, and blues recordings. So with the arrival of '60s pop, and its baby-boomer self-importance, Zappa was there preparing his arsenal to counter the love generation. "The problem with Americans is they have this self-image of 'We're so nice, we're so fair, we're so honest, we always take the high road,'" Zappa once remarked. "If only it were true, this would be Heaven on earth, but it's not true. And when you see 240 million people willingly deluding themselves with this idea that they're somehow God's chosen people. . . ."

Critic Greil Marcus confirms this view in *Mystery Train: Images of America in Rock 'n' Roll Music*. "The Puritans did not take their dreams from the land; they brought them along," Marcus writes. "They meant to build a community of piety and harmony. . . . The Puritans came here with a utopian vision they could not maintain; their idea was to do God's work, and they knew that if they failed, it would mean that their work had been the devil's. As they panicked at their failures, the devil was all they saw. . . . America is a trap: that its promises and dreams, all mixed up as love and politics and landscape, are too much to live up to and too much to escape." The American political landscape, embroidered with assassinations, deep racial divisions, religious zealotry, cultural elitism, and witch hunts, is deeply rooted in this Puritan heritage. Yet America's best music, movies, and paintings have always been an attempt to escape it.

Zappa also chose to identify that heritage. Whether it was in his most scatological songs like "Bobby Brown Goes Down," his political attacks like "Jesus Thinks You're a Jerk," or even his testimony before Congress fighting the censorship apparatus known as the Parents' Music Resource Center (PMRC), Zappa clearly identified the inherent contradictions in American democracy. "The major deficiency in the United States seems to be that it's got a history that only goes back a couple of hundred years and that history itself is riddled with corruption, it is riddled with exploitation," Zappa said. "You name it, we have exploited it and it's not exactly something to be proud of. If whatever we have achieved we had come by it honestly, we'd be in a lot better shape, but really we haven't. We've abused a lot of people not only here in our own country but around the world, and then gone to church to smooth it over and had some guy say, 'Yes, we're God's chosen people and this is our Manifest Destiny — to be the peacekeepers for the world.'"

With an eyebrow arched, Zappa began drawing moustaches on the faces of America's sacred cows, which made his work formidably political — even if the subject matter was sociological in nature. But where Woody Guthrie, Bob Dylan, U2, or Rage Against the Machine sometimes made their art explicitly partisan, Zappa's music was political in a manner that transcended the specifics of the lyrics. He understood how popular music, borne out of commercial and marketing demands, could always be co-opted by corporate interests to sell listeners anything. Rebellion could be packaged and co-opted just as easily as romance. For evidence, we need only look at how the Bank of Montreal altered Dylan's "The Times They Are a-Changin'" to promote their banking cards; or the way Ronald Reagan, during his 1984 presidential campaign, appropriated as his own anthem Bruce Springsteen's "Born in the USA," a scathing critique of America's treatment of Vietnam War vets. "Unlike Sting and U2, who ask us to admire their actions on our behalf, Zappa sets up a series of questions about meaning and its social control that encourage our speculation," critic Ben Watson wrote in *Frank Zappa's Negative Dialectics of Poodle Play*.

In some ways, it was Dylan who began to raise those very questions when he went electric at the Newport Folk Festival in 1965. In *Invisible Republic*, Greil Marcus aptly defines the folk revival as a paradigm of virtue overripe for subversion. He describes the movement as "a place of the spirit, where authenticity in song and manner, in being, was the highest value — the value against which all forms of discourse, all attributes inherited or assumed, were measured." It was also a blind stab at Utopia, "another country," where "values placed . . . the country over the city, labor over capital, sincerity over education . . . the natural expressiveness of the folk over the self-interest of the artist." Into this impersonal world walked Bob Dylan, who created "a persona that caught Charlie Chaplin, James Dean, and Lenny Bruce in talk and gesture, Woody Guthrie and the French Symbolists in writing. . . ."

The folk revival of the early '60s was also dramatically linked to the civil rights struggle. Though Dylan's early songs, like "Blowin' in the Wind," "A Hard Rain's a-Gonna Fall," and "The Times They Are a-Changin'," were an inexorable part of that struggle, the folk revival itself started to become, according to Marcus, "pageants of righteousness." And these pageants would appraise artists strictly by their political stance (only leftists need apply). Soon these musical coronations became places where, Marcus states, "life — a certain kind of life — equaled art, which ultimately meant that life replaced it."

It was into this socialist realist realm that Dylan, on July 25, 1965, at the Newport Folk Festival, strapped on an electric guitar. He made it clear to those who booed, and anyone who cared to listen, that folk music was "made less by history or circumstance than by particular people, for particular, unknowable reasons." Zappa would take all this a step further by writing songs about people that even Dylan might want to avoid.

5

When Zappa was a child, his father, Francis, a scientist and mathematician, wanted to write a history of the world — with Sicily as the hub. His basic thesis: all the old history was written for the amusement of the ruling classes. Since the lower classes couldn't read, their rulers didn't care about remembering what happened to them. Francis Zappa never got to write that book, but his son, in his own inimitable way, fulfilled his father's dream. The forgotten individuals that Frank Zappa chose to depict, however, weren't part of any noble tradition. He wrote songs about an armed robber who gave his female victims enemas ("The Legend of the Illinois Enema Bandit"), guys who flung their boogers on the bedroom window ("Let's Make the Water Turn Black"), and a menstruating groupie who got fucked by a fish ("The Mud Shark"). In 1993, Zappa told Nigel Leigh, "Many of the things that I've written have been true stories in song about obscure people who did obscure things, and they function in the same folk-music tradition, except that it's being performed on electric instruments."

In the case of Michael Kenyon, the enema bandit, his anal obsession resulted in the rape of several women. This is hardly a person worthy of "celebration" in a song — but that's part of the rub. Is Zappa actually endorsing the guy's behavior, or is he forcing us to confront something else? "[It] was the chance to do a folk song, especially since we were playing a lot of jobs in the Midwest," Zappa once remarked. "[Kenyon's] like a household word here, he should have a song. It's not exactly John Henry and the steamhammer, but, you know, he needs to have a song." Zappa considered the virtuousness attached to the folk tradition as largely counterfeit. If traditional Appalachian and Celtic folk songs could feature parricide, incest, and child murders, then why couldn't modern folk music render the horrific deeds of people like Michael Kenyon?

What bothers many people most is that Zappa doesn't identify with the "correct" view in many of these songs; instead, he creates a setting that lets listeners make up their own mind. Ben Watson says Zappa composed a kind of political music that becomes "an anathema to liberalism, which thinks that only commitment to certain pre-selected 'ideas' separates the saved from the damned." The liberalism Zappa attacked was the kind endorsed by the same people who came up with the counterculture, wrote for *Rolling Stone*, and latched onto Bruce Springsteen and U2. "They were very contemptuous of heavy metal and all those *lumpens* who liked their loud rock music," Watson said in an interview in *Menz* in 1996. "Then they attacked it, called it racist, sexist, and used all this left-wing-sounding language, but used it as a way to wash their hands of the white working-class in the United States. Zappa refused to do that. He had a strong underclass resentment in his music. He refused to indulge in ideal solutions that would be very nice to imagine."

Zappa picked subjects and people that unnerved listeners who wanted to strongly identify with the artist. Singing along happily with their idols' songs helped these fans believe they were becoming one with every word sung. Zappa countered this by including transgressive jolts in his work. Given that dynamic, it's hard to imagine songs like "The Legend of the Illinois Enema Bandit" or "Bobby Brown Goes Down" being happily crooned or, for that matter, used to sell running shoes. Zappa's rock songs, in particular, pointed out specific areas of sexual and political repression that left listeners questioning the very spectacle of what they were consuming. His instrumental work also brought a lurid vitality to orchestral and chamber music. Instead of underlining ideology, to paraphrase Watson, Zappa's music promoted consciousness. "Zappa understood from an aesthetic and intuitive point of view how the counterculture had gone wrong, and had become a new elitist form of liberalism that despised the masses down there," Watson explains.

Zappa didn't treat listeners, or fans, simply as consumers — he treated them as voyeurs, too. He understood that some of the record-buying public consumed music to reinforce their lifestyles. Therefore they became susceptible to trends. Zappa's rock music, on the other hand, forced the audience to confront ideas and thoughts they might not be comfortable accepting blindly.

NO NOT NOW

Yet his scathing lyrics did occasionally serve as a mantra for his legion of fans. Even so, within those words often lay doubt, self-incrimination, and a deep skepticism about political and cultural life. Singing his songs didn't absolve them from personal responsibility, or become mere wallpaper for their lifestyle. His songs forced listeners to constantly confront themselves — to make them think, not just accept. That gave his songs a highly political function, because they bred the desire to question what was considered acceptable.

Zappa's live performances also became an elaborate form of political entertainment. He developed into an enigmatic impresario (like the Joel Grey devil-doll of *Cabaret*) who provided a wry commentary on performer/audience relations. Some, however, found Zappa's role to be smugly condescending to his audience, but that's only if they thought of Zappa in a romantic vein. He never claimed to use music to reveal the sensitivities of his soul.

Zappa played a contrary role rather than the easily identifiable good guy. Whereas the Who, in their rock opera *Tommy*, cast lead singer Roger Daltry in the idealized role of the deaf, dumb, and blind victim, Zappa played the Central Scrutinizer, an authoritarian figure who enforced laws that outlawed music, in his rock opera *Joe's Garage*. Someone who felt superior to his audience would hardly cast himself in the least favorable role. But Zappa didn't cater to an audience's desire to identify with him.

Since many of his released recordings *were* live performances, though, we do get a fascinating view — over three decades' worth — of his relationship with his fans. The folklore concerning the band's escapades on the road, and their sexual proclivities, also became the subject material for songs (as well as Zappa's 1971 feature film, *200 Motels*). Zappa didn't create an illusion about who the performer was in his music. On the contrary, his music exposed his band members for *exactly* who they were. "He went after things that were important to him with a Zenlike absoluteness — and sex was only a little less important to him than his music was," Nigey Lennon writes. "Sexuality — *'those glands down there'* — unconsciously permeated everything he did, from his voice to his gestures to his guitar playing. He was serious-minded, even solemn, and yet at the same time I distinctly sensed that there was an element of madness in his refusal to accept any boundaries whatsoever, sexually or otherwise. He could find erotic possibilities in the least likely situations — the more absurd, the better; the further he could push the envelope, the better he liked it. And all the while he was pushing it, he was laughing . . . not too loud, but very deeply."

Using the lurid backdrop of rock as the foreground of some of his songs, Zappa provoked liberal sensibilities — just as Lenny Bruce had done when he used the milieu of vaudeville comedy to tweak social norms. Zappa's strategy of putting listeners at odds with the content of his songs did, however, sometimes backfire. Riots broke out in Berlin in the late '60s and Sicily during the '80s, sometimes forcing the group to abandon the stage. Playing on the volatile relationship between fans and their music was very much a part of Zappa's Dangerous Kitchen. What nourished you could also hurt you.

There were other, more candid, aspects of Zappa's political work. This included the voter registration booths he set up at concert venues during his last tour in 1988. He'd already led the fight against the PMRC's censoring of rock lyrics, and that ultimately led to his aborted run for president in 1991, until cancer started to debilitate him. Near the end of his life, which coincided with the fall of communism, Zappa developed business relations with the participants of the "Velvet Revolution" in the Czech Republic (President Vaclav Havel was a huge Zappa fan) and attempted to create entrepreneurial interests in the former Soviet Union.

In the end, though, it was Zappa's compositions that became the subliminally subversive force in popular music — despite attempts to both censor and restrict him. Frank Zappa was part of an ongoing iconoclastic tradition in American culture that constantly sought to deviate from the norm.

6

When the Orchestra of Our Time began the *Zappa's Universe* program each evening with Satie's *Socrate*, the concert had special significance. Erik Satie had been the unruly spirit that lit the fuse for Zappa's intercontinental absurdities, while the persecution of Socrates, held accountable for corrupting the minds of the young, was something Zappa understood through the systematic censorship of his records on North American radio. The combined beauty and sudden mortality Satie evoked in *Socrate* brought an inescapable air of poignancy to the Ritz Theatre. As the celebrations went on, Zappa was at his home in Los Angeles continuing to work and recover. Maybe his time had finally come. Perhaps his music was at last being celebrated. But for Frank Zappa, time was starting to run out.

CHAPTER TWO

YOU'RE PROBABLY WONDERING WHY I'M HERE

(1940-1964)

I never had any intention of writing rock music. I always wanted to compose more serious music and have it be performed in concert halls, but I knew no one would play it. So I figured that if anyone was ever going to hear anything I composed, I'd have to get a band together and play rock music. That's how I got started.

FRANK ZAPPA

A creator is not in advance of his generation but he is the first of his contemporaries to be conscious of what is happening to his generation.

GERTRUDE STEIN

1

Since Los Angeles has always habitually drawn dreamers and experimenters, it's a natural assumption that Frank Zappa hailed from Southern California. Frank Vincent Zappa, however, was born at the Mercy Hospital in Baltimore on December 21, 1940, to Sicilian-Italian parents. His last name translates into English as "plow" or "hoe." Frank's father, Francis, was a graduate in engineering, born in Partinico, Sicily, on May 7, 1905, of Greek-Arab ancestry. Francis had come to America on an immigrant boat when he was just a boy. Frank's mother,

Rosemarie, born in 1912, was a first-generation Italian-American. Her mother's mother was French and Sicilian, and her father was Italian from Naples. Rosemarie was both a librarian and a housewife. She and Francis had three children besides Frank. There was Carl, Bobby, and a sister, Patrice Joanne (Candy). Francis also had a daughter, Ann, from a previous marriage.

While in college, Francis developed versatile work habits. He earned money as a barber in his father's shop on the Maryland waterfront while performing as a guitarist in a serenading trio with banjo player Jack Wardlaw, who owned a local insurance company. Once Francis finished his education, he took a position at Loyola University, in Maryland, where he taught history. Francis became a good mathematician, which inspired him to write a small book on gambling probabilities. However, Francis's teaching position helped him cultivate a background as a metallurgist and meteorologist, rather than posting odds in Las Vegas. His scientific background, with the risks it entailed and its spirit of experimentation, deeply appealed to his eldest son. From an early age, Frank Zappa was interested in astronomy and chemistry.

Frank also spent his early youth conducting puppet shows. "My first appearance on television was a show called *Your Make-Believe Ballroom* where I was doing hand puppets," Zappa told Vicki Gabereau on CBC Radio's *Variety Tonight*. "I did it as a hobby because the kid who lived across the street from me had a father who was a carpenter. He built this little portable stage, and we made puppets and did little neighborhood shows." Yet he also found time for building plane models — and experimenting with explosives. "I think if I weren't in music," Zappa said many years later, "I would probably be in science. That's how I started off — in chemistry, when I was six. I always liked that. But I think music is probably less harmful." Zappa began his novice fascination with demolition at age five, when he offered his father an original design for a warhead. It was politely refused. "If they would have gotten me a chemistry set when I asked them to, I would have been a fucking scientist right now," Zappa explained.

During Frank's early childhood, the Zappa family lived at the Edgewood Arsenal Army installation in Edgewood, Maryland. Since their house, with its thin walls and improper insulation, was ill-equipped to handle the cold winters, Frank suffered from asthma and sinus problems. "Sicilian parents do things *differently*," Zappa wrote. "If I said I had an earache, my parents would heat up some olive oil and pour it in my ear — *which hurts like a motherfucker* — but they tell you it's supposed to make it feel better. When you're a kid you don't get to argue about it."

YOU'RE PROBABLY WONDERING

The proximity of their home to the arsenal's mustard-gas tanks also meant they were issued gas masks. "I just took it as a fact of life," Zappa told *Playboy* in 1993. "We lived in a place where we were obliged to have gas masks hanging on the wall in case the tanks broke, because you could die. Thinking back on it, if those tanks had broken, those gas masks wouldn't have saved us." Frank preferred to think of his gas mask as a space helmet. One time, he explored the contents of the can that hung at the end of the nose. He saw within it a collection of crystals and charcoal. He was thrilled to find detaching the can improved the space helmet. "My father got very upset when I opened it because I broke it and he would have to get me another one, which he never did. I was defenseless."

His son's poor health forced Francis to take a job in Florida near the Miami Canal in Opa-Locka. Although Frank's condition did improve, it turned out to be a brief reprieve because Rosemarie became homesick. The next move led to a new position in Pikesville, Maryland. Frank's health was the main factor in his father not taking a job at the Dugway Proving Ground nerve-gas production facility near Salt Lake City, Utah.

The Zappa family was devoutly Catholic, and though Francis and Rosemarie tried to put their son in a parochial school, Frank's attendance there was brief. "I used to have to go to catechism class and the nuns would show you charts of hell," Zappa recalled in *High Times*. "They would flip the page back and show you the fire and monsters and shit in there that could happen to you if you do all this stuff." Zappa attended church until he was eighteen, when it dawned on him that it was a perpetuation of suffering. "Suddenly, the light bulb went on over my head," Zappa told journalist David Sheff. "All the mindless morbidity and discipline was pretty sick — bleeding this, painful that, and no meat on Friday. What is this shit?"

In later years, Zappa developed the skepticism of a seasoned scientist. He dabbled in Zen Buddhism and tai chi, but saw Christianity as a faith whose tenets encouraged people to close their minds and accept professed dogma, which ran contrary to Zappa's hunger for knowledge. "This country has an anti-intellectual history that goes back to the first bundling board," he said. "You know, thinking is bad for you. As a matter of fact, you can trace it back to the beginning of Christian doctrine. The whole foundation of Christianity is based on the idea that intellectualism is the work of the Devil."

Zappa expanded on this in 1991 in *Spin*, talking about how the Christian doctrine was intrinsically linked to the American Way: "To the right-wing guys, there's nothing more dangerous than free access to information. And you know where that stems from? It stems from the beginning of Christian theology. When Adam and Eve were in the garden, how did we get in trouble? It wasn't because it was an apple, it was the fruit of the tree of knowledge, so the essence of Christianity is, nobody gets to be smarter than God, and access to knowledge and ownership of knowledge damns you. Knowledge itself is the work of the devil. We must not have knowledge, and what leads to knowledge? Information. Nip it right there, nip it in the bud." Zappa came to see any fundamentalist creed as a system of belief that created more discord and violence than peace and brotherhood. "Take the *Kama Sutra*. How many people died from the *Kama Sutra* as opposed to the Bible? Who wins?" Zappa asked the BBC's Nigel Leigh.

In November 1950, Francis took a metallurgy teaching position at the Naval Post-Graduate School in Monterey, California, where Candy was born a year later. In 1953, the family headed to Pacific Grove on the South Peninsula. Francis figured the West Coast climate would be so warm that he gave the family's winter clothing to a poor black family they met on the journey. But Monterey turned out to be cold and damp in the winter months. Money was also in short supply, so Francis often resorted to desperate measures. Each week, he took part in three or four top-secret government chemical test injections at $10 a shot, to make some extra money. Francis also exposed his family to a *Grapes of Wrath* lifestyle by taking to the road and picking up lettuce that had fallen from produce trucks.

While still entertaining ideas of becoming a scientist, Frank was also fascinated with music. "I went to my grandmother's funeral when I was little," he told *Playboy*. "I sat there looking at the candles. The choir was singing, and when they would hit a note, the candles would respond to it. I didn't know why . . . but it was a physical manifestation of a sound. . . . I put it in the memory bank to see what I could do with it later." He was also intrigued by the way music looked on the page. "It was fascinating to me that you could see the notes and somebody who knew what they were doing would look at them and music would come out," Zappa remarked. To stoke his fascination, Frank's parents let him attend a summer-school course for kids eager to join the drum and bugle brigade. The instructor, Keith McKillop, introduced Frank to the drums — his first musical instrument of choice — at age twelve. Initially, the family became alarmed when they witnessed the budding percussionist enthusiastically whacking the hell out of their furniture. In a desperate measure to save their kitchen table, they rented a snare drum so Frank could freely pound away in the garage. There, he composed his first percussion piece, "Mice," for a junior high school competition.

YOU'RE PROBABLY WONDERING

By the time he turned thirteen, Frank had moved six times. In 1953, the family lived in Pomona, California, where his father got a job as a metallurgist with the airplane manufacturer Convair. The next year, they were on the road again, traveling to El Cajon, where the elder Zappa worked on the Atlas guided missile system while Frank attended Grossamont High School. Even though he continued to experiment with explosives, Frank won the grand prize for his school's Fire Prevention Week poster in Grade 9. The design, which displayed an early example of Zappa's droll wit, featured three young faces (resembling the simple cartoon drawings of the kids from *South Park*) standing behind a fence with deeply disappointed and angry expressions. Above their heads were the words "NO PICNIC." Written along the fence was "WHY?" Beneath the fence lay the answer: "NO WOODS. Prevent Forest Fire."

Frank Zappa never developed any long-term friendships; he often referred to his bandmates as "employees" whose checks he had to sign. The constantly changing social circumstances in his youth greatly contributed to his need to become a homebody in his adult life. "There was little time to form friendships in the anonymous housing projects in which the family lived," Zappa told Nigel Leigh. "I never had the ethnic neighborhood upbringing experience. I was moving all the time and living in mixed company, so I never had that real strong meatball-sandwich identity."

Zappa would find an identity of his own through the music he encountered. His first discovery was the avant-garde composer Edgard Varèse.

2

I dream of instruments obedient to my thought and which with their contribution of a whole new world of unsuspected sounds will lend themselves to the exigencies of my inner rhythm.

EDGARD VARÈSE, 1917

On the night of May 29, 1913, Edgard Varèse sat in attendance at the Théâtre des Champs Elysées in Paris watching the infamous premiere performance of Stravinsky's *The Rite of Spring*. This was an evening considered by many to mark the spiritual birth of the 20th century. While abuse was being hurled at the stage, and indignation toward this "barbaric" music raged around him, Varèse calmly wondered what all the fuss was about. At the turn of the 20th century, many composers were growing tired of tonality. They resented its adherence to a single key as the only accepted foundation for musical composition. Arnold Schoenberg, the Austro-Hungarian composer born in 1874, developed the twelve-tone system, an approach allowing all twelve notes of the chromatic scale to be played before the first note is played again. This open-ended arrangement offered composers the opportunity to compose disciplined atonal music that would be equivalent to the more traditional tonal system.

Anton Webern, an Austrian composer who studied with Schoenberg, re-interpreted the twelve-tone form, writing with an abstract sparseness that influenced a whole generation of 20th-century composers, including Pierre Boulez and Karlheinz Stockhausen.

Igor Stravinsky headed in a different direction. He was less interested in harmony and more dedicated to what Frank Rossiter describes as "a return to the artistic ideals (and often to the specific musical forms) of the pre-romantic era." According to Rossiter, Stravinsky's music was "more objective and less personal, more concerned with form and less with content, more abstract and less programmatic, more craftsmanlike and less Byronic."

Varèse took an even more radical route. Born in France in 1883, he questioned the very principles of Western music altogether. He embarked on a search for a new music filled with the sounds of sirens, woodblocks, and eventually electronic tape. His influence was so deeply felt within the musical community that jazz saxophonist Charlie Parker once wanted Varèse to take him on as a student. Avant-garde composers John Cage and Stockhausen sought out his work. By the late '60s, progressive rock groups like King Crimson and Pink Floyd utilized Varèse's tape experiments, as did John Lennon and Yoko Ono in their tape collage "Revolution 9," from the Beatles' *White Album*. Even the rock band Chicago chipped in with "A Hit for Varèse" in 1971.

For Varèse, music was a scientific construct of sounds where the score sheets served as his simulated laboratory. He even had the wild and frizzy hair of those mad scientists from horror movies. Edgard Varèse wanted instruments that offered what he called "a whole new world of unsuspecting sounds." Like Zappa, Varèse developed a scientific approach to music. Much of his career was taken up with pure sound. In 1907, Varèse encountered pianist Ferruccio Busoni and his book *Sketch of a New Aesthetic of Music*. Varèse later wrote: "I had read his remarkable little book . . . and when I came across his dictum 'Music was born free and

YOU'RE PROBABLY WONDERING

to win freedom is its destiny,' I was amazed and very much excited to find that there was someone besides myself — and a musician at that — who believed this. It gave me courage to go on with my ideas and my scores."

From there, Varèse set out on his quest for "the bomb that would explode the musical world and allow all the sounds to come rushing into it through the resulting breach." In July 1921, Varèse organized an International Composers Guild dedicated to the presentation of works by Stravinsky, Schoenberg, and Webern, and wrote a manifesto that laid out the goals of the Guild. Nearly half a century later, these aspirations would be invoked as a clarion call by Frank Zappa. "Dying is the privilege of the weary," it reads in part. "The present-day composer refuses to die. They have realized the necessity of banding together and fighting for the right of the individual to secure a fair and free presentation of his work. . . . It is out of such collective will that the International Composers Guild was born."

Despite sufficient financial support, however, Varèse could not find a mass audience for this difficult music — he couldn't even find musicians eager to play the highly technical scores. The Guild's first concert at the Greenwich Village Theatre drew only three hundred people. The Guild soon splintered over which compositions to use, and Varèse's tendency to ruthlessly dominate the group. Eventually, Varèse decided to start composing material himself. He embarked on his first work, *Ameriques*, and declared, "I refuse to limit myself to sounds that have already been heard." In the piece, a solo flute is constantly interrupted by loud blasts from the orchestra, which sets up a significant tension between the solitary sound of the wind instrument and the larger instrumental projections. Another piece, *Ionisation*, requires a group of thirteen musicians who can play a total of thirty-seven percussion instruments, including a gong, Chinese blocks, tam-tams, snare drums, and Cuban claves. What Varèse was after with this bevy of percussive toys was timbre — sound in its purest form — rather than pitch. Zappa would draw on many of these innovations in dozens of his own compositions. (His most humorous nod to *Ionisation* is his low-rent homage "The Clap," from his 1970 album *Chunga's Revenge*. Zappa performs solo on a selection of woodblocks, tam-tams, temple blocks, and a miniature drum set.)

In 1925, Varèse moved to Greenwich Village, where he began work on his boldest score. *Arcana* needed an orchestra of 120 musicians, over seventy strings, along with eight percussionists playing close to forty percussion instruments. It received its premiere in 1927, with Leopold Stokowski conducting. In the '30s and '40s, Varèse explored numerous electro-mechanical devices, plus instruments such as the theremin and the Ondes Martenot that predated the Moog synthesizer. In addition to composing his magnetic-tape masterpiece *Deserts* in 1955, Varèse ventured further into electronic music. He wanted to find — and invent — instruments that would best articulate the sounds he heard in his head.

But Varèse couldn't get grants from the Guggenheim Foundation to help finance his search. American musical circles had become progressively conventional and conservative, driving the American avant-garde underground. Although he continued to believe that new instruments were necessary to free the composer, Varèse grew depressed. He would still compose scores, but only to destroy them in despair.

Frank Zappa told *Downbeat* in 1981 that it was significant that Varèse never received the acclaim in America that he had found in Europe. "He did go to Europe for a while and achieved more success in France during the '30s than he had in the United States," Zappa explained. "Even the critics that didn't like his music didn't dismiss him as a buffoon.... He was written about in the United States like he was some kind of quack who didn't know what he was doing." Zappa, who soon enough would also be considered a quack, knew exactly what Varèse was doing. And like his idol, he would chart his own form of musical expression and freedom.

3

Zappa asserted that he first discovered Edgard Varèse in an article about him in a 1950 issue of *Look*, where Sam Goody, a popular record merchant, claimed he could sell anyone a recording of Varèse's *Ionisation*. According to Greg Russo, in his thorough Frank Zappa encyclopedia, *Cosmik Debris*, Zappa's memory is faulty on this detail. Russo says it was Joseph Roddy's "Record Guide" column in *Look* that discussed the Varèse LP. Russo says there was no mention of Sam Goody, because Samuel Gutowitz (Goody's real name) did not start operations until 1951 — the year after the article was published. Russo figures Zappa saw a mention of the Varèse album in one of Goody's catalogs for record buyers from 1953 or 1954.

In any event, the title of the album was *Complete Works of Edgard Varèse, Volume 1*, on the obscure Elaine Music Store label. Although Zappa didn't purchase the record just yet, he set his sights on acquiring it. During this time, Zappa was also becoming an avid collector of R&B and blues 45s. While visiting his friend Dave Franken in La Mesa, California, Frank ventured into a store having a sale on singles. After selecting some R&B numbers by Joe Houston, he took a look in the LP section and found a scratched demo copy of the Varèse album. Zappa didn't have enough money to purchase this treasure, so he returned Houston to the bin and convinced the store owner to lower the price of the LP from $5.95 to $3.75.

As the proud new owner of the long-sought Varèse album, Zappa proceeded to play the LP on the family record player in the living room. "I had a genuine lo-fi," Zappa recalled in *Stereo Review* in 1971. "It was a little box about four inches deep with imitation wrought-iron legs at each corner. . . . My mother kept it near the ironing board. She used to listen to a 78 of 'The Little Shoemaker' on it." Zappa took his mother's favorite tune off the turntable, changed the speed from 78 rpm to 33 rpm, turned up the volume, and suddenly Varèse's *Ionisation* filled the room. It so upset his mother that he could only listen to it in his own room. "I have a nice Catholic mother who likes roller derby," Zappa once remarked wryly. "Edgard Varèse does not get her off, even to this day. I was forbidden to play that record in the living room ever again."

What Frank heard that day changed his life. This music had sirens and lots of drums. "The way I perceived the dissonance was, these chords are really mean," Zappa told Nigel Leigh. "I like these chords. And the drums are playing loud in this music and you can hear the drums often in this music, which is something that you could not experience in other types of classical music." Zappa may not have yet understood the particular forces that created a composer like Varèse, but the sounds were startlingly fresh.

Zappa played the record repeatedly, even if only in his bedroom — saving the best parts for his friends. "What I used to do was play them parts of the Varèse album and then play them Lightnin' Slim things like 'My Starter Won't Work' or 'Have Your Way,'" Zappa recalled. "Or I'd play them some Howlin' Wolf. . . . Usually that would get rid of the girls and the ignorant boys, and what was left over was somebody you could have a conversation with."

He started visiting his local library to find out everything he could about Varèse. Zappa discovered the Juilliard Percussion Orchestra's performance of *Ionisation*, which became his favorite track. The New York Wind Ensemble accompanied the orchestra for *Intégrales*, Varèse's largest ensemble piece for winds and percussion. The Wind Ensemble also performed solo on *Octandre*, the softest of Varèse's scores for horns and woodwinds. Flautist René Le Roy handled *Density 21.5*, a quiet and contemplative piece for solo flute.

Zappa was impressed that the record, although conducted by Frédéric Waldman, was recorded under the supervision of Varèse himself. "The thing I liked about that music was the arrogance that a person could make that kind of break with tradition," Zappa told Karen Gordon in 1991. "The twelve-tone composers made a break with tradition, but it was done in a very mathematical, calculating, and philosophical way that evolved out of a romantic tradition. It rebelled against that tradition in a certain way — in a part of the world that was stewing in this other kind of music. And so, there was a different motivation for Schoenberg, Berg, and Webern to go in the direction they went. But Varèse was out on a limb. The ultimate arrogance to turn to the whole musical world and say, 'Okay, look at this!' He flopped it right out there. Here comes *Ionisation*. Pretty bold."

In 1955, while attending Mission Bay High School in San Diego, fourteen-year-old Frank joined his first band, the Ramblers, led by Elwood Jr. Madeo and pianist Stuart Congdon. Zappa's parents bought him a second-hand drum kit. It was in San Diego that Zappa first absorbed some of the arcane aspects of '50s American pop culture. For instance, knowing how key owning a particular car was in picking up girls. Such esoteric details decorated many of Zappa's later songs like "Dog Breath, in the Year of the Plague" and "Cruising for Burgers." "In San Diego, where I was growing up, there were some very ferocious car clubs with these plaques that would drag on the pavement because the cars were lowered all the way around," Zappa told Pasadena DJ Les Carter in 1967. "The status car then was an icebox-white '39 Chevy with primer spots. But the customs and folklore of the American teenager are very curious in that they vary so much from area to area." A female gang called the Blue Velvets sponsored the Ramblers' first gig at the Uptown Hall in San Diego. They earned a hefty seven dollars for their effort. Unfortunately, Zappa forgot his drumsticks at home.

Zappa got fired by Madeo, though, for a different reason — he overworked the cymbals. This left the rejected percussionist practising alone in the high school's band room. "My main drawback," Zappa told David Mead of *Guitarist* in 1993, "was that I didn't have good hand-to-foot coordination. I could play a lot of stuff on the snare and the tom-toms and the cymbal and everything, but I couldn't keep an even beat on the kick drum. That was the reason I became no longer employed as a drummer — nobody could dance to it!"

Ruth Underwood, who became a percussionist in Zappa's band in the '70s, agreed with Zappa's assessment of his drumming style — even while she enjoyed the spectacle of his performance. "I loved watching him play the drums because he had a very unorthodox way of holding the sticks, sitting, flailing away — somehow everything came out great, but he looked ridiculous," she told *Musician*. "He came

YOU'RE PROBABLY WONDERING

up with some remarkable percussion writing because of his insight, his experience, in addition to his ears."

As fate would have it, Zappa ran into another drummer, Vic Mortenson, along with trumpet player Alex Snouffer, both of whom would later be founding members of Captain Beefheart and His Magic Band. After a few weeks of playing with these guys, and realizing that Mortenson was the more seasoned drummer, Zappa decided to learn to play his father's guitar. "My father had a guitar he kept in a closet, a round-hole guitar of anonymous make, and I stuck one of those DeArmond sound-hole pickups in that, so it wasn't a *real* electric guitar," Zappa told David Mead. "There was a music store not far from my house, and I rented this Telecaster for fifteen dollars a month. Eventually I had to give it back, because I couldn't make the repayments on it." On his fifteenth birthday, Frank's parents offered him a gift of five dollars toward the payments on the guitar. He told his mother, though, that he'd rather make a long-distance call to New York in an attempt to find Edgard Varèse.

Since Varèse looked like a "mad scientist," Zappa assumed he must live in the bohemian enclave of Greenwich Village. On the day Zappa called, Varèse's wife, Louise, told him Varèse was in Brussels, working on his *Poème Electronique* for the World's Fair. Varèse and Zappa spoke when the composer returned, and they agreed to meet soon. Zappa wrote a letter to Varèse in 1957; he would be visiting his Aunt Mary in Baltimore and hoped to make a trip to New York to meet Varèse. Varèse wrote back: "Dear Mr. Zappa. I am sorry not to be able to grant you your request. I am leaving for Europe next week and will be gone until next spring. I am hoping to see you on my return. With best wishes...." They never did get together. Varèse died on November 6, 1965. Zappa met Louise in 1974 and took part in a tribute to Varèse on April 17, 1981, at the Palladium in New York. This concert, part of a program selected by Louise, was performed by the Orchestra of Our Time, conducted by Joel Thome. As a memento of their brief encounter on the phone, Zappa framed the letter and hung it in his workroom in Laurel Canyon, where it remains.

4

By the mid-'50s, Frank Zappa encountered another style of music that would have an indelible effect on him. Doo-wop was a form of R&B rooted in the black gospel quartets. The new vocal harmony groups, like the Spaniels and the Crows, bridged both the gospel and secular worlds. They were quintets who perched on street corners and integrated nonsense syllables into wildly passionate love ballads.

Zappa responded to the complex vocal textures and the authentic attitude of the performers. He saw no difference between the popular sounds of R&B and the intricate orchestrations of Edgard Varèse.

What Zappa heard in "I" by the Velvets was some of the most innovative R&B singing for 1953. The Velvets, who came from Harlem, turned a simple plea for a girl's love into an elaborate tightrope walk. Charles Sampson, the lead singer, took the word *I* and drew out every kernel of longing he could find in it. While the backbeat propped him up, Sampson stretched out each syllable until you thought the yearning alone would collapse his lungs. "I" anticipated some of the vocal pyrotechnics to come in the late '50s. "Gee," by the Crows, was also released in 1953. This affectionately buoyant song — composed in ten minutes — opens with the singer professing his never-ending love by playfully bouncing over the lyrics. The words are basic romance fare, but Zappa was probably astonished by the way the vocalist tap-danced all over the word *so* when he proclaimed, "I love her so-oh-ohh-oh-oh."

"It was records — not TV, which I didn't watch — that brainwashed me," Zappa said in *Evergreen* in 1970, describing his mounting obsession with R&B and doo-wop. "I'd listen to them over and over again. The ones I couldn't buy, I'd steal, and the ones I couldn't steal, I'd borrow, but I'd get them somehow. I had about six hundred records — 45s — at one time."

Although music was consuming most of his time and interest, Zappa hadn't given up his love for things that detonated. One day, he and a friend filled a large glass jar with a combination of zinc, sulfur, and stink-bomb powder. They then collected a supply of paper cups and proceeded to disrupt an open-house night with a series of fires that gave off a pungent odor. The next day, Zappa and his friend received a stern lecture from the principal and a fire officer. They were punished by having to write a two-thousand-word essay during a two-week suspension. Zappa took the two weeks and came back not with an essay, but a list of his R&B records by song title, artist, and label, plus those he expected to buy in the not-too-distant future.

In 1956, Frank had reached his sophomore year, and the family moved to Lancaster in the Antelope Valley, north of Los Angeles. While his father worked at Edwards Air Force Base, Zappa attended Antelope Valley Joint Union High School. Lancaster was a desert town once known for the cultivation of alfalfa before the aerospace industry arrived. In his sublime Zappa biography, *Electric Don Quixote*, Neil Slaven gives a vivid description of this arid borough. "As the town grew, its

YOU'RE PROBABLY WONDERING

streets were laid out on a geometric grid, with the odd bend to keep drunk drivers alert. To this day, many outlying roads only exist as 'Avenue F-10' or 'G-14.' Downtown hides amongst the endless rows of anonymous streets. Dust from the Mohave makes Lancaster an arid, shabby town of pastel colors."

Euclid James Sherwood, a childhood friend and future band member in the Mothers of Invention, remembered Lancaster all too well. "Lancaster was just a barren town," Sherwood told Nigel Leigh. "It seems like all the misfits from Los Angeles and San Bernardino counties were sent up there to get out of everybody else's face. There wasn't really anything to do there. You spent most of your time just wandering around through the desert, trying to occupy yourself with anything. That's probably why most people got into music or drinking all the time. On weekends that's about all there was to do." It was out of that culturally barren climate that Zappa became enthralled with the neoclassical work of Igor Stravinsky, and, in particular, *The Rite of Spring*. Zappa purchased an LP of the score by the World Wide Symphony Orchestra on RCA Victor's Camden budget label. What Zappa didn't know was that there was a misprint on the album. It was really performed by the Boston Symphony Orchestra, conducted by Pierre Monteux. Monteux just happened to be the guy standing on the podium, waving his wand desperately, at the work's riot-filled premiere in Paris on May 29, 1913.

5

People always expect the wrong thing of me. They think they have pinned me down and then all of a sudden — au revoir!

IGOR STRAVINSKY

Looking back, it comes as no surprise that if any one composer in the 20th century could cause a riot, it would be Igor Stravinsky. Unpredictable in nature, and comparable in stature to painter Pablo Picasso, Stravinsky was an enigmatic figure who moved like a chameleon through the cultural world. He made his reputation with his erotically charged masterpieces *The Firebird*, *Petrushka*, and *The Rite of Spring*. Through these works, Stravinsky had forsaken the world of romanticism and forged a new style of neoclassicism. Yet right at the moment when he was pioneering that phase of his musical career, he joined forces with his serialist adversaries, Webern and Schoenberg, who had abandoned classicism altogether.

Stravinsky was born in St. Petersburg in 1882, and from a very early age showed a great aptitude for music. In 1903, he met the colorful Russian composer Nikolai Rimsky-Korsakov, who took him on as a pupil. In his biography of Stravinsky, Eric Walter White says that Rimsky-Korsakov had "become a sort of father-figure in his life following the death of [Stravinsky's] father in 1902." The only other figure Stravinsky admired more than his father was Pyotr Ilich Tchaikovsky. Tchaikovsky was revered in Russia, and his ballet *Sleeping Beauty* became one of Stravinsky's favorites — despite the sweepingly romantic character of the music.

In the early 19th century, due to its isolation and nationalistic fervor, Russia drew more on its own folk tradition than any other type of European "art" music. And still its folk music found its way into other cultures. Mikhail Glinka borrowed numerous Russian folk tunes for his first major work, *A Life for the Tsar*, while he was living in Berlin and Paris. Its international success in 1822 had a huge impact on Russian society. "Soon after the appearance of *A Life for the Tsar*, it became apparent that two philosophies of music were emerging which reflected the age-old division of Russian thought on everything ranging from art to politics," Joan Peyser writes in *To Boulez and Beyond*. "One group was committed to a Pan-Slavic orientation that precluded Western influences; the other was in favor of assimilating the wealth of the West."

The composers favoring the Pan-Slavic orientation called themselves the Nationalist Five. They included prominent 19th-century composers like Modest Mussorgsky, Alexander Borodin, and Nikolai Rimsky-Korsakov. They sought to "make art the servant of the people" and resist the pull of Western influences. That changed with the arrival of Tchaikovsky later in the century. He blended Russian folk melodies into the European classical tradition to enormous international success. According to Peyser, Stravinsky belonged to an era when the West and Russia had a mutual cultural identification.

In 1909, Russia's top impresario, Serge Diaghilev, heard two of Stravinsky's first compositions, *Scherzo fantastique* and *Feu d'artifice*, at a concert in St. Petersburg. Diaghilev was so impressed that he commissioned Stravinsky to write a couple of numbers for a ballet he was producing. Out of that encounter came *The Firebird* (1910), which was an overnight success. While not as daring or innovative as his later ballet scores, *The Firebird* still had something more foreboding than the exotic colors of Rimsky-Korsakov. Diaghilev could see that Stravinsky's work had "a latent barbarism" where he reveled in "an unusual combination of rhythms."

YOU'RE PROBABLY WONDERING

That "latent barbarism" would become more explicit in his next work for Diaghilev, *Petrushka* (1911). This piece, with its polytonality and sharper rhythms, caused something of a small commotion.

Petrushka, the story of a puppet who is bestowed with life, premiered in 1911, with the legendary dancer Nijinsky in the title role. At that time, Nijinsky was revolutionizing ballet dancing in much the same way Stravinsky was revolutionizing music. They both were taking the formal decorum out of their respective art forms and releasing the inherent primal impulses in their pieces. The ballet had parodic elements, repetitive rhythms, and passages where Stravinsky echoed the mechanical and soulless world in which Petrushka found himself. The composer also included a bitonal effect that illuminated the dual elements in Petrushka's character — both his mechanical and human sides. "I had conceived of the music in two keys in the second tableau as Petrushka's insult to the public," Stravinsky remarked, "and I wanted the dialogue for trumpets in two keys at the end to show that his ghost is still insulting the public."

Though *Petrushka* caused some controversy, it was nothing compared to Stravinsky's next score, *The Rite of Spring* (1913). This startling new piece was a culmination of what Stravinsky was working toward in *The Firebird* and *Petrushka*. The idea for the music and story had come to him a few years earlier. "One day, when I was finishing the last pages of *The Firebird* in St. Petersburg, I had a fleeting vision," Stravinsky recalled. "I saw in my imagination a solemn pagan rite: sage elders, seated in a circle, watching a young girl dance herself to death. They were sacrificing her to propitiate the god of spring." The score called for the largest orchestra Stravinsky had ever assembled (and with plenty of percussion). This was no romantic piece about the genial spirit within nature, or the renewing elements of the seasons; *The Rite of Spring* was about the scourge of dehumanization. Russian and Hungarian folk tunes were introduced in *The Rite of Spring*, but even if the themes were familiar, the instruments played them in unfamiliar registers. Stravinsky had the time signatures change rapidly after each bar. The bassoon sounded like it had a bad cold. Arpeggios blurted from wood instruments. Meanwhile, the pizzicato of the first violins set the pace, with running sequences filled with squawks, trills, and shrieks. The music prodded with an erotic force.

On the night of the infamous premiere at the Théâtre des Champs Elysées on May 29, 1913, Stravinsky could sense trouble in the audience right from the opening notes. Paul Kennedy, a writer/broadcaster on the Canadian Broadcasting

Corporation's *Ideas* radio program, remarks that "the smart audience in tails and jewels were interspersed with the aesthetic crowd — the latter would clap just to show contempt for the rich folks in the boxes. Snobbery of all kinds was present. . . . [T]iaras sparkled and silk flowed. In addition to lavishly attired snobs, there were aesthetic snobs too, who had come in ordinary suits, some with *bandeaux*, some with soft hats of one sort or another, which were considered a mark of revolt against the stiff toppers and bowlers of the upper classes."

It was an audience that historian Modris Eksteins describes in *Rites of Spring*, his illuminating study of the birth of the modern age, as one "to be scandalized, of course, but equally to scandalize. The brouhaha . . . was to be as much in audience reactions to their fellows as in the work itself. The dancers on-stage must have wondered at times who was performing and who was in the audience."

Stravinsky recalled the first stirrings of dissension: "I heard Florent Schmitt shout, 'Taisez-vous garces du seizieme'; the 'garces' of the 16th arrondissement were, of course, the most elegant ladies in Paris. The uproar continued, however, and a few minutes later I left the hall in a rage; I was sitting on the right near the orchestra and I remember slamming the door. I have never been that angry." The music he created and loved was being ridiculed. The piece was called "monstrous," a "massacre," and the choreography compared to "epileptic seizures."

As Kennedy points out, *The Rite of Spring* represented the violence of birth *and* death. It was the wiping out of an idealized past of romance and pining — with the modernist sensibility of a James Joyce lurking right around the corner. As choreographer, Nijinsky was after the true essence of the body's gestures. He wanted the ensemble work of groups stomping about in unison, their movements brutal and harsh, the rhythms complex. The conventions of beauty were revealed to be dying, and the serenity of those conventions were rendered obsolete. *The Rite of Spring* broke through into an ugliness that evolved into a new beauty. Within the piece, one could hear the primitive forces that anticipated the savagery of the world wars, which would kill millions; the brutality of the Russian Revolution, which would turn the world upside down and force Stravinsky from his homeland; the Holocaust; the carnage of famines; and the inflamed passions of nationalism that would unleash massacres around the world.

Even though Stravinsky and *The Rite of Spring* would gain acceptance in the coming years, he continued to experiment and challenge musical conventions. He broke with the Russian orchestral school during World War I and started working

YOU'RE PROBABLY WONDERING

with smaller ensembles. Stravinsky settled in Paris after the Russian Revolution, and, beginning with *Pulcinella* (1920), started his foray into neoclassicism. In the '30s, with the death of his wife and his child from tuberculosis, and World War II imminent, Stravinsky left Paris. He eventually settled in the United States, where he was introduced to the work of Anton Webern. Because of Webern, Stravinsky embraced the twelve-tone techniques of his former musical sparring partners.

The impact of Igor Stravinsky on Frank Zappa was nearly as great as that of Edgard Varèse. The orchestral color of *Hot Rats* (1969) owes a great deal to Stravinsky; the *Cruising With Ruben & the Jets* (1968) doo-wop album was Zappa's own nod to neoclassicism; "Igor's Boogie," from *Burnt Weeny Sandwich* (1970), was an affectionate tribute to Stravinsky; "Invocation and Ritual Dance of the Young Pumpkin," from *Absolutely Free* (1967), and "Drowning Witch," from *Ship Arriving Too Late to Save a Drowning Witch* (1982), are unthinkable without *The Rite of Spring*; and "Titties 'n Beer," from *Zappa in New York* (1978), is a recasting of Stravinsky's *L'Histoire du soldat* in a modern American idiom. Ben Watson points out that Stravinsky's pounding rhythms gave Zappa another key to orchestration. "Where Varèse achieves shock," Watson writes, "Stravinsky achieves splendor. . . . Zappa saw something in Stravinsky's exotic 'Eastern' barbarity that corresponded with elements of R&B." This convergence became nothing less than an astonishing epiphany for Zappa.

6

Frank Zappa was becoming deeply influenced by the black R&B and blues records he was collecting. "I had been raised in an environment where there wasn't a lot of music in the house," Zappa told Nigel Leigh. "This couple that owned the chili place, Opal and Chester, agreed to ask the man who serviced the jukebox to put in some of the song titles that I liked, because I promised that I would dutifully keep pumping quarters into this thing so I could listen to them. So I had the ability to eat good chili, and listen to 'Three Hours Past Midnight' by Johnny 'Guitar' Watson, for most of my junior and senior years."

Johnny "Guitar" Watson was one of the hottest blues guitarists on the West Coast during the '50s — even though his roots were in the blues environment of Houston, Texas, where he was born in 1935. At fifteen, Watson headed to Los Angeles, eventually playing piano and singing in saxophonist Chuck Higgins' band in 1952. He signed with Federal Records in 1953 as Young John Watson, and continued to develop into a fine singer. The next year, Watson switched from the piano to the guitar and came up with the rapid-fire instrumental "Space Guitar."

What distinguished Watson's playing (and no doubt impressed Zappa) was his quick and truculent attack on the notes. "One of the things I admired about him was his tone," Zappa told *Guitarist*, "this wiry, kind of nasty, aggressive, and penetrating tone, and another was the fact that the things he would play would often come out as rhythmic outbursts over the constant beat of the accompaniment.... It seemed to me that was the correct way to approach it, because it was like talking or singing over a background. There was a speech influence to the rhythm." (A good example of that "spoken" style of playing can be found on Zappa's guitar contribution to Jeff Simmons' version of "Lucille Has Messed My Mind Up" in 1969.)

In 1955, Watson signed with the RPM label, where he cut some of his most distinctive records: "Hot Little Mama," the gospel-influenced "Someone Cares for Me," the ripping "Three Hours Past Midnight," and his dynamic cover of the blues guitarist Earl King's "Those Lonely Lonely Nights." By the '60s, Watson hooked up with the Johnny Otis Band and cut his signature song, "Gangster of Love"; in 1962, he made the R&B charts with his soulful "Cuttin' In." After doing some jazz sides and moving to Britain, Watson eventually met Zappa in the mid-'70s and played on a number of his albums. The two stayed good friends until Zappa's death. Watson himself died of heart failure, while performing onstage, during his opening number in Yokohama, Japan, in 1996.

If Johnny "Guitar" Watson influenced the timbre of Zappa's guitar playing, "Guitar" Slim, and especially his song "The Story of My Life," inspired the attitude of Zappa's sound. "When I first heard ["The Story of My Life"], I thought, '*What the fuck is he doing? He really gets pissed off at it,*'" Zappa wrote in *The Real Frank Zappa Book*. "His style of playing seemed to be 'beyond the notes' — it had more to do with the 'attitude' with which he was mangling his instrument."

Born Edward (Eddie) Jones, in 1926, "Guitar" Slim hailed from Mississippi. Like many other rural blacks from that area, Slim migrated — but instead of heading north, he went to New Orleans. He patterned his style on Clarence "Gatemouth" Brown, and became a sensation covering many of Brown's great songs, including "My Time Is Expensive" and "Gatemouth Boogie." By 1951, Slim started recording for Imperial Records, but his first songs, "Bad Luck Is on Me" and "New Arrival," sold poorly.

In 1953, Slim became a hot item on the R&B circuit in the South. It was during those tours that Johnny Vincent, an A&R man from Specialty Records, heard him

YOU'RE PROBABLY WONDERING

and convinced label head Art Rube that Slim should be signed to a contract. The first song he recorded, the dynamic hit "The Things That I Used to Do," was augmented by none other than Ray Charles at the keyboards.

"Slim was very hard to record," Vincent remembered. "It took all night to record 'The Things That I Used to Do.'" Apparently, every time they did a take and Slim laid down a beautiful solo, he'd stop cold and turn to the band and say, "Gentlemen, did you hear that!" By the end of the day, when the take was finally completed, Charles could be heard at the end, no doubt out of exhaustion, sighing, "Yeah!" The record was the biggest R&B single of 1954.

What made the song so distinctive is exactly what most impressed Frank Zappa — the raw sound of Slim's guitar. "Slim was getting a fuzz-tone distortion way before anyone else was," Earl King once remarked. "You didn't hear it again until Jimi Hendrix came along." Slim's follow-up songs, "The Story of My Life" and "A Letter to My Girlfriend," were worthy successors to "The Things That I Used to Do," but they didn't chart. In an effort to make his songs more commercial, Rube started overdubbing an organ and burying Slim's aggressive guitar tone, but the plan backfired and sales began to slip badly.

Rube continued to record Slim anyway, and in his last session for Specialty in 1956, they restored his loud and distorted guitar. His last tracks for the label, "Something to Remember You By" and "You Give Me Nothing but the Blues," echoed his early work. Specialty failed to renew his contract in 1957, though, and Slim continued to work the road until his hard living — which included heavy drinking — caught up with him. He collapsed while playing in Rochester, New York, in 1959. After just barely making it through the performance, he was taken to the hospital, and died of bronchial pneumonia. After being flown back to Mississippi for a huge funeral, "Guitar" Slim was buried in an unmarked grave — with his trusty guitar right alongside him.

Zappa was also fond of Clarence "Gatemouth" Brown and Howlin' Wolf. "For my taste, [their] solos are exemplary because what is being played is honest and, in a musical way, a direct extension of the personality of the men who played them," Zappa told *Guitar Player* in 1977. "If I were a music critic, I would have to say that these values for me mean more than the ability to execute clean lines or clouds of educated gnat-notes."

Zappa's extensive knowledge of R&B and blues came from his frequent visits to Gilbert's Dime Store in Lancaster. Mr. Gilbert had a rack of jukebox records that he sold for a dime apiece, but he only ever stocked the shelf with popular tunes.

Zappa and his friends raided Gilbert's inventory on a daily basis, wanting to see what else arrived along with the current hits. Suddenly Zappa was getting records like Slim Harpo's majestic "I'm a King Bee" and recordings by the Orchids, the Spaniels, the Paragons, the Penguins, and other great West Coast doo-wop groups.

One of Zappa's frantic disc searches at Gilbert's led him to the R&B duo Don & Dewey. Starting out in 1955, Don & Dewey sat in with various doo-wop groups, such as the Squires from Pasadena, California. By 1956, Sonny Bono, who in those pre-Cher days was an A&R guy from Specialty Records, discovered Don & Dewey and signed them. Their first single was the self-penned "Leavin' It All Up to You" in 1957. "[Don] would play on electric violin and double on guitar, and the other one would play organ and sometimes bass, and they had this special type of vocal harmony which was very individualistic," Zappa told Les Carter.

They followed up "Leavin' It All Up to You" with Bono's "Koko Joe," and the radiant "Justine" in 1958. Their last big hit for Specialty was "Farmer John" the next year. "They had these gala costumes which were sort of Day-Glo rayon with bolero balls hanging all over their chest, phenomenally huge processed pompadours going up about two and a half feet from the top of their heads, and they really had it together," Zappa recalled gleefully. "Then the Righteous Brothers came along and borrowed their whole number and, because they were white, became very rich. Meanwhile, Don & Dewey don't function anymore." But many years later, Don Harris, who was now nicknamed "Sugarcane," continued to function somehow, and even joined Frank Zappa's band to perform on some memorable songs. During the '70s, he was in high demand, playing with blues artists John Mayall and Sonny Terry & Brownie McGhee. Harris died of pulmonary disease in 1996.

The other important R&B artist who helped inspire Zappa's career turned out to be one of Los Angeles' most influential performers: Richard Berry, who recorded blues and R&B tracks throughout the '50s. The one seminal song that touched off a storm, and dogged his career, was a lovely calypso tune that became an American frat-house classic — "Louie Louie."

7

Frank Rossiter writes that Thoreau believed an American popular tune could be quoted meaningfully in a symphony in the same way that an American colloquialism could work in a sentence. But it's unlikely Thoreau would have considered "Louie Louie" a worthy example. Frank Zappa, on the other hand, did. "Louie

YOU'RE PROBABLY WONDERING

Louie," the ultimate sex-joke song, was considered obscene because of its barely intelligible lyrics, yet it was still recorded by just about everyone: Iggy Pop, Barry White, Paul Revere & the Raiders, Julie London — even the Beach Boys. The version most people recognize is performed by the Kingsmen, a Top 40 cover band from Portland, Oregon.

One night in 1963, during a concert date, Kingsmen lead singer Jack Ely witnessed a group of people dancing in orgiastic ecstasy around the jukebox before the band hit the stage. The song playing was something called "Louie Louie," by the Wailers (no relation to Bob Marley). The Kingsmen decided they wanted some of that same action, and so they set out to learn the song. Ely made a mistake, however, by giving the band the wrong arrangement of the Wailers' interpretation. "Louie Louie" became something altogether different from the lilting calypso song Richard Berry had composed. The arrangement was more crude, with a relentlessly thumping beat pounded out on the guitar and organ. Nevertheless, the song had the desired effect at the Kingsmen's concerts. The band cut a single in May 1963, with the hope of having their first hit song. With its famous opening notes of DUH-DUH-DUH — DA-DA — DUH-DUH-DUH — DA-DA, and Ely slurring every insinuating word he could dream up, the only recognizable lyrics were simply "Louie Louie."

By September, the song was slowly climbing the charts (it was No. 94 in *Billboard*) when a rumor got started that it was obscene, and that Ely's mangled vocals were masking unimaginable sexual fantasies. By the end of the year, the song was banned from some radio stations in Indiana. The FBI and the Federal Communications Commission (FCC) even conducted an investigation in which they played the song at various speeds to determine what the lyrics meant. Many heard words much farther out than anything in Jack Ely's imagination:

At night at ten/I lay her again
Fuck you, girl/ Oh, all the way
Oh, my bed/And I lay her there
I meet a rose in her hair.

Oh, Louie Louie/Get her down low.

In the end, the FCC determined that they "found the record to be unintelligible at any speed." But the notoriety sent the song soaring up the charts, where it sold more than 8 million copies. Rock critic Dave Marsh, in his quirky book *Louie Louie: The History and Mythology of the World's Most Famous Rock 'n' Roll Song*, notes that the song's disrepute and success comes right out of America's divided consciousness:

> We're dealing with the concept of someone actually (well, possibly) singing about sex (sort of) in a nation that still goes into a giggling spasm when someone makes a fart joke, a society that tried to put a TV star, [Pee Wee Herman], in jail for jacking off at an adult film. America needs to foster panics like the ones over "Louie" and Pee Wee from time to time in order to have a way of releasing the tensions caused by so many self-consciously tightened sphincters, artificially dehydrated vulvas, and wilfully suppressed erections. In a culture that interprets puberty as a tragedy of lost innocence rather than as a triumphal entry into adulthood, the possibility of someone actually giving vent to sexual feeling remains deliriously scandalous. Sex is bad, and somebody singing about it would be really bad.

Richard Berry, the song's author and original performer, didn't foresee his soon-to-be-salacious tune ever turning into the monster hit adopted by bar bands across America. He was so certain, in fact, that years earlier, he had sold the rights to pay for his wedding.

Berry was born in 1935 in Extension, Louisiana, but when he was a year old, he was brought to Los Angeles, where he lived most of his life. At Jefferson High School, Berry was a respected member of the local doo-wop community. He played with the Flamingos and the Flairs, and recorded with reputable labels like Dolphin's of Hollywood, Flair Records, and Modern Records. Berry first made his mark providing the uncredited lead vocal on Leiber and Stoller's comic mini-opera "Riot in Cell Block #9" with the Robins (who later became the Coasters, a group critic Greil Marcus describes as sounding like "Stepin Fetchit as [an] advance man for black revolt"). Berry did his own sequel for "Riot" called "The Big Break" in 1954. He also provided the male counterpart voice for Etta James' recording of "Roll With Me, Henry," the sexual reply to Hank Ballard & the Midnighters' "Work With Me, Annie." Berry's vocal style was crazily dramatic, filled with affectation, and about as sly as a riverboat gambler. "I was always singing songs in different styles — Fats [Domino], Willie Mabon, [and] Johnny Ace," Berry explained. "I was like the Rich Little of Modern Records, a chameleon."

Berry wrote "Louie Louie" in 1955 and released it as a single two years later on Flip Records. The story behind its inception is legendary. Berry was playing with a local Latin R&B band known as Rick Rivera & the Rhythm Rockers, who performed a song called "El Loco Cha Cha Cha." The salsa-flavored tune had a persistent *dut-dut-dut* musical figure weaving through it. Berry couldn't get the notes out of his head and, waiting to perform at the Harmony Club Ballroom, superimposed new words over this riff. His other inspiration came from "One for My Baby," a song related from the viewpoint of a customer at a bar. The singer says to a bartender, "One for my baby, one for the road, set 'em up, Joe." In Berry's composition, however, the bartender is Louie, and the customer is telling Louie how he intends to sail to Jamaica. Even though it still has the DUH-DUH-DUH opening of Jack Ely's arrangement, the lyrics are far more intelligible:

Louie Louie/Me gotta go
Three nights and days/Me sail the sea
Me think of girl/constantly
On the ship/I dream she there
I smell the roses/in her hair.

The flavor of the song was cured by both his current Latin band and Chuck Berry's beautifully lilting "Havana Moon." Not much was expected from "Louie Louie" — in fact, it was recorded with the Pharaohs as a slow, seductive calypso number. "Louie Louie," intended as the B-side for the more popular standard "You Are My Sunshine," might well have fallen into obscurity were it not for the Kingsmen. "I was also in bands [playing] 'Louie Louie,' before the Kingsmen made it into the joke that everybody recognizes now," Zappa told Denn Simms of the Zappa fanzine *Society Pages*. "'Louie Louie' used to be a cool tune, the Richard Berry version of it. It had, y'know, a nice arrangement, and a whole different feel to it."

Zappa incorporated "Louie Louie" as a stock idiom in just about every album he recorded, and it wasn't out of malice toward Richard Berry. On the contrary, it was included as a snide indictment of how a lovely R&B song got turned into a ridiculous frat-house joke. Zappa was making a statement about the distinctly American method of cheapening an art form — and he extended that view beyond the world of rock. "When a guest conductor comes to town, he is not usually giving a performance of something by a living composer — because he can warm it up in one afternoon and make it sound okay," he wrote. "This makes the accountants happy, and allows the audience to concentrate on his choreography (which is really why they bought the tickets in the first place). Why is that any better than a bunch of guys in a bar band jamming on 'Louie Louie' or 'Midnight Hour'?"

For Zappa, it wasn't any better. He first transformed "Louie Louie" into "Plastic People," his attack on conformist freaks, on *Absolutely Free*. When he played Royal Albert Hall, in London, keyboardist Don Preston unleashed "Louie Louie" from their illustrious pipe organ. On album after album, "Louie Louie" would pop up at any moment to completely destroy an intricately beautiful piece of music, or to symbolize desperate acts of sexual incompetency. Zappa never resisted reminding the audience that the transformation of Richard Berry's "Louie Louie" stood for the idea of turning music into a stock cliché about sex.

8

While at Antelope Valley High School in 1956, Frank Zappa encountered vice-principal Ernest Tossi, who was in charge of enforcing discipline. The first task Tossi set for himself was to straighten out the fiercely independent Zappa. Tossi was "my favorite confrontation with authority," Zappa would recall. Yet, despite their differences, they had a mutual respect for each other. "Frank was an independent thinker who couldn't accept the Establishment's set of rules," Tossi told David Walley in *No Commercial Potential: The Saga of Frank Zappa*. "To make progress you've got to be creative. In my mind, if Frank chose to go academic to a university and get a PhD, he could. I saw his test scores and I know Frank has the talent of a genius."

William Ballard was Antelope Valley's music instructor and band director. To placate Zappa, he allowed him to write his experimental music, then had the school band attempt to play it. "He saved me a lot of effort in later life by letting me hear things like that," Zappa told *Q* magazine's Andy Gill. "Of course, the other people in the orchestra thought that I was out of my fucking mind." One of the orchestral compositions performed, "The String Quartet," contained two sections of what would later be titled "Sleeping in a Jar" and "A Pound for a Brown (On the Bus)" on the *Uncle Meat* album in 1969.

Zappa's sole musical outlet was the school band, but he managed to get kicked out for smoking under the bleachers — in uniform — during a break in a football

YOU'RE PROBABLY WONDERING

game. "When I was in senior high school, I was an incorrigible student," Zappa told *Guitarist*, "and one of the people in the office decided that maybe I would be socially better adjusted if I was given the opportunity to study something that I was actually interested in. So they arranged for me to go to the junior college to take a harmony course [for] one hour a week." Mr. Russell, a part-time jazz trumpeter and Zappa's harmony instructor, gave his student Walter Piston's *Harmony* to study. Piston wrote symphonies and taught such musicians as Leonard Bernstein and Elliott Carter. As Zappa told *Pulse*'s Dan Ouelette in 1993, "I was wondering why a person would really want to devote a lifetime to doing this, because after you complete [Piston's *Harmony*] you'll sound like everybody else who used the same rules. . . . I got the concept of what harmony was supposed to do, what voice leading was supposed to do, how melody was supposed to function in a harmonic climate. . . . I learned all of that and then chucked the rest of it."

Fortunately for us, Zappa's type of nonconformity found more comfortable expression in music rather than juvenile gang activity, and the new era of rock 'n' roll started to open up possibilities. "Rock music is a necessary element of contemporary society," Zappa wrote years later in *Life*. "It is functional. It is healthy and valid artistically. It is also educational (how to ask a girl for a date, what love is like). It has all the answers to what your mother and father won't tell you. It's also a big business." In that same article, "The Oracle Has It All Psyched Out," Zappa described his early reaction to hearing rock 'n' roll. "In my days of flaming youth, I was extremely suspect of any rock music played by white people. The sincerity and emotional intensity of their performances, when they sang about boyfriends and girlfriends and breaking up, etc., was nowhere when I compared it to my high school Negro R&B heroes like Johnny Otis, Howlin' Wolf, and Willie Mae Thornton."

Like many teenagers in 1955, though, Zappa happened into a theater where Richard Brooks' incendiary movie *The Blackboard Jungle* was playing. It was the story of a new teacher who begins a job at a school in the "wrong" part of town. Not only does he get a lot of grief from the underclass students he's trying to teach, one of his colleagues is trying to interest his charges in jazz. But the music of Stan Kenton and Bix Beiderbecke make no impressionable dent in their not-so-impressionable minds. (The poor teacher is forced to watch his prize collection of records get tossed around the room and smashed to bits.)

This film about juvenile delinquency hit the public nerve with the impact of an atom bomb — just as *The Wild One* had a year earlier and *Rebel Without a Cause* would the same year. All three movies dealt with adolescent angst and social unrest by making both issues vivid, real, and immediate — even identifiable to young audiences. Yet, in typical Hollywood fashion, these landmark films all tried to blunt their impact by candy-coating the stories in conventional melodrama. It didn't work, though. *The Blackboard Jungle* had introduced rock 'n' roll to mainstream audiences, through Bill Haley & the Comets' "Rock Around the Clock." This jumping tune, heard over the opening credits, got people in the audience hopping with an enthusiasm not seen since the beginning of the Swing Era. The movie — which featured the raw and exciting presence of Sidney Poitier — so startled the public that Clare Boothe Luce, the American ambassador to Italy, protested its inclusion in the Venice Film Festival that year because it incited people to violence.

"When the titles flashed up there on the screen, Bill Haley and his Comets started blurching 'One Two Three O'Clock [Four O'Clock] Rock . . . ,' it was the loudest rock sound kids had ever heard at that time," Zappa wrote. "I remember being inspired with awe. In cruddy little teenage rooms across America, kids had been huddling around old radios and cheap record players listening to the 'dirty music' of their lifestyle. . . . But in the theater, watching *The Blackboard Jungle*, [parents] couldn't tell you to turn it down." Suddenly, for Zappa, it didn't matter that Bill Haley & the Comets were a bunch of white guys singing black music: "He was playing the Teen-Age National Anthem, and it was so LOUD, I was jumping up and down. *The Blackboard Jungle*, despite the compromised storyline (which had the old people winning in the end), represented a strange sort of 'endorsement' of the teenage cause: 'They made a movie about us, therefore we exist. . . .'"

While *The Blackboard Jungle* opened Zappa's eyes to the early possibilities of rock, he formed a racially integrated R&B band called the Blackouts in 1956. The name came from the musicians' habit of passing out from the many peppermint schnapps they consumed. Zappa, who played drums, and pianist Terry Wimberly, were from white immigrant families, while Wayne Lyles and brothers Johnny and Carter Franklin were black, and the Salazar brothers (Fred on horn, and Wally on guitar) were Mexican-American. Their unofficial member was a new pal of Zappa's, Euclid James Sherwood, who would entertain the crowd with a dance dubbed "the Bug." This combo — and the music they played — was sure to offend the Ivy League elite of their school.

The Blackouts rehearsed in an all-black turkey-farming area outside Palmdale called Sun Village. They performed a ten-song set that included Andre Williams' "Bacon Fat," Little Richard's "Directly From My Heart to You," The Rockin' Brothers' "Behind the Sun," and Wilbert Harrison's hit, "Kansas City." Their most prominent

YOU'RE PROBABLY WONDERING

gig was at an NAACP benefit at Los Angeles Shrine Auditorium in 1958, where they opened for Earl Bostic and Louis Armstrong. They also had a successful spot, sponsored by the Eagles Lodge and entitled "the Summer Blowout," at the Lancaster Fairgrounds Exposition Hall. That night, the Blackouts shared the bill with Zappa's former band, the Ramblers. (This may explain why Zappa's field recording of the Blackouts talking about the gig on *The Lost Episodes* CD also features Elwood Jr. Madeo of the Ramblers. The tape may have been recorded after the show.)

Their most memorable concert, though, was one at the Lancaster Women's Club at a time when white people integrating with blacks was deeply frowned upon in Lancaster. The night before the show, Zappa was arrested for vagrancy and spent the night in jail. It turned out the arrest was calculated to prevent the dance from happening. But Zappa's parents bailed him out and the dance went on to be a success. After the show, some irate residents showed up itching for a fight just as the band were loading their stuff into Johnny Franklin's Studebaker. If it weren't for some supporters from Sun Village, armed with baseball bats, it might have turned ugly.

The Blackouts lasted a year and a half, breaking up when Zappa finished high school in June 1958. Years later, Zappa would commemorate those days with one of his few "sentimental" songs, "Village of the Sun," on the album *Roxy & Elsewhere* (1974). Zappa quit the drums and sold off his kit to another band. By December, he started to concentrate on playing the guitar. He wrote a piece called "Waltz for Guitar" that *Guitar Player* first published in their Zappa tribute issue in 1992.

In his last year of high school, Frank met a new friend — a young outcast named Don Vliet, whom Zappa would later reinvent as Captain Beefheart. Vliet was a kindred spirit in both his love of R&B and blues, as well as in being something of a misfit. "I met [him] in 1956," Zappa told British journalist Miles in 1970. "He was about to drop out of high school because his father was ill and he was going to take over his bread truck route to Mohave, driving a Helms Bread truck. He lived at home with his mother, and his grandmother, and he liked rhythm and blues records." Besides filling their ears with the great early work of Howlin' Wolf, "Guitar" Slim, and Sonny Boy Williamson, they filled their mouths with the partially stale leftover pastries from the Helms Bread truck. "I used to go over to his house, and we had all the used pineapple buns that we could ever wish for out of the truck," Zappa told Don Menn.

Don Vliet was born in 1941 in the Southern California town of Glendale. While his father, Glenn, did the deliveries for Helms Bread, Don's mother, Sue, worked as an Avon lady selling cologne door-to-door. (She would be immortalized by Zappa in the song "Debra Kadabra," which Don Vliet sang on the *Bongo Fury* album in 1975). An only child, Vliet had an unbridled independent streak, plus a real talent for both drawing and sculpting. Simultaneous with his interest in art, Vliet also developed a deep interest in music; his grandfather, Amos Warfield, was a blues musician who performed on a lap guitar — and played it with a pocketknife. Through Amos Warfield, Don Vliet acquired a natural feeling for blues music. "His grandfather had a plantation back in the South, and [Don] was tied to the South, he's got a lot of Southern blood in him," said Jerry Handley, the bass player who brought Don into his first band. "[Don] could whistle, that's all he could do at first. We'd be playing guitars and he'd come by, and he could whistle the blues, and he was damned good at it." When he turned thirteen, Vliet won a scholarship to study art in Europe, but his parents thought he would be corrupted by all the gay artists on the loose there. So, as if to build a protective wall around their son, they moved to the Mohave Desert and eventually settled in Lancaster.

While Don attended Lancaster High School, he started to hone his musical skills, which further alienated him from the white-bread community. The only person he could relate to turned out to be a spindly drummer/guitarist named Frank Zappa, to whom he gave a ride home one day in his '49 Oldsmobile 88 Coupe. "He spent most of his time, money, and effort in driving around the desert in [that] powder-blue Oldsmobile with a terra-cotta werewolf head that he had modeled himself, mounted either on his dashboard or underneath the blower of his horn on his steering wheel," Zappa remarked in 1970. "And he was very fond of wearing khakis and French-toed shoes and dressing in the latest pachuco fashion. It's a certain style of clothes that you had to wear to look like that type of teenager."

Bunk Gardner, a sax player with the Mothers of Invention, described what he saw — years later — as the fundamental difference between them. "I felt that Don had more dimensions and warmth to his playing and musical ideas," he told author Billy James. "Frank's playing was a little calculated, like a mathematician figuring a solution to a problem, and felt a little cold. Even looking at Frank's music you really had to break it down mathematically to figure it out and play it and memorize it."

Gardner's reaction, not an uncommon one, to Zappa's "cold" and "inhuman" approach to composition, is applicable only if Zappa treated music as a forum for his thoughts and feelings. Vliet may have had more "warmth" in his work because, quite simply, music *was* a vehicle for self-expression for him. In the conventional sense, Zappa didn't "pour his soul" into his work. He saw music as a series of complicated strategies with the aim of creating sounds yet unheard. Neil Slaven succinctly characterizes how the relationship between Zappa and Vliet would develop over the years. "Frank discovered Don was the only other teenager in Lancaster with an interest in blues and R&B. Music was their strongest point of contact. Both had grown up as loners, creating their own worlds to keep at bay a reality that each scorned. The difference was that Frank used his as a shield in order to pursue his own ends, while Don's was a living environment." Vliet would turn out to be an inhabitant of the edges of reality, while Zappa was a relentlessly curious explorer of those very edges.

In 1959, the first recording that Vliet and Zappa made was in an empty high school classroom with Frank's brother Bobby on rhythm guitar, Frank on lead, and Don singing a scatological blues called "Lost in a Whirlpool." "When we first started out doing it, his timing was definitely into the minus zero," Zappa recalled of the session. "The only things which we had cut were some tapes where I had conned him into doing a parody of a rhythm and blues vocal in one of the classrooms at the junior college. We borrowed a tape recorder from school and recorded . . . 'Lost in a Whirlpool,' about a guy who has been flushed down the toilet by his girlfriend and is confronted by a blind brown fish." The song had its origins in the cheerfully fetid imaginations of Zappa and his two schoolmates Jeff Harris and Larry Littlefield, kids he knew from Mission Bay High School in San Diego. "Lost in a Whirlpool," included on *The Lost Episodes* (1996), opens with Vliet singing in a Bessie Smith falsetto over the blues riff of the Zappa brothers. The lyrics had some of the outlandish improvisational qualities that Vliet would bring to his own records years later. In his natural growling tenor, Vliet yelps out in fear, "This big brown fish, lookin' at me/He ain't got no eyes." Before long, the rejected lover is swimming in piss, begging for Drano and a plunger: "I'll let you know a little secret, baby/I'm gettin' tired of all this pee." Hearing the recording many years later, Vliet would only comment, "Frank and I had a good time. We were just fooling around." Out of this fooling around, though, one could see the origins of Zappa's penchant for bawdy humor, and see Vliet's inspired vamping start to emerge.

That same year, with Don Vliet on vocals, guitarist Alex Snouffler, Doug Moon, Jerry Handley, drummer Vic Mortensen, and Euclid James Sherwood, Zappa formed a band called the Omens. "I was with them for quite a while," Sherwood remembers. "Frank had formed a few groups down in Ontario [California], and he would come up for battles of the bands all the time. It was kind of a kick." Frank Zappa now brought his guitar to school every day. "I know I was weird," Zappa remembered with a smile many years later. "You know the standard uniform that rap musicians wear [today] — the hooded parka with the hood up and sunglasses on — that's what I used to wear to school every day. I had a little goatee and a little moustache, and I used to take my guitar with me to school." Sherwood, who shared classes with Frank's brother Bobby and got to know him through the Blackouts, clearly remembers how they first met. "Frank used to sit out on the front lawn at the high school when I was a freshman and he had this old beat-up guitar," Sherwood told *T'Mershi Duween* magazine in 1993. "Bobby found out that I collected blues records and he introduced me to Frank, and Frank and I got together and swapped records. We've been friends ever since." When Zappa graduated from high school in June 1958, he didn't have all the credits he needed to graduate. The school, meanwhile, was more than happy to get rid of him.

By the spring of 1959, the Zappa family was on the road once again, to Claremont, California. Frank left home and moved into the Echo Park section of L.A. After doing a few musical gigs, he couldn't make enough money to survive on his own, so he moved back in with his parents. Given Zappa's unrelenting passion for music, Francis tried to get his oldest son to study at the Peabody Conservatory in Maryland, but Frank refused. According to Greg Russo, Zappa's attitude was "clinched by reading H.A. Clarke's [book] *Counterpoint: Strict and Free*. After noticing that Clarke's composing recommendations listed one rule after another, Zappa was determined to break every rule in Clarke's book. Decades before, American composer Charles Ives had the same disdain for regimented musical techniques. . . ." Whether he was conscious of it or not, Zappa's desire to reinvent the rules owed an immense debt to the musical crusade of Charles Ives.

9

Beauty in music is too often confused with something that lets the ears lie back in an easy chair.

CHARLES IVES, *Essays Before a Sonata*

Frank Zappa's contempt for the protocol of American musical education didn't emerge out of a vacuum. American composers, since the founding of the nation, had been battling over what American music should be or, at least, what it could be. "The quest for identity runs through American music like a leitmotif," writes

YOU'RE PROBABLY WONDERING

musicologist Veronica Slater. "Long before musical nationalism became an issue in Europe, native-born composers in the New World were trying to speak with a voice recognizably theirs, and theirs alone." Americans, says Slater, rebelled against the rules in both politics and music for good reason. They wanted an indigenous art borne of their own experiences of the new land, not what they inherited from the Old World.

William Billings, for instance, a Boston tanner who was part of the First New England School from 1746 to 1800, was one such breaker of rules. He even put together his own edict for the singing of psalms and hymns that broke free from the European liturgical chants. "Nature must lay the Foundation, Nature must inspire the thought," Billings wrote in *The New England Psalm Singer* in 1770. "For my own Part . . . I don't think myself confin'd to any Rules for Composition laid down by any that went before me. . . . Art is subservient to genius." And the music he composed, like the melodious *When Jesus Wept*, or his anthem *Be Glad Then America*, was filled with harsh discordances and abounding in parallel fifths. This primitivism, considered appallingly crude to the musically cultivated ears of his time, led to the short shelf life of Billings' music. Not surprisingly, he died in poverty.

Philadelphia lawyer Francis Hopkinson, on the other hand, a contemporary of Billings, wrote charming and ear-pleasing little hymns. Some even had alarmingly upbeat titles like "My Days Have Been So Wondrous Free" and were composed in the more acceptable British ballad style. His *Seven Songs for the Harpsichord* (1788), dedicated to George Washington, drew nothing but false modesty from its author, as well. "However small the Reputation may be that I shall derive from this Work, I cannot, I believe, be refused the Credit of being the first Native of the United States who has produced a Musical Composition," Hopkinson wrote.

"It was all very well," Slater comments, "for someone like George Washington's friend Francis Hopkinson — rich, cultured, educated — to write well-turned little airs in the manner of Arne; but William Billings, for instance — tanner by trade, musician by conviction, short, one-legged, one-eyed, and with an 'uncommon negligence of person' — had little time for the elegancies of late-18th-century music."

Charles Ives, born a century later, in 1874, in Danbury, Connecticut, also had little time for such elegancies. According to Slater, Ives had no patience for "sissies" and "lily-pads," or anyone who couldn't "take their dissonances like a man." In the America he envisioned, European decorum had no place to park. Ives was born into an America where the chasm between the "cultivating" arts and the "popular" arts was long and wide. Composers in the United States at this time were steeped in the European romantic sensibility that emphasized "the sublime and spiritually exalted in the arts," as Frank Rossiter puts it. This meant the cultural arbiters of taste in America wouldn't draw their inspiration from their new roots, but from the Old World values of Handel, Haydn, and Beethoven. These would be the role models for budding composers and musicians in the New Land.

By the time Ives arrived, American composers of classical music were either trained in European schools or by European teachers in America. "Lacking an American tradition of art music comparable to that of Germany or Italy," Rossiter writes, "they felt cut off from the popular culture of their own country. . . . Nor were they likely to have their compositions played, for there were no aristocratic patrons with court orchestras, and the audiences at public concerts found European composers more exotically appealing."

As a result, Ives' rebellion against European gentility took on an ebulliently harsh tone. His insurgence even contained specifically narrow sexual implications. "The artistic revolt in America has . . . always been masculine in character, with its emphasis on hardness, clarity, simplicity, boldness, difficulty, exploration, independence, and rebelliousness," writes Paul Seydor in *Peckinpah: The Western Films*. "Such an aesthetics reaches its culmination in Charles Ives, who, writing in the teens of [the 20th] century, when gentility was in its prime and about ready for collapse, defined the enemies of art as the 'ladies,' the 'sissies,' and the 'conservatives.'" Women in the 19th century were excluded from professional and prestigious positions in business, so those in the upper class turned to music for both leisure and a livelihood, embracing the cultivated music of Europe. Women soon made up the majority of audiences at operas and concerts, and the majority of music students, too, and even wrote most of what constituted music criticism. "Women became dominant in cultivated-tradition music because the European system of selecting out and educating a body of males to carry on artistic traditions had never caught hold in America," Frank Rossiter explains. "And as women's dominance grew, American men retreated from classical music as a threat to their masculinity."

"Women not only represented gentility," Paul Seydor points out, "but they cultivated the arts, and so in rebelling against the official culture an artist is necessarily going to find himself betraying or at least suppressing some of his deepest leanings towards art and expression." That suppression had an indelible affect on the life and career of Charles Ives. It was Ives' father, George, a former bandleader with the First Connecticut Heavy Artillery during the Civil War, who influenced his son's desire to break with the rules of etiquette in music.

YOU'RE PROBABLY WONDERING

George Ives initially attracted admiration from both President Lincoln and General Grant because of the dissonant musical innovations he incorporated into his compositions with the marching band. When George returned to Danbury, though, those discordant experiments could only be practiced in his marching unit. Band music was considered the lowest and most popular vernacular form, anyway, so Ives was limited in his desire to loosen the Anglo-Saxon grip on musical culture in Danbury. Ives came to see that cultivated music and its genteel attributes was a superficial masking of the true nature of the American character — and it still chained Americans to their colonial past. In the vernacular tradition, which was the common folkloric music of the daily life in Danbury, he found truly profound ideals.

His father's dreams for his son created an irreversible split for Charles Ives. It was an inconsolable divide between the musical foundations in which Ives would be schooled, the "feminine"-cultivated tradition, and his true love of the "masculine" vernacular music. This also had an impact on Ives' personal life. While asserting his masculinity as a young boy, excelling in sports like the other guys, he was terrified of being considered a "sissy" by his male friends. He couldn't show any interest in playing the music of Mozart or Haydn. "As a boy [I was] partially ashamed of it — an entirely wrong attitude, but it was strong — most boys in country towns, I think, felt the same," Ives writes in his autobiographical volume *Memos*. "When other boys . . . were out driving grocery carts, or doing chores, or playing ball, I felt all wrong [staying] in and [playing] piano. And there may be something in it. Hasn't music always been too much an emasculated art?"

Whether or not you accept Ives' ruggedly masculine assertions, which are not much different from Zappa's, they don't grow out of misogyny. Ives and Zappa didn't hate women, they hated gentility. Zappa had female musicians in his band, and his second wife, Gail, was a strong, assertive woman; Ives also married a wise and independent woman who was hardly a wallflower. Neither Ives nor Zappa saw elegance as part of the American character, because the land, and the foundations on which the country was founded, were anything but harmonious and sweet. Ives believed ruggedness was the only true response to the spiritual legacy of being an American. Allan Bloom declares in *The Closing of the American Mind*, in 1987, that "music is the soul's primitive and primary speech. . . . Civilization is the taming or domestication of the soul's raw passions." Zappa replied, in a piece published in *New Perspectives* the same year, "If one wants to be a real artist in the United States today and comment on our culture, one would be very far off the track if one did something delicate or sublime. This is not a noble, delicate, sublime country.... Performers who are doing the crude, vulgar, repulsive things Bloom doesn't enjoy are only commenting on that fact."

For Ives, the ideals of American culture were embedded in the work of transcendentalists like Emerson and Hawthorne. Formed in 1836 in Boston, the transcendentalists were noted for including male and female unitarians trying to find meaning and purpose in a universe that wasn't ruled by a genial or refined deity. Although the club met for only three years before disbanding, their influence was felt throughout the Civil War and into the late 19th century. Part of their appeal was the boundless range of subjects they explored, including mysticism, theology, pantheism, issues of law, individuality, and the nature of truth. They were an articulate group who not only tackled philosophical issues but also grappled with the very concept of what America was. "Our day of independence, our long apprenticeship to the learning of other lands, draws to a close," Emerson wrote in 1837 in his *American Scholar* address. "We have listened too long to the courtly muses of Europe.... We will walk on our own feet; we will work with our own hands; we will speak our own minds." Even if music would be the last American art form to walk on its own feet, Charles Ives certainly heard the call to speak his own mind. He put his own stamp on American music by combining the roots of American folk music — church hymns, campfire songs, popular ballads — with a complex and dissonant counterpoint that provided the supporting framework for all the melodic lines in the score.

Everything Ives heard made a lasting impression. He listened to the everyday sounds of his environment and experimented with its natural ambience — just as Edgard Varèse would years later. Ives wrote scores evoking the effect of two bands playing different pieces — in different keys — marching past each other. This peculiar matching of sounds was the precursor to Zappa's xenochronous compositions, like "Brown Shoes Don't Make It" (*Absolutely Free*, 1967), "Rubber Shirt" (*Sheik Yerbouti*, 1979), or most of the guitar solos on *Joe's Garage* (1979), where Zappa laid distinctly opposing musical pieces on top of each other. Ives also quoted popular songs in a satirical context within the score, as Zappa did years later. For instance, in his quietly ominous *Central Park in the Dark*, Ives suddenly incorporates the ragtime favorite "Hello My Baby," while Zappa superimposed "That Old Rugged Cross" over the melody of "Jesus Thinks You're a Jerk," on *Broadway the Hard Way* (1988).

YOU'RE PROBABLY WONDERING

Ives and Zappa were utopians with different aspirations. Ives dreamed of an America rooted in the past, in the small-town simplicities of Danbury; Zappa, in the City of Lost Angels, dreamed of an America in the future, one that hadn't happened yet, and maybe never would. Ives was optimistic about the intelligence and goodwill of people; Zappa believed we were Dumb All Over. They both envisioned an America that would largely ignore them, while finding themselves embraced by European modernists. Both Ives and Zappa were outsiders, excluded for most of their lives from the American cultural scene.

Ives' prudish attitudes toward sex and morality, and his contempt for new technology, left him a recluse — removed even from the avant-garde that worshipped him. Zappa, however, saw the peculiarity of American sexual attitudes as grist for his mill. He worked in the popular arena of rock 'n' roll, where he could freely mix musical genres and make his sociologically comic observations on absurd and bizarre behavior. Although he likely never studied, or embraced, the transcendentalists the way Ives did, Zappa still became a living embodiment of Thoreau's idea that "natural objects and phenomena are the original symbols or types which express our thoughts and feelings."

So, from this point on, in that expansive spirit of both Thoreau and Ives, Zappa began to mine natural objects and phenomena in an attempt to give voice to the "living speech" of the culturally disinherited.

10

Frank Zappa spent six months near the end of 1959 studying harmony at the Alta Loma, California, campus of Chaffey Junior College. He also snuck into a Pomona College composition course but soon lost interest. Once, in typical Zappa fashion, he showed up at the campus radio station and briefly did his own show — until the station staff discovered he wasn't a student. (A sample of this episode, called "Excerpt From The Uncle Frankie Show," turned up on the *Mystery Disc* CD, released in 1998.) While at Chaffey, Zappa met Kathryn J. (Kay) Sherman, who would become his first wife. That same year, he also established contact with his former high school English teacher, Don Cerveris, who had gone to Hollywood to be a screenwriter. Cerveris had written the screenplay for a low-budget Western, *Run Home Slow*, and had recommended Zappa to write the score. Because of inadequate financing, it would take three years before the movie would see the light of day. The plot, according to Zappa, involved "a nymphomaniac cowgirl [who] is getting plooked by a hunchback, next to the rotting carcass of a former donkey." Zappa's score included music that would later be the basis for the song "Duke of Prunes," from *Absolutely Free*.

On December 28, 1960, at the age of twenty, Zappa married the twenty-one-year-old Kay in San Bernardino County. They lived together in Alta Loma, while Kay worked as a secretary for the First National Bank of Ontario and Zappa started a job as a silk-screener and designer at the Nile Running Greeting Card Co. Zappa went on to other jobs as diverse as jewelry selling, window dressing, even becoming a door-to-door salesman for Collier's Encyclopedias, where he lasted about three days. In the early '60s, Zappa also continued to play in R&B bands on the cocktail circuit, including the Boogie Men, where Zappa played his first electric guitar. He had by this time printed up calling cards that read: *F.V. Zappa Composer — Master Blues Guitarist*. In the Boogie Men, Zappa played lead guitar and sang. One of their favorite numbers was a cover of Tony Allen & the Champs' exquisite "Nite Owl." (Zappa revived this song during one of his '80s touring bands, a version of which is included on the bootleg CD box *Apocrypha*.)

The most prominent local band Zappa played with was the San Bernardino–based Joe Perrino & the Mellotones, who became regulars at Tommy Sandi's Club Sahara on E. Street. A publicity photo of the band can be found in the *Mystery Disc* CD; the group is decked out in tuxedos and smiling — except for Zappa, who looks bored and disgusted. "I could tolerate that [only] for a short period of time," he told Nigel Leigh. "But eventually I hated it so much, I just put the guitar in the case, stuck it behind the sofa, and didn't play at all for about eight months." His ten months with Joe Perrino & the Mellotones, playing standards like "Anniversary Waltz," "Green Dolphin Street," and "Caravan" for drunk patrons, would be commemorated and satirized years later in "America Drinks and Goes Home," on *Absolutely Free*.

In 1961, more film work came Zappa's way. He began writing the music for *The World's Greatest Sinner*, which was written and directed by the star, character actor Tim Carey (*Paths of Glory*, *Echo Park*). The film was about an insurance salesman who, dissatisfied with his life, first turns to music, then religion, and finally politics. He also tries a stint at being God. "This was an absolutely ridiculous film," Zappa told Dave Marsden of CHUM-FM in Toronto in 1973. "It's about some guy who wants to find out if he's really God. His big test is to break into a Greco-Orthodox Church, steal a piece of communion bread, and stick a pin in it to see if it will bleed."

YOU'RE PROBABLY WONDERING

The World's Greatest Sinner was budgeted at $90,000, with most of the filming being done in Carey's garage in El Monte. "The score is unique," Zappa told the *Pomona Progress-Bulletin* in 1962. "It uses every type of music." Zappa's recording — including a small rock combo, a twenty-piece chamber ensemble, the fifty-five-piece Pomona Valley Symphony, augmented by musicians from Pomona High School and Chaffey Junior College — was completed in a twelve-hour session at the Chaffey Junior College Little Theatre. The score was indeed multi-textured, incorporating orchestral, jazz, and rock combo fragments (including a portion that would later become "Holiday in Berlin, Full Blown," on *Burnt Weeny Sandwich*). Instead of using the traditional method of leitmotif scoring, where developed themes consistently underscore the characters, their feelings, and their actions, Zappa came closer to the free-form, cartoon style of Carl Stalling's scores for Chuck Jones' Looney Tunes. It compares favorably to his comic oratorio "The Adventures of Greggery Peccary" from *Studio Tan* (1978). Since recording the score was a low-budget affair, using two microphones on portable equipment in a truck outside the theater and then later mixed to mono, Zappa described the results as "rancid." On top of that, he didn't get paid.

Zappa did manage to come up with three hundred dollars, however, to mount his first concert of his orchestral music, at Mount St. Mary's College. "It was a student orchestra," Zappa remarked in 1993. "There were probably fifty people in the audience and — for some strange reason — KPFK [Radio] taped it.... There was one thing called 'Opus 5,' and there were aleatoric compositions that involved a certain amount of improvisation, and there were some written sections that you actually had to play." Zappa had a tape of electronic music that accompanied the musicians, and he also featured some 8mm films taken from footage he shot of the L.A. County Fair carnival, with superimposed images of passing telephone polls, which he screened behind the musicians. (That footage, originally part of a 1957 work called "Piece No. 2 of Visual Music for Jazz Ensemble and 16mm Visual Projector," would also find its way into the video for Zappa's synclavier composition "G-Spot Tornado" in 1984.) An excerpt from KPFK's broadcast appears on *The Lost Episodes*, where you can also hear the beginnings of Zappa's comical interaction with the audience.

All was not comical, or harmonious, in Zappa's private life, however. His marriage was starting to come apart due to the couple's constant state of poverty. A chance meeting, though, provided a strange turn for Zappa, and it took him along Route 66 to Cucamonga. Zappa had already started developing his style as a composer, but he was still looking for subject matter that would give his work personality. If '60s folklore aimed at finding edifying individuals to celebrate, Zappa chose a different course. In 1960, he came into contact with two musician brothers, Kenny and Ronnie Williams, who had both dropped out of high school — and music wasn't their only claim to fame. Kenny and Ronnie's family resembled something out of a David Lynch film. Years later, Zappa would document their story in two songs, "Let's Make the Water Turn Black" and "The Idiot Bastard Son," on *We're Only in It for the Money* (1968). Their tale would be the template for a number of tunes about people who weren't typically commemorated in popular culture. Frank now made a conscious decision to document the lives of those left out of history simply because they didn't conform to standards of normalcy. Like the staid rules regarding musical composition, Zappa saw the rules regarding the content of American music worthy of revamping. And the story of the Williams family, every bit a part of the stained American fabric, was deserving of a song.

The brothers' father was a salesman named Dink, while their mother was a waitress at Ed's Cafe. As the parents earned a living to support their family, Kenny and Ronnie spent their time indulging in that great American male tradition of fart-burning. "They had this coordinated routine," Zappa recalled. "Ronnie and Kenny would come over to my house, and if one of them was stricken with gas pain, he would yell, 'I got one.' He would immediately hurl himself to the floor, stick his legs up in the air, and spread the Levi material that covered the special orifice designed for this purpose, and make it taut. The other assistant would lunge toward the orifice with a cigarette lighter. Then they would countdown, 3 . . . 2 . . . 1, and would emit enormous blue fireballs in the middle of my living room."

When Kenny went to jail for illegally selling homemade raisin wine to his fellow junior high school students, Dwight Bement (later a sax player in the '60s pop group Gary Puckett & the Union Gap) moved in with Ronnie. For about a year and a half, Ronnie and Dwight passed the time playing poker and flipping their boogers onto their bedroom window. Mrs. Williams, who one day discovered this "dysentery green" substance covering the once-transparent glass, demanded they clean it off. They ended up having to use a putty knife and Ajax because the snot had become so hard.

Euclid James Sherwood moved in with Ronnie and Kenny in 1962, when Kenny got out of jail and was living back at home. Kenny stayed in the garage, and the boys gathered to play poker and drink beer. Since it was too cold to use the outdoor bathroom (and they were probably too drunk, or lazy, to try), they would urinate in the Mason jars that Mrs. Williams used when making her homemade raisin wine. "It got to be a fetish with them as to how many of those jars they could fill up," Zappa told Dave Marsden. "As they would fill twenty or thirty of the little jars, they would pour it into bigger jars where they ended up with eight or nine gallons. Then they had these parties where everyone in the neighborhood would come over and whizz in these jars just to see how much they could save." However, they soon ran out of jars and poured all the putrefied liquid into their mother's crock, covering it with a board.

In 1964, Euclid left and Kenny moved back indoors. When Sherwood came back to visit Kenny a few months later, the two grew curious about the liquid excretions covered up in the garage. Lifting the lid, they discovered little tadpole-type critters swimming in the liquid. Kenny took one of them out, and Euclid poked it with a pin. Some clear, pus-like material emerged. The boys were so excited by their amateur scientific experiment that they couldn't wait to show their horrified father. He made them flush everything down the toilet. "When they weren't pissing in jars and saving their snot on the windows," Zappa told journalist Kurt Loder, "they were lighting each other's farts. So there it is. It's like a folk song."

Besides providing a bizarre story for Zappa's "folk song," however, meeting Ronnie served another important purpose. Ronnie was a guitarist in the band the Masters, who had released a single called "Break Time" on a small label owned by Cucamonga-based producer and recording engineer Paul Buff. It was Ronnie who introduced Frank to Buff. "[Zappa] just came in one day in 1960, when he was around twenty, as a person who wanted to record some jazz," Buff recalled. "He had some musicians, and wanted to rent a studio. Probably for the first year or so I was associated with him, he was doing a combination of recording jazz, producing some jazz records, and also writing some symphonic material for a local orchestra to record some of it." Zappa quickly summed Buff up as a genius. "He would listen to whatever was on the tracks and he would grasp what the hook element was, and then build his version of something that contained the same hook-type material," Zappa told *Goldmine*'s William Ruhlmann.

Buff, who today works as a record producer in Nashville, learned about electronics during a brief service in the U.S. Marine Corps, before he got out to become a songwriter and technical producer in the studio. He started by building the Pal Recording Studio in the industrial area of Cucamonga, running it as an offshoot of his parent's Pal-O-Mine music publishing company. In the control room, Buff built an eight-channel Presto stereo mixing desk, when the industry's standard was still mono. He also put together a five-track recorder that used half-inch tape, which in those days was usually reserved for film sound. This enabled him to overdub many tracks when cutting a record. Buff even had his own cutting lathe to make acetates, which gave Frank the opportunity to produce ready-made product for the record label.

Buff lived in the studio with two members of the Sonny Wilson Band. They were a local group who played sleazy bars and usually featured Buff on the drums. When studio clients would show up, he would have to quickly send the band members to the back room, so he could make the place look like a professional business establishment again. The studio's blacked-out windows gave the building an innocuous look. Folks in this conservative town had no idea about these self-styled freaks' outrageously creative activities.

Buff decided to organize all the musicians into a "Pal studio group" that included Zappa, Dave Aerni (who would later produce the Tornadoes, who had the early-'60s hit "Telstar"), and Ray Collins, a veteran R&B bar-band singer, plus many others. Collins, who had played with the Chicano doo-wop band Little Julian Herrera & the Tigers, met Zappa in a seedy Pomona bar called the Sportsman. "I was drinking . . . [and] Frank and his friends were playing," Collins recalled. "There wasn't even a stage. I figured that any band that played [Hank Ballard & the Midnighters'] 'Work With Me, Annie' was all right. They either asked me to sing with them, or I simply became too drunk, and wandered up there and asked to sing with them." Collins told Zappa about an idea he had for a song based on a favorite phrase of TV talk-show host Steve Allen. That song would become "How's Your Bird?," sung by Collins as part of the makeshift Pal band Baby Ray & the Ferns. While producing this tune, Buff introduced Zappa to multi-tracking, which Zappa would take full advantage of in his later studio albums. He also helped Zappa perfect the "close-miking" technique, giving each instrument a certain omnipresence by placing the microphone within a foot from whatever it was recording. Zappa applied that approach even to his voice in his albums *Over-nite Sensation* (1973) and *Apostrophe (')* (1974), and especially in the song "Po-Jama People," from *One Size Fits All* (1975).

"Because of having no money and having bad acoustics in the studio, I think myself and Frank and some other people in the studio did pioneer some of the close-miking techniques," Buff told Drew Wheeler of *Billboard*. "Everything was close-miked and we did definitely pioneer some multi-track recording techniques

YOU'RE PROBABLY WONDERING

and overdubbing." He and Frank issued ten singles on numerous labels in 1963, writing and producing songs for various groups. "[We were] a classic study in opposites," Buff told Bryan Thomas for the liner notes of *Cucamonga*, which collects much of Zappa and Buff's output at Pal. "But [we were] also, at the same time, incredibly alike. He was confident, outgoing, and an extremely gifted musician, while I was introverted and withdrawn, but equally gifted in the art of electronics. . . . We were both driven by necessity, with each of us using whatever tools were at hand to achieve whatever it was we were trying to achieve. When no tools were available — which was usually the case — we created them."

In the early '60s, novelty songs about monsters from horror movies were common, such as Bobby "Boris" Pickett's "Monster Mash." Buff and Zappa produced "Letter From Jeepers," featuring Bob Guy, an actor who introduced horror movies on a local television station. The song, a homage to John Zacherle's novelty single "Dinner With Drac," boasted many Zappa sound effects. Guy read fan letters with a droll Bela Lugosi–inspired delivery, plus a hearty laugh. On Buff's other label, Vigah!, he recorded a song by Brian Lord, a San Bernardino DJ who could do a killer imitation of John F. Kennedy. Performed with Lord's band, the Midnighters, "The Big Surfer" was sold to Capitol Records. The song was never issued, however, because a joke about the Peace Corps was deemed in bad taste after Medgar Evers, a field secretary in the National Association for the Advancement of Colored People, was assassinated in Jackson, Mississippi.

In order to get major labels interested in their R&B, surf rock, and novelty comedy, Zappa and Buff came up with a great scam. They pressed two hundred records and stocked them in San Bernardino record stores on consignment. Then some friendly DJ would play their records, and Zappa and Buff would buy all of the records from those stores. The stores would claim great sales for those titles, which would earn a healthy showing on the radio station's chart. When Zappa and Buff visited the major distributors in Hollywood, they boasted of the hot action they were getting on the San Bernardino charts, earning advances ranging from $500 to $1,000 when the major label released the local hit — only to watch it flop. Zappa and Buff put the money to good use before the major labels caught on to their game.

After releasing the "How's Your Bird?" single backed with a vocal version of Zappa's theme from *The World's Greatest Sinner*, Ray Collins and Zappa wrote "Memories of El Monte," an affectionate tribute to doo-wop, for Cleave Duncan, the former lead singer of the Penguins ("Earth Angel"). "Frank said he and a friend of his had thought of writing a song from that title, so I just sat down at the piano and said, 'Let's do it,'" Collins told David Porter of KPFK in Los Angeles. "We sat down, and I remember the first line coming out: 'I'm all alone, feeling so blue.' Then we wrote it." For Zappa, composing doo-wop music was closer to his field of interest than anything else he was writing and producing at Pal. "It's always been my contention that the music that was happening during the '50s has been one of the finest things that ever happened to American music, and I loved it," Zappa explained. "I could sit down and write a hundred more of the '50s-type songs right now and enjoy every minute of it."

But Zappa also played against the sentiment inherent in the song. "Memories of El Monte" opens with the narrator pining for the woman he once loved, and the memories they shared dancing to classic R&B at El Monte Legion Stadium. The first half of the song is pure doo-wop:

Remember the dance
I held you so tight
The Five Satins were singing
"In the Still of the Nite."

Cleave Duncan sings those lines wistfully, as his romantic aspirations turn to sorrow. "Now I'm alone/I'm sitting here crying," he continues. But midway through, he rouses from his despair and recalls the songs that made those dances at El Monte so grand. He lists the tunes as if scanning a jukebox full of favorites in his head: "You Cheated, You Lied" by the Shields, "You're a Thousand Miles Away" by the Heartbeats, Marvin and Johnny's "Cherry Pie," Tony Allen & the Champs' "Nite Owl." And suddenly he becomes Cleave Duncan of the Penguins singing "Earth Angel." Zappa and Collins cleverly work sections of these tunes into the song, making them all sound like choruses from the same number. This brilliant bit of arranging makes the listener aware of how important a song's hook is in making us pine for the past. In this way, "Memories of El Monte" strips away the song's nostalgic qualities, leaving only the beauty of the melodies it conjures up.

Around the time of *The World's Greatest Sinner*'s theatrical premiere, Frank appeared on television's *The Steve Allen Show* to play a concerto for two performers and a bicycle (which happened to belong to his sister, Candy). "I got on the show by just calling them up and saying that I play the bicycle," Zappa recalled in 1992. "They were booking all kinds of goofy things on there." Zappa called his bicycle-playing technique "cyclophony." It involved stroking the spokes with a violin bow as he twirled the pedals and blew the air through the tube of the handlebars. While Zappa demonstrated this to Allen, someone in the control room manipulated sounds from an audio tape and the house band supplied random background noise. "I congratulate you on your farsightedness," Allen told Zappa after the performance. "As for your music, don't do it around here again!" What many who watched the show that night might not have gathered was that Zappa was doing a low-rent variation on contemporary American avant-garde composers like Harry Partch, who invented his own instruments, and John Cage, who used the element of chance in his compositions.

In the spring of 1963, Paul Buff left Pal to construct a ten-track recorder for Art Laboe's Original Sound label, which had released some of the Pal singles. Laboe used to stage huge dances at the El Monte Legion Stadium and issued the first *Oldies But Goldies* LP compilation. Buff was in financial trouble, and Pal was on the verge of being lost. Fortunately, Zappa had finally been paid for his contributions to the film *Run Home Slow*, so he offered to buy the studio — he'd assume the debts and pay Buff a thousand dollars. By doing so, Zappa would also take over the lease, get two pianos (including a Steinway upright) and the recording equipment. The following summer, Buff signed the deal. He received, in lieu of cash, Zappa's Fender Jazzmaster guitar, his vibes, and an old set of drums. "I knew Frank intimately, and he was one of the least arrogant people I have ever known," Buff told Bryan Thomas. "He was revolted at the thought of idols, superstars, and those who manipulated the masses with such ideas. Indeed, Frank promoted, not arrogance, but pride in those who would escape from the 'human hydraulics' and utilize their own brains. He, like myself, was a believer in the power of the individual."

"[Paul Buff] showed me how to work the stuff," Zappa told William Ruhlmann, "and I went from being kind of an incompetent commercial artist to a full-time obsessive overdub maniac working in the studio." For twelve hours a day, Zappa laid the foundation for his project.

CHAPTER THREE

WHO NEEDS THE PEACE CORPS?

(1965-1969)

Most of the stuff that I did between '65 and '69 was directed toward an audience that was accustomed to accepting everything that was handed to them. I mean completely. It was amazing: politically, musically, socially — everything. Somebody would just hand it to them and they wouldn't question it. It was my campaign in those days to do things that would shake people out of that complacency, or that ignorance, and make them question things.

FRANK ZAPPA

Zappa's intention is to create a paranoid listener, who picks up with each new version some extra nuance, another hint.

JONATHAN JONES, *Eonta*, 1994

1

The night Frank Zappa took over the Pal studio, he renamed the place Studio Z and threw a party attended by Ray Collins, Euclid James Sherwood, and Don Vliet. Some of the party was recorded by Zappa and included on *Mystery Disc*, as an edited collage similar to some of the work he assembled later in 1967 as part of *Lumpy Gravy* (1968). Zappa redecorated the studio, painted "Studio Z" on the door, and placed a sign out front that read: *Record Your Band — $13.50 per hour*. "He turned the whole studio into his vision of the B-movie spaceship," Paul Buff told Bryan Thomas. "I remember him getting excited about it — asking for any junk electronics I had, and taking meters and painting them Day-Glo orange and putting knobs all over a board and painting it with different Day-Glo colors. That last time I was in Studio Z to go to the bathroom, you had to go out of the cockpit of this ship and crawl down tunnels underneath and come out in the bathroom. This again underscores necessity being the mother of invention."

During the summer of 1963, Zappa formed a band called the Soots, with Don Vliet, guitarist Alex Snouffler, and drummer Vic Mortenson. Their recordings included Little Richard's "Slippin' and Slidin'" ("as if sung by Howlin' Wolf," said Zappa) and "Metal Man Has Won His Wings," where, according to Zappa, "Vliet was 'singing' in the hallway outside the hallway outside the studio (our vocal booth) while the band played in the other room." The lyrics, apparently, were derived from a comic book pinned to a bulletin board near the door. "Tiger Roach," included on *The Lost Episodes*, opened with Vliet's prophetic words "This album is not available to the public. . . . Even if it were, you wouldn't want to listen to it!" Then, in between flatulent outbursts and hog squealing, Vliet does an amazing improvised riff while perusing an *X-Men* comic book.

That wasn't the only audacious thing about it. "It was my first attempt at stereo," Zappa told Rip Rense. "The band was in the studio mixed down to one track, and Don [was] in the hallway with just the leakage coming through the door. But finally I had a stereo mix." Zappa's guitar also had the hard-edged fuzz tone he admired in some of his blues heroes. "I had a Gibson amp. I plugged the guitar into the mike hole, and something bad happened. The fuzz tone was established this way."

Zappa sent these recordings for consideration to Dot Records, along with a Latin jazz instrumental called "Never on Sunday" (which would later be titled "Take Your Clothes Off When You Dance" on *We're Only in It for the Money*), and the demo for "Any Way the Wind Blows," under the name of the Soots. Milt Rogers, the A&R guy at Dot, wrote to Zappa in December 1963: "[Although] the material has merit, we don't feel strongly enough about its commercial potential. . . ." Zappa phoned Rogers for a further explanation and was told that Dot's lack of interest was due to the "distorted guitar."

Earlier that year, Zappa's marriage to Kay Sherman had completely fallen apart, his obsessive pursuit of his craft finally driving a wedge between them. He filed for divorce and moved into Studio Z. When the divorce became final, Zappa hung the

WHO NEEDS THE PEACE CORPS?

decree on the wall as he did all significant documents — such as the letter from Varèse. There were no facilities for personal hygiene in the studio, but that didn't stop Motorhead Sherwood (as Collins had dubbed Euclid) from moving in with Zappa. He helped fix cars, added sax stylings to various tracks, and scrounged for food. Their bachelor diet consisted of peanut butter, coffee, honey, instant mashed potatoes, and cigarettes (purchased regularly in exchange for empty soft-drink bottles). Before long, a number of women were moving in, including eighteen-year-old Lorraine Belcher, who would soon figure in the biggest pornography bust in the history of Cucamonga.

Zappa was working on a project called *I Was a Teenage Malt Shop*. This teen "rock opera," which Zappa termed "a stupid piece of trash," was being shopped around to various record companies. It was inspired by Paul Buff's first wife, Alison, a malt-shop waitress. Besides the title track, which is introduced by Vliet ("We've got a heck of a little teenage opera for you — really"), it features Zappa on piano, Motorhead on acoustic guitar, and Vic Mortenson on drums. Other tracks include "Ned the Mumbler," "Ned Has a Brainstorm," and "Status Back Baby." "It was the idea of an old man who has a daughter Nelda who was a cheerleader," Zappa told Michael Gray in *Mother! The Frank Zappa Story*. "The old man has a recording studio that hasn't hit and there's an evil landlord who's going to foreclose on him. So there's this group that comes in with a teenage hero that goes to the high school, a teenage Lone Ranger. It was just a fantasy-type thing with rock 'n' roll music on it." The project received little interest, but the title track was included on *Mystery Disc*. "Ned the Mumbler," "Status Back Baby," and the instrumental (which would later be re-recorded by the Mothers and named "Toads of the Short Forest" on *Weasels Ripped My Flesh* in 1970) were first aired on the radio in 1975. "Status Back Baby" was also re-recorded by the Mothers of Invention for *Absolutely Free*. The original version had backing vocals from Alison Buff and an unidentified woman (possibly Lorraine Belcher).

Zappa also utilized all the sci-fi sets he'd constructed, or acquired, for an aborted film project called *Captain Beefheart vs. the Grunt People*. This enterprise was mounted with Don Vliet in mind; he would play Captain Beefheart and eventually take on the name himself. "Captain Beefheart was a character I invented for the film," Zappa wrote in the liner notes to *Mystery Disc*. "His name derives from one of Don Vliet's relatives, who looked like Harry Truman. He used to piss with the door open when Don's girlfriend walked by, and [he'd] make comments about how his whizzer looked just like a beef heart." Zappa sent his film treatment to a CBS-TV repertoire workshop at a local station, KNXT, in December 1964. It went nowhere. Vliet, meanwhile, went on to form his own group, the Magic Band. "Frank and I would sit around the studio," Vic Mortensen remembers. "We got to talking about clever little band names like everyone does, and we got to playing on the character of Captain Beefheart.... [He] was supposed to be this magical character. His thing is he would drink the Pepsi Cola and he could make magic things happen, he could appear or disappear. I told Frank, 'Hey, wouldn't it be cool if Captain Beefheart had a Magic Band, and wherever he went, if he wanted the band to appear, he would take a drink of Pepsi, and — bingo — there's the band right behind him, jukin'?"

A few days later, Vic ran into Don, who asked him if he wanted to join his new group. When Mortensen quizzed him about the ensemble's name, Vliet told him — Captain Beefheart & His Magic Band. "And I said, 'Far out!' I didn't even discuss it. The only place he could have heard it was from Frank."

While Beefheart was out playing tricks with his Magic Band, Zappa was trying to find the easiest source of income for a musician playing the bars. It started with a weekend gig back in Sun Village at the Village Inn, a barbecue hut where he could make seven dollars a night. Zappa reunited with Johnny Franklin, of the Blackouts; tape from their gig at the Village Inn survived, and is included on *Mystery Disc*. An unnamed MC introduces the band, calling Zappa "Frankie Zappo." A singer named Corsa sat in with the band and sang "Steal Away," a 1962 hit for blues singer Jimmy Hughes. Zappa brought along Motorhead Sherwood to play tenor sax.

As if warming up for the Dadaist antics to come, Zappa and Ray Collins played a series of gigs satirically as a folk duo. In this age of earnest folk groups such as the Kingston Trio and the Lettermen, Zappa and Collins called themselves the Sin City Boys. "We sang 'Puff the Magic Dragon' as 'Joe the Puny Greaser,'" Zappa told *Pulse Magazine*. "And we played a perverted version of 'The Streets of Laredo' called 'The Streets of Fontana.' We weren't setting out to make any kind of impact on people. We were just doing it for a laugh, to have fun." One night they even appeared on Talent Night at the Troubadour in Los Angeles. They called themselves Loeb & Leopold, after the notorious Nathan Leopold Jr. and Richard Loeb, two gay Illinois men who were convicted of a 1924 thrill killing. When the Mothers of Invention were doing their stint at the Garrick Theatre in New York in 1967, two regular paying customers also called themselves Loeb & Leopold. According to Zappa, "they came to at least thirty shows."

Frank soon formed a power trio called the Muthers, with Paul Woods on bass and Les Papp on drums. They worked bars and clubs in Pomona, including the

WHO NEEDS THE PEACE CORPS?

Saints & Sinners in nearby Ontario. This rowdy saloon was particularly rough on the musicians; it was populated by very demanding Mexican laborers. "When they weren't ogling the dancers' latticed thighs, the audience looked askance at the group's appearance," Zappa told Nigel Leigh. "I was a mutant. . . . I was wearing striped shirts unheard-of to a population that thrives on the white short-sleeved T-shirt, because that's what you wore to work."

Studio Z ran into its first substantial dilemma when Zappa announced a casting call for *Captain Beefheart vs. the Grunt People* in the local paper, the *Ontario Daily Report*. The article profiled the studio, as well as Zappa's desire to make movies, calling him "the Movie King of Cucamonga." This drew the attention of the San Bernardino County Sheriff's Office vice squad, who feared Zappa was making porno films. Studio Z happened to be located across the street from a Holy Roller church, as well as the local courthouse. The county was a deeply conservative community with a population of about 7,500 — most of whom were growing suspicious of the fact that, as Zappa put it, music was coming out of that place thirty-six hours a day. "They did not approve of a recording studio in the middle of a town that boasted as its major industry wine-stomping and television repair work," Zappa explained. "So the neighbors started complaining. Also my hair was too long by Cucamonga standards."

Sgt. Jim Willis of the vice squad made his living by building entrapment cases against homosexuals getting it on in public toilets. In early 1963, Willis decided to "audition" for the film while his squad spied on Zappa through a hole in the studio wall. Another time, Willis came back disguised as a used-car salesman. He told Zappa that his friends were having a party and wanted a sex film for the occasion. Zappa told Willis it would probably be too expensive but that an audio tape might have the same effect — and cost only about $100. The bogus salesman agreed to the deal and suggested some of the sex acts they'd like to see included. Meanwhile, the conversation was being transmitted through a wristwatch transmitter Willis was wearing so his superiors could hear.

What Zappa did, with the help of Lorraine Belcher, was simulate sex acts on something resembling an audio party tape. He recorded the two of them jumping on the bed while making lewd noises. Zappa edited out their giggling and replaced it with some appropriate porno-movie music. The next day, Willis arrived to pick up the tape, but he offered only fifty dollars. Zappa requested the full amount. Before it could escalate into a full-blown argument, Willis pulled out his badge, slapped the cuffs on Zappa, and called out to his partners in a truck outside through his transmitter. Zappa and Belcher were booked for conspiracy to commit pornography. Since Motorhead was out scrounging for food, he avoided being arrested. Under California law, Zappa's crime was classified a misdemeanor, but since he had made the tape with Lorraine, the charge became conspiracy, which was a felony. Belcher and Zappa were jailed. Ontario police detectives Stan McCloskey, Phillip Ponders, and Jim Mayfield started preparing a case against Zappa that essentially labeled him a danger to the community. The *Ontario Daily Report* made the police raid its front-page story on March 27. It featured photos of Zappa, the studio, tapes being confiscated, and Zappa and Belcher embracing each other outside the studio. The headline read: 2 A-GO-GO TO JAIL — VICE SQUAD RAIDS LOCAL FILM STUDIO.

Francis Zappa, who at the time was recovering from a heart attack, took out a bank loan to pay his son's bail, while Paul Buff put up about eighty dollars. The following week, Frank was arraigned. On his release, Zappa got an advance against royalties for "Memories of El Monte" and another track called "Grunion Run" from Art Laboe of Original Sound. He used that money to get Lorraine Belcher out of jail and to secure an attorney. Before the trial, Zappa tried to get the American Civil Liberties Union interested in the case, but they refused, telling him there had been many cases of illegal entrapment in Cucamonga. The lawyer Zappa's father hired wanted Frank to plead no contest (which Zappa later translated as meaning, "I'm so broke I can't even buy justice in Cucamonga, so I'll just give a thousand bucks to this lawyer here and keep my fucking mouth shut, hoping you don't give me the death penalty"). His lawyer had expressed surprise that Zappa let Willis fool him, when everyone in town knew that Willis earned his living hanging out in public bathrooms. Zappa replied that he didn't stand around in toilets, and that he never heard of people being *paid* to stand around in toilets. As he wrote in his memoir, "[Was it] my fault that I never dreamed that scum like Willis existed, or that somebody in the government set aside tax dollars to provide guys like him with a salary and a 'research budget'?"

Covering the trial, the *Ontario Daily Report* reported mostly on Lorraine's appearance: "a buxom, red-haired girl of perfect physical dimensions." Eventually, the charges against her would be dropped. Zappa earned no description at all. While the prosecution was building its case, the judge requested to hear the evidence. As he listened to the offending tape in his chambers, he burst out laughing. The case would have been dropped, but the DA was a twenty-six-year-old building a reputation, so he desperately needed to nail Cucamonga's

WHO NEEDS THE PEACE CORPS?

reluctant pornographer. Zappa was given a sentence of six months in jail with all but ten days suspended, and three years' probation. He was also not to be seen in the company of an unmarried woman under the age of twenty-one — and wasn't to violate any of the traffic laws of the State of California.

The conviction had one benefit — it made Zappa ineligible for the Vietnam War draft. But his confiscated tapes were never returned. "At the time they raided the recording studio, they confiscated eighty hours of research tapes that I'd been doing on sociological subjects since 1955," Zappa told Dave Marsden years later. "Also some masters for tapes I'd recorded there at the studio." After he'd been hurled out of the courtroom into the retaining cell, Zappa was confronted by the district attorney and the secret investigator. They had offered him a deal: if he let the sheriff decide which tapes were obscene, they'd give him the rest of the tapes back — erased. Since Zappa didn't have the power to turn the sheriff into a judge who could deem the deal valid, Zappa demanded his tapes back. But he never did see (or hear) those recordings again. "They're probably still jerking off to them somewhere in San Bernardino."

2

Frank Zappa was now a convicted felon in Tank "C" of the San Bernardino County Jail. The facility had a scum-infested shower with one stall for forty-four men. It was summer, and with no ventilation in the cells, the temperature climbed to 104 degrees in the daytime. And the food was inedible. "I remember one day they handed me this aluminum bowl with some Cream of Wheat which fell out in one moulded helmet-like kind of thing, flipped over, and there was a cockroach stuck in the bottom," Zappa told Nigel Leigh. "So I pulled this out . . . saved the cockroach and put it in an envelope with a letter to Motorhead's mother. The jail censor caught it and threatened me with solitary confinement if I ever tried anything like that again." Besides the "educational" aspects of this experience, Zappa would use his incarceration to take jabs at authoritarian attitudes in songs like "San Ber'dino" from *One Size Fits All* and "Concentration Moon" from *We're Only in It for the Money*.

Once released from Tank "C," Zappa returned to Studio Z, where he'd fallen behind in his rent. A real estate development company was planning to widen the street and tear the building down. Zappa had to abandon his labored sets and colorful decorations. Since he wasn't welcome at his folks' place, he moved from

Cucamonga to Echo Park, in Los Angeles, in early 1964, taking a job at Wallich's Music City, a downtown record store where he worked as a salesman in the singles department.

Just when things were looking especially bleak, Zappa got a call from Ray Collins. Collins wanted him to join a band he'd been in for three months called the Soul Giants. According to Zappa, Collins had a fight with the Giants' guitar player, Ray Hunt, who apparently kept playing the wrong notes while Collins was singing. So Collins had him kicked out — and they needed a replacement. Collins, however, begged to differ with Zappa's version of the story. According to Collins, "Ray Hunt didn't want to be part of the band, so we just got together after the show one night, and said, 'Okay, Ray, you're not doing it right — don't do it.' So he said, 'Great, I'm leaving.' I said, 'Don't worry about it, 'cause I know a guy that I worked with before from Ontario/Cucamonga named Frank Zappa, and I think he'd like to be in the band.' So I called Frank and he became part of the band."

The Soul Giants played a pretty standard R&B repertoire in bars at the time, including chestnuts like "In the Midnight Hour," "Louie Louie," and "Gloria." The band had been formed by bass player Roy Estrada, a Mexican, who had been playing with R&B bands in L.A. for over ten years, and drummer James Inkinish Jr., also known as Jimmy Carl Black. Black, a Cherokee from El Paso, Texas, began his musical career as a twelve-year-old trumpet player, but once he joined the U.S. Air Force at twenty in 1958, he took an interest in the drums. That same year, after getting out of the Air Force, he started pumping gas in Wichita, Kansas, until he became the drummer for a local band that covered tunes by Jimmy Reed and Howlin' Wolf. Not long after forming his first band, the Keys, in 1962, Black moved to L.A., where he thought he could make a better living playing music. It was there that he met Roy Estrada.

Estrada was born in 1943 to a Mexican family in the bosom of deeply conservative Orange County. He drove a lumber truck part-time — which later provided the title of the instrumental "The Orange County Lumber Truck" on *Weasels Ripped My Flesh* (1970). Estrada's interest in music derived from spending time listening to a local orchestra in Santa Ana. In time, he took lessons playing bass guitar and learned to sing. Before long, Estrada jammed with friends until he and a friend formed a group called the Viscounts that played Latin music. Soon they started playing after-hours clubs, turning their music more toward blues and R&B.

One day, in 1964, while Black was busy pawning his cymbals to stave off starvation, he met Estrada. They decided to turn the Viscounts into the Soul Giants,

WHO NEEDS THE PEACE CORPS?

enlisting Hunt, Collins (who had been marking time as a part-time carpenter and bartender), and saxophonist Dave Coronado (who ran a bowling alley).

Black's brother-in-law got them their first audition at the Broadside in Inglewood. "It was a beer bar," remembered Estrada. "The atmosphere inside was like the docks by the sea. You know, they had cork and a lot of fishing nets hanging on the side of the wall — it had some atmosphere to it." When Zappa joined, the band was good enough to play the bar scene, but he thought they should do more original material. Frank had been writing songs at Studio Z and figured the group could probably learn them. He gathered the band together and told them he had a plan to make them rich. While most of the band bought this bit of naive whimsy, Coronado remained skeptical. He knew that if they played original music, they'd get fired from every bar in California. After all, if the crowd wasn't happy with the music, they wouldn't buy beer. And if they didn't buy beer, the bar owners wouldn't make any money. So while the Soul Giants sought fame and fortune, Coronado returned to the safe confines of his bowling alley.

At first, Zappa thought of changing the band's name to Captain Glasspack and His Magic Mufflers, and by playing his original material in local go-go bars, they'd find success. Coronado, however, turned out to be right. "We'd play something weird and we'd get fired," Zappa told *Rolling Stone*. "I'd say, 'Hang on,' and we'd move to another go-go bar — the Red Flame in Pomona, the Shack in Fontana, the Tom Cat in Torrence — [but] we even got thrown out of after-hours jam sessions."

If Zappa's idea wasn't exactly practical, it certainly set the tone for what was to come. Zappa wanted to work against the standard bar-band mentality of imitating both the image and success of other bands. For Zappa, being a musician meant being in the service of your muse, not at the mercy of the paying customer or the guy running the establishment. Yet Coronado had a point: they wouldn't get work with that attitude.

Zappa saw giving in to the norm as a concession to conformist attitudes. "The groups that got the most work were the ones who pretended to be English," he wrote. "Often they were surf bands who wore wigs so that they looked like they had long hair, or added the word *Beatles* somewhere in their band name. . . . We didn't have long hair, we didn't have band uniforms, and we were ugly as fuck. We were, in the Biblical sense of the word, UNEMPLOYABLE." Out of this desperate set of circumstances, Zappa developed a defiantly hostile stage presence to grab the audience's full attention. "We got into the habit of insulting the audience,"

Zappa wrote in *Hit Parader* in 1968. "We made a big reputation that way. Nobody came to hear us play, they came in to see how much abuse they could take.... We managed to get jobs on that basis, but it didn't last very long because we'd wind up abusing the owner of the club."

Undaunted, they headed back to the Broadside in Pomona. It was time to change their name to something that defined that "ugly as fuck" image. It was decided, on Mother's Day 1964, that they would become the Mothers. "At the time, if you were a good musician, you were a motherfucker," Zappa told Nigel Leigh. "And 'Mothers' was short for a collection of motherfuckers." The Mothers, according to Zappa, weren't quite good enough to earn the banner of "motherfucker." He knew, though, that they were light-years ahead of the competition in their environment. The so-called "project/object" was born. "The project was carefully planned," Zappa wrote in 1968. "I had been looking for the right people for a long time.... I composed a composite, gap-filling product that fills most of the gaps between so-called serious music and so-called popular music."

In a press kit issued six years later, Zappa elaborated on his strategy: "Perhaps the most unique aspect of the Mothers' work is the *conceptual continuity* of the group's *output macrostructure*. There is, and always has been, a conscious control of thematic and structural elements flowing through each album, live performance, and interview.... The *project/object* contains *plans* and *non-plans*, also precisely calculated *event-structures* designed to accommodate the mechanics of fate and all bonus statistical improbabilities thereto."

Neil Slaven comments on Zappa's ambitions: "The *project/object* was the means by which Zappa incorporated every aspect of his work into an undefined grand design. It meant that every record and performance, every musician and member of the audience, every critical reaction to each gig, record, video and interview was integrated into a unifiable whole. Beneath all this was the continuity of the compositions, which followed consistent themes and experiments that, in turn, were adapted and augmented by the influence of random events and circumstances chosen by him for being either opposite or contradictory."

Zappa's utopian synthesis couldn't have come along at a better time. The British Invasion of the Beatles and the Rolling Stones in 1964 sent American record companies into a panic trying to sign any band that could write music and strum a guitar. Out of all this hysteria, the freakish behavior of a counterculture started to emerge. The time had come for the Mothers to head for Los Angeles.

WHO NEEDS THE PEACE CORPS?

3

"American culture has a lot of great moustaches in its history," Matt Groening told Nigel Leigh. "Mark Twain had a great moustache. Charlie Chaplin, Ben Turpin... but Zappa, he's got the best moustache in American history... he's got that little thing on his chin... an imperial.... That's like one of the great icons of the 20th century."

Zappa grew his famous moustache, with the little imperial above the chin, to emulate '50s R&B band leader Johnny Otis, who was famous for the song "Willie and the Hand Jive." "I thought it looked good on bluesman Johnny Otis, so I grew it," Zappa said years later. "I talked to Johnny Otis when I was in high school. I went down and saw his studio on a field trip one day with a few of the guys from the Blackouts.... I saw his echo chamber, which was a cement room, and he was into overdubbing and a lot of that stuff even in the early days, and he gave us a bunch of records and talked about the business."

When the Mothers got to L.A., they incorporated a harsher blues sound into their music. First, they hired guitarist Alice Stuart. "She played guitar very well and sang well," Zappa recalled in *Hit Parader*. "I had an idea for combining certain modal influences into our basically country blues sound. We were playing a lot of Muddy Waters [and] Howlin' Wolf–type stuff. Alice played good fingerstyle guitar, but she couldn't play 'Louie Louie,' so I fired her." Zappa also picked up Henry Vestine, one of the West Coast's best blues guitarists, but when the music started to get weird, Vestine got going. Besides, he had a huge alcohol and drug problem that Zappa wouldn't tolerate. Vestine later joined the blues-rock ensemble Canned Heat, whom he played for — off and on — until his death in 1997.

Zappa also briefly hired James Guercio, who would later find fame managing Chad & Jeremy and producing groups like the Buckinghams, Chicago, and Blood, Sweat & Tears. Given Zappa's interest in the work of Ives, Satie, and Varèse, it's significant that he picked Guercio. A few years after they met, Guercio stuck a brief excerpt from Ives' *Central Park in the Dark* right in the middle of the Buckinghams' insipid love song "Susan." And Satie's *Gymnopédies* was included on the second Blood, Sweat & Tears album. Chicago's fourth LP, in 1971, opened with the appropriately cacophonic "A Hit for Varèse."

Once Guercio left, Zappa added a rhythm guitarist, Elliot Ingber. So the Mothers, circa 1965, consisted of Zappa on lead guitar, Ingber on rhythm guitar, vocalist Ray Collins, Roy Estrada on bass, and Jimmy Carl Black on drums. "In the case of Roy Estrada and Jimmy Carl Black, they knew unless their hair grew out they couldn't work in Hollywood," Zappa told *High Times*. "[But] they would still have to drive home to Orange County to their tract homes. They would have to tuck their hair inside their collar and pull it up so that nobody saw them driving down the street." Is it any wonder L.A. is known as "the City of Lost Angels"? Here's a place where sellouts go to bask in the sun, where shady deals are made under palm trees, and the hedonistic pleasures of the Beach Boys would give way to the apocalyptic horrors of Charles Manson. L.A. was the corruptible home of Raymond Chandler's incorruptible detective Philip Marlowe, and the place that seduced Annie Hall away from Alvy Singer in Woody Allen's hit comedy. It was the tinsel town where writer Nathanael West *(The Day of the Locust)* once said people "were stirred by the promise of miracles and then only to violence."

In the mid-'60s, L.A. was in a state of transition. There was much racial and social unrest, and an emerging freak scene, which evolved as a reaction to the perceived corruption and evil perpetrated by the city's inequities. This attitude was different from the hippie scene growing in San Francisco. "San Francisco in the mid-'60s was very chauvinistic, and ethnocentric," Zappa wrote. "To the *Friscoids*' way of thinking, everything that came from THEIR town *was really important Art*, and *anything* from *anyplace* else (especially L.A.) was dogshit. *Rolling Stone* magazine helped to promote this fiction, nationwide. . . . The scene in Los Angeles was far more bizarre. No matter how 'peace-love' the San Francisco bands might try to make themselves, they eventually had to come south to evil ol' Hollywood to get a record deal."

Neil Slaven expands more eloquently on the difference between the hippies and the freaks: "Hippies preached tolerance and love, fostered a herd instinct when it came to modes of dress and vocabulary, and turned begging (in the name of self-help) into a community service. Down in mercenary L.A., where they emphasized the second word of 'show business,' freaks were more individualistic and ego-driven, taking 'love' where they found it and equating 'tolerance' with 'every man for himself.'"

Zappa also told one interviewer, "In L.A. you had people freaking out; that is, making their own clothes, dressing however they wanted to dress, wearing their hair out; that is, being weird as they wanted to be in public and everybody going

WHO NEEDS THE PEACE CORPS?

in separate directions — I got to San Francisco and found everybody dressed up in 1890s garb, all pretty codified dress."

As the freak scene in L.A. grew, however, the police reaction to it did as well. Officers were tear-gassing kids and enforcing curfews. "People started looking as if they might want some of their rights back," Derek Taylor, the Beatles' press agent, told author David Walley. "Which they only just discovered they didn't have because the biggest deal up to then was getting girls in trouble, pimples, college, and getting busted for a six-pack."

Zappa was now living in a two-room apartment at 1819 Bellevue Avenue, which was parallel to the Hollywood Freeway in Echo Park. He had become deeply involved in the scene and was developing song ideas from what he was observing. Songs such as "Who Are the Brain Police," "Oh No," "Hungry Freaks, Daddy," and "Bow Tie Daddy," came out of the events of 1965.

One of those events was the August race riot in the inner city of Watts — a revolt of such magnitude that it gained worldwide attention. The casual arrest of a black motorist was the spark that set off a powder keg of frustration. This was an uprising brought on by neglect, black unemployment, discrimination, poverty, plus brutality by the L.A. police. For six days, 10,000 angry people turned Watts into an inferno. Rioters burned cars and buildings and looted stores while the riot police were pelted with stones, attacked with knives, and shot at. The National Guard was finally called in, and by the time order was restored, thirty-four people were dead, hundreds were injured, and over 4,000 were arrested. Out of this tragic event came Zappa's song "Trouble Every Day," or, as it came to be known, "The Watts Riot Song." Although the song shares some of the outrage and purpose of protest songs of the time, it is also a blistering blues number that spares neither side:

Well, I'm about to get sick
From watchin' my TV
Been checkin' out the news
Until my eyeballs fail to see
I mean to say that every day
Is just another rotten mess
And when it's gonna change, my friends
Is anybody's guess.

Even though the singer is watching the ugly scenario unfold on his television, Zappa provides little emotional distance for the listener. He puts us right in the center of the action:

> I seen the cops out on the street
> Watched 'em throwin' rocks and stuff
> And chokin' in the heat
> Listened to reports
> About the whiskey passin' round
> Seen the smoke and fire
> And the market burnin' down
> Watched while everybody
> On his street would take a turn
> To stomp, and smash, and bash, and crash
> And slash, and bust, and burn.

But as much as the singer pleads for sanity ("And I'm watchin'/And I'm waitin'/Hopin' for the best"), he also knows that circumstances have pushed this event beyond any facile solutions. The song is filled with irresolvable contradictions — the kind that deprive the listener of the satisfaction of pumping his fist in the air out of solidarity. The singer lashes out at his television: "Take your TV tube and eat it!" But, as Craig Werner points out in his luminous study of soul music, *A Change Is Gonna Come: Music, Race & the Soul of America*, television also made those feral images more real to us than a newspaper story might. "[Zappa] saw a televised world of smoke and fire, of women drivers machine-gunned from their seats, of drunken mobs waiting their turn," Werner writes. "He was well aware that images of fire in the street would continue to stoke the fires in our hearts." Zappa spends a lot of time at the end of the song talking about those fires burning, too, and the way everybody gets scorched by the flames.

When the Mothers started performing the song, it had a slow, tentative beat that suppressed some of its power. But when it finally appeared on the group's first album, *Freak Out!* (1966), the song had developed a force equal to Bob Dylan's "Like a Rolling Stone." Zappa would continue to perform "Trouble Every Day" right up until his last tour in 1988 (when he used it to strike out at disgraced televangelist Jimmy Swaggart), but it was never better than in its first recording. Listening to the version on *Freak Out!* today, it's just as relevant to the Rodney

WHO NEEDS THE PEACE CORPS?

King riots of the '90s as it was to the Watts riot of 1965. "Nothing has changed," Zappa told *Pulse* shortly before his death. "We have the same racial hatred, the same unwillingness to face the causes of racial unrest. We've had years to examine the causes of the Watts riots, but no one has done anything about it. There were studies and reports and conclusions then, just like there were studies and reports and conclusions reached after [the Rodney King] riots. There's a certain type of American adolescent behavior that hasn't gotten any better since the '60s."

While Zappa wrote about social unrest, he was also fending off starvation. He spent most of his time hanging out at Canter's Deli, a favorite hub for freaks that also drew such diverse company as record producer Phil Spector, folksinger Tim Hardin, and controversial comic Lenny Bruce. Although Zappa wouldn't actually meet and talk to Bruce until the Mothers opened for him at the Fillmore West in June 1966, his influence on the satirical content of Zappa's music was powerful.

4

People should be taught what is, not what should be. All my humor is based on destruction and despair. If the whole world were tranquil, without disease and violence, I'd be standing in the breadline — right back of J. Edgar Hoover.

LENNY BRUCE

If Edgard Varèse, Charles Ives, Igor Stravinsky, and "Guitar" Slim provided the musical foundation for Frank Zappa to synthesize his own meticulous sound, stand-up comedian Lenny Bruce gave him the satirical strategy. Bruce was a social satirist, often compared to Jonathan Swift and Mark Twain, who took on all the cultural taboos, including religion, sex, and drugs. He called his memoir *How to Talk Dirty and Influence People* — mocking the social etiquette guide by Dale Carnegie. When Bruce died in 1966, the *Washington Post* said in its editorial, "Lenny Bruce believed in free speech with a passion that was often masked by the jokes he told. He was . . . one of the boldest and one of the best." Jerry Tallmer is even more to the point in his eulogy in the *Evergreen Review*. "His gospel was freedom, sexual freedom, racial freedom . . . in short, happiness through truth. Bruce enraged many people, including some arresting officers and psychiatrists and judges and prosecutors and critics who by the record of their lives and deeds were as sick as he was. But wasn't that what his *shtick* was all about?" Bruce's *shtick*, as film critic Pauline Kael wrote, was being a comic who "took off on the whole straight world." The worldview he expressed, like Zappa's, "came from the cruddiness and corruption of show business."

In 1952, Bruce, then in his mid-twenties, moved to Los Angeles with his stripper wife, Honey, and started doing comedy bits opening for strippers. It was the perfect atmosphere to work his act because he could make cracks to the band and say whatever he wanted. Within a few years, Bruce had branched out to nightclubs, where he started to combine his burlesque-house act with social satire. In 1957, he was starting to build his reputation as the "King of the Sick Comics" by taking on everyone, from the Pope to Jesus and Jimmy Hoffa. Bruce was one of the first guests on Hugh Hefner's after-hours TV talk show, *Playboy Penthouse*, and he did a television first — he blew his nose on camera.

By 1961, Bruce was so popular that he sold out Carnegie Hall during one of New York City's worst blizzards. He had found an audience that wanted to see how far he might go. As Pauline Kael observed, "Bruce's hostility and obscenity were shortcuts to audience response; he could get and hold the audience's attention because they didn't know what or whom he was going to attack and degrade next, and they could sense he wasn't sure himself." Bruce also satirized — and tested — the prudishness of the audience.

One night in Philadelphia, a few months after his success at Carnegie Hall, Bruce got busted for narcotics. The next day, a bailbondsman suggested he pay off the judge so the charges would be dropped. Bruce went to the media and blew the whistle on everybody. As a result, the charges were dismissed. But what looked like a victory turned into the beginning of the end: the police and the courts weren't happy about being embarrassed by a sick comedian. From that moment forward, Bruce would continually get busted for obscenity. In Los Angeles, he was arrested for using the word *schmuck* onstage. In San Francisco, he was apprehended for using the word *cocksucker* during a routine. As much as he joked about it, the fact was, clubs were canceling engagements and Bruce was spending more money on legal fees than he was earning as a comic.

In 1964, at the Café Au Go Go in New York, he had sold out an April 3 performance. That night, he did a popular routine about the country's obsession with Eleanor Roosevelt's tits, and the club was cited for presenting an obscene show. Bruce was arrested and put on trial. During the hearing before a panel of judges, Bruce wanted to do his act so he could prove it wasn't obscene. The judges refused,

WHO NEEDS THE PEACE CORPS?

and Bruce was given four months in the workhouse and a $10,000 fine. Broke and defeated, he went back to L.A. It was during this period that Zappa encountered the fallen comedian at Canter's Deli.

What Zappa absorbed from Lenny Bruce was a fearless reproach of all that is sacred, combined with a performer's fervor in getting a rise out of the audience — making them the butt of the joke, as well as unwilling participants in it. Bruce, like Zappa, drew on the milieu around him for his material. "A lot of [Bruce's] humor came from hanging out with jazz musicians," recalled saxophonist Bunk Gardner. "He would do 'inside jokes' that only guys in the band would understand. . . . A true artist in the sense that he never stood idle — he always forged ahead regardless of whether it offended some people or not — especially religious people."

Sometimes Zappa drew explicitly from Bruce's routines. The "Don't come in me" section from "Harry, You're a Beast" on *We're Only in It for the Money* borrows directly from Bruce's "To Is a Preposition, Come Is a Verb." And in "Jewish Princess" from *Sheik Yerbouti* (1979) and the live versions of "Bobby Brown Goes Down" and "Cosmik Debris" on *You Can't Do That on Stage Anymore, Vol. 3* (1989), Zappa borrows material from Bruce's "Lone Ranger" bit.

Frank Zappa didn't become quite the counterculture hero that Lenny Bruce did, though. For one, many educated liberals liked to believe that Bruce's routines were "cleansing the national air," as Pauline Kael put it. People were also willing to accept Bruce's sleazy view of the show-business world as it pertained to stand-up comedy, but the counterculture audience saw rock 'n' roll as something beyond reproach. People who did romanticize the world of pop were bound to find Frank Zappa's satire smug or arrogant. In fact, many still believe Lenny Bruce's art grew specifically from his attack on the status quo, but he was also satirizing liberal hypocrisy, too. His tragic end from a drug overdose ultimately transformed him into a romantic myth. For some in the counterculture, though, Bruce's martyrdom was more appealing than the scowling image of Frank Zappa.

5

Lenny Bruce's roommate, John Judnich, earned a living by renting out PA systems to local groups, and he was the original recording engineer on the Mothers of Invention's first live recordings. One day, when Judnich was visiting Zappa, he introduced him to a guy named Crazy Jerry. Jerry was in his late forties and had been institutionalized for many years. He was also a speed freak who had become a bodybuilder after his mother bought him a copy of *Gray's Anatomy* when he was a youngster. Besides having a love for bending bars with various parts of his body, he was also addicted to electricity. Once he and a friend jumped a fence at a local power substation just to get juiced.

As if this wasn't enough, Jerry lived in Echo Park with a character who was even stranger. Wild Bill was a chemist who made the speed that kept Jerry going. But Wild Bill had another peculiar hobby involving mannequins he'd painted and fitted with rubber prosthetic devices so he could fuck them. While Zappa considered this a colorful era in Southern California, "a couple of Republican administrations and *poof*!" Ben Watson writes, "Zappa likes to focus on weirdness for its own sake, fashioning out of deviant behavior icons of protest against the homogenized lifestyle of postwar America." Simply put, Zappa decided to document the history of people that a homogenized society would rather not acknowledge. He was so deeply impressed by the freak culture in L.A. that he wanted to put it on the cultural map with his music.

Zappa was also impressed that drug use was far less important to the freaks than it was to the chemically refreshed hippies of San Francisco. Zappa was always adamantly antidrug. "The real freaks weren't using drugs at all," Zappa told Michael Gray. "Then there were the weekenders who would come in and stick anything in their mouth that they could find. And you were hearing about people freaking out on acid all over the place." Zappa felt that music provided a better imaginative stimulant than hallucinogens. "I don't use any and I've never encouraged it," Zappa told Ronnie Oberman of the *Washington Star*. "The same state of psychedelic happiness can be induced through dancing, listening to music, holding your breath and spinning around, and any number of the old, easy-to-perform and 100 per cent legal means — all of which I endorse."

Gray, though, felt Zappa's account was a sentimental, inaccurate reading of the freak scene: "Perhaps there *was*, for a short while, a kind of artsy freak scene only tangentially involved with the L.A. rock biz, and relatively pure in heart. But the rock biz, like capitalism generally, has a talent for co-option, and within a few months most freaks were caught up in the never-ending hustle for in-ness with the new rock 'n' roll musicians who passed through the L.A. clubs and the more established rock people — like Phil Spector — who lived in big houses up on the hills and hung around Canter's and the Trip and the Whisky looking cool. In the end, every one of us on the sidelines of rock becomes a groupie of one sort or another, and the L.A. freak people were not immune."

WHO NEEDS THE PEACE CORPS?

Almost every popular cultural movement that went against the grain of the mainstream, from Dada to surrealism, became endangered by co-option — and the '60s counterculture was no exception. Zappa's initial interest and enthusiasm wasn't naïveté but a utopian hope.

The leaders of the L.A. freak movement were an artist named Vito Paulekas and his hedonistic buddy, Carl Franzoni. Carl wore black tights, leopard-skin leotards, and a cape with an unambiguous *F* stitched on it, a designation for one of his predominant activities. David Walley describes Carl as one of the more extreme freaks: "He let his hair grow out in greasy curls. He wore leotards and crazy outfits and danced like mad. He used to have a band called the Wild Flowers but he never played an instrument. His thing was running the orchestra, playing the tambourine, and dancing." Zappa, who composed the song "Hungry Freaks, Daddy" for Carl, wrote about the effect Carl's dancing had on a teenage audience in Dallas. "Carl Franzoni [was] our 'go-go' boy," Zappa recalled. "He was wearing ballet tights, *frugging violently*. Carl has testicles which are bigger than a breadbox. *Much* bigger than a breadbox. The looks on the faces of the Baptist teens experiencing *their grandeur* is a treasured memory."

Vito was a fifty-four-year-old sculptor who led a troupe of dancers dedicated to shocking people with their complete lack of inhibitions. Pamela Des Barres, who would later become nanny to the Zappa children as well as a member of the first — and only — groupie rock band, the GTO's (Girls Together Outrageously), describes Vito in her memoir, *I'm With the Band*: "Vito [was] reclining on a rose-colored velvet couch, surrounded by lavishly decorated people of all ages and races who seemed to be paying him homage. He had long, graying, uncombed hair and a ragtag beard that looked like it had been dipped in a bottle of glitter; he was wearing only a lace loincloth, and his chest had been painted like a peacock feather." While Vito danced nude on a tabletop, his twenty-year-old wife, Szou (a former cheerleader), suckled their three-year-old son, Godot.

Vito was something of a patron saint for new rock groups in L.A., like the Byrds, Love, and the Leaves, who made "Hey Joe." Vito and his companions brought a sexual freedom that knew no moral bounds: public sex, underage sex, and multiple partners. Des Barres describes one such scene: "Vito invited a select few to come home with him to observe a tender fondling session. . . . It was such an odd occurrence; no one seemed to be getting off sexually by watching the pubescent girls, but everyone was silently observing the scene as if it were part of their necessary training by the headmaster, Vito."

Since one of the girls was only twelve, Vito was deported to Tahiti. His extreme form of hedonism — which could only happen in the sun-drenched climate of Southern California — pushed the boundaries of what many considered decent behavior. It was perfect folkloric material for Frank Zappa. But first, the Mothers had to find work, get an agent, and make a record.

6

While living in Echo Park in 1964, Zappa ran into Don Cerveris, the old friend and high school teacher who directed *Run Home Slow*. He introduced Zappa to his friend Mark Cheka, a fifty-year-old pop artist out of New York. "I came to the conclusion that the band needed a manager, and had thought (*Ow! Was I going to regret this one!*) that the person required for this important position needed to be someone with an 'artistic background,'" Zappa recalled. "Only then, I reasoned, would our aesthetic be properly understood, and, once we had acquired a manager of such sensitivity, our future success in show business would be assured." Cheka made a trip to Pomona to hear the Mothers at the Broadside. Although Cheka lacked skills in lining up gigs for the Mothers, he did bring on board Herb Cohen, who had plenty of experience booking bands.

Cohen, born in New York in 1933, became interested in music while he was in the army in San Francisco in the '50s. He began promoting the work of Odetta, a black folksinger he lived with at the time, as well as assisting troubadour Pete Seeger, who was being persecuted by the red-baiting Senator Joseph McCarthy. In 1956, after moving to L.A., Cohen ran a club called the Purple Onion, which featured folk and blues performers like Sonny Terry & Brownie McGhee and Theodore Bikel. However, Cohen didn't last there long — the club owner wanted him to wear a suit and tie. Cohen borrowed money from Bikel so he could open his own place on the Sunset Strip, the Unicorn.

Cohen developed a reputation for fighting the police over various issues, such as licensing for coffeehouses. In 1959, he featured Lenny Bruce and was busted for obscenity. Cohen got fed up with the business and left L.A. a couple of times, but he always returned.

By 1964, the Sunset Strip had become a folksinger's dream. Clubs like the New Balladeer, the Golden Bear, the Thirsty Ear, and the Troubadour were popping up everywhere. After the British Invasion made its impact in '64 and '65, rock bands with folk roots, like the Byrds, also began making waves, drawing attention with

WHO NEEDS THE PEACE CORPS?

an odd hybrid of electric blues and folk music soon to be dubbed "folk rock." In the midst of this radical change, Cohen met Zappa and the Mothers.

It wasn't hard to see why Zappa and Cohen would be drawn to each other. They were both fearless individualists who didn't follow trends — they set out to create them. Cohen encountered the band when Cheka arranged for the Mothers to appear at a party being filmed for a faux documentary called *Mondo Hollywood* (1965). The movie, produced in the same tabloid spirit as the Italian exploitation film *Mondo Cane* (1963), was supposed to be a revealing and shocking examination of the Hollywood freak scene. (It was also supposed to feature the Mothers, but they were cut from the film when Cohen became their manager and demanded too much money for their appearance.)

Cohen was both intrigued and perplexed by what he heard. He told David Walley, "They played all original material and they looked good. You're talking about five guys who weren't like teenage rock stars — who had enough things going to make it obvious there was a viable commodity." When Cohen met with Zappa, the first thing he was impressed by was the musician's intelligence. It was after a few meetings that Zappa told Cohen just what his project/object was. "I didn't quite understand at the time what he was talking about," Cohen told Mick Watts. But he was impressed enough to get them an audition at the Action in Hollywood.

The Mothers had been rejected by the Action seven months earlier because their hair wasn't long enough. This time, their hair was a little longer, and they wore purple shirts and black hats. They got the gig. "It was very tough getting the group together in the beginning," Zappa told Sally Kempton of *The Village Voice* in 1968. "They didn't like making themselves ugly, but they especially didn't like playing ugly. It's hard getting a musician to play ugly, it contradicts all his training. It's hard to make them understand that all that ugliness taken together can come out sounding quite beautiful." Just how ugly were the Mothers to look at? "There is nothing cute about us," Zappa told *High Times*' John Swenson. "But there was a market for people who bought monster magazines and things like that, and I assumed that people who went for ugly would go for us. We had a potential constituency — people who liked ugly things. This is not as large a market as people who liked cute things."

People who liked monster magazines were young adolescent males who felt like outcasts. They weren't necessarily malcontents, but they were the underclass with which Zappa identified. Their rage, which could turn explosive, could also be a force for cultural and political change. Since they both rejected the mainstream and were rejected by it, Zappa offered alternatives. He gave audiences an image different from those beautiful groups who were trying to lull everyone back into the Garden of Eden.

Since Zappa was trying to appeal to monster-magazine lovers, he decided to take an image right out of the graveyard. "We looked like Mafia undertakers," Zappa recalled in *Rolling Stone*. The packaging became just as important as the music; Zappa realized that in the world of popular music, a band's image determined its impact. Besides, he knew just how much Americans like to be *entertained*. "Americans hate music, but they love entertainment," Zappa once said. "The reason they hate music is that they've never stopped to listen to what the musical content is because they're so befuddled by the packaging and merchandising that surround the musical material they've been induced to buy." By creating an image that ran counter to popular taste, Zappa hoped audiences would stop to consider just what popular taste was, what made it popular, and why they were being induced to buy into it.

When Cohen took sole control over the Mothers, he booked the band at some of those popular clubs — including the Whisky A Go-Go and the Trip. As Zappa had promised, the band did original material like "Memories of El Monte" and some new songs, including an abstract number called "Help, I'm a Rock," which actually stopped the audience from hoofing on the dance floor. Instead, they started listening to this strangely absorbing music. The Trip might have found this acceptable, but the Whisky A Go-Go didn't. The owner, Elmer Valentine, who also owned the Trip, was more adamant that the bands that played the Whiskey play dance music because why else have "A Go-Go" in the title? "[Their] audience wasn't anything to brag about — they were just a bunch of drunk people in go-go boots," Zappa told Nigel Leigh. "But the money was a lot better than the Broadside, because we were actually making union scale." Since they insisted on playing their own songs, the Mothers didn't make union scale at the Whisky for long. One night, they played a complete hour of "Help, I'm a Rock" and "Memories of El Monte," and there wasn't a soul on the dance floor. They were fired, and the band found themselves "selling pop bottles for cigarettes and bologna," as Zappa told *Rolling Stone*.

When all hope of finding work seemed dim, a number of fortuitous episodes occurred that would help the Mothers land their first record contract. It all started with the appearance of eighteen-year-old Pamela Lee Zarubica, a young white

WHO NEEDS THE PEACE CORPS?

Pepperdine College student from the middle-class neighborhood of Inglewood. One day, she ventured into the city to visit the Sunset Strip, loved what she saw, and never turned back. While finishing college, Zarubica got a job as a part-time secretary at the Whisky A Go-Go and moved into a house with three other girls in the Kirkwood section of L.A. Zarubica first encountered Zappa and the Mothers while the band was sitting in with the Grass Roots (the precursor to Arthur Lee's psychedelic band Love) at the Trip in 1965. "[The Mothers] were rivaled by nothing we had seen to that date," she told Michael Gray. "This Indian drummer [Jimmy Carl Black] that was never without a bottle of beer in his hand.... The lead singer [Ray Collins] looked like an ex-Hell's Angel that would bash your head if you even talked to him, [though] he turned out to be the most peaceful person I know.... The bass player [Roy Estrada] was a Mexican who never said anything.... They played one song ['Help, I'm a Rock'] that lasted about twenty minutes, and they also did [Little Walter's] 'My Babe'.... As soon as their set was finished, Frank was standing in front of our table.... 'Good evening, ladies, I'm really glad you're here. Would you like to come down to our dressing room?' He looked terrifying...."

Soon Zarubica and Zappa had developed a deep, yet platonic, relationship. She was distressed to find that his one-room apartment was "thick with dust, old posters about El Monte Legion Stadium dances, music sheets, and records," so she was paid to come and clean the place. Many of the Mexican kids surrounding Zappa's apartment referred to him as Beardo Weirdo. Pam came to refer to Zappa as "Omar," after Omar Sharif in the film *Dr. Zhivago*, because of the huge fur coat Zappa often wore. (You can view it in all its gaudy splendor on the cover of *Freak Out!*) Zappa became both a mentor and confederate to Zarubica. "He used to come to my house all the time, bringing me those Chinese cookies from Greenblatts — the ones with the big chocolate drop on top," she recalled. "He was all the advice I could have needed.... He tried to teach me that sex didn't have to be dirty and that drugs were pointless.... My God, the boy had talent, was obviously brilliant yet warm and close." Zappa eventually moved in with Pamela at her apartment at 8404 Kirkwood.

Zappa may have found a new home, but he still didn't have a record contract. The Mothers did, however, finally record some demos at Original Sound Studios because of Zappa's connections with Art Laboe from the Studio Z days. These recordings, which included an early version of "Plastic People," were turned down by MGM and Columbia Records. Although MGM never bothered to get back to Zappa, Columbia's vice-president and general manager, Clive Davis, who today is the head of Arista Records, did. He called to say the band had "no commercial potential." Zappa would place that phrase on the inside cover of *Freak Out!* as a token of his scorn for a business to which he refused to ingratiate himself.

While the Mothers were playing at the Action on Halloween night, 1965, an unusual guest made an appearance. According to Zappa, the Action attracted celebrities, from Warren Beatty to Soupy Sales. But on this particular evening, a very drunken John Wayne turned up accompanied by two bodyguards. "He saw me," Zappa recalled with bemusement, "and picked me up and said, 'I saw you in Egypt and you were great . . . and then you blew me!' Onstage I said, 'Ladies and gentlemen, it's Halloween and we were going to have some important guests here tonight — like George Lincoln Rockwell, head of the American Nazi Party — but unfortunately all we could get was John Wayne.' He got up and made some drunken speech, and his bodyguards told me I'd better cool it." Zappa, who that evening dressed in khaki work pants, no shoes, an 1890s bathing suit, and a perfectly placed black homburg, had to pass the Duke on his way out. "As I went by, he got up and smashed my hat down on top of my head," Zappa continued. "I took it off and popped it back out. This apparently annoyed him, as he shouted, *'You don't like the way I fix hats? I've been fixin' hats for forty years.'* I put it back on my head and he smashed it down again. I said, *'I'm not even gonna give you a chance to apologize,'* and walked out."

That year, the Mothers' fortunes began to change. The catalyst of that change was one Tom Wilson. In 1954, Wilson had become one of the first blacks to graduate from Harvard with a degree in economics. Yet he had already developed an enormous interest in ground-breaking music, which he pursued with more zeal than his study of commerce. Shortly after his graduation, he produced some landmark jazz albums, including Cecil Taylor's *Jazz Advance* (1955), avant-gardist Sun Ra's *Sound of Joy* (1957), and John Coltrane's *Coltrane Time* (1958).

Wilson ventured into the counterculture when he became a producer at Columbia Records in the mid-'60s. He was behind the controls for Bob Dylan's *The Times They Are a-Changin'* (1964) and *Another Side of Bob Dylan* (1964), as well as 1965's *Bringing It All Back Home*, Dylan's first foray into electric music. Then Wilson moved on to another folk act that Columbia hoped he could mold into stars: Simon & Garfunkel. He had already produced their first album, *Wednesday Morning 3 A.M.* (1964), but Wilson came up with a radical idea for their first single. He took a simple acoustic track from the album, "The Sound of Silence," and added electric guitar, bass, and drums. The single became a hit, and Simon & Garfunkel completely changed their image and sound.

WHO NEEDS THE PEACE CORPS?

In November 1965, while the Mothers were playing at the Whisky, Herb Cohen got wind that Wilson was in town. Although Wilson was now the East Coast A&R man for the jazz label Verve, he had headed west to produce an album for a new client, the British rock band the Animals. Cohen talked Wilson into making a quick journey to the Trip to see the Mothers. By the time Wilson arrived, the Mothers were doing their Watts riot song, "Trouble Every Day." Wilson assumed they were yet another white R&B group. "He stayed for five minutes, said 'Yeah, yeah, yeah,' slapped me on the back, shook my hand and said, 'Wonderful. We're going to make a record of you. Goodbye,'" Zappa wrote. "I didn't see him again for four months. . . . He probably went back to New York and said, 'I signed me another rhythm and blues band from the Coast. We've got the Righteous Brothers. Now we're getting the Mothers.'" On March 1, 1966, Wilson returned with a contract that gave the Mothers a $2,500 advance plus a two-year, five-album deal with Verve/MGM. But before they could begin recording with Tom Wilson as producer, they would have to change their name. One executive at the label was aware of what "the Mothers" meant and the fuss it could cause. As the story goes: out of necessity, they became the Mothers of Invention.

"He was a fabulous guy," Zappa said of Wilson in *Billboard*. "I think they could use a guy like that in the business now because he was a real risk-taker. He put his ass on the line in order to sign us, and not just sign us, but after the first album was a complete flop, he pushed to make sure we could do album No. 2 and album No. 3. I definitely had the feeling that as a producer of those early records, he was in our corner." While Zappa and the band prepared the material for their debut album, Tim Sullivan (in lieu of money owed Zappa for his work composing the music on *Run Home Slow*) let them use his sound studio so they could rehearse. One recording from those sessions, "How Could I Be Such a Fool?," can be heard on *Mystery Disc*.

When Tom Wilson came back from New York, he and Zappa started to plot out what would become *Freak Out!*. "We had a little chat in his room and that was when he first discovered that R&B wasn't all we played," Zappa recalled. "Things started to change: we decided not to make a single, but an album instead." The first tune they recorded was an old Studio Z track called "Any Way the Wind Blows," with Wilson tapping his foot and nodding in rhythm to this relatively conventional R&B song. When it came time to record the spooky and comically ominous "Who Are the Brain Police?," Wilson's foot was no longer tapping. He was on the phone to the executives in New York trying to explain why this new band, the Mothers of Invention, wasn't . . . exactly . . . an R&B band.

7

When Edgard Varèse died on November 6, 1965, Frank Zappa seemed bound and determined to pick up his fallen torch. As Michael Gray writes, Varèse's death "galvanized Frank into a stronger-than-ever determination that he was not going to just make records, but change the face of music." *Freak Out!*, released in July 1966, didn't exactly change the face of music, but it had an incalculable influence on the pop scene. Until then, the only rock double album was Bob Dylan's *Blonde on Blonde* (which had come out only two months earlier). Yet, unlike *Blonde On Blonde, Freak Out!* was designed conceptually. The songs weren't randomly gathered in the traditional manner of making an album. There was a strategy at work on this debut. Zappa was presenting a whole new style of music that hadn't yet been heard in American pop.

The fundamental difference between the current rock scene and Zappa was that he considered the Mothers of Invention the ugly reminder that railed against the optimistic wave of hippie idealism. "We were well on our way to becoming the most despised musical group of all time," Zappa summed up in his liner notes to *Mystery Disc*, "partially for making noises like this . . . in an era when everyone else was stuffing flowers in the ends of policemen's guns." *Freak Out!* was far less solemn than those albums that promoted the dispensing of bouquets, and it was more lavishly deranged, too. The front cover featured a color negative of the band with a comic-strip balloon coming from Zappa's mouth shouting, "FREAK OUT!" On the back cover is a letter from one Suzy Creamcheese:

> These Mothers is crazy. You can tell by their clothes. One guy wears beads and they all smell bad. We were gonna get them for a dance after the basketball game but my best pal warned me you can never tell how many are going to show up . . . sometimes the guy in the fur-coat doesn't show up and sometimes he does show up only he brings a big bunch of crazy people with him and they dance all over he place. None of the kids at my school like these Mothers . . . especially since my teacher told us what the words to their songs meant.

WHO NEEDS THE PEACE CORPS?

Her address is listed as Salt Lake City, but the letter actually came from somewhere a lot closer: the mind of Frank Zappa. "Suzy Creamcheese was a girl named Jeannie Vassoir, and she was the voice on the *Freak Out!* album," Zappa told *Melody Maker*. "And the myth of Suzy Creamcheese, the letter on the album, I wrote myself. There never really was a Suzy Creamcheese. It was just a figment of my imagination until people started identifying with it heavily." Over the next few albums, Suzy Creamcheese would become the epitome of the Mothers of Invention groupie. She was free-thinking, open to sex, but also very much her own person. On the track "It Can't Happen Here," when Zappa tells her lewdly he's very interested in her development, she replies, "Forget it!" Hmmm . . . it can't happen here.

Inside the album's gatefold was a short biography of Zappa, plus some "relevant quotes." These words of wisdom included Varèse's "The present-day composer refuses to die!" and Zappa's closing message to tourists at the Whisky A Go-Go: "If your children ever find out how *lame* you really are, they'll murder you in your sleep." Each song came with background notes, above which was an enormous list of people who "contributed materially in many ways to make our music what it is. Please don't hold it against them." These figures formed a broadly based lexicon: Igor Stravinsky, Johnny "Guitar" Watson, Richard Berry, Charles Ives, Paul Buff, Lenny Bruce, Johnny Otis, and Anton Webern. Zappa also included old pals like Vic Mortenson and Johnny Franklin, his old high school teacher Mr. Tossi, and his ex-wife, Kay Sherman. No rock 'n' roll album had ever claimed such a varied catalog of influences, or promoted an image that most advertisers wouldn't dare try to market to the public. But Zappa was announcing that these sundry individuals were alive in his music.

Freak Out! opens with a prophetic anthem that sets the tone for both the record and Zappa's career. "Hungry Freaks, Daddy" begins with the inverse of the guitar chords that began the Stones' "(I Can't Get No) Satisfaction." While ingeniously turning Bob Dylan's nowhere man, Mr. Jones (from "Ballad of a Thin Man"), into Mr. America, Zappa launched a full-frontal attack on America's moribund culture:

> *Mr. America, walk on by, your schools that do not teach*
> *Mr. America, walk on by, the minds that won't be reached*
> *Mr. America, try to hide the emptiness that's you inside*
> *But once you find that the way you lied*
> *And all the corny tricks you tried*
> *Will not forestall the rising tide of* HUNGRY FREAKS, DADDY!

The song was written for Carl Franzoni and the rest of the freaks, but the ideas at work are much larger than any one group's theme song. As great a record as "(I Can't Get No) Satisfaction" is, it speaks basically to a state of alienation in the listener. Mick Jagger is frustrated at having been betrayed by the promises of consumer culture. He feels cheated because conforming to corporate ideals doesn't make him happy. "Hungry Freaks, Daddy," on the other hand, speaks directly to the disenfranchised listener rather than the alienated one. The singer isn't betrayed by the false blandishments offered by the culture because he's already rejected them: "Philosophy that turns away/From those who aren't afraid to say what's on their minds/ The left-behinds of the Great Society."

The Great Society (a term invented by President Lyndon Johnson in 1964 to describe his ideal America) is already deemed false, so there's no reason to feel forsaken. Which is why today, when the Rolling Stones, who are (at least) *financially* satisfied, perform "(I Can't Get No) Satisfaction," it's a mere echo of a great rock song, while "Hungry Freaks, Daddy," performed as recently as 1991 by *Zappa's Universe*, has lost none of its bite. "I don't think it's any accident that the educational system in America has been brought to its current state," Zappa told *Spin* in 1991. "Because only a totally uneducated mass of people will be baffled by balloons. And yellow ribbons and little flags and buzzwords and guys saying 'new world order' and shit like that. I mean, only a person who has been dissuaded from any kind of critical thinking and doesn't know geography, doesn't know the English language — I mean, if you can't speak English, then this stuff works on you."

In fact, the minds that were denied by the Great Society were left even more estranged in the New World Order of the '90s. "One of the things taken out of the curriculum was civics," Zappa explained. "Civics was a class that used to be required before you could graduate from high school. You were taught what was in the U.S. Constitution. And after all the student rebellions in the '60s, civics was banished from the student curriculum and was replaced by something called social studies. Here we live in a country that has a fabulous constitution and all these guarantees, a contract between the citizens and the government — nobody knows what's in it. . . . And so, if you don't know what your rights are, how can you stand up for them? And furthermore, if you don't know what's in the document, how can you care if someone is shredding it?"

"Hungry Freaks, Daddy" is followed by something completely different in tone and subject. "I Ain't Got No Heart," which Zappa called "a summary of my feelings in social-sexual relationships," is a warm-up for songs to come that dispensed with

WHO NEEDS THE PEACE CORPS?

the clichés of love lyrics ("No angels singing up above today"). It's also a cry of independence from the possessive aspects of romantic love ("Why should an embrace or two/Make me such a part of you?"), but it's not a self-righteous shout. In fact, at the end, the singer is practically retching rather than crying.

"Who Are the Brain Police?" follows, the album's first truly bizarre cut. Ray Collins groans portentously over a throbbing bass tone, while creaking doors open around him: "What will you do if we let you go home?/And the plastic's all melted and so is the chrome/Who are the brain police?" For the first (but not last) time, exploring the idea of plastic, including record vinyl, addresses the fetishizing of the product itself ("What will you do when the label comes off?"). Zappa is satirizing the manner by which listeners identify with the music on the album in their efforts to form an identity. Partway through the song — coming out of nowhere — voices start screaming in unison. Zappa edits in a portion of "Help, I'm a Rock," from Side 3, to jolt the listener out of any comfort brought on by identification with this music. In that same instant, Zappa is playing with our comfortable notion of linear time. "Go Cry on Somebody Else's Shoulder" is pure '50s grease. Zappa even claims in the album's notes, "You should not listen to it. You should wear it on your hair." It opens with a typical '50s love-song recitation:

A year ago today was when you went away
But now you come back knocking on my door
You say you're back to stay. . . . But I say
Go cry on somebody else's shoulder.

It was an R&B song from the Studio Z days, co-written by Collins. "I was thinking about my ex-wife, if I remember right," Collins told DJ David Porter at KPFK in 1989. "So Frank and I were in Cucamonga, and so I said, 'Oh, I've got this idea about, "Don't bother me, go away, go cry on somebody else's shoulder." He said, 'Great!' So I sat down at the piano and started playing it, and Frank joined in, and we created 'Go Cry on Somebody Else's Shoulder.' And then, of course, the spoken part that's on the Mothers' album is all ad-libbed, right in the studio." At the end of the song, Collins improvises a number of come-on lines that Zappa uses to make you conscious of the stock clichés that are supposed to make you swoon. He would parody these pickup lines in later songs, such as "Honey, Don't You Want a Man Like Me?" from *Zappa in New York* and "Dancin' Fool" on *Sheik Yerbouti*.

In the liner notes, Zappa describes "Motherly Love" as "a body commercial for the band." As commercials go, this one is a pretty conspicuous come-on to groupies. Women who worship at the altars of pop stars are hardly a new phenomenon, but there were few songs so blatantly devoted to them. "Motherly Love," with the clever double entendre of its title, puts its meaning right up front:

Nature's been good to this here band
Don't ever think we're shy
Send us up some little groupies
And we'll take their hands
And rock 'em till they sweat and cry
What you need is . . . motherly love.

The Rolling Stones were one of the few other bands of the '60s that depicted some of the lust that existed in relationships between rock stars and groupies, as they boldly demonstrated in "Stray Cat Blues," a lasciviously charged rocker from *Beggar's Banquet* (1968). Other groups, like Buffalo Springfield ("Rock and Roll Woman") and Chicago ("The Road"), treated the affairs between groupies and rock groups with more tender affection and sensitivity. Zappa, however, was drawn to the sexual dynamic that existed between bands and their female followers, rather than the romantic possibilities.

The first side of *Freak Out!* ends with "How Could I Be Such a Fool?," a pretty straightforward love ballad, except that it's based in what Zappa calls, "a nanigo rhythm. . . . We call it [a] Motown Waltz." Sometimes Zappa would create the basis of something familiar and then employ a rhythm completely foreign to the style of the song. Like Stravinsky, Zappa used the past merely as a foundation for something new.

"Wowie Zowie," a goofy doo-wop number that begins the second side, takes its title from one of Pamela Zarubica's favorite phrases. (Zarubica can be heard uttering the phrase a few years later on *Uncle Meat*, during the track "Ian Underwood Whips It Out." When Ian states he's the "straight member of the group," Pamela says dispassionately, "Wowie zowie!") The song mixes teeny-bopper corn with cleverly placed asides. In "Wowie Zowie," Zappa subverts the gooey lyrics of adolescent pop by inserting suggestive passages like, "Wowie zowie, baby, you're so neat/I don't even care if you shave your legs."

Most of the rest of Side 2, including "I'm Not Satisfied," "You Didn't Try to Call

WHO NEEDS THE PEACE CORPS?

Me," and "Any Way the Wind Blows," was composed at Studio Z. These are the straight-ahead R&B numbers that MGM/Verve and Tom Wilson thought they were getting. However, the last track, "You're Probably Wondering Why I'm Here," is the first sign of what Zappa's critics would later describe as "smugness." In the song, he attacks the very audience that comes to see him play, not to mention the record buyer:

You rise each day the same old way
And join your friends out on the street
Spray your hair, and think you're neat
I think your life is incomplete
But maybe that's not for me to say
They only pay me here to play.

As contemptuous as those words may seem, they are part of Zappa's strategy for treating the consumer as more than simply a compliant individual. In his mind, buying a record or going to hear the Mothers play was not a licence to be coddled by the band. "It should be done more often in pop music," Zappa told Martin Perlich in 1972. "It should be done in classical music, too, because if it's not done, the audience is going to continue to come to a performance saying, 'Merely entertain me. Just go up there and be a jukebox.' Unless you do something to alter that image, it'll just stay the same forever. People will just go down there and expect musicians to be robots spewing off some kind of little noise that they can identify with. I don't think that's what music's all about." Criticizing the audience was a means, for Zappa, of making them demand more from their favorite artists than they had come to accept.

On Side 3, "Trouble Every Day" comes out blazing and lays waste to the previous live performances. As Zappa finishes his lyric about disenfranchised blacks watching rats scurry across the floor while making up songs about being poor, he blurts out, "Blow your harmonica, son," a phrase often uttered by Lightnin' Slim. But here the phrase isn't used as a point of pride, instead it's a placebo, a blues cliché that's used to help you forget the misery around you. The next track, "Help, I'm a Rock," is the first real abstract bit of business on *Freak Out!* Although the piece is dedicated to Elvis Presley, it actually pays a debt to Simon & Garfunkel's "I Am a Rock," a song about one man's acceptance of alienation ("I have my books/And my poetry to protect me/I'm shielded in my armor") while finding personal comfort in isolation ("I am a rock/I am an island"). In contrast, "Help, I'm a Rock" is a satirical exploration of one alienated and isolated man's more desperate need to be accepted:

You know maybe if I practice, you know
Maybe if I pass my driving test
I could get a gig drivin' that bus and
Pick up some freaks up in front of Ben Franks.

Zappa is pointing out in this song that the need to be accepted holds the danger of wanting to conform. The protagonist of "Help, I'm a Rock" is initially caught up in a swirl of nonsense language, while a monotonous beat pounds away behind him. Just as he's about to tear off the cover of a matchbook, to send it away, hoping for something to help him be *anything* but a rock, we're suddenly confronted with that yelping we heard earlier on "Who Are the Brain Police?" It creates a startling connection between the two songs. They are both about the same thing: how self-censorship paves the ground for blind acceptance.

"It Can't Happen Here," which follows, is a bit of *a cappella* singing reminiscent of a barbershop quartet. But this doesn't sound like any barbershop quartet you've heard before. For one thing, there's nothing harmonious in the sound or in the content of the song. "It Can't Happen Here," not so accidently, was also the title of a 1935 anti-fascist novel by Sinclair Lewis. In the song, the tinge of paranoia is inseparable from the absurdity of the sound:

It won't happen here
You're safe, mama
You're safe, baby
You just cook a TV dinner
And you make it.

Just as he did on "Who Are the Brain Police?," midway through the number Zappa interjects a radically different piece of music, as if we've just changed stations. It's an atonal piano bridge, played by Zappa himself, that seems to come right out of Cecil Taylor, whose album *Jazz Advance* Wilson had produced years earlier. Before we can settle into the chopped rhythm of Zappa's playing and the percussion percolating behind him, the voices burst back in, asking, "Who can imagine?" By

WHO NEEDS THE PEACE CORPS?

the end of the song, Zappa introduces the character Suzy Creamcheese, who rejects his advances.

Their conversation continues, however, on Side 4, which again toys with the idea of time and space. Usually on vinyl, the end of a side meant the end. But Zappa continues the piece, breaking the imposed limitations of the record album.

"The Return of the Son of Monster Magnet" takes up all of Side 4. It is both Zappa's tribute to Varèse and a nod to Stravinsky (Part 1 of this bizarre ballet score is titled "Ritual Dance of the Child Killer"). Zappa, as "the voice of your conscience," asks Suzy Creamcheese what's got into her. Then a full twelve minutes are devoted to screams, yelps, electronic tapes filled with voices (that in one instance echo Lawrence Welk), nonsense syllables, and later shouts of "Creamcheese!" Zappa's casting of himself in the role of the "conscience" is the beginning of his self-examination as the authoritarian figure on his albums. He would expand on this further in his feature film, *200 Motels* (1971), and later in his opera *Joe's Garage* (1979), where he played the Central Scrutinizer. Zappa suggests that within the rock idol lies a dormant totalitarian. The ambiguous portrait he paints of himself as a rock star satirizes any desire the listener might have to identify with him. Even in the liner notes, Zappa is described mockingly as having a "personality so repellent that it's best he stay away . . . for the sake of impressionable minds who might not be prepared to cope with him." In Zappa's world, the listener is left with nobody to identify with but himself.

There hadn't been an album — until *Freak Out!* — that demonstrated such a range of musical diversity combined with such audacious impiety. Unlike other musical artists, who searched for a single unified sound to create a foundation for their audience appeal, Zappa continually pulled the rug out from under the listener. Just as you got comfortable with the style of one song, he'd suddenly confront you with something new. The music on *Freak Out!* didn't offer listeners a safety net to experience the multitude of new sounds. You either embraced it or you didn't. "The amazing thing about *Freak Out!* was that there was nothing quite like it in rock 'n' roll at the time," Matt Groening told Nigel Leigh. "It was really simultaneously crude and ugly, and incredibly sophisticated. The Beatles were funny, but there was nothing with the kind of sneer that you could feel in the music of Frank Zappa."

Instead of the usual three days to record an album in 1966, *Freak Out!* was recorded over three months, from November 1965 to January 1966, with an additional session in March to record "The Return of the Son of Monster Magnet."

"That's when we recorded Sides 3 and 4," remembered Jimmy Carl Black. "Mac Rebennack, who later became Dr. John, played keyboards on the album though he didn't get credit on the sleeve; Paul Butterfield came down and played with us; Kim Fowley sang 'Help, I'm a Rock' — it was a fun trip."

Abandoning stylistic unity, Zappa went after the much larger ambition of building a whole album around a unified *idea*. The utopian ideal behind his music could be stated simply: one size fits all. "If you were to graphically analyze the different types of directions of all the songs on the *Freak Out!* album," Zappa told Frank Kofsky, "there's a little something in there for everybody. At least one piece of material is slanted for every type of social orientation within our consumer group, which happens to be six to eighty. That whole *Freak Out!* album is to be accessible as possible to the people who [want] to take the time to make it accessible."

8

In April 1966, with *Freak Out!* finally finished, Herb Cohen sent the group to Hawaii for a two-week engagement at a club called Da Swamp, in Waikiki. There, Zappa found the time to write some of the material for the Mothers' follow-up album. When the band returned to the mainland, they did ten days of concerts in Texas. On May 3, the Mothers of Invention played their first truly controversial and high-profile gig, opening for Andy Warhol's Exploding Plastic Inevitable, which featured the Velvet Underground and Nico at the Trip in Los Angeles. Part of Zappa's stage rap was already designed to satirize and put down trendy attitudes, so the Velvet Underground, with their dark clothes and somber stage presence, became perfect targets for him. They just didn't fit the L.A. freak environment, and the audience knew it. From the stage, Zappa proclaimed to the crowd, "These guys really suck!" Lou Reed, the leader of the Velvets, later returned the insult. "He's probably the single most untalented person I've heard in my life," Reed sneered. "He's a two-bit, pretentious academic, and he can't play rock 'n' roll, because he's a loser. And that's why he dresses funny. He's not happy with himself and I think he's right." In truth, they *both* dressed funny. What became apparent was more a clash between two sets of temperamental talents. Both groups recorded on Verve/MGM and were produced by Tom Wilson. It was also an East Coast/West Coast rivalry between two fierce innovators who were figureheads for different aspects of the era's counterculture.

As Billy James points out, there were as many similarities as differences between Reed and Zappa. "Firstly, both Zappa and Lou Reed were equally single-minded

WHO NEEDS THE PEACE CORPS?

about the way they approached their material and the direction of their respective groups," James writes. "They were also both cynical about the whole new hippie scene." Chances are, the Velvet Underground were also considerably pissed off because they believed that their first album, *The Velvet Underground and Nico*, was held up due to the attention the Mothers of Invention were getting for *Freak Out!* The album was ready by April 1966, but didn't see the light of day until 1967, having been eclipsed by the Mothers. "I know what the problem was," the Velvet's guitarist Sterling Morrison said in 1981. "It was Frank Zappa and his manager, Herb Cohen. They sabotaged us in a number of ways because they wanted to be the first 'freak' release. And we were totally naive. We didn't have a manager who would go to the record company every day and just drag the whole thing through production."

Nevertheless, the two bands didn't have to share the stage for long, because the sheriff's office closed the Trip after three days. But both were still booked to play Bill Graham's West Coast rock palace, the Fillmore Auditorium, in San Francisco. The Fillmore, a legendary concert hall at the corner of Fillmore and Geary, had housed many great musical acts, from Duke Ellington to the Temptations. The May 1967 concerts at the Fillmore were designed as benefits for the San Francisco Mime Troupe, who were busted for performing without a permit in Lafayette Park. As part of a series of shows, the Velvets and the Mothers of Invention were set to perform on May 27–29. But before they even got to play a note, the Velvets got on Graham's bad side. Graham, who was temperamental at the best of times, took an instant dislike to the band. The Fillmore was famous for its light shows, with images projected behind the bands as they performed. When Lou Reed saw a slide of the Buddha, he told Graham bluntly that it had to go. Graham became angry at what he perceived to be the Velvets' low-class attitude. First he ejected guitarist Morrison from the building, then he told the band, as they mounted the stage, "You motherfuckers, I hope you bomb."

The Mothers of Invention returned to the Fillmore on June 24 and 25 to open for Lenny Bruce, who was in desperate shape from drug abuse and worn down by legal persecution. It was the first time Zappa talked to Bruce. "I met him in the lobby between sets and asked him to sign my draft card," Zappa recalled. "He said no — he didn't want to touch it." Bruce was, by now, a walking corpse, picked apart by legal and political machinations designed to bring him down. "It was the living death of a genius," Bill Graham writes in his autobiography. "He was a beaten soul and he was naked onstage." Graham felt the Mothers of Invention saved the show from being simply a ghoulish night of the living dead.

That same month, impressed by the strength of Zappa's musical orchestrations for the *Freak Out!* album, Tom Wilson hired Zappa to help arrange two songs on the Animals' album *Animalism*. "Zappa's a painstaking craftsman," Wilson told David Walley. "[And] in some ways it's a pity that the art of recording is not developed to the extent where you can really hear completely all the things he's doing, because sometimes one guitar part is buried and he might have three different-sounding guitars overplayed, all playing the same thing. . . . In the *Freak Out!* album he used a lot of chorus which was actually Frank overdubbed on himself. A lot of that took three weeks to complete." Zappa arranged a cover of folksinger Fred Neil's "The Other Side of This Life" and Harris Woody's R&B classic "All Night Long." With its infectiously chugging riff, "All Night Long" had been a big hit for singer Chuck Higgins back in the '50s. It was a standard dance favorite for many R&B bar bands. However, Eric Burdon, lead singer of the Animals, could care less about Zappa's technical prowess. He took issue with Zappa's "autocratic" behavior during the recording of those two songs, and told Wilson that "it was like working with Hitler."

Zappa was annoyed at the Animals' attitude toward the music. "I found out that not only were they not particularly original," he told Nigel Leigh, "[they] were hung up in that R&B bag, which is deadening when you get little white boys trying to be little black boys, screaming the blues and being funky and all — that's shitty." Although it may seem a double standard, since Zappa's previous bands also did R&B covers, Zappa felt Burdon (who was trying to impress Wilson with Ray Charles numbers) was putting on airs by *trying* to be black. For Zappa, this was nothing but disguised condescension. The Animals were playing music as a means to become something they weren't — black. Zappa's bands (which were racially integrated) set out to simply capture the essence of the music itself.

In July 1966, *Freak Out!* was released, and Verve/MGM didn't have a clue how to market it. In desperation, they put out as a single "How Could I Be Such a Fool?" improbably backed with the *a cappella* wonder of "It Can't Happen Here." When that failed to generate sales, they tried "Trouble Every Day" with "Who Are the Brain Police?" To no one's surprise, the results were not much better. The reviews for the album were also less than favorable. Pete Johnson of the *Los Angeles Times* called the Mothers of Invention "a talented but warped quintet" whose album "could be the greatest stimulus to the aspirin industry since income tax." Lorraine Alterman of the *Los Angeles Free Press* finished her pan by raising a loud warning to parents across the nation: "So, mothers and fathers, next time the Beatles, the

WHO NEEDS THE PEACE CORPS?

Stones, or Sonny and Cher come to town, welcome them with open arms. Next to the Mothers of Invention, the other groups come on like the Bobsey Twins."

Cash Box had the most positive comments: "A powerful rock outing on which the Mothers of Invention live up to their name by using such instruments as finger cymbals, bobby pins & tweezers and guitarron. . . . The album is colorfully packaged and contains extensive liner notes." But Zappa had complaints about how MGM handled the cover design. Although he had control over the exterior, the interior was another matter. While the Mothers of Invention were performing in Hawaii, MGM had developed graphics without consulting Zappa. "The result was a really ugly piece of graphic art," Zappa told Jerry Hopkins of *Rolling Stone* in 1968. "Some of the worst reproduction work I have ever seen. The picture in the lower right hand corner — it is a great panorama of all those people. They shrank it down and stuck it in the corner. I screamed all over the place."

The promotion of the album to radio stations was lame, too — the marketing division didn't know what they were selling. Besides printing up bumper stickers that read, "Suzy Creamcheese," they sent radio stations a jigsaw puzzle of the album's front cover. Zappa was exasperated.

MGM did, however, provide a handy mail-order offer for a poster map of all the best "freak out hot-spots." They also got some good coverage in *Record World*. "MGM Goes Way Out for *Freak Out!*" the headline read. But *Freak Out!* confounded MGM. It didn't fit any normal marketing pattern for a rock 'n' roll record. *Freak Out!* first appeared on the Billboard Chart on February 11, 1967, and got no higher than No. 130 in its twenty-three weeks of activity. All told, it sold close to 30,000 copies, which didn't please the label. And because the Mothers' royalty rate was just sixty to seventy cents a copy, they made only about $21,000. From a financial standpoint, *Freak Out!* was a bust. As a concept album, however, it was a pioneering work. *Freak Out!* helped dramatically change the belief that the success of American rock 'n' roll was solely dependent on the sale of singles — people started to consider the impact of albums.

In July, the Mothers of Invention did their first short tour to promote their radical debut. To offset the banalities of touring, they adapted a satirical stagecraft to match the unusual quality of their records. In Washington, D.C., for instance, they appeared on *Swingin' Time*, a television dance show similar to *American Bandstand*. The producers put together a "Freak Out Dance Contest" and invited the contestants to dress in a "freakish" manner. "The weirdest guy in the room wore two different-colored socks," Zappa recalled.

In Detroit, the band started to employ insurgent elements to promote their true image. When the producer of *Swingin' Time* asked Zappa about lip-synching their hit song, Zappa told him they didn't have a hit song. Zappa had a strategy in mind. "I gathered an assortment of random objects [from the prop department] and built a set," Zappa wrote. "We had been asked to pretend to play either 'How Could I Be Such a Fool?' or 'Who Are the Brain Police?' so I suggested that each member of the group choose a *repeatable physical action*, not necessarily in sync with (or even related to) the lyrics, and do it over and over until our spot on the show was concluded — Detroit's first whiff of homemade prime-time Dada." As for Dallas, Ray Collins remembers the fallout after a television performance there: "I recall them telling me afterwards that they were deluged with calls from irate parents saying, 'Get those guys off the air, out of town, off the planet!' We had a lot of fun."

When the tour returned to L.A., Pamela Zarubica and her friend Gail Sloatman met Zappa at the airport. Gail was a secretary in the same office where Pam worked. When Gail and Frank met that night, their attraction for each other was immediate. Gail told *Rock Wives* author Victoria Balfour years later, "I was just devastated. I didn't know what to do. It was like you were totally stripped of any preconceived notions about anything. . . . He probably scared the shit out of his mother, too." But she also told Drew Wheeler of *Billboard* that although Zappa was imposing, "he was compelling. He had a compelling glare. He had major magnetic charm."

Adelaide Gail Sloatman was born on January 1, 1945. Her father, a Navy scientist and nuclear physicist, was sent to London in 1959 and Gail was placed in what she called a "severely Catholic all-girls school" there. Gail's father had his heart set on sending her to college, but Gail left home instead and moved into a flat with a friend, Anya Butler. In 1962, she found a job as a secretary for the Office of Naval Research and Development. That year, the Beatles broke in England with their first single, "Love Me Do." This started a renaissance where other bands — like the Searchers and Gerry & the Pacemakers — followed suit. After hours, Gail started frequenting clubs.

In 1965, Gail's father was transferred back to New York, and because she could not obtain a work visa, she moved with her family. She started school at the Fashion Institute of Technology, and was soon followed to New York by Anya. Gail had already been scouting out the music scene in New York, hanging out with the Blues Project, which featured Al Kooper, who would later play organ on Bob Dylan's "Like a Rolling Stone" and become the songwriter and lead singer of Blood, Sweat &

WHO NEEDS THE PEACE CORPS?

Tears. Anya and Gail soon hitchhiked to Los Angeles, where they decided to become groupies. Although Gail never became a full-time freak, she went to concerts and dances with Vito and Carl. She only briefly experimented with drugs, and, like Frank, she didn't care for the trendier aspects of the hippie scene. "[I did not wear] a white John Lennon hat. And I never went near a go-go cage or burned a flag or helped anyone burn a draft card," she told Victoria Balfour.

When Gail met Zappa, he had already become a prominent figure on the groupie set. Pamela Zarubica remembers him shacking up with her friend Sally Anne Mann (until her dope smoking turned him off), the Cherry Sisters, and a hooker from San Francisco named Stephanie. His many sexual encounters led to an assortment of diseases, which would be passed on through his and Pamela's friends. "After he visited the doctor . . . he discovered that he had the crabs, too," Zarubica cited for Michael Gray. "He had been nurturing the little devils for some time without being aware of it, and he always used to sleep in my bed with his girlfriends. It took months to wipe out the epidemic. Frank wrote some delightful songs about it, and a lot of our dear friends got to share in something together."

Gail concurred with Pamela's observation. "He was infested, and so was his hair," she recalled. "He hadn't taken a bath for months. Or combed his hair. I think it was not so much rock 'n' roll and not so much the road as it is that nobody was taking care of him. You can always spot a bachelor!"

Before they pulled out of the parking lot at the airport, they were in love. This created a rift between Pamela and Frank, although they were not sexually involved. When Pamela left for a short trip to Europe in late 1966, Gail ended up moving into the 8404 Kirkwood apartment.

On July 23, the Mothers of Invention's appearance at the Great Underground Arts Masked Ball and Orgy (GUAMBO), a concert celebrating the second birthday of the *Los Angeles Free Press*, helped build the band's reputation. Jerry Hopkins of the *Free Press* described how the band encouraged others to "freak out":

> The Mothers of Invention go on. This is one of the truly wild scenes of the evening. Frank Zappa in his suit of flowers. His side men are garbed similarly, and behind them are five other musicians augmenting the group. Five short-haired American Federation of Musician types in black suits, white shirts and black ties. Just sitting there reading the charts, blowing with the

Mothers the Mother sound. And the Mothers' auxiliary dancing, dancing, dancing.

Carl, of "Hungry Freaks, Daddy" fame, is one of the featured dancers now. He is wearing what looks like zebra-skinned long johns with a pop art All American Superman bib. Two nice ladies are dancing with him, alternating with some of Vito's group . . . and from the dance floor comes a man in a mummy suit to join in.

GUAMBO introduced Zappa to a band called the Factory, formed by local guitarist and vocalist Lowell George, who would later form the rock band Little Feat. Perhaps they were fated to meet — when they were both kids, George and Zappa appeared on the same episode of the TV show *Your Make-Believe Ballroom*. Frank did a presentation of his hand puppets while Lowell performed on the harmonica.

George was also a misfit who brought an ingenious style to composing. "When Lowell lived in Benedict Canyon . . . he had a big piece of cardboard stuck to the wall, with chords written all over it at random," remembers Rick Harper, Little Feat's road manager. "He would sit a few feet away, and he'd throw a dart, write down the chord he hit, and play it. Then throw the dart again, write it down, and then play that chord. That was his idea of composing."

Zappa and Herb Cohen took an interest in Lowell George & the Factory. Martin Kibbee, a bass player who co-wrote songs with George, recalled that Zappa's influence on Lowell "can't be overestimated. Frank was so dedicated, so hardworking, such a no-bullshit guy, and that model of how the group ought to run was what Lowell aspired to." On August 18, the Factory recorded three oddly compelling demos, "Hey Girl!," "Changes," and "Candy Corn Madness," for Cohen. On the basis of those, Zappa decided to produce a single for them. "Lightnin' Rod Man" was a grinding R&B number that featured Zappa on piano and background vocals. Zappa provided some of those low grumbles you'd later hear on *Cruising With Ruben & the Jets* and *Uncle Meat*. George described the song as "a cross between 'They're Coming to Take Me Away' and Ian & Sylvia" — it had more in common with the early psychedelic blues of Captain Beefheart than the later Little Feat. The tune was based on a Herman Melville story about a man who sells lightning rods during a thunderstorm. But, Kibbee recalled, "Frank Zappa said, 'Forget Melville, sing it like Elvis. . . . Okay, now sing it like Little Richard'. . . ." The B-side, "The Loved

WHO NEEDS THE PEACE CORPS?

One," was a two-chord ditty about butterflies and helicopters. (Since Zappa had yet to form a separate label, these tracks went unreleased until 1993, when they were included on the CD *Lightnin' Rod Man* by Lowell George & the Factory.)

On August 3, 1966, Lenny Bruce died of a morphine overdose. Pamela remembered Zappa's reaction: "Frank asked me why I was crying. I guess he didn't think it did any good to cry. I told him that I cried because Lenny had wanted to talk to Frank and he never got the chance." The funeral was set for two days later, but Zappa was reluctant to go. Pamela was so distraught over Lenny's death, however, that he changed his mind. "By the time we got there, all there was was the dirt on top of the coffin, which was already in the ground," Zarubica told Michael Gray. "Frank, John [Judnich], Herbie [Cohen], and I all just stood there for a while. Then Frank and I went back to the car." There, Zappa reached into the glove compartment and pulled out a rock, which he handed to Pamela. On this small stone was painted "I Love You." "That rock," Pamela recalled, "made a lot of people happy." "Lenny was a saint," Zappa wrote in *Hit Parader*. "What the Big Machine of America did to Lenny Bruce was pretty disgusting. It ranks with civil rights as one of the big pimples on the face of American culture."

On August 13, the Mothers of Invention played at the Shrine Exposition Hall in Santa Monica. It was so successful that they returned four days later with a three-dollar admission charge. One of the problems the band was encountering was poor sound facilities in concert venues. Zappa was notorious for wanting the sound just right. He cancelled a gig at the Earl Warren Showgrounds in Santa Monica for just that reason. But the problems were solved by the end of October, and the Mothers began what would become a long tradition of Halloween concerts; the ads for the show read, "Legalize Therapeutic Abortion With The Mothers."

Things weren't going that well at home, though. As Zappa became more popular, he started bringing more people around to the house. Pamela got tired of the piles of clothes and dirty dishes. On top of that, Gail and Pamela had a further falling out. "The trouble began when Gail's roommate fucked [Zappa] and Gail made the mistake of telling me," Zarubica told Michael Gray. "Relationships were completely severed. Gail had stopped taking her birth control pills and had failed to tell Frank. I felt compelled to make him aware of the situation. It was over this issue plus the living condition [that the falling out occurred]." As Frank and Gail became more of a couple, Pamela and her friend

Vicki left on a trip to Europe. "When it was time to go in the morning, Pepper [a groupie] borrowed Frank's car to drive me to the airport where I would meet Vicki," Zarubica told Gray. "Frank and Gail were awake, but they never came outside to say goodbye.... Everything good can't last forever."

In November 1966, just as the Mothers of Invention were planning their second album, freak culture on the Sunset Strip was being put to the test. For three weeks, the police launched a campaign to destroy the culture by arresting teenagers on curfew violations. Demonstrators were arrested, beaten, and harassed by police in huge numbers. The largest disturbance took place at one popular club called Pandora's Box. Demonstrators destroyed buses and ripped down street signs, and finally a picket fence was erected around the club. Both sides taunted each other. The event, commemorated in Buffalo Springfield's hit song "For What It's Worth," forced Zappa to question not only the police actions, but also the ulterior motives of the counterculture of which he'd been part. (He later explored those motives in the song "Plastic People.") He suggested an alternative in the *Free Press* on December 30. "I would like to propose the Interested Party," Zappa told interviewer Liza Williams. "Posters, pins, a platform that was a little more logical ... a platform that stood for the re-evaluation of everything in light of, in terms of, the Constitution, not as it has been diluted ... and temper that with certain advancements in modern technology and certain advancements in sociological fields, take into consideration where we're really at in terms of the sexual revolution and just look at everything the way it actually is today and set it up all over again. That's your only chance to make it work."

Zappa was also becoming more outspoken about the rampant drug use in the L.A. counterculture. Carl Franzoni told the *Free Press* in October that he was a member of the Mothers of Invention, and that they extolled the use of LSD. The following week, Zappa issued a rebuttal: "Carl Franzoni is not a member of the Mothers of Invention.... *We*, as a group, agree with him in his plea for a sane drug policy ... we, as a group, do not recommend, verily, we repudiate any animal/mineral/vegetable/synthetic substance, vehicle and/or procedure which might tend to reduce the body, mind or spirit of an individual (any true individual) to a state of sub-awareness or insensitivity.... We are here to turn you loose, not turn you on. Turn yourself on." The trouble was, many of the Mothers were also turning themselves on.

Zappa recalled that at the band meeting where Mark Cheka was dismissed of his managerial duties, members of the Mothers wanted Zappa dismissed, too,

WHO NEEDS THE PEACE CORPS?

because he wasn't using drugs. Apparently, Ray Collins told Zappa to go to Big Sur and take acid with someone who believed in God. But Collins disputed Zappa's version of events. As far as he was concerned, the issue wasn't whether he did drugs — it was Zappa's desire to make the band his own that alienated him. "I didn't want Frank to be the leader of the Mothers of Invention because I didn't like what he was doing with the band, and his control," Collins explained. "I suggested at the meeting that we take any member of the band besides Frank or myself — [and make them] the leader. That way it would take the leadership away from him."

As for Zappa's coarse views of LSD, it amused Collins years later: "The first time I ever took LSD, Frank Zappa took me to get the LSD — in Hollywood on Sunset Boulevard. It was induced into my mouth by way of an eyedropper out of a vial. Frank didn't take any to my knowledge at the time. But he took me to get the LSD. So it seems a bit ironic that he should make this kind of statement about me."

Given the tensions between the police and the freaks — not to mention the subject matter of his songs — it isn't hard to see why Zappa didn't want to encourage unnecessary hostilities. Besides, given the complications of playing the music properly, he could ill afford to have band members busted. "Now if you go out there wrecked out of your mind, you're not going to be able to remember your sequence of events," Zappa told John Swenson. "You're going to make instrumental mistakes that are going to throw off the balance of everything else. The whole thing falls down like a stack of dominoes." In later years, when the group traveled abroad, Zappa also had to consider international drug laws that could impede the tour and cost him financially.

Frank Zappa had smoked marijuana — and inhaled — a few times, but he didn't understand what the fuss was all about. "Between 1962 and 1968, on maybe ten occasions, I experienced the *'joys'* of socially circulated marijuana," Zappa remarked. "It gave me a sore throat and made me sleepy. I couldn't understand why people liked it so much." Ironically, Zappa always attracted audiences to the concerts that were, as he put it, up to their eyebrows in chemical refreshment. In later years, they would even start throwing their used syringes up on the stage as "love offerings." They assumed that the only way Zappa could write and perform outrageous music was to be loaded himself. So, given the discontent between the authorities and the freaks, Zappa (under the pseudonym Suzy Creamcheese) laid out the working philosophy of the band in ads in the *Free Press*. These ads were permeated by a tone of skepticism about whether the freak culture could resist simply becoming fashionable:

> The Mothers' music is very new, and as their music is new, so is the intention of their music. As much as the Mothers put into their music, we must bring to it. The Mothers and what they represent as a group has attracted all the outcasts, the pariahs, the people who are angry and afraid and contemptuous of the existing social structure. The danger lies in the 'Freak Out' becoming an excuse instead of a reason. An excuse implies an end, a reason, a beginning. . . . 'Freaking Out' should presuppose an active freedom, freedom meaning a liberation from the control of some other person or persons. Unfortunately, reaction seems to have taken place of action. We SHOULD be as satisfied listening to the Mothers perform from a concert stage. If we could channel the energy expended in 'Freaking Out' physically into 'Freaking Out' intellectually, we might possibly be able to create something concrete out of ideological twilight of bizarre costumes and being seen being bizarre. Do we really listen? And if we really listen, do we really think? Freedom of thought, conversely, brings an awesome responsibility. Looking and acting eccentric IS NOT ENOUGH. . . . What WE must try to do then, is not only comment satirically on what's wrong, but try to CHANGE what's wrong. The Mothers are trying.

The Mothers personnel was also changing. Motorhead Sherwood, brought in initially as road manager, played tenor sax with the group. Rhythm guitarist Elliot Ingber was fired and left to join the Fraternity of Man. Their claim to fame, included in the 1969 film *Easy Rider* (1969), was the comic drug song "Don't Bogart That Joint." They also recorded the first version of Zappa's "Oh, No." "I think that Elliot Ingber was the only person who was ever fired," Ray Collins remembered in 1989. "He 'abused drugs.' . . . One night in particular, he was trying to tune his guitar, and his amplifier wasn't on. And Frank looked over at him, looked over at me, looked down at the amplifier, and I knew right then that was the last of Elliot Ingber in the band."

In addition to those personnel changes, Zappa wanted to form a touring electric chamber orchestra rather than hire studio musicians to play his charts, as he had on *Freak Out!* He decided to augment the band with keyboards and horns. He

WHO NEEDS THE PEACE CORPS?

brought in pianist Don Preston, horn man Bunk Gardner, and another drummer, Billy Mundi, who had been in a San Francisco band called Lamp of Childhood.

Preston, from Flint, Michigan, couldn't have been more of a kindred spirit. "I was affected early on by Boulez, Xenakis, Penderecki," Preston told *Downbeat Magazine* in 1987. "That's what I listened to more than anything, more than jazz . . . my ear was always trying to get something new." Even if Preston didn't listen to much jazz, he certainly played jazz piano. In the '50s, he performed with drummer Elvin Jones (who would later join John Coltrane's classic quartet), and he also played bass for flautist Herbie Mann. Preston ended up on the West Coast during the late '50s touring with Nat King Cole, and he eventually ran an L.A. club devoted to experimental music. There, he and Zappa played together. "We were improvising to films of microscopic life; [Zappa] had some real unusual films," Preston told Ben Watson. But years later, when Preston first auditioned to join the Mothers, he came up against Zappa's need for a diversified musician. "I auditioned and Frank said, 'I'm sorry, Don, you don't know anything about rock and roll' — which I didn't. I never played it and hardly ever listened to it. After that, I got a bunch of jobs in rock bands." Once well-versed in rock, Preston was set to play Zappa's unusually eclectic blend of musical styles and forms.

John Leon "Bunk" Gardner was a reed player, born in Cleveland, Ohio, in 1933. Along with his trumpet-playing brother, Buzz, he was brought into the band by Preston. Besides playing with the Cleveland Philharmonic, Bunk did session work with Baldwin Wallace, Freddie Slack, and Eartha Kitt. "As far as my earliest musical influences, well I guess having an older brother certainly helped," Gardner pondered. "From an early age, I was listening to Charlie Parker, Dizzy Gillespie, Miles Davis, and all the jazz greats. At the same time I loved classical music. . . . My brother was already playing trumpet, so I said I'd play clarinet. . . . Then later on in junior high school I got my first tenor sax. . . . Then right into high school, I started a combo with my brother. We'd play Stan Kenton arrangements and mix some be-bop jazz at dances. While still in high school, I started to play bassoon and got a scholarship from the Cleveland Institute of Music, and eventually started to play professionally with the Cleveland Philharmonic Orchestra."

Bunk first met Preston at a gig they were both playing in Italy. They got together again — with Zappa — at Preston's club, where Bunk joined in on their improvised jams. "I can remember going to Frank's house and spending just about the whole day auditioning for him," Gardner remembered. "He just kept handing out music for me to play: 'Play this — how fast can you play this?' I played my saxophone and soprano, I played my clarinet, I played my flute, my alto flute, my bass clarinet, and I played piano, it was just one thing after another. At one point he said, 'Well, we've got some dates coming up and might be touring, do you want to join the band?' This would be late 1965, early 1966."

By the time Zappa had added a contrabass, trumpet, and string quartet, he was ready to record the Mothers' second album. "When we finally became an eight-piece," Zappa told *Zig Zag*, "we finally had a very workable ensemble." Rehearsals became endurance tests lasting eight to twelve hours. "I always had my notebook and manuscript paper to take down notes and rhythms, but on a day-to-day basis the music always changed," Bunk recalled. "Because the rest of the band, other than myself and Don [Preston], could not read music, repetition was very necessary to memorize and retain all the notes and to remember the repertoire. . . . Nothing stayed constant. Parts were expected to be practised and learned before the rehearsals, so we could really make progress when we were together!"

It was with that sort of discipline that the Mothers went into the studio to record their second album, *Absolutely Free*.

9

If *Freak Out!* announced the arrival of the Mothers of Invention and their sublimely subversive intentions, *Absolutely Free* was the fulfillment of those ambitions. On the inside cover of *Freak Out!*, Frank Zappa listed all those who had an impact on his work. But it's on *Absolutely Free* that you can actually *hear* the presence of Charles Ives, Igor Stravinsky, Lenny Bruce, and Edgard Varèse. *Freak Out!* was a beautifully designed map for the Mothers' music, while *Absolutely Free* actually takes you places. Critic Greil Marcus wrote in *Stranded: Rock and Roll for a Desert Island*, that "on this early effort the wit was liberating, the noise of the band not merely Absurdist but actually absurd. . . ."

Absolutely Free was, in fact, an oratorio of ridiculous extremes — performed at breakneck speed. "We play the new free music — music as absolutely free, unencumbered by American cultural suppression," Zappa announced. "We are systematically trying to do away with the creative roadblocks that our helpful American educational system has installed to make sure nothing creative leaks through to mass audiences. . . . The same patriotic feeling expressed in songs like 'The Green Beret' and 'Day of Decision' are embodied in our every performance, only on a more abstract level. . . . We represent the only true patriotism left." This

WHO NEEDS THE PEACE CORPS?

abstract example of true patriotism barely leaves you time to catch your breath, and the musical quotes just go whizzing past. The album's title, though, turns out to be apt. All of Zappa's musical ideas happily and freely collide in the rush-hour traffic.

As a drumroll kicks in, Zappa introduces U.S. President Lyndon Johnson, just as Ray Collins, in the voice of LBJ, addresses the crowd: "Mah fella Americans . . ." Suddenly, we hear the intrusive opening notes of "Louie Louie." The President of the United States isn't safe from this pervasive song — and neither is the rest of the nation. Out of this preposterous fanfare, Zappa unveils "Plastic People." In part, the song (using a variation of the "Louie Louie" chords) addresses the conformity he saw creeping into the freak culture during the riots on the Strip. But the song is also an answer to Buffalo Springfield's "For What It's Worth," where singer-songwriter Steven Stills attempted to capture the division between the kids and the cops.

Stills, however, took refuge in the paranoia of the persecuted hippies. "Young people speaking their minds/Getting so much resistance from behind," Stills sang. "For What It's Worth" beautifully captured the mood, but didn't illuminate the hidden dynamics of the conflict. "Plastic People" spared neither side. As Neil Slaven deftly points out in *Electric Don Quixote*, "'Plastic People' began with a cryptic reference, 'There's this guy from the CIA and he's creeping around Laurel Canyon.' Later he intoned, 'I hear the sound of marching feet down Sunset Boulevard to Crescent Heights and there at Pandora's Box, we are confronted with a vast quantity of plastic people.' While Steven Stills' lyric about young people being attacked by 'the heat' fudged the issue, Frank called the police Nazis and criticized the conduct of those that allowed themselves to be manipulated."

Zappa didn't mince words about how dangerous succumbing to authoritarian ideas could be. Consider that these lyrics were written only a few years before American Nazis marched through the streets of Skokie, Illinois:

Take a day and walk around
Watch the Nazis run your town
Then go home and check yourself
You think we're singing 'bout someone else?

"Plastic People" addressed the failure of the freaks who refused to distinguish themselves from the trendsetters. Yet, the song would take on larger significance when countries behind the Iron Curtain adopted it as their anthem. "I had no idea that song made the impact it did there," Zappa said years later. "The album was smuggled into the [Eastern bloc] within a year of its 1967 release. I found out ten years later how powerful the song had become. We were touring heavily in Europe at the time, and a few Czechs had come across the Austrian border to hear our concert in Vienna. I talked with them after the show, and they told me that 'Plastic People' was responsible for a whole movement of dissidents within Czechoslovakia. It came as a shock to me to find out that there was a group called the Plastic People there and that a cult of followers had grown up around them."

Milan Hlavsa, a Czech rock star, was the co-founder of that underground band, Plastic People of the Universe. They supported various dissidents, including Vaclav Havel, during the '70s and '80s. The band was arrested in 1976, inspiring the formation of the human-rights group Charter 77 the next year. It was perhaps ironic that the two bands who became important symbols for democracy in Czechoslovakia in those years — the Mothers of Invention and the Velvet Underground — absolutely loathed one another.

After "Plastic People," the album took a sharp turn. "The Duke of Prunes" was partly a parody of Gene Chandler's doo-wop hit "Duke of Earl." The tune, however, was taken from a theme used in the film *Run Home Slow*. "Duke of Prunes," according to Zappa, was a surreal love song about lust. "[It uses] euphemistic sexual imagery popular in country blues tunes," Zappa remarked at the time. But no country blues tune ever featured sexual imagery as ridiculous as this:

> A moonbeam through the prune
> In June
> Reveals your chest
> I see your lovely beans
> And in that magic go-kart
> I bite your neck
> The cheese I have for you, my dear
> Is real and very new.

"Frank had this very beautiful tune called 'And Very True,' and when we went in to record it, being a little crazy at the time, I just ad-libbed on the spot," Ray Collins recalled. "The original lyrics I think were 'Moonbeam through the night,' something very loving — although Frank doesn't like love songs — and I said, 'Moonbeam through the prune, in June, I can see your tits.' So later, after we recorded it, you can hear Frank cracking up on the record." Collins, however,

WHO NEEDS THE PEACE CORPS?

didn't get a writing credit on the album. "I told Frank, 'Well, you know, I just made up those lyrics, as we went along, so if not money ... I should at least get an album credit for it.' So he says, 'Well, just tell me what you want to put on the album.' And so a couple of days later, I said, 'Well, just put 'Prune: Ray Collins.'"

"The Duke of Prunes" is spread out over three parts. "Amnesia Vivace" quotes Stravinsky's "Berceuse" from his *Firebird Suite*, and that melody floats — in Charles Ives fashion — over a theme from *The Rite of Spring*. In "The Duke Regains His Chops," as the singer's lust for his loved one reaches its peak, the group serves up a chorus of the Supremes' "Baby Love" (retitled "Baby Prunes"). The song ends with Collins' appropriate call of "cheesy, cheesy."

"Call Any Vegetable" immediately follows with the droll commercial announcement "This is a song about vegetables. They keep you regular. They're real good for you." Although in interviews Zappa referred to certain types of people as vegetables, here the vegetables are merely portraying themselves. "Call Any Vegetable" is about how vegetables can be useful in achieving sexual gratification: "Call any vegetable/And the chances are good/That the vegetable will respond to you." As the first part of "Call Any Vegetable" reaches its conclusion, Zappa moves into the instrumental "The Invocation and Ritual Dance of the Young Pumpkin" (which not only makes reference to Stravinsky's "Ritual Dance" from *The Rite of Spring*, but is also proceeded by a brief quote from "Jupiter, the Bringer of Jollity" from Gustav Holst's *The Planets*).

"Invocation" was the first extended guitar piece Zappa recorded that demonstrates both his agility and his ability to improvise. It turns into a beautiful duet between Zappa and Bunk Gardner. "[This piece] was a favorite of mine because I always got to play a solo and usually a long one," Gardner recalled. "I had a King Soprano that only went up to a concert high D — most sopranos now go up to a high concert E flat. ... The band was cooking and I was really pumped up and just kept playing and playing ... I thought it sounded great and I loved my solo! Then Frank said, 'Let's do another take.' So we went back out for take two. I didn't think we captured the excitement so well the second time, but I think Frank thought he played a better solo on take two. So that's the one that ended up on the album."

"Invocation" comes to a sudden end just as "Soft-Sell Conclusion" (the postscript for "Call Any Vegetable") starts up. While Zappa sells us the full value of vegetable gratification ("Standing there shiny and proud by your side/Holding your joint while your neighbor decides/Why is a vegetable something to hide?"), he plays sophisticated musical tricks to put it across, including another snatch of Stravinsky (the march from *L'Histoire du soldat*). Although the song appears to be a call of love to a pumpkin, "pumpkin" was Zappa's nickname for Gail Sloatman (on the inside cover, under an out-of-focus photo of her, are the words "my pumpkin").

Side 2 begins with the phrase "One, two, buckle my shoe," while nonsense syllables chime underneath. The cymbals, meanwhile, parody striptease music. The words themselves are from the Burt Bacharach and Hal David song "My Little Red Book." The song is the Mothers' "America Drinks," sung by Collins in the *sprechgesang* (or "speech-song") style developed by Arnold Schoenberg, a vocal technique that is a hybrid of speech and pure song. The singer performs a recitation on approximate pitches instead of the usual notes.

The melody of "America Drinks" parodies the lounge music Zappa played with Joe Perrino and the Mellowtones, but the lyrics are right out of '50s teen America:

> *I tried to find how my heart could be so blind*
> *How could I be fooled just like the rest*
> *You came on strong with your fast car*
> *and your class ring*
> *Soft voice, and your sad eyes*
> *I fell for the whole thing.*

As Collins performs the song, he often seems on the verge of cracking up (he even flubs a lyric partway through the song) and sometimes even lets you in on the joke (especially when he pauses lasciviously after the word "came"). Aside from trying to keep his composure, Collins sings as a man stripped of all romantic pretence, as if he's trying to remember why he fell in love in the first place. He recites words he's been taught by countless love songs, but they no longer hold meaning for him. By the end, his efforts are rendered ridiculous by the sudden intrusion of Julius Fucik's *Entry of the Gladiators*. "Status Back Baby" is the perfect follow-up to "America Drinks" — if the singer in that song was an automaton mouthing love lyrics, this one explores a whole group of people destined to become just as robotized. Zappa originally wrote "Status Back Baby" at Studio Z for his rock opera, *I Was a Teenage Malt Shop*. "[It's] a song about acne America and their daily trials and tribulations," Zappa explained. "It is unfortunate that many young Americans really do worry about losing status at their high school."

WHO NEEDS THE PEACE CORPS?

I'm losing status at the high school
I used to think that it was my school.
WAH WAH WAH WAH
I was the king of every school activity
But that's no more
Oh mama, what will come of me?

The tune lists the joys of a handsome football star who is happily painting posters, playing "records by the Coasters," and belonging to De Molay (a religious youth organization devoted to keeping kids on the "correct" moral path). But his status is slipping at the high school, and following De Molay's moral path has not made him happy. To drive that point home, Zappa includes — in the bridge of the song — the opening melody of Stravinsky's *Petrushka*, a ballet about a puppet longing to be human. Zappa reverses the meaning in "Status Back Baby." Here, a human being turns into a puppet.

"Uncle Bernie's Farm" is a straightforward critique of children's toys and their violent capabilities. It does, however, have a funny opening where the band vamps on Irving Berlin's "White Christmas."

"Son of Suzy Creamcheese," like "Plastic People," borrows from "Louie Louie" and tarnishes Suzy Creamcheese with the same conformist brush as Zappa used for the freaks. It's also his first anti-drug song:

Suzy you were such a sweetie
Yeah, yeah, yeah,
Once you were my one and only
Yeah, yeah, yeah
Blew your mind on too much Kool-Aid.

The reference to Kool-Aid comes from Ken Kesey's book *The Electric Kool-Aid Acid Test*, where he described how LSD was introduced to members of the counterculture and Grateful Dead fans by means of the popular instant drink. By the end of the next decade, though, the image of Kool-Aid would carry a much more sinister association. Reverend Jim Jones of the People's Temple in Jonestown, Guyana, would lead his followers to mass suicide by poisoned Kool-Aid. (Zappa commemorated this horrible event in his otherworldly composition "Jonestown," on *The Perfect Stranger: Boulez Conducts Zappa.*)

"Brown Shoes Don't Make It" is the premier cut on *Absolutely Free*. This mini-opera, said Zappa, is about "people who run the governments, the people who make the laws that keep you from living the kind of life you know you should lead." A seven-and-a-half minute opus paced at the speed of a Loony Tunes cartoon, the song is filled with enough musical quotes and references to inspire a dozen oratorios. It is about a middle-class American, just out of school and sitting at his pool. While calmly consuming a TV dinner, he's looking to make a career for himself at City Hall. What he finds is something less than benign: "A world of secret hungers/perverting the men who make your laws." Soon City Hall Fred, as he comes to be known, has philandered his way through the entire secretarial pool, until he finally finds his ideal fantasy:

> *We see in the back*
> *Of the City Hall mind*
> *The dream of a girl about thirteen*
> *Off with her clothes and into a bed*
> *Where she tickles his fancy*
> *All night long.*

But Zappa doesn't make this thirteen-year-old girl an innocent:

> *She bites his fat neck and it lights up his nose*
> *But he cannot be fooled*
> *Old City Hall Fred*
> *She's nasty, she's nasty*
> *She digs it in bed.*

Fred is ecstatic that "she's only thirteen and she knows how to nasty," and — to the tune of the Beach Boys' "Little Deuce Coupe" — he recites, "She's a dirty young mind, corrupted, corroded." Fred's desires get darker, however, when he starts to ask himself, "If she were my daughter, I'd . . ." and a young girl (played by Herb Cohen's daughter) asks, "What would you do, Daddy?" What does he do?

> *Smother my daughter in chocolate syrup*
> *And strap her on again, oh baby (repeat)*
> *She's my teenage baby*

WHO NEEDS THE PEACE CORPS?

And she turns me on
I'd like to make her do a nasty on the White House lawn
Smother my daughter in chocolate syrup
And boogie till the cows come home.

Zappa draws on a common blues motif to put across City Hall Fred's lecherous desires. In particular he quotes from blues singer Tampa Red's "Don't You Lie to Me": "I'll be with you till the cows come home/But mama, please don't you let me catch you/getting down wrong." "Brown Shoes Don't Make It" ends with divorce and disgrace, and Fred once again sitting by his pool, quietly eating his TV dinner and sizing up his situation: "Life is such a ball/I run the world from City Hall."

While "Brown Shoes Don't Make It" is a scathing indictment tracing how authoritarian attitudes are shaped, it is also a jab at the sexual revolution of the late '60s. "Zappa proposes a cultural politics: the explosion of sexual freedom that will topple the powers-that-be," writes Ben Watson. "As it dawned on him that it wasn't going to work, the stress on sexuality became instead a satirical slant, a litmus test on the freedoms of his audience and his society."

Zappa also deployed a complete storehouse of musical concepts in this song. "In 'Brown Shoes Don't Make It' most people hear only the words," Zappa told *Keyboard* magazine in 1987. "They don't realize that there is, in the middle of that song, a completely academic and rigorous twelve-tone string quartet going on in the background. The other thing that was funny about that song was that by playing 'God Bless America,' 'The Star-Spangled Banner,' and one or two other patriotic songs at the end, all at the same time, I was making a musical joke about [Charles] Ives."

"Brown Shoes Don't Make It" was the second song to bring an operatic structure to rock 'n' roll. Even before they made history with *Tommy*, the Who's first opera was the mini-epic "A Quick One While He's Away," from the *Happy Jack* album (1966). Because of the delay in the release of *Absolutely Free*, it's likely the Who were recording their opus at the same time the Mothers were recording theirs.

Absolutely Free concludes with "America Drinks and Goes Home," a Tin Pan Alley version of "America Drinks," complete with a loud boozing crowd and a horribly fatuous, ingratiating singer: "Last call for alcohol/Drink it up, folks/Wonderful." The song collapses in chaos, cash registers clanging, and a tidy "Night all." The song is a parody of lounge crooners, but it is also a comment on Zappa's contempt for the bars on the Sunset Strip where bands cater to the whims of the crowd. (The Rolling Stones tried to capture the same atmosphere in the limp "On With the Show" on their psychedelic indulgence, *Their Satanic Majesties Request*, in 1967.)

"America Drinks and Goes Home" is unmatched in the way it blends sardonic wit with scathing contempt for the bar crowd. "We used to work in cocktail lounges," Zappa said in *Melody Maker*. "I didn't think that anyone had really presented the horror of the cocktail lounge sufficiently and so we tried to relive a little of it. Everybody in the band at that time knew what the story was with the lounge musical life and they got off on making a parody of what they'd experienced in those lounges. All the clinking glasses and the fight that is going on in the background is specially staged. We had people all over the studio: a guy in the corner playing a cash register, another guy dropping broken glass into a garbage can and shaking it, and three people off in another booth having a fight over who was going to take this girl home, and it was all done simultaneously."

Absolutely Free took four double sessions to record, totaling twenty-five hours in November 1966, and was mixed at MGM Studios in New York. Finally released in May 1967, it was a stunning leap in musical prowess from *Freak Out!* — despite periodic sloppy playing. The album features a ragged charm, though, backed with a relentless intelligence. *Absolutely Free* embraced freedom so totally, that in its own vehement exuberance it couldn't help occasionally tripping over its own feet.

10

In 1966, the Mothers of Invention could get no work in Los Angeles — the club owners had shut their doors because of the riots. The Mothers went to New York City, where they were booked to play the Balloon Farm on Thanksgiving Day, November 26. There they performed a single piece of music, interrupted by dialogue and incorporating fragments from Mussorgsky's opera *Boris Godunov*. The Big Apple welcomed the kind of absurdism the Mothers displayed in performance. One critic said, "They are the perfect embodiment of all that is super-hyped and stunningly creative about West Coast rock." Robert Shelton raved in the *New York Times*, "The Mothers of Invention are primarily musical satirists. Beyond that, they are perhaps the first pop group to successfully amalgamate rock 'n' roll with the serious music of Stravinsky and others. . . . Compared to the Mothers of Invention, such big-beat groups as the Beatles and the Rolling Stones emerge as Boy Scouts with electric guitars."

WHO NEEDS THE PEACE CORPS?

In January, Zappa seriously entertained an offer from Nick Venet, a Capitol Records A&R man who originally signed the Beach Boys, to compose and conduct an original work. First, it could ward off starvation resulting from the lack of work in Los Angeles. Secondly, and more importantly, Zappa saw it as an opportunity to have some of his orchestral work recorded. He wrote what would become *Lumpy Gravy* in eleven days and started to record the album with a fifty-piece orchestra (dubbed the Abnuceals Emuukha Electric Symphony Orchestra & Chorus) that month at the Capitol Recording Studios in L.A., with an additional session at New York's Apostolic Studios in February 1967. Capitol was anticipating a summer release, but they immediately ran into problems with MGM. After Capitol spent over $40,000 on studio fees and artwork for the album, MGM voiced their disapproval. They threatened litigation, which lasted close to thirteen months, and settled with Capitol turning over the recording for an MGM release. Venet had mistakenly assumed that since Zappa was signed to Verve/MGM as a performer in the Mothers of Invention, he was free to record as a solo act for Capitol.

Back in November, the Mothers had played a week's residency at the Garrick Theatre, a small venue that seated about three hundred people, on Bleecker Street in Greenwich Village. The engagement was so successful that they were happily held over until New Year's Day. There hadn't been anything — in rock 'n' roll, at least — that came close to creating the type of atmosphere the Mothers brought to the live venue. "It began with the stage in total darkness except for the control lights on the amplifiers," journalist Miles writes in *Frank Zappa: A Visual Documentary*. "An imperceptible drumroll began, grew louder, and when everyone was fully focused on the stage, a dim light came back on at the back of the stage, growing brighter, silhouetting Frank who was standing at the rear of the sloping stage next to a huge gong, like the J. Arthur Rank trademark."

Zappa designed the show not only to blur the usual distinction between the performer and the audience, but to create areas of spontaneous improvisation where the audience could participate in the composition. "There were a lot of girls onstage, some playing tambourine, others being mauled by the group," Miles continues. "The Mothers threw a lot of vegetables about — particularly while playing 'Call Any Vegetable,' and the girls had brooms and would sweep the stage clean again. . . . The group was not particularly tight but they knew a lot of hand signals, some of which were virtually invisible. The group would be playing an extended rockout, seemingly . . . improvised, when suddenly they would all change tempo. It was all very impressive."

The Garrick shows would have been extended further, but the Mothers had booked two weeks of gigs in Montreal. That Canadian gig marked a deliberate turning point in their stage presentation. "We played a club called the New Penelope and it was twenty degrees below zero," Zappa remembered. "We walked from our hotel to the club and the snot had literally frozen in our noses by the time we got to work. The wind instruments got so cold that if you tried to play them, your lips and fingers would freeze to them. The instruments couldn't even be played until they were warmed up." Zappa had to come up with bizarre new ways to entertain the crowd while the horns thawed out — something he'd perfect next summer when they returned to the Garrick in New York.

After the Montreal gig, the Mothers went back to California — briefly — to play the Fillmore with Canned Heat (featuring former Mother Henry Vestine) and the Blues Project. They quickly returned to New York's Fillmore East in March, however, to play on a bill with blues artist Otis Rush and Morning Glory. On March 6, the Mothers made their first visit to Apostolic Studios in New York to cut a single. "Big Leg Emma" and "Why Don'tcha Do Me Right?" was issued in April 1967 but briskly vanished from the charts. While performing "Big Leg Emma" at the Ark in Boston a couple of years later, Zappa expressed mock astonishment at the song's inability to sell. "I can't understand why *that* didn't get on the radio," he told the audience. "It's just as imbecilic as 'Yummy, Yummy, Yummy.' I think the size of the woman's leg had something to do with it. A large stomach, that's one thing. Big legs — I don't know." "Big Leg Emma," which likely got its title from Champion Jack Dupree's 1956 hit "Big Leg Emma's," was part of a long tradition of anatomically silly love songs such as Larry Williams' "Bony Moronie" or "Short Fat Fannie," Louis Jordan's "Caldonia," and Joe Tex's "Skinny Legs and All." All these songs playfully fetishized female body parts in a crafty attempt to impart sexual innuendo. Zappa comprehended the commercial ploy often used to get various forms of carnal desire heard on the radio. He turned "Big Leg Emma" into something that was quite the opposite of those other songs. Instead of someone getting turned on by skinny legs, big feet, or a bony ass, Zappa's Emma created "a big dilemma" for the singer: "She used to knock me out/Until her face broke out." Sounding like a couple of drunk high-school dropouts hanging outside the graduation dance, Zappa and Collins reduce teenage lust to complete camp banality: "She was my steady date/Until she put on weight./Uh huh, oh yeah!" With a musical accompaniment right out of the Rudy Vallee era, "Big Leg Emma" would become the Mothers' signature "cheesy love

WHO NEEDS THE PEACE CORPS?

song" in the late '60s and early '70s; it was usually played before something really difficult that, according to Zappa, "was probably much better for you — in the long run."

"Why Don'tcha Do Me Right?" was your basic R&B love song that featured the kind of gut-bucket sound usually associated with early Captain Beefheart. Zappa, with a deep, gruff voice, sings the typically cliché love lyrics ("You got me beggin' on my knees/You're trying to wreck my life") in total sincerity, while breaking the song in half with a ripping guitar solo. Near the end, Zappa cleverly subverts the song by repeating the line "But baby, I think I love you" over a mock-psychedelic drone. Zappa takes the listener out of the driving rhythm of the song, revealing the total artifice of the tune's origins. A love lyric suddenly becomes nothing more than a common pickup line in a bar. The effect lasts only a few seconds before Zappa plunges back into a high-pitched plea of "Why don'tcha do me right?" But the point's been made. While we tap our feet to the grinding beat, we're aware of the monotony inherent in the song.

During the Mothers' second stint at the Garrick Theatre, during the 1967 Easter weekend, Gail and Frank decided to move to New York. So, along with the band, they found an apartment at 180 Thompson Street in Greenwich Village — just blocks from where Edgard Varèse had lived at 188 Sullivan Street. Zappa fashioned a show that he called "Pigs and Repugnant: Absolutely Free." He set the stage for what audiences could expect when he told Robert Shelton of the *New York Times*, "I am trying to use the weapons of a disoriented and unhappy society against itself. The Mothers of Invention are designed to come in the back door and kill you while you're sleeping."

Coming in the front door, however, weren't the same outrageous freaks who had populated the clubs in L.A. Zappa saw a profound difference between the people who wandered into the Garrick and those who once caught the band at the Whisky. "It's not like you'd go onstage and there would be a sea of people with long hair all decked out in '60s fashion, like the Time-Warner version of the '60s," Zappa told Nigel Leigh. "They were people who were from the suburbs, who were coming to this concert out of curiosity, weren't really part of any kind of a scene, except their local community, and basically stood there with their mouths open just going, 'Duh!'"

The reaction wasn't surprising considering the music's free-form structure and Zappa's unpredictable taunts. "We performed a couple of marriages onstage," he recalled. "We pulled people from the audience and made them make speeches.

One time we brought thirty people up onstage and some of them took our instruments and the rest of them sang 'Louie Louie' as we left."

Among the songs in their repertoire was "Hungry Freaks, Daddy," from *Freak Out!*, but there were also new songs like "Brown Shoes Don't Make It," "Call Any Vegetable," and "America Drinks and Goes Home." Some nights, the band did an extended jam on a theme that would later come to be known as "King Kong." The Mothers went to ridiculous extremes. They ran a wire from the light booth at the back of the theater to the stage. The lighting director sent a spread-eagled baby doll down the wire, followed by a huge piece of salami that would ram the baby doll in the ass — all skillfully choreographed to appropriate music. "We [also] had this big stuffed giraffe onstage, with a hose running up to a spot between the rear legs," Zappa explained. "Ray Collins would go up to the giraffe and massage it with a frog hand puppet . . . and then the giraffe's tail would stiffen and the first three rows of the audience would get sprayed with whipped cream shooting out of the hose." Apparently, this was one of the highlights of the show.

"You can't write a chord ugly enough to say what you want to say," Zappa once remarked. "Sometimes you have to rely on a giraffe filled with whipped cream." Sometimes, though, you have to rely on regulars. One regular was Mark Trottiner, who enjoyed running up the aisle, jumping onstage, grabbing the microphone, and screaming into it as loud as he could. If that didn't get the appropriate response, he would fall onto the stage and roll over like a dog and urge Zappa to spit Pepsi-Cola all over his body. Another habitual patron was a character named Louis Cuneo. Louis had a distinctive laugh that earned him the nickname "Louis the Turkey" and could be heard throughout the theater. Zappa would invite him onstage and stop the music. Louis would then sit on a stool, hold the mike, and just let out gales of mad laughter. Zappa would then thank him and Louis would return happily to his seat.

Sandy Hurvitz, a folksinger, was a Garrick regular who briefly joined the Mothers during their residency and also accompanied them on their speedy tour of Europe later that year. "One of Frank's jokes was that he liked to use opposites to call people," Hurvitz told Neil Slaven. "I was real nice and sweet, so he called me 'Uncle Meat.'" Ray Collins had come up with the name, but Zappa claimed it for Hurvitz. The claim was short-lived, however, because Hurvitz soon had no use for it. After a few days, according to Hurvitz, Zappa told her, "Okay, you don't have to be 'Uncle Meat.' If you don't want to make money out of the name, I will." He did, too. A couple of years later, Zappa titled his first film — and the soundtrack album — *Uncle Meat*.

WHO NEEDS THE PEACE CORPS?

When word got out about how Zappa coupled outrageous stagecraft with stunningly well-played music, more musicians began to turn up. Ian Underwood, a multitalented instrumentalist with music degrees from both Yale and Berkeley, was also an interested observer at the Garrick. After seeing the band twice in August, he went up to drummer Jimmy Carl Black and asked if he could play in the group. However, nothing came of it. That same year, Underwood showed up again, only this time in the studio. Zappa asked what he could do that was fantastic. When Ian said he played alto saxophone and piano, Zappa told him, in characteristic fashion, "Okay. Whip it out." (This story is sublimely recounted by Underwood on the *Uncle Meat* album on a track titled — appropriately — "Ian Underwood Whips It Out.")

Another satisfied Garrick customer was percussionist Ruth Komanoff, a graduate of Juilliard. "I went to college for seven years and did everything by the books until I met Frank," she told *Musician* in 1994. "His 'Absolutely Free' show at the Garrick Theatre changed my life. I no longer wanted to be a tympanist at the New York Philharmonic, or a virtuoso marimba soloist. All I wanted from that point on was to play Frank's music." Ruth got her chance one night when she and her brother were going to see Miles Davis at the Village Gate. While waiting outside for the concert to start, her brother saw Zappa walking down Bleecker Street. He waltzed up to him and said, "You should hear my sister play! She's a great marimbist!" While Ruth cowered in embarrassment, Zappa told her to bring her marimba set the next day, and he'd check her out. That audition led to some percussion work on *Uncle Meat*. Ruth would eventually marry (and later divorce) Ian Underwood, whom she met during those sessions. Then, in the early '70s, she would again join the Mothers on *200 Motels*, before becoming a full-time band member a couple of years later.

Attending the shows at the Garrick Theatre was a musical revelation for Ruth. "One never knew what to expect," she told Nigel Leigh. "There were some nights that you just heard pure music, and other nights, Motorhead would be talking about fixing his car with Jim Black's drumbeat in the background. Sometimes Frank would just sit in a chair and glower at the audience. Sometimes there were more people onstage than there were in the audience. And because of that, Frank got to know some of us by name. . . . I remember Stravinsky being played. . . . [Also] droning music going on for ages. . . . [Then] the song that became 'Oh No' breaking through the clouds. It just shocked me how beautiful music could come out of such bizarre-looking people."

How bizarre? Journalists Doon Arbus and Valerie Wilmer describe Zappa as a "wild [and] woodsy hermit, either very benign or very ferocious." His face was "made of planes and angles, like a house of cards, and is framed by a mantle of squiggly, black curls." Jimmy Carl Black resembled a "Mexican bandido"; Roy Estrada gave off the aura of "a Polish anarchist"; Ray Collins, with his thick, curly locks and beard, became "a high-browed Viking"; Bunk Gardner, on the other hand, with his trimmed gray beard, had "the unruffled elegance of a riverboat gambler"; and Billy Mundi looked like "a baker from the French Revolution."

"Music is always a commentary on society, and certainly the atrocities onstage are quite mild compared to those conducted on behalf of our government," Zappa told *Rolling Stone*. One such notorious example, where Zappa's remarks were severely put to the test, was about to take place. That summer, in 1967, the tension between the counterculture and authorities — particularly the military — reached a boiling point in the Village. A rumor circulated that the sudden death of a Marine had been caused by a hippie and that the boys were looking for payback. Though the Marine Corps never got their revenge, the paranoid residue of that event became part of a Zappa experiment at the Garrick.

Author David Walley recounts that two weeks after the rumor started to spread, three uniformed Marines walked into the Garrick while the Mothers were rehearsing before their evening show. Rather than stirring up trouble, they sat quietly listening. Afterward, they approached Zappa and told him that they had bought the *Freak Out!* album and had really enjoyed it. Surprised, Zappa thanked them and asked if they wanted to perform with the band that night. Sure, they said, they'd love to. When he asked what songs they knew, the soldiers responded that they were fond of Bob Dylan's "Rainy Day Women #12 & 35" and the Animals' "House of the Rising Sun." As the group went across the road for dinner, the three Marines gleefully warmed up in the Garrick. After supper, the Mothers returned to find the servicemen ready to go. Whereupon Zappa told them enthusiastically, "Now look, there's one little thing I want you to do. When I give you the signal, I want all three of you guys to lunge for the microphone and start screaming, 'Kill!'"

Zappa knew about the murder in the Village and felt he could tap into something primal in these young recruits, as well as in the audience. He wanted to test the servicemen's rage in the context of a live performance.

That evening, the boys in uniform started to perform their tunes to the obvious joy of the folks in the crowd, who no doubt were laughing in derision at these three tools of the Establishment making fools of themselves. Then the

WHO NEEDS THE PEACE CORPS?

Mothers started in with their usual dissonant material. Right in the middle of some atonal improvisation, Zappa cued the Marines to charge forward. As they thrust toward the crowd yelling "Kill!" the audience was horrified, and the disdainful chuckles were quickly stifled. A few audience members politely clapped, hoping to let the air out of the tension in the room. Zappa and Collins, having achieved their desired effect, said their thanks for the evening. But the Marines, caught up in the spirit of their scandalous debut, decided to take the concert to another realm.

"Eat the apple, fuck the corps," said the first Marine, who turned a salacious boot-camp rhyme into a provocative call and response. As the crowd sat stunned, the second Marine repeated the phrase. The third decided to build on what his comrades had started. "Hey, you know I feel the same way as my other buddies: Eat the apple, fuck the corps, some of us love our Mothers more!"

Zappa knew the Marines could get court-martialed for these remarks, but they didn't seem to care — they were in show business now. Zappa had a new idea for beginning the evening's second show. He sent Gail home to get a doll that they'd recently received as a present. She returned just before the Mothers were about to mount the stage for a second time. Zappa began the program by introducing the Marines to the new audience. "Hey, ladies an' gennelmen, the guys are, uh, going to sing 'Everybody Must Get Stoned.'" Once again, the boys performed the song with all the barroom gusto that the tune invites. After they finished, Zappa came back and informed the throng, "Now we're gonna have basic training." Zappa paused and reached for the little plastic doll. "Uh, ladies an' gennelmen, this is a gook baby."

He turned to the Marines and tossed them the docile toy, saying "Show us how we treat gooks in Vietnam." The Marines, caught off-guard, but without pause, began to zealously tear the doll to shreds. First, they ripped off the legs, then tore out the arms, and then completely mangled the toy. When they were finished, Zappa took back the plastic carcass and held it by the hair. He pointed to all the damaged parts as if he were holding a wounded child before the hushed crowd.

Zappa later told David Walley, "There was this one guy in the front row, a Negro cat just back from Vietnam, [who] was crying. It was awful. I decided to end the show there." For some, this perilous theater was insensitive, rude, perhaps even sadistic. But Zappa disagreed. "We were carrying on the forgotten tradition of Dada stagecraft," Zappa told *Playboy* in 1993. "The more absurd, the better I liked it."

11

It can probably be said for us that art is not an end in itself . . . but it is an opportunity for true perception and criticism of the times we live in. . . . What can a beautiful, harmonious poem say if nobody reads it because it has nothing to do with the feelings of the times? And what can a novel have to say when it is read for culture but is really a long way from even touching on culture? Our debates are a burning search, more blatant every day, for the specific rhythm and the buried face of this age.

HUGO BALL, *Flight Out of Time*, 1916

On February 5, 1916, while a world war raged around them, a group of artists had just landed in Zurich, Switzerland, to launch a club called the Cabaret Voltaire. Hugo Ball was a twenty-nine-year-old German poet and Catholic mystic. With him were his lover, cabaret singer Emmy Hennings; Tristan Tzara, a poet from Romania; painter Marcel Janco, Tzara's countryman; Alsatian artist Jean Arp; and a medical student named Richard Huelsenbeck, who had a thing for the drums. Ball was devoted to a philosophy called *Gesamtkunstwerk* ("total work of art") that was borrowed from Richard Wagner. Using this idea of the regeneration of a one-dimensional society through a totality combining all the arts, the Dadaists incorporated it into a similar idea for a totality of theater. The combination of poems being read, music performed, and songs sung would boost what had become a sagging clientele at the café, but Ball was looking for something more tantalizing — a new expressive art form that would put shock into entertainment.

"Dada is a new tendency in art," Ball wrote that year. "One can tell this from the fact that until now nobody knew anything about it, and tomorrow everyone in Zurich will be talking about it." Ball gave a deliberately loose definition of Dada. "Dada comes from the dictionary. It is terribly simple. In French, it means 'hobby horse.' In German, it means 'Goodbye,' 'Get off my back,' 'Be seeing you sometime.' In Romanian: 'Yes, indeed, you are right, that's it. But of course, yes, definitely right.' And so forth." Yet Dada was also something designed to shake an audience's neatly held assumptions about the state of the world. Ball saw a globe raging in chaos and blood, while a crowd, seeking comfort from that discord, came to the

WHO NEEDS THE PEACE CORPS? 127

cabaret expecting entertainment that would help them forget it all. Ball wasn't about to contribute to that style of amusement: "How does one achieve eternal bliss? By saying dada. How does one become famous? By saying dada. With a noble gesture and delicate propriety. Till one goes crazy. Till one loses consciousness. How can one get rid of everything that smacks of journalism, worms, everything nice and right, blinkered, moralistic, Europeanized, enervated? By saying dada. Dada is the world soul, dada is the pawnshop."

What Ball and his group performed nightly at the Cabaret Voltaire formed the basis for what Zappa brought to the Garrick in the late '60s. The German painter Hans Richter described the scene quite simply: "The Cabaret Voltaire was a six-piece band. Each played his own instrument, i.e., himself." Arp described their shows in even more graphic detail. "Total pandemonium. The people around us are shouting, laughing, and gesticulating. Our replies are sighs of love, volleys of hiccups, poems, moos, and miaowing of medieval Bruitists." The audience was shocked and outraged. There was no way for them to discern the difference between the outside world and the swirling upheaval surrounding them.

"Tzara is wiggling his behind like the belly of an Oriental dancer," Arp continued. "Janco is playing an invisible violin and bowing and scraping. Madame Hennings, with a Madonna face, is doing the splits. Huelsenbeck is banging away non-stop on the great drum, with Ball accompanying him on the piano, pale as a chalky ghost."

Ball, not satisfied, had something even more dramatic planned for the Cabaret. He'd been working on some phonetic verses that he called "*Lautgedichte*"; he wanted to shed the common dialect and communicate in pure vowels and syllables. "I shall be reading poems that are meant to dispense with conventional language, no less, and have done with it," Ball wrote in the Dada Manifesto. "I don't want words that other people have invented. . . . I want my own stuff, my own rhythm, and vowels and consonants too, matching the rhythm and all my own. If this pulsation is seven yards long, I want words that are seven yards long."

To premiere his first sound poem, Ball at first stood offstage, his legs covered in blue cardboard. He wore a collar that was gold on the outside and scarlet on the inside. Within a cubist mask that covered his face was a pale, distressed expression that soon fell into a deathly calm. As the lights went down, Ball's voice took on the age-old measure of a requiem:

gadji beri bimba
glandridi lauli lonni cadori
gadjama bim beri glassala
glandridi glassala tuffm i zimbrabim
blassa galassasa tuffm i zimbrabim . . .

The audience was spellbound, yet puzzled, deprived of a common reaction to this hedonistic embrace of the absurd. This wasn't a language that could be shared; it had to be heard, explored, and somehow made sense of. Ball had gone fearlessly into the source of language, the first guttural cries at birth, and the pain of waking into a new world. Clearly no one wanted to wake up — it was better to sleep, and to dream and forget.

Ball once described a Dadaist as someone "still so convinced of the unity of all beings, of the totality of all things, that he suffers from the dissonances." Frank Zappa believed that the universe worked beautifully, whether we understood it or not, and as a result, he didn't suffer those dissonances the way Ball did. If anything, Zappa gleefully utilized them in his work. When those Marines turned the Garrick stage into a makeshift war zone, Zappa found a radically seditious way to provide catharsis for an explosive situation. By 1967, the Vietnam War was already starting to divide the country, and television was bringing the daily horror of that conflict into people's homes. Taking a page from the Dadaists in Zurich, Zappa refused to allow the audience refuge. By not turning comfortably didactic, he adroitly illustrated the lines of demarcation that existed in the culture. For a short time in 1967, Zappa reached back across the century to borrow a performing trait from a group of rambunctious artists who had successfully turned a cabaret in Zurich upside down. Like that audience at the Cabaret Voltaire, the Garrick crowd had to make sense of the chaotic rage that swirled around them.

12

In May 1967, the Mothers of Invention's second album, *Absolutely Free,* named after the Garrick show, was finally released. It had been due out in January, but as usual, Zappa ran up against problems with his record company. First of all, MGM didn't like the fact that the artwork, which featured various advertising slogans, contained the phrase "War Means Work for All." This was an obvious comment on the crisis in Vietnam. These same executives also didn't want to publish the

WHO NEEDS THE PEACE CORPS?

libretto for the record because they found some of the words obscene. Apparently, they had legitimate legal grounds to prevent Zappa from including it in the record.

"There's a legal difference between what's on record and what's on paper," Zappa told a journalist. "You can sing it, and that's part of a work of art; but the liner notes to an album are not — you can't defend that in court as a work of art. MGM legal department decided that."

Also, the changes that the company wished to make were intolerable for Zappa — they altered the meaning of the songs. For instance, in "Brown Shoes Don't Make It," MGM wanted to censor the lyric "She's only thirteen and she knows how to nasty" by taking out the word "thirteen" rather than "nasty." They also wanted to change "I'd like to make her do a nasty on the White House lawn" to "I'd like to make her do the crossword puzzle on the back of *TV Guide*." What made matters even more frustrating for Zappa was that the label didn't even *understand* the lyrics they found offensive. One executive told the stupefied Zappa that he thought making her "do a nasty on the White House lawn" meant she was taking a shit on the grass.

Zappa wound up publishing the libretto himself, informing consumers on the album sleeve that if they sent in as much money as they could, he would mail them the lyrics. (When the CD of *Absolutely Free* was released in 1987 by Rykodisc, the libretto was finally included — uncensored.) During a short break from the Garrick in August, Zappa did some recording at the Apostolic Studios in New York. With MGM winning their lawsuit against Capitol Records, and garnering the right to release *Lumpy Gravy*, Zappa started preparing the album for a May 1968 release. It wasn't an easy task. Capitol Records hadn't taken the best care of the original tapes — in fact, they had attempted to haphazardly edit them. Zappa found a capable technician in Gary Kellgren, a gifted young engineer, who had just finished work on Jimi Hendrix's *Electric Ladyland*. At Mayfair Studios, they re-assembled the mess.

Zappa had an intriguing idea while restoring the tapes. "One day I decided to stuff a pair of U-87 [microphones] in the piano, cover it with a heavy drape, put a sandbag on the sustain pedal and invite anybody in the vicinity to stick their head inside and ramble incoherently about the various topics I would suggest to them via the studio talk-back system," Zappa recalled.

"[It] was a big grand piano, a nice instrument with remarkable resonance," recalled recording engineer Dick Kunc. "With the pedal held down it would just ring forever. Frank discovered by accident one day that when you spoke near it the appropriate sympathetic strings would resonate. So we clamped down the pedal and draped tarps and rugs over the open lid, sort of forming a little cave. Frank would put people in there and tell them to talk about various topics and we'd record it."

After setting this up in the studio, Zappa randomly recorded over several days. Some of the people who took up residence in the piano included Motorhead Sherwood and Roy Estrada of the Mothers; Spider Barbour, the lead singer of a band called Chrysalis; "All-Night" John, the studio manager; Gilly Townley, the sister of the guy who owned Apostolic Studios; the receptionist, Monica; and even Louis Cuneo, with his psychotic turkey laugh.

After about nine months of editing, he included portions of these absurd dialogues in between the orchestral music, *musique concrète*, electronic textures, and sound effects. By the time Zappa's first solo album finally hit record stores in October 1968, what had begun as a series of sessions to get some of Zappa's orchestral music recorded became an exquisite masterpiece of contemporary audio collage art.

13

Lumpy Gravy was a complete break from everything the Mothers of Invention had recorded. So when it came out in May 1968, listeners were baffled. (The album reached No. 159 — for one week — on the U.S. charts.) The title, from a commercial for Aloma Linda Gravy Quick, couldn't have been more fitting — there were a lot of lumps in this musical sauce. While *Freak Out!* and *Absolutely Free* were still ostensibly rock 'n' roll records, *Lumpy Gravy* had the textual quality of an avant-garde classical album by John Cage, or a Karlheinz Stockhausen patchwork. There were also elements in the work that couldn't be pigeonholed and put *Lumpy Gravy* in a category all its own. Listening to it was akin to spinning the dial on a radio — you might hear a snippet of dialogue, a bit of surf music, then suddenly a string quartet. In the blink of an eye, you could find yourself back to the station you started on.

With *Lumpy Gravy*, Zappa was exploring the meaning of sound. He took different musical genres, random dialogue, portions of songs — and created aural head-on collisions. Just as Varèse had tried to appropriate all the sounds he heard around him, Zappa, with his utopian lustre, incorporated anything he could find. The only difference was that Varèse would never have considered arcane elements of popular culture a part of his mosaic.

When a voice from inside a piano announces, "The way I see it, Barry, this

WHO NEEDS THE PEACE CORPS?

should be a very dynamite show," the album is off and running with a mighty gallop. This rousing main theme, "Duodenum," is a rollicking piece of orchestral cowboy music straight out of a 1940s adventure serial. As the theme fades, a bit of twelve-tone music (left over from the film *Run Home Slow*) leads us into an orchestral version of one of Zappa's loveliest pieces of music: "Oh No." Although written prior to the Watts riots in 1965, "Oh No" had yet to be recorded in any form. Just as its majestic elegance settles in, though, Zappa introduces his first bit of *musique concrète*, including the words "a little nostalgia for the old folks." With that comes a snippet from the surf-rock number "Hurricane," by Conrad & the Hurricanes, before we're led into a series of dialogues from inside the piano.

These randomly recorded conversations cover a variety of topics: Monica and Gilly discuss "living in a drum," Motorhead goes on about how his girlfriend gets boozed up and rips his car apart, and Louis Cuneo hysterically tells Roy Estrada about the horrible visions he has of "pigs and ponies." Breaking up all these seemingly nonsensical chats are a snatch of dixieland music, sped-up drums, strings, a cough, maybe a belch, or even a snork, and lots of percussion. *Lumpy Gravy* grabs you with both its randomness and the conscious purpose Zappa employs to create meaning out of such spare parts.

Much of that strategy Zappa owes to the American avant-garde composer John Cage. "Cage is a big influence," Zappa told Sally Kempton of *The Village Voice*. "We've done a thing with voices, with talking, that is very like one of his pieces — except that, of course, in our piece the guys are talking about working in an airplane factory, or their cars."

John Cage also developed a piano technique he learned from his esteemed teacher and colleague, Henry Cowell, where he made use of what he called "tone clusters." "I frequently held the piano pedal down while Henry would run behind and play his banshee," Cage said in 1982. "I also once saw him use a darning needle on the bass strings of the piano to get a glissandi of overtones. So it was perfectly reasonable for me, after he opened that door, to put screws and weather stripping between the piano strings. The only change was that all the things that Henry Cowell did were mobile on the strings, and the characteristic of the prepared piano is that they're stuck to the strings." In *Lumpy Gravy*, the timbre of the voices inside the piano created similar tone clusters.

Cage was also known to create musical happenings where he'd instruct the audience to participate randomly. One time, he had an audience go out to find garbage pails to bring back for use as percussion instruments — with or without the garbage. For Cage, sometimes the length of a composition was determined by the roll of dice — or a toss of *I Ching* coins. He would then explore (at random) acoustical pulses, noises, or the duration of a composition.

Zappa, too, was after a philosophical grasp of the meaning of music. At one point, one of the piano dwellers remarks, "Everything in the universe is made of one element which is a note, a single note." Zappa elaborated on this concept in his article "The Oracle Has It All Psyched Out," in *Life* in 1968. "One of the characters [in the piano] explains the concept of the Big Note: everything in the universe is composed basically of vibrations — light is a vibration, sound is a vibration, atoms are composed of vibrations — and all these vibrations just might be harmonics of some incomprehensible fundamental cosmic tone." *Lumpy Gravy* was an opportunity for Frank Zappa to experiment with the effect that different sounds in collaboration with one another have on the listener:

> Why does the sound of Eric Clapton's guitar give one girl a sensation which she describes as "Bone Conduction"? Would she still experience Bone Conduction if Eric, using the same extremely loud thick tone, played nothing but Hawaiian music? Which is more important: the timbre (color-texture) of a sound, the succession of intervals which make up the melody, the harmonic support (chords) which tells your ear "what the melody means" (Is it major or minor or neutral or what), the volume at which the sound is heard, the volume at which the sound is produced, the distance from source to ear, the density of the sound, the number of sounds per second or fraction thereof . . . and so on? Which of these would be the most important element in an audial experience which gave you a pleasurable sensation? An erotic sensation? Look at kids in school, tapping their feet, beating with their fingers. People try, unconsciously, to be in tune with their environment.

Zappa's experiments set out to unravel all the elusive mysteries contained in the world of sound. These quests into sonic possibilities would be worked on in more elaborate detail in the albums to follow. For now, *Lumpy Gravy*, with its concluding sentiment that "round things are . . . boring," served as a fascinating blueprint that was anything but dull.

WHO NEEDS THE PEACE CORPS?

14

The Mothers continued through early fall of 1967 recording material at Apostolic that would later surface on *We're Only in It for the Money*, *Cruising With Ruben & the Jets*, and *Uncle Meat*. Zappa was also planning, for the follow-up to *Absolutely Free*, an album that combined material by Lenny Bruce and music by the Mothers of Invention. It was to be titled *Our Man in Nirvana*. But the only people in Nirvana at this particular time were the Beatles. Once again, that summer, they had taken the world by storm with the release of their landmark psychedelic album, *Sgt. Pepper's Lonely Hearts Club Band*. Given the massive impact of the Beatles' latest hit, Zappa decided to change his plans. He dropped *Our Man in Nirvana* and concentrated his efforts on something to address the latest cultural upheaval by the Fab Four. That new project would turn into a scathing satirical attack on the hippie culture that *Sgt. Pepper* lauded in that Summer of Love.

Although the Beatles' album is certainly a lovely confection, "flower power" had evolved into a successful commercial fad. So Zappa went after the fad rather than the music. "*Sgt. Pepper* was okay," Zappa remarked to Kurt Loder in 1988. "But just the whole aroma of what the Beatles were was something that never really caught my fancy. I got the impression from what was going on at the time that they were only in it for the money — and that was a pretty unpopular view to hold." Like Lenny Bruce, Zappa saw duplicitous ideals as a worthy target to attack — and he saw it blossoming in the hippie culture. "While the world swooned in cosmic brotherhood and groups rushed to emulate the Beatles' studio-craft, Frank Zappa used *Sgt. Pepper* as a catalyst for a swinging attack on the meretriciousness and self-deception that he felt it embodied," Neil Slaven writes.

Incidentally, *Sgt. Pepper*, issued on June 2 in North America, came out a week after *Absolutely Free*. It was also being hailed as rock's first concept album — even though *Freak Out!* had already earned that honor a year earlier. In truth, *Freak Out!* demonstrated an enormous impact on *Sgt. Pepper*. For one, the way the Beatles used images of famous people on their cover resembled Zappa's list of influential artists on the gatefold of *Freak Out!* But where *Freak Out!* seemed to inspire *Sgt. Pepper* most was in creating an identity for itself. *Freak Out!* was a manifesto for the freak culture in Los Angeles, the way *Sgt. Pepper* was a proclamation for the hippie subculture of San Francisco the following year. As Slaven points out, however, *Sgt. Pepper* also shared something in common with *Absolutely Free*. "By coincidence, both albums made extensive use of the segue; the songs on each side ran in unbroken sequence," Slaven writes. But he points up a crucial difference when he adds, "But while Frank relied on sudden changes of tempo and precise editing to create his effect, the Beatles used cross-fades and bits of 'business' like the laughter at the end of 'Within You Without You' to make the transitions between songs. . . . *Sgt. Pepper* became a symbol of the mood of the time, encouraging both radicals and hippies to see it as an affirmation of their cause. *Absolutely Free* had a harder lesson to teach; it also spoke to the imagination, but its purpose was a call to action, not euphoria."

Dan Sullivan, in the *New York Times*, points up the discrepancy even more succinctly: "The most striking difference between [the Beatles and the Mothers of Invention] is not in their work but in their approach to their work — the Beatles' desire to please an audience versus the Mothers' basic distrust of one."

Sgt. Pepper was a beautiful, self-conscious neon sign that celebrated the romantic ideal, where the true possibility of love could transcend all our problems. *Absolutely Free* offered no such simple solution. Where *Sgt. Pepper* was self-satisfied and seamless, *Absolutely Free* was sharply funny — even ridiculous — daring you to laugh at what had already become a dark reflection of the counterculture. *Sgt. Pepper* set a mellifluous tone for that summer. The Monterey Pop Festival, which took place June 16–18, was America's answer to the Beatles' cry of love. Janis Joplin, the Byrds, the Jefferson Airplane, Canned Heat, the Grateful Dead, Ravi Shankar, Hugh Masekela, the Who, and Buffalo Springfield all attempted to create a solid foundation for the counterculture. Woodstock would build on those hopes, too, until Altamont ultimately crushed them in 1969.

So as the rock 'n' roll world moved and grooved to the cosmic sounds of universal brotherhood, Frank Zappa went to work on an album that tried to take out its underpinnings. Appropriately enough, it would eventually be titled *We're Only in It for the Money*.

While the album set out to create discord in the summer of harmony, discord extended to the group as well. Lead singer Ray Collins, for instance, briefly left the band. For Collins, *We're Only in It for the Money* was probably too much Penderecki and not enough Penguins. Yet even one of his more avant-garde colleagues, Don Preston, also decided to pack it in. "I decided, fuck all this shit in New York, I'm going back to L.A. to my wife and kids," Preston told *Mojo* magazine. "So I went back to L.A., found out where my wife was living, and this big guy answered. And I said, 'Fuck this shit, too.' So I called Frank and said, 'Let me back in the band,' and flew back to New York. I was gone for about a week."

WHO NEEDS THE PEACE CORPS?

For the recording of the album, Zappa took over lead vocals in Ray Collins' absence. He also hired Ian Underwood, who could read music, to play keyboards and wind instruments — even if he did look like the "straightest" member of the group. "Ian was an excellent musician who never really fit in with the band," Bunk Gardner recalled. "He tried real hard to be 'one of the guys' but never succeeded. He spent most of his time hanging out with Frank. There's really no area in Ian's personality that was bizarre or weird. He tried but he was never a source of laughs or genuine humor for the rest of the band, although he tried hard and wanted to be liked."

We're Only in It for the Money was the first Mothers album produced by Zappa. Tom Wilson, listed on the record as executive producer, would quit MGM at the end of 1967 to form Rasputin Productions.

In a sense, *We're Only in It for the Money* is a companion piece to all the experimental work started on *Lumpy Gravy*. When both albums were released, the front cover of *We're Only in It for the Money* had a cartoon bubble over Zappa that read, "Is This Phase One Of *Lumpy Gravy*?"; on the back cover of *Lumpy Gravy*, a cartoon bubble over Zappa reads, "Is This Phase 2 Of: *We're Only in It for the Money*?"

What Zappa accomplished with this razor-sharp appraisal of the counterculture was a perfect wedding of psychedelia, *musique concrète*, and a pop oratorio similar to the songs on *Absolutely Free*. Zappa described *We're Only in It for the Money* as a "monstrosity conceived and executed . . . as a result of some unpleasant premonitions, August through October 1967. All premonitions continuing to come true." Besides being a broadside against the Summer of Love, *We're Only in It for the Money* contained an uncanny number of accurate predictions.

A disembodied voice buried in various taped sound effects and a perpetual echo asks, "Are you hung up?" Meanwhile, guitarist Eric Clapton propositions a young woman, wondering if she *is* hung up, or maybe strung up, while she repeatedly tells him she doesn't understand a word he's saying. Clapton replies, "Yeah. Outtasight." He's totally oblivious to her confusion. Before the album is even a minute old, all the familiar terms of discourse are rendered unintelligible. Clapton and the woman are speaking, but no contact is being made, while chaos swirls around them. Then, out of the disarray comes another disembodied voice, but this one is speaking in a demonstrative whisper. Engineer Gary Kellgren, cast as Big Brother, is the man with his hands on the switch, recording this album. Regaling us with his omnipotence, Kellgren menacingly directs his comments to Zappa: "I know he's sitting in there now, listening to everything I say. But I really don't care.

Hello, Frank Zappa!" A whooshing sound resembling a spaceship is then coupled with feedback guitar, creating a mood of dire paranoia. *We're Only in It for the Money*, in its first two minutes, replaces any harmonious sentiment with an atmosphere of dread and misunderstanding. The spell is momentarily broken by the sound of drummer Jimmy Carl Black saying, "Hi, boys and girls, I'm Jimmy Carl Black. I'm the Indian of this group."

Before we can swallow the chuckle in our response, "Who Needs the Peace Corps" starts up, and the story of a hippie hopeful unfolds:

What's there to live for?
Who needs the peace corps?
Think I'll just drop out
I'll go to Frisco
Buy a wig and sleep on Owsley's floor.

The story resembles that of City Hall Fred from "Brown Shoes Don't Make It," except this guy wants no part of running the world from City Hall — he's dropping out. Yet they are both linked by their trust in values that turn out to be bankrupt:

I'm completely stoned
I'm hippy and I'm trippy
I'm a gypsy on my own
I'll stay a week & get the crabs
Take a bus back home
I'm really just a phony
But forgive me 'cause I'm stoned.

Before long, psychedelic dungeons are popping up everywhere, and our hippie is so blissed out that he's willing to accept anything: "I'll love everyone/I'll love the police as they kick the shit out of me on the street." "Who Needs the Peace Corps?" is one of the more powerful analysis of the '60s drug culture — Zappa boldly links the passivity of the hippie movement to its ultimate collusion with the authoritarian powers of the government. "The single most important [lesson of the '60s] is that LSD was a scam promoted by the CIA and that the people in Haight-Ashbury, who were idols of people across the world as examples of revolution and outrage and progress, were mere dupes of the CIA," Zappa told Neil Slaven.

WHO NEEDS THE PEACE CORPS?

While Zappa doesn't spare the hippie culture, he's no less harsh toward the government. "Concentration Moon" attacks the police for its blatant brutality against the hippies:

AMERICAN WAY
How did it start?
Thousands of creeps
Killed in the park.

These words were written a mere three years before the tragic shooting and killing of four students by National Guardsmen at Kent State University on May 4, 1970. Since Zappa attempts through his music to break our linear bond with time, his work always displays a certain prescience. Consider the following lyrics:

AMERICAN WAY
Threatened by us
Drag a few creeps
Away in a bus
AMERICAN WAY
Prisoner: lock
SMASH EVERY CREEP
IN THE FACE WITH A ROCK.

A couple of years later, in 1969, a parking lot at the University of California at Berkeley was turned into a "People's Park" by protesters. Governor Ronald Reagan ordered the National Guard to seize the park and shoot all resisters. Using saltpeter instead of bullets, they wounded many and killed one person. Later, after the "park" was reclaimed, several people were arrested, taken away in a bus to an internment camp in Santa Rita, and violently interrogated for a couple of days.

After the terror of "Concentration Moon," Zappa brings it all back home on "Mom & Dad." This song appears to continue the story — a man and woman, sitting at home drinking, learn that their daughter has been shot dead by police. Zappa finally takes some of the blame away from the hippies and the cops, and directs it at her folks:

Ever take a minute just to show a real emotion
In between the moisture cream and velvet facial lotion?
Ever tell your kids you're glad that they can think
Ever say you loved them? Ever let 'em watch you drink?

Zappa shows a naked ambivalence, leveling with every strata of society as he documents the cultural war of the '60s. The drinking parents, hiding behind their appearances, are irrevocably linked to their drug-addled kids. "Zappa . . . never found his emotions so mixed as when observing all those genuinely idealistic, authentically dumb kids trying to forge *something* positive out of the plastic catastrophic America they'd inherited," Dave Marsh writes in *Rock & Rap Confidential*. As we absorb the final blow of "they killed her, too," a telephone rings ominously. Zappa's voice calls out a number and then two women start talking about the FBI bumping someone off. According to Michael Gray, while in the studio, Gail had phoned up Pamela Zarubica and told her to contact Pam's sister Vicki, because their father had the FBI after her. Zappa recorded the conversation (in his usual manner of randomly documenting material he could incorporate into music) and placed it on the album.

The innocuous, Rudy Vallee–sounding "Bow Tie Daddy" follows before we get Zappa's views on female sexuality in "Harry, You're a Beast":

You paint your head
Your mind is dead
You don't even know what I just said
THAT'S YOU: AMERICAN WOMANHOOD.

Zappa would be attacked repeatedly by feminists for his portrayal of women in his songs, but as he often pointed out, most of his songs were about stupid men. "Harry, You're a Beast" isn't so much a gratuitous attack as it is an observation about male/female dynamics in an age many considered defined by the sexual revolution. In the song, Harry and his wife, Madge, live a sexless marriage until Harry attempts intercourse one night and Madge fights him off. Borrowing the words of Lenny Bruce, she cries, "Don't come in me/Don't come in me." (These lines were censored on the album's release, and restored only when the CD came out in 1986.) While it's obvious that Harry *did* indeed come in her, we head right into the real crime of the story, "What's the Ugliest Part of Your Body?":

WHO NEEDS THE PEACE CORPS?

Some say your nose
Some say your toes
But I think it's
YOUR MIND

As he did in "Brown Shoes Don't Make It," Zappa points to sexual repression. "Parents, unfortunately, have a tendency to misunderstand, misinterpret, and, worst of all, ridicule patterns of behavior which seem foreign to them," Zappa wrote in *Life* magazine. "When they noticed a growing interest among teenagers in matters pertaining to the pleasure-giving functions of the body, they felt threatened. Mom and Dad were sexually uninformed and inhibited (a lot of things wrong with society today are directly attributable to the fact that the people who make the laws are sexually maladjusted) and they saw no reason why their kids should be raised differently. (Why should those dirty teenagers have all the fun?) Sex is for making babies and it makes your body misshapen and ugly afterward and let's not talk about it, shall we?" Zappa, on the other hand, did talk about it:

ALL YOUR CHILDREN ARE POOR
UNFORTUNATE VICTIMS OF LIES YOU BELIEVE
A PLAGUE UPON YOUR
IGNORANCE THAT KEEPS
THE YOUNG FROM THE TRUTH
THEY DESERVE . . .

After Zappa identifies the scourge, he starts to point a way out. A lovely classical piano interlude (rudely interrupted by Pamela Zarubica intoning, "I don't do publicity balling for you anymore") leads into "Absolutely Free." Some, like Zappa biographer Ben Watson, have assumed that this song is making fun of psychedelic clichés, but Zappa actually uses those clichés to suggest a whole new freedom.

Unbind your mind
There is no time
To lick your stamps
And paste them in
Discorporate and we will begin.

Despite the cry of "Flower Power Sucks," the song is a mini-manifesto for absolute freedom. "Flower Punk" is a rewrite of the rock classic "Hey Joe" where a guy shoots his girlfriend and escapes to Mexico. Zappa turns Joe into a hippie with a flower rather than a gun. He's a lot like the guy in "Help, I'm a Rock," who's constantly looking for any group that will validate his existence. Zappa plays the tune at breakneck speed, using a wah-wah pedal on his guitar just before Jimi Hendrix started to make it a rock 'n' roll trademark.

Before Zappa presents his "folk" tale about Kenny and Ronnie Williams in "Let's Make the Water Turn Black" and "The Idiot Bastard Son," he presents his first truly sophisticated *musique concrète* composition. "Nasal Retentive Calliope Music" is an aural panorama of effects that also incorporates various voices, sped-up sounds of giggling, and, once again, Eric Clapton, who at one point cries out, "It's God. It's God. I see God." He actually asked to do a parody of Eric Burdon of the Animals on acid, but one can't help hearing his words in the context of the widely held worship of Clapton himself. Scrawled on walls in Britain at that time were slogans like, "Clapton is God!" Clapton, who eventually lost touch with Zappa, told *Guitarist* magazine in 1994 that Zappa's relationship with him was disingenuous to begin with: "He was very manipulative and knew how to appeal to my ego and my vanity and I put everything on this tape. I think he just had files and files of tapes of people and I was in there somewhere."

"Nasal Retentive Calliope Music" again drew attention to the record album as a fetish object. Near the end of the piece, we hear a few snippets from "Heavies" by the Rotations, which Zappa recorded at Studio Z in 1963. Just as the song begins, a needle scratches across it, jolting us out of our security that the album will continue on a linear path. "We took a Davy Jones record that the engineer happened to have sitting around, and put it on a Gerrard turntable," Zappa told David Marsden. "We spent approximately a half an hour trying to get the right kind of record scratch. Then when we got to the one that sounded good we panned it back and forth. If the studio cost eighty dollars an hour, that effect costs forty dollars."

"Take Your Clothes Off When You Dance," which dates back to the Dot demos of the early '60s (and borrows a theme from the Drifters' "True Love, True Love") restates the same hopes for a better culture as "Absolutely Free" had:

> *There will come a time when everybody who is lonely*
> *Will be free to sing and dance and love*
> *There will come a time when every evil that we know*

WHO NEEDS THE PEACE CORPS?

Will be an evil that we can rise above
Who cares if you're so poor you can't afford
To buy a pair of Mod A Go-Go stretch elastic pants
There will come a time when you can even take your clothes off when you dance.

After a reprise of "What's the Ugliest Part of Your Body?" Zappa presents the band's manifesto in "Mother People":

We are the other people
We are the other people
You're the other people, too
Found a way to get to you.

Again the needle scratches across a record, leading to an orchestral excerpt from *Lumpy Gravy*. Pete Johnson of the *Los Angeles Times* pointed out that this jarring effect inspired the Beatles' odd transitions in "I Am the Walrus," where radio static linked two different parts of the song. "I Am the Walrus" would be one of Zappa's favorite Beatles songs — he covered it, note for note, during his final rock tour in 1988.

We're Only in It for the Money's final track, "The Chrome Plated Megaphone of Destiny," a tour-de-force audio poem, mixes voice, tape, and instruments in a brilliantly paranoid collage suggested by Franz Kafka's short novel *In the Penal Colony*. Zappa advised record buyers to read Kafka's story — in which the victims of an authoritarian regime have their crime literally tattooed on their body — before listening to the piece. This stunning example of *musique concrète* possibly took its musical inspiration from the American electronic quintet MEV (Musica Electronica Viva), whose 1966 piece "Spaceship," according to co-founder Richard Teitelbaum, created a spontaneous electro-acoustic environment by mixing instruments that ranged from "homemade circuits to found objects like glass, springs, tin cans, amplified heartbeats, brain waves, acoustic instruments (cello, saxophone, trumpet), voice, and breath." The group's concerts sometimes lasted six hours. The sounds of their pieces ranged from the total cacophony of distortion to a contemplative pause that served as a short respite until the next outburst.

In "The Chrome Plated Megaphone of Destiny," Zappa prepared a similar stock of distorted instruments, sped-up (and slowed-down) voices, hysterical laughter, and acoustic instruments blending in and out of the orchestrated chaos.

"The percussive-type noises, the thing that sounds like little squirts and explosions, was done by using a box with three buttons on it," Zappa explained to Rick Davies of *Music Technology* magazine. "The console at the studio had three master faders — a separate fader for the left, the center, and the right. So these three buttons corresponded to inputs to the three master faders, and you could play it rhythmically. There's a tambora in there, a koto in there someplace. Some filtered tapes of industrial noises, horses, all collaged together."

"The Chrome Plated Megaphone of Destiny" was a more sophisticated version of "The Return of the Son of Monster Magnet." The title comes from — what else? — the anatomy of a doll. "Before they started making dolls with sexual organs, the only data you could get from your doll was looking between its legs and seeing that little chrome nozzle — if you squeezed the doll, it made a kind of whistling sound," Zappa told Kurt Loder. "That was the chrome plated megaphone of destiny."

We're Only in It for the Money eventually ushered in New Year 1968, reaching No. 30 in the U.S. charts, making the album a hit for Frank Zappa. But reception to it was mixed. In 1968, criticizing the hippie culture, as well as the status quo, and being vehemently anti-drugs, didn't make Zappa popular in the rock 'n' roll world. But the album not only painted an accurate portrait of the political and cultural realities of that era, it also had the uncanny ability to look ahead. After all, it would be a little over a decade later that many of those same hippies would become yuppies — folks who, without question, were *definitely* only in it for the money.

15

When the production on *We're Only in It for the Money* started in 1967, the Zappas' apartment on Thompson Street was becoming as overcrowded as a hippie commune. Camping out on the floor was Frank's brother, Bobby; the road manager, Dick "the Snorker" Barber; and now, a young visual designer named Calvin Schenkel. Cal, from Philadelphia, came recommended by his girlfriend, Sandy Hurvitz, who had joined the Mothers for the Garrick Theatre shows. "I lived with [Zappa] for a *very* brief period," Schenkel told *Seconds* magazine in 1995. "When I first met him in New York, the art studio was in his apartment." When Zappa saw Cal's portfolio, he hired him to help create the album cover for *We're Only in It for the Money*. "I don't think he was really studied in art or followed art trends, but he certainly was aware of basic art movements," Schenkel recalled. As Schenkel worked diligently on designs in the Zappa abode, Frank was in the

WHO NEEDS THE PEACE CORPS?

studio, working onstage, or sleeping it all off. "He wasn't the kind of guy where you would get together, go out, and have a couple of drinks," Schenkel told *Musician*. "He was always the person who was in control whenever you're around; everything revolved around what he was doing.... He had vision and he knew how to create it. On the other hand, I think he did allow for a lot of other input. He was able to draw out people's talents, but he knew how to put it all together."

Since the album was a satiric swipe at the values extolled by *Sgt. Pepper*, Zappa and Schenkel were after a cover that perfectly parodied in look and spirit Peter Blake's opulent design of that album. What they captured was a nightmarishly funny facsimile. "Where the Beatles' name was set out in a neat suburban herbaceous border, the Mothers' was spelt in vegetables," Neil Slaven explains. "Instead of brightly colored bandsmen's uniforms, the Mothers, never known for their physical beauty, wore dresses." The crowd gathered around the band in the photo featured character types that contrasted with the Beatles' album. "Where the Beatles had amassed portraits of their heroes, Frank was far more pointed in his choices, which ranged from Lyndon Johnson (twice) and Lee Harvey Oswald to Galileo, Beethoven, and Herb Cohen," Slaven continues. "Some, including the Statue of Liberty, Jimmy Reed, James Brown, Nancy Sinatra, and Eric Burdon, had their eyes blacked out — to protect their identities."

Like *Sgt. Pepper*, *We're Only in It for the Money* came with cutouts and an insert. But the Mothers included a Zappa moustache, a nipple badge, and a School Safety Patrol Lieutenant's badge bearing a photo of engineer Gary Kellgren. A back-cover photo of the band had Zappa, his hair in braids, looking like he just caught a whiff of something pungent. When Zappa sought permission from the Beatles to parody their cover, Paul McCartney told him he'd have to discuss it with their business managers. Zappa was stunned. Considering the clout the Beatles must have had, Zappa seemed surprised the Beatles didn't exert any influence here. He told McCartney that "business managers were there to be told what to do by their artists." In the end, Zappa reversed the gatefold images to avoid legal problems.

In September 1967, the Mothers did a short tour of the U.S. that included Detroit, Cincinnati, Miami, and New York. While in the Big Apple, Zappa met Simon & Garfunkel and discovered that they were once known as Tom & Jerry, a late-'50s rock duo who had a hit called "Hey Schoolgirl." While chatting with Zappa at a party, Simon & Garfunkel mentioned how much they missed being on the road, and Zappa suggested they come to Buffalo with the Mothers the next night.

They could open the show as Tom & Jerry, playing only their old tunes — no Simon & Garfunkel songs. The duo loved the idea, so the next evening in Buffalo, Tom & Jerry opened the show with "Hey Schoolgirl" and other old rock 'n' roll numbers. After the Mothers' set, Zappa came back out and announced to the audience that he'd like to bring back the special guests. Tom & Jerry returned and performed "The Sound of Silence." Finally, it dawned on the audience that this was actually Simon & Garfunkel. But apparently some folks in the crowd were not amused. "On the way out, after the show, a college-educated woman walked over to me and said, 'Why did you do that? What did you make fun of Simon & Garfunkel?' — as if I had pulled some kind of cruel joke on them," Zappa wrote in *The Real Frank Zappa Book*.

This episode illustrated the inexplicable way pop audiences get locked into personal identification with their favorite artists. What Simon & Garfunkel represented for the Buffalo crowd was a pop-culture abstraction defined by their socially conscious hit songs. Some fans couldn't accept that their folk idols were once Tom & Jerry, a teen rock combo. Zappa, with Simon & Garfunkel's assistance, had shattered that perception to the chagrin of those who felt he had only humiliated the duo. The subversion in Zappa's art stripped away the conventional links between the performer and the audience, so the audience could see the performers — and themselves — for who they truly were. "What the fuck did she think had just happened?" Zappa wrote about the angry woman. "That these two SUPERSTARS had dropped in out of nowhere and we had FORCED them to sing 'ooo-boppa-loochy-bah, she's mine!'?"

By the end of the fall, Zappa had become a fixture in New York, but a planned tour of Europe would establish him internationally. He had already taken a trip across the ocean in August to discuss the possibility of the Mothers making their debut at the Royal Albert Hall in England, as well as embarking on a short European tour that would take them to Sweden, Denmark, and Holland. While in Britain, Zappa introduced the power trio Cream at a club called the Speakeasy. After a few interviews where he put down Flower Power ("How can you love complete strangers," he asked Anne Nightingale of the *Daily Sketch*, "when a lot of them are unpleasant people?") and speculated on the Mothers' appeal in Britain ("Generally we seem to thrive in areas where there is unrest between the generations because we tend to pep things up!," he told Nick Jones in *Melody Maker*), Zappa came home to New York.

The tour plans didn't come at the most convenient time, however. *We're Only in It for the Money* hadn't yet been completed, and Gail was pregnant with their

WHO NEEDS THE PEACE CORPS?

first child. Pamela had just arrived back in California from her European trip to find that Zappa and entourage were now in New York. Zappa asked her to come to New York to watch over Gail while he was on tour. He mentioned that he needed to bring along some freaky female who could be Suzy Creamcheese, since Jeannie Vassoir, Suzy on the *Freak Out!* album, had disappeared. Pamela told Zappa that she was the only one who knew his work well enough to play the part, and Zappa agreed.

Frank and Gail (now nine months pregnant) decided to marry at New York's City Hall a couple of days before the Mothers left for Europe. Zappa didn't have a wedding ring so he went to a vending machine and bought a ballpoint pen that read, "Congratulations from Mayor Lindsay." After the ceremony, he pinned the pen on Gail's maternity dress. Before heading out the door to the airport two days later, Zappa told Gail, "If it's a girl, call it Moon, and if it's a boy, call it Motorhead."

When the group arrived in London, Zappa had a meeting with the rest of the Mothers. He told them they couldn't be holding any drugs, and that he alone would speak for the band. No one else would do interviews. After they checked in at the Royal Garden Hotel, the band went off to Piccadilly Circus. That evening they hit the clubs, and at the Marquee they witnessed the Crazy World of Arthur Brown, whose frenzied hit, "Fire," was riding high in the pop charts. Zappa also got to meet Pete Townshend of the Who, who had produced Brown's hit song. When they got to the Speakeasy, a popular London hot spot, Zappa shared scotch with Jeff Beck and finally got to meet Jimi Hendrix.

Zappa had only seen Hendrix perform once in New York, while the Mothers were at the Garrick — Hendrix even sat in one night with them. "Hendrix is one of the most revolutionary figures in today's pop culture, musically and sociologically," Zappa would write the following year in *Life*. "Hendrix's music is very interesting. The sound . . . is extremely symbolic: orgasmic grunts, tortured squeals, lascivious moans, electric disasters, and innumerable other audial curiosities are delivered to the sense mechanisms of the audience at an extremely high decibel level. In a live performance environment, it is impossible to merely listen to what the Hendrix group does . . . it eats you alive."

Zappa described just how gnawed to the bone he became in a 1987 interview with *Guitar World* magazine. "I had the incredible misfortune to be sitting real close to him at the Au Go Go in New York City, and he had a whole stack of Marshall [amplifiers], and I was right in front of it," Zappa recalled. "I was physically ill — I couldn't get out. It was packed and I couldn't escape. . . . I didn't see how anybody could inflict that type of volume on himself let alone other people. That particular show he ended by taking the guitar and impaling it in the low ceiling of the club. Just walked away and left it squealing." Zappa did figure out how to inflict that kind of volume by the time he hit Royal Albert Hall.

The Mothers rehearsed in a bingo parlor outside of London. They also filmed and took photos of the group in front of Buckingham Palace, with Zappa (a bowler hat on his head) carrying his trusty portable Uher tape deck recording and documenting the minutiae of the tour. Unfortunately, despite the publicity for the Royal Albert Hall debut, on September 23, *Absolutely Free* had yet to be released in the U.K. by MGM. Most of the press and the Mothers' fans in England assumed (just from hearing *Freak Out!*) that Frank was the ultimate hippie. One *Melody Maker* reader called him a product of "that rotten, commercial and crumbling society in America. . . . Thank heaven English society is not yet American enough to need 'flower power.'" Another reader said that Zappa was "horrid, vile, and disgusting." Zappa was baffled by the conclusion of the letter, which read, "effeminate flower power has turned our pop scene into a charade of rubbish." Zappa was also totally out of place among all the rock stars getting high on grass or hash. He even told Pamela that he found them "a nice little group of junkies." According to her, people seemed surprised that Zappa couldn't distinguish between the types of narcotics being imbibed.

When the Mothers finally hit the stage of the hallowed Royal Albert Hall, they put to rest any idea that they were some hippie invasion from America. Zappa's associates even released the now infamous PHI ZAPPA KRAPPA poster — featuring him sitting naked on a toilet. Zappa wanted to do something dynamic that night to overturn the false perceptions that dogged him in the press. It was Don Preston who gave him the great idea as to how that could be accomplished. "When we arrived at the Albert Hall, I noticed the pipe organ up behind the band," Don Preston told biographer Billy James. "I went over and looked at it and a person who worked there came over and said, 'Do you want to play it?' Stifling my urge to scream, 'Yes!' I mumbled, 'That would be nice.' He turned it on and left. I sat down and pressed a key on the second-largest organ in the world! A deep penetrating pure tone emanated from the ceiling. I looked at the five tiers of keyboards and all the tonal controls for each keyboard — I was in heaven! I spent the next four hours experimenting and figuring out how it worked."

When the Mothers mounted the stage, there were two devoted fans on hand who would — much later — become notorious talents in their own right. One of

WHO NEEDS THE PEACE CORPS?

them, Terry Gilliam, was an expatriate American living in England, waiting for his big break with the comedy troupe Monty Python's Flying Circus. The other, Salman Rushdie, was the future author of *The Satanic Verses* and *The Ground Beneath Her Feet*. Both men were affected so deeply by what occurred that night that they would passionately scrawl their responses years later. Yet, since it was the '60s, their powers of recollection were a little vague, differing in detail. Rushdie, for example, thought the concert was in the early '70s. But he also remembered facts that escaped Gilliam. While walking through Hyde Park the day of the concert, Gilliam ran into Herb Cohen, who he knew from Los Angeles. Cohen offered Gilliam tickets to see the show, and Gilliam saw this as a perfect opportunity to remind himself of the things he missed about America. "The Royal Albert Hall is a great Victorian monument," Gilliam remembers, "all red and gold and encrusted with elaborate decoration. With its tasteful boxes ringing the vast domed amphitheatre, it represented to me all that was cultured, refined, and civilized . . . the product of generations of decent British citizens and their gracious rulers. But that night this proud testimonial to respectability had been usurped by the Mothers of Invention . . . a hairy three-ringed circus with Frank as the ringmaster."

For his part, Rushdie describes an oddly funny moment about halfway through the concert. "An enormous black guy in a shiny purple shirt climbs onto the stage (security was lighter in those innocent days)," Rushdie recalls. "He starts swaying gently, and insists on playing with the band. Zappa, unfazed, asks gravely, 'Uh-huh, sir, and what is your instrument of choice?' 'Horn,' mumbles the Purple Shirt Guy. 'Give this man a horn,' Zappa commands. But the moment the Purple Shirt Guy blows his first terrible note, it's clear his horn skills leave much to be desired. Zappa looks lost in contemplation, chin in hand. 'Hmmm.' Then he moves to the mike. 'I wonder,' he muses, 'what we can think of to accompany this man on his horn.' He has a flash of mock inspiration. 'I know! The mighty [majestic] Albert Hall pipe organ!' As a roar came from the crowd, Zappa reminded them, 'You understand that you won't hear the organ once we turn our amplifiers up.'"

At which point, with sheer effervescence, Gilliam describes what he saw from the audience: "The keyboard player [Don Preston] abandoned his ivories and began to clamber up and over the speakers and other piles of electronic gear. An expectant ripple spread through the crowd. For a moment, he disappeared — lost in the darkness. Then a spotlight managed to pick him out — a small motley figure climbing onwards and upwards — up the back of the auditorium — towards the gigantic mountain of brass pipes that comprised the great Albert Hall organ. The audience cheered him as Frank cranked up the band.... With the mob chanting and clapping, this musical Quasimodo gained the summit and plunked himself down at the keyboard. There was a momentary hush as he grappled with the stops. And then the most glorious, outrageous sound ever heard erupted ... no ... it wasn't Elgar or Bach or even Saint-Saens.... It was a great thundering musical nose-thumbing fart. He was pounding out 'Louie Louie' on that great Victorian organ. The barbarians had taken over.... I decided it was worth staying in England."

In another part of the hall, as "Louie Louie" filled the air, Rushdie contemplates what it took to shake up the status quo. "I don't subscribe to the lyrics-are-poetry school of rock-aficionado overclaiming," Rushdie explains. "But I know I'd have been ridiculously proud to have written anything as good as this. And I'd loved to have had the talent, the humor, and speed of thought of Frank Zappa in the Albert Hall that night."

After the successful Royal Albert Hall show, the Mothers played Amsterdam to an enthusiastic reaction. But the enthusiasm was short lived: disaster started to strike. First, Ray Collins (who had rejoined the band for the tour) and Zappa had yet another dispute. Collins almost left the group again, but Tom Wilson stepped in to make the peace. The following day, the Mothers headed for Copenhagen while Wilson and Zappa took a detour to Rome to look into the possibility of scoring Roger Vadim's erotic science-fiction comedy, *Barbarella*, starring Jane Fonda. Vadim was interested in using portions of *Freak Out!* in the movie, but no definite arrangement was reached. While in Rome, though, Zappa made the mistake of drinking some tap water, which gave him a severe bout of gastroenteritis by the time he caught up with the band in Stockholm. Despite Zappa's illness, the show went on since it was being broadcast on Swedish radio, but Zappa was forced to leave in the second act. (The show can now be heard on the officially released bootleg CD, *'Tis the Season to Be Jelly*.)

Their first gig in Copenhagen was to follow the next day, but their equipment truck got stalled in a snowstorm. So for one night they became a semi-acoustic outfit (as they managed to borrow a few amps from the John Mayall Blues Band). The only good news, at this point, came from home — Gail had given birth to Moon Unit Zappa.

The morning after the Copenhagen concert, they took off for Lund to play a local college. That night Pamela and Zappa talked about the impact that being an international rock 'n' roll artist was having on him. She told Michael Gray, "He was

WHO NEEDS THE PEACE CORPS?

scared and he wasn't ready to leave the times we had in Europe." Zarubica asked him angrily, "How dare you be scared, you motherfucker. I mean, I gave up a lot just to come and go with you because you were the one who knew how democracy could work and could be president. And now when the responsibility is yours, and all these people look to you for answers, you realize that it isn't an easy job, that you're tired and that it could cost you more than your security."

What Pamela didn't understand was that Zappa's art wasn't about preparing political agendas for others to follow. He was interested in posing questions rather than providing answers: Who is my work attracting? What does the audience want from it? Why are they clapping after one piece, and acting quiet during the next? Like Erik Satie, Zappa was interested in the psychological impact music had on the performer and the audience, rather than a simple act of self-expression. As Neil Slaven remarked, "Whatever [Zappa] said by way of observation on the inequities he saw were almost a byproduct of a mind that was dedicated to music — and nothing else."

The first European tour might have ended with many of those questions left unanswered, but one thing was certain: Frank Zappa was now an international figure in popular music.

16

Returning to New York in late October 1967, Zappa had finally finished the production on *We're Only in It for the Money*. In November, he flew back to Los Angeles to do a cameo role in *Head*, the first (and last) film by the prefab four, the Monkees. *Head* was made by the team of producer Bert Schneider and director Bob Rafelson, who in 1970 would collaborate on the counterculture hit *Five Easy Pieces*. The Monkees' movie was a confusing pastiche that tried to copy the scattershot mood of Richard Lester's *A Hard Day's Night* (1964), but it failed to catch the charm of the Beatles' classic musical comedy. It had an odd ensemble cast, too, that included Annette Funicello, Timothy Carey (of *The World's Greatest Sinner*), and boxer Sonny Liston. None of it gelled. Zappa played a character called "the Critic." While leading a prize bull out of the studio, he's seen telling Monkee Davy Jones, "You should spend more time on your music because the youth of America depends on you to show the way." The film was released on December 14, 1968, but the youth of America didn't much care to have the Monkees show them the way.

Zappa produced a piece of music for a Luden's Cough Drops commercial, which won a Clio Award for Best Music for a Commercial. The ad, featuring just a squiggly line on the screen, took a piece of Zappa's *musique concrète* that incorporated a series of coughs, intercut with Zappa playing the celeste, kazoo, and percussion, while road manager Dick Barber produced a string of vocal snorks. Some of that snork/celeste combo, in fact, was an outtake from Part One of *Lumpy Gravy*. The full Luden's piece appears on the CD *The Lost Episodes*, under the title "The Big Squeeze."

Based on the success of the Luden's ad, Remington Electric Razor also commissioned Zappa to score one of their spots, paying him $1,000 for his services. In that ad, Zappa brought together Ian Underwood on keyboards and singer Linda Ronstadt (then lead vocalist of the Los Angeles band the Stone Poneys). It's a spiffy little jingle, not unlike *We're Only in It for the Money*'s "Bow Tie Daddy" and "Lonely Little Girl." While Ronstadt repeats the phrase "Remington Electric Razor," Zappa voices the line "thrills you and cleans you." Ronstadt's voice speeds up for the final section, where she sings, "Up go the shaving heads; down go the shaving heads," until Zappa finally announces, "Cleans you, thrills you, may even keep you from getting busted." In typical Zappa fashion, the piece both summons and satirizes many of the musical clichés found in sixty-second jingles. Perhaps that's why the ad never ran. When Matt Groening hired composer Danny Elfman to do the opening theme for *The Simpsons*, he suggested that Elfman listen to Zappa's Remington ad.

When Zappa returned to New York in December 1967, he discovered that MGM had made the mistake of not renewing the option on the Mothers' contract. The standard for most company contracts at that time was the five-year deal. Groups signed for one year with four options — to be picked up, or not, by the company. Zappa and Herb Cohen used the lapse as leverage to negotiate a deal with MGM to create a label within the company. It was to be called Bizarre Productions. They chose as their logo a picturesque 19th-century engraving of a vacuum pump. (Mothers' albums on Bizarre were released through MGM/Verve until 1969, when Warner Brothers acquired the production label.) Zappa and Cohen also formed Straight Records for the least "unconventional" artists managed by Cohen. Zappa wrote a mission statement that would be included as a sleeve note: "We make records that are a little different. We present musical and sociological material which the important record companies would probably not allow you to hear. Just what the world needs . . . another record company."

WHO NEEDS THE PEACE CORPS?

This strategy was partly precipitated by Zappa's growing disenchantment with MGM — especially their peculiar way of treating artists. During the recording of *Absolutely Free*, Zappa had heard about accounting problems within MGM that deprived musicians of their proper royalties. This dubious practice was called the "pressing plant overrun": the pressing plant would get an order to press a few thousand units of a record, and the press operator would be instructed to run off an extra thousand units. Someone would then pull up in the middle of the night and load those extra records in a car, drive to another state, and either sell the records to other dealers or trade them for furniture. The artist would get an accounting statement that showed sales to be only half of what they actually were.

This highly unethical procedure had a huge impact on Zappa's relationship with his label. As author David Walley points out, "Not only were Zappa's records being censored, but he was receiving no sales figures and losing control. It was determined publicly, three years later, that MGM executives had been stealing their company blind. In one year while Tom Wilson was working there, for instance, his products sold nearly 1,400,000 records. MGM executives claimed at the time the company was losing some $4 million. Someone was getting taken, and Zappa was tired of it being him." It took Zappa until 1976 to settle in court the royalty issue for his first two albums. He would encounter many more problems with the multinational record companies over the course of his career.

In January 1968, *We're Only in It for the Money*, the first album under the Bizarre imprint, was released in North America. Again, censorship problems arose. "They sent me a test pressing of *We're Only in It for the Money* that had a whole bunch of stuff censored out of it," Zappa said in 1968. "This is one line they cut: 'And I still remember Mama with her apron and her pad, feeding all the boys at Ed's Cafe' ['Let's Make the Water Turn Black']. Now, this not only didn't make sense to cut, it fucked up the piece of music by removing four bars before the bridge. . . . I called them up and said, 'You can't put this record out!' And they've already pressed 40,000 of them." Apparently, the line was censored because an MGM executive believed that the word "pad" referred to a sanitary napkin. In his twisted interpretation, some waitress in a little café in Ontario, California, was feeding her customers a daily ration of Kotex.

When the Mothers did their second European tour, later in 1968, *We're Only in It for the Money* won the Dutch equivalent of a Grammy. As Zappa accepted the award, the censored version of the album was playing. Zappa addressed the congregation: "I can't accept this statue. I prefer that the award be presented to the guy who modified the record, because what you're hearing is more reflective of *his* work than mine." Zappa then returned the prize.

After correcting the problems with *We're Only in It for the Money*, Zappa did some of the final editing to the vocal sections of *Lumpy Gravy* and began production on the soundtrack music for *Uncle Meat*, a movie he was planning for the Mothers of Invention. But before they finished recording the music, drummer Billy Mundi quit to join Rhinoceros, a psychedelic band that put out three albums before going the way of the dinosaur. An executive at Elektra Records had convinced Mundi to leave Zappa's comedy music behind. "He offered Billy Mundi a huge amount of money, a place to live — the whole package," Zappa told *Q* magazine. "We'll make you a star, you'll work with these top-grade musicians instead of those comedy guys.... And where the fuck is Rhinoceros now?" However, Zappa sympathized with Mundi's decision. After all, the Mothers were starving. "We were so poor, [Mundi] was living in the Albert Hotel and he couldn't get enough to eat — he used to come and tell us how he'd quell his appetite by drinking the hot water in the shower."

Zappa quickly found a replacement through recording engineer Dick Kunc. Arthur Dyer Tripp III was a percussionist who had spent time with the Cincinnati Philharmonic Orchestra and was familiar with the avant-garde, having played the music of Cage and Stockhausen. Tripp became familiar with Zappa when he read an article where Zappa had described his attraction to the work of Stravinsky and Varèse. "For years, Frank had lots of percussion ideas that no one could play," Tripp told Julien Colbeck in *Zappa: A Biography*. "Obviously from my background it was comparatively simple, I'd just make up a chart, or Frank would, and I'd learn it by heart."

"Art fit in right away," Bunk Gardner remembered. "He loved John Cage and true experimental music. He played drums and marimba equally well and really was an asset to the band." But Tripp also had some of those peculiarities that made him a perfect candidate for the band. "Art used to wear female panties over his head, dye his moustache green and wear wing-tip shoes — fairly unusual for a rock 'n' roll drummer!" Tripp was sensitive to the nuances in Zappa's music. "Art was always checking out percussion accessories," Gardner continued. "Anything that might make a weird or unusual sound, Art would buy it for the drum set. He would then try to figure out how to mount it so he could play it, or use it in a particular song in just one measure or beat."

WHO NEEDS THE PEACE CORPS?

Zappa confirmed Tripp's vast contributions to the group. "[Tripp's] a great musician, no doubt about it," Zappa told Steve Birchall of *Digital Audio* in 1984. "He was a little bit out of place in our band because he was so skilled. There were very few really skilled musicians in that group of early Mothers. Most of them were just rock 'n' roll guys. And Art pretty much outclassed them. He definitely knew about things in the musical world that Jimmy Carl Black and Roy Estrada had never considered before."

Simultaneously with the sessions for *Uncle Meat* at Apostolic Studios, Zappa began work on an album that would mirror Stravinsky's neoclassical period. The music Zappa revisited was the R&B doo-wop of his formative years. "When we were still in New York, I started working on the Ruben & the Jets story," Zappa told Miles in *Mojo Magazine*. "[It's] connected with the *Uncle Meat* story in which this old guy turns this teenage band into these dog-snout people. That came out of my love for comics and anthropomorphic animals." The result, *Cruising With Ruben & the Jets*, was a collection of what Zappa called in his liner notes "greasy love songs & other cretin simplicity." But there was something more significant going on here. "If [Stravinsky] could take the forms and clichés of the classical era and pervert *them*," Zappa wrote, "why not do the same with the rules and regulations that applied to doo-wop in the '50s?"

Zappa explained to Nigel Leigh that Stravinsky approached the classical period with a reverence that was also tinged with irony. "The music of the early '50s was characterized in that [complex] harmony group vocal stuff," Zappa said. "[But] the themes that went on in the background, the so-called words, were usually quite limited in scope." Zappa also wanted to do something that went against the current trend toward psychedelic rock. He even tried to shock those who came to love the sophisticated atonal material in his first two albums, introducing them to those complex vocal harmonies of R&B tinged with "imbecilic lyrics."

Zappa stated that besides being an album conceived in the manner of Stravinsky's neoclassical period, *Cruising With Ruben & the Jets* was also a satire about what he termed the "bad mental health" encouraged in certain love songs. "You're a young kid and you hear all those 'love lyrics,' right?" Zappa wrote in his autobiography. "Your parents aren't telling you the truth about love, and you can't really learn about it in school. You're getting the bulk of your 'behavior norms' mapped out for you in the lyrics to some dumb fucking love song. It's a subconscious training that creates a desire for an imaginary situation that will *never exist for you*. People who buy into that mythology go through life feeling that they got cheated out of something."

Although Zappa, like Satie and Ives before him, was revolting against the sentimentality of romantic art, it didn't mean he was anti-love. "For him, *love* was a transitive verb, not some flowery adjective," Nigey Lennon wrote in *Being Frank*. "*Lust* was a concept he understood perfectly; its adjunct was *improvisation*, and the desired result was *adventure*, or at least diversion. And yet he was far more giving than selfish. Being instinctively attentive to detail, he generally succeeded admirably."

Zappa told Michael Gray that, aside from some of the lyrical content, '50s rock was territory unexplored by the current groups. "Prior to the release of that *Ruben & the Jets* album, nobody in amplified music had even touched on that early aspect of early rock 'n' roll," Zappa explained. "Their idea of early rock 'n' roll was a pseudo–Chuck Berry song; and the college students and the generation that was our audience at that time didn't know from nothin' about group ballad vocals and things like that, or the context from which that flowed. And I thought that it might be a valuable public service to show them that some of that could be entertaining to listen to and could even make you feel good." Releasing an album of '50s doo-wop songs in 1968 was unquestionably a gutsy move. For one thing, there was nothing more "uncool" at this point in time than '50s rock. Even when it reared its greasy head (as Sha Na Na did at Woodstock in 1969), it was considered nothing more than a circus act for the hippies to laugh at. Zappa seemed to anticipate that hostility. He perceived that the music he loved was considered horribly retrograde to the very hip counterculture. So while that audience was looking for psychedelic morsels to feed their heads, Zappa provided a dish nobody was waiting to consume.

The front cover of *Cruising With Ruben & the Jets* featured a group of '50s musicians with dog noses and ears, and popular pompadour hairstyles, while a cartoon bubble above the lead guitarist's head asked us: "Is this the Mothers of Invention recording under a different name in a last-ditch attempt to get their cruddy music on the radio?" Inside the gatefold, Zappa laid a claim to his own rock 'n' roll roots: "We made it because we really like this kind of music (just a bunch of old men with rock & roll clothes on sitting around the studio, mumbling about the good old days). Ten years from now, you'll be sitting around with your friends someplace doing the same thing if there's anything left to sit on." With his high school graduation picture on the back, and assuming the persona of Ruben Sano, the leader of

WHO NEEDS THE PEACE CORPS?

the Jets, Frank Zappa decorated the album with finely etched details of some of the more delightfully esoteric aspects of that decade. He even had some fun at the expense of Varèse. Ruben Sano is quoted, from 1955, as saying, "The present-day Pachuco refuses to die!" The album featured a number of new compositions, but some of them ("Fountain of Love," "Deseri") were from the Studio Z days, and others ("I'm Not Satisfied," "Any Way the Wind Blows," "How Could I Be Such a Fool?" and "You Didn't Try to Call Me"), were new arrangements of songs from *Freak Out!* Even though the melodies were consistent with '50s doo-wop, including the vocal style, timbre, and melodies, the chord progressions certainly were not.

All through *Cruising With Ruben & the Jets*, the blocks of sound stood out as musical clichés from another time. The drums made large echoing snats and piano triplets rolled on redundantly. The singers sounded authentic one moment, and the next like a resurrection of Alvin & the Chipmunks. The album is a brilliant study in contrasts between the present and the past. "Cheap Thrills" opens the record with a typical '50s plea — "Darling/Darling/Please hear my plea/God only knows/What your loving does to me" — but the album ends with the despair of the singer killing himself in "Stuff Up the Cracks": "Stuff up the cracks/turn on the gas/I'm gonna take my life." This song ends with Zappa letting loose with one of his most beautifully stated guitar solos, but with a '60s era wah-wah pedal. This yanks us right out of the decade in which we've just been immersed. It's as if, when the singer sticks his head in that oven, we feel the '50s dying with him.

While perverting the norms of '50s doo-wop and keeping the listener alert, Zappa subtly weaves relevant quotes from period songs into the overall fabric. For instance, the "please hear my plea" line from "Cheap Thrills" originates with Vernon Green & the Medallions' "The Letter." The "story untold" quote in "Cheap Thrills" comes from the song of that title by the Nutmegs. If you listen carefully to the end of "Love of My Life," you'll hear the backing vocals to "Earth Angel." The ridiculously sublime "Jelly Roll Gum Drop" mentions the dance inspired by Chuck Higgins' hit "Pachuko Hop." In "Later That Night," when Ray Collins says, "I hold in my hands three letters from the stages of your fine, fine, superfine career," he's paying homage to the Velvetones' "Glory of Love." The direct nod to Stravinsky, though, heard within a Charles Ives sandwich, occurs in "Fountain of Love." At the end of this track, the background vocalists simultaneously sing the opening notes to *The Rite of Spring* and quote "Sincerely" by the Moonglows.

Cruising With Ruben & the Jets was built on some of the same musical ideas that Collins and Zappa put into their song "Memories of El Monte," where they stripped away the nostalgia from romantic longing. *Cruising* is a doo-wop hybrid, however, whereas "Memories of El Monte" was the real thing. The spirit of *Cruising* is also much more anarchic than that of "Memories of El Monte." Yet when the album came out, nobody (even the most staunch Mothers fans) liked it. Some didn't even believe that it *was* the Mothers of Invention.

By the '70s, because of movies like *American Graffiti* (1973) and television shows like *Happy Days,* people pined for the '50s, mistaking it for a simpler time. When he recorded *Cruising With Ruben & the Jets* in 1968, Zappa wasn't presenting the past as a refuge for those wishing to escape the present. He had set out to reinvent the music of the '50s for the time in which he lived. The rejection of the album and '50s rock 'n' roll by the counterculture audience illustrated how their form of cultural snobbery would inadvertently plant the seeds for a nostalgia wave in the '70s — when the counterculture itself was truly dead.

17

From October 1967 to February 1968, Zappa worked on *Uncle Meat,* one of his most ambitious projects (it wouldn't reach the public until April 1969). Unlike the broadly satirical and confrontational music he had already released, this was to be a largely instrumental album. It was also to be the soundtrack for the first Mothers of Invention movie, but Zappa never acquired the money to finish it in the manner he intended. Instead, *Uncle Meat* (the album) served as a surreal scrapbook history of the Mothers of Invention, documenting Pamela Zarubica talking about her bizarre friendship with Zappa, a parody of "God Bless America" from the Whisky, Don Preston's heroic climb to the Royal Albert Hall pipe organ to unleash "Louie Louie," Jimmy Carl Black complaining about his endless poverty, Ian Underwood whipping it out on sax from the Copenhagen show, and surreal doo-wop songs that didn't make the final cut of *Cruising With Ruben & the Jets.*

Uncle Meat, their second double-album set, would be the first work by the Mothers of Invention that was a remarkable technical achievement. "[It] was a leap forward in technology because Frank had more toys to play with," Jimmy Carl Black explained. "That [one] was on twelve-track as opposed to most of the eight-track studios." Don Preston also remembered some of the intricate work that went into producing this album: "One time, [Zappa] was listening to the group record parts for *Uncle Meat* and writing a harmony part for the song also, and if somebody made a mistake, he'd stop them and make them go over that. I always

WHO NEEDS THE PEACE CORPS?

thought that it was quite amazing that while he was writing another piece of music that he could still be listening to the one being recorded.... We'd do fifty takes of eight bars, and then fifty takes of another eight bars. I always liked to say that he was a compulsive editor. I saw him three months after an album was released, put that same album together in different ways, and re-editing the album when it's not even going to come out. He used to love to sit there and edit anything." Preston was absolutely right. Besides being an awesome display of musical and studio virtuosity, *Uncle Meat* is a marvelous tribute to editing.

"Uncle Meat: The Main Title Theme" isn't a typical movie theme. The lightning-quick motion of Art Tripp's marimba comes across in a spree, as the melody is doubled on the drums, until its concluding strain is finally resolved delicately by a harpsichord. As it fades, a brief section of *musique concrète* leads directly into the voice of the cheese herself. "Hello, teenage America," Pamela Zarubica intones gravely. "My name is Suzy Creamcheese. I'm Suzy Creamcheese because I've never worn fake eyelashes in my whole life. And I never made it on the surfing set. And I never made it on the beatnik set. And... actually I really fucked up in Europe." At that moment, Dick Barber lets out a few quick snorks. "Now that I've done it all over and no one else will accept me," Zarubica explains as Barber lets out another squawk, "I've come home to my Mothers." In the first three minutes of *Uncle Meat*, we can hear just how advanced Zappa's ability to integrate disparate parts had become since *Lumpy Gravy*.

"Nine Types of Industrial Pollution" is a guitar instrumental where Zappa changes the pitch of the solo by altering the speed of the tape. He attempted something similar in 1962 with "Speed-Freak Boogie" (available on the *Mystery Disc* CD), where he first experimented with half-speed recording. No doubt both of these efforts were inspired by hearing John Lee Hooker's legendary 1952 recording of "Walkin' the Boogie," where the bluesman overdubbed a sped-up guitar sound into his song. As for the title of Zappa's piece, it was another example of his usual prescience. "The funny thing about that song title is that, at the time that it was put on *Uncle Meat*, there was no such thing as a concern over industrial pollution," Zappa reminded journalist Bob Marshall in 1988. "It hadn't even been brought up as a topic. I put that on that song just as a joke after driving through New Jersey." On some early versions of the album, though, the song was called "400 Days of the Year."

The next tune, "Zolar Czakl," illustrated Zappa's growing efficiency in the studio. Besides his clever use of overdubbing, Zappa continued to experiment with different speeds and — taking up the challenge of Varèse — altering the sound of acoustic instruments. "Things that sound like trumpets are actually clarinets played through an electric device. . . . Other peculiar sounds were made on a *Kalamazoo* electric organ," Zappa wrote in the album's liner notes. "Zolar Czakl" is barely a minute long, yet it contains so many shifts in rhythm and texture that, in retrospect, it presages some of the electronic music Zappa would compose in the mid-'80s. A couple of other tracks, "We Can Shoot You" and "Project X," are also amazing innovations on Varèse soundscapes.

Although *Uncle Meat* was recorded on a twelve-track machine, it allowed Zappa infinite overdubbing possibilities. For instance, he was able to pile up forty tracks onto the next song, "Dog Breath, in the Year of the Plague." This doo-wop piece wouldn't have been out of place on *Cruising With Ruben & the Jets* (in fact, *Uncle Meat* and *Cruising* were once planned as a three-album set, *No Commercial Potential*). It's a hilariously surreal song, which mixes Spanish and English idioms and concerns itself with the usual male adolescent pastime of scoring ("Fuzzy dice/Bongos in the back/My ship of love/Ready to attack"). As in *Cruising*, Zappa inserts quotes and references to other R&B songs (the phrase "ship of love," for instance, is from the title of a Nutmegs song). Yet it's typical of Zappa's love of mixing genres (not to mention adding sexual confusion) that he has the operatic soprano Nelcy Walker sing that line. Besides recounting a young Spanish-American priming his '39 Chevy to pick up his girl by El Monte Legion Stadium, Zappa also delves into fashionable fetish objects from that period. "No car was complete without some fuzzy dice or bongos in the backseat," Zappa told Les Carter of KPPC in 1967. "And let's not forget the shrunken head — that was a big item."

Many of the R&B songs on *Uncle Meat*, including "The Air," "Electric Aunt Jemima" (an oblique song about a favorite amplifier), and "Cruising for Burgers," were steeped in '50s lore that appeared to bubble out of the group's collective unconscious. "The words to the songs on this album were scientifically prepared from a random series of syllables, dreams, neuroses & private jokes that nobody except the members of the band ever laugh at, and other irrelevant material," Zappa wrote in the gatefold. Unlike in many pop songs of the late '60s, the lyrics were not designed to instruct the listener in the ways of the world, instead they instigated associations and random responses. On this record, Zappa had much in common with the French Symbolists of the late 19th century, like Paul Verlaine and Arthur Rimbaud, who reacted against dominant realist and naturalist tendencies in literature. "Mr. Green Genes" was another song about vegetables ("Eat your greens/Don't forget your beans and celery/Don't forget to bring your fake ID/Eat a bunch of these/MAGNIFICENT"), but it's even more opaque in meaning than "Call Any Vegetable."

"The Legend of the Golden Arches," named after the McDonald's burger chain, is a slow movement from "A Pound for a Brown (On the Bus)." The music dates back to the string quartet Zappa wrote while in high school, but the title . . . well, that's another story. "Last year, before we did our Festival Hall show, we arrived at the airport and were provided with a touring bus with nice big windows so that everybody on the outside could see in and we could see out," Zappa recalled. "During this trip, a wager was made between Jimmy Carl Black, the Indian of the group, and Bunk Gardner, our silver-haired tenor saxophone virtuoso. Jimmy Carl Black turned to Bunk Gardner and said, 'I'll bet you a pound you won't 'brown-out' [moon] on this here bus.' Bunk Gardner, being the crafty silver-haired devil that he is, quickly computed the difference between a pound and a dollar and had his pants off before anybody knew what was happening."

The final side of *Uncle Meat* is taken up with the extraordinarily popular "King Kong." Not only did this piece provide instrumentalists with lots of improvisational room to move, it has a great single-chord drone that Zappa wrote to provide a foundation for outrageous soloing. A small sample of the theme from "King Kong" appeared on *Lumpy Gravy*, but on *Uncle Meat*, it gets a full workout by the entire group. When the band performed it during their European tour, Zappa often provided a prelude to the piece. "It's the story of a very large gorilla who lived in the jungle," Zappa told a hushed crowd in Stockholm in 1967. "He was doing okay until some Americans came by and thought that they could take him home with them. They took him to the United States, and they made some money — by using the gorilla — then they killed him."

"King Kong" is built on a series of astonishing extemporized sections. It begins with the Mothers in the studio establishing the theme of the composition, before Don Preston provides a melodious interpretation on the electric piano. Yet just as Preston draws us in with his understated yet dramatic rendering, the band changes gears. Motorhead Sherwood suddenly jumps forward with a tenor sax solo that is the musical equivalent of an epileptic fit. While Sherwood tears the notes out of his horn (you can hear him inhaling and exhaling), the band starts to set up the main movement for Bunk Gardner's solo on electric sax. Gardner's sound is uncanny, resembling a kazoo being blown into a sheet of wax paper. For over six minutes, he wails through short melodic lines until a startling piece of tape manipulation recreates the "King Kong" theme. Zappa varies the speed of the instruments to make it appear that the tune is being played on "three deranged Good Humor trucks," as he described it. Before the last deranged vehicle can finish speaking its piece, however, a gong ushers in yet another version of "King Kong," from a live performance at the Miami Pop Festival in September 1967, where Zappa and Ian Underwood take their solos.

Much of "King Kong" was probably inspired by the late '50s "free jazz" of Ornette Coleman, especially that of *The Shape of Jazz to Come* (1959). Yet the use of an electric jazz ensemble predates a similar path taken by jazz trumpeter Miles Davis on his landmark records *In a Silent Way* (1969) and *Bitches Brew* (1969). The music on *Uncle Meat* is visual, and the contrasting textures of the dialogue, or the tape-manipulated sounds, give the album an added element of virtuosity. *Uncle Meat* has the scope and dimension not only to transcend the limits of pop, but to open the way for a whole new music, played with skill, imagination, and, most importantly, humor. With the addition of Art Tripp, plus the other adept players who could read music, such as Underwood, Gardner, and Ruth Komanoff, the Mothers demonstrated an unrivaled versatility. They combined musicians who had roots in rock with players from the world of jazz and classical music.

With such an eclectic balance, the band started to draw a reputable crowd. "There was always somebody hanging around or near the band at that time — the Fugs, Blood, Sweat & Tears, Jimi Hendrix, Linda Ronstadt, Simon & Garfunkel," Gardner recalled. "I met Salvador Dali, Bob Downey the filmmaker, and Glenn Gould the piano player. It was a never-ending array of artists who wanted to see if we were as weird as everyone said we were, and if our music was as avant-garde and out there as they said it was! We played classical, R&B, jazz, rock, and made fun of everyone. We always combined satire and humor with the precision playing of Frank's tunes. People didn't know what to think of us at times, or take us seriously. We were like the Spike Jones of rock 'n' roll."

WHO NEEDS THE PEACE CORPS?

18

My father saw [Spike Jones] at the Michigan Theater in Detroit back in 1943: "They were crazy. . . . The stage went black and all these sirens and gunshots started going off. Then the stage lit up and it was Spike Jones and His City Slickers. . . . They had a guy playing a toilet seat with strings on it, people onstage wearing wigs and crazy outfits — oh, geez, they were nuts."

MICHAEL "CUB" KODA of Brownsville Station

If Frank Zappa wanted to find a homegrown popular artist with the same healthy appetite for hijinks as his own, he didn't have to look any farther than Spike Jones. From the early '40s to the mid-'50s, Spike Jones and His City Slickers tore into the pomposity of high culture with a savage intent. Jones implemented a storehouse of rude sounds that made Erik Satie's experiments in *Parade* seem polite. Jones featured gunshots, but he included gurgling noises, police sirens, and cash registers, too. He made a mockery of honored classics like Rossini's *William Tell Overture*, which he turned into a ridiculously hysterical horse race. The unbearably dippy standard "Love in Bloom" was torn to shreds in much the same way the Marx Brothers laid waste to *Il Trovatore* in *A Night at the Opera* (1935). Johann Strauss' delicate *Blue Danube* waltz was transformed into a drunken brawl (in contrast to Stanley Kubrick's lame reverence in *2001: A Space Odyssey*). In their assault on Bizet's *Carmen*, the group's "messy-soprano," Eileen Gallagher, is heard frightening off three bulls with the shriek of her opening aria. Spike Jones blew raspberries at high culture with an all-American gusto.

"I was a massive Spike Jones fan," Zappa told Charles Amirkhanian in *Society Pages*. "When I was six or seven years old, he had a hit record called 'All I Want for Christmas (Is My Two Front Teeth)' and I sent him a fan letter because of that." "All I Want for Christmas (Is My Two Front Teeth)" became one of the biggest holiday songs in 1947. George Rock, a six-foot giant, provided the pipsqueak voice of the little boy who loses his two front teeth after sliding down the bannister in his house. Whistling through the wide gap in his mouth, he asks for their prompt return.

"I used to really love to listen to all those records," Zappa told Nigel Leigh. "It seemed to me that if you could get a laugh out of something, that was good, and if you could make life more colorful than it actually was, that was good." As it turned out, Zappa and Jones had a lot more in common than just their love for low-rent Americana.

Lindley Armstrong Jones was born in 1911 in Long Beach, California. Living above a railway depot, Jones grew up hearing all sorts of clanging and whooshing; like Charles Ives, he incorporated the sounds of his environment into his psyche. Jones, who earned the nickname "Spike" from a railroad telegrapher, was from a family of staunch Methodists — the only music allowed in the home was religious hymns. However, thanks to some black railway workers who played washboards, Jones became enthralled with percussion. He began by putting together railway utensils, but by the time he was eleven, his father bought him a set of drums and signed him up for lessons. The next year, Jones formed his first band, the Caliptra Melody Four, and further pursued his interest in percussion by playing in the school orchestra.

A few years later, Jones put together a college dance band called Spike Jones and His Five Tacks, patterned after Red Nichols' Five Pennies. In 1936, Jones turned professional, becoming a session drummer. He worked with the Andrews Sisters and played on Bing Crosby's original recording of "White Christmas." Jones eventually grew tired of such earnest arrangements, and developed a notion of satirizing some of those stiff dance-band numbers that were boring him to pieces. It might have remained merely a whim if he hadn't met the multi-talented Del Porter, who played xylophone, violin, sax, and clarinet, and had hung out with the great impressionist Mel Blanc, who provided Porter with a blissfully maniacal sense of humor. Porter and Jones formed a novelty band called the Feather Merchants, with Porter the group's chief architect of musical mayhem.

By the end of the '30s, they had changed their name to Spike Jones and His City Slickers and caught the attention of RCA Victor. By this time, the group included violinist Carl Grayson, whose tenor vocal style displayed a twisted grin in songs like "Cocktails for Two"; Red Ingle, who mutilated the sentimental weepie "Chloe," turning it into a beautiful act of desperate desecration; Winstead "Doodles" Weaver, a former comedian who created the droll voice of the race-track announcer on *The William Tell Overture*"; Freddy Morgan, a goofy-faced, mad banjo player; "Babyface" George David Rock, a trumpet player with the sweet kid voice in "All I Want for Christmas"; and Dr. Horatio Q. Birdbath (a.k.a.

WHO NEEDS THE PEACE CORPS?

Purves Pullen), who contributed mightily to the massacre of "Love in Bloom." Sir Frederick Gas (a.k.a. Earle Bennett) replaced Red Ingle in 1947, providing ample demonstrations of his peculiar emissions on songs like "Happy New Year" and "Knock Knock." The band dressed like inebriated renegades out of a Preston Sturges comedy, with loud clothes and goofy hats. Their stage presence was a Dada explosion from Dogpatch.

Spike Jones, a hayseed Harry Partch, unleashed a vast assortment of homemade musical weapons on the public, including the latrinophone — a toilet seat strung with catgut — as well as bathroom plungers and bicycle horns. These appliances put across a multitude of rude noises.

The group had a string of hits until the mid-'50s — when Elvis entered the building. As Presley stole Spike's thunder at RCA, Jones candidly remarked, "I just resent it because I don't think it's music, and it's certainly hurt the record business from the artistic standpoint." By then, the City Slickers had parted company with him, and Jones signed a contract with Liberty Records in 1959, playing straightforward standards again. Jones died of emphysema in 1965 at the age of 53.

Zappa got the idea for using "stock modules" from Jones. "There's an assortment of 'stock modules' used in our stage arrangements," Zappa wrote in *The Real Frank Zappa Book*. "These 'stock modules' include the *Twilight Zone texture* ... the *Mister Rogers texture*, the *Jaws texture*. . . . Those are the *Archetypal American Musical Icons*, and their presence in an arrangement puts a spin on any lyric in their vicinity. When present, these modules 'suggest' that you interpret *those lyrics* within parentheses." Zappa also patterned the Mothers of Invention as an ugly group, just as Jones patterned his as barroom drunks. Spike Jones used cartoon balloons on his album covers (an idea Zappa borrowed for *Freak Out!*, *Lumpy Gravy*, *We're Only in It for the Money*, and *Cruising With Ruben & the Jets*) to spell out backhanded titles like *The Very Worst of Spike Jones* and *Spike Jones Is Murdering the Classics*. Zappa did the same with his remarks on the cover of *Cruising With Ruben & the Jets* about the Mothers' "cruddy music."

Despite their shared madness, however, there were major differences between them. Jazz critic Ralph J. Gleason wrote, "The Mothers were total where Jones was selective in his satire." Both Jones and Zappa were indeed part of a legacy of disrepute that was genuinely American in spirit. Their shared mission was to make outrageous noises in the church of good taste.

19

Who knows why the Mothers of Invention were asked to play at the pre-award ceremony for the ninth annual Grammy Awards at the Waldorf-Astoria Hotel in April 1968? Perhaps it was a concession to the youth market which, up to that time, had been ignored by the National Academy of Recording Arts and Sciences. The Academy probably didn't know anything about the Mothers, but they sure wouldn't forget them by the time the night was over. The program listed "Music by Woody Herman; Entertainment by the Mothers of Invention." Zappa wasn't sending flowers of affection to the recording industry, though. Instead he turned the evening into another version of the Garrick Theatre. Neil Slaven writes, "When the Mothers took the stage, Frank went for the fat cats' throats: 'All year long you people manufactured this crap, and one night a year you've got to listen to it! Your whole affair is nothing more than a lot of pompous hokum, and we're going to approach you on your own level.' The band then proceeded to ravish 'Satin Doll,' the tune with which the Woody Herman band had opened the evening, dismembering dolls and handing the limbs out to the stunned audience."

The New York chapter of the Academy was so appalled that it met the following week to discuss just how repugnant it found the whole affair. According to one member, Zappa was "a tasteless dope" who turned the hall "into a barroom." Many just didn't get the joke, but John McClure, the head of classical A&R for Columbia Masterworks, understood it all too well. His label had taken a huge risk by creating a market for listeners interested in 20th-century music, issuing recordings by Stravinsky, Ives, and Glenn Gould since the '50s. McClure approached Zappa after the show and told him, "When you get tired of that dipshit label you're on, why don't you come and make a deal with [us]?" In light of what was to come in the years ahead, perhaps Zappa should have taken him up on the offer.

In May 1968 *Lumpy Gravy* was released, but it wasn't well-received. Many critics hated that it didn't resemble a Mothers of Invention record. "*Lumpy Gravy* doesn't really come to life," wrote Jim Miller in *Rolling Stone*. "It is a strangely sterile recording, as though all the studio musicians reading their music could not do what a batch of well-rehearsed Mothers can do; furthermore, what Zappa has lost by not using the smaller Mothers, he has not gained back by using a huge orchestra." *Lumpy Gravy* charted for only five short weeks, peaking at No. 159.

WHO NEEDS THE PEACE CORPS?

In June, with *Cruising With Ruben & the Jets* and *Uncle Meat* in the can, the Zappa family and the band headed back to California. Gail had found a house at the corner of Laurel Canyon Boulevard and Lookout Mountain Drive. "The Log Cabin," which had once belonged to cowboy actor Tom Mix, quickly became a communal environment with over a dozen people living there. Besides Frank, Gail, and Moon, there was Pamela Zarubica; Cal Schenkel, who set up his art department in the house; his secretary, Pauline Butcher; Ian Underwood; Motorhead Sherwood; Dick Barber; Pamela Des Barres; and the Zappas' baby-sitter, Christine Frka. Frka and Des Barres were members of Vito's dance troupe, nicknamed the Laurel Canyon Ballet Company.

On June 5, the day Robert Kennedy was hit by an assassin's bullet at the Ambassador Hotel, Zappa, Art Tripp, Ian Underwood, and Don Preston went into the RCA studios in L.A. to record a track with Grace Slick of the Jefferson Airplane. It was an odd pairing since Zappa rarely had kind words for San Francisco bands. And, for her part, Slick had once referred to Zappa as "the most intelligent asshole I've ever met." Creative heads prevailed, though, and "Would You Like a Snack?" was recorded. The tune had nothing in common with the same-titled song featured on *200 Motels* and it remained unreleased until the Jefferson Airplane CD box set, *Jefferson Airplane Loves You*, in 1992. "Would You Like a Snack?" was reminiscent of some of the improvised material recorded by Beefheart and Zappa at Studio Z, like "Tiger Roach" and "Metal Man Has Won His Wings." Where those tracks drew on the sounds of surf rock, however, "Would You Like a Snack?" was a cockeyed oratorio out of Luciano Berio.

That same month, *Life* published Zappa's article on the genesis of rock, "The Oracle Has It All Psyched Out." It was a fascinating sociological study that not only traced the evolution of rock as a rebellious art form, but proficiently described how the business of rock would render its own rebellion superfluous. "It is something of a paradox that companies which manufacture and distribute this art form (strictly for profit) might one day be changed or controlled by young people who were motivated to action by the products these companies sell," Zappa wrote prophetically. He traced how radio, which censored certain rock songs by defanging them in the '50s, when Little Richard was neutered by Pat Boone, continued to do so in a different form in the '60s. "Suppression for racial and sexual reasons doesn't go on as much, but radio stations still do not program progressive rock in proportion to the market which exists for it," Zappa explained. "Specific songs which seem most threatening to the established order don't get on radio and TV. Example: 'Society's Child' by Janis

Ian about interracial dating. (Mass media does more to keep Americans stupid than even the whole U.S. school system, that vast industry which cranks out trained consumers and technician-pawns for the benefit of other vast industries.)"

It may seem odd that Zappa hailed "Society's Child" as "threatening to the established order." After all, "Society's Child" was one of those mid-'60s folk songs by a sensitive young girl with an acoustic guitar. But "Society's Child" cut far deeper than the more topical folk songs of the period. Ian's intelligent and sophisticated track is an accurate account of liberal condescension, and one young girl's honorable — yet failed — attempt to rise above it.

In 1963, Martin Luther King Jr. delivered his "I Have a Dream" speech, declaring that children wouldn't "be judged by the color of their skin but by the content of their character." The Freedom Movement, which fought the early battles for desegregation in the South and voter registration for black Americans, was extending a call for a shared vision of interracial harmony. King, the political and spiritual leader of the civil rights struggle in the United States, called for the country to abandon the bitter legacy of slavery. King's speech, that hot day in August, hit like a bolt of electricity, and suddenly a vision of hope and possibility spread throughout the country. Craig Werner persuasively describes that promise in his book *A Change Is Gonna Come: Music, Race & the Soul of America*.

> For people of all colors committed to racial justice, the '60s were a time of hope. You could hear it in the music: in the freedom songs that soared high above and sunk within the hearts of marchers at Selma and Montgomery; in the gospel inflections of Sam Cooke's teenage love songs; in Motown's self-proclaimed soundtrack for "young America"; in blue-eyed soul and English remakes of the Chicago blues; in Aretha Franklin's resounding call for respect; in Sly Stone's celebration of the everyday people and Jimi Hendrix's vision of an interracial tribe; in John Coltrane's celebration of a love supreme. For brief moments during the decade surrounding King's speech, many of us harbored real hopes that the racial nightmare might be coming to an end.

Janis Ian, a white Jewish girl who was born Janis Eddy Fink in New York City in 1951, was probably one of those touched by the hope that the racial night-

WHO NEEDS THE PEACE CORPS?

mare would end. However, by 1966, the war in Vietnam had taken priority over the war on poverty, and violent riots in black inner-city ghettoes every summer were reducing King's aspirations to ashes. Still, some American liberals wanted to see, in their films, television shows, and music, more racial harmony — despite evidence to the contrary. By the mid-'60s, more black actors were appearing on bland TV shows, such as Bill Cosby on *I Spy*, or in solemn exercises in maudlin melodrama, like *Guess Who's Coming to Dinner?*, where Sidney Poitier, who had electrified audiences a decade earlier in *The Blackboard Jungle*, was reduced to a black token of patronizing benevolence. Under that haze of white liberal denial about some ugly facts, fourteen-year-old Ian in 1966 wrote a song about interracial dating while she was waiting to see her guidance counselor. When "Society's Child" was recorded a year later, the tune stirred up a storm of reaction.

"Society's Child" begins innocently enough with a baroque melody played on a harpsichord before the full orchestra joins in. Ian's voice hovers over the arrangement, with a longing that feels beyond her early adolescent years, yet still has the buoyant anticipation of first love: "Come to my door, baby/Face is clean and shining black as night." Within moments, though, those eager yearnings start to crumble:

> *My mother went to answer, you know, that you looked so fine*
> *Now I could understand your tears and your shame*
> *She called you "boy" instead of your name*
> *When she wouldn't let you inside*
> *When she turned and said, "But, honey, he's not our kind."*

While she sings her mother's words to her black suitor, you can hear his response in the gospel organ crying out from behind her voice. Then the song turns into what we believe will be a story of defiant young lovers turning against the mendacity of their elders:

> *My teachers all laugh their smirking stares*
> *Cutting deep down in our affairs*
> *Preachers of equality*
> *If they can't believe it, then why can't they just let us be?*

Those were strong words for 1967. Ian was saying that all the talk of racial harmony was just platitudes — she was the one walking the talk. In the next verse, she stands up against the injustice:

One of these days, I'm gonna stop my listening
Gonna raise my head up high
One of these days, I'm gonna raise my glistening wings and fly.

But then, after she defiantly states her own values, the simple facts come crashing in:

But that day will have to wait for a while
Baby, I'm only society's child
When we're older things may change
But for now this is the way
THEY MUST REMAIN.

"Society's Child" was banned on radio stations in both the South and the North. What Zappa probably responded to in this tune was how the theme wasn't reduced to simple folk-music propaganda for racial harmony. Instead, Ian spelled out the basic facts that racism hadn't gone away. Thus she went against the romantic idea that protest songs should change the way people think and act. Janis Ian didn't make herself the proud spokesperson for the ideals of Lyndon Johnson's Great Society. She cut right to the bone of the very issues that culminated in Martin Luther King's assassination in 1968.

20

The year 1968 saw the escalation of the Vietnam War, the assassination of both Martin Luther King Jr. and presidential hopeful Robert Kennedy, and the widening of the divide between race, class, and age. "If in the past American political divisions had been primarily based on region and class and ethnicity," historian David Halberstam wrote, "a new ingredient had now been added, profound generational differences, not just region by region, but remarkably and often quite painfully, house by house." If King's credo of a land of racial and economic harmony had

WHO NEEDS THE PEACE CORPS?

raised hopes, the cry in the streets was now "Burn, Baby, Burn!" Violent confrontations took place in the home, the streets, and even at the Democratic National Convention in Chicago.

While many rock bands, from the MC5 to the Jefferson Airplane, kicked out the jams, there wasn't a whiff of support from Frank Zappa. Ed Sanders, from that other ugly, satirical rock group, the Fugs, appealed to Zappa to join them in Chicago. Zappa refused to get involved. "In the spring of 1968," Sanders recalled, "I went to his house in L.A. to ask him to perform in Chicago during the August Democratic Convention, and he turned me down. Later that year we were on a panel discussion about politics at the Essen Song Festival in Germany, and he again took a stance against overt political activity. To those of us who wanted him to perform at benefits and rallies, it was a maddening stance."

Instead, Zappa went to Chicago to open for the power rock trio Cream at the International Amphitheatre. Backstage, after the show, Eric Clapton asked Zappa if he had ever heard of the "Plaster-Casters." When Zappa replied that he hadn't, Clapton took him to his hotel, where two girls named Cynthia and Dianne were sitting in the lobby. One had a small suitcase with an oval cardboard emblem glued to the side that read "THE PLASTER-CASTERS OF CHICAGO," while the other had a brown paper bag. In Clapton's room, the girls opened the suitcase and pulled out a collection of plaster replicas of the penises of Jimi Hendrix, Noel Redding, and other rock stars. After politely refusing to be immortalized themselves, Zappa and Clapton investigated how these unusual groupies went about their task. They discovered that the girls created their bizarre little sculptures with alginate, the same material dentists use to take impressions of teeth. It's a powder which, when mixed with water, gets rubbery and hardens so that plaster can be poured into it. Cynthia, the originator of the concept, would mix the substance while Dianne blew the rock star so that he would be firmly erect. Dianne had to take her mouth off the rock star's dick at the precise moment Cynthia slammed the container full of glop onto the end of it, where she would hold it until it hardened enough to make a good mold. Meanwhile, the rock star had the strenuous job of maintaining his erection. According to Cynthia, Hendrix grew so smitten with the goop that he ended up fucking the mold.

Despite the commonly held view, gleaned from some of his lyrics, that Zappa had contempt for groupies, he saw them, on the contrary, as a socially and sexually positive phenomenon. "I appreciate what they're doing, both artistically and sociologically," Zappa told *Rolling Stone*. "I want to make one thing clear. The girls don't think this is the least bit creepy and neither do I. Pop stars are idolized the same way General Grant was. People put up statues to honor war heroes. The Plaster-Casters do the same thing for pop stars. What they are doing is making statues of the essential part of stars. It's the same motivation as making statues of Grant." The Mothers, like many other rock 'n' roll bands, got a lot of mileage while roaring their engines through the groupie culture. "I would have to say that touring with Frank in the '60s bordered on the incredible when it came to the groupie situation," Bunk Gardner remembered. "There was not only a sexual revolution, but social and political upheaval going on at the same time, which made things very interesting in more ways than I ever imagined." The road became one long party where band members were sated and worshipped for both their musical and sexual dexterity. "After every concert there was always somebody who wanted to take you to a party or just talk or hang out and see what developed," Gardner explained. "Groupies were a part of the scene and acceptable to all rock musicians as a bonus for playing rock music and being a 'star.'"

In November 1968, *Cruising With Ruben & the Jets* was the last official Mothers release by MGM/Verve, although in 1969 a "greatest hits" package, put together under Zappa's supervision, called *Mothermania*, included material from *Freak Out!*, *Absolutely Free*, and *We're Only in It for the Money*. *Cruising with Ruben & the Jets* was put out to fulfill the remainder of their contract. As for Zappa's '50s pastiche, it got deeply mixed reviews. *Billboard* called it "a great put-on record." Others took it too seriously. According to Zappa, one DJ in Philadelphia played the album consistently until informed that it was actually by the Mothers of Invention — and then he dropped it from the playlist.

Free of MGM/Verve, Zappa wanted to launch some new artists on Bizarre and Straight. Back in 1967, he was set to produce folksinger Sandy Hurvitz's first solo album, *Sandy's Album Is Here at Last!*, with the Mothers backing her. But Hurvitz argued with Zappa about a track ("Arch Godliness of Purplefull Magic") where she wanted Billy Mundi to play drums. When she stormed out of the studio, Zappa turned the production chores over to Ian Underwood, who reluctantly arranged and finished the album. "Ian just used to sit and put on horn parts and erase them on a daily basis," Hurvitz told Neil Slaven.

The first release on Bizarre for Warner Brothers, in the summer of 1968, was a collection of mostly *a cappella* folk songs by an aggressively disquieting busker named Larry "Wild Man" Fischer. Fischer, born in Los Angeles in 1945, was a familiar fixture along the Sunset Strip in the mid-'60s. He made his living by spontaneously composing songs for small change. Having been twice institutionalized by his mother, Fischer was essentially homeless and jobless, and hung out at clubs along the Strip. *An Evening With Wild Man Fischer* was a double-album collection of his street recordings, monologues in the studio, as well as songs featuring percussion overdubs by Art Tripp. The montage cover by Cal Schenkel featured the maniacal Fischer holding a knife to the throat of a cardboard-cutout woman who many assumed to be his mother. "I don't know if people will enjoy him, but for the first time in recording history you will have a chance to hear a man's thoughts as they happen," Zappa told Chris Welch. "You'll be laughing at home and saying, 'He's out of his mind,' but he's not out of his mind. You'll be hearing a person who has been stuck in an institution and told he is insane."

Recording engineer Dick Kunc told music producer Bill Lantz that trying to do the street recordings was particularly perilous. "My first task was to literally follow him around the streets for several days, carrying a Uher two-track, chronicling whatever madness he got into," Kunc recalled. "Parts of that mission were plain scary! Larry was truly certifiable then." The studio sessions weren't any less hazardous. "Frank was gentle, encouraging, yet demanding of Larry . . . as Frank was with all who toiled under his baton."

An Evening With Wild Man Fischer is a rock 'n' roll album designed as a piece of social anthropology. Fischer's songs might be simple, childlike tunes, but they are steeped in fantasy, violence, and family dysfunction. Zappa's voice can be heard threading through many of Fischer's songs like the omnipresent voice of Larry's conscience. "He needed some structuring," Zappa explained years later, "someone with an appreciation of what his craft was, to sit through the problems of making the album and then have the patience to put it together in the continuity the listener could pay attention to."

Some of the street compositions, "Merry Go Round," "Which Way Did the Freaks Go?" and the strangely haunting "Jennifer Jones," are intercut with conversations about growing up and being institutionalized. They blur the line between entertainment and psychodrama. Listening to *An Evening With Wild Man Fischer* is unsettling because it explodes the illusion that only pop stars make albums, not street performers with barely functioning lives. Zappa presents Fischer as a performer whose songs are his life, not illusory constructs designed to become hit records.

Zappa also released the double album *Lenny Bruce: The Berkeley Concert*, made up of material that was to be part of the aborted project *Our Man in Nirvana*. The 1966 concert features Bruce discussing his many arduous legal battles, something he did with great regularity in his last years. Zappa can be heard off-mike at the beginning of Bruce's opening routine reciting the opening line "Ladies and gentlemen, the President of the United States," from "Plastic People."

In the fall, the Mothers made their second trip to Europe, only this time without lead singer Ray Collins, who again left the band over a dispute with Zappa. America wasn't the only country torn by a violent summer in 1968. There was a revolution in France that almost toppled the government of Charles de Gaulle. The Soviet Union had put the boot to Alexander Dubcek's "socialism with a human face" in Czechoslovakia, turning the Prague Spring into a deep frost. The night the Mothers of Invention came to Berlin, on October 16, students were still in the mood for storming the barricades. They demanded that Zappa endorse their cause by inciting the audience to set fire to an Allied fuel dump. Zappa refused to play any part in this second coming of an October uprising, and within moments, he was greeted by pears and eggs flying at the stage.

"There was 10,000 people in the hall, and it was jam-packed," Jimmy Carl Black recalled. "After the pears came a can of green paint; it went all over my drums, all over me. Roy Estrada had this pair of white pants on which immediately turned green. It was then that they started ripping the iron railings from around the balconies, ready to throw those down onto the band." Neil Slaven quotes German journalist Helmut Kopetzky, who further described the crowd's insurgence: "The first missile . . . buzzed through the air. . . . For the moment unconcerned, the Mothers carried on removing sundry toys from a hatbox and symbolically destroying them. Then the first egg smashed to pieces on Zappa's yellow (Les Paul) guitar. The Mother Superior opined, 'You people act like pigs!' Battle lines were drawn: 'Evolution versus Revolution.' At twelve minutes past nine, the stage hangings were in tatters."

The Mothers decided to depart from the stage to their dressing room, but all seventy or eighty of the security guards hired for the evening were hiding there. A message was sent that if the band didn't finish the show, the crowd would come after them. Zappa decided to go back — but not sheepishly. "After telling the crowd that the band was there to play music, Frank said, 'Your situation in Berlin has got to be desperate for you to behave like this. You're behaving like Americans,'" Kopetzky reported. "The band with damaged equipment hammered out the 'Ho-Ho-Ho-Chi-Minh' chant of the stage occupiers, making it sound like the martial rhythm of a Nazi parade. Organizer [Fritz] Rau threw himself forlornly between the two camps, hoarse from imploring, 'Friends, let's talk . . .' But nothing came of

WHO NEEDS THE PEACE CORPS?

it. The police, who up until then had stayed discreetly in the background, gave both friend and foe ten minutes to leave the battlefield. The evacuation took place without any clashes." For surviving the event, Zappa gave everyone in the band a medal: the Berlin Survival Award, 1968.

The Mothers arrived in London a week before their October 28 gig at the Royal Albert Hall. Zappa had conjured up a play for the band to improvise onstage with the help of fourteen members of the BBC Orchestra. During the European tour, he'd been writing chamber-music pieces while waiting in airports or hotels. (These compositions would later form the basis for the score to his feature film, *200 Motels*.) Since the Mothers could hardly perform with this classical ensemble, Zappa constructed a little drama where the two could — in a word — commingle. Zappa provided the framework for the story, and the band members improvised their own lines. "The logistics were pretty ridiculous," Zappa recalled. "How were we going to rehearse a 'play' in the middle of the tour? Who was going to copy out all the sheet music for the BBC guys? How could Ian, Bunk and Art rehearse their solo parts? Who was going to pay for all this? Only the last question had an easy answer." Zappa laid out close to $7,000 to hire extra musicians, rent costumes, record the show, and hire a 16mm film crew to shoot the concert (this footage would turn up in the video release of *Uncle Meat*). Zappa still believed he could get a good live album out of it. That album, though, wouldn't be heard until 1993, when it was released on CD as *Ahead of Their Time*.

The show opened with the BBC Orchestra performing a piece that would later be titled "Bogus Pomp," but for that evening was part of a suite called "Music for the Queen's Circus." Joining them were the only three members of the Mothers who could read music: Underwood, Gardner, and Tripp. While they performed, Preston, dressed in a villain's cape and a top hat, crept onto the stage and whipped a bit of electronic music on them. The orchestra and the three Mothers protested, while Preston announced that there must be progress, "We're coming to the beginning of a new era," he shouted, "wherein the inner self is the most important thing." Preston tried unsuccessfully to convince them that diatonic music was archaic, and vegetarian living would lead to human growth. The result of Preston's exhortations was that Underwood, Gardner, and Tripp left the group to form their own disciplined band devoted to diatonic music. Along with the BBC Orchestra members, they dressed up in tuxedos and makeup. Once they were set, Motorhead Sherwood turned up banging a tambourine, wanting to join the orchestra. However, they turned him down because he couldn't read music. But

Motorhead forced himself into the group anyway, finding a crumpled tuxedo to call his own.

When Jimmy Carl Black ambled onto the stage and saw what was going on, he rebuked his three wayward colleagues: "If you wanna get laid after the show, you gotta play rock 'n' roll and drink beer." When he caught sight of Underwood in his new formal duds, he proceeded to remark, "You're not going to get laid anyway with those uniforms on!" Black then announced his departure from the band and set out to find some young ladies in the audience to hustle — but not before he was done up to look like Donovan in Jimi Hendrix's clothes. While Black bounded into the audience, Roy Estrada entered the stage in an elaborate Pope outfit, carrying a plastic pail with the inscription "NO MORE UGLY BABIES," while throwing Smarties (representing birth-control pills) and chanting Latin in his beautifully shrill voice. A few weeks before the concert, the Pope had announced a ban on birth-control pills. Estrada approached Underwood to join the new group as an opera singer, saying he had to leave the Mothers because he was Mexican and was holding the band back from success.

Underwood had Estrada audition a vocal piece later to be known as "Holiday in Berlin" (after the riot they had recently experienced). The group booed Estrada's effort, and he left the stage dejected. Meanwhile, Preston, through his macrobiotic food, was transformed into a monster. He attacked and strangled Underwood, who was seated at a grand piano, playing in a state of euphoria. With Underwood out of the way, Preston took over and forced electronic dissonance on the group. Then he unveiled a pop arrangement of a song called "Agency Man," about a CIA agent who devised a campaign to sell then-Governor Ronald Reagan as a presidential candidate. (In 1993, Zappa reflected on the significance of that song: "Since Bill Casey was Reagan's campaign manager, and later became head of the CIA, the idea of a political sales pitch emanating from an 'agency man' takes on a whole new dimension.") While Preston played, the band reunited, until Underwood came back to life, dispatched of Preston, and brought the orchestra back in for a rousing conclusion.

The rest of the concert featured only the Mothers, performing "King Kong," "Help, I'm a Rock," "Pound for a Brown," and an instrumental version of "Let's Make the Water Turn Black." They also premiered a guitar piece called "Transylvania Boogie" (which would be recorded for Zappa's solo album *Chunga's Revenge* in 1970) that drew on the kind of folk melodies that Béla Bartók had researched for his *Violin Duo, No. 44, "Transylvanian Dance."* "The Orange County

WHO NEEDS THE PEACE CORPS?

Lumber Truck," a big-band spectacular featuring one of Zappa's more driving guitar solos, would later be included in an abridged version on *Weasels Ripped My Flesh*. The concert was an elaborate exercise in absurdity that lacked the immediacy of the shows at the Garrick. At best, it gave Zappa a sense of what could be done with some of his orchestral scores.

England would again figure in his plans to hear them played once more — only next time, he'd live to regret it.

21

When Zappa returned to L.A., he needed a replacement for Ray Collins. After several auditions, he again came across Lowell George, who, since performing with the Factory, had recorded with the Standells, a local garage band that won brief acclaim during the psychedelic era. Like Collins, George had a genuine love — and feel — for R&B and a lilting tenor that caught the nuances and longings in the tunes. But Zappa used him more in the role of the band's rhythm guitarist. "I got into the Mothers to replace Ray — an impossible job because no one can replace Ray," George told *Zig Zag* in 1975. "He's a singer par excellence and has a sense of humor that I couldn't hope to get near." Nevertheless, George brought his own devilish impertinence that fit in perfectly with the group. His first assignment was to help Zappa work on the next release for Bizarre.

Christine Frka and Pamela Miller, Moon Unit's nannies, were members of the Laurel Canyon Ballet Company, which also included Miss Sandra, Miss Cinderella, and Miss Mercy. All of them were so dubbed by Tiny Tim, the freaky but prim performer of "Tip-Toe Through the Tulips With Me." On one occasion, while they were staying at the Log Cabin, Zappa told them, "As long as you're going to hang around, why don't you girls come up with some material?" The ladies put together a number of songs about their lifestyle and named themselves the GTO's — Girls Together Outrageously. "Frank was like the ruler of Laurel Canyon," Pamela Des Barres explains. "People would just congregate up there and, in his words, 'freak out.' And not only were you allowed to, but Frank would just pull that stuff out of people. He made them become their true, freaky selves. . . . It wasn't what you'd call normal but it wasn't what people thought either. It was a very free-form household — loose, but very loving and warm. He was very much a family man."

Yet this family man, with a particular appetite for the bizarre, saw something quaintly strange about the GTO's behavior. "They had an interesting lifestyle," Zappa told COQ magazine in 1974. "They used to write poetry and do little skits. . . . I thought it would be interesting to share their experiences with people who had never come in contact with anything like that. So I encouraged them to set music to their songs or get somebody to help them put their poems to music and I would record them. [The album *Permanent Damage*] was just a sampling of their lifestyle."

Des Barres recalled that having Zappa as their producer was nothing short of inspiring — the weirder they got, the more enthused he became. "Frank did everything in the studio, directing and producing," Des Barres told *Musician*. "He would point to us with his baton like we were an orchestra. We'd watch his response and it would encourage us so much because he loved it. The more he slapped his knee and laughed, the more nuts we'd get. And he wanted that. He wanted everyone to experience their creativity as far out as they could get it."

Permanent Damage, like *An Evening With Wild Man Fischer*, is a work of oddball sociology as much as it is a rock 'n' roll album. Zappa allowed the group, with their stories and songs, to define their personality. "The GTO's write all their own lyrics & no subject matter covered by these lyrics was suggested by any outside source," Zappa wrote in the liner notes. "The choice of subjects is a reflection of the girls' own attitudes toward their environment." To Zappa, making a record of the GTO's was documenting a folkloric aspect of American culture that would be frowned upon by cultural snobs who felt these women were not talented enough to record. Since Zappa treated subject matter, dialogue, and song as musical material, *Permanent Damage* is a beautiful piece of editing and production, merrily dancing along to its own nutty rhythm — even if the ladies' singing abilities were questionable. "We had serious trouble harmonizing," Des Barres remembers, "so we all sang together like a grade-school choir, which didn't faze Frank — he thought of us as a living, breathing documentary."

In songs like "The Captain's Fat Theresa Shoes" (about Captain Beefheart's footwear) and "Wouldn't It Be Sad If There Were No Cones?" (about some of L.A.'s soul brothers who came on to the ladies at the Whisky), the group brings to mind the Roches, an eccentric trio of musical sisters from New York who started recording in the '70s, but with a touch of the California surf in their voices. When the GTO's talk about their high school gym class and "having to take showers in front of the dyke gym teacher who drools at the sight of your pectoral muscles flexing, smelling of four laps around the track," they evoke the mordant adolescent chatter of the high school cafeteria. Miss Pamela also sings a rather spirited love song written by Lowell George, "Do Me in Once I'll Be Sad, Do Me in Twice

WHO NEEDS THE PEACE CORPS?

& I'll Know Better (Circular Circulation)." "The Moche Monster Review" describes the behavior of older men who hope they can score with these young nubile freaks, while "Rodney" is a brilliant little production number about Rodney Bingenheimer, a boy groupie who periodically makes his own comments on the song — which becomes an illuminating portrait of idol worship from a bisexual perspective:

> *I'm one with the Vanilla Fudge*
> *I know Sonny & Cher*
> *I meditated with George Harrison*
> *The Hollies are my best friends*
> *And I had lunch with Grace Slick yesterday*
> *You can ball Ringo Starr if you ball me first.*

Permanent Damage offers a revealing examination of pop-star fetishism in "Love on an Eleven Year Old Level," which deals with the girls' fascination with an eleven-year-old boy who looks like the Rolling Stones' late guitarist:

> *Do you realize this little eleven-year-old looks like Brian Jones?*
> *A kiss on the cheek would be enough*
> *But when he does more . . . wah! wah!*

"I'm in Love With the ooo-ooo Man," a love song about Miss Pamela's affection for Nicky St. Nicholas of the rock band Steppenwolf, contains probably the most revealing passage about how transient a groupie's love can be:

> *Even though he doesn't think of me*
> *Day & night, night & day (and probably barely)*
> *It doesn't mean I think of him less*
> *(In fact I think of other things rarely)*

Besides contributions by some of the Mothers, including George and Preston, *Permanent Damage* features the Jeff Beck Group (with Rod Stewart), and a young Ry Cooder. This confluence of real groupies and their idols, appearing on the same album, displays a great lack of self-consciousness. As Zappa biographer Ben Watson points out, "[The] GTO's pursued hedonism with discernment and anti-authoritarian wit." *Permanent Damage* is one of the more honest records that tries to capture perhaps the least documented aspect of the '60s sexual revolution.

One day Christine Frka introduced Zappa to a bunch of guys from Arizona who were part of a band named after the 17th-century witch Alice Cooper. The lead singer, Vincent Furnier, declared himself her reincarnation. Frka had spotted them playing the bar scene. Their wildly androgynous costumery and their totally macabre stage manner became their trademark in the years to follow. Alice Cooper opened for the Mothers, along with Wild Man Fischer and the GTO's, on December 6 and 7 at the Shrine Exposition Hall in L.A. They recorded two commercially unsuccessful albums for Zappa's Straight label, *Pretties for You* (1969) and *Easy Action* (1970), before jumping to Warner Brothers in 1971 and launching a lucrative career with the playfully necrophilic *Love It to Death*, which spawned the hit single "I'm Eighteen."

"I remember Frank came to only one recording session for the *Pretties for You* album," Alice Cooper guitarist Michael Bruce told author Billy James. "He was so bored with the project that he turned it over to Ian Underwood, who did the rest of the producing, even though he didn't receive credit on the album." Drummer Neal Smith gave *Goldmine* a different take on those sessions: "Frank Zappa said he wanted the album to sound like a car driving past a garage while a band was playing. That was his goal, and I think he more or less achieved it. He had us set up our amps around the drum set, so there was total leakage. We would run down the song — setting the dials on our amps and stuff, just trying to get a proper sound going so that we could record — and Zappa would say, 'We got a take.' We would be like, 'What? We didn't even play the song yet.'"

By the end of 1968, Zappa had put together a book called *The Groupie Papers*, commissioned by publishers Stein & Day. For reasons unknown, they decided not to publish it, but portions of the book were included in the album package of the GTO's *Permanent Damage*. "They really would make a fantastic book," Zappa said with regret in 1975. "There are Cynthia [Plaster-Caster's] diaries and Noel Redding's diaries. . . . It's a dramatic factual insight into the '60s and rock hysteria. . . . There's a sequence when Pamela falls in love with Cynthia. The problem is that Cynthia isn't the least bisexual. Pamela hocks her record player and, without any real idea of what it's like, goes to Chicago in the middle of winter, to get into Cynthia's pants. . . . Cynthia's diaries are quite incredible. She makes strange clinical notes about who she balled, and if she casted them. . . . It would make one hell of a movie."

WHO NEEDS THE PEACE CORPS?

The darker side of the hippie subculture was starting to rear its head, reaching its nadir by the beginning of 1969. It attained its culmination, however, in August with the savage murder spree by Charles Manson and his Family. Film critic Jake Horsley accurately captured their impact: "Manson and the clan gave the world a shocking reminder of the darker, more aberrational potential of this revolution — namely, chaos and destruction, for its own sake. By attempting to turn an artistic rebellion into a social and even a political one, Manson pulled the rug out from under the '60s. The murders shattered the foundation of a counterculture, and left nothing but the ruins." Manson wasn't alone, however. There were other extremists on the political fringe, including the Motherfuckers, the Molotov Cocktail Party, and the Weathermen. Ian MacDonald, in *Revolution in the Head*, echoed Horsley's sentiments: "The sad fact was that LSD could turn its users into anything from florally bedecked peaceniks to gun-brandishing urban guerrillas."

As if to foreshadow what was once a benign freakishness in L.A., an odd stranger found his way into Zappa's Log Cabin. While Zappa was hanging out with Wild Man Fischer and some of the GTO's, a guy who introduced himself as "the Raven" wandered through the front door. "First he handed me a bottle of fake blood with a rag in it," Zappa wrote. "[He said], 'I have isolated The Specimen!' and pulled out an Army .45." While everyone — including Wild Man Fischer — was looking for a place to hide, Zappa tried to be helpful. "You know what? If the police see you with that gun around here, you're going to be in a lot of trouble." Zappa got everyone in the house involved in trying to help the Raven hide his gun. It was placed in a well with stagnant water out back. Once he left, Zappa and company started looking for a new place to live.

In early 1969, the Zappas bought a large house on Woodrow Wilson Drive, off of Mulholland Drive, in the Santa Monica mountains overlooking Laurel Canyon. In February, the Mothers toured the East Coast, bringing engineer Dick Kunc to do some live recordings. He put together a portable recording studio consisting of his Uher two-track tape machine and a stereo microphone that he attached to a small eight-channel Shure mixing console in a little attaché case. Kunc recalled recently to Billy James, "I got a call from Frank saying, 'I want you to come and record the rest of this tour.' . . . To him it was buy a screwdriver and a pair of pliers and that's it — you're off, what else do you need?" Most of those recordings found their way into Zappa's mammoth concert retrospective, *You Can't Do That on Stage Anymore*. "There wasn't much recording going on at that time," Zappa told Neil Slaven. "Today, you take it for granted that you can take a little pocket cassette machine with you and bootleg yourself anyplace. But portable recording gear at that time didn't exist. So, if you were going to make a recording someplace, you really had to make some special arrangements to do it."

By now, the Mothers had brought their particular form of stagecraft, with its nightly improvisations, to a new level. But audiences were so inundated by the psychedelic sounds of bands like Vanilla Fudge that they grew impatient with the Mothers' absurdist posturing. And according to Zappa, the audiences were "clapping for the wrong reasons." They were cheering on the ritual without understanding what they were taking in. The fact that the crowds were up to their eyebrows in hallucinogens didn't help. "The best responses we get from an audience are when we do our worst material," Zappa told Larry Kart in *Downbeat*. He was even more precise with Richard Green of *New Music Express*: "We had developed the music of the group to a stage where it had really evolved. We would go onstage and we didn't need to play any specific repertoire. I could just conduct the group and we could make up an hour's worth of music that I thought was valid. On the spot it would be spontaneous and new and interesting. It would be creative because the personalities of the people in the group were contributing just as much as their musicianship. [But] nobody knew how to take the band; they didn't know if we were Spike Jones with electronic music or whether it was serious or what it was."

MGM/Verve washed their hands of Frank Zappa's contract when, in March, they issued *Mothermania*, whose inside gatefold featured each band member's teeth. On the back cover was a photo of the riot from the Berlin concert in a German newspaper with the coverage in German. Aside from the familiar tracks from the first three albums, Zappa included an uncensored version of "Mother People," a demo version of "Idiot Bastard Son," a re-edited version of "It Can't Happen Here" with the piano bridge removed and some dialogue added, plus better mixes of songs from *Freak Out!* and *Absolutely Free*. Meanwhile, *Uncle Meat* was released by Bizarre/Reprise in April with a booklet filled with photos, the plot of the movie, and some of Zappa's written scores of pieces like the title track and "King Kong." Cal Schenkel's album cover also made use of dental charts, and a skull with the Year of the Black Plague (1348) stamped on its forehead. "That was coincidental," Schenkel said with a laugh. "I noticed myself some time after completing the cover . . . the Plague, of course, lasted for quite some time, but 1348 has some special significance."

Straight Records started putting out more records by artists managed by Herb Cohen, like folksingers Tim Dawe (*Penrod*), Tim Buckley (*Blue Afternoon*), and

WHO NEEDS THE PEACE CORPS?

Judy Henske and Jerry Yester (*Farewell Aldebaran*). Zappa also had an interest in the late hipster jazz poet Lord Buckley, who had an enormous impact on Lenny Bruce. *A Most Immaculately Hip Aristocrat* contains six performance pieces originally recorded in 1956 by Lyle Griffen; Zappa edited a selection for the album.

Also in the winter of 1969, Zappa ran into Captain Beefheart for the first time since their days together at Studio Z. While Zappa took off to find glory in L.A., Beefheart had stayed in Lancaster to start the first incarnation of his Magic Band in 1964. With Alex Snouffer and Doug Moon on guitars, Jerry Handley on bass, and Paul Blakely on drums, they signed a deal with A&M Records in 1965.

Beefheart, unlike Zappa, was a musical primitive. His integration of free jazz, Delta blues, Dada absurdism, and idiosyncratic verse was much more instinctual than that of Zappa, who mixed his musical colors with more deliberate intent. This is perhaps why Zappa and Beefheart are at opposite poles of the same beguiling yardstick. As Beefheart remarked to a radio interviewer in 1987, "I was never influenced . . . possessed, but never influenced." Although their stage appearance and costumery would prove even more outlandish than the Mothers', Captain Beefheart & His Magic Band in 1966 appeared to be a straight-ahead blues band. Their first single for A&M was a cover of Bo Diddley's "Diddy Wah Diddy." (The producer was David Gates, an aspiring songwriter/producer who would later form the soft-rock band Bread.) This foot-stomping blues, featuring Beefheart's wailing harp and deep, growling vocal, wasn't the chart success it deserved to be, although it did sell well in California.

When Beefheart delivered his first album, *Safe as Milk* (1967), to Jerry Moss of A&M, Moss was probably as shocked as his MGM/Verve counterpart had been with Zappa's *Freak Out!* With the addition of a young and talented L.A. slide guitarist, Ry Cooder, and new drummer John French, as well as producers Richard Perry and Bob Krasnow, Beefheart shot far beyond the conventional blues of "Diddy Wah Diddy." "Sure 'Nuff and Yes I Do" had that snake-moan sound of his early material. The theremin-driven psychedelic rock of "Electricity," however, carried a different jolt. The white-soul balladry of "Call on Me" was Beefheart at his most seductive. And the Hindu-influenced rhythms of "Abba Zaba" were simply transfixing. The lyrics came across as dense abstractions: syntax was altered, nouns were transformed into verbs, and verse structure was shattered into free-form shouting. It's doubtful this is what A&M had in mind for a debut album.

The record company hoped to get some mileage out of the band playing the Monterey Pop Festival, but a gig at a "love-in" at Mt. Tamalpais in San Francisco changed all that. Dressed in natty suits, like gangsters instead of hippies, they mounted the stage. Beefheart was on edge to begin with, feeling the anxiety of performing in front of a large audience, as well as tripping from heavy LSD usage. As they started to play "Electricity," the second song in their set, Beefheart froze, turned around, and walked off the back of the ten-foot platform. French recalled the event with horror: "He told me later what happened. He said he looked down at a girl right after he sang ["Electricity"] and she turned into a fish and bubbles came out of her mouth." Beefheart added another perspective: "An audience can really lift you right off the stage. . . . I walked right off the stage about ten feet in midair. Then fell down about six feet, got up, and ran back up on the stage and asked them, 'Why did you drop me?'"

That evening, Ry Cooder left the band. His assessment of Beefheart? "He's a Nazi. It makes you feel like Anne Frank to be around him." Thanks to Beefheart's meltdown, the Monterey Pop Festival was definitely out. By the time his second album, *Strictly Personal*, arrived in 1968, producer Krasnow decided to move on to Kama Sutra Records, and brought Beefheart with him. He signed him to yet another contract, even though Beefheart was still legally tied to A&M. Since A&M wouldn't release *Strictly Personal* because Jerry Moss deemed it "too negative," Krasnow had Kama Sutra put it out. While the band was touring Europe, however, Krasnow took the master tapes and littered the album with phasing effects and other psychedelic sounds — to make it saleable — without permission from Beefheart. While on tour, Beefheart heard the album and was outraged. He immediately disowned it. The tour was aborted and the band was in disarray.

While wandering in his musical limbo, Beefheart ran into his old friend Frank Zappa at a Kentucky Fried Chicken in L.A. just after the Straight label was launched. "He was in contractual bondage all over the place," Zappa wrote. "Companies weren't paying him, but the contracts were written in such a way that he was precluded from recording — they had him tied up for years."

Zappa promised Beefheart what no other recording executive would — the freedom to come up with whatever he wanted. Beefheart had added some new members to the Magic Band. Guitarist Bill Harkleroad, a fan of Beefheart & the Magic Band, replaced Snouffler. Blues musician Mark Boston was added on bass. And Beefheart's cousin, Victor Heyden, rounded out this version of the group on bass clarinet and vocals. Beefheart also decided to rename the members: Harkleroad became Zoot Horn Rollo, Boston was Rockette Morton, French was simply Drumbo, new member Jeff Cotton was Antennae Jimmy Semens, and

WHO NEEDS THE PEACE CORPS?

Heyden was the Mascara Snake. The first tracks they laid down at Sunset Sound in Hollywood were "Moonlight on Vermont," a twisted hybrid of Delta blues and roof-raising gospel, and the poignant antiwar song "Veteran's Day Poppy."

Within nine months, in the spring of 1969, these two songs plus twenty-one others were included on a landmark avant-garde rock album called *Trout Mask Replica*. Of all the albums Zappa released on Straight Records, only Beefheart's is still available, despite having less widespread airplay on North American radio than any of Zappa's records. It never sold well. Its jagged rhythms and sharply atonal melodies shocked many listeners. Only those who would later create punk rock found a kindred spirit in the Captain's fearless originality.

The popular myth was that Beefheart composed all the songs on *Trout Mask Replica* at a piano in a remarkable eight-day span. Harkleroad begs to differ. "There were days and days when [Beefheart] and John French were pounding out parts," he recalls. "I don't mean to diminish [Beefheart]'s creativity or his view of the big picture, but he would play something and couldn't repeat it ten minutes later.... John would try to make him do that so he could write it. [Beefheart] was chiseling away at rhythmic shapes and sounds, and it wasn't done in any concise way where he had a direct vision of what he was going to come up with, other than the parts that the band was going to put together." Most of the control over how the music would be played came from French. Beefheart, who didn't attend rehearsals, would hear the parts and either express satisfaction over what he heard or tell the band to "fix it."

The band lived together in a house on Entrada Drive in the San Fernando Valley; they were so poor, they stole food. One time, they got caught and Zappa bailed them out of jail. Beefheart drove the guys hard, making them play twelve to fourteen hours a day. He was also "brainwashing" the band by keeping them talking for thirty-six hours straight. Zappa wanted to approach the album as an anthropological field recording, just as he had done with *An Evening With Wild Man Fischer*. Since Dick Kunc had a portable recording unit, they could treat the band's home as their studio. "I thought it would be great to go to Don's house with this portable rig and put the drums in the bedroom, the bass clarinet in the kitchen, and the vocals in the bathroom, complete isolation just like in a studio — except that the band members probably would feel more at home, since they *were* at home," Zappa recalled.

Some of the selections were recorded that way, but Beefheart accused Zappa — who was pleased with the recordings — of being cheap and demanded to use a studio. So Zappa moved the operation to Glendale, where they recorded the balance of the album in Whitney Studios. (Some of the "house" recordings were used on *Trout Mask*; the complete set is included in the five-disc rarities box set *Grow Fins*.) But the problems didn't end there. "The basic tracks were cut — now it was time for Don's vocals," Zappa wrote. "Ordinarily a singer goes in the studio, puts earphones on, listens to the track, tries to sing in time with it, and away you go. Don couldn't tolerate the earphones. He wanted to stand in the studio and sing as loud as he could — singing along with the audio leakage coming through the three panes of glass which comprised the control-room window. The chances of him staying in sync were nil — but that's the way the vocals were done."

Zappa described the sound as "claustrophobic." By Easter Sunday 1969, the album was edited and mixed. "I think that if he had been produced by any professional famous producer, there could have been a number of suicides involved," Zappa told Nigel Leigh. "I called him up and I said, 'The album's done,' and he made all the guys in the band get dressed up and they came over here early in the morning and sat in this [living] room and listened to it. And loved it."

Despite the frustrations of putting the album together, Zappa responded to the fusion of avant-garde jazz and Delta blues in Beefheart's sound. "You can really hear that influence," he told Dick Lawson of *Zig Zag*. "And it's perfectly blended into a new musical language. It's all his. And it bears no resemblance to anything anybody else is doing."

22

Trout Mask Replica begins with a charging guitar riff that crumbles the moment Beefheart breaks into song. "My smile is stuck/I cannot go back to yer frownland," he shouts in "Frownland." As he states his intentions for a new world, and a new music, the guitar notes fall aimlessly like raindrops to the ground:

> *My spirit's made up of the ocean*
> *And the sky 'n' the sun 'n' the moon*
> *'n' all my eye can see*
> *I cannot go back to yer land of gloom*
> *Where black jagged shadows*
> *Remind me of the comin' of yer doom.*

WHO NEEDS THE PEACE CORPS?

Beefheart's band doesn't give you melodies on which to hang your hat. "If the purpose of a phonograph record is to soothe us, to provide a beat for dancing, a pulse for making love, a set of themes to reassure us in the joys and troubles of life's daily commerce, then *Trout Mask* fails utterly," music critic Langdon Winner writes in *Stranded: Rock and Roll for a Desert Island*. "But if a record is legitimate in trying to overthrow our somnambulistic habits of hearing, seeing, and touching things, if it is valid in seeking to jolt our sensibilities and restructure the way we experience music and everything else, then Beefheart's strange collection of songs begins to make sense." *Trout Mask Replica* puts demands on the listener that go beyond mere taste — it demands a whole new way of listening. A song like "Steal Softly Thru Snow" has as romantic a sentiment as anything popular music could dream up:

The black paper between a mirror breaks my heart
The moon frayed thru dark velvet lightly apart
Steal softly thru sunshine
Steal softly thru snow.

Yet Beefheart doesn't provide a lulling melody to draw the listener into the meaning of the song; his tunes are boldly dissonant statements from a romantic who doesn't feel part of a harmonious landscape. "Beefheart's notion of musical liberty, however, requires the transcendence of all deeply rooted habits," Winner writes. "He refuses to use them in his playing. More importantly, he will not allow listeners to depend on them for satisfaction. . . . Is there *nothing* we can hold on to?" Well, there are plenty of things actually. The abstract recitations of "The Dust Blows Forward 'n' The Dust Blows Back" suggest Walt Whitman after a jug of hillbilly booze; "Orange Claw Hammer" is a wild and surreal sea chantey about familial longing; "Hair Pie: Bake 1," a slang reference to cunnilingus, is a free-form instrumental for sparring saxophones that owes something to Ornette Coleman's initial experiments in "free jazz." And "Ant Man Bee" is an ode to nature's cruel hierarchy:

Now the bee takes the honey
Then he sets the flower free
But in God's garden only
Man 'n' the ants
They won't let each other be.

Even though Zappa produced *Trout Mask Replica*, the only track that resembles anything by the Mothers is "The Blimp." While Zappa was in the studio, working on a piece of music by the Mothers, he received a phone call from Antennae Jimmy Semens, who wanted to recite some of Beefheart's lyrics. Zappa recorded the phone call while simultaneously laying Semens' voice over the Mothers' music. The effect of his slightly distorted, hyperbolic delivery brings to mind the famous radio report of the crash of that other blimp — the *Hindenburg*. But the lyrics themselves are another story:

The sumptin' hoop the sumptin' hoop
The blimp the blimp
The drazy hoops the drazy hoops
They're camp they're camp
Tits tits the blimp the blimp

The music Zappa laid these words over was a 1969 live recording of a new piece that featured a small quote from Charles Ives' *The Unanswered Question*. Another live version eventually showed up as an unreleased coda to the track, "Didja Get Any Onya?" on the CD release of *Weasels Ripped My Flesh* in 1990. A different rendition appears on Zappa's compendium, *You Can't Do That on Stage Anymore, Vol. 5*, under the title "Charles Ives." What Zappa did in the studio with Beefheart's "The Blimp" was nothing short of a Charles Ives musical meld.

Although as a producer, Zappa stayed out of Beefheart's way, he still managed to shape the album into a unified whole. Essentially, it's in the same sociological collage style as *An Evening With Wild Man Fischer* and *Permanent Damage*. These three albums represent far-ranging anthropological documentaries in which the music and the lifestyle of the artist are intertwined. Unlike conventional pop artists, who use music to carve their niche in the charts, Wild Man Fischer, the GTO's, and Captain Beefheart reveal themselves for who they truly are. *Trout Mask Replica*, however, is such a powerful individual statement about music, and Beefheart's own place in it, that it makes Fischer and the GTO's seem pleasantly capricious by comparison.

Zappa told *New Musical Express* in 1975 that Beefheart's approach to language was unique. "Of course, he has problems", said Zappa. "His memory causes him trouble. He won't be separated from his sheets of paper that have his words written

WHO NEEDS THE PEACE CORPS?

on. He clings to them for dear life . . . he does have this thing inside him. It's dynamic and he wants to express it. In a voice like Howlin' Wolf."

Trout Mask Replica was issued as a two-LP set in June 1969. Cal Schenkel's cover art, featuring Vliet with a mammoth hat and a fish face, was something of a collaborative effort. "I went and found this carp head at some fish market," Schenkel explained to Steven Cerio in *Seconds* magazine. "We took it back to my studio, which was the same place that I did the *Uncle Meat* cover . . . and I took this trout head and hollowed it out — the thing stank like hell — and Don had to hold it up to his face for a couple of hours while we shot."

Despite Beefheart's professed love of the album, though, he told the press he resented being marketed by Zappa "as a freak," alongside Wild Man Fischer and Alice Cooper. He also didn't think Zappa offered much support as a producer. But Zappa, who had tried to accommodate Beefheart in every way, defended his deference to Beefheart's demands. "[It] was difficult to produce because you couldn't explain, from a technical standpoint, anything to Don," Zappa told Nigel Leigh. "You couldn't tell him why things ought to be such and such a way. And it seemed to me that if he was going to create such a unique object, that the easiest thing for me to do was keep my mouth shut as much as possible, and just let him do whatever he wanted to do, whether I thought it was wrong or not."

On January 31, 1969, the Mothers had appeared on the first night of the Boston Globe Jazz Festival at the War Memorial Auditorium, on the same bill as B.B. King, Nina Simone, and Sun Ra. Zappa appeared with the blind jazz flautist and saxophonist Rahsaan Roland Kirk. Blinded shortly after his birth in 1936, Kirk had still managed to learn the clarinet and saxophone. As a teenager, Kirk developed a method by which he could play three reed instruments simultaneously. In time, Kirk would incorporate whistles, sirens, car horns, and other natural instruments into his compositions. Even if his roots were in New Orleans, he moved through swing and bebop into something completely his own. Zappa found Kirk's defiant individualism much to his liking. "We began our set, wending our atonal way toward a medley of 1950s-style honking, saxophone numbers," Zappa recalled. "During this fairly complicated, choreographed routine, [Roland], assisted by his helper . . . decided to join in." A reviewer for *Downbeat* was knocked out by the results: "Kirk sounded as raspy and earthy as he ever has. Zappa instantly picking up Kirk's concepts and playing telepathic guitar counterpoint . . . the audience was close to berserk.... Kirk and Zappa are crazy if they don't make a record together." Sadly, they never would.

In late May, the Mothers toured Europe again. This time they played venues throughout England, including Birmingham, Bristol, Portsmouth, Newcastle, and once again, the Royal Albert Hall. Pye Records, which distributed Warner Brothers albums in the U.K., refused to release *Uncle Meat* or *Lenny Bruce: The Berkeley Concert* because of "obscene" language. TransAtlantic Records ended up issuing both recordings but not until months after the Mothers had returned home. The botched distribution hurt the sales of both albums. As for the tour itself, from the moment Zappa and the Mothers touched ground in Great Britain, the disputatious residue of their last European tour followed them from town to town. On May 27, Zappa spoke to students at the London School of Economics, where he faced the same type of hostile reaction the band had received in Berlin a year earlier. "So here's a bunch of youthful British Leftists who take the same youthful Leftist view that is popular the world over," Zappa recalled. "It's like belonging to a car club... basing their principles on Marxist doctrine... and Mao ZeDong.... And they think that's the basis for conducting a revolution that's going to liberate the common man. Meanwhile, they don't even know any common men.... I told them what they were into was just the equivalent of this year's flower power. A couple of years before those same schmucks were wandering around with incense and bells in the park... because they heard that that was what was happening in San Francisco."

The students weren't impressed that, although Zappa was sympathetic to the concerns of young people, he was vehemently antidrugs. They were also shocked to discover his support of advertising. "Today, a revolution can be accomplished by means of mass media, with technical advances that Madison Avenue is using to sell you washing machines and a loaf of bread," Zappa informed them. "This can be used to change the world around — painlessly."

In the *Daily Mail*, columnist Victoria Ironside eloquently expressed the divergence between Zappa and the students in Britain: "In the States, the Mothers, for all their freakishness, are dug by middle-class kids with short hair who rebel against their parents. Here, misled by their appearance and their music which is definitely in the progressive pop bag, they're heroes of the Underground who are fast getting confused [about] where their loyalties lie."

That confusion continued when the Mothers reached Royal Albert Hall on June 6, and the audience was restless throughout the concert. At the end of the

WHO NEEDS THE PEACE CORPS?

show, after performing a hurdy-gurdy version of a chamber work called "Aybe Sea," Zappa informed the crowd that if they sat down and kept quiet, the group would do a version of "Brown Shoes Don't Make It." While some in the audience applauded, small skirmishes started to break out as the attendants urged people back to their seats. One guy yelled abuse at the band, annoyed that Zappa was reluctant to do anything about the uniforms guarding the stage. Zappa calmly pointed out, "Everyone in this room is wearing a uniform and don't kid yourself." Yet the guy continued to complain — in even more exasperating tones. Zappa finally replied, "You'll hurt your throat. Stop it!" (This exchange would be included a year later *Burnt Weeny Sandwich*.)

"The same kids who a year ago were wandering around with beads and all that gear are now yelling 'Kick out the jams!' Zappa told *Beat Instrumental*. "They are at the mercy of the establishment when they act like that. The establishment looks at these kids and sees they are not going to do anything, but if a guy comes into the office and acts on his choice to try and change it, they are going to be hard-pressed to stop it."

Zappa also had business-related difficulties as the '60s drew to a close. Besides the problem of distribution in England, Straight was having similar headaches in the U.S. An independent company, they were finding that their product was difficult to locate in many record stores. By December, Straight and Bizarre had to rely completely on Warner Brothers and its subsidiary label, Reprise Records, for all production and distribution rights. Zappa was also frustrated that his songs were not getting played on the radio.

The Mothers spent some studio time at Criteria in Miami recording potential singles, including the shimmering pop beauty "My Guitar Wants to Kill Your Mama," plus an exquisite cover of Jackie & the Starlites' early-'60s doo-wop weepie, "Valerie," for the B-side. They also put together some tracks that didn't arrive until years later — "Chucha," "German Lunch" (a colorful and amusing piece with Lowell George imitating a German border guard interrogating the band as they enter the country), and "Right There," a gleefully ribald song featuring Roy Estrada's high falsetto in blissful abandon.

The genesis of "Right There" started with Bunk Gardner, who followed his boss's example of social documentation. Gardner had made a field recording of himself having sex with a young woman he met on tour. "While in Columbus, Ohio, and playing a club called the High Low Spot, I met a couple of young girls, Sandy and Peggy, and we became good friends," Gardner remembered fondly.

"After I left Ohio, I found out Peggy was living in Florida. I don't remember how many times I went down to see her. She was pretty vocal, and it was just a lark that I recorded it." When Zappa heard the tape, it must have brought back a host of memories from his Cucamonga bust with Lorraine Belcher at Studio Z. He configured an existing piece called "Skweezit Skweezit Skweezit" (found on the *Mystery Disc* CD) around Bunk's sex tape by adding Estrada's ecstatic vocals.

When they performed "Right There" live, Estrada would add new phrases to "Skweezit Skweezit Skweezit" like "Right there, Bunk!, Oh God, right there, oh God, Bunk! Yes! Yes!" The piece was performed live during the Mothers' 1969 tour. It was a close cousin to "Prelude to the Afternoon of a Sexually Aroused Gas Mask," later featured on *Weasels Ripped My Flesh*.

After the 1969 tour, there was much ill will in the band. Many in the group felt that it wasn't really the Mothers of Invention — it was just Zappa and his backup band. "Frank borrows a lot of music from a lot of players that are in the group," a disenchanted Lowell George told author David Walley. "Don [Preston] has been ripped off all along. A lot of the chord passages are Donny's concepts that Frank borrowed. Frank's attitude is, 'The guy plays in my group . . . sure I can borrow anything from him.'" George would be fired by Zappa later that year over his drug use. But friend Bill Payne, future keyboard player for Little Feat, cited another reason. Lowell had written a song about a trucker's ode to the road that also celebrated the narcotics needed to make the journey. "Lowell was taken out of the Mothers because of the song 'Willin',"' Payne explained. "I think Frank was both impressed and put off by the song, because of the drug reference — he was somewhat conservative on certain levels. He was afraid of the very thing that bit the hippie movement in the ass, which was the craziness of what would happen to people when they got fried on drugs — like Charles Manson."

Art Tripp was also growing fed up with what he saw as Zappa's autocratic nature. "His entire hazy half-assed concept is the sum total of each individual thievery," Tripp told Walley. Zappa, however, was becoming unhappy for a whole other set of reasons. Paying each member of the group a $200 weekly salary fell completely on his shoulders. And since the band wasn't getting any airplay on the radio or royalties from MGM/Verve, Zappa found himself $10,000 in the red. It also didn't help that album sales were bad due to poor distribution. This all came to a head that summer during a short East Coast tour organized by George Wein, the former organizer of the Newport Jazz Festival, who teamed the Mothers once again with Roland Kirk, Gary Burton, and Duke Ellington.

WHO NEEDS THE PEACE CORPS?

On a hot June day in South Carolina, Zappa suddenly realized that the Mothers were being used as bait to get the young audience out to hear jazz. They were playing venues where the best amplification they could get was small jukebox speakers with thirty-watt capacity circling the audience. It was also 95 degrees outside, with 200 per cent humidity inside. But the worst indignation for Zappa, as an artist and composer, was watching Ellington backstage begging the road manager for a ten-dollar advance.

After that show, Zappa told the group he'd had enough. "I was paying everybody in the band a weekly salary of two hundred dollars — all year round, whether we were working or not, along with all hotel and travel expenses when we did get work," Zappa recalled. "The guys in the band were pissed off — as if their welfare had been cancelled." Don Preston felt there were much deeper artistic reasons for Zappa's decision to dissolve the group. "I think Zappa was dissatisfied with some of the performances of the band, the limited nature of some of the people like Roy Estrada and Jimmy Carl Black who couldn't read music. They did play some very complicated stuff, but it just wasn't complicated enough. Zappa wanted the very best sight-readers in the world to read his music."

Zappa's assessment of the group was more generous and thoughtful in a piece he wrote for *Hit Parader* in April 1970:

> The Mothers set new standards for performance. In terms of pure musicianship, theatrical presentation, formal concept, and sheer absurdity, this one ugly band demonstrated to the music industry that it was indeed possible to make the performance of electric music a valid artistic expression. The Mothers managed to perform in alien time signatures and bizarre harmonic climates with a subtle ease that led many to believe it was all happening in 4/4 with a teenage backbeat.... It is possible that, at a later date, when audiences have properly assimilated the recorded work of the group, a reformation might take place.

Motorhead Sherwood, whose friendship with Zappa dated back to the early experiments in Studio Z, elaborated on Zappa's sentiment. "It was getting to the point that I think Frank wasn't going in the direction he wanted to, wasn't being as creative as he wanted to," Motorhead told Nigel Leigh. "So that's basically how we disbanded. He just got tired and said, 'Hey, guys, let's go out into other groups, let's infiltrate other bands, and let's get some fresh ideas. You guys come back, and maybe we'll get together three or four years down the line, bring in your ideas from the groups you have, and let's get back together and do something.' But it just never happened."

The former Mothers tried to reform without Zappa in early 1970, even hiring Tom Wilson to produce, but the session went nowhere. Don Preston went on to work with performance artist Meredith Monk; Jimmy Carl Black formed the rock band Geronimo Black with Bunk and Buzz Gardner, releasing a solid album called *Geronimo Black* for Uni Records; Art Tripp joined Captain Beefheart's Magic Band under the name Ed Marimba; and Roy Estrada joined Lowell George in forming Little Feat.

"When a guy is in the band, he's got a little something going for him," Zappa explained philosophically in 1982 while in the middle of a lawsuit launched by the ex-Mothers for perceived royalties owed. "He's got the security of the band paying his salary, he's got a licence to be as weird as he can be onstage because he knows that his ass is covered — because I take the rap for what's going on there. . . . When a guy leaves the band, he loses that licence. He has to take the rap for his own behavior. . . . Now they have to take responsibility for who they actually are. And who and what they actually are is not what they were." Which is why there would be no Mothers of Invention reunion. Those unshorn days of the '60s, filled with utopian dreams and satirized by the Mothers with razor-sharp precision, had come to an end. The '70s would become something of a shell-shocked decade, or maybe a hangover from the heady '60s.

Many tried to escape the fallout from the crash of the counterculture by retreating, recanting, or retiring permanently. Zappa would be there — through it all — to account for all the casualties. Even if, in a certain sense, he'd end up becoming one himself.

CHAPTER FOUR

I'M THE SLIME

(1969-1980)

I have been called a misanthrope, but I prefer curmudgeon; it's folksier and less threatening. Misanthrope sounds like you'd have to have gone to college to be one.

FRANK ZAPPA

What in the '60s looked like a chance to find new forms of political life, has been replaced by a flight to privacy and cynicism; the shared culture that grew out of a love affair with the Beatles has collapsed . . . into nostalgia and crackpot religion . . . within such a culture there are many choices: cynicism, which is a smug, fraudulent kind of pessimism; the sort of camp sensibility that puts all feeling at a distance, or a culture that re-assures counterfeit excitement and adventure, and is safe . . . sometimes though, you want something more: work so intense and compelling you will risk chaos to get close to it.

GREIL MARCUS, *Mystery Train*

1

Frank Zappa wrote in his liner notes for *We're Only in It for the Money*: "The whole monstrosity was conceived and edited by Frank Zappa as a result of some unpleasant premonitions . . . all premonitions continuing to come true." In 1968, could Zappa have anticipated the sinister aura that would encompass the Nixon years in America during the '70s? Those years carried an acrid aroma of paranoia and dread, making a travesty of the democratic process. If the Lyndon Johnson era bore witness to a country splintering over Vietnam, racial inequity, and assassination, Richard Nixon was the duplicitous force who brought in severely repressive measures under the guise of law and order. He also played, rather shrewdly, into the latent fears of the middle class by appealing to those he called the "Silent Majority." These ordinary Americans, disenchanted with the excesses of the counterculture, had grown tired of the violence and chaos and wanted order restored at any cost. Yet it was Nixon who would continue the Vietnam War, order the bombing of Cambodia, and, by 1973, create COINTELPRO. This highly elaborate intelligence network was designed to spy on citizens suspected of having connections to subversive political organizations. Its mission was to infiltrate those groups and create dissent and disloyalty.

"There were police spies constantly," poet and political activist Allen Ginsberg told this author in 1982. "They were spreading disinformation. If there was going to be a peace march, the spy would call in and report that it was happening at a different time, and in a different place. There were anonymous letters sent from a 'concerned taxpayer' or a 'concerned citizen' — or even better — a 'concerned student.' *The Great Speckled Bird*, an underground newspaper in Atlanta, was put on trial for obscenity. They won the case but it drained the paper of money because they were operating on a shoestring. The FBI also had landlords raise the rent for these places by telling them that subversives lived and worked there. It was a great network of conspiracy which reduced the number of underground publications from four hundred in 1968 to sixty in 1975."

Zappa would tell Don Menn in 1993 that concealing COINTELPRO was the real purpose of the Watergate break-in on June 17, 1972. "It wasn't just breaking into the Democratic headquarters," Zappa explained. "What they were trying to cover up is the fact that Nixon had decided to create a secret police. There was no legal authority to spy on U.S. citizens. He felt he had enemies everywhere, so he created a program called COINTELPRO."

Before the pervading gloom of the '70s settled in, however, Zappa still had some unfinished business with the '60s. There remained recordings by the Mothers of Invention yet to be issued. Initially, he tried to work out a deal with *Playboy* for the creation of a Mothers of Invention Record Club. Zappa would put out twelve albums — both studio and live material — ranging from the days at Studio Z to the present. The titles included *Before the Beginning, The Cucamonga*

I'M THE SLIME

Era, Show and Tell, What Does It All Mean, Rustic Protrusion, Several Boogie, The Merely Entertaining Mothers of Invention Record, The Heavy Business Record, Soup and Old Clothes, Hotel Dixie, The Orange County Lumber Truck, and *The Weasel Music*. The deal fell through, even though much of the material was eventually released.

Back in Los Angeles in August 1969, after the ill-fated tour that broke up the band, Zappa focused his attention on the production of his second solo album. He first called Ian Underwood to help out. Underwood, who had recently married Ruth Komanoff, had been looking to form a jazz band, but he changed gear with Zappa's request. Zappa also contacted veteran West Coast session men like bass player Max Bennett, and drummers John Guerin and Paul Humphrey, as well as Shuggie Otis, an accomplished blues guitarist who happened to be the son of bandleader Johnny Otis. Violinist Don "Sugarcane" Harris, late of Don & Dewey and a friend of the Otis clan, also joined up. "To me, he was a legend," Zappa told Rip Rense for the liner notes to *The Lost Episodes*. "I had records he made in high school. 'Soul Motion,' a favorite of mine, had a mean-ass blues violin solo. While making the *Hot Rats* LP, I thought, 'Wouldn't it be great if I could find that guy and put him on the album?' Since Johnny Otis was a DJ from that period and music, I called him. He found Harris in jail — he was in on a drug bust — and we bailed him out."

The other violinist who would make a cameo appearance on the album was Jean-Luc Ponty. While on tour in the U.S. in 1969, the French-born Ponty formed a small band that recorded two albums on World Pacific Jazz. "The producer, [Dick Bock], wanted me to do something different," Ponty recalled in *Le Jazz*. "He was a very open-minded man, a Buddhist before it was trendy. He introduced me to Ravi Shankar's music, for example, but he had also signed all the West Coast jazz musicians. He decided he wanted me to meet musicians from outside the jazz world — [like Frank Zappa] for example."

"I'd heard more and more about Frank Zappa in jazz circles," recalled Bock. "Then Frank played me some of the *Hot Rats* album, which he was still working on. It was hard to pigeonhole; just fascinating instrumental music. Then I took an acetate of Jean-Luc to Frank's house. A few days later Jean-Luc played on a *Hot Rats* track ['It Must Be a Camel']."

Hot Rats surprisingly abandoned the *musique concrète* and Dada intrusions of the previous Mothers albums, perhaps as a result of the influence on Zappa of Roland Kirk. It is a vibrant and stunningly rich rock 'n' roll album that not only highlighted Zappa's immense skill as a guitarist, but also emphasized the gifted soloists he brought on board. The record would, in time, achieve the dubious honor of being considered the first Frank Zappa album bought by those who didn't like Frank Zappa albums.

"The real reason for *Hot Rats* was to do the overdubbing," Zappa told Neil Slaven, "because I don't think there'd been anything outside the early experiments of [guitarist] Les Paul where there was that much overdubbage applied to a piece of tape. We were using a primitive, maybe even a prototype 16-track recorder for that. So it was the first time we could really pile on tracks. I think that that album is more about overdubbing that it is about anything else."

Hot Rats was a masterpiece of overdubbing — Zappa created the illusion of having a whole rock orchestra backing him, when most of the instruments were played by him and Underwood. Zappa described *Hot Rats* as "a movie for the ears," but as fitting as that description is, the album also captures much of the rhythmic sophistication and color of Stravinsky's scores. The sonic complexities in the overdubbing, barely perceivable on the LP, wouldn't be fully appreciated until the remixed CD arrived in 1987. Opening track "Peaches en Regalia," featuring Shuggie Otis on bass, is a kaleidoscopic merry-go-round with horns, keyboards, and percussion happily interacting. The tune became so popular that Zappa released it on two subsequent live albums, *Fillmore East, June 1971* and *Tinsel Town Rebellion* (1981). "Willie the Pimp" is a powerfully compelling blues song — and the only vocal track on the album. Given that it *is* a blues number, it seemed only natural that it should feature Captain Beefheart. A solo violin intro by Sugarcane Harris quickly states the theme, as Zappa's churning guitar checks in underneath. Captain Beefheart, with his characteristic growl, introduces Willie:

> *I'm a little pimp with my hair gassed back*
> *Pair of khaki pants and my shoes shined black.*
> *Got a little lady, walk that street*
> *Telling all the boys, she can't be beat.*
> *Twenny dollar bill, I can set you straight*
> *Meet me on the corner, boy, and don't be late.*

Willie is a slick figure standing in front of the Lido Hotel in New York, commenting on how "the floozies love the way I sell: HOT MEAT, HOT RATS, HOT ZITS, HOT WRISTS. . . ." Beefheart's voice is filled with libidinous glee when he sings, "Man in a

I'M THE SLIME

suit with a bow-tie neck/Want to buy a grunt with a third-party check." The Captain's appearance is only a brief cameo (featuring in the first two minutes of this nine-minute tour de force) — the remainder is the first full-blown platform for Zappa's guitar pyrotechnics since "Invocation and Ritual Dance of the Young Pumpkin," on *Absolutely Free*. What makes "Willie the Pimp" so astonishingly fresh and inventive, though, is the way Zappa builds the solo on a variety of conceptual ideas rather than just jamming endlessly.

"Son of Mr. Green Genes" is an augmented instrumental version of "Mr. Green Genes" from *Uncle Meat*, but it's played at a quicker tempo, and the orchestral cast is more spirited. This highly contrapuntal piece sustains itself purely on its own momentum and invention. Zappa and Underwood push it forward by piling endless musical bricks on a deep rhythmic foundation. "Little Umbrellas," propelled by Underwood's elegant keyboard work, is a lovely, quaint ballad, with some of the shimmering beauty of one of Erik Satie's piano pieces. The title comes from a bowl of umbrellas Zappa saw in the Royal Garden Hotel in London, but it may also be a tribute to Satie's vast collection.

"The Gumbo Variations" is a vehicle for some energetic soloing — bubbling with drive and enthusiasm for over sixteen minutes. The main theme is stated by both Zappa and Underwood (alto sax), before Underwood grunts and growls, as if tearing through the sheets of music. When Sugarcane Harris joins in, "The Gumbo Variations" starts to soar on waves of harshly played notes cascading over Paul Humphrey's polyrhythmic drumming. Harris had never played with more force than he did on Zappa's recordings. The rough, piercing quality of his performances here were in sharp contrast to the sweet, lyrical recordings he did with blues artists like John Mayall and Sonny Terry & Brownie McGhee. For Zappa, Harris worked with all the force of a hurricane determined to blow a house down.

"It Must Be a Camel" has some of the same grandeur of "Little Umbrellas." Although Jean-Luc-Ponty's contributions are small, he provides a beautifully serene tone that contrasts with the Varèsian percussion surrounding him.

The cover art by Cal Schenkel (done in the same psychedelic pinks he used on Beefheart's *Trout Mask Replica*) features Christine Frka climbing out of a pit in a backyard. On the inside cover, among the many Zappa photos, is a shot of Beefheart holding a portable vacuum cleaner. (His fascination with this household appliance apparently derives from a time when he worked as a door-to-door Hoover salesman. In his brief tenure in this odd occupation, he once successfully sold a new model to novelist Aldous Huxley. When Huxley initially expressed ambivalence about purchasing one of these beauties, Beefheart told him simply, "I can assure you, sir, that these things really suck.") *Hot Rats* is a breathtaking fusion of musical genres. There's no doubt its pure invention made the album a success in the end. When it was released in October 1969, it reached only No. 99 in the charts, but over the years its popularity has been sustained by the many who feel it's Zappa's best work.

2

On September 5, 1969, the second Zappa child, Dweezil, named after the designation for one of Gail's toes, came into the world. He might have had an easy delivery — if not for the problems that arose because of his name. Gail had opted for natural childbirth, and the only facility in Los Angeles to offer this (with Frank present in the delivery room) was the Hollywood Presbyterian Hospital. They were filling out an endless series of forms when they ran into serious difficulties. The admitting nurse simply wouldn't accept the Zappas giving their child such an unusual name. With Gail going through the agony of labor pains, the nurse just stood there pleading with them to reconsider. To get Gail admitted, Zappa reluctantly put down the names Ian Donald Calvin Euclid (after band members and associates), and the nurse was finally content. At the age of five, Dweezil would demand that his birth certificate contain his real name. "People make a lot of fuss about my kids having such supposedly 'strange names,'" Zappa wrote. "But the fact is that no matter what first names I might have given them, it's *the last name* that is going to get them in trouble."

After *Hot Rats* came out, Zappa served as road manager for Captain Beefheart & His Magic Band at the Amougies Pop Festival in the fall of 1969. After numerous festival sites were rejected, it was finally held in a turnip field near Amougies, just across the border in Belgium. The three-day festival featured a wide variety of artists including Soft Machine, jazz saxophonist Archie Shepp (who in 1984 would appear live with Zappa in Amherst, Massachusetts), Terry Riley, the Aynsley Dunbar Retaliation, and Pink Floyd (who Zappa would jam with on their guitar-driven "Interstellar Overdrive"). Zappa had the honor of acting as an MC, in the freezing cold, introducing and playing with several bands. Late into the evening, while the crowd was huddled and snoozing in sleeping bags, the Art Ensemble of Chicago decided to give everyone a wakeup call. "Here comes the Art Ensemble of

I'M THE SLIME

Chicago, [and] one guy lights a highway flare, they start playing, and he throws it in the middle of these sleeping people," Zappa told Neil Slaven. "And a few of them woke up because their things were on fire. . . . I think the real reason I ended up going there in a cosmic sense was to finally wind up with [drummer] Aynsley Dunbar in the band." Zappa sat in with Dunbar's band and compared notes on other groups. It would be another year, though, before they'd play together again. (footage from Amougies of Captain Beefheart's devastating version of "My Human Gets Me Blues" appears on the box set *Grow Fins*.)

November saw the release (on Straight Records) of the GTO's *Permanent Damage*, and Jeff Simmons' *Lucille Has Messed My Mind Up*. Simmons was the former bass player with a Seattle bar band called Easy Chair. Zappa produced *Lucille*, writing the title song, as well as playing some stinging Johnny "Guitar" Watson licks on the track. He also co-wrote with Simmons the song "Wonderful Wino," which Zappa would also include on his solo album *Zoot Allures* (1976). In his rock opera *Joe's Garage*, Zappa would rearrange "Lucille Has Messed My Mind Up" from its bluesy origins into a reggae waltz. Simmons would also join Zappa's band, along with Aynsley Dunbar, within the year.

Zappa finally began shooting footage for *Uncle Meat*. During the previous summer, he had abandoned the plot that was included in the album's liner notes when he couldn't get the financial backing to do the special effects in Japan. As an alternative, he came up with the idea of doing a chronicle of the group, exploring why it developed its following and mythology. The film would include footage from the Berlin riot in 1968, excerpts from the Festival Hall concert from the same tour, and home-movie footage of the Mothers on the road. Zappa also devised a "plot" that involved Don Preston, as the Monster from Festival Hall, becoming the obsession of Phyllis Altenhous, the film's assistant editor. There were also scenes shot of Zolar Czakl (Cal Schenkel) and Motorhead Sherwood jamming on appliances in a supermarket, a pool game between some band members, and Zappa's brother Carl (who inexplicably keeps reminding everyone that he's using the "[rubber] chicken to measure it."). That material was shot — free of cost — by legendary cinematographer Haskell Wexler.

By the time *Uncle Meat* was released on home video in 1987, it was a rambling, inchoate work. Where Zappa's music would become a movie for your ears, his films didn't become music for your eyes. His visual imagination worked most strongly in his scores, where he could animate the sound of the instrumentalists and the timbre of the vocalists. The scope of his musical arrangements gave the work a powerfully distinct vitality. Using the musicians as "dramatic" characters just didn't create the same force on the screen that the sound of their performing did on record. It might be argued that the *Uncle Meat* album is the *real* movie. (*200 Motels*, his first theatrical feature, would be plagued with some of the same problems in 1971.)

The movie *Uncle Meat* did have one thing going for it: an examination of Zappa's idea that time was a continuum. But the failed ambition of the film was simply a matter of content that couldn't carry the weight of the audacious conceptual ideas Zappa brought to the work.

Another obvious problem that hampered the production was the acrimonious breakup of the band. Few members of the original group (except for Preston and Sherwood) wanted to be interviewed on-camera. "Four of the guys decided they wanted to have nothing whatsoever to do with any of the projects," Zappa recalled. "That radically changed my plans for that week's shooting, which I had all blocked out. So two days before we were supposed to go — we had already hired the crew and I had the lights and the [film] stock bought and all that shit — to the tune of maybe $12,000 for the week. Even though Haskell was free, the stuff that goes with him costs you some money." Because of that lack of funding, only forty minutes of material was assembled, the rest to be completed in the early '80s.

In January 1970, Jean-Luc Ponty released an album of Frank Zappa's music on the World Pacific Jazz label. *King Kong: Jean-Luc Ponty Plays the Music of Frank Zappa* was recorded during the *Hot Rats* sessions conceived as an instrumental record. "Thanks to my classical background, I had no trouble with any of the written music," Ponty told *Le Jazz*. "It was a very interesting experience. [Zappa and I] were curious about each other. He was interested in jazz and above all in contemporary classical music. He was very interested by my mix of a classical background and the ability to improvise. That's why he called me later to ask me to join his group."

King Kong featured the title track, "Idiot Bastard Son," "America Drinks and Goes Home," and the unreleased "Twenty Small Cigars." Ponty wrote one track called "How Would You Like to Have a Head Like That?" that featured a cameo appearance by Zappa on guitar. A long orchestral piece, integrating quotes from "Duke of Prunes" and "A Pound for a Brown (On the Bus)," was also included. Zappa had asked Dick Bock for a ninety-seven-piece orchestra to play it, but the budget would allow for only eleven musicians. As a result, the scaled-down epic would be titled "Music for Electric Violin and Low Budget Orchestra."

I'M THE SLIME

King Kong did more than just kickstart a temporary mutual admiration society between Ponty and Zappa — it also introduced Zappa to a few players who would later join his band: first and foremost, jazz pianist George Duke. Duke had led a vocal group during the late '60s called the Third Wave, and had further honed his skills with seasoned pros like Dizzy Gillespie and vibes wizard Bobby Hutcherson. Duke's first solo album was *Presented by the Jazz Workshop* (1966), a smooth Latin-flavored record that lacked the R&B direction of his later work. Once Duke heard Ponty playing at a Los Angeles nightclub, he bombarded him with tapes and letters expressing his interest. They first worked together in 1969, when Ponty joined the George Duke Trio to record *Live in Los Angeles*. Zappa jammed with Duke and Ponty at Thee Experience club in L.A., just before *Hot Rats*, so it was a natural for Zappa and Ponty to suggest Duke for *King Kong* when the sessions were planned.

Zappa had also asked for bass player Buell Neidlinger, who had built his reputation in the '50s with avant-garde jazz pianist Cecil Taylor and arranger Gil Evans. The opening bassoon ostinato in "Music for Electric Violin and Low Budget Orchestra" is by Don Christlieb, "one of the best bassoonists around, especially for the avant-garde," Zappa recalled. "He has played Stockhausen and does regular concerts of contemporary music." They also brought seasoned West Coast session men on board, like sax player Ernie Watts (who would later play on Zappa's *Grand Wazoo*) and drummer John Guerin. Zappa included a couple of ex-Mothers, Art Tripp and Ian Underwood.

The resulting fusion made for a lively and skillfully performed record — even if it lacked the edge and excitement of a Mothers album. Duke's playing has some great swing, and Ponty performs a couple of solos that really sing (especially on "Idiot Bastard Son"). The album, though, has an impersonal studio-session quality, creating the impression of a group of talented people who don't want to risk stepping on each other's toes.

After the release of *King Kong*, Zappa put together a small touring ensemble consisting of Max Bennett on bass, Ian Underwood on saxes, Sugarcane Harris on violin, and Aynsley Dunbar on drums. Dunbar had played in a variety of bands, including Jeff Beck and the John Mayall Blues Band, before forming the Aynsley Dunbar Retaliation. "Aynsley has a rhythmic concept that none of my other drummers have had," Zappa told Kathy Orloff of *The Hollywood Reporter* in 1970. "If I get it off, then he's with me and the others just stand there."

In the pursuit of that dynamic rhythm section, Dunbar found in Zappa a willing participant. "He liked fire in playing, and when I was playing there was always fire — I was always moving and always kicking ass," Dunbar recalled. "When Frank took off, I took off."

That same month, Zappa screened a twenty-minute film called *Burnt Weeny Sandwich* at San Fernando Valley State College. The movie, featuring the Mothers in Germany during their 1968 tour, inspired Zappa to again try to resuscitate *Captain Beefheart vs. the Grunt People*, but he got only as far as recording some recitations with Beefheart. These included a hilariously self-mocking turn called "I'm a Band Leader," which parodied Zappa's days in the lounge clubs. Beefheart also read a piece called "The Grand Wazoo," which poked fun at what Zappa called "anybody in those lodge organizations with a stupid hat on." Both of these tracks would eventually appear on *The Lost Episodes*, with "The *Grand Wazoo*" reading wedded to a synclavier composition recorded in 1992.

After playing the San Diego Sports Arena in late February, the combo performed the Los Angeles Olympic Auditorium on March 7, where a bootlegger recorded the show. Two tracks from this show appear on the bootleg CD box set *Apocrypha*. The first is the achingly beautiful "Directly From My Heart to You," a cover of one of Little Richard's best (and least known) '50s R&B numbers. The version performed in Los Angeles is slower, but Sugarcane Harris captures the longing in Richard's voice, and the scratching sound of his electric violin echoes the song's passionate pleas. The second track from *Apocrypha* is "Twinkle Tits," essentially a variation on "Return of the Hunch-Back Duke," an unreleased piece from the 1969 Mothers' live repertoire. It resembles some of the music on *Hot Rats* — its ingeniousness comes from the way the performers' solos are orchestrated. "Twinkle Tits" would soon find a new identity as "Little House I Used to Live In" on the first posthumously released Mothers of Invention record named — after Zappa's short film — *Burnt Weeny Sandwich*.

Burnt Weeny Sandwich, released in February 1970, is one of the more underrated Mothers albums. Like *Uncle Meat*, it is basically an instrumental collection with a couple of doo-wop songs thrown in, but it doesn't have the same dramatic shifts in texture that *Uncle Meat* has. The pleasures found in *Burnt Weeny Sandwich* are more subtle, which may be why it's rarely mentioned and generally dismissed. It possesses some of the elegance of a chamber work, but without sacrificing any of Zappa's proclivity for musical satire.

Zappa opens and closes *Burnt Weeny Sandwich* with two classic doo-wop songs that — literally — sandwich some of the Mothers' more dexterous workouts. "WPLJ" is a cover of the 1955 R&B hit by the Four Deuces. The song's title stands

I'M THE SLIME

for "white port lemon juice", a potent West Coast beverage used to achieve quick and cheap sexual stimulation. Ironically, Swiss Colony, a wine company, had adopted it as a jingle to sell their product. Even if the company didn't fully get the meaning of the tune, "WPLJ" has all the rousing gaiety of a party singalong. In the Mothers' version, Zappa takes the lead vocal (along with the uncredited Lowell George) while the band does the doo-wop backing — Roy Estrada answers Zappa's exclamations with his beautifully wacky falsettos. At the conclusion of the song, Estrada launches into a patter of nonstop Spanish, gleefully exhorting his buddy, Motorhead, to try the drink. "Why don't you buy a wine to make you more attractive to fuck?" Estrada asks in his native tongue with ticklish merriment.

"Igor's Boogie, Phase One" is a brief horn ostinato that serves as a playful homage to Igor Stravinsky (the repeating melodic figure of the ostinato played a huge part in *The Rite of Spring*). Given Zappa's love of trashy horror movies, the title might also suggest Dr. Frankenstein's pet assistant — either way, the track stubbornly mates high and low culture. "Overture to a Holiday in Berlin" is a refurbished excerpt from Zappa's score to *The World's Greatest Sinner*, arranged here into a twisted tribute to Kurt Weill. The piece also ironically references the Berlin riots during the 1968 European tour.

"Theme From Burnt Weeny Sandwich," written for his short film, abruptly breaks into the conclusion of the "Overture" with the percussive sound of a wooden spatula hitting a pan. Zappa's electric guitar rises slowly out of the mix, while the percussion instruments battle for space around him. The collision of the various types of drums are reminiscent of "Nine Types of Industrial Pollution" from *Uncle Meat*, but Zappa's use of the wah-wah pedal gives the piece a texture closer in spirit to *Hot Rats*.

A very brief reprise of "Igor's Boogie, Phase Two" (including beeping horns and squawking dolls in honor of Spike Jones) follows before the band segues into the fully orchestrated version of "Holiday in Berlin, Full Blown." The composition is picturesque and hilarious, with the band sounding like they are drunkenly entertaining patrons in a German beer hall. Halfway through, the song settles into a lengthy guitar solo that was obviously recorded from a live event. Up until now, Zappa had included concert recordings only on *Uncle Meat*, and they were kept separate from the studio material. Here, for the first time, he mixes the live and studio recordings in the same piece of music. "Holiday in Berlin, Full Blown" moves seamlessly from the full band in the studio to Zappa's live solo, creating the effect of melting away time and location.

At the conclusion of the piece, Zappa, onstage, calls out to the band for the next track, "Aybe Sea." But what follows is not the live version of "Aybe Sea," but a studio recording. "Aybe Sea" is a beautiful chamber piece for harpsichord, piano, and acoustic guitar that features some lovely interplay between Zappa and Underwood. The tone is entirely different from their energetic work on *Hot Rats*. The piece ends with Underwood's solo piano tinkling into the higher registers until the ear can barely acknowledge its presence — and then Underwood and his piano abruptly vanish.

"The Little House I Used to Live In," an epic that runs close to twenty minutes, picks up where "Aybe Sea" left off. Underwood does a solo introduction on the piano, until the band (again from a live recording) state the main theme, known as "The Return of the Hunchback Duke." As this bouncing melody ends in slowly drawn-out feedback, Sugarcane Harris brings it all back together with a billowing solo that's matched only by the polish of Don Preston's brief piano improvisation. After a short but stately interlude by the band, a wild organ solo by Zappa finally delivers that live version of "Aybe Sea" that we heard him announce earlier. As it concludes, Zappa has a discursive exchange with a fan, promising that the group will attempt a version of "Brown Shoes Don't Make It." We never get to hear it. Instead, we're bounced right back into the studio — and back in time — to a cover of Jackie & the Starlites' 1960 doo-wop gem, "Valerie."

When Jackie & the Starlites performed "Valerie" in the early '60s, at the Apollo Theatre in Harlem, lead singer Jackie Rue would fall to his knees, delivering the tune with melodramatic histrionics. The band members would cover him with capes and carry him from the stage, while the crowd went wild. Zappa's version is done without the tears and hyperbole. He sings the lead with much more earnest emotion than Jackie Rue, and his crisp electric guitar traces the melody with a pure reverence. Roy Estrada's falsettos don't parody Jackie Rue's tears, either; they contrast Zappa's plaintive reading of the song. Although the tune was released as a single, it vanished. With proper attention, it could have been a commercial hit.

Burnt Weeny Sandwich features one of Cal Schenkel's customary collage covers, with bits and pieces of electronic and hand-painted objects, but this art was originally intended for a different album. "*Burnt Weeny Sandwich* was done much earlier for another project when we were still in New York," Schenkel told *Seconds* in 1995. "[Zappa and I] were going to be supplying advertising and packaging for a little label that Alan Douglas was starting [called] Moop. There were some ads done —

I'M THE SLIME

crazy comic-strip stuff, very surrealistic. *Burnt Weeny Sandwich* was originally done for an Eric Dolphy album. Then at the last minute Alan Douglas backed out. . . . I was out of the picture and [Zappa] had this nice piece of art and decided to use it for *Burnt Weeny Sandwich*."

3

In May, Zappa finally had the opportunity to get a symphony orchestra to perform his music. It was arranged through a friend, the gifted film composer David Raksin (*Laura, The Bad and the Beautiful*). Earlier that year, Zappa had discussed with Raksin his difficulties in getting his orchestral music performed. As a way to open up an opportunity, Raksin had Zappa join him as he interviewed conductor Zubin Mehta of the Los Angeles Philharmonic Orchestra for KPFK-FM in Los Angeles. After the interview, Raksin introduced Zappa to Mehta, and Mehta commissioned Zappa to write something for the orchestra's 1971 program. Mehta was becoming something of a pop star in his own milieu, having already performed concerts with Jethro Tull and other bands, and collaborated on a show with teen heartthrob Bobby Sherman. Yet he took a particular interest in Zappa. "Most rock musicians could not do this sort of thing because they cannot read music," Mehta explained. "Frank Zappa, on the other hand, is one of the few rock musicians who knows my language."

Zappa had arranged for a May 15 concert at the Pauley Pavilion, a mammoth basketball stadium on the campus of UCLA that seated 14,000 people and was noted for its terrible acoustics. Zappa proposed that Mehta conduct the LAPO in some of the orchestral pieces he was preparing for *200 Motels*. The organizers agreed — as long as the Mothers of Invention were also on the bill. There were three problems, though. First, the orchestra didn't want to play Zappa's music. They wanted a commercial spectacle like the popular rock band/orchestra combos featuring Deep Purple or the Moody Blues. In other words, they wanted to let their hair down and rock out. Second, there was no longer any Mothers of Invention. Third, since the score needed to be copied for the orchestra, they asked that Zappa swallow the $7,000 expense. He ultimately agreed. On top of all this, Zappa had asked that he be able to tape the show so he could hear what the music sounded like, but the Musicians' Union wouldn't allow it. "They told me that if I turned the tape on, I would have to pay the whole Musicians' Union scale," he told Don Menn. In the end, the show was bootlegged by a fan with a portable tape deck. He released it as an album and never had to pay a cent to the Musicians' Union — or to Zappa.

Zappa put together a makeshift Mothers of Invention band to do a short tour before the Pauley gig. He brought back Ray Collins for the lead vocals; Aynsley Dunbar and Billy Mundi shared the chore of the drums; and Jeff Simmons played bass. For the Pauley show itself, Zappa added Ian Underwood on reeds and Don Preston on keyboards, with the dependable Motorhead Sherwood on baritone sax. The show was part of the Pauley Pavilion's sold-out *Contempo 70* festival, which was also supposed to include composer Mel Powell's *Immobiles 1-4*, plus Zappa's arrangement of Varèse's *Intégrales*, but Powell, dean of the California Institute of the Arts' School of Music, was appalled by the inclusion of a rock band in a symphonic concert. He pulled his piece as the concert was in progress.

Powell's musical world had always expressed contempt for the blatant lasciviousness of rock 'n' roll, but Powell also believed that, in this case, rock fans were being hoodwinked by the greedy ambitions of people from his own cultural camp. "The very hypocrisy young people abhor is at work ensnaring them, seducing them," Powell told Michael Gray. "Pop music . . . is manifestly in the wrong zone when set beside a symphony orchestra." He recognized the pure commercial expedience of the whole enterprise. On the other hand, Zappa didn't pander to the consistent bickering between these two incompatible groups. He preferred perfectly executed satire as a means to integrating the battling genres. As David Felton of *Rolling Stone* wrote, "Mehta and the Philharmonic were simply new lab toys for [Zappa's] mad genius and they became better people for it."

Zappa began his segment by explaining to the audience that he'd made numerous errors in the *200 Motels* score — mistakes he couldn't correct before the show. He then turned to Mehta and said, "All right, Zubin, hit it!" What Zubin and the orchestra actually hit was the orchestral arrangement for "A Pound for a Brown (On the Bus)," before shifting into "Bogus Pomp," which combined a number of themes that would be part of *200 Motels*, along with "Holiday in Berlin" "Duke of Prunes," and "Who Needs the Peace Corps?" As the concert went on, Zappa started incorporating some of the absurdities from the Garrick Theatre shows. One such bit of nonsense involved having a toy giraffe stuffed under the dress of clarinetist Michele Zukovsky during an encore of "King Kong." By the time Zappa called for a chorus to blow bubbles through straws, and the soprano to start singing, "Munchkins get me hot," Mehta swiftly dropped it from the program.

I'M THE SLIME

Two enthusiastic fans in the audience that evening were Howard Kaylan and Mark Volman, the lead singers of the Turtles, who had their first big hit in 1965 with a rave-up version of Bob Dylan's "It Ain't Me, Babe." They put out a number of popular singles over the next couple of years, but really hit paydirt in 1967 with "Happy Together." This perennial favorite at high school dances became the eighth-best-selling song that year, launching the Turtles into superstar status. The band started to come apart by 1969, after a concert at the White House playing alongside the Temptations. They finally broke up, embroiled in legal problems. Because they were being sued by their record label, White Whale, they couldn't work under their real names. So they took on the names "the Phlorescent Leech and Eddie," or Flo & Eddie. In June 1970, they played a few gigs in England with Zappa, and filmed a TV documentary in Holland. While in England they laid some tracks down at Trident Studios with engineer Roy Thomas Baker (who would later produce Queen) that appeared on *Chunga's Revenge*.

Before Zappa completed his next solo album, he assembled the last of the '60s Mothers of Invention recordings that were to be part of the *Playboy* Record Club. That album, released in August, was *Weasels Ripped My Flesh*. It was a terrific coda for the now defunct band. Part of its brilliance was the precipitous editing techniques Zappa employed to create a fascinating overview of their live and studio work between 1967 and 1969. "I was interested in the juxtaposition of various musical textures — pieces of recordings from different times — one from now, one from a few years ago," Zappa told *New Music Express*. "At the same time, I got interested in the editing technique. All the albums were heavily edited to make abrupt changes, then we were faced with the problems of duplicating that onstage. So I devised the hand signals that would allow things to change, and so we rehearsed in such a way that it was a question of . . . keep your eyes open for a signal once in a while . . . so that when it comes, it will sound just like an edit onstage."

Weasels Ripped My Flesh is a masterpiece of collage art that brings together every element of the Mothers of Invention's diverse abilities. Zappa's experiments go much farther in combining live and studio material than they did on *Burnt Weeny Sandwich*. Where that album smoothly glided from one source to the next, *Weasels Ripped My Flesh* features shockingly sudden shifts in tone and genre. The album not only rips your flesh, it also tears the rug right out from under you. "Didja Get Any Onya?" recorded live at the Philadelphia Arena in 1969, leads off with a sharp barrage of notes from Buzz Gardner's trumpet, just before Lowell George stifles Buzz with his own vocal honking. As the Mothers make their way through some atonal blowing, George begins speaking in an exaggerated German accent that creates disquieting echoes of the *Reichstag*:

> Years ago in Germany, when I was a very small boy . . . there was lots of people standing around on zee corner, asking questions: "Why are you standing on the corner, acting the way you act, looking like you look? Why do you look that way?"

Roy Estrada rides in under George's narration with some operatic falsettos, until Gardner's trumpet, hilariously borrowing from Charles Ives' *The Unanswered Question*, harmonizes with Estrada's aria. At that point, George and Estrada sing in doo-wop chorus, "Didja get any onya, onya, onya, onya, onya. . . . " The phrase is inspired by Lenny Bruce's celebrated routine about pissing on the audience.

Zappa first staged a variation on Bruce's bit at the Garrick Theatre, when a toy giraffe (stuffed with whipped cream) blew up and sprayed the audience. He would in the '80s reprise the phrase "Didja get any onya" in his stage musical *Thing-Fish*, when an incontinent group of Mammy Nuns start whizzing on the first-nighters in the audience.

While "Didja Get Any Onya?" dissolves to its raucous conclusion, Sugarcane Harris' violin comes screaming in and introduces a studio cover of Little Richard's "Directly From My Heart to You" that is much snappier than the rendition Harris performed with Zappa earlier in the year. His voice perfectly matches the yearning and passion Little Richard had given to the song. Following an abstraction like "Didja Get Any Onya?" with "Directly From My Heart to You" is a tribute to Zappa's great skill at contrasting conflicting pieces to create a different notion of harmony. "Dissonance when it's unresolved is like having a headache for life," Zappa once told journalist Bob Marshall. "So, the most interesting music, as far as I'm concerned, is music in which dissonance is created, sustained for the proper amount of time, and resolved."

Those happily grooving to the blistering blues of "Directly From My Heart to You" don't groove for long when the next track, "Prelude to the Afternoon of a Sexually Aroused Gas Mask," comes knocking at the door. Recorded at the Festival Hall show with the BBC Orchestra, "Prelude" is *all* Roy Estrada. Hitting nothing but high notes with full abandon while laughing as maniacally as Louis the Turkey

I'M THE SLIME

at the Garrick, Estrada takes the song to the furthest extreme of silliness. The title of this splendidly improvised piece alludes to the mustard-gas masks of Zappa's childhood, but it also refers more explicitly to Claude Debussy's *Prélude à l'après-midi d'un faune* ("Prelude to the Afternoon of a Faun"), from 1894.

Debussy, born in France in 1862, had great ambitions to be a radical thinker. A dazzling pianist who invented harmonies and chords that continually questioned and reinterpreted tonality, he both fascinated and horrified contemporary critics and audiences. Debussy rejected Wagner's German romanticism; his interests lay more in Russian folk melodies and the gamelan music he had heard in his youth. Debussy became fascinated with the different ways to explore timbre and harmony. He was after the evocative rather than the bombastic. *Prélude à l'après-midi d'un faune* takes place on a summer afternoon, when a half-asleep faun dreams of nymphs. When he wakes up, he fashions a flute to attract them, but the sound drives them away. The faun then imagines he's holding Venus in his arms and falls back into slumber, once again dreaming of nymphs. In "Prelude to the Afternoon of a Sexually Aroused Gas Mask," there is no flute (although Zappa at one point remarks, "Play your harmonica, son"). Estrada's voice, which could probably scare many a nymph, is the dominating force in the song. By the time Estrada's faun falls into slumber, Zappa cleverly has the band play a portion of Tchaikovsky's Sixth Symphony (*Pathetique*), perfectly evoking Debussy's love of Russian melodies.

The next track, "Toads of the Short Forest," is broken into two parts. The first section, recorded at Whitney Studios in 1969, is a piece of instrumental jazz from Zappa's aborted opera, *I Was a Teenage Malt Shop*, that hastily cuts to a live performance from Thee Image in Miami that same year. The band does some insane horn blowing that obliterates the melodic harmonies of the previous studio section. Partway through, however, Zappa addresses the audience on two of his favorite subjects — time and sinuses: "At this very moment onstage, we have drummer A playing in 7/8, drummer B playing in 3/4, the bass playing in 3/4, the organ playing in 5/8, the tambourine playing in 3/4 . . . and the alto sax is blowing its nose." The track ends with a brief bit of Motorhead Sherwood, whose brief recitation is possibly an outtake from one of his monologues on *Lumpy Gravy*. He once again combines his interest in cars and sex. "It was really hot, and everybody working," Motorhead begins as an unidentified voice coughs uncontrollably behind him, "so I figured I'd rip off her drawers and get a little . . ." The word "pussy" is inserted by some tape manipulation that takes us directly into the next track, "Get a Little," a short guitar solo creeping out of a bed of insistent feedback, recorded live at the Factory in 1969. Zappa's solo is a beautifully sustained tightrope walk above waves of shrieking from his amplifier. Where some guitarists would give up in embarrassment, Zappa uses the feedback as if he's playing with a randomly found object.

"The Eric Dolphy Memorial Barbecue" is a marvelous piece of solo horn work by Underwood and the Gardner brothers. Dedicated to the jazz flautist and saxophonist Eric Dolphy, the piece's theme is quickly discarded before the saxes start to improvise in a free jazz form. "I used to listen to Eric Dolphy albums and I really liked 'em," Zappa told *Downbeat*. "Most of the people I knew didn't. And then, he was dead. So, it's a memorial barbecue for Eric." Dolphy was a multi-instrumentalist who recorded in the late '50s and early '60s, and died of a brain tumor in 1964 at the age of thirty-six. He was the first jazz player who used the bass clarinet as a solo instrument. Perhaps what Zappa liked in Dolphy's playing was the way his tone and phrasing resembled the patterns of human speech. The saxophones in Zappa's opus carry on a running dialogue for just under seven glorious minutes.

"Dwarf Nebula Processional March & Dwarf Nebula" is like a confrontation between Stravinsky and Cage. Just like "Toads of the Short Forest," the composition is broken into two radically different pieces. The first is a royal march out of Stravinsky that's decorated with a touch of the baroque. The second — dwarf nebula itself — is an audio collage that resembles some of Cage's tape mixes, or perhaps the audio manipulations of modern French sound poets Henri Chopin and Bernard Heidsieck. It concludes with one of Motorhead Sherwood's frenzied baritone sax notes bleating away until he breathes in the opening sounds of "My Guitar Wants to Kill Your Mama."

"My Guitar" jumps out with the same force as "Directly From My Heart to You," resolving the previous dissonance while providing an appealing momentum. It's a classic rock song with an infectious hook and lyrics that mockingly play up the ugly side of the Mothers' persona:

You know, your mama and your daddy
Sayin' I'm no good for you
They call me dirty from the alley
Till I don't know what to do

I'M THE SLIME

I get so tired of sneaking around
Just to get to your back door
I crawl past the garbage and your mama jumps out
Screamin', "Don't come back no more."
I can't take it

My guitar wants to kill your mama
My guitar wants to burn your dad
I get real mean when it makes me mad.

Besides the deep-fried boogie of Zappa's electric guitar, partway through the instrumental bridge he provides an obbligato on acoustic guitar that's so beautifully stated it sharply contrasts with everything else in the song. Yet it belongs. Zappa seems to be saying that as much as we may think he plays a mean guitar, he can also make one sound like a thing of beauty, too.

The following track, "Oh No," dates back to the Garrick Theatre; in instrumental form, it was featured on *Lumpy Gravy*. On *Weasels*, it finally has words — and they're good words, sung beautifully by Collins. "Oh No" was written in response to John Lennon's "All You Need Is Love" and the Beatles' simplistic cry for universal brotherhood. Zappa didn't see how positive anthems trumpeting the virtues of love could change the volatile political climate around him:

Oh no, I don't believe it
You say that you think you know the meaning of love
You say love is all we need
You say with your love you can change
All of the fools, all of the hate
I think that you're probably out to lunch.

Zappa's dismissal of the privileged Lennon's plea for peace is more than a simple act of cynicism, it's a recognition that self-righteous bromides — even well-intentioned ones — won't plumb the depths of human iniquity. "I think it's easier to make somebody mad than to make somebody love," Zappa told Frank Kofsky in *The Age of Rock*. "And seeing as how hate is the absolute negative of love, if you can evoke hate and it's really there, you can polarize it, and then you really could have love."

"The Orange County Lumber Truck," from the Festival Hall show, is an exciting instrumental driven by great propulsion, but just as Zappa's guitar solo starts cooking, the sound of laughter breaks in, as if someone in the room has just yanked the needle off the record, and we are inundated with the overwhelming sound of feedback.

With the fury of a thousand vacuum cleaners going full-tilt, "Weasels Ripped My Flesh," the concluding piece on the album (and the last number at the 1969 Birmingham show), is the exact opposite of "Get a Little." While the latter played with feedback as part of its overall texture, "Weasels" is a full assault on the senses. Yet the ugly noise it emits, which got the jump on Lou Reed's cacophonous *Metal Machine Music* (1975), was Zappa's answer to the album's opening question: Didja get any onya? At the song's conclusion, when Zappa says, "Good night, boys and girls," there's scattered applause, a chorus of boos, and a voice coming out of the mix, yelling, "Go home!" With *Weasels Ripped My Flesh*, the Mothers of Invention had proudly and promptly left the building.

Weasels Ripped My Flesh is graced with perhaps the most disturbing of conceptual album covers. Zappa and Cal Schenkel had had a brief falling-out, so Zappa brought in Martin Muller, a young poster artist from San Francisco who went by the name of Neon Park. The illustration Park came up with features a man in a suit with a detached, otherworldly expression on his face. While staring off in the distance, he's shaving with a razor made of a live weasel. As the appliance rips a large hole in his face, a cartoon balloon from the weasel announces, "Weasels Ripped My Flesh," while the shaver simply goes, "RZZZZZ!" In the distance, another balloon announces, in bold letters, "The Mothers of Invention."

Park earned $250 for this painting, which would eventually be No. 30 in *Rolling Stone*'s 100 Greatest Album Covers of All Time. The illustration caused turmoil at Zappa's record company, Warner Brothers. Zappa and art director John Williams originally requested that the painting only have the "RZZZZZ!" printed on it. But the executives were adamant that the band's name be included on the cover. Williams fought the bigwigs on this concept until they agreed to his terms. But they reneged and included the band name and album title, without consulting Williams or Zappa.

Park said he was inspired by the cover of a 1956 edition of *Man's Life*, depicting a man, naked to the waist and standing in a river, being assaulted by small, flesh-eating mammals. "The printer was greatly offended [by my work]," Park told

I'M THE SLIME

Rolling Stone in 1991. "The girl who worked for him, his assistant, she wouldn't touch the painting. She wouldn't pick it up with her hands. . . . It was an infamous cover, although I guess by today's standards, it's pretty tame. It's not like eating liver in Milwaukee."

4

By the fall, Zappa decided to reform the Mothers of Invention — only not with the same players he had cut loose a year earlier. He enlisted Mark Volman and Howard Kaylan on vocals; Jeff Simmons on bass; Ian Underwood on keyboards and winds; George Duke on keyboards; and Aynsley Dunbar on drums. With this ensemble, Zappa was after something vaudevillian. The new group would act out scatological routines and satirize the very rock milieu of which they were a part. As Ben Watson writes, "The Flo & Eddie edition of the Mothers was designed to expose backstage events at precisely the time when rock was turning into a patronizing spectacle of cosmic proportions. Whereas the original Mothers were presented as some kind of alternative — a band of genuine freaks who would improvise 'genuine' atonal piano backstage — Flo & Eddie were presented as sweaty, horny pop stars whose main interest was getting laid."

By the '70s, rock had become a monolithic corporate entity with very few of the subversive qualities it possessed in the '50s and '60s. Zappa chose to reveal the true underpinnings of rock's fad-driven spectacle. Flo & Eddie didn't possess the outrageous impulses of a Roy Estrada or Jimmy Carl Black. As the former lead singers of the Turtles, they were the personification of pop. Who better to have in this group than guys who had once been driven to become No. 1 in the charts?

As Lenny Bruce once brought the backstage sleaze of the stand-up world into his routines, Zappa would chronicle the current state of the rock 'n' roll business, including the desperation for sex and the megalomaniacal qualities of both stars and promoters. This new stance would be as politically formidable as the early work of the Mothers — entertainment that still raised questions about what the audience was consuming, and why they were consuming it. Rock critics who received perks from the industry for buying into an exalted view of rock dismissed Zappa's new interests as juvenile. But Zappa saw uncovering the reality of rock's low road as a way of exposing some of the hypocrisies in taking the high road.

A great example of this happened when the refurbished Mothers played a venue in Florida in September 1970. A little over a year earlier, Jim Morrison of the

Doors had caused a riot in Miami by inciting the crowd to revolt, and demonstrated his good faith in leading the charge by exposing himself onstage. This episode swelled into a scandal that brought about the demise of the Lizard King and his band. Yet, despite Morrison's self-indulgence, many saw his actions as political, even radical — as if his rambling incoherence, induced by bourbon and mescaline, was a powerful bit of agitprop. The only residue it left behind, though, was a fear in rock promoters of booking *anyone* in the business — because *they* might whip it out onstage, too.

The day the Mothers arrived, they were threatened by what Zappa called "a blobulent redneck with a shotgun in his hand, demanding assurances that none of us would commit such an evil act within the hallowed halls of his miserable venue." As the band took to the stage, an enthusiastic crowd was shouting out various Mothers lyrics. Zappa addressed the crowd. "Your attention — please — for this important public announcement," he began, as the band tuned up. "It is necessary for me to tell you at this point that there's a clause in our contract here tonight that says if anything nasty happens onstage, terrible things happen to us. So . . ." Zappa paused for the audience's unhappy response. "We just want to assure you that our only interest here is doing a swell job for you. However, it is also necessary to prove our good intentions before we begin by reciting our Mothers of Invention Anti-Smut Loyalty Oath." As the crowd began to cheer, Zappa gathered the band around him, and they proceeded to offer *their* idea of good faith.

"I, Frank Zappa, Jeff Simmons, Howard Kaylan, Mark Volman, Ian Underwood, George Duke, Aynsley Dunbar, do hereby solemnly swear, in accordance with the regulations of the contract with this here rock 'n' roll establishment; and the imbecilic laws of the state of Florida; and the respective regulations perpetuated by rednecks everywhere!" By now the band was shouting their pledge over the cheering throngs. "[We] do solemnly swear: Under no circumstances to reveal my tube, wad, dingus, wee-wee, and/or penis, anyplace on this stage." This does not include private showings in the motel room however . . ." And here Kaylan concluded Zappa's sentence: ". . . which is the Ramada Inn."

While Zappa's oath may lack the dynamic charge of a manifesto, or the hell-raising acrimony of Morrison's drunken cry for open revolution, it was still subversive. Rather than martyr himself by playing to the crowd (as Morrison did) and indulge some need to be deified as a pop star, Zappa turned the conflict into a piece of musical theater that forced the audience to confront their own prurient fantasies. He diffused, through comedy, the sexual taboo that Morrison could only exploit. The reference to "private showings" makes it clear that beyond the public stage lies the private world of the rock musician. This assertion puts the power of the taboo back where it belongs — in the listener's imagination.

"Unfortunately, some people have a peculiar attitude toward things of a glandular nature connected to things of a musical nature and they say, 'Well, music is so far as here and glands are way down there,'" Zappa told radio journalist Martin Perlich in 1972. "We can't really get them together . . . [so] a group comes in and doesn't sing overtly about those things, but couches their language a little bit, and does it with a little choreography. They think that's great, and that's real rock 'n' roll. I maintain there's no difference. We were just honest enough to go out there and say, 'This is this, and that's that, and here you are. Respond to it.' And the response to that was, 'I'm hip, but of course, I'm offended.'"

What offended many in the American avant-garde was that Zappa had abandoned the atonal compositions and *musique concrète* of his earlier albums. But Zappa wanted to see if he could, with a live stage band, replicate the shifts in texture and tempo he once achieved through editing tape in the studio.

Zappa also loved the wide harmonic qualities in Kaylan and Volman's voices — something he couldn't get out of Ray Collins in the original Mothers. "For the first time the melodic content of those songs can come out — 'cause I was never a good singer, and Ray Collins, at the time he was the lead singer, was not very fond of harmonizing with anybody else," Zappa told Mike Bourne of *Downbeat*. "So we couldn't get into any of the stuff that we're doing now: the three- and four-part vocals, which I enjoy doing. I don't mind singing those same songs over and over again."

Kaylan and Volman also added to the commercial appeal of Zappa's music. This was partly due to the bad-boy humor in the lyrics, but it was also because of the pure theatricality of their shows. "They were very strong on the vaudeville," Zappa told COQ in 1974. "It was more rustic bumpkin. If they did choreography or anything onstage it wasn't controlled. It was spur-of-the-moment random weirdness. It was okay for working in a three-hundred-seat theater, but little actions with dolls and things like that are invisible when you start working four-thousand- or three-thousand-seat auditoriums. You just can't get it across. So you need large gestures, and Mark and Howard of the Turtles were good at large gestures."

More young people were starting to attend Mothers' concerts (while the early fans started to turn away). "He felt it was silly to have just a small band of committed, active followers when, by changing his approach just a bit, he could attract a larger audience," Kaylan told *Zig Zag* in 1972. "Then, when they're not looking, he can give them what he wanted to play in the first place." By 1972, they would be selling out in halls with a capacity of 10,000.

In October 1970, the listening public was about to be introduced to this newly invented band on a record called *Chunga's Revenge*. The new record was a hodgepodge of material left over from *Hot Rats*, as well as the new recordings featuring Flo & Eddie. It also previewed some of the themes that would be part of *200 Motels*. On the inside cover of *Chunga's Revenge*, once again designed by Cal Schenkel (who was brought back into the fold), is, as Zappa describes, "a Gypsy mutant industrial vacuum cleaner [that] dances about a mysterious night time camp fire ... [with] dozens of imported castanets, clutched by the horrible suction of its heavy duty hose, waving with marginal erotic abandon in the midnight autumn air." The image neatly ties into the opener, "Transylvania Boogie," a solo guitar track that borrows from the folk idiom of Bartók (hence the title). Since Transylvania was also the home of Dracula, it brought Zappa's love of horror into the mix. The number was first performed by the Mothers in 1969, but Zappa adds more boogie rhythmic invention in this version. The second track, "Road Ladies," the first song featuring Flo & Eddie, is a blues about groupies that reveals a very different attitude than the one displayed on "Motherly Love."

In "Motherly Love," a novice band was happy to receive female affection and adulation, but on "Road Ladies," some wear and tear starts to show. Amid an onslaught of sexually communicable diseases, plus homesickness, the song demonstrates just how lonely and miserable this life can be: "You got nothing but groupies and promoters to love you/And a pile of laundry by the hotel door." As if to make his break with the teen-pop market of the Turtles truly final, Kaylan lets loose with a hilarious invective about his time on the road:

> *I know someday I will never*
> *I ain't going to roam the countryside no more*
> *I'm going to hang up them ol' Holiday Inns*
> *And heal my knees from when I was doin' it on the floor.*
> *See me doin' it, see me doin' it on the floor!*

Flo & Eddie had the perfect personalities for the song. "They had the 'road rat' mentality," Zappa told Neil Slaven. "In order to tour, you really have to have a special mentality. No matter how good a player is, if he doesn't have that 'road rat' sense, he'll die out there." Zappa had no time for musicians who could play the notes, but not negotiate the psychological landscape of touring. In the chorus, Zappa can be heard longing for a time away from the road. He explores what it does to a musician's home life — especially a musician with a wife and kids:

> *Don't you ever miss your house in the country*
> *And your hot little mama, too*
> *Don't you better get your shot from the Doc*
> *For what the road ladies do to you.*

In 1971, an interviewer asked Zappa how Gail liked the idea of him sleeping with groupies on the road. "She's grown accustomed to it over a period of years," Zappa replied. "I mean, you have to be realistic about these things — you go out on the road [and] you strap on a bunch of girls, [then] you come back to the house, [you] find out you've got the clap, what are you gonna do? Keep it a secret from your wife? So I come back there and I say, 'Look, I've got the clap' . . . so she gets some penicillin tablets, we both take 'em and that's it."

The song "Twenty Small Cigars" was left over from the *Hot Rats* sessions (although it was premiered on Jean Luc-Ponty's *King Kong* album). It's a short but captivating piece for guitar and harpsichord that rivals "Aybe Sea" in its Satie-like delicacy. "The Nancy & Mary Music" is a live track from a concert at the Tyrone Guthrie Theatre in Minneapolis that features the Flo & Eddie band, though the music has more in common with *Hot Rats*. Essentially an instrumental, it's built on several elements: a bluesy guitar solo by Zappa, George Duke taking flight on the electric piano, a flamboyant drum solo by Aynsley Dunbar, and finally Flo & Eddie (joining Duke) on some improvised scat singing at the end. Although not well-recorded, it's a spirited track with some impressive free-form improvisations. "Tell Me You Love Me" is a simple rock 'n' roll song with Flo & Eddie providing dynamic vocals that verge on the hysterical. Driven by Zappa's guitar work, the song reaches a certain grandeur at the end when Ian Underwood comes in with the melody on the pipe organ. Again, Zappa demonstrates a sensitivity to using instruments not traditional for the style of the song. "Would You Go All the Way?" combines Zappa's love of '50s sci-fi with the sexual anxieties of teen lovers groping in the darkness of a movie theater. Freddie and Joe go to a monster movie, and as the suspense increases, Joe decides to relieve the tension by putting the moves on Freddie — and within seconds her brassiere is missing:

The monster came out
Everybody shout
People all around you
Screaming at the monster
The monster from the USO.

Zappa often referred to the sexual frustrations of American servicemen, and this song was the first to fully express it. The song, led by Duke performing a quasi-march on the trombone, comes on like a recruitment ad, similar to the tongue-in-cheek endorsements of the Village People on "YMCA":

Would you go all the way for the USO?
Would you go all the way for the USA?
Would you go all the way for the USO?

Lift up your dress if the answer is no!

The title track, "Chunga's Revenge," like "Twenty Small Cigars," features many of the musicians from the *Hot Rats* sessions. Besides being another great vehicle for soloists, it has the distinction of featuring Underwood playing an alto sax solo with a wah-wah pedal. Sugarcane Harris provides a solid organ drone that rides under the probing notes of Underwood's sax, and Zappa bursts in with a blistering guitar solo that continues to build until it's interrupted abruptly by "The Clap," a solo percussion piece where Zappa reimagines Varèse's *Ionisation* in a miniature form.

"Rudy Wants to Buy Yez a Drink" is Zappa's first anti-union song. His views on organized labor (more explicitly expressed in the '80s with "Stick Together") take issue with the idea that unions still represent the interests of working people. Zappa felt they do more to promote bureaucracy and protect mediocrity. "The union mentality means that too many people do too little work for too much money and then go on strike in order to get more days off," Zappa told a journalist in 1984. "And there are a lot of people like this in the world who think that that's the way things ought to be. My attitude is this: I pay money to have a service performed for me on

I'M THE SLIME

behalf of an audience that pays money for a service performed for them and I'm there to make sure that if somebody buys a ticket to my show they're not going to be disappointed in it. They're going to see a band that knows what they're doing, that does it well and delivers entertainment for the money that's spent." "Rudy Wants to Buy Yez a Drink," however, is about the musicians' union and suggests the involvement of organized crime:

> *Hi and howdy doody.*
> *I'm a union man*
> *You can call me Rudy*
> *Any you boys not paid up on your cards?*

Rudy carries a gun, demands his pay, and departs as quickly as he arrived. Flo & Eddie sing in a mock '50s R&B style (even imitating Elvis at one point), perhaps to remind us again that even the King wasn't immune to the shady practices of the rock 'n' roll business.

The album's final track, "Sharleena," is pure '50s R&B, though, and one of Zappa's more enduring love songs. In spirit, it has a lot in common with Jackie & the Starlites' "Valerie," but it's less dramatic and more confessional. The tune is about losing someone, but unlike most heartbreak songs that wallow in despair, "Sharleena" puts the singer's true desires first:

> *Ten long years, I've been loving her*
> *Ten long years, and I thought deep down in my heart she was mine.*
> *Ten long years, I've been loving her*
> *Ten long years, and I would call her my baby and now*
> *I'm always crying.*

The longing at the end is sincere and deeply felt, when Flo & Eddie plead for Sharleena's return. Sharleena (sometimes spelled Charlena) is a popular name in '50s R&B songs, and Zappa evokes her like a ghost. Ian Underwood, as he did in "Tell Me You Love Me," adds poignancy to the singer's pleas with lovely arpeggios on the grand piano. The first version of "Sharleena," which appears on *The Lost Episodes*, was recorded just before Flo & Eddie joined the group, and features Sugarcane Harris on vocals and electric violin. That version includes some great solos by Harris and Zappa, and Harris' heartfelt reading of the song equals his performance on

"Directly From My Heart to You." Zappa also rearranged "Sharleena" into a reggae song in 1984, including it on the *Them or Us* album. Even though *Chunga's Revenge* is a transitional album, caught between the fusion rock of *Hot Rats* and the new vaudevillian routines with Flo & Eddie, its sundry pleasures are plentiful.

In November, the Mothers played a couple of nights at the Fillmore East. It was there that they had a surprise guest: folksinger Joni Mitchell. Unlikely as it may seem, Mitchell had been Motorhead's girlfriend back in 1967. "Yeah, he picked her up in New York someplace and brought her to the house," Zappa told Michael Gray. "And I remember her sitting in the corner, playing guitar, singing to herself; she had a beret on the first time I saw her and she was leaning over the guitar and she was drooling. That was before she had a record contract." Gray was skeptical that Zappa had *anything* in common with a sensitive singer-songwriter like Mitchell, but Zappa disagreed. "Actually I have a great respect for what she does," Zappa said. "The thing I like is her melisma — I think that it's well executed and I think that it's interesting, from a musical standpoint. I'm not too enthralled by the lyrics, because I'm not into love songs."

As he demonstrated in his episode with Simon & Garfunkel in 1967, Zappa was fully prepared to explode the Fillmore audience's baffled expectations. He wanted them to witness the incongruity of Joni Mitchell performing with the Mothers of Invention. Zappa told *New Musical Review*, "She is very shy and we had to lead her on eventually. Then I said to her, 'Look, we don't play any of your songs and you don't sing any of ours, so just make up some lyrics and we'll follow you.'" Mitchell walked up to the microphone, and the first lyrics that tumbled out of her mouth were, "Penelope wants to fuck the sea." The crowd was astonished. What had happened to the lovely, fragile Joni Mitchell?

"We ended it with her singing 'Duke of Earl,'" Zappa recalled. He realized that the hierarchy of popular music left some people, like Mitchell, exalted and pigeonholed. Since her work was confessional in nature, the audience had built a strong personal identification with her songs. Zappa, on the other hand, continually shocked and outraged audiences, so he was often dismissed as a deviant element. By skillfully stripping away the edifying image of a Simon & Garfunkel, or a Joni Mitchell, he confronted the elitism being cultivated in the pop audience.

On January 11, 1971, Zappa announced at a London press conference a project to confront that elitism head on. He was finally ready to launch his film *200 Motels*, about life on the road for the Mothers of Invention. Even though the surreal

I'M THE SLIME

themes of *200 Motels* had already been previewed on *Chunga's Revenge*, the orchestral score had been years in the making. During the first five years of the Mothers of Invention's existence, Zappa had carried with him, on the road, masses of manuscript paper, and whenever he had an opportunity he scribbled music on it. This material eventually became the score for *200 Motels*. The title came from an estimate of the number of concerts the band played in their first five years, based on forty jobs per year. "It was more of a musical diary," Zappa told COQ. "So I devised a screenplay that chronicled in an abstract way the activities of the group on the road for a certain period of time and used the music that had been written in the motels as the scoring for the film."

The idea for the movie had come together quickly after the Pauley Pavilion concert. When Zappa invited Kaylan and Volman to join the band after that show, he told them there was a movie in the works. Zappa and Herb Cohen, as part of Bizarre Productions, approached David Picker, an executive producer at United Artists, with a ten-page synopsis of the film. They struck a deal where Bizarre would sell the movie and the subsequent soundtrack album to United Artists. It was stipulated that the film not be X-rated. The budget for both the movie and the soundtrack was about $600,000 — even though Zappa would end up spending close to $679,000. As the band toured during the spring and summer of 1970, they rehearsed and performed many of the songs intended for the film. Meanwhile, Zappa wanted to use an orchestra in the movie. Since he had decided to use the Royal Philharmonic Orchestra in England, it made sense to save money by moving the production overseas to Pinewood Studios. It was decided that *200 Motels* would be shot on videotape — it would be cheaper than film and offer immediate playback of the scenes shot. The footage would be edited on videotape before being transferred to 16mm film stock. *200 Motels* was the first feature film made in this fashion.

By Christmas 1970, the script's continuity problems had been resolved, and Zappa had moved his family over to England. He also brought Lucy Offerrall ("Miss Lucy") of the GTO's, who would look after Dweezil and Moon Unit, and portray one of the groupies in the movie. While set construction was underway at Pinewood, the casting was completed. The Mothers would play themselves: folksinger Theodore Bikel (who was managed by Herb Cohen) would play Rance Muhammitz, the MC and possibly the Devil — posing in a military uniform; Ringo Starr would be Zappa (under the pseudonym Larry the Dwarf); Keith Moon, the drummer in the Who, turned up as Pamela, a hot nun; Motorhead

Sherwood would run a ranch full of newts while pining for the affections of road manager Dick Barber (who wore the mutant vacuum cleaner featured on the inside cover of *Chunga's Revenge*). Don Preston reprised his role as the mad scientist from *Uncle Meat*, with his vile foamy liquids; Jimmy Carl Black, for the moment at least, buried his grudges against Zappa and portrayed the redneck Lonesome Cowboy Burt; Pamela Des Barres ("Miss Pamela") of the GTO's would play a rock journalist.

Zappa also needed an assistant director. He turned to Tony Palmer, a film director who had introduced video technology to Cohen. Palmer was already a familiar chronicler of popular culture in England. Besides directing Cream's farewell concert at Albert Hall, he had made the documentary feature *All My Loving* for the BBC. The film was an examination of pop music that incorporated footage of cataclysmic world events. Palmer had also written a book on pop music called *Born Under a Bad Sign* that had illustrations by Ralph Steadman and a foreword by John Lennon. However, problems began from the moment shooting started on January 28. Because of the short shooting schedule, Zappa had tailored the script so the characters could be themselves, rather than playing dramatic parts.

Given the outrageous characterizations, though, how could anyone even begin to figure out what being themselves really meant? Since the inner logic of *200 Motels* came from Zappa's personal observations of a rock band on the road, the Royal Philharmonic would certainly be at a loss — as would everybody else. To paraphrase Neil Slaven: What does a newt rancher falling in love with an electric vacuum cleaner really mean? How can a town become a sealed tuna sandwich? And why do rock stars steal towels from their hotel rooms?

Palmer was annoyed that he was only the *assistant* director. When he discovered Zappa would be directing the actors and he would only be in charge of the effects, he almost walked. "Maybe this was the role of the electronic director of the future, happy enough to point the electronic cameras in the right direction and push the buttons," Palmer wrote later in the *Observer*. "I was persuaded that this was a sufficiently complicated job to warrant my staying with the picture and who was I to complain?" According to Zappa, Palmer found plenty of things to complain about. He told Slaven that Palmer had a full plate of his own personal turmoil outside of the film set. "He was on the verge of a divorce, he had the flu, and he seemed to be a fairly ill-tempered individual even on a good day," Zappa remarked. At the completion of principal photography, Palmer demanded his

I'M THE SLIME

name be removed from the credits for fear it would damage his career. Gail Zappa even overheard Palmer telling someone on the set he would erase all the master tapes if the film wasn't done to his satisfaction.

Zappa still needed Palmer, though, because he'd never edited video before, and in that pre-computer era, it was all done manually. It would take long days in a frigid room to accomplish the task. "It was like guerrilla warfare to put this film together," Zappa recalled. Problems also erupted during the first read-through of the script. While reading a scene where the band is heard complaining that Zappa, with his hidden tape recorder, steals all his best ideas from the group, bass player Jeff Simmons started to get cold feet. The scene was based on conversations Zappa had heard — and recorded — over the years. "That was Frank's special talent for taking bits and pieces from all over the place and incorporating them into his own work," Motorhead Sherwood told Pete Feenstra of *Real Music*. "Don Preston had taped lots of things; any little thing, like a saying on the bus or an in-joke, [and that] became part of the compositional project." But Simmons felt uneasy reading lines — attributed to him — where he described Zappa as "too old" and suggested his retirement ("Let's buy him a watch!"). In the script, as in life, Simmons also questioned whether Zappa was even taken seriously anymore as a musician, and boasted about forming his own band. Simmons' girlfriend told him he was too "heavy" to be working in a "comedy group" and that he should be a blues musician. He decided to walk from the band — and the film.

Noel Redding, the bass guitarist for the Jimi Hendrix Experience, was the first applicant to replace Simmons. Zappa thought he didn't have the necessary acting skills. Up next was British actor Wilfrid Brambell, best known for playing Paul McCartney's grandfather in *A Hard Day's Night*. Despite his age and his inability to play bass guitar, he had a terrific audition. Although Brambell was more than a little baffled by the story; he decided to take the role. Once they started rehearsals, though, he had trouble remembering his lines. And the ones he did remember (like "Zappa's fucked!") left him less than pleased with his decision. On the last day of rehearsal, Brambell had had enough. He took off down the hall screaming "This is crazy!" and never came back.

Zappa told the group that the next person who walked in the room was going to be the faux Jeff Simmons. That person turned out to be Martin Lickert, Ringo Starr's chauffeur. And not only did he have an appealing Liverpudlian accent, Lickert was a young pretty-boy who looked like a pop star. He was also a competent bass player.

Meanwhile, the Royal Philharmonic wasn't any more enthusiastic about being in the movie than Simmons. These practitioners of symphonic sounds had very little regard for a weird-looking guy with a goatee who resided in the world of rock 'n' roll — and was a rock 'n' roller who wrote orchestral music. But Zappa was not pleased with the orchestra, either. "It's one thing to say, 'Oh, look at this weird guy and what does he want now? 'Course, he's paying us to do this,'" Zappa told Neil Slaven. "Then suddenly, they get a piece of paper that they can't really play. And then you compound that with the fact that there was never enough rehearsal time to teach them how to play it to make it sound right. So the level of commitment to a proper musical performance simply wasn't there."

The principal photography was shot over fifty-six hours, with only a third of the script done. This meant Zappa had to shape the plot in the editing room. Although video was still in its infancy, Zappa assumed that this form of production could revolutionize making movies. Zappa and his crew had used four cameras for every scene. Palmer set up the shots, did the blocking, and conducted the rehearsals. In the morning, the band would pre-record the music. After lunch, the shooting would begin. The cast sat in their dressing rooms until their scene numbers were called, bringing them to the set. At the dinner hour, a loud buzzer ended work for the union members (which excluded Zappa and his band). There was no money in the budget to have the technicians do overtime.

Five days into production, disagreements forced Zappa to delete from the shooting script scenes that would affect the story's continuity. Zappa and Palmer were constantly huddling to concentrate on the scenes that were absolutely essential, as well as the cutaways they needed for editing the movie. "With Frank, nobody knew what was gonna happen from one night to the next, which was one of the reasons it was exciting and challenging," road manager Dick Barber told Bruce Burnett of *Society Pages*. "Now, I think Frank . . . approached the making of *200 Motels* the same way. . . . We got this script, but the script was being rewritten by the minute, and I think that was a little frustrating for Tony Palmer. You really can't, and shouldn't, for the most part, make movies on that basis."

As usual for Zappa, time started to become an albatross. He couldn't finish all the additions, deletions, and modifications needed for his story to make sense. So, by the completion date of February 5, it barely did.

I'M THE SLIME

5

In the press kit, Zappa described his film this way:

> As far as I'm concerned, *200 Motels* is a SURREALISTIC DOCUMENTARY. The film is at once a reportage of real events and an extrapolation of them. Other elements include 'conceptual by-products' of the extrapolated 'real event.' In some ways, the contents of the film are autobiographical. . . . *200 Motels* is a SURREALISTIC DOCUMENTARY, but it might also be helpful to think of the overall 'shape' of the film in the same way you might think of the 'shape' of a piece of orchestral music, with leitmotifs, harmonic transpositions, slightly altered repetitions, cadences, atonal areas, counterpoint, polyrhythmic textures, onomatopoeic imitations, etc. . . .

The problem, as with *Uncle Meat*, is that *200 Motels* the album works better as a movie than the *200 Motels* film.

The soundtrack, released simultaneously with the film in October 1971, opens with the hilariously bombastic "Semi-Fraudulent/Direct-From-Hollywood Overture," an orchestral rearrangement of "Holiday in Berlin, Full Blown" that sounds as if film composer Miklos Rozsa was on hand to resurrect *Ben-Hur*. In the film, as the heavenly choirs and horns chime gloriously, Rance Muhammitz (Theodore Bikel), with the same German accent Lowell George summoned in "Didja Get Any Onya?," announces the arrival of Larry the Dwarf (Ringo Starr), who appears on a game-show set suspended in a harness. As Varèse-like percussion takes us out of the archaic sounds of a Biblical epic and into the absurdly modern world of Frank Zappa, a chorus of munchkin voices proclaim, "Two hundred motels!" As Larry lands on the podium, Muhammitz, in an aside to the audience, whispers, "Larry likes to dress up funny. Tonight he's dressed up like Frank Zappa. Let's ask him: What's the deal?" On the album, the Mothers kick into the rock number "Mystery Roach." Just as he did on *Weasels Ripped My Flesh*, Zappa juxtaposes different musical genres — and it also fits beautifully here. "Mystery Roach," a song about the craving for the potent aroma of those small, stubby marijuana butts, could very well be for Jeff Simmons, who was reportedly the major pothead in the band.

After the short orchestral burst of "Dance of the Rock 'n' Roll Interviewers," "Tuna Fish Promenade" follows. This is a Kurt Weill/Bertolt Brecht–inspired number about the trappings of small American towns (represented by Centerville in the film) from the point of view of touring bands used to big cities: "This town we're in is just a sealed tuna sandwich/With the wrapper glued." Howard Kaylan and Mark Volman were perfect for this material because it required singers with a more dynamic range than Ray Collins had. Besides, the style of the music, patterned after *The Rise and Fall of the City of Mahogany*, written by Weill and Brecht in 1930 as an attack on social corruption, wouldn't have suited Collins' taste. The instrumental "Dance of the Just Plain Folks" is a small section from "Bogus Pomp," which the BBC Orchestra first performed back at the Festival Hall shows. Out of the reprise to "Tuna Fish," which is done as a bolero in moderate triple time, Flo & Eddie introduce us to the town redneck, Lonesome Cowboy Burt (Jimmy Carl Black). This mock country-and-western tune fixes Burt with a vast number of country-music clichés. He's a unionized roofer who hates hippies, wears a fringy shirt, loves to get drunk — and he despises communists:

> *When I get off, I get plastered*
> *I drink till I fall on the floor*
> *Find me some Communist bastard*
> *And I'll stomp on his face till he don't move no more.*

Burt also loves to get laid, but Zappa doesn't empathize with Burt's sexual frustrations:

> *Come on in this place*
> *And I'll buy you a taste*
> *You can sit on my face*
> *Where's my waitress?*

Although Zappa had plenty of compassion for dispossessed blacks, Mexicans, and other minorities he saw suffer the abuses of racism, he never extended the same sympathy to the rootless whites whose melancholic search for roots found expression in country-and-western music. Nigey Lennon observes this trait: "In the Antelope Valley of the '50s, [Zappa] had been jailed the night before a dance because he led a racially mixed R&B band; the local Okies thought all niggers were dope

I'M THE SLIME

fiends and gangsters," Lennon writes. "Italians were considered pretty alien by the hayseeds in Lancaster, and Frank had suffered miserably in high school at the hands of the second-generation Okie and Arkie students. There was no point in my trying to explain to him that there were plenty of outcasts in places like Texas and Oklahoma, and as much innovation in Spade Cooley as there was in Anton Webern."

Zappa didn't have many blind spots, but when it came to country music (or, as he called it, "cowboy music"), he regarded the genre's performers in the same way that the jazz elite (who Zappa also despised) sneered at the R&B and blues artists he loved. Zappa failed to recognize that not all country singers, or country fans, were rednecks out to kill hippies.

200 Motels also features a trio of songs about groupies that sets out to examine both the desperation and loneliness of their lifestyle. Many rock stars, in typically narcissistic fashion, have written melancholic songs about being alone on the road. But in "Half a Dozen Provocative Squats," Zappa examined this from the female groupie's perspective:

She's just twenty-four and she can't get off
A sad, but typical case
The last dude to do her got in and got soft
She blew it and laughed in his face.

In the song "Shove It Right In," Zappa zeroes in on the bar scene, where the sexual desperation between the star and the worshipper is just about equal:

Somewhat desirable boys there
Dressed really spiffy with long hair
Looking for girls they can shove it right in.

Zappa's "tribute" to Jeff Simmons — who quit playing in a "comedy" group to join a "heavy" band — is depicted in the film's animated sequence, "Dental Hygiene Dilemma." In this brutally comic satire, Jeff (Martin Lickert) is torn between his good conscience — a female who describes herself as "a cosmic love pulse matrix becoming a technicolor interpositive guiding light" — and his bad conscience — a little devil with a pitchfork. This miniature Lucifer prompts Simmons to rip off the hotel towels, and poses the key question of his dilemma: Why are you wasting your life, night after night, playing Zappa's comedy music?

Simmons agrees. While all he ever gets to do is play this ridiculous music, Zappa actually eats. Before long, the whirling dervish gets Jeff to try an elixir that inspires him to steal more towels and rip off ashtrays — and eventually leave the group to become big like Grand Funk Railroad or Black Sabbath. Since *200 Motels* also toys with the notion that Zappa is a tyrant who controls the band while defining every aspect of the group's identity, Simmons' escape isn't just an inspired bolt for freedom. It's a futile attempt to be a big star in his own right.

Simmons' dementia is evoked further in "Does This Kind of Life Look Interesting to You?" where he frantically lists the benefits of being in Zappa's band — and they amount to very few. The song, delivered in a furiously paced rant by the cartoon voice of Simmons' bad conscience, would inspire "What Do You Want From Life?" by the '70s concept band the Tubes.

"Daddy, Daddy, Daddy" is an R&B number about a whole different class of groupie:

> *She's such a dignified lady*
> *She's so pretty and soft*
> *If you call her a groupie*
> *It just pisses her off*
> *She's got diamonds and jewelry*
> *She's got lotsa new clothes*
> *She ain't hurtin' nobody*
> *So that everyone knows that she knows what she wants*
> *She knows what she likes*
> *Daddy, Daddy, Daddy.*

Besides her wealth, which sets her apart from the desperately lonely groupie of "She Painted Up Her Face," she judges success by the size of the male organ:

> *They want a guy from a group*
> *That's got a thing in the charts*
> *If his dick is a monster*
> *They will give him their hearts.*

Zappa follows this song with the oratorio "Penis Dimension," where the rock star is plagued by anxieties about whether his cock is large enough to fulfill the wildest

I'M THE SLIME

fantasies of this obsessed and obscenely wealthy woman. As the chorus sings the title phrase, the orchestral score builds triumphantly — only to collapse suddenly like an erection turned to flab. Mark Volman follows with a benediction that connects a liturgical thread that began with the battle over Jeff Simmons' soul a few songs earlier:

> Hiya, friends. Now just be honest about it. Did you ever consider the possibility that your penis, and in the case of many dignified ladies, that the size of the titties themselves might provide elements of subconscious tension? Weird, twisted anxieties that could force a human being to become a politician, a policeman, a Jesuit monk, a rock 'n' roll guitar player, a wino, you name it.

At this moment, Zappa returns to areas of sexual dysfunction he touched on back in "Brown Shoes Don't Make It." "Penis Dimension," though, is also inspired by Lenny Bruce's classic routine "Tits and Ass," where the comic launched an inspired attack on our concept of obscenity. Zappa does a variation on that theme by not only including guys who measure their manhood by the size of their dick, but also ladies who have what Zappa calls "munchkin tits" and who are ultimately doomed to become "the writers of hot books." Howard Kaylan proceeds to read sections that resemble *Lady Chatterley's Lover* through the sensibility of Terry Southern. Kaylan and Volman provide reassuring words to those women "who can't afford a silicone beef-up," by quoting some schoolyard wisdom: Anything over a mouthful is wasted.

"Penis Dimension" reveals how the very guys who worry about whether they're hot enough to score on the road are also the ones singing about it. Zappa doesn't so much gratuitously attack the men or women, as he exposes the absurd length to which both sexes go to prove their sexual worth. These anxious thoughts about having the proper equipment leads directly into "What Will This Evening Bring Me This Morning?" Here, the rock star is faced with the possibility of having an uproarious time:

> *What will this evening bring me this morning?*
> *A succulent fat one!*
> *A mod little flat one!*

Maybe a hot one to give me the clap!
Maybe a freak who gets off with a strap!

But he's also caught in the dilemma of the morning after:

What will I say the next day
To whatever I drag to my hotel tonight?

Zappa points out that even though the road brings wild, unconventional, and unattached groping, the sexual frustrations of being human don't disappear — if anything, they are magnified. You might get your fantasies fulfilled during the night, but the morning always follows, and you still have to face the person you chose, as well as the person you are.

"A Nun Suit Painted on Some Old Boxes" begins a series of songs (including "Motorhead's Midnight Ranch," "The Lad Searches the Night For His Newts," and "Little Green Scratchy Sweaters & Corduroy Ponce") that are performed by the Top Score Singers, in the style of Schoenberg's *Pierrot Lunaire*. "A Nun Suit" features the soprano desperately wrapping her lips around such tasty phrases as "pink gums" and "stumpy gray teeth," while the chorus talks about getting "hot and horny" over cardboard boxes. Zappa includes some of the dialogue from the play "Progress" that the Mothers performed with the BBC Orchestra at Festival Hall in 1968. "A Nun's Suit" segues directly into "Magic Fingers" (the album's single), a straightforward rock 'n' roll song in the same vein as "Tell Me You Love Me." The subject of the tune is the Magic Fingers, an automatic bed-vibrator, used here to increase the pleasure of sex. Kaylan and Volman pair off as a man and woman to act out the conflicts in the song and subtly evoke the homoeroticism inherent in male rockers bonding on the road.

The final track, "Strictly Genteel," begins with Theodore Bikel assembling the cast at the Centerville Recreational Facility, which is decorated like a concentration camp, to bid the audience a sentimental farewell:

Lord, have mercy on the people in England
For the terrible food these people must eat
And may the Lord have mercy on the fate of this movie
And God bless the mind of the man in the street.

I'M THE SLIME

The song, once called "Every Poor Soul Who's Adrift In the Storm," is a tribute to the everyman. In spirit, it's not unlike Aaron Copland's *Fanfare for the Common Man*, except Zappa's composition includes individuals probably considered by some as less than common:

> God help the winos, the junkies, and the weirdos
> And every poor soul who's adrift in the storm
> Help everybody so they all get some action
> Some love on the weekend, some real satisfaction.

After everyone has received benediction, Flo & Eddie turn the conclusion into a gospel hoedown about tearing down the fake sets of the movie, until they're faced with the specter of their boss. "He's making me do all this," Kaylan screams to the audience, pointing toward Zappa. "He is over there. He is the guy that is making me do all this shit.... I can't even believe the guy sometimes! But we gotta watch him, after all, we said, 'It's Frank's movie. We're the Mothers — but it's still Frank's movie." Even though the illusion of life on the road is created in the movie, the group's relationship to their creative boss becomes the true bone of contention by the end of *200 Motels*.

The film doesn't hold together nearly as strongly as the album. Some of the set pieces, like "Penis Dimension" (featuring Flo & Eddie in a line of figures who carry torches like ancient monks), the dance of the ordinary folks of Centerville, and the animated cartoon "Dental Hygiene Dilemma," are brilliantly conceived. But the band, even playing themselves, can't bring their deepest fantasies and anxieties to life — they're too self-conscious, and since they're not actors, they don't know how to invent characters who could. Yet the idea behind the movie is a fascinating, original pop concept. "Building junk sculpture out of the banal sleaze around him, Zappa made of *200 Motels* a social microcosm: it turns work and sex, limits and desire into specific questions unresolvable in abstract moral terms," Ben Watson writes. "The chaos and competition of life on the road becomes a metaphor for capitalism: people reduced to puppets within a schema they can't understand."

Whether the film worked as well as the album was of little concern to Zappa. "It's still a composition," Zappa told Tim Keele of CFNY-FM in the early '80s. "If you take the contents of this ashtray and you move it around, that's a composition. It just depends on what materials you're using.... If you do it one way, you're a playwright or a screenwriter; if you do it the way I do it, you're still a composer."

On February 8, three days after principal photography for *200 Motels* was completed, the Mothers turned up at the Royal Albert Hall to rehearse for an evening concert with the Royal Philharmonic Orchestra. To their surprise, the doors were locked and the concert cancelled.

On January 18, Marion Herrod, the orchestra's secretary and lettings manager, had requested the libretto for the performance. It wasn't until February 5 that some of the lyrics crossed her desk. Songs about a rock star's obsession with his penis, or brash sailors desperate to stick their hands down some girl's pants, likely didn't sit well with someone attuned to the pastoral beauty of Delius. She canceled the concert because "there were words I did not want to be spoken in Albert Hall."

Zappa was stunned. "It was all right for us to appear at Albert Hall in 1968, when the place was black and dirty. Now they've had the place cleaned up, [and] they don't want to know us," he told the *Daily Express*. The show had been sold out with over 4,000 tickets sold, and the concert had cost £5,000 to put together. After the ticket holders were given their money back, Zappa and Herb Cohen announced at a press conference outside the Royal Albert that they were suing the hall for breach of contract. The case would take three years to get to court. In the meantime, it was Yankee Go Home.

While Zappa prepared the *200 Motels* soundtrack in April and May, George Duke had left the Mothers because of commitments to Cannonball Adderley's band. Zappa hired session man Bob Harris to fill in on keyboards. With Jeff Simmons off trying to find a band to express his own brand of heaviness, Jim Pons became the new bass player in the group. Pons was co-founder of the West Coast psychedelic band the Leaves ("Hey Joe"), as well as the former bass guitarist in the Turtles. This version of the Mothers began their tour on May 18 with a show at the Bridges Auditorium in Claremont, California. It was there that the band premiered Zappa's epic adventure "Billy the Mountain," a piece that would take up a whole side on a future live album, *Just Another Band From L.A.* (1972). After concerts in Chicago, Middleport, and Columbus, the band was booked into the Fillmore East in New York for two nights in June. Fillmore impresario Bill Graham had decided he was losing too much money carrying two venues, so he decided to close the East Coast branch, and the Mothers — one of the first bands to play both locations — were slated to help close out the place. Both afternoon and evening performances on June 4, 1971, were recorded for the first official live Mothers of Invention album, called simply *Fillmore East, June 1971*.

I'M THE SLIME

The front cover of the Fillmore East album was white, with the words "The Mothers" scratched in pencil, and the date underneath. Designed either as a mock bootleg or a sly parody of the Beatles' *White Album*, it was Cal Schenkel's least ostentatious design. The album itself earned Zappa some of his worst reviews. Since *200 Motels* wasn't due out for a few months, most critics had heard Flo & Eddie only on *Chunga's Revenge*. *Fillmore East, June 1971*, which arrived in August, brought out — in full bloom — the bawdy vaudeville humor of the new group.

A more compact version of "Little House I Used to Live In" opens the record in an arrangement borrowed from "Twinkle Tits." The stripped-down sound of this band takes some of the sonic color out of the original arrangement on *Burnt Weeny Sandwich*. But "Little House" is merely a setup for another piece of amateur anthropology from the road. "The Mud Shark" is an oratorio that recounts a sordid story about a rock band, a groupie, a hotel in Seattle, and a strange little fish called a mud shark. The song tells of a hotel in Seattle, Washington, called the Edgewater Inn, located on a pier. The hotel has a bait and tackle shop where guests could rent fishing poles, and fish from their hotel windows. Apparently, the psychedelic rock group Vanilla Fudge told Don Preston about a home movie they had made depicting some pretty unusual stuff with a fish and a young woman they had procured for their pleasure. While Zappa doesn't go into graphic detail about the event, former Led Zeppelin road manager Richard Cole, the author of *Stairway to Heaven: Led Zeppelin Uncensored*, certainly does.

"So the next time I was in Seattle was with Led Zeppelin and Vanilla Fudge, and we started to catch sharks out the window," Cole writes. "By this time, the tours were becoming more and more risqué, and you could do what you liked with the girls who showed up at the hotel." While Cole and Zeppelin drummer John Bonham were catching fish, they were interrupted by a young groupie out for sex. "But the true shark story was that it wasn't even a shark," Cole adds. "It was a red snapper and the chick happened to be a fucking redheaded broad with a ginger pussy.... Bonzo was in the room, but I did it. Mark Stein [of Vanilla Fudge] filmed the whole thing. And she loved it.... It was the nose of the fish, and that girl must have come twenty times. I'm not saying the chick wasn't drunk, I'm not saying that any of us weren't drunk. But it was nothing malicious or harmful, no way! No one was ever hurt. She might have been hit by the shark a few times for disobeying orders, but she didn't get hurt."

Some of the seedier behavior of rock bands on the road either gets sanitized and sentimentalized in the music, or triumphantly glorified (as in Grand Funk

Railroad's pleasantly goofy hit, "We're an American Band"). In Cameron Crowe's sweet but self-serving film, *Almost Famous*, he treats his own experiences on the road as a novice rock journalist as a rite of passage. The main character is congratulated for dictating the ethics of behavior to misbehaving rockers. Zappa takes no such moral high ground. He digs his hands right into the muck and puts it out there as entertainment. Zappa transforms "The Mud Shark" event into a perverse dance lesson. The genius of depicting the squalid incident in this manner is that the song parodies how sexual positions were once turned into popular dances.

"What Kind of Girl Do You Think We Are?" is a further exploration into the bizarre dating rituals that take place between rock stars and groupies in American bars. Again Volman and Kaylan take on the dual male and female roles. Asked why she hangs out at the bar, the Volman persona tells Kaylan exactly what she has in mind:

> *I get off bein' juked with a baby octopus*
> *And spewed upon with creamed corn*
> *And my girlfriend digs it with a hot Yoo-Hoo bottle*
> *While somebody's screaming, corks and safeties, pigs and donkeys . . .*
> *Alice Cooper, baby!*

The next song, "Bwana Dik," which uses a speeded-up arrangement of the *Lumpy Gravy* theme, "Duodenum," continues the "Penis Dimension" motif from *200 Motels*:

> *My dick is a monster*
> *Give me your heart*
> *My dick is a Harley*
> *You kick it to start*
> *Bwana Dik speaks*
> *The heavens will part.*

"Latex Solar Beef" is one of many Zappa songs fixated on anal sex ("Acetylene Nirvana/Talkin' bout your hemorrhoids, baby"). "The only conceptual connection to the two above-mentioned hemorrhoid references is from whence they sprang," Kaylan remarked. "Those silly words made Frank laugh . . . need I say more."

On the LP, an instrumental version of "Willie the Pimp" is divided into two parts to conclude one side of the record, and then begin the next (the CD release

I'M THE SLIME

features only the first part). It's the one time on the album that Zappa and the group really cut loose. Just as they start to cook, though, the album delves back into more groupie burlesque with "Do You Like My New Car?" The piece is based on the time Kaylan, then with the Turtles, had to sing "Happy Together" before a groupie would sleep with him. But Zappa takes it further when the groupie taunts him with a variety of perverse suggestions:

> Picture this if you can
> Bead jobs, knotted nylons,
> Bamboo canes, three unreleased recordings of Crosby, Stills & Nash
> fighting in the dressing room of the Fillmore East!

She demands to hear his big hit record "with a bullet." The bullet, which in radio parlance means the speed of the song shooting up the charts, gets transformed into Kaylan's sexual prowess:

> Well, I know when I'm licked . . . all over
> Okay, baby, bend over and spread 'em
> Here comes my bullet!

Suddenly the band launches into a deliriously infectious performance of "Happy Together."

"Lonesome Electric Turkey" is a moog synthesizer solo from "King Kong" played by Preston (who sat in for the encore), and "Peaches en Regalia" is given a spunky but unimaginative reading. However, the album's final song, "Tears Began to Fall," is another of Zappa's beautifully rendered R&B songs that perfectly suits the flamboyant vocal stylings of Flo & Eddie. Like "Sharleena," "Love of My Life," and "You Didn't Try to Call Me," "Tears Began to Fall" showcases all of those perfect — and very American — '50s romantic phrases: "Tears began to fall down my shirt/Cause I feel so hurt/Since my baby drove away."

Fillmore East, June 1971 became a favorite party album among adolescent males who never gave Zappa's other music a moment's notice. Meanwhile, critics, like Lester Bangs at *Rolling Stone*, acted betrayed. "The sometime ribaldry of the early albums has finally been allowed to bloom like a Clearasil jack-off fantasy," Bangs writes, "resulting in two sides mostly filled with a lot of inanity about groupies and exotic fuck-props." Comparing the album to the lewd comedy of Redd Foxx and

Rusty Warren, Bangs concludes with the notion that since Zappa's work has always been "calculated," it lacked any relationship to the true form of rock 'n' roll. "In the end, the most pertinent thing you can say about Frank Zappa is probably that for all he knows about music, he lacks the talent to write a song like, oh, say 'Louie Louie.'"

But Bangs' dismissal doesn't take into account the evolving theatrical aspect of the Mothers' work rooted in the Garrick shows (not to mention the strategies of the Dadaists). Bangs — one of the last great romantics of rock criticism — didn't like to see the music he loved tarnished by Zappa's irreverence. It's not that Bangs was naive about the behavior of the artists he admired, he just wasn't entertained by hearing their dirty laundry aired.

"Judging from the quality of the rock 'n' roll writers that are appearing in rock 'n' roll publications I would say they're not doing quite as good as the people who are actually making the records," Zappa told Martin Perlich in 1972. "So therefore, in a hundred years if people want to find out what was going on during this period of time they'd be better off listening to the source rather than to read the thing in print. Therefore, if we are involved in things that occur on the road with groupies and assorted weird events of a sexual nature, it's better that we tell about it ourselves in a musical format and do it with the people that it occurred to than have somebody else say, 'And then in 1971 one time when they were out on the road at the Mudshark hotel . . .' You know, it's better to do it that way."

Regarding his preoccupation with groupies, Zappa's views are no less harsh, or as dismissive, as those expressed in songs like "Stay With Me" by Rod Stewart & the Faces. "To me, groupies are girls you meet on the road," Zappa said. "Some are nice, some are nasty, some have a sense of humor, some have none, some are smart, and some are dumb. They're just people." Zappa recognized the changes in the rock 'n' roll culture and its folklore since the mid-'60s and was determined to write about it. "The content of the music that the Mothers play is not 100 per cent the result of me making people do things," Zappa pointed out. "The reason we're performing ["Do You Like My New Car?"] is because it was a true story, it actually happened to Howard Kaylan. It was just a process of commemorating a piece of folklore that was peculiar to the group and there was no reason why that shouldn't be saved. I think that other groups who ignore the folklore that happens to the members within the group are missing a good shot for preserving a little history, because I also take the position that contemporary history is going to be retained on records more accurately than it is going to be within history books."

I'M THE SLIME

A surprise awaited the audience at the end of the Saturday-evening concert at Fillmore East. As the Mothers were in the midst of their encore, Zappa introduced two guests: John Lennon and Yoko Ono. Considering that Zappa had skewered the Beatles in *We're Only In it for the Money*, and blatantly snubbed the sentiments of Lennon's anthem "All You Need Is Love" with "Oh No" on *Weasels Ripped My Flesh*, it may have looked oddly incongruous to have them sharing a stage. Lennon, however, had a fawning respect for Zappa. After all, by 1971, Lennon was tired of being a rock idol, of being a Beatle. He expressed admiration for Zappa's independence to Jann Wenner, editor of *Rolling Stone*, in *Lennon Remembers*. "I've decided I'm sick of . . . reading things about Paul [McCartney being] the musician, and George [Harrison being] the philosopher. I wonder where I fit in," Lennon told Wenner. "So I'd sooner be like Zappa and say, 'Listen, you fuckers, this is what I did, and I don't care whether you like my attitude saying it, but that's what I am . . . I'm a fuckin' artist, and I'm not a fuckin' PR agent, or the product of some other person's imagination.'"

The genesis of Zappa and Lennon's encounter began earlier in the day, thanks to journalist Howard Smith. Since November 1970, when Lennon and Ono first landed in the Big Apple from England, Smith was their constant escort. When Smith told Lennon he was off to interview Zappa for his *Village Voice* column, Lennon jumped with joy. "He's at least *trying* to do something different with the form," Lennon explained to Smith. "It's incredible how he has his band as tight as a real orchestra. I'm very impressed by the kind of discipline he can bring to rock that nobody else can seem to bring to it." Sensing Lennon's enthusiasm, Smith invited him to the interview. When they met, Smith recalled, Lennon was in awe of Zappa. Zappa, meanwhile, just waking up, was greeted by the pop star with "You're not as ugly as you are in your pictures."

"Lennon was very deferential to Frank," Smith told Albert Goldman in *The Lives of John Lennon*. "John acted like, 'I may be popular, but *this* is the real thing.'" It was Smith who suggested to John and Yoko that they join the Mothers onstage that night. Zappa wasn't immediately impressed, but the band certainly was. Zappa agreed and told Lennon and Ono to appear at the end of the second show, around two in the morning. But, according to Smith, Lennon and Ono fell to pieces with bad nerves: "John and Yoko were nervous wrecks. It was like young kids going on with the big boys for the first time. . . . She was nervous about getting up with a band as artistic as that."

The irony is that Lennon and Ono had acquired the kind of public acclaim

Zappa would never know. Yet they also recognized that in the flirtatious world of pop, stardom was fleeting next to artistic accomplishment. While Zappa's band, unconcerned about public appeal, dressed however they pleased, Lennon and Ono, trapped by the idolatry they'd helped create, worried desperately about what to wear — and also needed a gram of cocaine to calm their nerves. When the two walked onstage that night, the crowd roared their approval. Zappa, writes Goldman, "stood scowling at the house, obviously thinking: 'These scumbags! What the hell do they know about music?'"

The first song the band performed with their guests, "Well (Baby, Please Don't Go)," was one from Lennon's Beatles days at the Cavern in the early '60s. This faithful cover of the Olympics' late-'50s hit started a little rough, but Lennon's voice quickly became confident. While Yoko periodically wailed, the band provided a steady groove until Lennon yelled out, "ZAP-PAH!" At which point, Zappa provided a tasty blues solo. The next song, titled "Jam Rag" on the Lennon/Ono album *Sometime in New York City*, was a loose jam. On the album, writing credits went to Lennon and Ono, even though the song was Zappa's.

"During our time onstage, a number of pieces were improvised, but a number of pieces that were played were absolutely written compositions that had already been on other albums — namely a song of mine called 'King Kong,'" Zappa told Kurt Loder years later. "The deal that I made with John and Yoko was that we were both to have access to the tapes and could deploy them any way we wanted. They got a duplicate copy of the master, and I was gonna mix it and put it out as part of this Mothers album. They put out this record and took 'King Kong' — which obviously had a tune, and a rhythm, and chord changes — and they called it 'Jam Rag,' and accredited the writing and publishing to themselves." When Zappa eventually questioned Yoko about the issue, she merely told him she was suing their label.

"The other thing that was sad was, there's a song on there called 'Scumbag,'" Zappa continued, "but the way they mixed it, you can't hear what Mark and Howard are singing. There's a reason for that. They're singing, 'Now Yoko's in the scumbag, we're putting Yoko in a scumbag.'" Zappa restored that omission when he included their live session on his *Playground Psychotics* CD (1992).

In June, the Mothers again faced charges of obscenity, this time at the Dome, in Virginia Beach, Virginia. The police had warned the band about using four-letter words onstage, but given the freedom of speech practiced by the band, Flo & Eddie dared to utter the word "fuck." It earned them a night in jail. But that wasn't the

I'M THE SLIME

only significant aspect of the show. Opening for the Mothers was a black *a cappella* group called the Persuasions. Back in 1969, David Dashev, a *Los Angeles Times* rock critic, was in New York. He ran into Stan Krause, a promoter who staged *a cappella* concerts in Jersey City. Krause played Dashev a tape of the Persuasions, five singers who worked the streets of New York: Jerry Lawson, Jayotis Washington, "Sweet Joe" Russell, Jimmy Hayes, and Toubo Rhoad. To finance their music, the group worked part-time jobs for the Bedford-Stuyvesant Restoration; a federal program to restore the rapidly dilapidating Brooklyn neighborhood. After spending their days helping to rebuild Bed-Stuy, they sang at fundraisers at night.

Dashev phoned Zappa in L.A., knowing that he was signing unconventionally talented artists to the Straight label. Frank and Gail got to hear a song, recorded live, called "Searchin' for My Baby," and by the fall of 1970, the Persuasions had their first album on the Straight label, titled *Acappella*. The first side consisted of the field recording tape, while the rest was done in a studio. But the Persuasions hadn't met Zappa until that night at Virginia Beach.

The evening was fraught with tension simply because the Persuasions were crossing a color barrier that divided the black beach from the white. Jimmy Hayes later told journalist Rip Rense, "We were the first black group to play in Virginia Beach, when we opened for Frank. Everybody was tense and nervous and shit. . . . Blacks just didn't go to Virginia Beach. I remember when we opened, man, a state trooper came up to us and said, 'You guys got huge balls to go up onstage with no instruments at all and do what you did. Huge balls.'" The Persuasions would open for the Mothers one last time in the much more comfortable confines of New York's Carnegie Hall in October.

On August 7, the Mothers played the Pauley Pavilion, the site of the Zubin Mehta extravaganza in May 1970. Jimmy Carl Black joined the band on this night to sing "Lonesome Cowboy Burt" from *200 Motels*, his last appearance with Zappa until *You Are What You Is* in 1981 (where he would sing another "cowboy" song, "Harder Than Your Husband"). Zappa had purchased a Scully four-track to replace the two-track recording device that Dick Kunc had operated from his suitcase back in the '60s. Excerpts from the Pauley show would make up the entirety of their next album, *Just Another Band From L.A.*.

The epic tale "Billy the Mountain," which opens the album, is filled with the kind of in-jokes only a person from Southern California would understand. Even so, it is a brilliantly constructed and beautifully performed piece of musical theater. The storyline concerns Billy the Mountain and his lovely wife, Ethel (a tree that grew out of his shoulder), who reside between Rosamond and Gorman, just a few miles from where Zappa spent his youth in Lancaster. Billy and Ethel make their living posing for postcards. One day, Billy gets a royalty check and they decide to take a holiday to New York (the *Tonight Show* theme is heard every time New York is mentioned). Unfortunately, Billy innocently levels every piece of real estate he crosses. In Columbus, Ohio, he receives his draft notice. Since Ethel doesn't want him to go, she is called a communist by the media. As Billy and Ethel continue their destructive journey across America, the government turns to Studebaker Hoch, a "fantastic new hero of the current economic slump." Sent to stop Billy, he pastes on wings, pulls down his pants, and applies generous amounts of Aunt Jemima syrup that attracts thousands of flies, and then . . . up, up, and away! While standing on the bulging giant's mouth, Studebaker confronts Billy about serving his country, but Billy laughs and sends Studebaker falling into the rubble below. The song's simple motto: A mountain is something you don't want to fuck with.

The story of Billy the Mountain is slight, but what brings it to life is the quick shifts in pace and the free-associative references quoted by the band. Throughout the oratorio they work in allusions to numerous pop songs ("Suite: Judy Blues Eyes" by Crosby, Stills & Nash; the phrase "canyons of your mind" from the song "Elusive Butterfly" by Bob Lind; and, in one hilarious moment, when Billy causes a fissure in the Earth's crust, those punsters Flo & Eddie sing Eddie Fisher's "Oh Mein Papa"). Zappa also includes pop references to everyone from Bullwinkle to L. Ron Hubbard, fully expecting the listener to pick up on them.

With "Billy the Mountain," Zappa finally achieves — onstage — a live representation of what he'd only been able to do by editing tape in the studio. "Call Any Vegetable" is close to the original — except during "Soft-Sell Conclusion," where Flo & Eddie riff on various TV commercials. And "Eddie, Are You Kidding?" is inspired by a Zachary All menswear commercial. Mark Volman sings the song's key lines:

> *I'm coming over shortly*
> *Because I am a portly*
> *You promised you could fit me in a fifty-dollar suit*
> *Eddie, are you kidding?*

By the end, the song quotes the Crests' 1958 hit "Sixteen Candles."

I'M THE SLIME

"Zappa frames his ideas in ways that work like anti-adverts," Ben Watson said in 1996. "He uses advertising techniques that are appetizing in terms of pithy slogans, along with humorous phrases and running jokes — but with Zappa, there's no product being pushed. There's no strategy of being bound into anything. It's there for its own sake. So he latches himself to the most degrading part of commercialism, and then he turns those techniques on their head. This is what makes Zappa subversive."

"Magdalena" is an incest song about a French-Canadian lumberjack who abuses his daughter. Done in a faux French-Canadian folk style, with a sample quote of Stravinsky's violin capriccio from his *Violin Concerto in D*, the song is a catalog of clichés redeemed by the vigorous humor of the performance:

My daughter dear, do not be concerned
When your Canadian daddy comes near
I work so hard don't you understand making maple syrup
For the pancakes of our land.

A rousing version of "Dog Breath" ends the album and amply demonstrates why Zappa remarked that Flo & Eddie brought new spirit and energy to the older material. Despite renunciations by critics, *Just Another Band From L.A.* is musically much fuller than *Fillmore East, June 1971* simply because of the expansiveness of its material.

In October, *200 Motels*, the movie and the soundtrack, were released to mixed reviews. Vincent Canby, in the *New York Times*, didn't hate it, but he said it became exhausting too quickly, and that it had "several dozen potentially funny ideas that are never developed, since the movie has the attention span of a speed freak." Robert Hilburn of the *Los Angeles Times* was positive. He thought the record had "a sense of vitality and excitement akin to some of the feelings generated by the early rock records."

Zappa himself assessed the work with characteristic modesty. "Within the scope of the budget that we were given, I'd say I got maybe 40 to 50 per cent of what I wanted to get out of it," he said. "You just have to kiss the rest of it goodbye because there's not enough time or money to do it perfect."

The rest of the year would be considered anything *but* perfect. After *200 Motels* opened, the band began a European tour in November, playing two shows at the

Konserthuset in Stockholm. After the second show, two kids asked Zappa a favor. Their younger brother, Hannes, couldn't stay for the second show because he had school the next morning. So they asked Zappa if he'd come to their home, wake up Hannes, and surprise him. Zappa agreed, and indeed, Hannes was surprised. That turned out to be the highlight of the tour. On December 4, they played the Casino in Montreux, Switzerland. It was a pretty lively show, including "Peaches en Regalia," "Anyway the Wind Blows," "Call Any Vegetable," "Magdelena," and a new piece called "Sofa," another epic story. Neil Slaven describes the twisted plot (which had formed the original prelude to "Billy the Mountain") succinctly: "God, along with his faithful Saint Bernard, Wendell, decides to make a raunchy home movie with an unnamed small girl, Squat the Magic Pig, and a fat, floating sofa . . . the everyday story of a girl and a magic pig sharing an intimate experience on a sofa — without soiling it — has its moments."

The most memorable moment in the concert, however, came during the encore while Don Preston was playing his customary mini-Moog solo during "King Kong." As Preston reached his peak, an overexuberant fan fired a flare into the ceiling of the hall. Within moments, the rattan that covered the ceiling started to burn and the room was filling with smoke. Zappa quickly tried to urge the capacity crowd of close to three thousand people out of the hall. Since the front door was too narrow for a crowd this size, they escaped through a big window that a roadie smashed. The group, meanwhile, escaped through an underground tunnel. No one was seriously injured, but the building — and the Mothers' equipment — was destroyed. Although this event didn't end up in the Zappa folkloric canon, it did take residence in the repertoire of a middling hard-rock band named Deep Purple. Their lead singer, Ian Gillian, was in the audience when the fire broke out. "Everyone was a bit dazed," Gillian told Q. "We went back to the hotel and sat in the restaurant watching this beautiful building blaze. Flames were shooting two, three hundred feet, and the wind coming down the mountains blew the smoke across Lake Geneva. . . . And [bass player] Roger Glover came up with the idea of 'Smoke On the Water,' and scribbled it down on a napkin." It became Deep Purple's biggest hit on their album *Machine Head* (1972).

With Christmas coming, the Mothers voted to finish the ten remaining tour dates. They canceled a week of concerts in Paris, Lyons, and Brussels, so they could gather some equipment. They had a gig at the Rainbow Theatre in London, and Zappa wanted to get there early enough to rehearse so the band would be at ease with the new gear. On December 10, they performed the first of four shows there

I'M THE SLIME

with little problem. For the encore, they performed "I Want to Hold Your Hand." When the band left the stage, Zappa returned to introduce the next number. Suddenly a man in the audience ran onto the stage and pushed Zappa into the orchestra pit — it was a fifteen-foot drop. Some roadies grabbed the assailant, while the band returned to the stage not knowing what had happened. Mark Volman was the first to see him. "I remember looking down at him from the top of the pit," Volman told *Musician*. "His leg was bent underneath him like a Barbie doll; his eyes were open but there was no life in them. Two or three of us were cradling him in the pit and the blood was running from his head to his knees. We weren't sure if he'd live through the night."

The injuries were serious. Besides gashes and contusions to his head, Zappa had also had a broken leg and rib, a fractured ankle, and a paralyzed arm caused by damage to his spine. He also had a crushed larynx — the pitch of his voice dropped a full third as a result. An ambulance took him to Royal Northern Hospital, while the police identified the suspected assailant as Trevor Charles Howell, a twenty-four-year-old manual laborer from London. He was arraigned at North London Court, charged with causing grievous bodily harm, and remanded on bail. When Howell was released, Zappa hired a round-the-clock bodyguard. Zappa spent the next month recovering at the Weymouth Street Clinic. At his arraignment, Howell said he'd attacked Zappa because Zappa was "making eyes" at his girlfriend. He also claimed she was in love with Zappa. But at his trial in March, Howell changed his testimony, now claiming that the show didn't give him value for his money. He was sentenced to a year in jail for maliciously inflicting grievous bodily harm.

With his leg in a cast for four months, and confined to a wheelchair, Zappa headed off to Hawaii to recuperate. When he eventually healed, one leg would be shorter than the other and slightly crooked (something he'd commemorate in the songs "Zomby Woof" and "Dancin' Fool"). Zappa may not have been able to perform, but his injuries didn't stop him from working. Quite the contrary, he wrote a science-fiction musical called *Hunchentoot*, a venture that never came to fruition, except as part of the plot to *Them or Us (The Book)*. A few of the songs were later included on *Sleep Dirt* (1979). Zappa also composed a Stravinsky-inspired musical fairy tale about the tribulations of time and trends called "The Adventures of Greggery Peccary," which would be featured on *Studio Tan*.

One of the first major projects that appealed to Zappa was an album of R&B songs by a real group that called itself Ruben & the Jets. Ruben Ladron de Guevara, a Mexican R&B singer, had approached Zappa while he was recuperating — Guevara wanted to form a band using the name of the fictional group created by the Mothers. Zappa was not only enthusiastic about the idea, he also offered to arrange some of the songs, contribute a track, and produce the album. "Oh, Frank loved the idea. It was the kind of thing we did in high school," Motorhead Sherwood told Pete Feenstra of *Real Music*. "We played rock 'n' roll, R&B, and all that stuff, before we joined the Mothers. So when Ruben came up with the idea to start a band that was going to play that old-time R&B, Frank was very interested." Not surprisingly, the first thing Zappa told Guevara to do was call Motorhead to play baritone sax. Motorhead then introduced Zappa to a terrific slide guitar player named Tony Duran. The group was then filled out with talented sidemen like Robert "Frog" Camarena on rhythm guitar; Johnny Martinez on bass, keyboards, and vocals; Robert "Buffalo" Roberts on tenor sax; Bill Wild on bass; and Bob Zamora on drums. Their album, *For Real*, would be released in 1973, featuring spirited covers of "Dedicated to the One I Love," "Charlena," and "All Night Long." Zappa contributed a song of his own, "If I Could Only Be Your Love Again," which contained some of his intricately arranged vocal harmonies.

The latest chapter of the Mothers was concluded with the release of *Just Another Band From L.A.* in May 1972. Even if the reviews were tepid, the album made No. 85 on the charts. Those who missed the more instrumental side of Zappa, however, didn't have long to wait. Zappa booked some session work at Paramount Studios in Hollywood that spring. He was looking to create a follow-up to *Hot Rats* with music that would feature more extended soloing, only this time with a big-band sound rather than the small combo concertos of *Hot Rats*. Zappa decided to bring back some old friends. George Duke returned from his tour with Cannonball Adderley; Don Preston sat in again with his mini-Moog synthesizer; Aynsley Dunbar was back on the drums; Alex Dmochowski, the bass player in the Aynsley Dunbar Retaliation, went billed as "Erroneous." A large brass section included some seasoned West Coast session men like Sal Marquez, Bill Byers, Joel Peskin, Ken Shroyer, and Mike Altschul.

They ended up recording enough material to fill two albums. The first would be called *Waka/Jawaka* and the follow-up, *The Grand Wazoo*. "On the *Waka/Jawaka* and *Grand Wazoo* albums I ended up writing and arranging all the horn parts and giving [Zappa] ideas . . . and he was very accepting," trumpeter Sal Marquez told *Musician*. "We had a good chemistry, maybe because we shared the same birthday." Marquez was most impressed by Zappa's musical stringency. "We may have looked

I'M THE SLIME

like freaks, but everyone had the intellect to carry it through, musically and otherwise," he recalled. The evidence of that is obvious on both albums. *Waka/Jawaka*, released in July 1972, was designed as a sequel to *Hot Rats* (the album cover features a sink with the taps labeled Hot and Rats), but if the music lacked the snap that Underwood and Zappa concocted in 1969, there's still some very fine material on this album.

"Big Swifty" opens *Waka/Jawaka* in a flurry of electronic jazz that resembles some of Miles Davis' early-'70s experiments. The theme is taken from "The Adventures of Greggery Peccary" (Greggery works for the trendsetting company Big Swifty), but most of this near-twenty-minute piece is improvisations between Sal Marquez on trumpet and Zappa on guitar, while Duke sets loose a swirling ambience of electronic keyboard noodling. "Your Mouth" comes from a long folk and blues tradition of songs like "Delia's Gone," "Sleeping in the Ground," and "I Can't Be Satisfied," about jealous men who kill their wives or lovers. In "Your Mouth," the singer faces a lover who's been unfaithful and not the least bit understanding:

> *I heard your story when you come home*
> *You said you went to see your sister last night*
> *Well, you might lose a bunch of teeth*
> *And find a funeral wreath*
> *While you're laying in the ground all alone.*

What runs against the grain of the song, though, is the peppy blues arrangement and the lively vocal by Chris Peterson. Listeners not truly paying attention might find themselves singing along to lines like this:

> *So tell me where are you comin' from with all them lines*
> *As you stumble in at breakin' of the day*
> *Where are you comin' from, my shotgun say*
> *Because he just might want to blow you away.*

"It Just Might Be a One-Shot Deal" is a rare country song by Zappa that isn't a snide put-down of rednecks. By the '70s, the Flying Burrito Brothers, the Eagles, Little Feat, and Linda Ronstadt had created a fusion of country and rock that was becoming a genre of its own. "It Just Might Be a One-Shot Deal" is something else again, though. It's a paranoid hallucination sung — in a conspiratorial whisper —

by Janet Neville-Ferguson (who played a groupie in *200 Motels*) and Sal Marquez, about a frog with a satchel and some sand, who starts to grow an unusual garden in an apartment hallway:

> *You can be lost and you can wanna be found*
> *But keep an eye on that frog*
> *Whenever he jump around*
> *You keep a watchin' him.*

Jeff Simmons returns to play Hawaiian guitar, while Zappa performs on an instrument of his own creation: the electric bedsprings. "Sneaky Pete" Kleinow of the Flying Burrito Brothers has a marvelous pedal steel solo (the first for a Zappa song).

"Waka Jawaka" is a brisk big-band number that showcases a great Don Preston mini-Moog solo and an imaginatively precise drum solo by Anysley Dunbar. The idea of a Moog synthesizer in the middle of a big-band composition is yet another example of Zappa's brilliantly incongruous concepts. During the early '70s, the Moog was popularized by musicians such as Walter (soon to be Wendy) Carlos (*Switched-On Bach*) and Tomita (*The Planets, The Firebird*), who treated the instrument as a flash-in-the-pan commercial gimmick. Preston, on "Waka Jawaka," explores some of the serious musical possibilities inherent in this electronic keyboard.

The Grand Wazoo, which came out the following December, has more variety and more frolic than *Waka/Jawaka*. "For Calvin (and His Next Two Hitchhikers)" is another surreal tale based on a true story. The saga concerns how illustrator Cal Schenkel, driving a 1959 white Mark VIIII Jaguar that he borrowed from Zappa, ended up with two hippie hitchhikers in his backseat. Schenkel didn't invite them in the car, and neither would they tell him where they were going. They didn't even answer any of his questions. When Schenkel arrived at his studio (where he was working on the *Uncle Meat* cover), he asked them to leave and still they didn't reply. Schenkel figured they were probably on acid and left them in the car while he went to work. Every now and again he would look out the window, and they would still be sitting there. After an hour, it appeared they had finally left. "Then shortly afterwards," Schenkel recalled, "I saw that they were back! They went to the supermarket for a loaf of bread and lunch meat and started making sandwiches in the back of the car. They were eating their lunch!" When they were through, they mysteriously departed.

I'M THE SLIME

"For Calvin (and His Next Two Hitchhikers)" again features Neville-Ferguson and Marquez, using the same creepily soft vocals that added the comic paranoia to "It Just Might Be a One-Shot Deal." But, like Captain Beefheart's role in "Willie the Pimp," they serve only to introduce the tune because, for the most part, it's a prolonged instrumental. One portion of the composition is music lifted from the "New Brown Clouds" section of "The Adventures of Greggery Peccary."

"The Grand Wazoo" (which bears no resemblance to Captain Beefheart's recitation of a few years earlier) is a big-band swing number in the same vein as "Waka Jawaka." It's essentially a vehicle for some heavy blowing. Using as its main theme an instrumental version of "Think It Over," from the unreleased *Hunchentoot*, "The Grand Wazoo" also features a stinging slide guitar solo from Tony Duran, the lead guitarist of Ruben & the Jets.

"Cleetus Awreetus-Awrightus" is a cartoon jamboree — part Carl Stalling and part Keystone Kops — that takes its title from the zany short story Zappa concocted in the album's liner notes. Uncle Meat (first name: Stu) sits in his laboratory twiddling knobs and comes up with a replica of ancient Rome, where the Funky Emperor, Cleetus Awreetus-Awrightus, leads an army of unemployed musicians against arch-villains the Mediocrates of Pedestrium. They apparently duke it out every Monday night, with their battles recorded on everything from telephone poles to spray-painted aqueducts. "Cleetus Awreetus-Awrightus" may be brief, but like "Zolar Czakl," from *Uncle Meat*, it contains a multitude of musical ideas and fragments. Duke plays a maniacal solo on a honky-tonk piano that evokes car chases from Mack Sennett comedies. After Ernie Watts plays a stuttering sax solo that sounds like a quick series of sneezes, Zappa, Duke, and a woman identified as "Chunky" sing the tune in a la-la-la chorus, like happy drunks closing a bar.

"Cleetus Awreetus-Awrightus" races by until it collides with the slow, building melody of "Eat That Question." In Zappa's story, Questions are "a grotesque cult of masochistic ascetic fanatics who don't like music." Just like the Christians of old, they are marched to the arena. "The word 'Questions' used in that story was instead of 'Christians.'" Zappa told journalist Bob Marshall. "The original name of that song was 'Eat that Christian.' "Eat That Question" is primarily a platform for Duke's enormous abilities. His electric piano opens the song tentatively searching for the melody. When he finds it, the song lifts into the spheres until Zappa's electric guitar solo answers Duke's piano runs. While Dunbar's rhythm section powers the song forward, Duke (multi-tracked on the organ) grinds the song to a halt, where Zappa mirrors the tune's opening with a hesitant search for the lost melody.

After a brief pause, the horns join in with a triumphant finale that confirms the song's melodic march. "Blessed Relief," the album's final track, is aptly named. A beautifully relaxed ballad along the lines of "Little Umbrellas" or "Twenty Small Cigars," "Blessed Relief" features a softly muted trumpet solo from Marquez, plus some fine rhythm guitar work from Duran and a pleasantly bouncing solo from Zappa.

The Grand Wazoo doesn't have the far-reaching experimental textures of the early Mothers, or the bad-boy hijinks of the Flo & Eddie group, yet it was still a solid piece of ensemble work — and it served as an energetic warm-up for what was to come.

6

While Zappa was recording his big-band material, ex-Mothers Flo & Eddie and Jim Pons were waiting to see if the band would ever get back together. But they might as well have waited in line behind the '60s edition of the Mothers, because it wasn't going to happen. As *Waka/Jawaka* hit the record stores, Kaylan, Volman, Pons, Preston, and Dunbar created their own band. They signed with Reprise Records and released the album *The Phlorescent Leech & Eddie* in August 1972. Essentially Flo & Eddie felt abandoned, while Zappa thought they were using him as a way to promote their own group. In short, neither Zappa nor Flo & Eddie were happy with each other. "Flo & Eddie, like the Mothers before them, had ended up feeling exploited," author Neil Slaven writes. "Frank had assumed ownership of their contributions to the band's records and gigs. Frank's idea of friendship seemed to include the right to incorporate the bands' characteristics and adventures into his material, blurring the line between salaried employees and acknowledged collaborators."

Zappa's first live venture out of his wheelchair was as a reciter in a performance of Stravinsky's *L'Histoire du soldat*, conducted by Lukas Foss, at the Hollywood Bowl. Zappa also put together a slightly altered touring version of the *Grand Wazoo* band. After taking in Berlin and Holland, Zappa brought the band to London, the city of his recent nightmares. At a press conference for the show at the Oval Cricket Ground on September 16, a truly bizarre occurrence took place. A young girl entered the room, gave Zappa a bouquet of flowers, and walked away. She had told reporters she was the girlfriend of Trevor Charles Howell, the guy who had knocked Zappa off the stage, and that she had brought the flowers as a gesture of remorse. Zappa discovered later that the promoter had hired her as a publicity stunt.

The band finished its remaining dates in New York and Boston, and officially broke up on September 24. In November, the Zappas received bad news. Christine Frka, former GTO and governess to their children, had died of a heroin overdose in Massachusetts. She had been trying to put together a modeling career.

At the end of 1972, Zappa announced a new Mothers of Invention lineup and a new label, DiscReet. The label was named after one of jazz performer Slim Gaillard's favorite phrases, but it also referred to a quadraphonic sound system that had just been invented. This revolutionary stereo technology allowed the listener, through additional speakers, to hear four-channel sound. Poor album distribution had finally forced Zappa and Herb Cohen to dismantle Bizarre/Straight. Cohen also believed the cast of characters they had signed didn't help, either. Wild Man Fischer, for instance, didn't exactly tear up the charts. "I don't think we sold more than six thousand copies [of *An Evening With Wild Man Fischer*]," Cohen told Michael Gray. "And Frank had been in the studio with the guy for three months.... You know, Bizarre/Straight [was] not as rich as Columbia or Capitol or Kinney or whoever it is, and we can't afford to subsidize indefinitely."

Even Beefheart, with the cult success of *Trout Mask Replica*, couldn't placate Cohen. "First off, it took us six months to get him out of all the legal entanglements he was in. So we spent a *lot* of time and money just on the legal end of things before we could even start with him properly," Cohen said. "When we went to do [*Trout Mask*], I asked him how much it was gonna cost, to give me a budget for rehearsals and production and so on, and he gave me a list of expenses, and in there he had $800 for a tree surgeon. And when I asked him what the tree surgeon was for, he said, well, the band rehearses out at his house, and there's this tree out in the front yard that overhangs the house and he wanted to make sure that the vibrations from the amplifiers didn't disturb the tree. [He felt] the tree would get angry and the overhanging branch would fall on the house in retaliation.... I'll be goddamned if I didn't get a bill for $240 which I *paid*, which was for a tree surgeon, at the end of that session."

It was obvious that the days of fronting money for such outlandish extravagances were coming to an end. Zappa often lamented that one of the better things that happened during the '60s was that at least some experimental music got recorded. "So, who *were* those wise, incredibly creative executives that made this Golden Era possible? Hip young guys with Perrier breath?" Zappa asked rhetorically. "No — they were old cigar-chomper guys who listened to the tapes and said, 'I dunno. Who knows what the fuck it is? G'head — put it out there! Who knows? I dunno.'" Looking ahead into the future, Zappa remarked, "We were better off with that attitude than we are now. The 'bright young men' are far more conservative — and more dangerous than the old guys ever were."

The truly insurgent aspects of the '60s were now over. In the early '70s, after the Manson Family massacres and the Kent State shootings, the counterculture had either turned ugly, turned to Jesus, turned to self-help therapy, or turned away altogether. As Ben Watson aptly points out, the last time the Bizarre logo made an appearance on the cover of a Mothers' album was *The Grand Wazoo* — and it appeared as "a petrified urn on a column being toppled by [the] Mediocrates of Pedestrium's army, an excellent image for the state of the counterculture."

Now Zappa wanted a band that had a more polished sound. He veered toward creating a proficient group filled with virtuoso performers, knowing he'd sacrifice some of the more outrageous aspects of what the Mothers used to be. "There are plenty of people interested in playing with the group and there are good musicians among them," Zappa told NME in 1974. "But the ones who are technically skilled don't have a sense of humor. And the ones who have a sense of humor usually don't have the technical chops." For those technical chops, he again recruited George Duke on keyboards; Ian Underwood on winds; Ruth Underwood on marimba and percussion; Sal Marquez on trumpet; and Jean-Luc Ponty on violin. "It was again a very interesting experience at the beginning," Ponty told *Le Jazz*, "because Zappa took out all the very complex instrumental music that he had stashed in his desk for a long time since it was too sophisticated for the previous members of the Mothers."

Zappa also added Bruce Fowler, a trombone player who had performed with the Petit Wazoo (a smaller version of the Grand Wazoo), and his brother Tom Fowler on bass, and drummer Ralph Humphrey. The first thing Bruce Fowler became aware of when he joined the group was the rigorous work ethic involved. "He was completely tireless," Fowler told *Musician*. "In a sense, he never stopped.... Also, he was really open-minded. He wanted to learn. He was the kind of guy who didn't stop learning at the age of twenty-five like everyone else. His vocabulary did increase and he did keep getting aware of new musicians and things."

In February 1973, the new band kicked off a U.S. tour at the Cumberland County Auditorium, in Fayetteville, North Carolina, to sharpen the new material for their debut on DiscReet, *Over-nite Sensation*. Recording had already started

Erik Satie, the eccentric 19th century composer, inspired Zappa with his own revolt against the excesses of Romanticism.
(Bettmann/CORBIS/MAGMA)

Edgard Varèse, who was Frank Zappa's musical mentor, questioned the very principles of Western music.
(Edward Gaittans/Chou Wen-Chung)

The music of Igor Stravinsky, the flamboyant Russian composer, offered Zappa a map to explore the musical past.
(Metro Toronto Library Board)

Charles Ives, the dynamic American composer, shared with Zappa a dislike for gentility. (Bettmann/CORBIS/MAGMA)

Zappa in one of his first bands, the Blackouts. Left to right, Dwight Bement, Ernie Thomas, Terry Wimberly, John Franklin, Wayne Lyles, Zappa. (MICHAEL OCHS ARCHIVES.COM)

Lenny Bruce, the controversial comic, provided Zappa with a strategy for his satire.
(© Kai Shuman/MICHAEL OCHS ARCHIVES.COM)

Frank Zappa participates in one of L.A.'s "freak outs" in 1966.
(MICHAEL OCHS ARCHIVES.COM)

An early 1965 performance of the Mothers of Invention in Los Angeles, with Ray Collins on tambourine. (MICHAEL OCHS ARCHIVES.COM)

The Mothers of Invention celebrate the release of their first album, *Freak Out!* in 1966. Left to right, Roy Estrada, Jimmy Carl Black, Carl Franzoni, unidentified woman, Elliot Ingber, Zappa, Ray Collins. (MICHAEL OCHS ARCHIVES.COM)

The cover of the Mothers' third album parodies The Beatles' *Sgt. Pepper's Lonely Hearts Club Band* in 1968. (MICHAEL OCHS ARCHIVES.COM)

Frank Zappa and his wife Gail, who was pregnant with Moon Unit in 1967. (©Alice Ochs/michael ochs archives.com)

Frank, Gail, and Moon Unit in 1968. (michael ochs archives.com)

The Mothers of Invention circa 1968 — not one of the "beautiful" groups. Left to right, Art Tripp, Roy Estrada, Jimmy Carl Black, Ian Underwood, Motorhead Sherwood, Zappa, Don Preston, Bunk Gardner.
(MICHAEL OCHS ARCHIVES.COM)

Captain Beefheart (a.k.a. Don Vliet), in fur coat and top hat, observes his Magic Band during the recording of *Trout Mask Replica* (1969).
(MICHAEL OCHS ARCHIVES.COM)

The Flo & Eddie version of the Mothers in 1971. (Henry Diltz/CORBIS/MAGMA)

Composer Frank Zappa turned movie director with *200 Motels* (1971). (CORBIS/MAGMA)

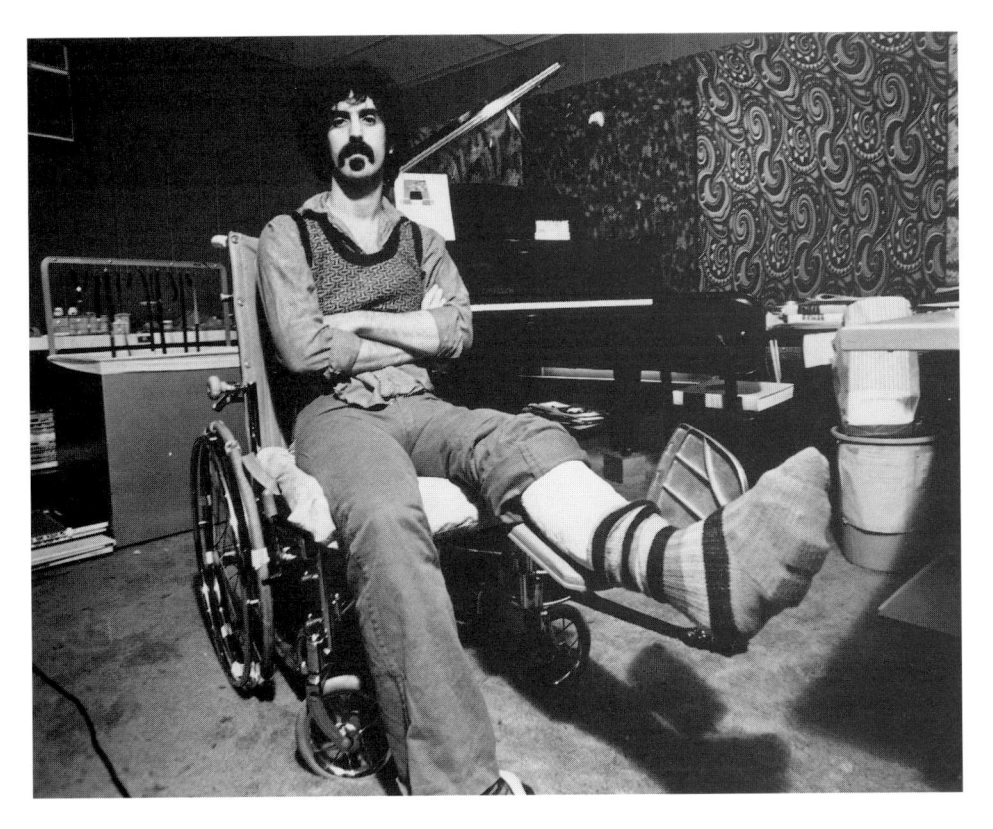

Zappa spent a good part of 1971 in a wheelchair after an overzealous fan threw him off the stage in England. (MICHAEL OCHS ARCHIVES.COM)

In 1976, Zappa produced Grand Funk Railroad's *Good Singin', Good Playin'*. Left to right, Mark Farner, Don Brewer, Zappa, Craig Frost, and Mel Schacher. (Lynn Goldsmith/CORBIS/MAGMA)

Frank Zappa hosted the popular TV show, *Saturday Night Live,* in 1978, shown here with Laraine Newman and Dan Aykroyd. (Lynn Goldsmith/CORBIS/MAGMA)

In 1979, Zappa unveiled his own Zappa Records with the release of his hit album, *Sheik Yerbouti.* (Neal Preston/CORBIS/MAGMA)

The 1974 edition of the Mothers of Invention. Left to right, Tom Fowler, Napoleon Murphy Brock, Zappa, George Duke, Ruth Underwood, Chester Thompson. (MICHAEL OCHS ARCHIVES.COM)

Frank Zappa sued Royal Albert Hall in 1975 for breach of contract. (Paul Canty/London Features International)

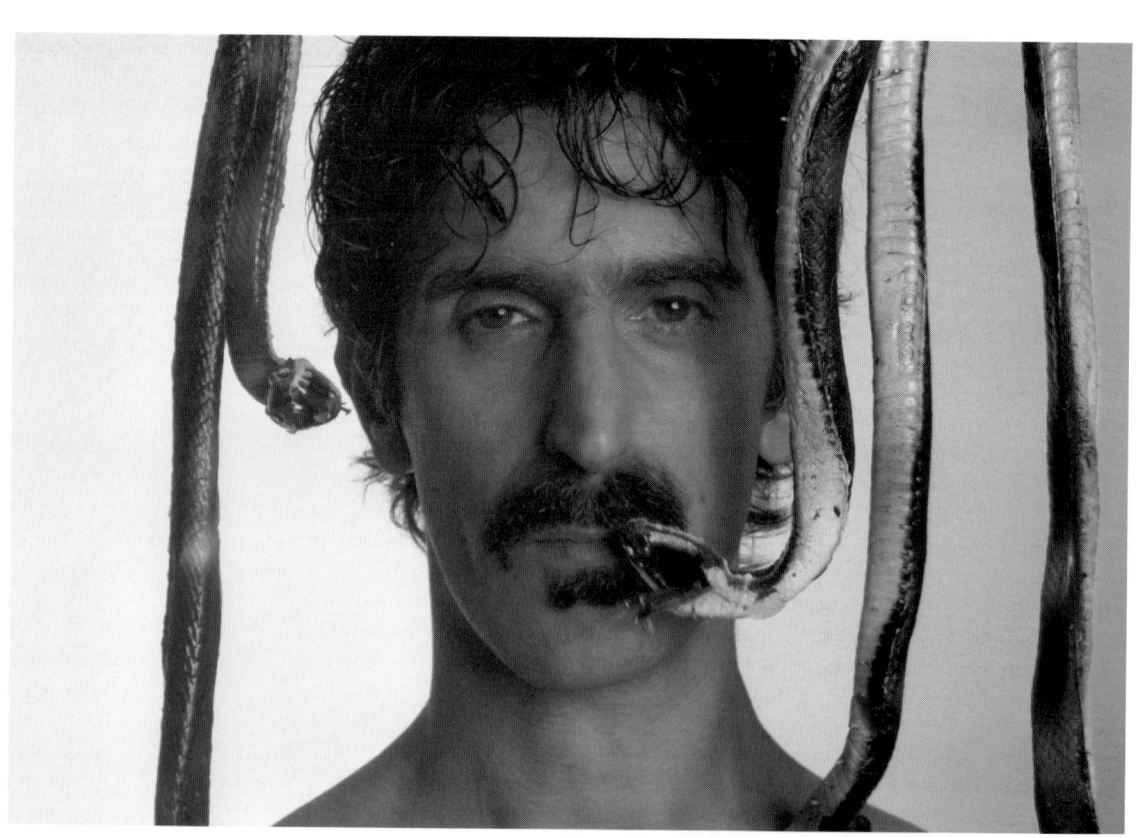

Frank Zappa's Halloween 1977 concert at the Palladium in New York became the source of his film, *Baby Snakes*. (Lynn Goldsmith/CORBIS/MAGMA)

The Zappa family (Dweezil, Gail, Ahmet, Frank, Moon Unit) relax in their home studio.
(Neal Preston/CORBIS/MAGMA)

Daughter Moon Unit Zappa penned the lyrics to the Zappa hit "Valley Girl."
(CORBIS/MAGMA)

Zappa conducting rehearsals with the London Symphony Orchestra in 1983.
(Michael Putland/Retna UK/ PONOPRESSE)

The tempestuous French composer Pierre Boulez conducted Zappa's orchestral work, *The Perfect Stranger*.
(Neal Preston/CORBIS/MAGMA)

Frank Zappa testifies before the Maryland State Senate Judiciary, which was modifying the pornographic statutes. (Wally McNamee/CORBIS/MAGMA)

In 1988, Frank Zappa took on TV evangelists and Republicans in a series of concerts. (Lynn Goldsmith/CORBIS/MAGMA)

The ill-fated 1988 Big Band tour ended after only five months.
(CORBIS/MAGMA)

Retired from rock and roll, Frank Zappa reads the American Constitution to his kids.
(Lynn Goldsmith/CORBIS/MAGMA)

I'M THE SLIME

that year at Bolic Sound in Inglewood, Paramount in L.A., and Whitney Studios in Glendale.

The first track, "Camarillo Brillo," cuts loose from the shaggy elements of the previous decade, when the singer meets a hippie Earth Mother from Camarillo, California, with wild, frizzy hair and a poncho. She may have green skin, a snake for a pet, and a doll with a pin, but she is a holdover from the late, lamented '60s counterculture:

> *She said she was a Magic Mama*
> *And she could throw a mean Tarot*
> *And carried on without a comma*
> *That she was someone I should know.*

Even though they engage in the kind of unbridled wild sex associated with the '60s, the singer eventually asks if she's wearing a *real* Mexican poncho, or is it a Sears poncho? Zappa was already identifying the co-option of the '60s. The change of era is also signaled when she tells the singer her new stereo is four-way. She's eagerly promoting the new quadraphonic system into which she's bought.

"I'm the Slime" is Zappa's second assault on television, after "Trouble Every Day." The song is a funky blues led by the pouring lava of Zappa's guitar, while Duke's electric keyboard bubbles underneath. Many listeners thought the song's target was far too easy, and that the song lacked complexity. But in "I'm the Slime," Zappa identifies himself with the very object he's criticizing. He creates ambiguity by portraying *himself* as the slime (even on the front cover of the album, his scowling face is seen dripping from a TV tube). Singing in a menacing and reverberating whisper, Zappa plays havoc with the listener by assuming a role many had already created for him:

> *I am gross and perverted*
> *I'm obsessed and deranged*
> *I have existed for years*
> *But very little has changed*
> *I am the tool of the government*
> *And industry too*
> *For I am destined to rule*
> *And regulate you.*

If Zappa is identifying himself with television, could that medium's nefarious goals also apply to the album? "The influence of television as a negative sociological element in the hands of big business and big government is a complicated thing to think about," Zappa told Dave Marsden. "It's not just what it can do to you to make you vote for somebody who shouldn't be in office, but it's all the horrible things it sells to you and the lifestyle that it merchandises to you. It makes you want things that aren't really necessary. So politics is only one aspect of the oozing."

"Dirty Love" is a straightforward piece of rock 'n' roll about lust with some nice harmonizing between Duke's piano and Ponty's violin. It's also one of Zappa's more rousing rejections of romantic illusion:

I don't need your sweet devotion
I don't want your cheap emotion
Just whip me up some dragon lotion
For your dirty love.

While existing somewhere on the far end of something sentimental like Dan Hill's "Sometimes When We Touch," "Dirty Love" also adds the perverse touch of a poodle into the equation:

Give me your dirty love
Like your mama make her fuzzy poodle do
Give me your dirty love
The way your mama make that nasty poodle chew.

Zappa was used to people taking issue with the lack of romanticism in his songs, but when he started including acts of bestiality, many thought he'd gone too far. Yet, as he told Robert O'Brian of *RockBill* in 1984, "If somebody writes a song that says, 'Fuck me, suck me, baby,' it's accepted as great American art. But you can't talk about people on either sides of the sexual fence doing strange things to each other, or to . . . dogs, or whatever. I didn't make it up. This is all real shit. People do this stuff. Why not do a song about that? It's the real world just as much as 'Fuck me, suck me, baby.' So why pick on me?"

"Fifty-Fifty" is a great rocking number where Zappa continues his diatribe against love songs and artists who set out to share their hearts with you:

I'M THE SLIME

Ain't gonna sing you no love song
How my heart is all sore
Will not beg your indulgence
'Cause you heard it before.

For lead vocals on "Fifty-Fifty," he found singer Ricky Lancelotti, who had the kind of frenzied voice not heard (in the vicinity of Frank Zappa) since Wild Man Fischer. There are moments when he sounds like Wolfman Jack after a toke of helium. Lancelotti, who had a huge mane of golden hair, had originally auditioned for the band in 1972. He got to play one show with the Mothers at the Hollywood Palladium, where he sang a little ditty (as yet unreleased) called "Smog Sucker." His personal life, however, was a hazard to his professional one. "He auditioned for the band, passed, went home and got ripped, and broke his arm," Zappa told Rip Rense for the *Lost Episodes* liner notes. "I said, 'Rick, you're not going to make the tour.' He used to carry a .45. He had a cassette in which he imitated one hundred cartoon voices in sixty seconds. I thought he was really talented. He wanted to get work as a cartoon-voice guy, but never did. OD'd. An old New Jersey tough guy." Besides Lancelotti's "ants in the pants" vocal, "Fifty-Fifty" also features a mammoth solo by Duke on the pipe organ, followed by a brief statement by Ponty before Zappa kicks in with a stinging solo choking on the strings.

"Zomby Woof," an extraordinarily complex piece of music, suggests a heavy-metal hybrid of Louis Jordan and Fats Waller. Like "Dirty Love," it's a song about carnal desire out of Howlin' Wolf, but sprinkled with horror-movie references that spice up the trashy aspects of the American kitsch that Zappa serves up:

I got a great big pointed fang
Which is my Zomby Toof
My right foot's bigger than my other one is
Like a reg'lar Zomby Hoof
If I raid your dormitorium
Don't try to remain aloof . . .

I might snatch you up screamin' through the window all nekkid
An' do it to you up on the roof, don't mess with the
ZOMBY WOOF.

Lancelotti again helps bring a certain comic hysteria to the piece, which also features some nifty horn playing by Sal Marquez, Ian Underwood, and Bruce Fowler. The reference to the right foot relates to Zappa's near-fatal accident at the Rainbow, which left him with one leg shorter than the other.

"Dinah-Moe Humm" is the song Zappa said paid the bills for years to come, and made it possible for him to mount many of his orchestral compositions. The track could probably qualify as one of Zappa's loopier folk songs — like "Camarillo Brillo" — about a boisterous sexual adventure. In this case, it's a woman who bets the singer forty dollars that he can't make her come. The singer is getting nowhere "applying rotation on her sugar plum," when suddenly Dinah-Moe's sister enters the scene to hold the bet. The singer decides to give the sister a try, which leads to Dinah-Moe squealing in ecstasy, especially when the singer starts to utilize zircon-encrusted tweezers. The specially adorned utensil, according to Dan Rabin of the computer science program at Yale University, has a prominent place in the Old West, where prestige was attached to gold-covered ornaments. In "Dinah-Moe Humm," Zappa connects that stature to sexual prowess. The name Dinah-Moe Humm first came up in the story booklet for *Uncle Meat*: "It's quiet except for a little light wind. We are traveling across the wasteland toward a huge hydro-electric dam. Dynamo hum increases as we near it."

It was easy for women to attack the song for its "sexist" attitudes, but Zappa again defended himself from simple interpretations. "I don't think there's anything wrong with depicting women the way I depict them," Zappa told *Spin*. "I think I depict them in a rather accurate way because women are not perfect. But the bulk of my songs are about men and the stupid things that men do. And they never complain. So, is it because the men are so inferior — which then proves the women's point, that they're so fucking stupid they don't know what to do, or they're too lazy to complain — or is it because the women think they really should get special treatment and they should be treated with kid gloves. . . . Rock 'n' roll is a journalistic medium as well as a musical medium."

In "Dinah-Moe Humm," Zappa was perfectly parodying the seductive crooning of many current — and popular — R&B songs. Performers who feminists never attacked, like Isaac Hayes on *Hot Buttered Soul*, or Barry White or Donna Summer, during the disco era, made consciously designed make-out music as home entertainment. With "Dinah-Moe Humm," Zappa created a piece that went to uproariously silly lengths to satirize the salacious techniques Hayes and Co. deliberately employed to have a hit record. And "Dinah-Moe Humm" not only became

I'M THE SLIME

a concert favorite, it also inspired other songs about sexual pursuit, like Meat Loaf's "Paradise by the Dashboard Light," from *Bat Out of Hell* (1977). In that operatic number, New York Yankee broadcaster Phil Rizzuto describes a boy's seduction of his girlfriend as if he was doing the play-by-play of a ballgame.

"Montana" is one of Zappa's best "cowboy" songs, reveling in the clichés with which it is having fun. "'Montana,' which is, in part, about a man who dreams of raising dental floss on a ranch in Montana, started out this way," Zappa remembered. "I got up one day, looked at a box of dental floss, and said, hmmm. I assumed that nobody had done the same thing and I felt it was my duty as an observer of floss to express my relationship to the package. . . . I've never been to Montana, but I understand there's only 450,000 people in the whole state. It has lots of space going for it, plenty of space for the production of dental floss . . . and the idea of traveling along the empty wasteland with a very short horse and a very large tweezer, grabbing the dental floss sprout as it pooches up from the bush . . . grabbing it with your tweezers and towing it all the way back to the bunkhouse . . . would be something good to imagine."

"Montana" has plenty of cowboy imagery and even a few Yippy-Ty-O-Ty-Ay's thrown in for good measure. What was a bigger surprise, however, was the participation of Tina Turner and some of the Ikettes on the bridge (they also appear briefly on "I'm the Slime," "Dirty Love," and "Dinah-Moe Humm"). They weren't credited on the album, though, because Ike Turner was less than impressed with having his wife singing about raising dental floss, or people having massive orgasms with zircon-encrusted tweezers. "Tina was so pleased that she was able to sing this thing ["Montana"] that she went into the next studio where Ike was working and dragged him into the studio to hear the results of her labor," Zappa said. "He listened to the tape and he goes, 'What is this shit?' and walked out. I don't know how she managed to stick with that guy for so long. He treated her terribly and she's a really nice lady."

Over-nite Sensation, like its title, was devoted to fleeting sensual appetites, and the tumescent sounds were more sinuous than any arrangements Zappa had yet come up with. Somehow he sensed that the quest for sexual freedom, which grew out of the '60s counterculture, had turned into something perversely mechanical.

When the album was released, in September 1973, its "slickness" divided audiences and critics. The avant-garde aspects of the '60s Mothers, with their cut-and-paste collage style, was no longer in evidence, and the vaudevillian theatrics of Flo & Eddie were also gone. *Over-nite Sensation* shimmered with a virtuosity that many felt grew from — God forbid — commercial aspirations. The music was audience-friendly, even if the lyrics were overtly lewd. Zappa had consciously set himself up as a dubious Master of Ceremonies. His closely miked voice echoed show-biz insincerity, making his satire more biting at a time when the utopian hopes of the '60s had collapsed. "It's a curious paradox," Zappa told Dave Marsden. "We have an album now that a lot of people seem to like, and it's selling very well.... It's already a No.1 album in Finland. It sold more copies in Finland than any record ever released there."

Ben Watson is the most clear-headed critic about Zappa's new direction. "*Over-nite Sensation*, in all its neon-lit brashness, was an atrocity committed on a counterculture now revealed as hypocritical and collusive," he writes. "*Over-nite Sensation* declared bankrupt the consumer-defined movement that at one time thought it could overturn governments and stop wars: explicit trash for the market, mechanical sex-substitutes on the display racks. Actually predicting many of the shock tactics of punk . . . art rock it was not."

The album cover, designed by David B. McMacken, depicted a hotel room right out of *200 Motels*, filled with discarded food, maps, stage passes, a half-fucked grapefruit (considered a roadie's delight), and road manager Marty Perellis (in a Jekyll/Hyde expression) playfully holding a fire-extinguisher hose. A frame filled with gargoyles being "cornholed" (fucked in the ass) surrounds the whole outlandish affair. *Over-nite Sensation* was exactly that — a profoundly direct study of surreal gratification.

7

Compared to the Bizarre/Straight collection of artists, DiscReet didn't have anywhere near the outrageous (or talented) clientele. Aside from Ted Nugent & the Amboy Dukes, at that time shifting from the psychedelic rock of the late '60s to heavy rock, and the quickly fading folk artist Tim Buckley, none of the artists had distinguishable talent. It didn't seem to matter, anyway. Zappa had no interest in the production end, or even the matters of business. He would defer only to company president Harold Berkman. Herb Cohen, on the other hand, simply used the label to record artists that he represented. As for Cohen's batting average, who today even remembers the Whizz Kids or Christopher Bond & the Bond? While Cohen filled DiscReet's dubious roster, Zappa and the Mothers continued to tour.

In April 1973, while Zappa was in Phoenix, playing the Circle Star Theatre, Francis Zappa died of a heart attack. Gail made the funeral arrangements while

I'M THE SLIME

Zappa was on the road. "I think my dad was an interesting man — even if I didn't get along all that well with him," Zappa wrote in *The Real Frank Zappa Book*. "Mostly I tried to stay out of his way — and I think he tried to stay out of mine as much as he could." However, Francis did more than stay out of Frank's way. When biographer David Walley talked to Francis Zappa the year before his heart attack, Frank's dad expressed an almost secret pride in his son. "I was very much aware of what his activities were in school, and Frank didn't like the damn situation at all," Francis said. "They don't like anybody to make waves because in making waves it means that these people have to think and try to ameliorate the situation . . . so Frank gave them hell from one end to the other. . . . I don't know whether it's good to tell you, but Frank's a genius. He's totally aware of who he is."

As the latest incarnation of the Mothers played together, it was obvious they were a band with great musical proficiency. "At [this] time the band wasn't grungy anymore . . . so we're not talking about bizarre-looking animals," Ruth Underwood recalled in *Musician* in 1994. "I was ready to dedicate myself completely to Frank's music. He really knew what buttons to push, emotionally and musically. . . . He knew how to synthesize people's personalities and talents. That's a very rare gift. He wasn't just a conductor standing up there waving his arms; he was playing us as people." One might think that being the only woman in the band would lend Underwood another perspective from that of the guys, but that wasn't the case. "Being the only woman was something I rarely noticed because I didn't feel particularly womanly, I just felt like one of the guys, a musician," Underwood explained. "Where it did distinguish itself was I saw the road personas of guys in the band who had wives and kids. And the wives were my friends. That sometimes was uncomfortable."

Nigey Lennon, who became very familiar with the Zappa entourage in 1971, discusses the road personas of the band members in her memoir, *Being Frank*. "The guys, most of them pretty typical rock musicians, were a bunch of pathological socializers, and I wasn't," Lennon writes. "Worse, my presence as understudy made the dissolute among them, knowing why I was there, regard me with hostility as a prig and a scab. Besides, I was a girl trying to infiltrate their male ranks. Their stage shtick revolved around road humor and groupie jokes — so where did I fit in?"

If that was the behavior of the band, what was the persona of Zappa, the composer who chronicled their activities? "He'd hang out with the guys after a show the way somebody else might attend the office cocktail party — although when the action got hot and heavy (as it inevitably did), he rarely took an active role, preferring to leave that to the others," Lennon writes. "It wasn't that he was beyond arousal — in fact, he walked around in a perpetual state of multidimensional sexual awareness that was actually far more dangerous than even the most incorrigible cocksman in the band could conceive of — but he had his own distinct way of viewing things, and in his mind these semi-public orgies were part of his supra-musical megastructure."

That megastructure — which included anything and everything — was always translated into music. "He just devoured music; that was all he thought about," Ruth Underwood explained. "We listened to his music on the bus, we rehearsed it at sound checks, we played it that night, we analyzed it the next day. I've got some original sketches, pieces he composed for me sitting in an airport waiting to board! I always meant to ask Frank: What was this for? Everything was music."

Touring took the band to Europe and Australia, and when they returned to America, Zappa found that playing music was easier than playing people. First, he fired Sal Marquez from the band. "I felt bad about leaving the group, but we were broke," Marquez told *Musician*. "One day I called Frank and tried to get him to give us a per diem. And he got all upset, claiming he never paid his groups that way. 'Not even fifteen dollars?' And he said, 'No, man, I've never done it and I'm not going to start. You can just hand in your music, too.' And that was it. I was shocked."

Then, Jean-Luc Ponty decided to leave the band, expressing misgivings about the music the Mothers were performing. "[Zappa] had written music that was very influenced by Stravinsky, so he wanted to put together a group of excellent instrumentalists," Ponty explained to *Le Jazz*. "But the public lost interest quickly, and he had to go back to satire and more commercial rock. That wasn't what I wanted to do, so I left after only seven months. He didn't take it well at all and we parted on very bad terms."

Finally, veteran Mother Ian Underwood, who had lasted through the many permutations of Zappa's bands, felt it was time to finally move on. He became involved in synthesizer programming and doing arrangements for Hollywood film scores, which is he still does to this day.

During a brief vacation, Zappa discovered a new virtuoso singer to handle the difficult songs — Napoleon Murphy Brock, a black soul singer and saxophone player. "I went to a bar called the New Red Noodle Club in Honolulu and saw Napoleon Murphy Brock playing there, and I tried to get him to be in the band,"

I'M THE SLIME

Zappa told Vicki Gabereau of CBC Radio. "That was the real reason I was meant to take that vacation — to meet him." After watching a set, Zappa asked Brock to join the band for their August 1973 European tour. Brock was tied up, but eventually joined the group for a three-day stint at the Roxy Theatre in L.A. The lineup consisted of George Duke on keyboards; Ruth Underwood on percussion; Bruce and Walt Fowler on trumpets; Tom Fowler on bass; Brock on sax, flute and vocals; the dual drums of Ralph Humphrey and Chester Thompson; Jeff Simmons on rhythm guitar; and even the stalwart Don Preston on synthesizer. This tremendously gifted group of performers also had a willingness to "put on the lampshade." Even so, that didn't mean the music was any easier to play. Nevertheless, the pleasure they took playing off one another was evident. Duke and Brock exchanged jive talk that added texture to each piece. Zappa's outrageous humor didn't drive this band; he was just another passenger within the vehicle, and the evidence could be heard on the pristine sixteen-track recordings of the show, called *Roxy & Elsewhere*.

The Mothers were scheduled to play three nights — December 10–12, 1973 — at the Roxy, where the show was being filmed. *Roxy & Elsewhere* was mostly made up of material from those concerts, with the rest coming from a Mother's Day event at the Auditorium Theatre in Chicago in 1974, and the Edinboro State College, in Edinboro, Pennsylvania, on May 8, 1974. The Roxy shows seemed to complement the band's intimacy. After all, this was a nightclub, as opposed to the concert halls and auditoriums in which Zappa was used to playing. As tight as the group was, there was also a looser, more affectionate dynamic than in any other configuration of the Mothers. Zappa wrote more intricate melodies for Ruth Underwood's marimba, and inspired George Duke to start singing along with the synthesized sounds he'd cook up. Zappa seemed happy and no longer scowled at the audience. But even if he was in a more amiable frame of mind, it didn't mean he'd abandoned the Master of Ceremony demeanor.

Zappa began each side of the double LP *Roxy & Elsewhere* with lengthy spoken introductions. "Penguin in Bondage," which opens the set, continues Zappa's fascination with contemporary attitudes toward the mechanics of sex — only this time practiced by those involved in S&M. Unlike the Velvet Underground's "Venus in Furs," which categorizes various sadomasochistic activities, "Penguin in Bondage" is a symbolist poem filled with autoerotic imagery and castration anxiety. Since the show was being filmed, however, Zappa had to introduce the song in a more implicit manner: "The procedure . . . I am circumlocuting at this present time in order to get this text on television." Throughout the song, though, Zappa mentions numerous "devices" designed to achieve sexual arousal, all couched in playfully suggestive imagery:

> *She's just like a Penguin in Bondage, boy*
> *Shake up the pale-dry*
> *Ginger ale*
> *Tremblin' like a penguin*
> *When the battery fail*
>
> *Lord, you must be havin' her jumpin' through*
> *a hoopa real fire*
> *With some Kleenex wrapped around a coat-hang wire.*
> *She's just like a Penguin in Bondage, boy.*

The story, as strange as "The Mud Shark," leaves much more to the imagination. The penguin is no doubt a chilled female who, in her bound state, has aroused her male partner. But if he "leaves her straps too loose," she will leave him impotent,

> *'Cause she just might box yer dog*
> *She just might box yer doggie*
> *An' leave you a dried-up dog biscuit.*

"Penguin in Bondage" is a medium-tempo blues that beautifully utilizes Duke's electric keyboards and features a grungy wah-wah solo from Zappa. A fan favorite, in 1988 the song would find the perfect subject. Disgraced televangelist Jimmy Swaggart had been found indulging in bizarre sexual practices with a prostitute. "Penguin in Bondage" seemed to have caught up to Swaggart's plight. It proves again how peculiarity functions so presciently in Zappa's music.

"Pygmy Twylyte" is a surreal drug song that rips by at the speed of light. Even so, Napoleon Murphy Brock manages to create something soulful out of some very hallucinogenic lyrics:

> *Crankin' an' a-coke'n*
> *In the Winchell's do-nut Midnite*

I'M THE SLIME

Out of his deep on a 'fore day run
Hurtin' for sleep in the Quaalude Midnight.

This song leads into an improvised theatrical bit, "Dummy Up," that would become common with this particular band. Jeff Simmons resurrects the role he abandoned in *200 Motels*, attempting to push some very strange drugs on Brock, just as the Devil tried to get him to rip off the ashtrays in "Dental Hygiene Dilemma." Simmons begins by having Brock smoke a damp gym sock (called "the Desenex Burger," after the foot deodorant) once worn by Frank's brother, Carl. Eventually this sock is stuffed in a diploma that provides instant knowledge with just a simple toke. Brock ultimately discovers that "you get nothing with a college degree," then comes to realize that "nothing is what I want." Zappa tweaks the institutions that promise *higher* education.

"Village of the Sun" takes us out of the abstract and into a direct, almost nostalgic, portrait from Zappa's adolescence. As music critic Greg Russo points out in *Cosmik Debris*, Zappa deliberately chose a racially and sexually integrated band to perform this very autobiographical tune. This song laments the days of Zappa's R&B band the Blackouts. Since Zappa never wrote sentimental songs, "Village of the Sun" is an oddity, its realism contrasting to the elliptical lyrics of Zappa's earlier work:

Goin' back home
To the Village of the Sun
Out in the back of Palmdale
Where the turkey farmers run.

Zappa describes how the wind used to take the paint right off cars. "The wind was a constant factor," Zappa wrote in *The Real Frank Zappa Book*, "and so were the microscopic particles of sand it carried, capable of pitting a windshield till you couldn't see out of it anymore, simultaneously reducing the finest custom paint job to garbage in an amazingly short period of time." In this faintly romantic song, Zappa also refers to "the stumblers" — these were dancers at the Village Inn who worshipped the jukebox and would "bob and weave and grovel in front of it." One night, out of curiosity, Zappa approached a stumbler (assuming he was "some kind of space-wino") and found someone not unlike himself:

> After the gig, I followed him out into the desert a few miles, to a small turkey ranch. There was a handmade sort of house with cinder-block steps. The light was on in the front window. I followed him in. In spite of the shabby exterior, the living room was pleasant, with new furniture and a very large, very new Magnavox stereo. Apparently he'd been listening to some records before his evening romp in front of the jukebox — maybe a pregame warm-up. The album on the turntable was Stravinsky's *Firebird Suite*.

"Echidna's Arf (of You)," named after an anteater in the L.A. zoo, is a dazzling display of Ruth Underwood's dexterity. The marimba had been used to great effect in the early '60s, on pop songs like Betty Everett's irresistible "The Shoop Shoop Song (It's in His Kiss)" and Chuck Jackson's splendid "I Keep Forgetting." But nobody found a way to make it sound more demonstrative than Underwood. She could madly hammer notes that still managed to warmly embrace the sinewy sound of Duke's synthesizer. The next track, "Don't You Ever Wash That Thing?" is an extended instrumental that highlights Bruce Fowler's marvelous trombone playing and features a stunning drum duet between Chester Thompson and Ralph Humphrey.

While "Cheepnis" is Zappa's tour de force tribute to the cheap sci-fi films of the '50s, it also shrewdly integrates the raw elements of the genre with the potent sexual anxieties of the period (as he also did in "Would You Go All the Way?" from *Chunga's Revenge*). In the story, Frunobulax — the name of one of the Zappa family's dogs — is a large poodle that is lured to a cave where the National Guard hope to kill it with napalm. Besides resurrecting the sexually aroused poodle from "Dirty Love," the monster is the same phallic beast the USO guy unleashed from his pants in "Would You Go All the Way?":

> GOT A GREAT BIG SLIMEY THING
> GOT A GREAT BIG HEAVY THING
> GOT A GREAT BIG POODLE THING
> GOT A GREAT BIG HAIRY THING.

Zappa is quick to point out that humor helps us come to terms with the dread of the "great big slimey thing":

I'M THE SLIME

Can y'laugh till yer weak on yer knees
If you can't, I'm sorry 'cause that's all I wanna know
I need a little more cheepnis please.

The band plays the song at a furious pace with flash-card references to cheesy monster-movie music and sound effects. "Cheepnis" begins with the singer eating a burnt weeny sandwich before watching a horror movie that features — in the end — a bigger weeny. "Monster movies are the present-day offspring of romantic tales of the unnatural," Ben Watson writes. "Zappa makes explicit the shoddiness of the illusion, as well as the crude sexual point around which the tawdry facades revolve."

But the image of napalm in "Cheepnis" is not tawdry or associated with '50s monster movies — it is tied to the modern horror of the Vietnam War, a conflict that continued to rage under Richard Nixon.

"Son of Orange County" follows "Cheepnis," combining the conclusion of "Oh No" with "The Orange County Lumber Truck." This time, however, "Oh No" is not about John Lennon, but Nixon. It aims at the heart of the Watergate crisis, with Zappa even reciting Nixon's "I am not a crook," after the line "The words from your lips." Zappa had already composed and performed another Watergate song at the Roxy show, "Dickie's Such an Asshole," but it wasn't included on the *Roxy & Elsewhere* album (it would turn up in 1989 on the CD compilation *You Can't Do That on Stage Anymore, Vol. 3*). Zappa follows "Son of Orange County" with an R&B version of the Watts riot song "More Trouble Every Day" that only includes the first third of the original lyrics. However, in this context, it's hard not to hear the song as an indictment of the Nixon administration.

"The Be-Bop Tango (of the Old Jazzmen's Church)" is an augmented number that satirizes both the tango and modern jazz, but then turns into a combination of complex rhythmic arrangements (out of *Uncle Meat*) and audience participation (a perverse shadow of *American Bandstand*, guest dancers from the audience, and a stripper). In the spoken introduction, Zappa calls the piece "a perverse tango" that's "hard to play." He is careful to inform the band that he wants all "the right notes on the tape." Portions of "The Be-Bop Tango" once formed a small part of a piece called "Farther Oblivion," which the 1973 band performed in Europe. During a show in Stockholm, the band played some of the more difficult sections so badly that Zappa forced them to do the piece again.

"The Be-Bop Tango" playfully quotes from Charles Mingus' "Trio and Group Dancers," and, at one point, Duke scats a hilarious version of Thelonious Monk's signature composition, "Straight, No Chaser." Yet despite Zappa's vast knowledge of jazz and his use of jazz musicians, his feelings about the music were always contradictory. "I came into contact with Charlie Parker records and things like that, but they didn't hold my interest," Zappa told Nigel Leigh. "I just couldn't follow it." But much of Zappa's distaste for jazz came from aficionados who considered the genre to be an exalted form of American music. Naturally, after twisting bebop conventions in knots, Zappa concludes "The Be-Bop Tango" with some straight ahead R&B. *Roxy & Elsewhere* would be released in September 1974 and peak at No. 26 in the charts.

During January and February 1974, Zappa took a break from the road and went back into the studio to record some tracks that would be part of his next solo album, *Apostrophe (')*. The sessions also produced a bicentennial parody, "200 Years Old," an autobiographical companion to "Village of the Sun" called "Cucamonga," and the opening intro to "Muffin Man." These songs would appear on *Bongo Fury*. *Apostrophe (')*, like *Weasels Ripped My Flesh*, was a compilation of material collected over a couple of years. But unlike *Weasels*, the incongruity wasn't built into the theme of the album: it had a seamless spirit closer to its predecessor, *Over-nite Sensation*. (When Rykodisc first released the album on CD in 1986, it was actually teamed with *Over-nite Sensation*.)

Apostrophe (') covers a wide variety of typical Zappa subjects, including masturbation, civil rights, religious cults, cosmology, and foot odor. "Don't Eat the Yellow Snow," a fairy tale in four parts, resembles Prokofiev's *Peter and the Wolf*, especially in the way it integrates recitation with music. While Prokofiev's story is about a young boy who fools a wolf, Zappa's ribald fantasy is essentially about a young Inuit named Nanook who tries to fool a fur trapper. It is an absurdist allegory about masturbation and sex done up in a colorful array of symbolist imagery. The name Nanook is derived from Robert J. Flaherty's 1922 silent documentary *Nanook of the North*, a fascinating early account of Inuit life in the Hudson Bay region of Northern Quebec.

As we hear the cold northerly winds blow, Zappa relates a dream in which he was an Eskimo whose mother warns him against wasting his money and, more importantly (at least in that part of the world), "Watch out where the huskies go/An' don't you eat that yellow snow." Ben Watson is quick to point out that the advice about thriftiness resembles parental warnings about masturbation:

I'M THE SLIME

"Parental threats about the danger of sex suggest anal retention and restriction of spending (a Victorian term for orgasm)."

In "Nanook Rubs It," Nanook encounters an evil fur trapper "who was strictly from commercial" (here, Zappa nimbly quotes Lionel Hampton's 1946 hit "Midnight Sun") who starts attacking his favorite baby seal with a lead-filled snowshoe. Employing the deadly yellow snow crystals his mother warned him against, Nanook starts rubbing tainted snow cones in the fur trapper's eyes. He employs them with "a vigorous circular motion hitherto unknown to the people in this area, but destined to take the place of the mud shark in your mythology." The "mud shark" reference draws a direct line to masturbatory thoughts, and Nanook's action, which deprives the fur trapper of his sight, follows through on that idea. In the dream, the identities of Nanook and the fur trapper are virtually interchangeable, Zappa using the first person initially for Nanook, then shifting it to the fur trapper.

The blinded trapper turns on Nanook with snow cones of his own that consist primarily of dogshit. Watson, citing Freudian psychoanalyst Norman O. Brown, suggests that "parental threats about sexuality cause regression from the genital to the anal stage, a fascination with faeces that finds its sublimation in moneymaking and capital formation." Which is why, after the trapper has escaped Nanook's clutches, he remembers an "Eskimo legend" that says he can seek repair at the parish of St. Alfonzo. "Having suffered the traditional punishment for masturbation — blindness — the fur trapper meets someone involved in the mass production of pancakes," Watson writes. "St. Alfonzo's Pancake Breakfast," which opens with a flurry from Ruth Underwood on the vibes, has the trapper trying to recover his sight by covering his eyes with margarine. After pissing on bingo cards ("in lieu of the latrine"), he regains his sight and witnesses the first example of moral piety. A handsome parish lady makes her "entrance like a queen," but she is flanked by her lover — a marine — whose genitals she abuses for her amusement ("Why don't you treat me mean? Hurt me, hurt me, oooooh!"). Zappa asserts that underneath middle-class decorum and gentility lies more perverse sexual fantasies that equate masochism with pleasure.

In "Father O'Blivion," we are introduced to the Grand Wazoo himself, Father Vivian O'Blivion, who is "whipping up the batter for the pancakes of his flock." Zappa makes it clear the pancakes symbolize O'Blivion's semen, and it's his sublimated sexuality — in essence, he invites his followers to eat his come — that he uses to control the flock. In a stroke of mad genius, Zappa has O'Blivion sing

"Lock Around the Crock," a twisted variation on Bill Haley & the Comets' "Rock Around the Clock," the very song that set off a wave of teenage rebellion in *Blackboard Jungle*. "Rock 'n' roll is delinquent music that proposes immediate pleasure against the deferred gratification of school and work," Ben Watson remarks. With his cheery, sacrilegious behavior, Zappa, who regarded fellatio as either an act of unbridled pleasure or enforced subjugation, uses that metaphor to show how religious leaders can make their followers servile: "Won't you eat my sleazy pancakes . . . they're so light 'n fluffy white/We'll raise a fortune by tonite." In the end, Father O'Blivion makes himself servile by offering a snowshoe to the parish lady, while quoting an Imperial Margarine ad ("Good morning, your Highness/Ooo-ooo-ooo"). In this heretical religious parable, Zappa exposes the devious psychology of fundamentalism.

After exposing one form of carny tent-show theology, he shifts into satirizing another in "Cosmik Debris." During the early '70s, following in the misguided footsteps of the Beatles and the Beach Boys with their zealous deference to the Maharishi Yogi, several rock and jazz performers had turned their attention to a perverse bastardization of Eastern religion. Sri Chinmoy was the latest religious idol to snare the attention — and loot — of talented musicians like guitarists John McLaughlin and Carlos Santana. McLaughlin's Mahavishnu Orchestra had toured with the Mothers in 1973, so it's likely that Zappa wrote this song after coming into contact with this brilliant band and their newfound state of nirvana.

"Cosmik Debris" is a slow blues that is peppered with appropriate Spike Jones–inspired sound effects. The song introduces a guru, the Mystery Man, who makes Zappa an offer:

> *If I was ready, willing 'n' able*
> *To pay him his regular fee*
> *He would drop all the rest of his pressing affairs*
> *And devote His Attention to me*

Zappa advises this counterfeit deity to quit "jivin' with that Cosmik Debris" after he attempts to show Zappa just how he "could reach *nervonna* t'nite." To remove the mystical aura from this charlatan, Zappa snatches away his crystal ball and reveals it as nothing more than a circus trick. He hypnotizes the guru and puts him to sleep, while "robbing his rings an' pocket watch." As he tells the self-appointed divinity his future, Zappa sings, referring to Maharishi Yogi's indiscretions with

I'M THE SLIME

female followers, "The price of meat has just gone up/An' yer ol' lady has just gone down. . . ." When Zappa asks the Mystery Man, as he did of Camarillo Brillo, whether he's wearing a real poncho or a Sears poncho, he (not so subtly) connects the failed '60s counterculture to the faddish religious cults that grew from its ashes. As a final benediction, "Cosmik Debris" finishes with the phrase *om shanti*, Sanskrit for "peace."

Perhaps offering an alternative to those cults, "Excentrifugal Forz" is a brief introduction to Zappa's own personal cosmology. His worldview is shaped by a scientific perspective rather than a spiritual one. It doesn't rely on religious figureheads, but is based on Zappa's elaborate connection between music, mathematics, and the stars. Zappa adds an oblique reference to the turban-wearing Hammond organ player Korla Pandit (named "Korla Plankton" in the song), who did the music for Chandu the Magician's radio episodes in the late '40s.

> *Him 'n me can play the blues*
> *An' then I'll watch him buff that tiny ruby*
> *That he use*
> *He'll straighten up his turban*
> *An' eject a little ooze*
> *Along a one-celled Hammond Organism.*

Zappa obviously trusts the more kitsch-laden Korla Pandit, with his clichéd Arabian keyboard riffs, than any religious idol promising him Heaven — for Zappa, playing the blues with Korla would be Heaven. Zappa also includes a character named Pup Tentacle who crosses the galaxy between the past and the future ("I'll find out how the future is/Because that's where he's been") and reinforces his belief in a time continuum ("The time he crossed the line/From LATER ON to WAY BACK WHEN").

The title track, "Apostrophe,'" which Ben Watson sees as a nod to Thelonious Monk's "Epistrophy," is a rare Zappa jam session featuring former Cream bass guitarist Jack Bruce, session drummer Jim Gordon, rhythm guitarist Tony Duran (from *The Grand Wazoo* and the band Ruben & the Jets), and Zappa. It showcases some nifty soloing from Zappa, who was annoyed by Bruce's obtrusive bass — which was "too busy" for his taste.

"Uncle Remus," a gospel-blues written with Duke, depicts the state of the Civil Rights struggle in the '70s. The tune is a warm-up for attitudes Zappa would explore in more savage detail in "You Are What You Is" in 1981. The character Uncle Remus, from the tales of Joel Chandler Harris in 1880, was also featured in Disney's cloying film *Song of the South* (1946). In the movie, a lonely boy living on a plantation finds his only solace in the stories told him by Uncle Remus. For Zappa and Duke (who is black), Uncle Remus is an emblem of black servitude. The song's opening line suggests that since Martin Luther King's assassination in 1968, the Civil Rights struggle has become a trendy affectation marked by obsequious assimilation:

> *Wo, are we movin' too slow?*
> *Have you seen us, Uncle Remus?*
> *We look pretty sharp in these clothes (yes, we do)*
> *Unless we get sprayed with a hose.*

Zappa was equating black liberation with fashion attitudes (is that a *real* Afro, or is it a Sears Afro?), making "Uncle Remus" a far cry from "Trouble Every Day" in its outlook. The most effective action taken by the character in the song, who has shed his "'fro" and "doo-rag," is to drive to Beverly Hills to knock "the little jockeys off the rich folks' lawn." (In his book *Waiting for the Sun*, Barney Hoskyns tells of jazz artist Charles Mingus acting out this exact stunt.) Those hideously racist statues, depicting a spooked black jockey with a lantern, represent everything militant blacks rejected in characters like Uncle Remus. The protagonist becomes merely one symbol knocking over another, rather than significantly changing society's racist attitudes.

The album's final track, "Stinkfoot," inspired by a Mennen foot-spray commercial, was the first song to introduce listeners to Zappa's idea of conceptual continuity. "There is a concept to what I'm doing and there is a continuity to the concept, and I happen to be living inside of the concept. I'm a participant in it," Zappa told journalist Bob Marshall in 1988. "The conceptual continuity is this: everything, even this interview, is part of what I do for, let's call it, my entertainment work. And there's a big difference between sitting here and talking about this kind of stuff, and writing a song like 'Titties 'n Beer.' But as far as I'm concerned, it's all part of the same continuity. It's all one piece. It all relates in some weird way back to the focal point of what's going on."

The focal point of "Stinkfoot" is initially the singer's "exquisite little inconvenience." As in the album's opening track, we are taken "out through the night an' the

I'M THE SLIME

whispering breezes." When the singer orders his dog, Fido, to get his slippers and the dog barfs all over them, the song is linked to the huskies and their yellow snow. After an immaculate Zappa guitar solo, the second half of the song is a philosophical dialogue between the singer and the pooch. It's likely not coincidental that the name Fido evokes Phaedo, one of Socrates' favorite disciples, who told Plato of his mentor's death Just as Plato's *Phaedo* is about the immortality of the soul, as expressed through a dialogue concerning Socrates' demise, Zappa's Fido tells the singer about the continuity of time:

> *Once upon a time*
> *Somebody said to me*
> *(This is the dog talkin' now)*
> *What is your conceptual continuity*
> *Well I told him right then* (Fido said)
> *It should be easy to see*
> *The crux of the biscuit*
> *Is the Apostrophe (')*

By the end of the song, the chorus sings, "The poodle bites/The poodle chews it," echoing "Dirty Love" from *Over-nite Sensation*. *Apostrophe (')* is a masterful medley of diverse themes given a sublime structural unity.

The phrase "strictly commercial," heard in "Nanook Rubs It," is fitting. *Apostrophe (')*, released in the doomed quadraphonic sound format in March 1974, became the first Zappa album to make the Top 10 in the American charts (it peaked at No. 10 after eleven weeks) and go gold. Zappa was so surprised — and pleased — that he hired a fifty-piece marching band to wind their way past the Warner Brothers office to thank them. The group carried a sign that read, "Anyone who can get Frank Zappa even to the bottom of the Top Ten is OK in my booklet." Zappa and Cal Schenkel used their current notoriety to do some television spots, one of which involved a hysterical DJ promoting the record over the animated images of a cheap monster movie.

What truly made *Apostrophe (')* a success, though, was the industrious efforts of a Pittsburgh DJ. "[He] took 'Don't Eat the Yellow Snow,' cut it down ... to three minutes and put it on the station," Zappa told William Ruhlmann. "[He] perceived it as a modern-day novelty record and put it on right alongside of 'Teeny Weeny Bikini' and it became a hit." So while the song won Zappa an audience that, in the past, had stayed clear of him, it also created a pop image that distorted the nature of his work. He was now perceived as a novelty act worthy of Dr. Demento, not an irreverently serious American composer. Ben Watson nails the point eloquently. "To build a surrealist documentary of modern life, one that challenges *Finnegans Wake* for scale, complexity, and breadth of reference, and explicitly site it in the marketplace is cultural outrage of the highest order," he writes. "It is a blow to hierarchies of value that moralism, no matter how well intentioned, can never achieve, because moralism relies on a notion of the few who are saved percolating truth to the damned below." It's significant that Watson cites *Finnegans Wake* — James Joyce's reinvention of language, which tore apart conventional narrative, is now considered by many to be of great literary value. In the world of pop, though, some critics confer merit on music by taking it out of the realm of adolescent disrepute, to make it appear more socially significant. What other reason could there be for the proliferation of so many rock benefits, during the '70s and '80s, for a variety of social causes? Rarely did these bloated events ever aid the victims they sought to assist; it was a blanket attempt to legitimize music that the high-culture commissars had already dismissed.

8

The Mothers of Invention celebrated their tenth anniversary in 1974, even though Frank Zappa was the only original member left from 1964. During their celebratory tour, they played Chicago's Auditorium Theater on May 11, the same date the band was named (a poorly recorded bootleg, *Unmitigated Audacity*, captured the occasion). That night, Zappa did a whole set of early songs from *Freak Out!* What he discovered on this commemorative evening was just how far the Mothers had come in ten years. For pure ability to play difficult and uncompromising scores, the current ensemble was light years ahead of the original group. In fact, this band learned all the songs from *Freak Out!* in only a few days. Zappa had once told a journalist the '60s Mothers sometimes took weeks to master *one* song.

On May 15, as Zappa was mixing and editing *Roxy & Elsewhere*, his third child, Ahmet Rodan Zappa, was born. He was named after both Ahmet Ertegun, the esteemed co-founder of Atlantic Records, and Rodan the giant pterodactyl, who terrorized Japan in sci-fi movies of the late '50s. Ahmet was prematurely delivered by C-section and had hyaline membrane disease, a lung disorder. While visiting the hospital, Zappa noticed that Ahmet wasn't breathing. When he informed the nurse, they discovered that one of the child's lungs had collapsed. Yet despite Ahmet's fragile beginnings, he would start to challenge his namesake — in height, at least — by the time he was a teenager. Zappa continued to get grief about the names for his kids. First Moon Unit, then Dweezil, and now Ahmet Rodan! When comedienne Joan Rivers raised the issue on her talk show in 1986, Zappa replied, "Well, consider the beauty of a name like Ralph."

While the Mothers toured Europe in September, *Roxy & Elsewhere* was issued as a double album. By the time they hit the road, the band knew the *Roxy* material so well that the tempo grew quicker and more fluid. Ralph Humphrey had left the group, leaving Chester Thompson as the sole drummer. On September 17, the Mothers played a concert in Helsinki, Finland, which — released in 1988 as the second volume of the six-volume live omnibus *You Can't Do That on Stage Anymore* — proved just how skilled these musicians had become at playing Zappa's scores. Besides performing many of the songs on *Roxy & Elsewhere*, like "Village of the Sun," "Echidna's Arf (of You)," "Pygmy Twylyte," "Don't You Ever Wash That Thing?" and "Cheepnis," the group introduced some new material. "Inca Roads" and "RDNZL" were dynamic showcases for Ruth Underwood's and George Duke's talents. "Room Service" was mostly an improvised theatrical piece that incorporated the events of a party at the Hotel Hesperia the night before — the festivities had been interrupted by the Finnish police, who maced Coy Featherstone, the band's lighting director.

"Dupree's Paradise," which eventually found a new life as an orchestral piece (under the baton of conductor Pierre Boulez on *The Perfect Stranger: Boulez Conducts Zappa*), was mostly a platform for Duke's eclectic skills on the keyboards. "T'Mershi Duween," named after a character in a childhood story created by Moon Unit, became a compact polka gone amok. The band also provided a promenade with a Finnish tango called "Satumaa." During the encore, the Mothers were about to play "Montana," when a fan yelled out for "Whippin' Post." Why this individual assumed that Zappa and Co. would know this 1969 blues song from The Allman Brothers Band we'll never know. Zappa certainly didn't recognize it, but within ten years he would, and the song became another gem in his repertoire. The Helsinki concert was a spirited showcase for the band, despite the macing and Napoleon Murphy Brock's bout of pneumonia.

On Halloween, Zappa threw a tenth anniversary party at the Blue Hawaii Room at the Roosevelt Hotel in New York. A wide assortment of guests appeared, including soul singer Patti Labelle (who sang "Happy Birthday"), James Taylor, Carly

Simon, Dory Previn, and Bianca Jagger. In December, Zappa worked out a deal with KCET-TV in L.A. for a television special entitled *A Token of His Extreme*, which was essentially a Mothers concert with a live studio audience. Besides using tracks from this show ("Inca Roads" and "Florentine Pogen") for a new album to be called *One Size Fits All*, Zappa did some additional recording at James Guercio's studio in Colorado. This included "The Adventures of Greggery Peccary," "Revised Music for Guitar and Low-Budget Orchestra" (a more compact reworking of the extended orchestral piece from Jean-Luc Ponty's *King Kong* album), and "RDNZL." Those numbers would comprise a section of an aborted project called *Läther* (1977), and later the entire album *Studio Tan*. Another track from this period was the demo of "A Little Green Rosetta," eventually the conclusion of *Joe's Garage Acts II & III*, which featured George Duke on piano with Zappa playfully singing some moronic lyrics about "making a muffin betta." (This demo had also been meant for *Läther*.)

Putting together *One Size Fits All* while simultaneously working on *A Token of His Extreme* was arduous enough, but then bass player Tom Fowler broke his left hand while playing touch football. Zappa brought in James "Bird Legs" Youmans to replace him (he plays on "Can't Afford No Shoes" from *One Size Fits All* and other tracks released later). Zappa canceled tour dates to accommodate the completion of the album, the special, and the broken hand.

Zappa also lost Chester Thompson to the jazz fusion group Weather Report, which meant holding auditions for a new percussionist. Terry Bozzio, a drummer from San Francisco, flew to L.A. to discover a roomful of eager candidates — and some frightfully difficult sheet music. To make matters worse, he wasn't very familiar with Zappa's music. "Yeah, I'd never heard his music before," Bozzio confessed to Howard Shih in *The Rutgers Review*. "Three days before the audition, I bought a couple of his albums and it scared me sleepless." At the audition, Bozzio saw a huge soundstage with a complete band setup, plus a huge pile of sheet music and two drum kits. Zappa had one drummer play, while the other set up the second kit. "I did the best I could," Bozzio told journalist Andy Greenaway. "[I was] sight-reading a very difficult piece . . . jamming in a very odd time signature — like 19/16 — and then playing a blues shuffle." After he finished, Bozzio turned to road manager Marty Perellis. Perellis looked at the other assembled percussionists; none wanted to follow Bozzio. At which point, Zappa glanced at Bozzio and said, "Looks like you've got the gig if you want it."

Zappa also added slide guitarist Denny Walley, who came from Geronimo Black. By spring, Tom Fowler's hand was healed, and his brother Bruce returned

I'M THE SLIME

with his trombone. The biggest surprise, though, was the sight of Captain Beefheart. Back in February 1972, while Zappa was still in his wheelchair, Beefheart was in pretty good spirits. After all, he was enjoying greater popularity and critical success than ever. He had followed up *Trout Mask Replica* with two superb records, *Lick My Decals Off, Baby* (1970) and *The Spotlight Kid* (1972), and he was working on *Clear Spot* (1972), when he inexplicably unloaded a barrage of invective on Zappa. "Zappa was an oaf," he told one reporter. "All he wanted to do was make me into a horrible freak. I'm not a freak, I am an artist. . . . Zappa uses people." Yet Beefheart's status wouldn't have been possible without his work with Zappa. Despite the hard work Beefheart & His Magic Band put into the luminous *Clear Spot*, it was a disaster, charting at No. 191.

In a mad attempt to go commercial, Beefheart had signed with Mercury Records in 1974, along with a manager, Andy DiMartino, whose claim to fame was producing the 1963 hit "Rhythm of the Rain," by the Cascades. Beefheart's first album on Mercury was *Unconditionally Guaranteed*, a record that took the magic right out of the band by trying to duplicate more conventional jazz/pop arrangements and burying Beefheart's growl in the mix. The cover showed Beefheart grabbing a fistful of money. There wasn't an embarrassment of riches on the record, however, as Beefheart sounded tired, strained, and ultimately ridiculous. *Unconditionally Guaranteed* charted even worse than *Clear Spot*. The original Magic Band members, appalled, left the group. Then Beefheart's audience started to abandon him as well. At one concert, the audience booed him, and Beefheart shouted back, "I've got a right to win a Grammy!"

Beefheart followed *Unconditionally Guaranteed* with the lacklustre, *Bluejeans & Moonbeams* (1974). If *Unconditionally Guaranteed* had Beefheart sounding awkward and sluggish, on the new record he came across as beaten and broken. His recording career was in tatters, too — he was in complete contractual bondage due to all the agreements he had signed with different labels. This was the point at which Zappa again encountered Captain Beefheart.

After Beefheart had apologized for all the bad blood, Zappa asked if he wanted to join the fall rehearsals. Beefheart showed up just before the Halloween shows at the Felt Forum in New York — but he flunked the audition. "See, he had a problem with rhythm, and we were very rhythm-oriented," Zappa told Steve Weitzman of *Rolling Stone*. "Things have to happen on the beat. I had him come up on the bandstand at our rehearsal hall and try to sing 'Willie the Pimp' and he couldn't get through it. I figured if he couldn't get through that, I didn't stand much of a chance in teaching him the other stuff." By the following spring, Beefheart managed to nail a spot in the band before their April 11 gig at Pomona College in Claremont. He appeared on a few tracks on *One Size Fits All*, billed as "Bloodshot Rollin' Red."

Despite this taxing period, Zappa remained enthusiastic about *One Size Fits All*. "I spent a long time on this album," he said. "I was in the studio for four months, ten to twelve hours a day, and by God I want people to hear the thing." But the record didn't fare as well commercially as its predecessors, though it exceeded *Over-nite Sensation* and *Apostrophe (')* in both production and performance. "It has some story-type songs," Zappa said. "But it's pretty much rock 'n' roll-oriented. You could actually dance to this record."

One Size Fits All, which would be released in June 1975, is named for Zappa's most cherished cosmological belief: "the universe is one size — it fits all." Cal Schenkel's cover design gives not only a vast view of the solar system, but also the hand of God (with his burning cigar) and his fat, floating divan from the song "Sofa" (first performed by the Mothers during the Flo & Eddie period). On the back, a constellation of stars appears over a large anthill, some suburban homes, and what appears to be the collapsing San Andreas, while the fault line consumes Beverly Hills. Befitting the genial spirit of this album, the stars are named after a variety of friends, family, and familiar objects. Besides Gail (Pumpkin) and the kids, Zubin Mehta can be found, along with Zircon (of tweezer fame), Billy the Mountain, the Sheraton Hotel chain, "Chunky" (the vocalist from "Cleetus Awreetus-Awrightus"), swimmer Mark Spitz (who had won seven gold medals in the 1972 Olympic Games), and Asparagus, representing the vegetable kingdom.

"Inca Roads," one of Zappa's most popular tunes, began as an instrumental performed by the 1972 Mothers. The song was recorded by that ensemble at a more methodical pace and later included on *The Lost Episodes*. "I'd write lyrics when I was traveling," Zappa told *Pulse Magazine*. "The reverse of [starting with the lyrics] happened with 'Inca Roads.' I came up with the melody first. I took it as a challenge to find words to go with it. A lot of songs may start with one or two words. You hear a funny expression and away you go." "Inca Roads" is a seamless marriage between sci-fi and group folklore. The tune begins with a repetitive phrase on the marimbas by Ruth Underwood, while George Duke (who sings lead for the first time on a Zappa record) surrounds her with swirling spaceship noises from his synthesizer. As Duke sings, "Did a vehicle come from somewhere out there just to land in the Andes?" he calls up images from Erik Von Däniken's best-selling book *Chariots of the Gods?* Von Däniken claimed that flying saucers from outer space landed in the

I'M THE SLIME

Andes and developed the underpinnings of Western civilization. But then Duke adds, "Or was it something different?" The tune, as it turns out, is about "booger bears," slang for the genitals of female groupies ("Did a booger bear come from somewhere out there just to land in the Andes?"). Zappa mocks Von Däniken by suggesting that if aliens built those nifty pyramids, it was only to have band members score on them.

Zappa mixed live and studio material into each song, just as he had on *Burnt Weeny Sandwich*. While the basic tracks of "Inca Roads" and "Florentine Pogen" came from *A Token of His Extreme*, the guitar solo on "Inca Roads" was from the Helsinki concert. Besides the spotless insertion of the solo, the song also features the right-hand tapping technique known as Zappa's "Bulgarian bagpipe" maneuver. Zappa learned this style in 1972 from drummer Jim Gordon, who played on *Apostrophe (')*. Zappa would employ this method later on "Po-Jama People" and "City of Tiny Lites" ("Variations on the Carlos Santana Secret Chord Progression" on *Shut Up 'n' Play Yer Guitar*). "I'm biologically disposed to Bulgarian folk music," Zappa once told *High Times*. "It cracks me up every time I hear it."

"Can't Afford No Shoes" is a no-nonsense rock 'n' roll song that addresses the 1975 economic recession. After the prosperous '60s gave baby boomers avenues to explore their desires in life, the '70s generation was just looking to survive:

Went to buy some cheap detergent
Some emergent nation got my load
Got my load
Got my toad
That I stowed.

The mention of an "emergent" nation tapped a new and growing attitude in the '70s. As productivity started to shift to Third World nations, a source of cheap labor, the U.S. was becoming poorer:

Hey anybody,
Nothin' we can buy
Chump Hare Rama
Ain't no good to try
Recession
Depression.

Zappa's salvo directed at the Hare Krishna movement reflects his strong belief that religious organizations — like drugs — keep people docile rather than aware of their circumstances.

"Sofa No. 1" is an exquisite instrumental taken from Zappa's perversely entertaining story of how the universe was created. "Po-Jama People," however, deals with a universe Zappa has no deep affinity with. While performing with the large jazz ensembles he assembled for *Waka/Jawaka* and *The Grand Wazoo*, Zappa deeply admired the musicians' abilities. Their company, however, was less than thrilling. "I think the overall impact of that group would be that it was between pseudo-jazzette and cranial," Zappa told NME in 1976. "And the people who were in the band at the time — with a couple of exceptions — were genuinely boring people. I mean — I don't appreciate a band that likes to play chess in their off-stage hours. If you have to spend a lot of time with people who are interested in their chessboards and little card games and shite like that, it can drive you nuts." Since Zappa's art was fueled by the unconventional behavior of the people he both encountered and performed with, he likely found the hair-shirt tastes of sedentary artists suffocating:

> *The pyjama people are boring me to pieces*
> *They make me feel like I am wasting my time*
> *They all got flannel up 'n down 'em*
> *A little trapdoor back aroun' 'em*
> *An' some cozy little* footies *on their mind.*

"Florentine Pogen" might be named after a Swedish biscuit, but this vivacious song is about a rich woman ("She was the daughter of a wealthy Florentine Pogen") who is hidden behind the symbolist imagery of an organ ("She didn't like it when her fan belt/Shrunk and got shorter"). Zappa fills the song with striking imagery that evokes the '50s American culture that spawned him:

> *She was a debutante daisy*
> *With a color-note organ*
> *Deep in the street*
> *She drove a '59 Morgan.*

The poetic deviations in the narrative are balanced by quick shifts in pace and time signatures allowing for short bursts of spontaneity. For instance, if we miss some of the sexual connotations in the song, right after the line "She didn't want to stay home an' watch her pestle go mortar," we hear a brisk musical quote from "Louie Louie."

Many such folkloric clues are peppered throughout the song. Road manager Marty Perellis (who was featured with a fire extinguisher on the cover of *Over-nite Sensation*), is mentioned ("Later she speaks/On how Perellis might court her"), as well as drummer Chester Thompson ("Chester's go-rilla/She go quack"). "Florentine Pogen" is a tribute to a woman of privilege who has no problem getting lowdown.

"Evelyn, a Modified Dog" is another canine tribute that features Zappa delivering a poetic recitation over Duke's cabaret-style solo piano. The song provides a peculiar perspective from the dog's-eye view:

Evelyn, a dog, having undergone
Further modification
Pondered the significance of short-person behavior
In pedal-depressed panchromatic resonance
And other highly ambient domains . . .

"Pedal-depressed panchromatic resonance" refers to the *Lumpy Gravy* sessions, where people gathered inside the grand piano to speak. A large weight kept the piano's sustain pedal always depressed, setting up the special "ambient domains" where the piano strings would vibrate — as one — sympathetically. They were panchromatic, since all the chromatic tones were heard. If the universe was one size that could fit all, so too could all the chromatic tones in the scale. As for Evelyn's response to this startling revelation — "Arf," she said.

"San Ber'dino," a rollicking number that holds many surprises, is partly a genial portrait of a trailer-park couple, rodeo worker Bobby (who "looks like a potato") and his girlfriend, who lives in a Winnebago in the Mojave Desert. It's also a glimpse into Zappa's jail term after his mock-pornography bust in 1963 ("Potato-headed" Bobby gets busted for being drunk and does thirty days in Tank C). Since the tune takes Zappa back to his early days at Studio Z, "San Ber'dino" fittingly features a guest appearance from Captain Beefheart on blues harp, plus Zappa's boyhood hero, Johnny "Guitar" Watson, on "flambe vocals" during the out-chorus. (George Duke had enlisted Watson, who had expressed surprise at Zappa's thorough knowledge of blues and R&B.)

"Andy" is about personal disillusionment ("Is there anything good inside of you/If there is, I really want to know") with a possible drug burnout ("Have I aligned/With a blown mind/Wasted my time/On a drawn blind"). Zappa employs some of his absurdist wit in assessing the character in question:

Andy de vine
Had a thong rind
It was sublime
But the wrong kind.

The references here are perhaps esoteric. Andy Devine was a whiny-voiced character actor in Westerns, and a "thong rind" is a callus that builds up when breaking in thong sandals. "Andy" features, once again, Duke's light tenor taking the lead, and Watson on the out-chorus.

"Sofa No. 2" is the vocal version of "Sofa" (sung in both English and German). The arrangement, very close to the Flo & Eddie rendering, has a beer-barrel loopiness that doesn't conceal the song's utopian yearnings:

I am the heaven
I am the water
I am the dirt beneath your rollers
I am your secret smut and lost money down your cracks
I am your cracks and crannies.

Even though the song has a European dancehall aura, there is a truly American sensibility at work in the content: "I am The Chrome Dinette/I am eggs of all persuasions." Here, Zappa embraces the universe and all that the world had to offer, no matter how palatable the planet is.

One Size Fits All is a joyous record despite the effort taken to produce it. Zappa appears totally at ease with the world around him ("I am here/And you are my sofa"). As the decade wore down, however, this state of bliss turned out to have been merely a respite.

9

"Breach of contract, that's what the whole lawsuit was really about," Zappa told reporters in April about his fight with the Royal Albert Hall. "[It was] not about whether *200 Motels* was obscene or not." However, the three-day trial beginning on

I'M THE SLIME

April 14 in Court No. 7 of the Law Courts in the Strand did become farcically obscene. Besides the obvious issues being contested, what turned the events mulishly comic was the colloquial gap between American and British culture. Mr. Justice Mocatta, who heard the case, was a caricatured patrician right out of a British costume drama. Zappa's satire, which is peppered with American slang and idiomatic expressions, evokes graphically what was being parodied. These parochial references were largely what baffled Justice Mocatta during the trial. "Bwana Dik," for example, was the name given to the band member who fucked the most women while on the road. This piece of folklore whizzed right over the head of the justice. When he asked Zappa what a "bunna" was, Zappa had to correct him with "bwana." But that didn't help, because Justice Mocatta hadn't seen those Hollywood grade-B jungle movies where the subservient black African guide had to call the white man in the pith helmet "Bwana." But Americans, who grew up hearing that ridiculous term, understood the satirically pointed reasons Zappa would employ it.

The song "Lonesome Cowboy Burt," Zappa's scathing portrait of a redneck cowboy, was completely out of the cultural jurisdiction of the court. When Burt demands that the waitress "sit on my face," it conjured up a most literal image for the court.

> *Mr. Justice Mocatta:* A very unpleasant occupation for the person whose face is being sat upon, is it not?
> *Mr. Zappa:* Well, this is an unusual character, this Cowboy Burt.

In confronting "She Painted Up Her Face," Justice Mocatta didn't even understand what a groupie was. "Is a groupie a girl who is a member of a group?" he asked. "No," Zappa replied. "She is a girl who likes members of a rock 'n' roll band." The word "members" certainly resounded far beyond being a benign expression for the people who belong to the band, but that, too, had no impact on the staid British justice or the counsel for the Royal Albert Hall.

Zappa's idioms of low-rent Americana, though, weren't confined to verbal remarks. As he explained succinctly in *The Real Frank Zappa Book*, there were also musical idioms that transcended their original context: "There's an assortment of 'stock modules' used in our stage arrangements . . . these 'stock modules' include the *Twilight Zone* texture (which may not be the actual *Twilight Zone* notes, but the same 'texture'), the Mister Rogers texture, the Jaws texture . . . and things that sound either *exactly like* or *very similar to* 'Louie Louie.'" Sometimes these "stock modules" say more than mere words — and much better, too.

In the final verdict, on June 10, 1975, Justice Mocatta decided the material was not obscene. He also stated that the Royal Albert Hall had breached its contract. But since the Royal Albert Hall was also a *royal* institution, a lawsuit would stand little chance of succeeding. "In [an American court] it would have been a jury trial," Zappa told Neil Slaven years later. "And for another thing, the whole rules of evidence are different in court here. And I think that it's demonstrably ludicrous that this spinster [Marion Herrod] closed the door on us because of words like 'brassiere.' And I think that, as long as you can point out to a jury that this is a breach of contract suit, not an obscenity trial, did she or did she not breach the contract?"

For Zappa, the only obscenity was the breach of contract. A mutually held agreement was inviolate to him. Besides, how could the British legal system judge whether material was obscene when it didn't truly understand it from a linguistic or musical perspective? After the trial, Justice Mocatta remarked, "When I started this case, I knew very little about pop and beat music. I knew it was to do with rhythm, banging, and an infectious atmosphere. I didn't know it was anything to do with sex or drugs." Zappa informed him that — as every American knows — most pop music has some kind of sexual connotation.

Throughout April and May, the Mothers, along with Captain Beefheart, toured the U.S. The group now included new drummer Terry Bozzio; Denny Walley on slide guitar; Tom Fowler on bass; Bruce Fowler on trombone; George Duke on keyboards; and Napoleon Murphy Brock on sax and vocals. The Captain, who was more than a little absent-minded, created havoc for the road manager and the group. "All the other musicians in the band were well-seasoned road rats," Zappa told Nigel Leigh. "They knew how to pack up and get out of a motel; they knew how to show up at the sound check on time; they knew how to live that life on the road. . . . [Beefheart] carried his possessions in a shopping bag, including his soprano sax . . . and was forever leaving it in hallways and not knowing where he was or what he was doing."

Walley also agreed. "Don was very hard to handle, but Frank had a way of keeping things going without any friction," he told Barry Alfonso in the liner notes to the Beefheart CD box set *The Dust Blows Forward*. "Don would be there for the entire set, but mostly he'd sit on a bench toward the back of the stage and

I'M THE SLIME

draw — sometimes he'd draw Frank as the devil. I don't think Frank was real pleased about that. But on the whole, Don was a pro — he could really sell a song."

When the band performed in Austin, Texas, at the Armadillo on May 20 and 21, they recorded what was to be the next Zappa album, *Bongo Fury*.

Despite the acrimonious relationship that had developed over the years between Beefheart and Zappa, *Bongo Fury* is a wonderfully affectionate memoir about their friendship. They trade songs, exchange experiences, and, without getting maudlin, reminisce about their days in Lancaster. "Debra Kadabra" is an outlandishly funny composition that manages to be a homage to both Beefheart's mother (who sold Avon cologne door to door) and cheesy '50s sci-fi — in this case, the Mexican classic *Brainiac*. "It's one of the worst movies ever made," Zappa explained, "and when the monster appears, not only is the monster cheap, he's got a rubber mask that you can see over the collar of the guy's jacket." The hyper-scary notes that Bruce Fowler plays over Beefheart's excited tones as he yelps "Make me grow Brainiac fingers" come directly from the movie. There was a connection between the monster and Avon products involving the time Beefheart decided to try out his mother's beauty aids. "One day, he made the unfortunate mistake of taking some Avon cologne and putting it in his hair, which made it start falling out," Zappa told *Society Pages* in 1991. "He also put some kind of Avon cream on his face, which made him break out in this giant rash. His face looked like an alligator."

"Carolina Hard-Core Ecstasy," one of the few songs on *Bongo Fury* that's not about Zappa and Beefheart's shared folklore, is in the S&M vein of "Dinah-Moe Humm" and "Penguin in Bondage." It begins innocently enough with a passionate round of sex (reminiscent of "Camarillo Brillo") between the singer and Carolina, a woman he's just met. After she puts on the Doobie Brothers' "Listen to the Music," and the singer mounts her with a Roger Daltry cape on, the song turns into a strange erotic episode involving a pair of plastic leather fourteen-triple-D shoes:

> I said I wonder what's the shoes for
> She told me, "Don't you worry no more"
> And got right down there on the tile floor
> "Now darling stomp all over me"
> Carolina Hard-Core Ecstasy.

"Sam With the Showing Scalp Flat Top" is a typical Beefheart composition that features a recitation over the music. It's a proudly confessional tune about the music he chooses to play:

> *I usually played such things as roughneck and thug*
> *Opaque melodies that would bug most people*
> *Music from the other side of the fence.*

As Greil Marcus writes in *Ranters & Crowd Pleasers*, Beefheart tries to live out the role of the difficult and hermetic artist — who occupies "the other side of that fence" — but at the heart of his work is the accessible romantic with a total lack of self-consciousness. "Beefheart's songs," writes Marcus, "may not be accessible — that is, conventional — but anyone's terrors, and anyone's delight at seeing them plain, are accessible through his songs. Van Vliet's version of freedom is the mastery of a man who cannot make anyone else's music. As he proved in the past, a man who can't make anyone else's music is not the same as a man who won't." By the end of his elliptical poem, Beefheart starts to cry out — in a voice that resembles *no one* else's music — for some bongos ("I wish I had a pair o' bongos/Bongo Fury!") while the band accompanies him with a little "Louie Louie."

Since the concert took place one year before the American bicentennial, Zappa prepared a country song to mark the occasion. "Poofter's Froth Wyoming Plans Ahead," sung by Beefheart, even though it's written by Zappa (in the spirit of Beefheart), is loosely based on the song "Set Up Two Glasses, Joe," recorded by Ferlin Huskey and Simon Crum (and written by Cindy Walker and Ernest Tubb). Huskey and Crum's song is a relaxed sentimental country tune about two old codgers sitting at a bar and going over their shared past. "Poofter's Froth Wyoming Plans Ahead" has two old friends going over the checkered history of the entire country, leading up to its current economic malaise:

> *The entire stock is slipping*
> *Oh our shod is hardly slipping*
> *To the markets of the world*
> *Our wrinkled pennants are unfurled!*

Beefheart and Zappa satirize America's zealous need to sell a proud image of itself at moments when it feels the least distinguished:

I'M THE SLIME

Everything a nation needs
For making hoopla while it feeds
The trash compactors, small reactors,
Mowers, blowers, throwers & the glowers:

This is Buy-Cent-Any-All Salute
Two hundred years have gone ka-put!
Ah, but we have been astute!

This theme continues in "200 Years Old," where America has become so mean that it can't "grow no lips."

"Cucamonga" recounts the early days of Studio Z, where Zappa and Beefheart dream of making it big (at which point we hear the voice of Nanook's mother once again warning, "Nanook, no-no"), while "Advance Romance" is a terrific blues number that perfectly integrates both artists' temperaments. While this latter song appears to be about seeking illicit sex when one is broke, it features some of Beefheart's oddly romantic yearnings, which are expressed in highly conceptual imagery. Given that it's a Zappa composition, though, the story is told with direct idiomatic expressions. Denny Walley provides a great slide guitar solo that prompts Beefheart to sing a bar of "All Night Long."

"Man With the Woman Head" is one of Beefheart's intangible compositions, with roots in early Beat poetry, especially Gregory Corso's harsh abstractions. Sings Beefheart:

Dark circles collected under the wrinkled, folded eyes,
Map-like from too much turquoise eyepaint
He showed his old tongue through ill-fitting wooden teeth
Stained from too much opium, chipped from the years.

Zappa precedes "Muffin Man" with a recitation over George Duke's piano, which perfectly mimics silent-movie music. Though likely recorded at the same session that produced "Evelyn, a Modified Dog," it serves as an introduction to the live track. Zappa describes the activities of the Muffin Man, who sits in the laboratory of the Utility Muffin Research Kitchen, gathering quantities of dried muffin remnants. (Since he brushes "his scapular aside," he may be related to Father O'Blivion from "St. Alfonzo's Pancake Breakfast.") While "pooting forth a quarter ounce green rosette" on the muffin, he describes his distaste for cupcakes. He praises the muffin as "that prince of foods," and the live band launches into a blues about a man who may not actually be one:

> *Girl, you thought he was a man*
> *But he was a muffin*
> *He hung around till you found*
> *That he didn't know nothin'.*

Zappa merely suggests that the Muffin Man could actually be a woman — a theory bolstered by the fact that the previous song was "Man With the Woman Head." The sexual ambiguity at work in "Muffin Man" is similar to that in Ewan McColl and A.L. Lloyd's sea chantey "The Handsome Cabin Boy," the story of a woman who disguises herself as a male sailor on a ship. When "she" becomes pregnant, it raises suspicions about not only who the father is, but why there would even *be* a father.

After an extended guitar solo by Zappa concludes "Muffin Man," he introduces the band and bids farewell: "Good night Austin, Texas, wherever you are," paraphrasing Jimmy Durante's customary good-night wish to Mrs. Calabash. Sadly, *Bongo Fury* would be the last collaboration between Zappa and Beefheart. Despite suspicions by many Zappa fans that Beefheart was only along for the ride, *Bongo Fury* was a dazzling celebration of American ingenuity by two wildly iconoclastic artists fighting for the freedom to play, as Beefheart put it, "opaque melodies that would bug most people." Even though it didn't make a dent in the U.S. charts when it was released in October 1975, the album did have one special fan: Vaclav Havel, a highly opinionated Czech playwright fighting for his country's freedom. He cited *Bongo Fury* as his favorite Zappa album when the two met in 1989.

On June 25, *One Size Fits All* was released to general disinterest from both the public and critics — it reached only No. 26 in the charts. Michael Watts of *Melody Maker* described Zappa's lyrics as having "an irrelevancy that's Dadaist and a detachment that's Bunuelian," as if that's a crime.

In September, Zappa was determined to record more of his orchestral work. Having already been thwarted at the Pauley Pavilion and the Royal Albert Hall, he made an arrangement with Royce Hall on the UCLA campus. On September 17–18, Michael Zearott conducted the thirty-seven-piece Abnuceals Emuukha Electric

I'M THE SLIME

Orchestra, which was augmented by a small combo that included Zappa on electric guitar, Terry Bozzio on drums, Dave Parlato (of the Petit Wazoo) on bass, and Emil Richards on percussion.

They recorded a wide selection of material, including newly orchestrated versions of "Dog Breath Variations," "Uncle Meat," "Duke of Prunes," and "Bogus Pomp." They also did new pieces, among them "Pedro's Dowry," "Naval Aviation in Art?" and a guitar ballad first performed in 1974 called "Black Napkins." Selections of these recordings would appear in 1979 on the unofficial release *Orchestral Favorites*. "Strictly Genteel" was a lively instrumental version of the finale from *200 Motels*, while "Naval Aviation in Art?" was a short and lean piece for strings that contained some of the taut spareness of Anton Webern. "Duke of Prunes" had a ripe grandeur in this orchestral setting, sharply contrasted by Zappa's guitar solo, which drips with feedback. "Bogus Pomp" featured selections from the orchestral music to *200 Motels* welded together into one piece. *Orchestral Favorites* illustrated — even better than the evening with Zubin Mehta — how a rock ensemble could enhance and complement an orchestra.

When *Bongo Fury* came out in October, Captain Beefheart's legal problems held up the release of the record in England, where he was signed to the independent Virgin label. Virgin issued an injunction against Warner Brothers releasing the album in the U.K., which wouldn't be settled until 1989. Beefheart's comments about his British label? "Who are they kidding with a name like that? There are no more virgins, we all know that. The Dance of the Seven Veils is over!"

That fall, Zappa put together a new lineup for the road. Aside from regulars Napoleon Murphy Brock and Terry Bozzio, he added Andre Lewis on keyboards and ex-Mother Roy Estrada on bass and vocals. At a Halloween concert at the Felt Forum, the band was joined by singer/saxophonist Norma Jean Bell, who then accompanied the band on a two-concert trip to Yugoslavia in late November. Back in the U.S., Norma Bell started dipping into narcotics, which got her fired before the New Year had even arrived. In January, the band launched a world tour, which took in Japan, Vienna, Germany, Denmark, Norway, Finland, France, Italy, and Spain. Zappa returned in May to start recording a new album.

Zoot Allures, a pun on the French phrase *zut alors* (meaning loosely "dammit"), was a stripped-down-for-action rock 'n' roll record. With Zappa playing guitar, synthesizers, and drums, augmented by overdubs by assorted band members, the album was a hodgepodge of fascinating material. Originally to be a two-LP set called *Night of the Iron Sausage* (after a line in a new track called "The Torture

Never Stops"), *Zoot Allures* (October 1976) collected both new studio material and some of the live recordings from the world tour.

The album kicks off with a drum flurry by Terry Bozzio, as Zappa churlishly sings, "This here song might offend you some/If it does, it's because you're dumb." The song is "Wind Up Working in a Gas Station," which suggests both the fate of those not educated enough to fulfill their talent and perhaps the destiny of Americans who'll fall victim to the upcoming gas shortage:

> *Hey now, better make a decision*
> *Be a moron, and keep your position*
> *You oughta know now, all your education*
> *Won't help you no-how*
> *You're gonna wind up workin' in a gas station.*

When Zappa asks, "Show me your thumb if you're really dumb," he draws on a schoolyard rhyme from the '50s. Recording engineer Davey Moire, who has a desperately high voice up in the Roy Estrada decibel range, joins Zappa on lead vocals. They both fanatically drive home the title of the song. At the end, Zappa sings (inexplicably in a German accent), "Manny de camper wants to buy some white." The white refers to white gas, a fuel used in camp stoves and lanterns — maybe all that many feared would be left in this '70s recession.

"Black Napkins," a lovely guitar instrumental recorded live in Osaka, Japan, has some of the Latin blues sound of Carlos Santana. "In my opinion, in a sense, it's old-school in the way that it's bluesy," guitarist Steve Vai, who played with Zappa in the '80s, told Nigel Leigh. "I mean, he has very many different sides. He can just play over a real heavy rock vamp . . . and he's got these blues runs and stuff that . . . have a lot of balls or grip to them, like, they have a lot of cayenne pepper or something." The cayenne pepper reference is apt — "Black Napkins" has its roots in food preparation. "We were having this horrible Thanksgiving dinner in Milwaukee," Zappa recalled. "Sliced turkey roll with the fucking preservatives just gleaming off of it, and this beat-up cranberry material. The final stroke to this ridiculous dinner was the black napkins, sitting next to the dishes. That really said the most about the dinner." "The Torture Never Stops" was originally a slow blues, with a melody based on Howlin' Wolf's "Smokestack Lightnin'." It was first performed by Captain Beefheart during the *Bongo Fury* shows as "Why Doesn't Someone Get Him a Pepsi?" In this sinewy rendition, which features Zappa playing bass, lead guitar, and keyboards, and singing in a deep, whispery voice, the song at first evokes images of Third World dungeons of iniquity:

Knives and spikes, and guns and the likes
Of every tool of pain
And a sinister midget, with a bucket and a mop
Where the blood goes down the drain.

And it stinks so bad, the stones been chokin'
And weepin' greenish drops
In the room where the giant fire puffer works
And the torture never stops.

However, the song's backing track features the sounds of a woman experiencing orgasmic pleasure. The tension between the violent lyrics and the clamor of ecstasy builds a powerfully lurid contrast between desire and dread. This use of erotic voices is a brilliant parody of artists like Donna Summer ("Love to Love You Baby") or Sylvia ("Pillow Talk"), who used the sound of women moaning in ecstasy throughout their songs as a soft-core come-on. Zappa locates our prurient interest and puts it right at the center of "The Torture Never Stops." As Ben Watson points out, "Zappa challenges us not to find the girl's squeals alluring. . . . To turn Donna Summer's moans of ecstasy into screams of torture is a masterstroke." The sound effects — reminiscent of Bunk Gardner's sex recordings for "Right There" and Zappa's mock-pornographic tape at Studio Z — were created in Zappa's bedroom, as Gail, Frank, and another woman participated in a four-hour session of simulated sex that was edited down to ten minutes.

A final joyous scream takes us right into "Ms. Pinky," a song about what Zappa describes as a "lonely person device." While the band was in Finland that year, a fan named Eric showed up with presents, which included his favorite pornographic magazine. Within its pages were ads for lonely-person products that included a rubber girl named Ms. Pinky. She was nothing more than a large head with a very small body. With her mouth wide open and her eyes closed shut, she offered mechanical blow jobs to the lonely consumer who purchased her.

When the group arrived in Amsterdam, Zappa purchased a Ms. Pinky for the show — it cost $69.95. "It was worse than I imagined," Zappa recalled. "Not only is it a head, it's the size of a child's head. The throat is sponge rubber and it's got a vibrator in it with a battery pack and a two-speed motor. Sticking out of its neck is a nozzle with a squeeze-bulb that makes the throat contract." These details, reminiscent of Wild Bill's painted mannequins with the prosthetic devices that Zappa encountered in Echo Park in the mid-'60s, would lead to another "folk" song. "I thought: Hmmmmm, anyone who's gonna buy a plastic head just to give himself a gum job is right out there," Zappa said.

Given the synthetic decade of the '70s, "Ms. Pinky" was a song about a different kind of plastic person from the Sunset Strip conformists Zappa depicted in *Absolutely Free*. The song borrows its main theme from Van Morrison's "Gloria," but instead of his cry of adolescent lust, the tune is sung from the point of view of a sex-starved, middle-aged man who is craving for an inanimate sex toy:

> *Her eye's all shut in an ecstasy face*
> *You can cram it down her throat, people, any old place*
> *Throw a little switch on her battery pack*
> *You can poot it, you can shoot it till your wife gets back.*

Although it traffics in the same areas of counterfeit love that Roxy Music's "In Every Dream Home a Heartache" did in 1973, Zappa's song goes directly to the source of the man's desires, pulling no punches.

"Find Her Finer" is a grinding blues tune that expresses cynicism about dating rituals. Here, Zappa appears to suggest that guys who initially act "dumb" will get the women of their choice:

> *Find her finer, sneak up behind her*
> *Unwrap like a mummy 'til you finally unwind her*
> *Find her, blind her, see who designed her*
> *Act like a dummy 'til you finally grind her.*

The song assumes that guys who depict themselves as dumb do so only as a pretense to pick up girls:

> *Don't never let her know you are smart*
> *The universe is no place to start*
> *You gotta play it straight from the heart*
> *She gwine renunciate you.*

I'M THE SLIME

"Find Her Finer" plays out the hunt for a mate in a manner completely opposed to conventional pop songs on the same subject. In other words, Zappa is hardly endorsing being stupid. He elaborated on this to journalist Bob Marshall in 1991:

> I say choose to be smart. It ain't as bad as you think. The problem is most people choose to be stupid because there's a social stigma attached to being smart. If you're smart, you don't get laid. That's something every kid learns in school. The other thing that used to be true, it's not so true anymore, is nobody wants to fuck a comedian. Now it's different, a little bit. That used to be an axiom. Nobody wants to fuck a mad scientist either. So, Americans have steered themselves away from intellectual pursuits because they want to have a social life. And the ones that have been the most victimized by it are the women who have made themselves stupid. I think there's probably a lot of smart women in the United States. . . . But women are pathetic when they make themselves stupid. There's even more of a stigma to being a smart girl than there is to being a smart guy.

"Friendly Little Finger" is a further example of Zappa's xenochronous experiments (or strange synchronizations), where he pairs disparate musical elements from different sources. The song opens with a Balinese-sounding melody played in the studio by Ruth Underwood on the marimba. As she repeats this quaint, lovely motif, a raging Zappa guitar solo comes out of the mix and buries the marimba. The time signatures of the two threads are incompatible, but by contrasting them so dramatically, Zappa creates an entirely atypical piece of music.

As his solo winds down, like a racing car desperately revving its engines, a much more familiar piece of music arises from the mix, leading into the next song — a synthesizer quotes the hymn "Bringing in the Sheaves" just before "Wonderful Wino" starts up. Zappa's musical joke, besides bookending the song, identifies the Salvation Army's relationship to recovering alcoholics. He also offers another friendly nod to Charles Ives, whose *Third Symphony* (1904) incorporated camp-hymn tunes. But while Ives aimed at spiritual revival, Zappa reaches for satire. The character in "Wonderful Wino," after all, is *anything* but a candidate for spiritual revival:

I've been drinking all night until my eyes got red
Stumbled on the gutter and busted my head
Bugs in my zoot suit and I'm scratching like a dog
I can't stand no water and I stink like a hog.

Originally cowritten with Jeff Simmons for his 1969 album *Lucille Has Messed My Mind Up*, "Wonderful Wino" has been revived many times. Zappa later performed the song with Flo & Eddie (who added "Bringing in the Sheaves"), and eventually recorded a version during the *Over-nite Sensation* sessions with the verbally spastic Ricky Lancelotti handling vocals.

On "Zoot Allures," Zappa builds the melody on drawn-out sheets of sound, as if he were taking a long drag on one of his Winstons. It's hard to imagine any other guitarist creating such beautiful air sculptures using feedback, except maybe Jimi Hendrix. "Zoot Allures" is a lovely instrumental ballad featuring a beautiful harp overdub by Louanne Neil and quietly pensive percussion by Ruth Underwood. In most live versions of "Zoot Allures," Zappa performs an expanded solo, but on the album version, the song fades out just as he begins improvising.

The album concludes with "Disco Boy," Zappa's first missive at an emerging new cultural phenomenon. During the '60s, dance clubs hired live bands, and groups could earn their living and get signed to record labels. In the far less affluent '70s, clubs looked for new ways to save money, so they hired disc jockeys to spin records. The record industry followed suit by creating a new genre of music designed especially for those wanting only to shake their booty. Though discotheques were popular in the '60s, disco represented a whole different phenomenon, as music critic Tom Smucker points out in *The Rolling Stone Illustrated History of Rock & Roll*:

> It was about ecstasy: a place where the DJ choreographed music and lighting to manipulate the mood on the dance floor until everyone was lost in movement. It was a strange new brew of '70s self-absorption with '60s communalism: a mix of jogging, the swinging bar, the drug high, and the light show, in which who was playing the records was often more important than what the records were.

As someone who cared more about what the records were than who was playing them, Zappa found disco intolerable. He first encountered the culture that year in

I'M THE SLIME

Denmark. "We went to a place there called the Disc Club, and it was really poot," Zappa told British journalist Miles in 1977. "It was so make-believe sophisticated that it was embarrassing. The place was decorated like a playboy-type living room would sorta be like — low-boy chairs and snackettes on the table, and everybody drinks and dances to these robot-beat records."

Yet the trend made sense. First, dance music is always popular in times of economic gloom (hence the emergence of the swing era during the Depression years). Second, rock music was growing more monolithic — that is, white-male monolithic. The disco era ushered in a racially and sexually diverse panorama of performers: black talent like Donna Summer, Gloria Gaynor, and George McCrae, and gay groups like the Village People, suddenly found avenues to larger audiences. It's safe to say that '70s rock denied a voice to these marginalized groups.

Zappa liked a rough polyrhythmic sound, so he resented the synthetic repetitive din being peddled in these hot nightspots. *Zoot Allures*, with its emphasis on the synthesizer pumping out robotic notes, parodies what was taking place in music. The song "Disco Boy" begins with a synthesizer spitting out one of those "robot beats" Zappa complained about. Guest vocalist Roy Estrada leads off with a high, wheezing chirp of "Disco Boy-oy-oy-oyyyy!" while Zappa spins into a full-scale portrait of a lonely guy different from the one in "Ms. Pinky":

Disco boy
Run to the toilet and comb your hair
Disco boy
Pucker your lip and check your shoulders
'Cause some dandruff might be hiding there.

Zappa mocks the romantic hopes of this aspiring hoofer who anticipates some of the characteristics of John Travolta's Tony Manero in *Saturday Night Fever* (1977):

Disco boy, you're the Disco King.
Aw, the disco thing makes you think that you just might go somewhere
Disco girl, you're outtasight
You need a disco boy to treat you right
He'll do the dance
Take you home tonight
(Leave his hair alone, but you can kiss his comb).

Zappa attacks disco not simply as a musical form, but as a fashion statement. For him, disco was too demure, and caught up in its own fantasy image of pristine sexiness. He suggested that despite the vigorous efforts to "pump your booty," the disco couple were denying their own bodies — denying even the dark realities of excrement: "You never go doody!/(That's what you think)." By the end of the song, the disco boy has lost his disco girl to his best friend, leaving him still alone, and going home to spank his monkey. Zappa sums up his views in the song's last lines (hilariously recited to the tune of George Harrison's "Here Comes the Sun"): "It's disco love tonight/Make sure you look alright."

"Disco fulfills a social function," Zappa told TV host Dick Cavett in 1980. "As long as people want to get laid, there will be something like a disco, because that's the main social function of a discotheque. People go there to pick each other up."

With its emphasis on recession, impersonal sex, and disco glamor, *Zoot Allures* vividly seized on the decade's nascent narcissism. The libidinal obsessions of the '60s had grown sterile and ritualistic. Zappa sang these new songs in the same low whisper you could identify in the purring, seductive tracks by Isaac Hayes and Barry White — only Zappa wasn't selling seduction. *Zoot Allures* said that, in the '70s, there was little difference between working in a gas station and disco love tonight.

In August 1975, Zappa had sued MGM/Verve Records for $2 million for unpaid royalties on his first records. He wound up receiving $100,000 and the master tapes, but found they had deteriorated due to poor storage. Zappa decided to sever his relationship with Herb Cohen, as well. He alleged that Cohen and his attorney brother Martin had misled him in the three-way agreement they signed for DiscReet, which ostensibly put Zappa's master recordings in the hands of Warner Brothers.

Under the terms of that deal, Zappa was paid 12 per cent of the total retail price royalty, while the rest reverted to the coffers of DiscReet. Zappa argued that he and Cohen each had fifty shares of DiscReet stock, which were the only shares delegated. He went on to claim that Cohen misused the funds: a bookkeeper with DiscReet was given $2,500 to pay personal bills; advance rental fees of $15,000 were paid to for office space where Cohen conducted his own personal business; the legal firm of Irmas, Simke & Chodos was paid $10,000 out of DiscReet assets to finance the litigation against Zappa.

Zappa set out to dissolve the corporation with a receiver appointed so that he could get his share of the money; and he began to end his relationship with Cohen in March 1976, while performing in Spain.

I'M THE SLIME

As Cohen continued unilaterally signing artists to DiscReet, Zappa launched the lawsuit against him and negotiated a deal with Warner Brothers to distribute *Zoot Allures*. Zappa was to receive a royalty allowance payment from Warner Brothers of $60,000 for each release, but he ended up receiving nothing. Even the money he obtained from MGM/Verve was inaccessible, because his lawsuit with Cohen had frozen his assets. Zappa couldn't even access his tape and film archives until 1982. And Zappa had also ceded the entire Bizarre/Straight catalog to Cohen, with the exception of the Mothers' recordings.

Finally, the suit prevented Zappa from securing the master tapes to *Zoot Allures*, unless he indemnified Warner Brothers from any legal action Cohen might take against them. "Can you believe it?" Zappa asked incredulously. "An individual artist having to indemnify one of the biggest record companies in the world so that they can bring his record out."

While his business dealings continued to get more bizarre, Zappa decided to take an unusual detour away from the fray.

10

In the animated sequence "Dental Hygiene Dilemma," from *200 Motels*, Jeff Simmons is tempted by the Devil to quit the Mothers and join one of the heavy groups, like Black Sabbath . . . or Grand Funk Railroad. During the summer of 1976, during his own season of hell, Frank Zappa *did* join Grand Funk — to produce their next album. This came as something of a shock — or a sick joke — to many people in the industry, as well as to fans of both artists. If Zappa was considered a weird yet serious musician, Grand Funk Railroad were regarded as a bloated garage band from Flint, Michigan, who made it big only due to shrewd marketing. The trio, singer/guitarist Mark Farner, bass player Mel Schacher, and drummer Don Brewer, began in 1969 as a powerhouse hard-rock combo. They took that basic garage-band sound and overamplified it, so the end result would be overwhelming. If you responded to Grand Funk at all, it wasn't because you were seduced — you were slain. Terry Knight, their producer, was a low-rent Colonel Parker, carving a niche for the band in a market where rock fans, glutted by the corporate promotion of hard rock, were desperate to be bowled over. Rock journalists, however, saw the band as a prefab nightmare — a heavy-metal version of the Monkees. Yet Knight managed to get ten consecutive platinum albums out of this critically despised group.

How despised were they? John Mendelsohn, in *Rolling Stone* in 1972, laid down his cards firmly: "What the Frankies and Bobbies and Fabes of the late '50s were to Elvis, so were Grand Funk, a decade later, to Cream/Hendrix." Mendelsohn characterized their music as "worthless rubbish" and warned the rock audience to "let none of the pathologically insecure dingbats, who forced themselves to like it for fear of losing touch with the mass rock audience, convince you otherwise." He might as well have thrown in the death penalty free of charge. Lester Bangs, writing in the same magazine, was a little more solicitous in reviewing their 1971 release, *Survival*: "Grand Funk are one of the very few groups rising recently that *do* reflect the aspirations and attitudes of their audience in the most basic way." Bangs hit on the very thing that made this group more popular with audiences than critics. They positioned themselves as a "people's band" — a bunch of regular guys who played music because they liked it, not because they wanted to be hip.

By the time Zappa caught up with them, they barely wanted to play music anymore. Just a few years earlier they'd had huge hits with their wonderfully corny "We're an American Band," a sluggish cover of Little Eva's "The Loco-Motion," and a rousing version of that great Soul Brothers Six tune, "Some Kind of Wonderful." But in 1976, with the sudden emergence of disco, and with rock getting buried in a faceless corporate culture nosediving in cocaine, Grand Funk didn't even measure up to being a joke anymore. They were quickly becoming an anachronism.

Many internal problems were tearing up the band as well. After extensive touring, they were completely burned out. After the release of their desperately titled *All the Girls in the World Beware!!!* in 1975, it appeared Grand Funk was heading for a fall (even as the album became their eleventh straight platinum record). They fired their manager and retreated to their rehearsal studio on Farner's farm in a tiny Michigan suburb. There they started working on the songs that would make up *Good Singin' Good Playin'*. Their new manager, Andy Cavaliere, suggested Frank Zappa as a producer. It puzzled the band. "It was such a contrast," Brewer told Don Pullen of the *Flint Journal* in 1999. "Frank Zappa producing Grand Funk! It was the weirdest combination ever." Farner was petrified by the idea. "I can't play in front of Zappa," he remarked with dread. But when they finally met, the combination seemed to make sense.

First, both Zappa and Grand Funk had been roasted by the elites in the rock press. They shared a simple love of the kind of rock that was either born in a suburban garage or out on the street. So not only did they get along well, Zappa also knew exactly how the group should be produced: without any special studio effects. He approached the band just as he did when he worked the board for Wild Man Fischer, Captain Beefheart, and the GTO's, stripping away the artifice to reveal the personality of the band and, more importantly, their music. "His whole viewpoint on what rock 'n' roll is about is basically the same as ours," Brewer explained. "You go in and do exactly what you do live, without overproduction. Keep it as simple as possible and really bring the balls out of this thing." Zappa, meanwhile, was most humble. "All I did was in a documentary way make a record which tells you exactly what they really sound like," he explained. "For the first time on record, you can hear Grand Funk Railroad."

From the joyous opening notes of *Good Singin' Good Playin'*, it's evident what he means. "Just Couldn't Wait," for instance, is a wonderful showcase for Farner's muscular tenor voice, and the background vocals show some of the sophistication and affectionate leanings of the best '50s R&B. The music comes across as very clear, and not at all bombastic. Grand Funk Railroad sounds like a group of talented musicians rather than an entity. Zappa jams with the band on the instrumental "Out to Get You," and the group never flinches. Just as he did on the Captain Beefheart and Wild Man Fischer albums, Zappa includes the band's warm-ups, flubs, and improvisations (including the raunchy *a cappella* cameo "Big Buns," sent out to Farner's then-girlfriend, actress Suzanne Sommers).

Captain Beefheart's next opus, *Bat Chain Puller*, which Zappa considered "his best album since *Trout Mask Replica*," also became a casualty of the lawsuit with Herb Cohen. It was to be released on the DiscReet label, but got caught in the legal crossfire. "One of the reasons I argued with Herbie was because he used my royalty checks to pay for the production costs of Beefheart's album while I was away on tour," Zappa explained. The album had been produced by Beefheart, using Zappa's engineer Kenny McNabb, who had worked wonders on *One Size Fits All*. As a result, Zappa had the master tapes languishing in his basement studio. Beefheart wanted the tapes delivered to Virgin in the U.K. so the album could be released there, but Zappa refused — he was afraid that Beefheart and Virgin would be sued by Cohen if the album ever came out. Cohen was after any advance money from Virgin Records, if the album saw the light of day. Since it was Zappa's cash that had made the album possible, he thought he should be paid. *Bat Chain Puller* was never released (although some songs would be re-recorded and put out on Beefheart's next three albums on Virgin), and it brought on the final falling-out between Zappa and Beefheart.

When Zappa eventually gained the rights to the *Bat Chain Puller* tapes from Cohen in 1982, Beefheart and Gary Lucas, a guitarist in Beefheart's new band, apparently visited Zappa with the intent of using outtakes from that session to fill out what would be Beefheart's last album, *Ice Cream for Crow*. But, according to Lucas, Zappa changed his mind; he wasn't in the mood to negotiate.

"Frank says, 'Don, what do you want?' real nasty and kind of hostile," Lucas told Magic Band drummer John French in a 1999 interview. "Don says, 'Gary?' and I go into my rap: 'Listen, we called your manager about getting these tracks, we have a whole fifteen minutes on this record we're doing predicated on getting these tracks. You didn't call back. What's the story? I thought we could get them.' . . . [Zappa] says, 'Yeah, well I thought about it. I thought there might be a higher market in Beefheartland if I didn't split up the set.' I asked, 'Do you think with this recording budget we have with Virgin, we could afford to buy the whole record back?' Don starts reciting his poem 'There Ain't No Santa Claus on the Evening Stage,' which was about, among other things, the music business, intending to bum Frank out. Then I hammered Frank. 'We don't have the money. What are you doing to us?' Then he asked, 'How many minutes do you need to fill?' I said, 'About fifteen.' He says, 'Well, I got a track about twelve minutes long called 'Why Doesn't Someone Get Him a Pepsi?' Don sings on it. I wrote it. It's one of my tunes.' I said, 'You really think we want to put a Frank Zappa tune on a Captain Beefheart album?' That was it. He just said, 'I don't know what to say. I've gotta go drink my coffee now.'"

This episode illustrates how the legal battles heightened the competitiveness between Beefheart and Zappa. Since Beefheart didn't want the song, Zappa eventually released it on Vol. 4 of *You Can't Do That on Stage Anymore*. Zappa and Beefheart would never work together again.

The lawsuit also put the Mothers officially to rest. The only way for Zappa to perform without being blocked by Cohen was to go it alone, under his own name. It was also a way to make the band truly his alone. "I get cassettes, letters, musical scores, from all over the world," Zappa told Michael Gray. "I have the only group which is important and long-lasting, which anybody can join if they're good enough. I audition everybody who comes up, and I'm the only one who offers this opportunity. There's no way you could join a band like Led Zeppelin, but musicians know that my door is always open."

He went further in explaining the benefits of working this way to Nigel Leigh. "I like to find players that have unique abilities that haven't been challenged on

I'M THE SLIME

other types of music," Zappa said. "I mean, a good example would be a guy like Bruce Fowler, who has an incredible range on the trombone. When he plays the trombone, you hardly recognize it as a trombone because his technique is so bizarre. Or Terry Bozzio, whose idea of constructions for drum solos was in a whole musical realm that nobody had touched before.... How often do you get a chance to apply these unusual skills on other types of music?"

During September 1976, Zappa put together the first touring ensemble to bear only his name. He brought in a newcomer, Ray White, a black gospel singer who played guitar, kept Terry Bozzio on drums, replaced George Duke with Eddie Jobson (late of Roxy Music) on keyboards, and enlisted Patrick O'Hearn (an old friend of Bozzio's) on bass. That tour also included Bianca Thornton on keyboards and vocals, but constant requests from the crowd for her to whip off her clothes forced her to bail out.

In November, the band played Maple Leaf Gardens in Toronto. While there, Zappa dropped in on radio station CHUM-FM for an interview. In the booth, he noticed that the *Zoot Allures* album had white stickers over the songs "Black Napkins" and "The Torture Never Stops." Zappa challenged the interviewer, asking who did this, and why. The host tap-danced around the questions until the music director, Benjamin Karsh, stormed in to defend the station's policy.

This fascinating interview served as a warm-up for the PMRC hearings on music censorship that Zappa would address in the '80s. A simple promotional junket for an album suddenly turned into a lively debate that exposed the typical and tired annoyance Zappa always had to confront. Most music programmers had no clue about the sophistication and range of Zappa's music; they saw him as nothing more than an obscene novelty act. Zappa asked what was offensive about "Black Napkins," an instrumental. Nothing apparently, but the song segued into one they did take issue with. "The Torture Never Stops" was no more sexually explicit than Donna Summer's "Love to Love You Baby." But, Karsh told Zappa, "The Torture Never Stops" was "hard to get into."

"The only thing a radio station really cares about is ratings, which in turn jack up the value of the airtime that they charge for people who are buying commercial spots," Zappa told listeners. "The more people who listen to a station, the more they can charge for the time that the commercial people want to buy. That's the way the business works. However, it's a subterfuge to have to do this using music. People make music because it's an artistic expression . . . and the radio station is playing certain types of music in order to boost their ratings, so consequently they're always tempted to take the easy way out. Just format everything and stick the whole day's worth of programming on cartridges and let it rip."

Karsh countered that this may be true for AM radio, but not for FM. Zappa replied, "You haven't put your whole day on carts yet, but give it another couple of years. As the ratings wars go on, you'll have to worry about who's selling what and who's doing what to whom. And I don't like to get stuck in the middle of that."

Within a few years, Zappa's words would turn out to be prophetic. The FM radio format would become just as rigid as AM. "I think that it's difficult for kids listening to the radio to understand what radio is really all about," Zappa said. "They listen to radio like it's their little friend . . . but it's a grubby business. And people who make records, and want to have those records on the radio, have to eventually come face-to-face with things like white stickers on albums. And if you wink your eye and ignore it and walk away, there's going to be two more stickers on the next album." Meanwhile, the song CHUM-FM did play was "Ms. Pinky" — the one tune on the album that *would* offend people!

The tour that set out to herald the Motherless version of Frank Zappa started to turn into a Mothers of Invention reunion. For instance, in Detroit at Cobo Hall on November 19, Flo & Eddie opened for Zappa in their first appearance with him since his accident. The duo were recording for Columbia Records and promoting their new album, *Moving Targets*. When their guitarist Phil Reed fell to his death from a hotel window, Flo & Eddie joined Zappa for the rest of his tour. Playing in the group was ex-Zappa sidemen Walt and Bruce Fowler (Ian Underwood would join the lineup once they got to L.A. to play the Roxy). By the end of the evening in Detroit, there was a jam session featuring Ralph Armstrong of the Mahavishnu Orchestra and Don Brewer of the now-defunct Grand Funk Railroad.

Five days after the Cobo Hall show, Zappa guested on the highly rated NBC late-night comedy show *Saturday Night Live*. With the *Saturday Night Live* band, he performed a new song, "Dancin' Fool," yet another parody of the disco culture. He also did the old favorite "Peaches en Regalia," as well as "I'm the Slime," which had the added bonus of featuring the usually invisible NBC emcee, Don Pardo, who battled Zappa for the title of the *real* slime. The sheer ironic power of hearing Pardo's booming voice yelling out that *he* was the slime moved Zappa to ask him to take part in the band's concert at New York's Palladium Theatre at the end of December. The band also debuted an instrumental number, "The Purple Lagoon," a big-band track dating from *The Grand Wazoo* days. What distinguished the piece on this particular evening was the participation of the wildman comic John

I'M THE SLIME

Belushi, who portrayed a samurai bebop musician (complete with jazzbo yelps). This performance is best appreciated on the Italian bootleg CD box set *Apocrypha*.

For the Palladium shows, Zappa added a five-piece brass section — Mike Brecker on tenor sax and flute; Randy Brecker on trumpet; Lou Marini on alto sax and flute; Ronnie Cuber on baritone sax and clarinet; Tom Malone on trombone, trumpet, and piccolo — plus David Samuels on timpani and vibes. The touring band consisted of White, Jobson, O'Hearn, Underwood, and Bozzio. Zappa put together selections from both the Palladium and Felt Forum shows for a new live album to be called simply *Zappa in New York*. To complete his contract with DiscReet, Zappa brought Warner Brothers tapes three months ahead of schedule. These recordings included the music for the albums *Orchestral Favorites*, *Studio Tan*, and *Sleep Dirt* (which included pieces that were to have been on the aborted *Night of the Iron Sausage* double album, which had become *Zoot Allures*). He also included the new recording, *Zappa in New York*. But since all of Zappa's assets — including advances for his albums — were frozen due to the ongoing suit, *Zappa in New York* (and any other recordings) would be in limbo. The appeal of the Royal Albert Hall breach of contract case also had to be dropped. There was nothing left for Zappa to do but tour.

Ruth Underwood left the group after the Palladium concerts, and Ray White, a devout Christian, departed because he had moral qualms about the material. So the touring band consisted of the core group that performed at the Palladium, minus the augmented sections. A European tour was planned for early 1977. Zappa acquired a new manager, Bennett Glotzer, who had managed Procol Harum, Janis Joplin, and Blood, Sweat & Tears. It also seemed like a good idea to hire a personal bodyguard, so no repeat of the Rainbow could take place. He found John Smothers, a huge black gentleman who was bald and built like Mr. Clean. Smothers was a fan of classical music, so he was uncertain about the job until he recognized the scope of Zappa's work. Smothers had an unusual habit of mangling the English language, which Zappa would put to good use in a song called "Dong Work for Yuda" (later featured in *Joe's Garage*). In a live version (heard on *Apocrypha*) from February 1977, Terry Bozzio leads the band *a cappella*. Bozzio affectionately imitated Smothers' pronunciation of words like saliva, which he would call *salima*; water would be referred to as *HtO*; *McDonalds* became *McDoogles*.

The touring group disbanded after they returned to North America at the end of February, and by the summer, Zappa started looking for new blood. He conscripted percussionist Ed Mann to fill Ruth Underwood's shoes, and singer/guitarist Adrian Belew, who played in Sweetheart, a Top 40 cover band Zappa's chauffeur talked him into catching one night at Fanny's Bar in Nashville. Belew was certainly aware he had a special guest in the audience that night. "You could almost tell from the audience that something unusual was happening; there was a real buzz in the air," Belew recalled in *T'Mershi Duween* in 1994. "Frank sat and listened to us for about forty minutes, then he came up and shook my hand in the middle of a song, 'Gimme Shelter.' He said he would get my number from his chauffeur and audition me sometime later. It was about six months before he called me and I thought he had forgotten about me, but he'd been finishing off the tour. So then I auditioned at his house, and the rest is history."

Belew, born in Kentucky, came from a family with absolutely no musical abilities. But, like Zappa, he developed an interest in the drums. He also wanted to be a songwriter, though, so he took up the guitar at sixteen. The British Invasion had inspired him to become a recording artist.

Within a few years, the psychedelic era hit and Belew became immersed in the music of Jimi Hendrix and King Crimson (a band he would join years later). By the '70s, Belew worked in a number of groups that played Hendrix, Elvis, and the Beatles. "Even when I was in my little Beatles copy band, I was already listening to Zappa's music," Belew remembered. "My manager gave me the *Freak Out!* album and said I was the only person he knew who might enjoy this music." Within a year of Belew's meeting Zappa in that Nashville bar, Sweetheart broke up. Zappa called the same week, asking him to audition. "I was always kind of the theatrical element [in the group] because I don't read music," Belew recalled in a discussion with ex-Zappa sideman Steve Vai in 1994. "So I would go to Frank's house over the weekends to prepare for the next week. He would show me things kind of by rote. I would have to start learning them. Meanwhile on Monday morning, Terry Bozzio and everyone else would be sitting there sweating out some new charts."

Another of Zappa's new recruits was German keyboard player Peter Wolf, a founding member of the rock band Gypsy Love. Wolf, whose father was a musician, became a pianist by age four. But at sixteen, he dropped all of his conservatory studies — especially classical music. "A classical player can't turn around and whip into a jazz club and wail, because his head will be in a different space entirely," Wolf told *Keyboard*. Wolf formed Gypsy Love with Carl Ratzer, and recorded a couple of albums. As Ratzer became more jazz-oriented, though, Wolf started a new group with the improbable name of the Objective Truth Orchestra. They played jazz-rock fusion, until gigs became sparse. Then Wolf headed for

I'M THE SLIME

America and played bebop in Atlanta and Birmingham until he joined Zappa's ensemble. "Working with Frank makes you aware of a lot of things," said Wolf. "I've learned more with him than I have at any schools or during any other gig. . . . You play '50s rock 'n' roll and you play total jazz and you play Schoenberg — or Webern–oriented stuff — and to pull that off in one concert is what Frank loves to do."

Also aboard was Tommy Mars, a keyboard player who performed in the kinds of lounges that Zappa loathed back in his youth. "I was getting incredibly distressed playing for men and women who would come in as perfect ladies and gentlemen and leave as animals," Mars told Ben Watson. "They would be sitting as close to me as we are sitting now and I could not resist the temptation to start singing to you, and to you, and telling to you, how fucked up you are. And what the hell are you doing to her? I was putting on the wrong mask for that gig, and it was just perfect that Frank needed somebody to put on that mask for him."

With Bozzio and O'Hearn the only holdovers from the Palladium shows, the new band did a warm-up concert at the University of California in San Diego on September 9. Two days later, the first night of the tour, in Las Vegas, a bad omen occurred. Ron Nehoda, the road manager, committed suicide after spending close to $10,000 on drugs and gambling at the Aladdin Casino. Glotzer brought in the veteran Phil Kaufman to take over.

The group returned to the Palladium for four shows concluding on Halloween, and that Halloween concert would be the source for the next Zappa film, *Baby Snakes*. Unlike *Uncle Meat* and *200 Motels*, *Baby Snakes* was, for the most part, was less a conceptual movie than a straightforward performance film. Yet it, too, featured people "who do stuff that is not normal." There was ex-Mother Roy Estrada, reprising his operatic Pope from the Royal Albert Hall show, as well as getting himself acquainted with Ms. Pinky; Phil Kaufman demonstrating an unusual method for extracting trombone-like sounds; bodyguard John Smothers taking an active interest in Terry Bozzio's "poop chute"; and claymation designer Bruce Bickford creating some fascinating and distorted narratives that Zappa set to music. *Baby Snakes* would be released on Zappa's birthday in Times Square on December 1979. The soundtrack album, a picture disc, wouldn't make the record racks until 1983.

Close to twenty-seven years after its initial release, Finnadar Records reissued the original Edgard Varèse album on EMS that started Zappa on his musical quest. So it seemed fitting that they would include in the liner notes an article Zappa wrote for *Stereo Review* in June 1971, "Edgard Varèse: The Idol of My Youth." But while the late Varèse was finding a new life on a new label, the very much alive Frank Zappa couldn't find a record company that would take him. At first, he approached Capitol Records, but that deal fell through when Zappa discovered that Capitol was represented by the same law firm as Warner Brothers. Capitol used the same record pressing plant as Warners. He then turned to Mercury Records with an idea to release a four-record box set titled *Läther* (but pronounced "Leather").

Läther contained tracks recorded between 1973 and 1977 that were part of the package of albums Zappa had delivered to Warner Brothers, plus some new songs. This included the complete *Studio Tan* and selected tracks from *Orchestral Favorites* and *Sleep Dirt*. Zappa also threw in a few pieces from *Zappa in New York*. But that's where the trouble came in. While Mercury was definitely interested, and had three hundred box sets produced and ready for release for Halloween in 1977, Warner Brothers still held the rights to *Zappa in New York*. Even if they refused to release it, Mercury was prevented from putting it out.

Zappa told Den Simms in *Society Pages* that his career was in limbo. "They made it impossible for me to get a record contract with anyone," he said. "There was a period of time where I was kind of locked out of the music business, and since I didn't have a recording studio at that time, and since I didn't have a contract, and I couldn't go into a recording studio... I took my four-track and hooked up a bunch of little dip-shit equipment here in [my] basement, just like every other garage band guy would do, and I was making some one-man tapes here."

An example of those homemade efforts was "Basement Music #1," which turned up on *The Lost Episodes*. This very basic track, which consists of a Rhythm Ace being fed into a flanger, was done on a Synkey synthesizer with no overdubs. In a way, this bouncy little tune with some nice variations on the simple chord progression served as a precursor to the synclavier recordings Zappa would produce in the '80s.

In an act of desperation and self-preservation, Zappa appeared on Pasedena radio station KROQ and brought the complete three-and-a-half-hour *Läther* album with him. "The way it stands now is my future as a recording artist is dangling in midair, pending court procedures which in California can take anywhere from three to five years for civil cases just to get a day in court and get your case heard," Zappa told listeners. "So, since I don't think anybody wants to wait three to five years to hear my wonderful music, I've taken it upon myself to come down here and advise anybody interested in the stuff I do to get a cassette machine and tape the album. You can have it for free, just take it right off the radio. Don't buy it, tape it."

This was the first — and last— time Zappa would be so generous toward bootleggers. Those who had their tape recorders ready were treated to a magnum opus that revealed the full range of Zappa's "project/object," and it wouldn't be officially available to the public for another twenty years.

11

In the film *Uncle Meat*, mad scientist Biff Debris (Don Preston) gives his own particular definition of music. "We're coming to the beginning of a new era, wherein the development of the inner self is the most important thing," he says. "We have to train ourselves so that we can improvise on anything . . . a bird, a sock, a fuming beaker. This, too, can be music. Anything can be music." *Läther* would be the litmus test for Biff Debris' theory.

The album is a continuation of Zappa's pursuit of the Big Note that he started in *Lumpy Gravy*, while it further develops elements from *Uncle Meat* and *Weasels Ripped My Flesh*. Like *Uncle Meat*, it surveys a wide range of Zappa's work: *musique concrète*, orchestral, rock oratorios, and jazz. But like *Weasels*, the material is a masterfully edited non-chronological collection of live and studio recordings made over a period of years. Its vast diversity seems built on the assumption that Zappa's listeners are not your average passive consumers. "It's participatory," Zappa told John Stix of *Guitar World* in 1980. "The music should interact with the person that's listening to it. What I do isn't designed to reinforce your lifestyle. It's coming from a different place; it's not product. Ultimately everything that gets released by a record company turns into product, but the intent of what I do is not product-oriented."

That participatory aspect is built right into the set. A bit of *musique concrète* incorporates speaking voices that resemble the piano conversations Zappa wove into the score of *Lumpy Gravy*. The first voice we hear is someone confessing their sins. "Father, I'm glad you're here . . . I want you to hear this . . . I have a confession to make." After being encouraged to "spit it out," the voice cries out, "LEATHER!" The second voice replies, "Well, don't be ashamed. . . ." Just as he did in "St. Alfonzo's Pancake Breakfast," Zappa strips away the moral confines dictated by religion and social stigma, attempting to probe the hidden desires that these enforced precepts mask. Zappa overturns the hierarchies of musical taste, the homoeroticism of life on the road, and the margins of time itself. As Ben Watson writes, *Läther* is about "the frenzy of forbidden practices, and the grotesque shock of revealing private matters on the public stage."

"Regyptian Strut" is a glorious instrumental march complete with brassy horns (courtesy of Bruce Fowler), a nimbly added bass line by James "Bird Legs" Youman, stately percussion by Chester Thompson and Ruth Underwood, and elegant cabaret piano work by George Duke. Composed around the time of *The Grand Wazoo*, "Regyptian Strut" opens the album with a perfect combination of vivacious bombast and cheesy pomp. "Naval Aviation in Art?" which immediately follows, is Zappa's masterpiece of taut sparseness from the *Orchestral Favorites* sessions. Coming as it does right after the anthemic "Regyptian Strut," "Naval Aviation in Art?" dramatically shifts the mood into something more contemplative, until an abrupt portion of *musique concrète* (which includes a voice remarking, "God, that was really beautiful") breaks in and leads directly into the corniness of "A Little Green Rosetta."

This cabaret number is a duet between Zappa and Duke likely recorded at the same session as "Evelyn, a Modified Dog" and the introductory section to "Muffin Man." Although the song would be re-recorded as the concluding number on *Joe's Garage*, here it's an edited section from "Muffin Man," who works in the Utility Muffin Research Kitchen making muffins ("A little green rosetta/You'll make a muffin betta"). The song ends briskly with Zappa saying, "Whereupon the door closes violently," and a burst of guitar takes us into "Duck Duck Goose," a hodgepodge of random happenings. The first portion is a short outtake from a performance of "Zoot Allures" recorded in Tokyo during Zappa's 1976 world tour (it later turns up on *Shut Up 'n Play Yer Guitar* as "Ship Ahoy"), more *musique concrète*, some of Roy Estrada's high-decibel singing, plus another live hard-rock guitar solo that sounds like a variant of Led Zeppelin's "Whole Lotta Love."

"Down in de Dew" is an instrumental duet between Zappa (playing guitar and bass) and drummer Jim Gordon that was likely recorded during the *Apostrophe (')* sessions. The song, which originally appeared on a cassette included in *Guitar World*, gets its title from a line in "Uncle Remus": "I'll be knockin' the jockeys off the lawn/Down in the dew." It features some of the delicate playing of "Toads of the Short Forest" from *Weasels Ripped My Flesh*. "For the Young Sophisticate," on the other hand, is an indelicate blues that tackles our preoccupation with looking beautiful. Recorded during the *Over-nite Sensation* sessions, it features the frenzied vocal stylings of Ricky Lancelotti (who trades off lead vocals with Zappa); a different version of the track would be included on *Tinsel Town Rebellion*.

I'M THE SLIME

In just over seventeen minutes, Zappa sets up the strategy of *Läther*. This album will take us on a panoramic tour of different musical styles and ideas, and still fit magically together. Once we become comfortable with the contrasts in music, Zappa zeros in on his first theme — anxieties about the body — beginning with "For the Young Sophisticate." The motif continues with "Tryin' to Grow a Chin," a rollicking rock song about adolescent angst with a delirious vocal by drummer Terry Bozzio. "The song was constructed using every kind of cliché that folk-rock brought to the world — all those stupid bass lines," Zappa explained. "And it's sung by the drummer who has a squeaky little teenage voice." Unlike "For the Young Sophisticate," where the protagonist craves to look beautiful, this is a song about a teenager who suffers the indifference of his folks and takes refuge in feeling repulsive. Zappa anticipates the ugly refusal of punk rock in this song:

I'm horny 'n' lonely
'N' I wish I was dead
Why am I livin'?
I wanna be dead instead.

Since "Tryin' to Grow a Chin" concerns someone who turns anal-retentive, the next one, "Broken Hearts Are for Assholes," makes that fact the point of the tune:

Some of you might not agree
'Cause you probably like a lot of misery
But think a while and you will see . . .
Broken hearts are for assholes
Are you an asshole, too?
Whatcha gonna do, 'cause you're an asshole.

The song follows a fascinating bit of *musique concrète* where a brief conversation evokes the homoeroticism that underscores the buddy atmosphere of guys on the road:

Voice one: Whaddya say we go down the street for a few minutes?
Voice two: No . . . no go on that. . . . I don't like fag bars.
Voice one: No . . . we'll, try 'em . . .

"Broken Hearts Are for Assholes" starts with Bozzio (using the same hysterical voice from "Tryin' to Grow a Chin") taking us into the gay-bar scene. Zappa surveys how hard, impersonal sex becomes sentimentalized while bass player O'Hearn answers back as the club's emcee:

> FZ: HIS WHISKERS STICKING OUT FROM UNDERNEATH HIS PAN-
> CAKE MAKEUP
> O'Hearn: Alive and living in leather
> FZ: NEARLY DROVE YOU INSANE
> O'Hearn: Alright
> FZ: YOU SNIFFED THE REEKING BUNS OF ANGEL
> O'Hearn: Formerly Buddy Love, the Baron of Beef
> FZ: AND ACTED LIKE IT WAS COCAINE
> O'Hearn: And next week, a Grape salute to S&M.

While the first half of the song satirizes the "sensitivities" of gay men, by the end, Zappa turns his attention to the "gentility" of women:

> *You say you can't live with what you've been through*
> *Well, ladies, you can be an asshole, too*
> *You might pretend you ain't got one on the bottom of you.*

Zappa is saying that, in our culture, seeking personal reassurance in love is tantamount to taking it up the ass. Where most popular love songs fetishize the broken heart (as in, say, the Bee Gees' "How Can You Mend a Broken Heart?"), Zappa brings this romantic notion right back to the glands.

His exploration of anal sadism is followed by another song of the same specimen, "The Legend of the Illinois Enema Bandit." This one tells the story of Michael Kenyon, a thirty-year-old armed robber who, from the late '60s to the early '70s, terrorized coeds at the University of Illinois, administering enemas to several of them. Recorded at the Palladium on Halloween, 1976, "The Legend of the Illinois Enema Bandit" is a classic blues sung (with a gospel urgency) by Ray White. The song completely subverts the folk tradition, which usually celebrates the lives of noble people or documents injustice. Instead, "The Legend of the Illinois Enema Bandit" is an outrageous bit of underclass resentment where Kenyon's heinous acts are portrayed as attacks on "college-educated women."

I'M THE SLIME

Since Kenyon was never charged for the sexual violations, Zappa imagines what would have happened if he had been put on trial. Zappa invokes circumstances right out of "Back Door Man," Willie Dixon's famous blues about anal sex. As the Back Door Man stands before a judge for his sexual proclivities, the women in the courthouse plea for his release. The suggestion is that despite the strong taboo around anal sex, these women — and their secret craving — overturns the court's judgment. In "The Legend of the Illinois Enema Bandit," some of his victims yell, "Let the fiend go free!" which leads Kenyon to believe that his acts liberated their libidos ("It must be just what they all needs . . . "). Zappa bravely puts that bit of male posturing from "Back Door Man" right at the heart of the questionable activities of a sexual deviant. This clever transposition subverts the blues tradition of sexual bravado, as well as the noble folk legacy. Since the song is introduced by NBC voice Don Pardo in the manner of a true-crime documentary, Zappa also satirizes our fascination with aberrant figures on sensationalized TV shows.

While many critics took issue with Zappa's "infantile" preoccupations (Chip Stern of *Downbeat* wrote that "The Legend of the Illinois Enema Bandit" elevated "the doody joke to Wagnerian proportions"), Zappa raises key questions about the very spectacle of the folk and blues traditions, and the whole idea of representation. Zappa suggests that if America commemorates in song a heroic figure like Joe Hill, why not the ignoble deeds of Michael Kenyon, equally a product of American culture?

The next three studio-recorded songs illustrate Zappa's frivolous side. "Lemme Take You to the Beach" is an animated bit of surfer music performed in a wild contralto style by Davey Moire. With Eddie Jobson's bubbling synthesizer pumping the song along, and Don Brewer's hilariously frantic bongo playing in the bridge, the track is a delirious surf send-up. "Revised Music for Guitar & Low Budget Orchestra" is a reduced version of the piece performed by Jean-Luc Ponty on *King Kong*, but done in the same cartoonish fashion as "Lemme Take You to the Beach." "RDNZL" is a glittering instrumental that goes off like a chain of fireworks, highlighted by Ruth Underwood's percussion and synthesizer solos, and George Duke's luxurious lounge piano work, with Zappa performing a ripping solo that is underscored by Underwood's lovely, Latin-flavored marimba.

With "Honey, Don't You Want a Man Like Me?" — a live recording from the *Zappa in New York* show — Zappa returns to documentation of socio-sexual behavior. Churlishly, he depicts a date between two very uptight middle-class folks. He's a "playboy type," who smokes a pipe, owns an Irish setter, and loves to say, "Outtasight!" She's an office girl named Betty, whose favorite performer is Helen Reddy ("I Am Woman"), out for fun at a singles bar. After they enjoy eating brown rice (served by "a real hippie") in a quiet restaurant, he takes her home to her motor court. When she won't kiss him, he shows his true colors by calling her a slut and other invectives. While she runs inside, weeping hysterically, he tries to start his car, only to find the battery dead. When he comes in to use her phone, she ends up performing fellatio on him. That's pretty much the whole story in what Zappa describes as "just another love song." "Everybody else writes songs about beautiful girls who make you fall in love, and groovy guys that are so wonderful, and heartbreak and all that shit — that's everybody else's department," Zappa told *Trouser Press* in 1980. "I'm alternative information on specimen behavior." However, not everyone in the audience appreciated the "alternative information." At one point, someone yells, "Fuck you!" to which Zappa replies (without missing a beat in the song), "Fuck you, too, buddy. You know what I mean? Fuck you very much." In this song, Zappa demonstrates that the assumed sensitivity of the couple is undermined by their hidden fears and desires. In "Honey, Don't You Want a Man Like Me?" Zappa is critical of dating patterns that create false impressions of what true love can be. "I'm making comments about society, and the society I was commenting on was engaged in what they love to describe as the Sexual Revolution — a world of sexual incompetents encountering each other under disco circumstances," Zappa told Nigel Leigh. "Now can't you do songs about that?"

Zappa called the instrumental "The Black Page" a "melody that sounds like the missing link between 'Uncle Meat' and 'The Be-Bop Tango.'" Originated as a drum solo for Bozzio, "The Black Page" is a lovely syncopated work for percussion that, in this live performance (intended for *Zappa in New York*), features Ruth Underwood and Bozzio, with punctuated overdubs by percussionists Ed Mann and John Bergamo and delicate harp work by Louanne Neil.

A rousing big-band version of "Big Leg Emma," from the same Palladium show as "The Black Page," was included not only as "a stupid song to tap your foot to in the middle of this other stuff," Zappa said, but also "for nostalgic purposes, as this was one of the pieces regularly performed when we lived in New York and worked at the Garrick Theatre in 1967." What follows is an oratorio, also from the Palladium — and introduced by Don Pardo — called "Punky's Whips." In a

I'M THE SLIME

Japanese music magazine, drummer Terry Bozzio had encountered a photo centerspread of a musician named Edwin "Punky" Meadows, lead singer of a band called Angel. Angel, all dressed in white, represented the forces of Goodness. "Punky's Whips" is about "Terry's litheroticization" of Punky Meadows, with his pompadour hairdo and huge pouting lips. Zappa wrote this hilarious oratorio to explore a heterosexual man's desperate attempt to deal with his erotic fascination with the photo of another man.

"Flambé" is a studio instrumental originally intended — with lyrics — for the science-fiction musical *Hunchentoot*, where the Queen of Cosmic Greed sings of her love to Hunchentoot, a giant spider. It's a slow blues with lovely lounge piano by Duke, gorgeous marimba lines by Underwood, and a subtle pulsating bass line by O'Hearn. "The Purple Lagoon" is the full-blown version of what Zappa performed on *Saturday Night Live* (with John Belushi). In this Palladium recording, Zappa has the band play two themes against each other. One of them, "Approximate" (written around the time of *The Grand Wazoo*), was a piece where "each musician can choose the tone pitch they want to play." While usually played separately, the two pieces are connected here to create a wonderful piece of jazz soloing.

"Pedro's Dowry," from the *Orchestral Favorites* sessions at Royce Hall, is a merry-go-round of diverse musical fragments done up like a Carl Stalling score to a Looney Tunes cartoon. The story that inspired the piece, which Zappa related at the session, could also be considered something of a cartoon:

> A woman with oceanfront property waits for someone named Pedro. She will launder his burlap shirt in a splendid sunset. He will play an inexpensive guitar. She will make him a stimulating drink. While he drinks it, she will put on more lipstick. Later, they'll have a cheap little fuck and accidently knock over an ashtray. In the confusion, she might have misplaced her necklace. Within moments, Earl has cleaned her up.

"Läther" is a lovely instrumental from the Palladium concert that earns a place beside "Little Umbrellas," "Aybe Sea," and "Twenty Small Cigars" as one of Zappa's more delicate pieces described as a "ballad for late-nite easy listening." "Spider of Destiny" is another piece from *Hunchentoot* (minus the lyrics), and "Duke of Orchestral Prunes" is "Duke of Prunes" given a full orchestral rendering, from the *Orchestral Favorites* sessions.

The rock instrumental "Filthy Habits" is a studio recording filled with the foreboding shrieks of loud guitars (some playing backwards through tape manipulation) and a driving percussion track by Bozzio. Zappa plays an extended solo that toys with the grungiest of feedback in the manner of "Zoot Allures" or "Get a Little." After a brief bit of *musique concrète*, where some band members wonder, "What has happened to all the fun in the world?" the next song tells you. "Titties 'n Beer" is another oratorio, live from the Palladium, that features Bozzio. This gaudy number about a biker, his girlfriend Chrissy, and a confrontation with the Devil is a rewrite of Stravinsky's *L'Histoire du soldat*.

In Stravinsky's tale, a soldier meets the Devil in disguise along a road. He tries to push an old book, which holds the promise of attaining great wealth, on the soldier in exchange for his violin. When the soldier agrees, it brings him more grief than he could imagine, and he spends the rest of the piece attempting to outwit the Devil. In "Titties 'n Beer," the Devil swallows up the biker's girlfriend and his beer. In exchange for the biker's "titties and beer," the Devil wants him to sign a contract. To the Devil's surprise, the biker can't wait to get his pen. While the Devil is reeling with confusion, Chrissy jumps out of his mouth, saying, "I've got three beers 'n a fistful of downs." While she goes to get wrecked, the biker discovers she's at his pad and the whole episode was nothing more than a dream.

In *L'Histoire du Soldat*, the soldier stays beholden to the Devil because no matter how often he fools the Devil, his desires always lead to his undoing. In "Titties 'n Beer," the biker (played by Zappa) outfoxes the Devil (Bozzio) because he keeps his desires pretty basic (titties and beer) and will sign anything to have those needs fulfilled. The Devil ultimately has no soul to rob since the biker doesn't believe in the Devil's power over him. "Titties 'n Beer" is a witty example of Zappa's belief that total freedom comes through unchaining oneself from the hypocrisies found in the loftier definitions of moral turpitude.

Out of this oratorio, we're thrust into "The Ocean Is the Ultimate Solution," a chugging instrumental from the studio that resembles "The Gumbo Variations" from *Hot Rats* with its high-energy playing. There's an electrifying guitar solo from Zappa and some great acoustic bass from O'Hearn with repetitive thumping that sounds like heavy rain hitting a roof. "I stopped by at about 2:30 in the morning," O'Hearn recalled for *Keyboard* in 1994. "Not being one to leave my upright bass in the car, I carted it into the studio. Frank, upon seeing me with this bass, remarked, 'Do you play that doghouse, fella?' I said, 'Sure do.' Then, without even a formal

I'M THE SLIME

introduction, he said, 'Well how would you like to put some acoustic bass on this track?' I said, 'Let's do it.'" O'Hearn, in the spirit of Ian Underwood, proceeded to whip it out.

The epic story "The Adventures of Greggery Peccary" completes the album by encapsulating all of *Läther*'s themes in one long, virtuoso piece that implicitly echoes Stravinsky. While more imaginative than "Billy the Mountain" (who makes a cameo appearance) and filled with more complex orchestrations than "Don't Eat the Yellow Snow," its storyline is far simpler. It's about a little pig, Greggery Peccary (an obvious play on actor Gregory Peck), who works for Big Swifty Associates, a firm that creates trends. One morning, Peccary comes up with the idea of creating a calendar so that everyone can keep track of time. Unfortunately, although people plan their lives by this nifty invention, they also discover how old they are. "What hath God wrought?" Peccary asks himself in horror. He ends up being pursued by angry Hunchmen and hides in the mouth of Billy the Mountain. When the Hunchmen disappear, he seeks the advice of a philosopher and attends a lecture by Quentin Robert DeNameland, "the greatest living philosopher known to mankind." Greggery discovers that "time is an affliction" and that "the eons are closing." Although DeNameland is right about the fragility of the hardware (clocks and calendars), Greggery concludes that even the world's greatest living philosopher can be a trend all to himself: "If you ask a philosopher/He'll see that you pays."

Within this wonderfully innovative piece, Zappa includes numerous musical quotes and conceptual continuity clues that connect to the larger meaning of *Läther*. When Greggery enters Big Swifty, we hear the musical theme "Big Swifty," from *Waka/Jawaka*. With "What hath God wrought?" he's quoting Samuel Morse's first words after laying down the first complete message (a Morse code) over a telegraph line. When Zappa describes the rage of the Hunchmen, he quotes musically from Elmore James' "Dust My Broom." As Greggery tries to escape the clutches of the Hunchmen, a snatch of "Chameleon" from Herbie Hancock's *Headhunter* album follows. Peccary also takes "the short forest exit" to escape, echoing *Weasels*' "Toads of the Short Forest." When the Hunchmen and Hunchwomen have a "love-in," they dance "with depraved abandon in the vicinity of a six-foot pile of transistor radios each one tuned to a different station," evoking John Cage, who once performed a piece for six radios tuned to different stations. When Greggery asks, "Who is making these new brown clouds?" (it's Billy the Mountain), Zappa quotes "For Calvin (and

His Next Two Hitch-Hikers)" from *The Grand Wazoo*. "The Adventures of Greggery Peccary," like *Läther* itself, is an elaborate mobile construction where all the elements of Zappa's project/object hang in the balance.

Zappa spent the last part of 1977 touring, since it was virtually impossible for him to continue making records. During a stop in Paris, he took a hike into the Métro to find a harmonica player he'd read about in the *New York Herald Tribune*. At the Odéon station, he encountered a rather soulful musician who went by the name of Sugar Blue, playing his harp and accompanied by his girlfriend Cécile. Zappa invited him to play with the band at the Nouvel Hippodrome that night in front of 10,000 people. To the surprise of no one, Sugar Blue fit in perfectly with the group. "I could feel his heart beating while we were playing," Zappa told *New Musical Express*. Within the year, the Rolling Stones would also discover just how much soul Sugar Blue possessed — it was his harp that adorned their hit single "Miss You," from *Some Girls* (1978).

In March 1978, Warner Brothers finally released *Zappa in New York*. But, after all this time, it caused more grief than relief. The company had several objections and took it upon themselves to edit the album without Zappa's consent. First, they took exception to the improvised banter between Bozzio and Zappa during "Titties 'n Beer," so they trimmed it. Second, they cut "Punky's Whips" altogether, leaving the double album twelve minutes shorter than planned. Even though Punky Meadows was pleased with the dubious tribute, Warner Brothers wouldn't take any chances. *Zappa in New York* came out truncated, and critics and fans used this as a reason to jump on Zappa. "There was something in one of the papers over here complaining about how short the album was," Zappa explained to journalist Miles in 1978. "It wasn't my fault. I didn't have any control over it. I think Herb Cohen was the one who took it out." The cuts may have also been an ominous sign of a changing of the guard in the record industry.

The marketing people who began to infiltrate the rock 'n' roll industry in the '70s had not developed their chops through the music business — had no real interest in music, for that matter. Their prime goal was to make money for the corporations who hired them so they could rise up the corporate ladder. As conglomerates usurped various record labels, the companies became less willing to risk signing talented bands who possessed an original sound. This insidiously corporate thinking that emanated from the boardroom created the punk backlash in the late '70s (even if punk, too, would itself become co-opted). "Now, how did

I'M THE SLIME

they earn the *right* to be the gods of the record industry?" Zappa asked Matt Resnicoff of *Musician* in 1991. "These fuckers came from the shoe business, a lot of them. And they are the ones who finally made the decision of who gets the zillion-dollar push, the big endorsements. . . . These esteemed gentlemen, based on advice received from hip magazines that tell you what's hot, will then reshape the size and texture of American musical culture in their own pinhead image."

It was one thing for the executives in the music industry to turn into expedient careerists, but the critics were also getting drawn in by the glamour, the power, and the rubbing of shoulders with the glitterati. Zappa offered a famous definition of rock journalism in the '70s (which was stolen for George Cukor's final film, *Rich and Famous*, in 1981): "Rock journalism is people who can't write interviewing people who can't talk for people who can't read." In 1991, Zappa would elaborate further on this for Matt Resnicoff of *Musician*. "I lived as an entertainer through one era of rock 'n' roll where the rock press was *absolutely* the blowboy of the industry," Zappa recalled. "In the '70s, when corporate rock really blossomed into this stinking apparition it became, companies were giving cocaine, girls, money, junkets, and all this stuff to famous rock writers, just greasing them from one end to the other so they would write nonstop, wonderful glowing articles about groups that needed to be promoted."

Zappa in New York was obviously not worthy of even being promoted by the record company or critics, possibly because it sounded its own clarion call against the encroaching pinhead culture. Besides the tracks that were included on the aborted *Läther*, *Zappa in New York* featured "Läther," under the indiscreet title of "I Promise Not to Come in Your Mouth"; a wonderful big-band arrangement of "Sofa"; a take of "Honey, Don't You Want a Man Like Me?" (minus the heckler); and Bozzio's original drum solo of "The Black Page," plus the more accessible, "teenage New York version" of "The Black Page #2."

Zappa toured Europe in the summer and early fall of 1978, even as his headaches with Warner Brothers continued. Touring was his only source of income. While on tour in Germany, Adrian Belew was lured away by David Bowie — in mid-concert. "There was a segment of the show where Frank did an extended solo and I think Patrick O'Hearn and Terry Bozzio accompanied him and the rest of the band could leave," Belew recalled. "I looked off to the side of the stage and there was David Bowie and Iggy Pop. I walked over and said, 'Hey, David, I've always appreciated your music.' And he said, 'How would you like to join my band?' I said, 'I'm in a band right now with this guy here,' and pointed to Frank. It worked out later that Frank was sort of finished with his thing and it was time for me to go do something else." Zappa seldom forgot episodes like this, which would become valuable folkloric material. "I remember one night we were playing the song 'Yo' Mama,'" Belew said. "Frank changed the words to 'I think maybe you should stay with your *David*.' Apart from that, he never gave me grief about it."

Much later, in 1993, when Zappa was ill with cancer, Belew got back in touch with him after waking up dramatically from a dream one night. "In the dream, it was simply Frank and I together having a conversation," Belew told *T'Mershi Duween*. "We were talking about his music and I told him what I was doing. When I woke up from it, I realized that I had never really genuinely thanked Frank for helping me out and giving me a start, so I sat down at my computer and wrote up a little fax. I then faxed it off to him and he faxed me back saying, 'Call me.' I called him and we had a great conversation and he said, 'That was very sweet of you, Adrian, to say thanks.' And that's an unusual word, 'sweet,' for him to say. It made me feel great."

But if Zappa didn't give Adrian Belew any more grief about running off with the Thin White Duke, that didn't mean other band members would be spared. Guitarist Steve Vai, who would join the group a few years later, became the subject of a practical joke inspired by Bowie's poaching from the band. "Scott Thunes was the bass player when we toured Europe and we played the same hall that David Bowie had come to in Germany to meet you," Vai told Adrian Belew in an interview. "We received this note after the show and it said, 'Dear Scott and Steve: I really like the way you guys play and I'd really be interested if you want to join my band and stop playing this comedy music.' It was a really long note and it was signed, 'David Bowie.' It was something that [Tommy] Mars and Frank put together! It had phone numbers and fax numbers — I thought it was real."

By 1978, drummer Terry Bozzio had also decided to move on. "At that point, I went back and studied a lot of the rock music that I had missed while I was being a jazzer and classical artist," Bozzio told Howard Shih.

Bozzio was replaced by Vinnie Colaiuta, a former high school flautist who just couldn't keep his hands off the drums. When he finished school, he left Boston for New York and joined up briefly with a band headed by Al Kooper. In 1977, not entirely happy with his career, Colaiuta returned to Boston before making his way to Los Angeles. It was there in 1978, where he played a gig with Tom Fowler, that he discovered that Zappa was looking for a new drummer. "I auditioned on Bozzio's drums," Colaiuta recalled. "I had never played on two bass drums before,

I'M THE SLIME

but I said, 'Screw it — I'm going for it!' He put this thing in front of me, 'Pedro's Dowry', and it was the melodic part that I had to sight-read in unison with the marimba. So I sight-read a little bit of that . . . and I guess he heard enough because he said, 'Okay, yes, you can read.' Then he started playing this thing in 21/16 and he wanted me to play along. I grasped it."

Zappa agreed with Colaiuta's assessment. "You can rely on him — you know that he knows where he is and knows where he's going and will come back," Zappa told *Guitar Player*. "He's not just piddling around out there. And unless you're playing with a drummer who understands that type of rhythm and can stretch it to the max, then you're not going to get the same effect."

Arthur Barrow, a fan for many years, had long wanted to play in Zappa's band. Barrow began his pilgrimage by auditioning as a bass player for Top 40 groups. He was surprised to discover that the keyboard player in one of those bands was ex-Mother Don Preston. Through Preston, Barrow met other ex-Mothers like Bruce and Tom Fowler. In the late '70s, Preston and Barrow put together a jazz group called Loose Connection. "When a friend called to tell me that Zappa was auditioning drummers and bass players, I got up the nerve to call Frank on the phone, and I told him that I had learned the melody to 'Inca Roads' by ear from the record to use as a bass exercise," Barrow recalled.

"I think he did not believe me at first. He asked if I was familiar with the instrumental melody in the middle of ['St. Alfonzo's Pancake Breakfast']. When I said yes, he told me to learn it off the record and then play it for him at an audition in two days." First, Barrow made a reel-to-reel recording of the cut from *Apostrophe (')*. He then slowed it down to half speed so he could pick out all the fast and funny little notes, and then he wrote the score down. "I got to the audition early and . . . when Frank came in, I introduced myself and said, 'Here's that melody from "Saint Alfonzo" that you asked me to learn,' and then I 'whipped it out,'" Barrow explained. "Zappa said, 'Well, you got a few wrong notes in there, but you show promise.' . . . Frank asked me to join on a trial basis — I was to rehearse for a week, and then he would decide if I made the grade. . . . I must have done pretty well, because after a couple of hours, he took me aside, smiled broadly, shook my hand, and said, 'You don't have to wait until the end of the week — you're hired. You are one of the best bass players I've ever played with.' I was so thrilled I remember feeling like I could have jumped thirty feet into the air!"

Within a year, Barrow would also become the "clonemeister." "This was Zappa's term for the rehearsal director," Barrow explained. "I guess the term 'clone' in the word 'clonemeister' refers to one aspect of the job which was to transcribe from the albums and perfectly teach to the band the songs that Frank wanted to perform." Rehearsals would last eight to ten hours a day, with the clonemeister running things for the first half and Zappa taking over when he arrived for the second half. "I still had to worry about my own bass and vocal parts, but as clonemeister, I had to know everyone else's parts as well," Barrow recalled. "It was quite a difficult job, especially when I first took over. I had a portable cassette recorder and taped the parts of rehearsal when Frank was there. At night, after rehearsal, I would listen to the tapes and make notes or transcriptions of what Frank had come up with that day. The next day I would drill the band on the previous day's changes and additions. Frank changed his mind a lot, so it was hard to keep up with all of that constantly shifting information."

When Zappa would show up for the final four hours of rehearsal, Barrow taped it. He then made notes about what each musician carried out during a show. "It was like being a drill sergeant," Barrow said. Barrow was amazed at how Zappa played the band the way an artist would use paint on a canvas. "When Frank was there at the rehearsal and inspired, he would write with the band the way someone else might write at the piano, or with a piece of score paper, or at a computer," Barrow told journalist Ernie Rideout in 1994. "It was really amazing how quickly he could get stuff together, and get really good players to interpret it and make it sound like Frank Zappa music."

During the American end of the tour, in late September and October, Zappa's band played a number of East Coast gigs, including their annual appearance at the Palladium on Halloween. That night, the band was joined by Lakshminarayna Shankar (whom Zappa dubbed "Larry" for short), a violinist from Madras who had studied ethnomusicology at Wesleyan University in 1969. In 1973, Shankar met jazz guitarist John McLaughlin, and within four years created the quartet, Shakti. This acoustic band developed a wonderfully adept fusion of jazz and Indian music and made three stunning albums before breaking up in 1978. Shankar and Zappa would have an intermittent, but fruitful, musical relationship right up to Zappa's death. At the Palladium, they did a complicated but sonorous number in 13/8 called "Thirteen" and a rousing instrumental version of "Take Your Clothes Off When You Dance." Both numbers would be included on *You Can't Do That on Stage Anymore, Vol. 6* (1992).

Also on hand was guitarist Warren Cucurullo, a friend of Davey Moire, who, like Barrow, was a huge Zappa follower. Within the year, he'd audition for — and

I'M THE SLIME

become a new addition to — the Zappa band. "I met Frank, and he said, 'Come up to the sound check,' and I kind of followed him around," Cucurullo told *T'Mershi Duween* in 1994. "He told me he was putting another band together — the one with the horn section used on the *In New York* album. That's when our friendship really started to develop." On Cucurullo's birthday, Zappa took him and a friend out to dinner. "We were in this little place in New York and William Burroughs and Allen Ginsberg were at the next table. Frank introduced us: 'This is Malcolm, he's a taxi driver. And this is Warren, he's a guitar player . . .' And I thought, 'Fuuuck!' Two weeks later he asked me to play on his European tour."

Zappa had also met a promising young vocalist named Ike Willis. "I met Ike at an outdoor college concert we did in St. Louis," Zappa told *Sounds* magazine. Willis, a native of St. Louis, had first seen Zappa's band in 1974. While studying at Washington University three years later, he caught the group again. This time, he approached Zappa after the sound check and auditioned for him in the dressing room.

"He was one of the student roadies," Zappa recalled. "He had a summer job on a garbage truck and played on the football team. He said he played guitar and sang, and the guy was great! He just sings his ass off, it's fantastic. I told him at that time that when we were having auditions, I'd bring him out." Willis made his debut with the group in September 1978, in England at Knebworth, singing lead on a new Zappa song about jealousy and murder called "Bamboozled by Love." By 1979, he'd become a key figure in Zappa's musical plans.

Meanwhile, Warner Brothers had finally released *Studio Tan* on September 15, without any liner notes or credits. The slipshod packaging featured a gaudy cover drawing by cartoonist Gary Panter, who designed *Raw Comix*. The mixes of the pieces weren't to Zappa's satisfaction, either. To add insult to injury, "RDNZL" was misspelled on the back cover as "Redunzl." On October 21, Zappa returned to *Saturday Night Live*, only this time as both musical guest and host. One sketch had Zappa performing with the Coneheads, pointy-headed aliens from the planet Remulak. These large-domed creatures, Beldar (Dan Aykroyd) and Prymaat (Jane Curtin), had advanced intelligence and (like Earthling jocks) an unquenchable appetite for beer and potato chips. In the sketch, Zappa arrives at their house to go on a date with their daughter, Connie (Laraine Newman). After consuming much beer and potato chips with Beldar while waiting for Connie to get ready, Zappa gives the family a copy of his new album, *Studio Tan*. Appropriately enough, perhaps as a comment to Warner Brothers, they chew it to pieces.

Zappa and the band performed some new material on the show, including "Dancin' Fool," which would soon appear on *Sheik Yerbouti* (1979), "The Meek Shall Inherit Nothing," which would turn up on *You Are What You Is* (1981), and "Rollo," which is the unreleased coda for the "Don't Eat the Yellow Snow" suite from *Apostrophe (')*. Given the spontaneity of live television, Zappa managed to handle it pretty well, but there were a few close calls. "An interesting thing happened during the live telecast," Arthur Barrow recalled. "Before the show, we were given copies of the schedule of events — which skit was coming next and when we were to play our songs. As the show was getting near the end, I looked at the schedule and noted that there was to be one more sketch, then we were to play 'Rollo.' I was looking around, trying to see which stage the skit was to be on, and Vinnie [Colaiuta] had just lit a cigarette, when suddenly Frank came running up to the stage, baton in hand! The lights came on, Frank leapt onto the stage, baton raised high, and when the baton came down and his feet hit the floor, we launched into 'Rollo.' We are on the air! It turns out the show was running too long so the producers had cut out that sketch, but nobody had bothered to tell us."

The experience of doing *Saturday Night Live* put Zappa in the middle of the type of organized chaos he was always subjecting his band to. Only Zappa wasn't pleased to be standing in their beleaguered shoes. "It's a very difficult thing to do," Zappa told Steve Simels of *Stereo Review*. "They never make it easy on anyone who hosts the show. All the direction and attention goes to the sketches . . . and it's all designed to accommodate the people who are regulars on the show. So anybody who goes on there to host is at a severe disadvantage. They never tell you what camera is on, and you're not supposed to memorize your script because they're rewriting right up to show time. And so you're looking at the cue cards, and unless you're used to acting live on TV, you haven't got a prayer; you'll be looking at the wrong camera. It was really hard."

Over the years, Zappa's relationship with his audience was at best ambivalent. "These are the people who have made it possible for me to stay in music through the years — and I thank them for it," Zappa wrote in *The Real Frank Zappa Book*. But he also pushed that audience, subjecting them to hostile treatment that grew out of his belief that they were basically ignorant about music and always clapping for the wrong reasons. "Unless you're one of these ass-licking pop performers that must always do a song that people enjoy in the traditional sense of enjoyment . . . then you really have to be a lot more pandering to an audience," Zappa told Neil Slaven. "But if you're doing something — I hate to use the word 'experimental,' but

I'M THE SLIME

it was at the time — if you're doing something experimental, then you have to take the attitude that the audience is part of the experiment, and they're not necessarily there to engage in the same sort of 'enjoyment' exercise that they would be getting from something from *Top of the Pops*." Experiments, however, can also backfire.

In the '70s and '80s, Zappa's audience became less and less willing participants in the band's stage antics. As a result, aggressive episodes at concerts, much different from the political turmoil he wrestled with during the '60s, became more frequent. Arthur Barrow recalled one such incident in Maine that December. "I was standing near Frank on the stage and he was playing one of his long guitar solos," Barrow told Dave Dimartino of *MOJO*. "He was just there enjoying himself. He had his eyes closed, playing away. And I look at him, and all of a sudden he's knocked back. I think, Oh my God, he's been shot or something. He almost fell over." As Zappa was performing, a beer bottle came flying down from a balcony, hitting him in the shoulder. At which point, Zappa halted the show and announced, "Now, I'm not going to start playing again 'til that asshole is taken away."

"He was so great at this," Barrow continued. "I guess all those years of handling an audience. He really knew how to do it. . . . It didn't hurt him, but it scared him." After his brush with death at the Rainbow back in 1971, it was certainly understandable. The "asshole" turned out to be twenty-three-year-old James Collins, who was charged with reckless conduct. He pleaded not guilty and was later remanded. A couple of years later, at the Santa Monica Civic Center in December 1981, just before Zappa could launch into the last verse of "Broken Hearts Are for Assholes," someone from the audience tossed a bag of popcorn onto the stage. Again, Zappa stopped the song and deployed John Smothers to go into the crowd, round up the culprit, and bring him back to clean it up. After being interrogated by Zappa, the guy was ordered to lap up the popcorn. "Step right up, introduce yourself, and prepare to dine as you've never dined before," Zappa told him. Once the stage was deemed clean enough to perform on, Zappa launched right into the last verse of that appropriately titled song.

The interruption served a significant purpose for Zappa. He found a way to confront the potential for danger by working it into the fabric of the composition.

By January 1979, Zappa had finally found a way out of the legal mess with Warner Brothers and DiscReet Records. He negotiated a deal with Polygram Records that set up distribution for his own label, Zappa Records. The deal gave Zappa a budget that enabled him to run his own office and sign new recording artists. He would also get more money himself. At a press conference announcing the deal, Zappa made a clear point about the way record companies treat artists. While stressing that he was a businessman, as well as a musician, who hired musicians to play his music, he explained how *he* treated musicians.

First, he always paid them on time. Zappa described how record companies found ways to defer royalty payments. As an example, he said, an artist comes to town and is invited with his band to dinner. After thirty bottles of champagne are ordered and consumed, the artist discovers that he will be footing the bill for this opulent feast, while the label deducts the costs from his royalties. Zappa said firmly that he would do business differently. "Nowhere in the contract is there the provision that a record company can take out of your royalties expenses that you never agreed to, or don't even know about at the time," Zappa said. He also made clear that the accounting of records sold, and how many are pressed, would be done fairly by his label. While no doubt thinking about his experiences with MGM/Verve, he told the reporters stories about how middle-management record executives order overruns on record pressings to trade the surplus albums for personal profit without the artist seeing a dime.

Before Zappa could launch a single record on his new label, Warners put out the second of their unofficial releases, *Sleep Dirt*, on January 19, 1979. Most of *Sleep Dirt*'s tracks were part of the unreleased *Läther* project, except for "Time Is Money," which was from *Hunchentoot*, and the title track, "Sleep Dirt," a lovely acoustic guitar duet between Zappa and James "Bird Legs" Youman.

Zappa turned up in London in mid-January to look into the possibility of recording some orchestral work, but ended up producing L. Shankar's debut solo album, *Touch Me There*, which would be the first release on Zappa Records that spring. The record was a combination of pop and elaborate orchestrations featuring Shankar's phenomenal talent on the violin. On one track, "Dead Girls of London," Zappa managed to get Van Morrison to sing the lead vocal, until Morrison's label, Warner Brothers, caught wind of the deal and nixed it. Ike Willis and Zappa took over the lead vocals for the album.

One year after Warner Brothers had put out their edited and poorly sequenced version of *Zappa in New York*, Zappa released his first official album on the new label. It was immediately obvious that he was making up for lost time. His desire to outrage couldn't have been sharper, more vicious, or more spiked with salacious drollery. Appearing on the cover in a hooded cloak and looking like an Arab prince charging home from the desert digs, Zappa called this two-record set *Sheik Yerbouti*. The title, while hardly a subtle swipe at disco, was also a play on K.C. & the Sunshine Band's hit song "Shake Your Booty." If ever a record expressed the mounting frustration of an angry artist whose career had been sabotaged, this was it. Zappa not only took on disco, but didn't spare punk, nor feminism, Jewish princesses, gay promiscuousness, unions, and teenage angst. Even if it alienated more rock critics than any other previous Zappa album (one scribe described it as "wall-to-wall four-sided dreck"), it would become one of his biggest international best-sellers (the album made No. 21 on the American charts and sold 1.6 million units worldwide). Released on March 3, 1979, it would also be one of his most controversial.

12

Sheik Yerbouti is made up of recordings from the European tour — with numerous studio overdubs — that Zappa did with Terry Bozzio, Patrick O'Hearn, Adrian Belew, Ed Mann, and Peter Wolf in 1978. Some of the songs, including "Broken Hearts Are for Assholes" and "Tryin' to Grow a Chin," are different performances of songs that had been included on the unreleased *Läther*, while a number of the *musique concrète* moments ("What Ever Happened to All the Fun in the World?" "Wait a Minute") are the original pieces from *Läther*. The humor on the two-record set is both harsh and unforgiving. Former band member George Duke noticed a shift in Zappa's satire in the few years since he had played in the band. "The only change I saw in Frank over those years was that he went from being funny/sarcastic to being almost serious/sarcastic," Duke told *Keyboard*. "The latter part of the time I was in the band, his sense of humor became kind of vindictive."

The opening track, "I Have Been in You," was a case in point. The title is a play on British pop star Peter Frampton's hit "I'm in You." Frampton, who earned his reputation in the late '60s as the lead guitarist in the hard rock band Humble Pie, later went through a transformation to teen pop idol, reaching his zenith in 1976 with the overnight success of *Frampton Comes Alive!*, a live album that sold over 8 million copies. Within a year, though, Frampton's cloying persona hit a speed bump with *I'm in You* (1977), featuring a title song that defined insipidness. Zappa wrote an answer to Frampton's blatant attempt to outdo Dan Hill's simpering style of pop singing by composing "I Have Been in You." Where Frampton sang with an earnest sensitivity ("I'm in you/You're in me"), Zappa stripped away the sentiment and went for the gonads:

> *I have been in you, baby*
> *You have been in me*
> *Aw' little girl, there ain't no time*
> *To wash yer stinky hand*
> *Go 'head 'n' roll over*
> *I'm goin' in you again.*

The falsetto vocals of this slow R&B number only enhance its salaciousness. When Zappa took on Frampton, he was commenting on the budding narcissism in rock stars who masked their solipsism in tenderness. In 1920, Charles Ives had made a similar criticism of artistic posturing in his *Essays Before a Sonata*: "The pose of self-absorption, which some men . . . put into their photographs or the portraits of themselves, while all dolled up in their purple dressing-gowns, in their twofold wealth of golden hair, in their sissy-like postures over the piano keys — this pose of 'manner' sometimes sounds so loud that the more their music is played, the less it is heard. . . ."

"Flakes" is an attack on the service-industry incompetents who are protected by unions, and the suburban "morons" who hire them to repair things. Besides its easy target, the only noteworthy element in the song is Belew's uncanny Bob Dylan impersonation partway through. "[Zappa] would arrange a song about five or six different ways before he finally arrived at it," Belew told *T'Mershi Duween*. "When Frank showed ['Flakes'] to me at home one night on a weekend, when he sat and played it on guitar, it sounded like a lousy folk song, so I started kidding about it, singing it like Bob Dylan, and he said, 'That's in the show. You're going to do it that way.'" It was an inspired decision because Dylan is reduced to protesting poor building maintenance rather than significant human deeds. "I'm So Cute," frantically sung by Bozzio, is Zappa's punk song, and a perfect companion to the adolescent angst of "Tryin' to Grow a Chin":

> *Feelin' sorry*
> *Feelin' sad*
> *So many ugly people*

I'M THE SLIME

I feel bad
I'm so cute.

"Jones Crusher" is a straight-ahead rock 'n' roll number about castration anxieties, sung by Belew with a mixture of allure and dread:

She don't ever want to leave it alone
She can push; she can shove
Till it's just a nub
Just a nub.

A bit of *musique concrète* ("What Ever Happened to All the Fun in the World?") from *Läther* leads into the guitar instrumental "Rat Tomago." "A tomago is a stuffed omelette in a Japanese restaurant," Zappa explained to journalist Miles. "You take an egg and beat it up, and I think it's got some sugar in it. Then they make a little brick out of it, and make a slit in the side and stuff it with rice. That's a tomago. A Rat Tomago is different." The solo, recorded live at the Deutschland Halle in Berlin, is lifted from a performance of "The Torture Never Stops." This is one of the first occasions (prior to *Shut Up 'n Play Yer Guitar*) where Zappa takes a guitar solo from another song and labels it a separate composition.

"Bobby Brown Goes Down" is a disputable bit of social commentary about sexual confusion that would probably have fit perfectly on *Läther*. While some have called this song anti-gay, it's not an indictment of homosexuality, but a blatant attack on careerism. Bobby Brown is a preppy, privileged guy who thinks he's "the cutest boy in town." He drives a fast car and dresses sharp and acts cool. He gets the attention of all the cheerleaders. When one such lucky damsel helps him with a paper, he — as a way of showing his appreciation — contemplates raping her. Bobby Brown has a simple outlook on his life that could have been shaped by the white-bread values of the '50s:

Oh God, I am the American Dream
I do not think I'm too extreme
An' I'm a handsome sonofabitch
I'm gonna get a good job 'n' be real rich.

But it's not the '50s anymore — it's the '70s. The emergence of feminism and gay rights has overturned the dominant social order. The road to wealth and power is no longer a sure thing, and Bobby Brown's dreams of getting ahead end up, instead, with him helplessly *giving* head. His first encounter with a lesbian leaves him desperately unsure of his masculinity:

> *I tell you people I was not ready*
> *When I fucked this dyke by the name of Freddie*
> *She made a little speech then,*
> *Aw, she tried to make me say* when
> *She had my balls in a vice, but she left the dick*
> *I guess it's still hooked on, but now it shoots too quick.*

Suddenly, Bobby Brown's means to achieving success come from acts he finds degrading ("I can take about an hour on the tower of power/'Long as I get a little golden shower"). Zappa is saying that Bobby Brown's hyper-aggressive masculinity ("I tell all the girls they can kiss my heinie") was just a cover for his submissive personality ("With a spindle up my butt till it makes me scream/An' I'll do anything to get ahead"). Rather than being a smug assault on homosexuality, Zappa's song confronts our culture's masculine ideals:

> *Oh God, I am the American Dream*
> *But now I smell like Vaseline*
> *An' I'm a miserable sonofabitch*
> *Am I a boy or a lady . . . I don't know which.*

When the band performed the song during the 1984 tour, lead vocalist Ike Willis inserted a "Hi-ho, Silver!" partway through. This reference to the Lone Ranger, which cracked up Zappa to the degree that he could barely sing, was an observant bit of improvisation. It came from Lenny Bruce's classic routine "The Lone Ranger," a satiric jab at the personification of masculine ideals in our heroes. Bruce suggested that once the Lone Ranger doubted his powers, he revealed a submissive side. This leads the townsfolk to speculate that "the Masked Man's a fag!" Despite its contentious content, "Bobby Brown Goes Down" became a huge hit in dance clubs overseas. "'Bobby Brown' was the largest-selling record in CBS's history in all of Scandinavia," Zappa remarked proudly to *RockBill*. "It was a big hit in Germany, too. But these people don't hear the music the same way that Americans do, because they don't know what it means. They may respect it and they may like it — but they haven't the faintest idea what a hamburger is."

"Rubber Shirt," an apt title for both a condom and this instrumental, is a beautiful example of Zappa's xenochronous compositions. It features relaxed interplay between drummer Bozzio and bass player O'Hearn, though neither are playing in the same room, the same time signature — or even the same point in time. Zappa had taken a recording of O'Hearn from a performance in Göteborg, Sweden, where he was playing in 4/4, removed the bass track, and transferred it onto another tape, where he had a Bozzio drum track playing in 11/4 in the studio. By resynchronizing them, Zappa came up with a simulated piece of music. "Rubber Shirt" is more daring than even the xenochronous experiment he tried on "Friendly Little Finger" from *Zoot Allures*. It is an astonishing piece of music that, in Zappa's view, could never take place in the real world. "Suppose you were a composer and you had the idea that you wanted to have a drum set playing expressively and intuitively at a certain tempo while an electric bass player is doing exactly the same thing in another tempo, in another time signature, and you want them to do this live onstage and get a good performance," Zappa proposed to journalist Bob Marshall. "You won't get it. You can't. You can ask for it, but it won't happen. There's only one way to hear that, and that's to do what I did. I put two pieces of tape together."

"Baby Snakes" is a peppy little song that echoes some of the short, funny moments from *We're Only in It for the Money* and shares some of the cartoon flavor of "Cleetus Awreetus-Awrightus" from *The Grand Wazoo*. Nobody is quite sure what this song is about, although a few folks have ventured a theory. Dweezil Zappa delightfully recalled his first impression. "When I was little and first heard it, I thought it was a little cute song about baby snakes," Dweezil laughed. "I didn't know about all of the other stuff that was going on in it, like the SMPTE code things. That stuff goes right over your head when you're little. Now that I know what SMPTE is, I'm going, 'Oh great. He made a little jingle for the Society of Motion Picture and Television Engineers out of a stupid little hideous code that goes on your tape to keep you in sync.' All these things that are on these records each year make more and more sense."

The opening falsetto in "Baby Snakes" might remind listeners of the happy shrills of Roy Estrada, but they actually belong to Tommy Mars. "I was watching a *Twilight Zone* on TV late one night and I got this phone call from Frank," Mars told

Keyboard. "He said, 'Hi, Tommy, how are you? Feel like doing a little singing tonight?' And I said, 'Sure.' I came down to [Village Recorders] and did 'Baby Snakes' that night about six times, my own voice on one line, no harmonies, just a straight linear thing."

"City of Tiny Lites" is another oblique song about drugs — like "Pygmy Twylyte," only with a Latin flavor providing the musical blanket for its surreal imagery:

> *When you get the squints*
> *From your downers and your wine*
> *You're so big*
> *It's so tiny*
> *Every cloud is silver line-y.*

Given the seasoning of the tune, it's not surprising that a guitar solo from another version of this song would eventually form the basis of "Variations on the Carlos Santana Secret Chord Progression" on *Shut Up 'n Play Yer Guitar*.

"Dancin' Fool," which earned for Zappa his first Grammy nomination for Best Rock Vocal, was another shot at the disco culture. But, unlike in "Disco Boy," Zappa also pokes fun at himself:

> *Don't know much about dancin'*
> *That's why I got this song*
> *One of my legs is shorter than the other*
> *'N' both my feet's too long.*

Most of the song is another hilarious blast at the disco culture's underlying social and sexual incompetence ("The beat goes on/'N' I'm so wrong"). By the end of the track, Zappa makes a direct link between the disco automaton who dances "to give 'em all a thrill" and the same entertainer who tries to please the girls with his synthetic come-on lines:

> *Hey darlin'. . . . can I buy ya a drink?*
> *Lookin' for Mister Goodbar? Here he is . . .*
> *Wait a minute . . . I've got it . . . You're an Italian*
> *Hah?*

I'M THE SLIME

Yer Jewish?
Love your nails . . . you must be a Libra . . .
Your place or mine?

If "Dancin' Fool" earned Zappa his first Grammy nomination, the next song, "Jewish Princess," earned Zappa his first major storm of protest. The Anti-Defamation League of B'nai B'rith filed a formal protest letter requesting that the Federal Communications Commission ban the song, which they said contained "vulgar, sexual, and anti-Semitic references which leave very little to the imagination." Well, the last part is certainly true. "Jewish Princess" *doesn't* leave much to the imagination, but then again, Zappa's satire is often bitingly direct. But is it anti-Semitic? Not at all. Besides being an equal opportunity offender, Zappa tries to get at certain basic themes in his satire. With "Jewish Princess," he attempts to get beneath the self-appointed noble privilege of the princess mentality, and digs into underlying desires that he finds more alluring:

I want a nasty little Jewish Princess
With long phony nails and a hairdo that rinses
A horny little Jewish princess
With a garlic aroma that could level Takoma.

Zappa doesn't buy the affectation of putting on airs within one's ethnic community (he would soon write a song about Italian princesses called "Catholic Girls") any more than he does a Dancin' Fool, or that hopeless careerist, Bobby Brown. "I'm an artist and I have a right to express my opinion," Zappa said at the time of the controversy. "I'm not anti-Semitic. The Jewish princesses I've played this song for think it's funny. . . . Producing satire is kind of hopeless because of the literacy rate of the American public."

The American public's inability to comprehend what Zappa's parodying points to our failed concept of democracy, which doesn't allow ideas to be debated. What Zappa did in his music was to test democracy. If a culture needs to censor its critics, then how can it lay claim to the most cherished of democratic principles? "[The Jewish Anti-Defamation League] wanted to convince the world that there's no such thing as a Jewish princess, but I'm sorry, the facts speak for themselves," Zappa told *The Observer*. "They asked me to apologize and I refused. . . . Well, I didn't make up the idea of a Jewish princess. They exist, so I wrote a song about them. If they don't like it, so what?" Zappa raises the issue of how organized ethnic PR groups use censorship to try to sanctify certain thoughts and ideas that prevent the diversity of the individuals within each culture. "[The Anti-Defamation League's] job is to make sure that everybody who is not a Jew will always perceive Jews in just this one special, perfect way," Zappa explained to *Relix*. "This is wrong. It's as wrong as your assuming that all musicians are the same. There's all different kinds of Jews, too."

The next track, "Wild Love," is what biographer Ben Watson calls "a reflection on changed sexual customs, delivered with documentary objectivity":

Many well-dressed people
In several locations
Are kissing quite a bit
Later in the evening
Leaves will fall
Tears will flow
Wind will blow
Some rain; some snow
A fireplace maybe
A kiss or two
And down they'll go
But that's the way it goes sometimes
You just might find yerself in the clutches
Of some wild love.

Zappa contrasts this matter-of-fact information with rhythmically complicated music featuring dexterous percussion work by Ed Mann and some uncharacteristic wild blowing on the clarinet by David Ocker. The beginning of the song deals with the postwar generation trying to cope with its raging libido. By the end, Zappa brings us up to date with a young hip couple trying to get hot and bothered while having no guarantees: "A frantic pace maybe/But who's to say/Where it will go?" Zappa suggests that wild love can unhinge those who are repressed, just as repression can sneak up on those who think they are sexually liberated.

"Yo' Mama" probably draws its musical inspiration from Billy Mirandi's hilarious late-'50s R&B single, "Go Ahead." Mirandi, who sounds like the mutated offspring of Screamin' Jay Hawkins and James Brown, stridently tells off his girlfriend — but then collapses in hysterical grief:

I'M THE SLIME

Go ahead
Go on home to yo' mama
That's where you oughta be
Home with yo' mama.

In Zappa's more vitriolic song, his target isn't exactly a romantic partner:

Maybe you should stay with yo' mama
She could do your laundry 'n' cook for you
Maybe you should stay with yo' mama
You're really kinda stupid 'n' ugly too.

Some believed it was written for a former road manager, but keyboard player Tommy Mars thought he was the bull's-eye for the song's wrath. "Frank wrote that song at the very beginning of the '77 tour," Mars recalled for *Keyboard*. "We were doing this rehearsal in London and Frank was getting very tense. I got fined because I hadn't memorized this little piece called 'Little House I Used to Live In.' I hadn't realized he wanted it totally memorized. So this rehearsal ended in a total fiasco. The next day, he came in with this lyrics: 'Maybe you should stay with yo' mama. . . .' It was really autobiographic; that's how things evolve with Frank."

If Zappa did intend this epic — over twelve minutes — song for Mars, it's odd (or perversely fitting) that Mars ended up orchestrating a perfectly majestic keyboard overdub that helped link *three* Zappa guitar solos taken from different locations and xenochronously welded into the track. "I couldn't believe that I was a compositional part of this!" Mars told Ben Watson. "It's like when you put a freeway together, you have to chop down this section of woods, you have to drill through that granite, you have to cross this water to get where you're going. [Zappa] just had this idea of these three guitar solos and it was just like that." Despite the vicious putdowns in the song ("Maybe you'll return to Managua/You could go unnoticed in such a place"), "Yo' Mama" is an extraordinarily beautiful piece of music that transcends its own mean-spiritedness.

Once *Sheik Yerbouti* was out, so was Zappa, back on the road and storing up tracks for future albums. In April, as he started recording some new material, Warners finally divested itself of Zappa with the release of *Orchestral Favorites*. The five pieces on the album — "Strictly Genteel," "Pedro's Dowry," "Naval Aviation in Art?" "Duke of Prunes," and "Bogus Pomp" — were all from the 1975 Royce Hall recordings with Michael Zearott conducting the Abnuceals Emuukha Electric Orchestra. The cover bore the same type of garish Gary Panter cover art as *Sleep Dirt* and *Studio Tan*.

In June, Zappa suffered the frustration of having a proposed concert of his orchestral music by the Vienna Symphony Orchestra fall through, due to poor funding and production fee disagreements over televised rights. Feeling the effects of exhaustion, Zappa returned to the studio to work on a new album. Given his sixteen-hour-a-day rehearsal schedule, plus touring, no one was surprised that he was dropping from fatigue. But this hardly meant that it was a restful summer. Instead of resting, Zappa decided to build his own studio.

In August, Gail gave birth to another daughter. Her name, Diva, grew out of distinct circumstances. Zappa had told the press, while having his little joke at the expense of those who ridicule his kids' names, that "if it's a boy we'll call him Burt Reynolds, and if it's a girl she'll be called Clint Eastwood." She ended up with the name Diva because "she had the loudest scream in the hospital." Gail claimed in *Rock Wives*, "Diva has this incredible voice and she can knock you over from a distance of thirty feet."

As the decade was coming to an end in 1979, the American economy continued to slump, and the forces of right-wing reaction were building, especially after Americans were taken hostage in their embassy in Iran on November 4, by radical fundamentalist Muslims led by the Ayatollah Khomeini. Zappa then began work on what would become the prescient opera *Joe's Garage*. "I know the world isn't ready for me, so I'll just stay in my basement," Zappa told reporters that year. "But the world may be ready for *Joe's Garage*. It started out to be just a bunch of songs. But together, they looked like they had continuity. So I went home one night midway through recording, wrote the story, and changed it into an opera.... When we went into the studio to cut 'Joe's Garage' as a single and 'Catholic Girls' as the B-side, we stayed in there and cut about sixteen tracks. Then I figured out a story that would hold 'em together ... it's like doing crossword puzzles. In looking at it, I saw that not only did it make a continuous story, but it made a good continuous story."

Joe's Garage is a comic parody of the type of high school pageant where civics lessons were taught. But the instruction conveyed here is delivered by an authoritarian figure known as the Central Scrutinizer. His message is simple: Music is an evil that needs to be banned. The victim of the Scrutinizer's new legislation is a poor schlep named Joe, who has just started his first garage band. Before the end of the opera, Joe would get to play his song, but at a horrible price. He loses his girl

I'M THE SLIME

Mary to a rival band (and their crew), gets the clap, develops an erotic dependence on an electrical appliance, gets imprisoned and gang-banged by powder-snorting record executives, imagines guitar solos in his mind, and in the end, gives up music and produces little green rosettas in the Utility Muffin Research Kitchen.

The theme of *Joe's Garage*, a world where anything to do with music is deemed a crime, anticipated Zappa's battles with censorship in the mid-'80s. But Zappa had to do some censoring of his own when he was recording the album. "The first few sessions were very chaotic," Zappa explained to *Keyboard*. "I hate to have to act like an umpire or referee and go scream at everybody because they're jamming. I don't pay $200 an hour studio time to have guys go in there and jazz out." In particular, Zappa found that as good a keyboard player as Tommy Mars was, he couldn't play a simple melody. On the other hand, Peter Wolf turned out to be far more disciplined. As a result, Mars played on the first act, and Wolf was featured on the remainder of the album. The first act would hit the record stores in the fall of 1979.

Joe's Garage is an autobiographical work that represents a distinct mixture of Zappa's contempt for the music industry combined with his deep love of music. There's probably no other Zappa album where both sides commingle as they do here. There are moments of genuine joy, typically bawdy humor, uncharacteristic wistfulness, and even melancholy. It's possible that *Joe's Garage* represented a culmination of both his rage toward Warner Brothers and Herb Cohen and how they had sabotaged his career, and his recent positive experience with Grand Funk Railroad. Whatever the reasons, Zappa found a new passion on this record that gave his satiric edge vitality.

Zappa called *Joe's Garage* "a stupid story about how the government is going to try to do away with music (a prime cause of unwanted mass behavior). It's a really cheap kind of high school play." Before he launches into his low-grade production, Zappa reminds us of the opera's political intent:

> Environmental laws were not passed to protect our air and water ... they were passed to get votes. Seasonal anti-smut campaigns are not conducted to rid our communities of moral rot ... they are conducted to give an aura of saintliness to the office-seekers who demand them.... All governments perpetuate themselves through the daily commission of acts which a rational person might find to be stupid or dangerous (or both).... If the plot of

the story seems just a bit preposterous, and if the idea of the Central Scrutinizer enforcing laws that haven't been passed yet makes you giggle, just be glad you don't live in one of the cheerful little countries where, at this very moment, music is either severely restricted . . . or, as it is in Iran, totally illegal.

The Central Scrutinizer, an update of engineer Gary Kellgren's ominously whispering voice from *We're Only in It for the Money*, is a forbidding authority figure who's a cross between the Grand Inquisitor in Dostoevsky's *The Brothers Karamazov* and the Wizard of Oz. Only, unlike in *Money*, this time Zappa himself steps into the limelight as the totalitarian figure. "Sometimes when you're not looking he just sneaks up on you," Zappa writes in the plot notes. "He looks like a cheap sort of flying saucer about five feet across with a snout-like megaphone apparatus in the front with two big eyes mounted like Appletons with miniature motorized frowning chrome eyebrows on them." As he steps into view, we hear his voice telling us that it's his responsibility to warn us about music, "a horrible force [so] dangerous to society at large that laws are being drawn up at this very moment to stop it forever!" This means administering punishments so subtle that "they won't conflict with the Constitution (which, itself, is being modified in order to accommodate THE FUTURE)."

It's neither a great stretch nor a simple coincidence that the political paranoia and dread raised here resembles that of Kafka's *In the Penal Colony* (where people had their crimes literally tattooed on their bodies). Zappa drew on the theme from that novella on *We're Only in It for the Money*, but he elaborated further in this album's liner notes. One day, God decided that he didn't want humankind to be uniform, Zappa explained. Governments depended on uniformity to "make the future work." They were going to have to find a way to create a sameness and decided to institute total criminalization based on the idea that if we are all deemed criminals, we would also be so in the eyes of the law. Most of us, however, are too passive (or ethical) to commit a crime, so certain laws had to be created that could be broken in a variety of ways. Those who didn't want to be outlaws had to be *fooled* into committing crimes. This is where the notion of outlawing music comes into being. Although Zappa introduced the idea in *200 Motels*, where the orchestra was housed in the government's Reorientation Facility as part of "the final solution to the orchestra question," this would be the first time the ban would involve a rock 'n' roll band.

I'M THE SLIME

Joe's Garage, Act I, released as a single album in September 1979, opens with Joe (Ike Willis), a teenager living in a residential area, who is putting together his first band in his garage. His best friend, Larry Fanoga (Zappa), joins him in the opening song, "Joe's Garage":

We could jam in Joe's Garage
His mama was screamin'
His dad was mad
We was playin' the same old song
In the afternoon 'n' sometimes we would
Play it all night long.

The sentiments seem to stretch back to Zappa's early days in Studio Z — in fact, Larry Fanoga was a pseudonym that Motorhead Sherwood used while in the Mothers. At one point in the song, Zappa even inserts a brief snatch of the Surfaris' "Wipeout," which was recorded at Studio Z when it was under Paul Buff's ownership. "Joe's Garage" is pure '50s R&B with a lonely harmonica added that calls out in mock nostalgia for the good ol' days. As the band envisions being signed by "a company we can't name," their thunderous playing catches the attention of neighbor Mrs. Borg (Denny Walley), who calls the police. Since this is a first offense for Joe, the police give him a doughnut and advise him to "stick closer to church-oriented social activities."

Meanwhile, Joe's girlfriend, Mary (Dale Bozzio), is at a Catholic Youth Organization party in the rectory basement where, instead of "taking the vow" with Father Riley (who's exposed as gay), doing the "Hokey Pokey," and eating baked goods, they're learning to "blow all the Catholic boys." The tune "Catholic Girls" is Zappa's answer to the wave of dissent caused by "Jewish Princess." It's a catchy song with a rocking electric sitar — echoing the melody of "Jewish Princess" — punctuating the lyrics: "Catholic girls . . . /With a tongue like a cow/She could make you go WOW!"

One night, Mary doesn't meet Joe at the social club, but instead is backstage at the local armory performing fellatio on Larry Fanoga, who has become a roadie with a band called Toad-O (a swipe at the bland, commercial rock group Toto). Larry invites Mary to be their "crew slut." "Crew Slut" is a slow blues with a pungency that pulses:

I know yer prob'ly gettin' tired
Of all the guys out there
You always wondered what it's like
To go from place to place
So, darlin,' take a little ride
On the mixer's face.

Walley provides a tasty slide guitar solo that underlines the comically sordid behavior in the song. After the entire crew have their way with Mary, she is dumped in Miami with no money. She tries to earn cash to get home by working in a local bar and participating in a wet T-shirt contest, where the sexually starved men in the crowd vote for the girl with the best "mammalian protuberances."

The idea for the song "Wet T-Shirt Nite" didn't just come out of Zappa's imagination. "I thought that the one I saw, at the Brasserie in Miami, was so sickening that I didn't even stay to see the T-shirts get wet," Zappa told Michael Branton of BAM magazine in 1979. This establishment had a two-hundred-pound girl with enormous breasts who went under the name of the Good Fairy. "She came out in a ballet skirt with these big jellyroll legs and a man's T-shirt, with these biiiiig tits hanging down and a magic wand," Zappa recalled. "When they announce the contest, the dance floor fills up with guys sitting on the floor — they're all sitting right up to the edge of the stage. And what happens is, the regular contestants would come out and the emcee would be talking to them, and the Good Fairy would jump out with her wand and whip up her T-shirt and hit guys in the head with her tits and then jump back on the stage. I mean, it was really carnival time."

"Wet T-Shirt Nite" (titled "Fembots in a Wet T-Shirt" on the 1987 CD release) definitely creates a carnival atmosphere, even if Zappa provides an upbeat jazzy arrangement with beautifully complex percussion patterns for Ed Mann to negotiate on the marimba. The sleazy contest emcee, Buddy Jones (Zappa), who is actually the defrocked Father Riley, introduces Mary to a crowd of excited, red-blooded American guys. After winning fifty bucks, she finds herself on a bus back home.

The next track, "Toad-O Line" ("On the Bus" on the CD), is the album's first guitar solo, revealing another singular strategy on Zappa's part. "All the guitar solos on *Joe's Garage* came from the European tour in 1979," Zappa said in 1984. "They were recorded on a two-track Nagra, just two microphones in front of my guitar amplifier, and every time I played a solo the guy turned it on and recorded just the guitar. And when we did the *Joe's Garage* album, I found the solos I liked

I'M THE SLIME

and put them on top of the studio tracks and that's what's in there." This became a further variation on the xenochronous experiments of *Zoot Allures* and *Sheik Yerbouti*. "When I suggested doing it, the engineer I was working with [Joe Chicarelli] looked at me like I was really nuts," Zappa told John Swenson of *Guitar World* in 1981. "When we were working on the album he called it the Ampex guitar, 'cause when it came time for a solo all I did was play the master tape and sit by the ATR and when it was time I pushed the button and the guitar solo would go on." The solo, which begins with the main theme of Toto's "Hold the Line" (hence the original title, "Toad-O Line"), snakes its way through the melody into something startlingly fresh.

Joe soon finds out about Mary's exploits, and in a fit of jealousy and depression gets seduced by a girl named Lucille, who works at a Jack in the Box. He ends up getting a dose of the clap, which leads him to a profound question that provides the title of the next song: "Why Does It Hurt When I Pee?" This song originates from a bit of folklore on the road provided by Phil Kaufman, Zappa's road manager in 1979. "We got stuck in a bus on the way to a huge concert in Saarbrücken, Germany," Kaufman wrote in his memoir, *Road Mangler Deluxe*. "I was sitting in the back and having a little drink. I went into the toilet, which was located in the middle of the bus. Halfway through my piss, I jokingly start screaming and everybody was looking at me. I cried, 'Frank, why does it hurt when I pee?' and everybody laughed. By the time we had gotten through the crowd to the venue, he had written a song called 'Why Does It Hurt When I Pee?' scored all the parts, given it out to all the guys in the band, and made them play it that day. Needless to say, the band told me to shut my fucking mouth in the future."

The song is a hilarious litany of myth ("I got it from the toilet seat/It jumped right up and grabbed my meat") and metaphor ("My balls feel like a pair of maracas") that ultimately leads into a slow reggae version of "Lucille Has Messed My Mind Up." Unlike the hard blues arrangement Zappa wrote for this track on Jeff Simmons' album of the same title, Zappa rearranged the song as a delicate waltz, sung beautifully with a soft pining by Willis. By the end of Act I, the Central Scrutinizer puts forth his dubious thesis about the inherent dangers of music:

> Joe says Lucille has messed his mind up, but was it the girl or was it the music? As you can see . . . girls, music, disease, heartbreak . . . they all go together. Joe found out the hard way, but his troubles were just beginning.

Those troubles wouldn't be exposed to the public for another couple of months when the two-album set *Joe's Garage, Acts II & III* finally hit the record stores. Zappa broke up the set for very pragmatic reasons. "*Joe's Garage* was supposed to be a single three-record set, but I changed it into two releases because the cost of a three-record package might be hard on people the way the world is today," he remarked in *Frank Zappa: A Visual Documentary by Miles*.

Joe's Garage, Acts II & III opens with Joe in a "cesspool of his own steaming devices." To find a way out, he pays money to L. Ron Hoover of the First Church of Appliantology, who introduces him to the "token of his extreme." Besides cleverly invoking L. Ron Hubbard's Church of Scientology and his cultish sci-fi philosophy, the song also parallels Greggery Peccary's fate when he seeks the help of the philosopher Quentin Robert De Nameland ("If you ask a philosopher/He'll see that you pays"). Zappa's distrust of cosmic prophets comes from the pure expedience of their goals. In "The Token of My Extreme," Zappa gives the diabolical philosopher a psychological dimension:

Don't you be Tarot-fied
It's just a token of my extreme
Don't you never try to look behind my eyes
You don't wanna know what they have seen.

The song was first performed as an instrumental show opener by the 1974 band (a version appears on *You Can't Do That on Stage Anymore, Vol. 2, The Helsinki Concert*). Captain Beefheart also sang a rough version of the tune with the '74 band in Bologna, Italy. On *Joe's Garage*, the song goes further to include Joe discovering that he is a "latent appliance fetishist" who seeks sexual gratification through the use of a machine. He even acquires a really good one by learning the perfect operatic language for such mechanical romanticism: German. Hoover leads him into a club called the Closet, where he imparts his final benediction to Joe. Joe's transformation is complete as he gives into his deeper impulses.

If you been
Mod-o-fied,
It's an illusion, an' yer in between Don't you be
Tarot-fied

I'M THE SLIME

It's just a lot of nothin'
So what can it mean?

What can it mean? Ben Watson thinks it's a comment on Zappa's work. "Zappa advises us to be neither terrified nor mystified by his art," Watson writes. "[It's] something that is meant to provoke questions and then self-destruct."

During Joe's time at the Closet, he sees numerous appliances dancing with each other. Dressed as a housewife, with a napkin on his head and a yellow chiffon apron, Joe becomes smitten with an apparatus that "looks like it's a cross between an industrial vacuum cleaner and a chrome piggy bank with marital aids stuck all over its body." Joe starts to sing "Stick It Out," a song that dates back to the Flo & Eddie era. Originally, the tune was part of the "Sofa" routine, where God's girlfriend sings to Squat, the Magical Pig. On *Joe's Garage*, Joe screams out in German (using deep masculine tones), asking the appliance known as Sy Borg (Warren Cucurullo and Ed Mann) to fuck him senseless. In response, Sy Borg recites the same lines used by the bar sleaze in "Dancin' Fool" ("I've got it . . . You're an Italian/What? You're Jewish/Love your nails") and by Flo & Eddie in the anal-sex classic "Latex Solar Beef" ("Touch the chrome/Heal the chrome/See the screaming/Hot black steaming/Iridescent naugahyde python screaming/Steam Roller!").

If the idea of human beings getting turned on by mechanical devices seems farfetched, one need only consider our relationship today to mechanical contraptions. Whether it's the emotional gratification we receive from listening to our CD player or radio, watching television, or using cellphones, technology often lets us avoid any meaningful contact with actual human beings. Zappa reveals in the song that true romance has become an impersonal ritual, even an acting out of a fetish. It also examines Zappa's own ambivalences in this area — especially given his desire to sometimes have machines play his music rather than human beings, who make mistakes and have to be paid.

Joe goes to Sy Borg's apartment where he croons in the voice of the singer of the '70s novelty song, "Gimme Dat Ding," by the Pipkins ("Gimme dat, Gimme dat/Sy Borg/Gimme dat, give me de chromium leg"). When Sy Borg invites him to meet his roommate, "a modified gay Bob doll," Joe's sexual vacillations draw him to the Bob replica whom he begs for a blow job, and Peter Wolf provides a tasty synthesizer solo that manages to be both beguiling and sanguine. Since Bob is tired, Joe "plooks" Sy Borg until he shorts out and is destroyed. Having given all his cash to L. Ron Hoover, Joe can't afford to repair him so the Central Scrutinizer sends him to a special prison for criminals from the music business.

There, watching "musicians and former executives [taking] turns snorting detergent and plooking each other," Joe meets Bald-Headed John (Terry Bozzio), who used to be a promo man for a major label. "Dong Work for Yuda," written for Zappa's bodyguard John Smothers, had been a concert favorite since 1977, when it was premiered. On *Joe's Garage*, Zappa rearranges the tune to incorporate Obie Jessie's '50s R&B song "Mary Lou." But instead of stealing a watch and chain, a diamond ring, and a Cadillac, Bald-Headed John (besides mangling the English language) introduces us to "a sausage that will break your heart." When John says, "Make way for the iron *shaschige*," he's echoing the threats on "The Torture Never Stops" during the "night of the iron sausage." Ultimately Joe is gang-banged by the record executives to the tune of "Keep It Greasy."

At the end of his ordeal, Joe is driven to imagining guitar notes that take him outside of his confinement. "Outside Now" perfectly weds Zappa's recent rage toward the music business and his deeper desire to just play music. While imagining low, dissonant guitar notes "that would irritate an executive kind of guy," Joe decides to play outside of time as well as outside the prison. He sees that the imagination isn't restricted by the boundaries of time. As if to prove the point, Zappa has his xenochronous guitar solo play in a different time than the backing track — just like in jazz performances, where being "outside" means playing outside of the acceptable chord changes.

When Joe leaves jail, he wanders through his old neighborhood playing guitar solos in his head. Along the way he imagines the reviews he will get from rock critics. "Packard Goose" is Zappa's gratuitous attack on the writers who panned him over the years. Although perhaps justified, there's also something self-aggrandizing in his tone ("Fuck all them writers with the pen in their hand/I will be more specific so they might understand/They can all kiss my ass/But because it's so grand/They best just stay away"). He does, however, foresee the media's collusion with the government during the Gulf War, still more than a decade away:

> Who do you write for?
> I wanna know
> I believe you is the government's whore
> And keeping peoples dumb is where you're coming from.

I'M THE SLIME

Aside from demonstrating Zappa's blatant hostility towards the press, this song also explores the fabricated formality required by the media to solicit information from someone. "The journalistic profession is a highly overrated piece of fantasy," Zappa told Clark Peterson of *Relix*. "The reason you're here is because this is your job; and the reason I'm here is because this is my job. Aside from that, the process of being interviewed is highly unnatural. . . . Most of it is totally irrelevant to who and what I am. They walk in the door seeking a method by which they can reinforce conclusions they've already arrived at." When a vision of Mary appears to Joe, she echoes Zappa's sentiments about the nature of information:

> *Information is not knowledge*
> *Knowledge is not wisdom*
> *Wisdom is not truth*
> *Truth is not beauty*
> *Beauty is not love*
> *Love is not music*
> *Music is* THE BEST

Zappa explained this bit of philosophical discourse to journalist Bob Marshall in 1988:

> I walk up to you and say, "Two and two is eleven." That's some information. It's bad information, but it's information. Now, if somebody comes up to you and says, "Two and two is eleven," and they have the Presidential Seal on their coat, and they got bunting waving in the background, and balloons go up, you might consider it for a minute. So, that's information. Information is not knowledge. Knowledge is the point at which you know something, okay? Now, wisdom is the idea that you have a bank of facts. To behave wisely, you have to deploy those facts in some way. You can deploy them stupidly or you can deploy them wisely. So, information is not knowledge. Knowledge is not wisdom. Wisdom is not truth. You can take all the sorted pieces of information which gives you a knowledge base. You can act in what you believe is a wise procedure, but that is not necessarily any ultimate truth. And just because

something is an ultimate truth doesn't mean it's beautiful. And just because something is beautiful certainly doesn't mean you have to love it. Because there's lots of ugly stuff that you could love, too.

Zappa doesn't address why "music is THE BEST," but he's obviously alluding to its transcendent qualities. Those very attributes are present in the next track, "Watermelon in Easter Hay." Essentially an exquisite guitar solo, the song is also shadowed by Joe's realization that "imaginary guitar notes exist in the mind of the Imaginer . . . and . . . ultimately who gives a fuck anyway?" It's the first — and only — guitar solo on the album that isn't a xenochronous one. Although the full title of the track is "Playing a Guitar Solo With This Band Is Like Trying to Grow a Watermelon in Easter Hay," he does succeed in pulling it off.

The melody has a pensive quality that Zappa plays with great delicacy, until the solo jumps on the notes with passion and regret. "It's the best song on the album," Zappa told Neil Slaven. "But *Downbeat* didn't think so. The review in *Downbeat* was so unfavorable toward *Joe's Garage* and especially 'Watermelon in Easter Hay.' The jazzbo reviewer of that album just hated that song. It was supposed to be that character's last imaginary guitar solo before he quits the music business. So it's a sad song."

Having persevered when Warner Brothers and Cohen had him tied up in legal knots, he imagined the fate of those who might be forced to abandon the music business in "A Little Green Rosetta." This song, which was in its demo form on *Läther*, is the final track on *Joe's Garage*. Here, the Central Scrutinizer (minus his whispering megaphone) details Joe's fate — hocking his guitar and getting a job working the day shift (beside the neutered Muffin Man) at the Utility Muffin Research Kitchen ("A Little Green Rosetta/You'll make a muffin betta"). Ben Watson points out, "'A Little Green Rosetta' is like 'Return of the Son of Monster Magnet' thirteen years later: this time the massed extras don't freak out, they sing along like a muppet chorus." The age of open-ended alternative rebellion that Joe imagined has now been passed over in order to learn how to "make a muffin betta."

By the time Zappa's exercise in monotonous free association reaches its conclusion — with the hideous victory of the Central Scrutinizer — he claims that no one cares if there are good musicians on this album because "this is a stupid song/AND THAT'S THE WAY I LIKE IT." Yet the stupidity has a clear purpose. "Zappa's 'stupid songs' betray an attitude that is stronger than technique," Ben Watson writes. "It is the way it rubs against his musicians' skills that produces great music, just as the way his jokes and obscenities rub the listener the wrong way and generate sociological perceptions." *Joe's Garage* is a wealth of perceptions that pointed the way to events of the '80s that would bear out many of Zappa's stinging observations.

In December, Zappa launched his concert film, *Baby Snakes*, at the Victoria Theatre in Times Square. Although the film won the Premier Grand Prix for a musical film at the First International Music Film Festival in Paris in 1981, it received mainly bad reviews. It was even put in the same company as Bob Dylan's moribund concert extravaganza, *Renaldo and Clara* (1978). Tom Carson, in the *Village Voice*, was the most perplexingly savage. He wrote that Zappa was "still trying to act as if he symbolizes a whole culture, but the culture isn't there anymore."

Part of what confounded critics (and audiences alike) was that Zappa refused to be a symbol of anything. His art examined the symbols both imposed on, and imagined about, pop culture. "Zappa built a satirist's career on the idea that all of life was just like high school," Carson wrote. "Now it turns out that all he ever wanted, apparently, was a high school clique of his very own." Carson, of course, was suggesting that Zappa's fan base had become what Zappa once despised in rock audiences. But these fans, unlike the conformist cliques that desperately cling to security, were celebrating the wide spectrum of weirdness on a Halloween night at the Palladium in New York City. Although they were merely an echo of L.A.'s once disenfranchised freaks, they were still willing to let American normalcy just walk on by. So, as the tumult of the '70s turned into the nostalgia-draped Reagan '80s, Zappa began to prepare his defiant response to the next decade.

CHAPTER FIVE

THE MEEK SHALL INHERIT NOTHING
(1980-1988)

> *Some scientists say that a major building block of the universe is hydrogen because it's the most plentiful element. But my theory is that the universe is made out of stupidity because it is more plentiful than hydrogen. Since it is more plentiful, why shouldn't we talk about it?*
>
> FRANK ZAPPA

> *Democracy is the theory that holds that the common people know what they want, and deserve to get it good and hard.*
>
> H.L. MENCKEN

1

Many people came to believe that the '60s came to an end with two events that occurred in 1980. First, there was the November election of Ronald Reagan as the new President of the United States. Second, a month later, John Lennon was gunned down by a crazed fan in front of his home. Although it would appear that these two events had little in common, Greil Marcus, writing in *Rolling Stone*'s tribute issue to John Lennon, saw a certain symbolic connection:

> The secret message behind the election of Ronald Reagan on November 4 was that some people belong in this country, and some people don't; that some people are worthy, and some are worthless; that certain opinions are sanctified, and some are evil; and that, with the blessing of God, God's messengers will separate one from the other. It's as if the Puritans have reached across three hundred years of American history to reclaim the society they once founded — accepting the worst vulgarization of their beliefs if it means that, once again, God and his servants will be able to look upon America and tell the elect from the reprobate, the redeemed from the damned.

It's highly doubtful, as Marcus acknowledged, that the meaning behind the November election inspired John Lennon's assassin to "attach a private madness to its public justification." But if Ronald Reagan's ascendancy was an attempt to blot out any memory of the '60s, what it stood for, and the utopian hopes it once encouraged (hopes that were hopelessly dashed), Lennon's murder began to make some horrible metaphorical sense.

One thing had certainly become clear. As Marcus stated, "[A] radical change in the nature of public discourse in the United States" had taken place. Political columnist Haynes Johnson, in his lucid book *Sleepwalking Through History*, expands on the implications of that radical change when he describes the Reagan era as a period that brought together "two contradictory but complementary strains of pessimism and optimism":

> By the time the American people granted Reagan the ultimate democratic gift of national power, the country had weathered a period of instability and failure. President after president had come and gone in swift succession, leaving in their wakes the wreckage of four straight failed presidencies and an underlying current of doubt about America's purpose and future.

The '60s had been a decade during which national leaders were removed violently from the political scene. John and Robert Kennedy, Medgar Evers, Malcolm X, and Martin Luther King had died by assassins' bullets. The turn to the apparent sunny optimism of Ronald Reagan came specifically from "Americans [who] became

THE MEEK SHALL INHERIT NOTHING

conditioned to expect less of their leaders and personally invest[ed] less emotion in them," writes Johnson. An omnipresent fear existed that the "person in whom they placed trust could suddenly be taken away, leaving a sense of hurt, unfulfillment, or betrayal — or all three."

But there were other dramatic forces at work. During the '60s and '70s, the early stages of Frank Zappa's career, the barriers between what was considered high and low culture had begun to wither. It was possible to be simultaneously open to the classical Indian sounds of Ravi Shankar and still be in tune with the driving force of the Rolling Stones — without being considered a snob or somebody lacking in taste. The prosperity of the time had brought a wealth of cultural alternatives to the mainstream. When the affluence of the '60s turned into the severely pinched '70s, our culture moved dangerously inward. Before long, our reality wasn't shaped by the outside world we wished to experience. The only reality considered worth recognizing was ourselves. Our self-worth was no longer determined by our ideas and thoughts, but by our celebrity status. Worthiness was earned by emulating whoever was considered hot — and ignoring whoever wasn't. A social amnesia (where a celebrity was popular one minute and forgotten the next) evolved from this stargazing. By the '80s, solipsism became the yardstick by which politics, art, and popular culture were measured.

The upheaval of the '60s and early '70s had sought alternatives to conformity by encouraging individual dissent within the boundaries of a collective culture. By the '80s, a desperate need in the middle-class to survive — at any cost — created a generation of yuppie careerists. They began looking to the self-serving banalities of pop psychologists for answers. The spoken goal of this was self-knowledge, but the hidden desire was to find "enlightened" ways to regain lost prosperity.

What was sacrificed in that process was a more complex understanding of behavior, provided by hundreds of years of literature, philosophy, and psychology. A generosity of spirit that comprised a worldview wider than the contours of our own navels was deemed expendable. Diversity of opinion began to dissolve as well, in favor of a bland homogeneity that could shape the public's taste into something that could make dollars rather than sense. When the latest fad stopped proving lucrative, it was forgotten. We witnessed a crippling recession that narrowed not only the pocketbook, but also the tolerance for free and open debate about important issues.

The '80s were often defined by the entrepreneurial phrase "Go for it!" This particular kind of junk-bond philosophy, which ate away at our economic infrastructure, extended itself, as well, to how we thought. Out of a need to put the turmoil of Vietnam in the past, Americans began to connect to a mythology from their Puritan history. According to Haynes Johnson, Ronald Reagan fed into this desire for nostalgia by creating a public aura that differed greatly from the reality of his life.

Frank Zappa was a different kind of walking contradiction. Although often associated with the '60s counterculture because of his long hair and weird music, he was a self-described "practical conservative." In *The Real Frank Zappa Book*, he devoted a whole chapter to the subject of practical conservatism. "I want a smaller, less intrusive government, and lower taxes," he wrote. Yet in the '80s, under what was understood to be three consecutive "conservative" administrations, Zappa became a political activist against them. By the end of this decade, he would oppose the American government not only through his music, but by fighting music censorship, setting up voter registration booths at his concerts, and, at the conclusion of the Cold War, becoming a self-appointed ambassador of goodwill and business opportunity.

"I don't think that Americans, in the way they think of themselves as being nice, kind, free, fair, good-natured, jolly little individuals, would willingly opt for fascism, but they could easily be tricked into it," Zappa told journalist Bob Marshall about the state of American political discourse. "All you have to do is tell them that it's a candy apple, or whatever the lies are that are going on right now. Literally, they are being molded into something that is as potentially dangerous to the rest of the world as Nazi Germany was in the '30s and '40s. But tricked into it by people who have just lulled them into this false sense of security, and they wave a little American flag over it and everybody just has this knee-jerk reaction that they've got to buy it."

Zappa's art and political activism over this decade would be devoted to shaking people out of this false sense of security.

2

Zappa began the '80s on a benign note by building his own home studio, "Utility Muffin Research Kitchen" (named after the reform facility in *Joe's Garage*). He tried to utilize every technological advancement to improve both the sound of his music and his capacity to record and perform it. The '80s were about to become the new age of digital audio — compact discs would replace the record album and computer technology would give composers the software to produce music

THE MEEK SHALL INHERIT NOTHING

that humans couldn't play. This would bring Zappa into further conflict with critics who felt that his preoccupations with electronic technology created a dehumanizing quality in his music. "People who worry about that are worried about their own image as a person performing on the instrument," Zappa told Tim Schneckloth of *Downbeat*. "In other words, the instrument is merely a subterfuge in order for the musician to communicate his own personal, succulent grandeur to the audience, which to me is a disservice to music as an art form." Zappa's dedication to music was set apart from the performer's ego. It was an adherence to the classical origins of music, rather than the romantic derivation where music expresses the performer's personal feelings. As Varèse had attempted years before him, Zappa sought to acquire whatever technology was necessary to create the sounds he needed for his work.

The first Zappa composition to come out of the new UMRK studio was a single. "I Don't Wanna Get Drafted" had actually been recorded in 1979, but it wasn't released until May 1980. The song had grown innocently out of a rehearsal where a typical Zappa guitar riff evolved into something more. "One day we were taking a dinner break from rehearsals, and Ike Willis started talking about a news broadcast about [the possibility of reinstating] the draft," Tommy Mars said in the liner notes to *The Lost Episodes*. "And it just infuriated Frank into talking politics. And when he talked politics, you'd better hold on tight. We had such a history lesson about the draft in other countries, in World War II. . . . And from out of nowhere, about a half-hour later — he said, 'That's it — rehearsals over.' And goddamn it, the next day he comes in with this song, 'I Don't Wanna Get Drafted.' The baby was delivered." This particular infant, by Zappa standards, seemed pretty benign. Aside from some lovely piano arpeggios by Mars, the song was your basic protest tune against the draft told from the viewpoint of an adolescent:

Roller skates 'n disco
It's a lot of fun
I'm too young and stupid
To operate a gun.

CBS Records distributed the single in England, but Mercury-Phonogram declined to do so in the United States, which led Zappa to drop Mercury as his distributor and pick up CBS in the U.S. as well. Zappa was naturally surprised at Mercury-Phonogram's reaction to the single, especially given their support of his last few albums. Yet it was a sign of things to come. Pop music, now turning more vapid and less inclined to make any relevant comment on the culture, had little time for political commentary. "Every once in a while somebody will say 'War is hell' or 'Save the whales' or something bland," Zappa told *The Wire*. "But if you talk about pop music as a medium for expressing social attitudes, the medium expresses the social attitude perfectly by avoiding contact with things that are really there. That is the telling point about the society that is consuming the product. If society wanted to hear information of a specific nature in songs, about controversial topics, they would buy them. But they don't. You are talking about a record-buying audience which is interested in their personal health and well-being, their ability to earn a living, their ability to stay young at all costs forever, and not much else."

"I Don't Wanna Get Drafted" was a contender for inclusion on a three-record set Zappa was putting together called *Warts and All*. The material came from live recordings at the October 1978 Palladium shows, as well as the February 1979 concerts at the Odeon Hammersmith. But the project became too unwieldy and financially unfeasible, so Zappa would later reconfigure it. In the meantime, he created another record label, Barking Pumpkin Records, which would be distributed by CBS Records. The company name got its title from a bad cough Gail had developed from smoking. Since Zappa called Gail his "pumpkin," when she hacked, she was a "barking pumpkin." The logo design, which continued his interest in anthropomorphism, featured a Halloween pumpkin barking "Arf!" at a startled cat, who responds (in Chinese), "Holy shit!"

There had also been a change in band personnel. Warren Cucurullo left to work with Terry and Dale Bozzio in their new band, Missing Persons. "It was the hardest decision of my life," Cucurullo told *T'Mershi Duween* in 1994. "But there were always so many band changes and it got so I wanted a more permanent situation. I had been hanging out with Terry and Dale and we'd made up about ten songs together. We thought we had something special and Frank liked it." With Zappa's blessing, Cucurullo moved on. Zappa put together a new group consisting of Ike Willis, Vinnie Colaiuta, Ray White, Arthur Barrow, and Tommy Mars for studio rehearsals for some upcoming recordings and a tour. He also recruited a young new guitarist from Carleplace, Long Island, named Steve Vai.

Steve Vai was born in 1960 and acquired a taste for music when he started playing the accordion at age eleven. After moving on to a five-dollar Tempo electric, he took lessons and studied music theory, while performing in various rock bands. In high school, a friend introduced Vai to Zappa's music. "He played me

THE MEEK SHALL INHERIT NOTHING

'Muffin Man' from *Bongo Fury*, and it was like an epiphany," Vai recalled in *Guitar Player*. "The song contained a lot of different musical elements that I loved, all rolled into one song: crazy, wacky guitar playing with cool notes all over the place, and it managed to be arranged and well thought out, yet improvisational, too. It also had comedy, which was so rare."

When Vai graduated from high school, he moved to Boston and attended the Berklee College of Music, where he happened onto the art of transcribing music. "I had a roommate who transcribed a Larry Carlton solo, and I'd never heard of transcribing," Vai said. "He showed it to me and I said, 'You figured this out from the record?' I thought it was a neat idea, so I started transcribing all kinds of stuff."

The "stuff" included guitarist Allan Holdsworth's solo from "In the Dead of the Night" and Carlos Santana's glorious "Europa (Earth's Cry Heaven's Smile)." When he heard Frank Zappa's "The Black Page," he was hooked. "I was awed by it, and I tried to transcribe it," Vai explained. After a few months, he created a rough copy he could continuously amend. Once finished, Vai sent it to Zappa. Zappa wrote back, telling Vai how much he liked it, and offering him a job transcribing.

Vai was eighteen and in his fourth semester at Berklee when Zappa gave him the call. He knew that if he took this job, he'd have to quit college. "I was transcribing anywhere between thirteen and fifteen hours a day," Vai explained. "At the beginning, I was getting paid nothing — like ten dollars a page, which is what a lead sheet transcriber would get. And I used to cram this stuff on the page, and cram all the staffs so that Frank would see that I wasn't trying to rip him off." The first piece Vai transcribed while on salary was "Outside Now" from *Joe's Garage*, and he followed that with "He Used to Cut the Grass."

What made Vai's job difficult was that he had to use a cassette recorder. "I used to sit and listen to one bar of music maybe a hundred times — hours and hours of music. But it was fun; I enjoyed it. . . . I think that transcribing is one of the biggest learning experiences for a musician." This assignment led Vai to do all the transcriptions for *The Frank Zappa Guitar Book*, and it also paved the road for him to become a member of Zappa's touring ensemble.

"I transcribed a song called 'The Deathless Horsie,' and Frank asked me to learn it on the guitar," Vai told *Guitar Player*. "He knew I played guitar because I'd sent him a tape he'd said he'd liked. So I told him I'd try. I learned the song, and I guess it was pretty good because he used it on the record and went into the studio and doubled the original guitar part." This piece turned into "The Second Movement of Sinister Footwear," which would be released later on *You Are What You Is*. "So, he asked me if I'd do some overdubs for *You Are What You Is*. I ended up redoing about 80 per cent of the guitars on the album. He had me down to rehearsal, and I got the gig." From then on, Vai became known by Zappa as "our little Italian virtuoso."

"I could tell that he had a superior musical intelligence and very great guitar chops," Zappa told *Guitar Player*. "And this showed me that there was a possibility to write things that were even harder for that instrument than what had already been used in the band. That's why he got the job."

Vai discovered in Frank Zappa's music something kindred to his own disenfranchisement. "I felt that I'd found something that I could really relate to," Vai recalled fondly. "As an adolescent, I think one can often feel alone and misunderstood . . . like there's no one more out-there than thou. And when you find something that you can latch onto, it's like a revelation."

Before heading out on tour, Zappa also added keyboardist Bob Harris (not the Bob Harris from *Fillmore East, June 1971*), who had a pitched falsetto so strong he was dubbed the "boy soprano." According to author Greg Russo, Zappa tried some new experiments during the rehearsals, where he would layer tunes overtop of one another. For instance, while singing the Thurston Harris R&B hit "Little Bitty Pretty One," the band would play a new Zappa track, "Mudd Club." They also attempted another recent composition called "Mo's Vacation" (which would turn up on *London Symphony Orchestra, Vol. 1*). Zappa also tried for a simultaneous mix of "Mudd Club" and his old chestnut "I Ain't Got No Heart."

Besides the obvious influence of Ives in his compositional style, Zappa was also attempting to discover whether his new band could perform — live — even quicker rhythmic changes than what his earlier '70s groups accomplished. It was part of Zappa's quixotic desire to transcend the synthetic capabilities achieved by overdubbing and other studio effects while playing concerts on the road. Zappa wanted to hear shifting and colliding time signatures in *real* time. Oddly, most of the live material they played that spring wasn't drawn from those rehearsal experiments. Instead the band used the skills they had honed to recreate the sound of old studio tracks like "Brown Shoes Don't Make It" and "I Ain't Got No Heart." The results were heard in May on a new live double album called *Tinsel Town Rebellion*, the first offering from Barking Pumpkin Records.

Although the record consisted of live tracks recorded at the Odeon Hammersmith in London and the Berkeley Community Theatre, the opening song came from the studio. Zappa described "Fine Girl" as a song that's "included so that conservative radio stations can play something on the air, thereby alerting

THE MEEK SHALL INHERIT NOTHING

people to the fact that this album exists." It's doubtful the tune received much airplay — it was hardly a song conservative radio stations would consider. "Fine Girl" is a mock celebration of strong and noble servant women, sung in the same underclass Negro dialect that Amos & Andy used in their radio programs:

> *She was a fine girl*
> *She could get down wit de get down*
> *All de way down*
> *She do yer laundry*
> *She change a tire*
> *Chop a little wood for de fire*
> *Poke it around . . . if it died down.*

Despite its gleeful descriptions of the girl's acquiescent behavior, the song is a beautiful composition. It features a light reggae arrangement with doo-wop background vocals and a tasteful synthesizer section that provides a lovely bridge. At the end of the song, the voices echo, with a stunning canon, their dubious endorsement ("We all need some more like dat/In dis kinda town").

"Easy Meat," on the other hand, celebrates a whole other kind of girl — the kind that walks the street:

> *This girl is easy meat*
> *I seen her on the street*
> *See-thru blouse an' a tiny little dress*
> *Her manner indiscreet.*

Although the song dates back to the early '70s and was often performed by the Flo & Eddie edition of the band, this was the first time it had appeared on record. While the term "easy meat" no doubt rankled many feminists, it's not so much a sign of misogyny as Zappa's insistent love of '50s R&B slang. He may have borrowed the phrase from the Clovers' 1951 doo-wop hit, "Fool Fool Fool":

> *The first time that I met you*
> *You looked so doggone sweet*
> *When you walked down the street*
> *I said, There goes my meat.*

But Zappa adds more a level of absurdity to the song, which ridicules the singer's obsession:

She wanna take me home
Make me sweat and moan
Rub my head and beat me off
With a copy of Rollin' Stone.

Zappa was now growing more confident in mixing together different performances of the same song. The opening of "Easy Meat" is from a performance recorded at the Tower Theatre in Philadelphia, while the out-chorus comes from a concert at the Santa Monica Civic Auditorium. As in "Yo' Mama," Tommy Mars provides a fabulous classical section with massively over-dubbed synthesizers leading into an extended Zappa guitar solo.

"For the Young Sophisticate" is pretty much the same arrangement from *Läther*, except that Zappa spends some of the song tweaking a possibly heartbroken Vinnie Colaiuta ("I thought you were in love, Vinnie?"). After lively covers of "Love of My Life" and "I Ain't Got No Heart," Zappa launches into "Panty Rap," in which he solicits females' undergarments. Although this is a theatrical piece designed to provide gratification for some of the panty fetishists in the group, the request also had a practical angle. Emily James, an artist from Lyons, Colorado, wished to make a quilt of panties and brassieres collected at Zappa shows. She insisted that the contributions not be washed so she could, as Zappa remarked, "[maintain] some exquisite sort of miasma in the vicinity of the finished work of art."

While some may see this as a further example of Zappa looking for gratuitous laughs, Jonathan Jones, writing in a 1994 edition of the cultural magazine *Eonta*, offers a more incisive view: "Looking back over twenty years, what has [Zappa's work] been but a public display of America's dirty linen. But it is also worth considering the nature of a quilt, a fabric which is stitched together out of leftovers, discarded bits and pieces, remnants and scraps. Zappa's music is just such a heterogeneous assembly." The completed quilt, which resembles a huge playing card featuring Zappa's head instead of a Jack, can be seen on the Internet at www.arf.ru/misc/Quilt.

"Tell Me You Love Me" is a much slower version of this hard-rock classic from *Chunga's Revenge*. "Now You See It — Now You Don't," which follows, is an adroit guitar solo from a performance of "King Kong." From the sublime to the ridiculous,

THE MEEK SHALL INHERIT NOTHING

Zappa continues with a "dance contest" staged at the Palladium in New York. During the live segment, we catch him nervously dealing with an overzealous fan named Butch (who is dying to hear "Dinah-Moe Humm"), as Zappa chooses a subdued Lena to be Butch's dance partner. But as Zappa looks for other contestants, chaos ensues to the point that one guy is heard screaming that he isn't queer and another fan cries out in support of ugliness. In this moment of utter disarray, Zappa finally gets to focus on perhaps the true purpose of this track. "I have an important message to deliver to all the cute people all over the world," Zappa announces to the frenzied crowd. "If you're out there and you're not cute, maybe you're beautiful, I just want to tell you somethin' — there's more of us ugly motherfuckers than you are." Zappa satirizes the very nature of the dance contest — to pick the most beautiful couple — using it instead to celebrate genuine ugliness.

"The Blue Light" is an amazing bit of *sprechgesang* that examines the failed '60s counterculture, and the rubble that's been left behind. The song not only explores a wasteland of ecological pollution, but also faceless pizza parlors and impersonal nightclubs. Zappa suggests bluntly that the once clearly defined revolt against the status quo has become an empty gesture of self-gratification:

You'll do anything
Just so you can hang out with the others
The others just like you
Afraid of the future
(Death Valley Days, straight ahead).

The allusion to *Death Valley Days* is a forewarning of Ronald Reagan, who hosted this '50s television Western. If surviving hippies felt slighted by "The Blue Light," the punks didn't fare much better in "Tinsel Town Rebellion." While punk rock was perceived as a new revolt against the established order, Zappa saw it as just another version of flower power. "As far as I'm concerned, this has nothing to do with music," Zappa told *Telos* magazine. "I am glad that someone sneaks in there and makes a mockery of the business. But how much of a mockery is it if they wind up being sold and distributed by the same business that they intend to mock?" "Tinsel Town Rebellion" addresses this co-option of rebellion. "Today record companies don't even listen to your tape," Zappa told *The Wire* in 1986. "They look at your publicity photo. They look at your hair. They look at your zippers. How gay do you look? And if you've got the look then it really doesn't make a fucking bit of difference what's on the tape — they can always hire somebody to fix that. And they don't expect you to be around for twenty years. The business is not interested in developing artists. They want that fast buck because they realize that next week there's going to be another hairdo and another zipper. And they realize that the people are not listening, they're dancing, or they're driving, or something else. The business is more geared to expendability today."

"Pick Me, I'm Clean" is a song from band folklore based on a groupie's desperate attempts to be with the band. It lists, in detail, her relationship with each of them:

> *Vinnie goes bare-back*
> *Peter goes wet-back*
> *Denny goes way back*
> *Eddie should get back*
> *Pick me, I'm clean.*

Zappa doesn't extend sympathy or put her down, he merely presents the material as found subject matter. "Sometimes you get it from chicken. Sometimes from coffee. Sometimes from an ashtray and sometimes from a napkin. . . . Or you hear somebody say something and it's just perfect. It becomes the whole song. Like 'Pick Me, I'm Clean.' Somebody really said that. Seriously. She was a girl in France."

"Bamboozled by Love" is a whole other kind of love story — one that drips with acrimony. This slow blues, which traffics in similar territory as "Your Mouth" from *Waka/Jawaka*, doesn't delve into heartache or pain. The singer (who has found his girlfriend "sucking off some other man") states his case clearly and coldly:

> *I ain't the type for beggin'*
> *I ain't the type to plead*
> *If she don't change those evil ways*
> *I'm gonna make her bleed.*

Ike Willis sings this song passionately, but without a whisper of compassion. Zappa doesn't romanticize the circumstances, either, as many songs about infidelity do. He designs the song as a statement of this guy's mind and leaves it to listeners to form their own conclusions.

THE MEEK SHALL INHERIT NOTHING

Tinsel Town Rebellion concludes with a rousing version of "Brown Shoes Don't Make It" and a Devo-like rendering of "Peaches en Regalia," titled here "Peaches III." *Tinsel Town Rebellion* is basically a mixed sampling of live material conceived as a thank-you letter to Zappa's fans. It is a quick warm-up for his charge on the new decade.

The inner sleeve of *Tinsel Town Rebellion* contained an ad for a very unusual Zappa project that would be available only by mail order — an album made up of nothing but guitar solos from various concerts, sound checks, and studio jams. The idea of using a mail-order company was inspired, especially given Zappa's legal battles with record labels. "We were virtually prevented from having an income by them," Gail Zappa told Don Menn in the 1992 tribute magazine *Zappa!*. "We were an insignificant entity facing this huge corporation. They had Frank's earnings tied up in order to prevent us from fighting them, and on top of that we were fighting old managers. I realized we were going to be in a position where we weren't going to have a lot of money because the legal fees at that point were just phenomenal. Plus we had a lot of money tied up with the current management. So I started the mail-order company."

The mail-order albums went under three different titles that snidely addressed the protests of fans who didn't like his satirical lyrics. Hence, *Shut Up 'n Play Yer Guitar*, *Shut Up 'n Play Yer Guitar Some More*, and *Return of the Son of Shut Up 'n Play Yer Guitar*. In contrast to the wide spectrum of music Zappa usually included on his albums, these three have a much more narrow focus. The only material that separates the different solos is a bit of *musique concrète* made up of pieces from the unreleased *Läther*. "There were a lot of requests from a certain group of fans that we have for an album that just had a lot of guitar solos on it," Zappa told *Guitar Player* in 1982. "Although I play maybe anywhere from five to eight extended solos during a concert, the basic style of the show that we take on the road is not guitar-spectacular oriented. There is *some* guitar playing, and some people really like that stuff. And so to accommodate them, I put it together."

Despite the lack of variety on the trilogy, there is a great difference in the style of the solos. For instance, "Shut Up 'n Play Yer Guitar," "Gee, I Like Your Pants," "Shut Up 'n Play Yer Guitar Some More," and "Return of the Son of Shut Up 'n Play Yer Guitar" are all solos taken from different performances of "Inca Roads" — and none of them sound the same. Zappa was going against the grain of easily pleasing the crowd by merely duplicating his solos. "Most guys who go onstage are going to replicate the solo that was on the record, because the audience must hear that in order to think that the guitar player is good," Zappa told Matt Resnicoff of *Musician*. "'Can he play exactly what he did on the record? Okay, he's good.'" The grungy "Hog Heaven" is from a 1980 performance of "Easy Meat" in Tulsa. The bluesy "Soup 'n Old Clothes" is from "The Legend of the Illinois Enema Bandit" in Santa Monica, 1980. The Latin-tinged "Variations on the Carlos Santana Secret Chord Progression" comes from a performance of "City of Tiny Lites." "Pink Napkins" is simply a 1977 performance of "Black Napkins" from the Hammersmith Odeon.

The albums also contain a few stand-alone tracks. "Treacherous Cretins" is an eerie piece of music that features a sinuous electric sitar. "Heavy Duty Judy" is a great guitar showcase first performed in 1980 in Pittsburgh, with improvised vocals by Ike Willis and Ray White; here, the track simply has Zappa's guitar ripping through a funky melody. "The Deathless Horsie" is a spiritual cousin to the mournfully beautiful "Outside Now," where Zappa's solo is played over a slowly repetitive drone on the keyboard. "Canard du Jour" is a startlingly fresh duet between Jean-Luc Ponty on baritone violin and Zappa on bouzouki, recorded in the early '70s. The piece resembles a jazzy hybrid of Stravinsky and Bartok, with the buoyancy of Stephane Grapelli. "While You Were Out" is a beautifully stated duet between Zappa and Warren Cucurullo from a 1979 studio recording, similar to the sensitive interplay of "Rubber Shirt."

"Canard du Jour" and "While You Were Out" are the only two studio cuts on the three-album set. "First of all, I find it very difficult to play in the studio," Zappa explained to *Guitar Player*. "I don't think that I've ever played a good solo of any description in the recording studio. I just don't have the feeling for it. And up until the time that I got my own studio, I was working in commercial ones where you have to pay anywhere from a hundred to two hundred dollars an hour for the time. There you don't have the luxury of sitting and perfecting what it is that you're going to play, whereas if you have a collection of tapes made over the period of a few years — which I do — you can go through that stuff and find musical examples that achieve some aesthetic goal that you're interested in achieving. Then you collect those together and make the best possible performance out of that."

3

In April 1981, just as Zappa's guitar solo collection was being prepared for the U.S. mail, he received a special invitation. Joel Thome, the conductor of the classical ensemble the Orchestra of Our Time, was participating in a tribute to Edgard

THE MEEK SHALL INHERIT NOTHING

Varèse at the Whitney Museum in New York on April 17 and wondered if Zappa would be interested in taking part. Not only was Zappa interested in performing, he also got involved by changing the location of the event to the more capacious Palladium, a former opera house Zappa had played many times.

Once again, the appeal for Zappa was the idea of creating a hybrid between the boisterous sphere of rock 'n' roll and the more staid classical world. "[This event might draw] the kids so they could hear Varèse's music and come to love it," Zappa remarked at the time. "They may be a little rambunctious, but I've always had a good rapport with them and talked to them like they were my neighbors." Zappa wore a suit and tie for the occasion, and he played emcee, a role he described as "comic relief." The pieces performed that night were *Déserts*, *Intégrales*, and *Ionisation*. The program was also selected by Varèse's widow, the ninety-one-year-old Louise Varèse. While Zappa had met her once before at a Halloween show the Mothers gave at New York's Felt Forum in 1974, this was a much more special event because it was a tribute to Zappa's mentor, her husband. After the concert, she described Zappa as "a lovely person" who's "very serious about Varèse's music."

On May 3, Zappa and the band played Boston's Music Hall, and before performing the last tune of the concert, he introduced a new song. Zappa always liked the element of surprise, for both the audience and the band. "Here's the deal," Zappa told the crowd. "We have a new song here — we have this song that was written about three days ago and we rehearsed it this afternoon. We're getting it together, you know what I mean? We've never played it for anybody before. You guys'll be the first people on the face of the Earth to hear it." The song turned out to be a number called "You Are What You Is," which explored the racial confusion of whites trying to act black, and vice versa, as a means to gain personal acceptance. Like "Fine Girl," it was sung in the speech patterns of the black caricatures created on the '40s radio show *Amos & Andy*, but the song was also a full-frontal attack on the yuppie conformism growing under the burgeoning Reagan administration. The many facets of that acquiescence became the subject of the next album.

You Are What You Is is indeed a worthy sequel to *We're Only in It for the Money* with its sociopolitical insights and musical impertinence. Zappa traces a path that illustrates how the hippies of the late '60s became the yuppies of the early '80s. He told journalist Bob Marshall:

> I can see that there's a logical continuum because the hippie culture was not anything divine to begin with. Most of the people who joined that were just chumps looking for a good time — just like the people who become yuppies. The reason they join any kind of a movement, or a culture, is because they're looking for a home, they want to belong to something. Now, a lot of the people who became hippies, maybe they knew that they didn't look good in paisley and long hair, with joints dangling out of their mouth. Maybe they knew that was stupid, but they did it anyway because that was the only way they were going to get a blow job that season. Now the yuppies have gone beyond that. They have to have a Rolex, they have to have a Porsche, but they don't even care about the blow job anymore because it's just about the dollars. Now, that's a mutation.

Although it doesn't feature any of the Dadaist absurdities of *Money*, this double-record song cycle still tells a seamless story of that mutation from the '60s. The album opens with the same howling wind we heard at the beginning of "Don't Eat the Yellow Snow." Only this time, it's not Nanook trying to save his money. It's a suburban teenager (in the wining voice of Bob Harris) complaining — like the character in "Tryin' to Grow a Chin" — that he's miserable and lonely and only wants to get ripped and see the Grateful Dead. "Teen-age Wind" is a caustic song that spells out how the teenager of the '80s defines his freedom and personal priorities:

> *Free is when you don't have to pay for nothing*
> *Or do nothing*
> *We want to be free*
> *Free as the wind.*

Zappa illustrates that the current crop of rebellious youngsters have no claim on social change, just a desire to climb the social ladder. But Zappa doesn't just satirize the late, lamented hippie in this song, he includes some of his own fans, as well:

> *I could tighten my headband for an extra rush*
> *During Jerry's guitar solo*
> *Then I could go to a midnite show of* 200 Motels.

THE MEEK SHALL INHERIT NOTHING

The song came about when Arthur Barrow heard his childhood friend Christopher Cross' 1980 hit "Ride Like the Wind" on the radio while driving to rehearsal. "I went up to Frank when I got to rehearsal and I said, 'I can't believe it! This guy I went to high school with has got a song on the radio.' And I started playing it on the radio and singing as much of it as I could remember. Frank says, 'Aw, gimme a pencil and paper and I could write a song like that in five minutes,' and he whipped out the lyrics to 'Teen-age Wind.'" Apparently, when Cross discovered that Zappa had written a takeoff on his song, and perhaps remembering Zappa's parody of Peter Frampton's "I'm in You," he told Barrow, "Oh God, I hope he doesn't release it when I'm peaking!"

The counterfeit freedom of "Teen-age Wind" leads right into another track about achieving independence — "Harder Than Your Husband." This country tune, sung by ex-Mother Jimmy Carl Black, is a terrific song about the end of a love affair:

Our affair has been quite heated
You thought I was what you needed
But the time has come, my darlin'
To set things right, 'cause
I'll be harder than yer husband
To get along with
Harder than yer husband every night.

Despite the double entendre, one can easily imagine Johnny Cash taking a crack at this one. (Talented actress Beverly D'Angelo, a friend of the Zappa family, covered the song in Jack Fisk's little-seen 1990 film *Daddy's Dyin' . . . Who's Got the Will?*)

"Doreen" is classic R&B doo-wop that features a powerful performance by Ray White, plus a stinging guitar solo over some masterfully overdubbed background vocals. The next track, "Goblin Girl," is a coarse tribute to the ladies in the audience who appear in costume during the band's Halloween concerts. As with "Harder Than Your Husband," the double entendre in the title is intentional:

When they're a goblin
There ain't a problin
When they're a goblin
I start a-wobblin'.

At the end of the song, Zappa does a lovely Ivesian meld of a verse from "Doreen" and the out-chorus to "Goblin Girl."

"Theme From the 3rd Movement of Sinister Footwear" is an instrumental orchestral piece scored and arranged for the rock band. The melody played on guitar is doubled on David Ocker's clarinet and Ed Mann's marimba to create a stunning distillation of rhythmic sophistication and energetic rock.

"Society Pages" starts a series of songs examining the yuppie phenomenon. This piece explores small-town careerism in the form of an entrepreneur who owns the paper "and a bunch of other stuff" to promote her own success while enhancing her status in her community: "You ran the paper 'n the Charity Ball/Every day on third or fourth page/There you was . . . you was *quite the rage.*" *Society Pages* would soon become the name of a future Zappa fanzine. "I'm a Beautiful Guy," "Beauty Knows No Pain," "Charlie's Enormous Mouth," and "Any Downers" look at the yuppie narcissism of a couple obsessed with looking good while living the high life and snorting cocaine. The parallels between the "beautiful people" of the '60s dropping acid and these new artificial models are bold and fascinating.

"You Are What You Is" is an update of "Uncle Remus" where both black and white individuals try to be who they are not. The white guy, from a middle-class family, wants to sing the blues because he thinks it's "manly," but he's left talking like the stereotypical Kingfish, a character from the '30s radio show *Amos & Andy*. The black guy, meanwhile, trades his *dashiki* for Jordache Jeans and learns to play golf. His final comment (daringly voiced by Zappa himself) is simply, "I ain't no nigger no more!" As the song devolves into semantic confusion, Ray White sets up a gospel call and response that winds up with the singer desperately searching for personal gratification at the Mudd Club.

"Mudd Club" has Zappa using a whispering megaphone tone similar to the one he used as the Central Scrutinizer in *Joe's Garage*. He examines the same sado-masochistic dating rituals ("from the ruins of Studio 54") he first explored in "Broken Hearts Are for Assholes." "The Meek Shall Inherit Nothing" is the first in a series of songs addressing another preoccupation of the '80s: fundamentalist Christianity. Zappa is quick to point out that there was a complete transformation from the hippies he satirized on *Money* to the Jesus freaks who appeared in the '70s:

Those Jesus Freaks
Well, they're friendly but
The shit they believe

THE MEEK SHALL INHERIT NOTHING

Has got their minds all shut
An' they don't even care
When the church takes a cut
Ain't it bleak when you got so much nothin'.

There had always been a strain of messianic preoccupation in the counterculture (expressed in films like *Easy Rider*). Jesus had become a symbolic hippie doomed to crucifixion by the power structure, as in the rock opera *Jesus Christ Superstar* and songs like "Put Your Hand in the Hand" by Ocean, "Day by Day" from *Godspell*, "Signs" by the Five Man Electrical Band, and "Spirit in the Sky" by Norman Greenbaum. Zappa overturns this hippie romanticism by suggesting that, in the '80s, the hippie Christ had been swallowed whole by the yuppie Christ. Those born again had found salvation in the mighty dollar:

Some take the Bible for what it's worth
When it says that the meek shall inherit the Earth
Well, I heard that some sheik has bought New Jersey last week
'N you suckers ain't getting nothin'.

"Dumb All Over" is a rap song about how religion has done little to foster world harmony, but instead has created a litany of bloodshed. Once again using the Central Scrutinizer voice, Zappa savages the hypocrisy of using religious faith to justify murder:

You can't run a country
By a book of religion
Not by a heap
Or a lump or a smidgen
Of foolish rules
Of ancient date
Designed to make
You all feel great
While you fold, spindle
And mutilate
Those unbelievers
From a neighboring state.

In "Heavenly Bank Account," Zappa takes his first swipe at the Moral Majority. This group, whose name was drawn from Richard Nixon's silently conservative constituents, was founded in 1979, dedicated to aligning the Church with the State. They infiltrated the Republican Party and began dictating policies that bore the influence of fundamentalist Christianity:

> *When some man comes along and claims a godly need*
> *He will clean you out right through your tweed*
> *He's got twenty million dollars*
> *In his Heavenly Bank Account*
> *All from those chumps who were born again.*

Zappa gives the song a classic gospel arrangement with a final benediction: "You ain't got nothin', people/Thank the man . . . oh, yeah."

The next track, "Suicide Chump," borrows a tune from the Doors' "Roadhouse Blues" to examine suicide as yet another form of self-absorption:

> *Now maybe you're scared of jumpin'*
> *'N poison makes you sick*
> *'N you want a little attention*
> *'N you need it pretty quick*
> *Don't want to mess your face up*
> *Or we won't know if it's you*
> *Aw, there's just so much to worry about*
> *Now what you gonna do?*

"Jumbo, Go Away" is the only truly crass number on the album. Here, a groupie is given an ugly send-off that buoys the arrogant attitudes of the boys in the band. Based on an incident where guitarist Denny Walley threatened a female fan with a black eye if she didn't back off, the song merely indulges the sexism inherent in the episode. Although Zappa defended the song as a mere recounting of a true event, he also blames Jumbo for her fate, as if not "washing her pie" was good reason for Walley's threats.

"If Only She Woulda," which also draws from the Doors (the uncredited Arthur Barrow does a perfect Ray Manzarek organ meltdown), is a mocking turn on the travails of doomed romance, while "Drafted Again" is simply another

THE MEEK SHALL INHERIT NOTHING

recording of the single "I Don't Wanna Get Drafted" that links perfectly into the medley of songs that conclude the album.

The gatefold of *You Are What You Is* included an article by Zappa intended for *Newsweek*. Using the metaphor of cheese, Zappa scrutinizes how American culture, in its embrace of religious fundamentalism, disparages intelligent critical thinking. "Modern Americans behave as if intelligence were some sort of hideous deformity," Zappa wrote. "To cosmeticize it, many otherwise normal citizens attempt a peculiar type of self-inflicted homemade *mental nose-job* (designed to lower the recipient's socio-intellectual profile to the point where the ability to communicate on the most mongolian level provides the necessary *certification* to become ONE OF THE GUYS). Let's face it . . . nobody wants to hang out with somebody who is smarter than they are. This is not FUN."

Newsweek was neither amused by, nor interested in, the piece. "They told me it was too idiosyncratic," Zappa told CBC Radio's Vicki Gabereau in 1984. "But I think the reason they didn't run it was that the United States had taken this unbelievable turn to the right. Everybody wanted to be a video Christian and they all wanted to have fiscal responsibility, and that Ronald Reagan was going to save them. So everyone was scared to say anything about unions, about religion, they wouldn't touch it."

You Are What You Is, released in September 1981, died a miserable death. "It was listed by *People* magazine as the Worst Album of the Year," Zappa told Gabereau. "I don't expect everybody to love what I do, but c'mon, there *had* to have been something less desirable than an album that would tell you the truth about video religion and race relations in songs that were about something. . . . But I still think it stands as one of the best albums that I've made, yet at the time it was released no one would touch it."

4

Radio host Vicki Gabereau asked Zappa who, if he were given the chance to host her show, he would have as a guest. Zappa, without a moment's hesitation, told her, "Nicolas Slonimsky." Taken aback, Gabereau asked just who Slonimsky was.

Three years earlier, at a Santa Monica gig, Zappa had introduced the elderly Nicolas Slonimsky during a performance of "A Pound for a Brown (on the Bus)." He called Slonimsky "our national treasure" and enthusiastically filled the audience in on the man's accomplishments. Zappa then announced that this octogenarian would play the piano. What the rock audience perhaps failed to grasp was that without Slonimsky, there might not have been a Frank Zappa. For Nicolas Slonimsky was the closest that Zappa ever got to his idol Edgard Varèse. It was Slonimsky who had conducted the premiere of Varèse's *Ionisation* in 1931 (with Varèse churning the sirens) and who had overseen the world premiere of Ives' symphonic works, as well as Bartók's *First Piano Concerto* (featuring Béla at the keyboards).

Born in St. Petersburg, Russia, in 1894, Slonimsky had studied harmony and orchestration with two of Rimsky-Korsakov's students. After the 1917 revolution, Slonimsky became a rehearsal pianist in Yalta, accompanying displaced Russian singers. In 1923, he made his way to the United States and became a vocal coach in the opera department of the Eastman School of Music in Rochester, New York, where he first started studying conducting and composition. By 1927, Slonimsky established the Chamber Orchestra of Boston with the aim of performing modern music. It was with this group that Slonimsky presented those first performances of Ives, Edgard Varèse, and Henry Cowell.

Slonimsky's own compositions were often studies in miniature, including his *Studies in Black and White* for piano, which he wrote in 1928. *Gravestones* (1945) was a song cycle that took its texts from tombstones found in an old cemetery in New Hampshire. The orchestral work *My Toy Balloon* (1942) presented a set of variations on a Brazilian song that included one hundred balloons exploded multifortissimo at the climax. Slonimsky demonstrated his total disregard for academic decorum when he published his *Thesaurus of Scales and Melodic Patterns* (1947), which collected an index of all tonal combinations — both probable and improbable. He also edited and updated three editions of the mammoth musical anthology *The Baker's Biographical Dictionary of Musicians*, which features close to 13,000 entries.

It was Slonimsky's book of scales that inspired Zappa to contact him that spring in 1981. Zappa was surprised that Slonimsky even lived in L.A., while Slonimsky was surprised to receive a phone call from Frank Zappa. "Frank Zappa was the last person who, to my mind, could be interested in my theoretico-musical inventions," Slonimsky wrote in his memoir, *Perfect Pitch* (1988). "His name was familiar to me from a promotional record jacket showing him seated on the john with his denuded left thigh in view, and a legend in large letters: PHI ZAPPA KRAPPA" The two met the following week. Zappa told Slonimsky he was a huge admirer of Varèse and gave the older composer some of the scores he'd written. Slonimsky was impressed, but even more so with the fact that Zappa had learned his technique of composition from texts rather than through conservatory schooling.

THE MEEK SHALL INHERIT NOTHING

When Slonimsky admired Zappa's Bosendorfer piano, Zappa invited him to play it. He began with the coronation scene from *Boris Godunov*, and eventually played his own *Minutudes*. Zappa asked Slonimsky if he'd play this piece at the Santa Monica concert the next evening. Slonimsky reluctantly agreed, wondering what a rock audience would make of his intricate piano composition. The next night, as the arena filled, Slonimsky was given earplugs to protect him from the amplified sound. From the sidelines, he heard Zappa's rock band begin to play. A guest soprano, Lisa Popeil, started singing a song called "Teenage Prostitute," and soon enough it was Slonimsky's turn:

> Balancing a cigarette between his lips, Zappa introduced me to the audience as "our national treasure." I pulled out the earplugs and sat down at the electric piano. With demoniac energy, Zappa launched us into my piece. To my surprise I sensed a growing consanguinity with my youthful audience as I played. My fortissimo ending brought out screams and whistles the like of which I never imagined possible. Dancing Zappa, wild audience, and befuddled me — I felt like an intruder in a mad scene from *Alice in Wonderland*. I had entered my Age of Absurdity.

Slonimsky had experienced something Varèse and Ives had dreamed of earlier in the century when they began exposing audiences to their new brand of American music. Since there was no popular forum for their demanding compositions, these composers existed in an artistic ghetto. But Zappa, who had built a career in popular music, introduced his fans to a hidden musical tradition, creating a bridge between pop and the avant-garde. "It has been my luck to have lived to see the emergence of this totally new type of music which a hundred years ago didn't exist," Slonimsky recalled happily a few years after his rock debut. Slonimsky, who died in 1996 at 101, outlived his contemporaries to perform for a popular audience. He would also outlive the man who made it possible.

5

The lineup for the group changed drastically in the fall of 1981 when they started their U.S. tour. Arthur Barrow was replaced on bass by a former parking-lot attendant from San Francisco named Scott Thunes. Thunes had been playing the bass since he was ten. At fifteen, he studied jazz and the work of Béla Bartók at the College of Marin. But as immersed as he was in the higher arts, Thunes also became infatuated with the music of the new wave band Devo. In the late '70s, Thunes failed to get into the San Francisco Conservatory of Music, and he started parking cars while doing club work with local bands.

Bobby Martin took over from both Peter Wolf and Bob Harris on keyboards, sax, and vocals; Martin was a Curtis Institute graduate with a powerful singing voice. Drummer Vinnie Colaiuta, meanwhile, tired of being on the road, moved on. The rest of the band now consisted of Ray White on rhythm guitar and vocals; Steve Vai on "stunt" guitar; Ed Mann on percussion; Tommy Mars on keyboards; and, replacing Colaiuta on the stool and drum kit, Chad Wackerman. "I knew the reputation of how difficult Frank's music was to play and I wasn't disappointed when I saw the music," Wackerman told *Musician*. "It was extremely intricate and detailed." Zappa could now present those intricate and detailed arrangements more clearly with a twenty-four-track portable recording facility that captured the performances in a much larger grandeur than the old days with Dick Kunc and his trusty two-track analog briefcase.

On Halloween, the band played their usual Palladium gig, but this time it was simulcast on the new twenty-four-hour rock-video network, MTV. Promotional rock films had been created during the late '60s by the music industry as a way to promote and sell bands. The MTV ethos cut into the quality of the music and concentrated on the "hot" look of the video. If you weren't suitably primed with a terrific video, you could hardly expect to be signed by a record company just because you were a good musician. "The record companies thought it was the greatest thing that ever happened to them, because it was a way for them to get cheap commercials," Zappa explained. "And so the tail started wagging the dog. The record companies stopped signing groups that could play in favor of groups that looked good in pictures, because they figured we could always get a producer to sing their songs."

MTV irreparably changed how the music industry worked. In the past, talent scouts scoured the clubs looking for promising talent, based on the musical ability of the band. Now a television network could deem what could — and would — sell. "Before MTV, if you wanted a hit record, there were probably 10,000 stations in America where you could break something regionally and have it spread," Zappa said many years later. "Now there is one MTV, with one playlist, and because of that the record companies put their own balls into the bear trap and

THE MEEK SHALL INHERIT NOTHING

sprung it on themselves. Now they can't make a move without calling MTV and getting permission. They call up in advance to say, 'We are getting ready to make a video, we're going to have such and such pictures in it, what do you think?' And MTV is a total censorship organization and it has all the major record companies at its mercy."

Videos also changed the way the rock audience experienced music. Now, more important than the music was how the group looked. "A young audience who never experienced any music to speak of started watching MTV the same way they watched Saturday-morning cartoons. And it caught on. There was no competition," Zappa explained.

The October 31, 1981, show would be Zappa's last from the Palladium — the historic hall was about to become a disco. Although the concert itself was a success, Zappa ran into problems. Westwood One broadcast the concert live on the radio, while MTV ran the video and audio for television, while Zappa's recording truck carried the feed. The Palladium, however, billed both Zappa and Westwood One $9,000 — 100 per cent extra — for what it called "stagehand costs." Even though Zappa's own road crew had taken care of everything, he also had to pay for the unionized crew of the Palladium to stand around. Zappa reluctantly agreed to the amount, but was emphatic that he would never come back.

On November 17, Zappa played the Ritz with Al DiMeola, the virtuoso jazz guitarist, who joined in on a ripping rendition of "Clowns on Velvet" (heard on the bootleg box set *Apocrypha*) and Christopher Cross' "Ride Like the Wind," the pop song that caused the fuss that led to "Teen-age Wind" on *You Are What You Is*. "[Zappa] tended to change things all the time," Wackerman recalled in *Musician*. "A piece we might have learned as a heavy-metal song, he'd give the cue and it might become a reggae song, just spontaneously. So every show was completely different. . . . Even if you heard the same piece two nights in a row — which was rare — it might be ska one day and a Weather Report–style the next."

Despite the fabulous shows, though, concert attendance was down. (In fact, when Zappa launched the 1982 tour, he avoided the U.S. and concentrated on Europe, where his fan base had always been large.) But Zappa's fortune was about to change, thanks to an accident that gave birth to Zappa's first big hit single, "Valley Girl."

The main guitar line of "Valley Girl" arose from a sound check in 1980, and Zappa continued to play with it. One day, while recording a drum track with Wackerman, Zappa tried out a background riff that he taped so that he wouldn't forget it. Within a few weeks, he decided to have Moon Unit provide a monologue overtop of it. The notion of including his daughter came from a note she slipped under Zappa's door when she was thirteen. The note shyly stated that "until now I have been trying to stay out of your way while you record." Now she wanted to sing on one of his albums. Moon wrote that she "would love to do my 'Encino Accent' or 'Surfer Dood Talk.'"

According to Moon, she had always had an interest in language and words, teaching herself as a two-year-old to read by copying letters from magazines and books. Now, in the tenth grade, she was ready for her recording debut. Moon would adorn "Valley Girl" with the language and lifestyle of some privileged kids from the San Fernando Valley. "I spent a lot of time back then going to bar mitzvahs," Moon Unit remembers. "There would be all these kids out there whose lifestyle was so different from mine — this beer-drinking, rebellious, tortured existence, plus a funny way to talk that went along with it. So I would listen and pick up the dialogue, the lingo, the information, everything. I was fascinated by it. I would do it around the house and make everybody laugh."

Much to Moon's surprise, Zappa woke her up one night to come into the studio and do her "Surfer Dood Talk." "I managed to improvise several tracks saying the first thing that came into my head, reciting things I'd heard people *really* talk about . . . elaborating on subjects which really amused my father," she writes in the liner notes to the CD *Ship Arriving Too Late to Save a Drowning Witch*. "He edited the tracks together and my life has never been quite the same."

Zappa's life was never quite the same, either. "We went off on a tour in 1982," Zappa told *Society Pages*. "We're in Europe, touring around, and I find out that I've got a hit record . . . by accident." Moon Unit had brought an acetate of the song to a radio interview, they played "Valley Girl," and the phones went crazy. It became such a novelty hit that other radio stations taped it off the air and played the tune in their regular rotation. "It didn't sell a lot — maybe 350,000 copies — and the album . . . maybe did 125,000 units," Zappa told Charles Shaar Murray. "But sociologically it was the most important record of 1982 in the United States."

Zappa was hardly exaggerating. Valley Girl lunch boxes started to appear, plus *The Official Valley Girl Coloring Book* (written by Moon and edited by Dad), even a Valley Girl doll that said, "Bag your face." In 1983, director Martha Coolidge released a quaint little romantic film, *Valley Girl*, starring Nicolas Cage in his movie debut. Zappa tried to legally prevent the film from being released because he felt that it would diffuse the meaning of the song and dilute its intent. However,

THE MEEK SHALL INHERIT NOTHING

he lost the lawsuit. "I'm not too thrilled about the [San Fernando] Valley as an aesthetic concept," Zappa told Michael Goldberg in *Creem* in 1982. "To me, [it] represents a number of very evil things."

It might be overstating the point to describe phrases like "barf me out" and "gag me with a spoon" as evil, but Zappa's satire was a pointed attempt to rip away the facade that surrounds lifestyle trends. The song "Valley Girl" became a hit because the public could hear, in Moon Unit's voice, an affectionate jibe at a way of life her father would prefer to snarl at. "Valley Girl" appeared on Zappa's next album, *Ship Arriving Too Late to Save a Drowning Witch*, in May 1982. No doubt its inclusion helped the record reach No. 23 in the charts — the rest of the album contains some of Zappa's most demanding scores.

Just over a half-hour in length, it's a wickedly paced record. Without a wasted second, each song segues into the next, and a maniacal laugh track from a mechanical toy periodically leaps into the mix like a twisted leitmotif. "No Not Now" is a mutant country-and-western track that features Roy Estrada's pachuco falsettos dubbed into three-part harmonies. Given the subject matter of a trucker "driving string beans to Utah," it could be Zappa's contorted version of Lowell George's "Willin'." Since Utah is the home state of Donny and Marie Osmond, Zappa couldn't resist making fun of their Hawaiian Punch commercial, while Ike Willis chimed in with "Boog 'em, Dano — Murder One," a reference to the *Hawaii Five-O* police drama. Zappa's random shifting through popular culture always created openings for such absurd free associating.

"I Come From Nowhere" is another Estrada showcase where he does a vocal meltdown similar to Zappa's *sprechgesang* on "The Blue Light." What starts out as a pulsating rock 'n' roll song begins to disintegrate into a passionate attack on those with duplicitous "happy" faces:

> *Their eyes are all frozen over*
> *The sides of their faces pooch out at the corners*
> *Because that's what happens when their mouths turn up*
> *On both sides*
> *Which is why we can tell they're smiling.*

The title track on *Ship Arriving Too Late to Save a Drowning Witch* extends that theme of decomposition. "Drowning Witch" is one of Zappa's most intricate scores — and apparently none of Zappa's touring bands ever performed it correctly. Zappa weds a contemporary ecological catastrophe to both '50s sci-fi and Igor Stravinsky. A sorceress swims to a ship to meet a wealthy marine, but gets caught in "America's spew-infested waterways." But rather than drown, she mutates (as does the music) into a monster out of a bad sci-fi film, with "lobsters up 'n down her forehead . . . smelling very bad . . . and DANGEROUS." By the time she's brought home by the Navy, she's prepared for a ritual sacrifice — just like the virgin in Stravinsky's *The Rite of Spring*.

"Drowning Witch" has some of the primitive thrust of Stravinsky's score, but now it's reimagined for a rock band. And thanks to some masterful editing, the group sounds adept at performing the quickly changing tempos. "Do you know how many edits there are in 'Drowning Witch'?" Zappa asked *Guitar* magazine. "Fifteen! That song is a basic track from fifteen different cities. And some of the edits are like two bars long. And they're written parts — all that fast stuff. It was very difficult for all the guys to play that correctly. . . . So there was no one perfect performance from any city. What I did was go through a whole tour's worth of tape and listen to every version of it and grab every second that was reasonably correct, put together a basic track, and then added the rest of the orchestration to it in the studio."

"Envelopes" is an elaborate instrumental featuring some brittle glissandos from keyboardist Mars that mirror Ruth Underwood's nimble work on "RDNZL." "Teenage Prostitute" is essentially the same story as "Easy Meat," told in the same objective tone. But, as sung by Lisa Popeil, the song takes on a tragic urgency not found in the lyrics alone:

> She ran away from home
> Her mom was destitute
> Her daddy doesn't care
> She's a teenage prostitute.

The power in Popeil's voice is matched by Steve Vai's machine-gun-paced guitar, which owes no small debt to composer Henry Mancini's *Peter Gunn* theme. "The lick is *Peter Gunn*, and when I went in to record it, the part was overdubbed," Vai told *Guitar Player*. "When I heard it on the record, I was really shocked because the sound is completely a result of processing. I played my Strat through a couple of effects — nothing really serious — but when [engineer] Mark Pinske and Frank Zappa got done with it, it sounded like *Peter Gunn*." As live applause greets the

THE MEEK SHALL INHERIT NOTHING

conclusion of both "Teenage Prostitute" and the album, you can almost hear the band (and the listener) finally catching its collective breath.

Ship Arriving Too Late to Save a Drowning Witch came complete with a marketing spreadsheet prepared by Zappa with his usual self-deprecating humor. "Now that programmers have chosen to go with concepts prevalent in the industry twenty years ago," Zappa wrote, "the release of a single would seem to be a waste of money ... and that's all we really care about (*it's the thing that sort of sets us apart from the Communists*)."

Unfortunately, the 1982 tour that followed the release of the album turned into a ship of fools. While they made their way across Europe, if it didn't rain syringes on the stage (thanks to the drug users in the audience), it poured actual rain. The show at the Rhein-Neckar-Stadion in Mannheim, Germany, took place under a downpour so heavy that it was cancelled after ten minutes. And when the band got to Geneva on June 30, Zappa had had enough of objects being tossed on the stage, so he ended the show after only fifteen minutes with an abrupt "House lights — concert's over!" What made this particularly frustrating for Zappa was that the 1982 band was a skilled, versatile touring unit. On Vol. 5 of his live omnibus, *You Can't Do That on Stage Anymore*, he dedicated an entire disc to that group. "The '82 band could play beautifully when it wanted to," Zappa wrote in the liner notes. "It is unfortunate that the audiences of the time didn't understand that we had no intention of posing as targets for their assorted 'love offerings' cast onto the stage."

When they arrived in Palermo, Sicily, on July 14, the band got more than just "love offerings." "I wanted to see the town that my father was born in and I went there and I saw it and then we played the concert and the next thing you know, you have the army and the police; each with their own general telling them what to do; an audience that had brought their own guns; and they're shooting tear gas and tearing up this stadium that we were playing in," Zappa said in 1984. "We played for an hour and a half in this riot with tear gas in our face and everything else, and when it was all over we went off the stage and we were trapped inside this place. The audience was circling around outside shooting at the police and the police were shooting back. . . . Well, I got a pretty good idea of what my Sicilian roots are like after seeing the town of Partinico — it was pretty bleak."

Thirty minutes into the show, while the band was playing a new song called "Cocaine Decisions," a tear-gas canister was launched into the crowd by the police. "We couldn't see what was going on in the middle of the soccer field. The army and the local police (who didn't like each other, and who were completely uncoordinated) began a random process of blasting these little presents into the crowd," Zappa recalled. He desperately appealed for calm, but it was futile. Yet the show went on as planned. The band shifted into another new song called "Nig Biz." As Ray White tried to sing, with all his soul, a song about a black man selling his soul, another black man, John Smothers, wiped the tears from White's stinging eyes. All the while, the police and the crowd continued to pummel each other. The 1982 tour was now officially over.

During the last part of the year, Zappa went into the studio to finish recording the material for two rock albums, *The Man From Utopia* and *Them or Us*. Once those sessions were done, Steve Vai left the band and started a successful solo career.

The Man From Utopia sported an album cover that suggested anything *but* Utopia. The graphic, by Italian artist Tanino Liberatore, depicted Zappa battling mosquitoes with a flyswatter at a concert in Milan during the ill-fated 1982 tour, at the Parco Redecesio, where they had played near a mosquito-infested lake in an industrial neighborhood. Zappa's half-clothed body, with muscular arms that are stitched together like Frankenstein's monster, is squeezing the guitar neck until it breaks. The characterization is based on an Italian comic hero named Ranxerox, who Liberatore created with Stefano Tamburini. The back cover shows Zappa from behind examining the tear-gas-enshrouded crowd at the Palermo concert — the gathered throng includes the Pope, bodyguard John Smothers (who's breaking a photographer's neck), a bare-breasted woman holding aloft the magazine *Frigidaire*, a banner commemorating Italy's 3–1 defeat of Germany in the World Cup soccer tournament, and two guys snorting cocaine. The only one who seems to be enjoying the concert is the moon, huge and yellow in the background, smiling while the tumult rages below.

Fittingly, "Cocaine Decisions" leads off the album — cocaine had become the most popular drug of the '80s. Cultural critic Camille Paglia, in *Sex, Art, and American Culture*, examines the role of cocaine in the new yuppie revolution. "In the '60s, LSD gave vision, while marijuana gave community," Paglia writes. "But coke, pricey and jealously hoarded, is the power drug, giving a rush of omnipotent self-assurance. Work done under its influence is manic, febrile, choppy, disconnected. Coke was responsible for the plot incoherence of fifteen years of TV sitcoms and glitzy 'high-concept' Hollywood movies." In the opening verse of his song, Zappa identifies the omnipotent culprit behind that incoherence:

THE MEEK SHALL INHERIT NOTHING

You are a person with a snow-job
You got a fancy gotta go job
Where the cocaine decision that you make today
Will mean nothing later on
When you get nose decay.

Although Zappa had no problem dealing with Ronnie and Kenny Williams' nasal contents in "Let's Make the Water Turn Black," it was quite another story with the high-class folks tooting nose candy. Zappa was aware that cocaine dealing, besides producing "expensive ugliness," was shaping the nature of political power and policy in underdeveloped countries. "This friend of mine who's spent some time in Brazil verifies the fact that the cocaine cartels have gone into the worst slums in Brazil and played Robin Hood to the people there," Zappa told journalist Bob Marshall. "They're [using] cocaine profits to give them clothes and setting up these little fiefdoms. Basically what they've created is an army of people who are willing to protect them...."

"Think of every place in the world where you have an underclass — it's poor and it's being pushed down by the middle-class, directly above in the case of the United States, or the upper crust that does all their bad stuff. Who is going to take care of these people?" Zappa pointed to the unprecedented homeless underclass that had developed in the U.S. in the '80s. What if the cocaine cartel came into the U.S. and helped the homeless? What would happen then to the War on Drugs?

But Zappa was quick to remind Marshall that the people who make billions from cocaine distribution also finance right-wing governments. "As long as the right-wing governments are in operation, their drugs are going to be illegal and as long as they're illegal, they're going to make more profits. It is so twisted."

"The Dangerous Kitchen," the track that follows, is yet another *sprechgesang* meltdown. In this song, Zappa lists the ways in which the sources of nourishment in your kitchen can turn on you:

Sometimes the milk can hurt you
(If you put it on your cereal
Before you smell the plastic container)
And the stuff in the strainer
Has a mind of its own

*So be very careful
In the dangerous kitchen.*

Describing this catalog of horrors, Zappa asks the key question: Who the fuck wants to clean it? Peter Occhiogrosso, who worked with Zappa on his memoir, recalled for Zappologist Vladimir Sovetov an episode in the Zappa household in 1988 that perfectly mirrored the events in the song. "One night before we went to work, we were hanging out in the kitchen, and Gail was relating some story about some food that went bad in the refrigerator. The kids were milling around and Frank was trying to find some peanut butter and jelly to make a sandwich, and nothing seemed to be going right. Frank turned to me and said, 'That's why I call it the Dangerous Kitchen.' [His] songs come from close observation of the small absurdities of life."

"Tink Walks Amok," with its trashy sci-fi title, is named for Arthur Barrow, whose agile fingers worked some nifty figure eights around Chad Wackerman's staccato drumrolls. "Frank was literally making up the arrangement as we were recording," Barrow recalled with amusement. "I was overdubbing to some kind of click track, and as the tape was rolling, Frank would say something like 'Okay, now move up two frets . . . now move to the A string . . .' — what fun!"

"The Radio Is Broken," like "Debra Kadabra," is a tribute to '50s sci-fi kitsch. Zappa and Estrada perform an exaggerated and affectionate vocal duet, both parodying the appallingly stiff actors — Richard Basehart, John Agar, and Jackie Coogan — who made appearances in those chintzy films, and paying tribute to the films themselves (especially *Queen of Outer Space*, from 1958, which starred Zsa Zsa Gabor). Zappa and Estrada practically crack each other up with talk of the "blobulent suits," "pointed brassieres," and finally, in reference to Zappa himself, "dwarf nebula." Again, a Zappa track features a musical figure borrowed from the Doors — this time a chord progression from "Love Street," played by Barrow.

"Moggio" offers some familiar snorks that evoke fond memories of former road manager Dick Barber. The bouncy tune is a beautiful keyboard and percussion exercise in the manner of "RDNZL." Then, Side 2 opens with one of Zappa's typical nods to '50s R&B, a medley called "The Man From Utopia Meets Mary Lou." His renditions of R&B in the '80s had become more reverential, and less experimental, than they were with the Mothers of Invention in the '60s, perhaps because of the lack of incongruity in his '80s bands. The Mothers had been an odd

THE MEEK SHALL INHERIT NOTHING

mixture of R&B musicians and those who were trained in modern classical music. His musicians in the early '80s tended to blend in, rather than conflict.

"Stick Together," Zappa's anti-union song, is done in a bionic arrangement of an old pro-union protest number. His anti-union sentiment was not based on the hatred of workers, or those who protect their rights. "Unions, through their PR firms, perpetuate the myth that America is a *unionized country*, and that all the unions are there to *fight for the working man and woman*," Zappa wrote in *The Real Frank Zappa Book*. "Maybe in the beginning the unions did support the workers — but what they have turned into is a network of organizations that take money from working-class people to finance a banking scheme which often benefits organized crime." Zappa had endured endless conflicts with the musicians union (commemorated in "Rudy Wants to Buy Yez a Drink" on *Chunga's Revenge*) where he had to pay stagehands astronomical fees for doing virtually nothing at his concerts. "Stick Together" is *his* protest song about that treatment, and how those union locals often used extortion, subjecting "touring groups to interpretations of regulations that border on science-fiction":

> *Don't be no fool, don't be no dope*
> *Common sense is your only hope*
> *When the union tells you it's time to strike*
> *Tell the motherfucker to take a hike*
> *You know we gotta stick together.*

In *The Real Frank Zappa Book*, Zappa explains that his hostility to unions does not discount the state of affairs that would exist if unions were nullified. "Some people fear that if unions were to vanish, the labor situation would return to the way it was in the beginning, with child labor and the sweatshops," Zappa wrote. "*I agree with them*. Large employers *do* tend toward unscrupulous behavior when nobody is looking over their shoulder."

"Sex" is a lewd tribute to the act that (thanks to newly hatched sexually transmittable diseases and right-wing moralists) was starting to again earn a bad name. Zappa gleefully — and metaphorically — celebrates the urge:

> *Watch the scenery while you ride*
> *You can be very warm inside*

DANGEROUS KITCHEN

'N when the train goes around the bend
Check the shrub'ry on the other end.

The urge depicted in "The Jazz Discharge Party Hats," however, is quite another matter. Similar to the speech-song manner of "The Dangerous Kitchen," this track is essentially about panty fetishism. Based on an incident that took place in Albuquerque, New Mexico, it's about some guys in the group (they remain nameless) who got together with three local girls to go skinny-dipping in the motel pool after midnight. One of the band members spotted an abandoned pair of panties by the edge of the pool, and when the owner wasn't looking, he started "sniffing the fudge and sniffing the glue." This resourceful individual then wore them on his head (hence the song's title). Zappa described the activities in this song as "a great American tradition." He was right. Female undergarments had graced the stage for years where pop singers like Tom Jones or Engelbert Humperdinck performed. Furthermore (for those who think Zappa is merely peddling smut in this song), James Joyce had already made an art out of panty fetishism in his novel *Ulysses*, especially the scene where Leopold Bloom masturbates while Gertie McDowell flirtatiously exposes her knickers to him. The only reason Zappa's work is condemned as filth while Joyce's is lauded as art is that Zappa focuses his obsession in American vernacular rather than lyrical prose. "A few years ago, in Philadelphia, a girl approached the stage and pitched up this little pair of blue panties," Zappa told *Relix*. "I knew the drummer and one of the other guys in the band liked to sniff girls' underpants, so as soon as she pitched them up, I made the drummer get off the stand and come down and sniff them. He did and immediately pretended to gag and faint and rolled all over the stage. The audience loved it. The girl, however, was somewhat chagrined, but I have it on good authority that the panties were semi-lethal."

The track's musical arrangement is clever given the pun on the word *jizz*, and the jazz-like score that accompanies the recitation. Steve Vai essentially traces the notes in Zappa's voice — with his guitar — throughout the whole song. "On ['The Jazz Discharge Party Hats'], Frank does a part that's half talk and half singing," Vai explained to *Guitar Player*. "And I transcribed that part and doubled it on guitar. And it sounds really weird — like George Benson from Venus. It sounds so bizarre. If you listen hard enough after you write down the notes in each syllable, and use the right articulation markings to phrase the notes so that they sound like they're in a sentence, you'll come out with some really strange effects."

THE MEEK SHALL INHERIT NOTHING

"We Are Not Alone," the concluding track, is a saxophone-driven instrumental with the transcendently pure '60s energy of beach-bum tunes like Dick Dale & His Del-Tones' "Misirlou," Link Wray's "Rumble," and the Bar-Kays' majestic "Soul Finger." As if to make a more direct link with the past, the track features infamous West Coast session man Marty Krystall on tenor sax. Krystall had played on recordings by Charlie Haden, bassist Buell Neidlinger's String Jazz, Aretha Franklin, and Jaco Pastorious. "We Are Not Alone" is also a brighter, cleaner-sounding version of those great good-time instrumentals Zappa had produced with Paul Buff at Pal Recording.

In March 1983, Zappa also released the soundtrack album to his 1979 film, *Baby Snakes*. Most noteworthy was the cover, featuring a lascivious-looking Zappa and a partial view of a woman's face, her tongue teasingly licking her lips. After Warren Cucurullo reminds listeners that audiences don't realize there are "a lot of notes involved" in Frank Zappa's music, Zappa kicks the record off with the *Sheik Yerbouti* version of "Baby Snakes." The rest of the album consists of excerpts from the Palladium concert that formed the basis for the movie. "Titties 'n Beer" is pretty much the same as the *Zappa in New York* version except that Zappa inserts some up-to-date dialogue. The Devil (Terry Bozzio) mentions "the Ayatollah and Falwell" as the souls he's taken rather than "Milhous Nixon and Agnew, too." Zappa, to great cheers from the crowd, tells the Devil he's already done time in Hell after being signed to Warner Brothers "for nine fucking years!"

"Jones Crusher" is also similar to the *Sheik Yerbouti* version. "Disco Boy" has a much quicker tempo than the original studio take from *Zoot Allures*, while "Dinah-Moe Humm" is presented as the crowd-pleasing encore. The biggest revelation may be the inclusion of "Punky's Whips," a song fans heard on record for the first time since it was censored by Warner Brothers on *Zappa in New York*. It's a lively performance, yet a bit thin without the glorious horn section used on the earlier recording. *Baby Snakes* is a small and tasty sample from a much larger meal — check out the movie.

When Zappa started to concentrate on performing his orchestral work, he didn't realize that the state of modern classical music was in the same poor shape as that of the rock world. But the venture certainly began on the right note. One of his pieces, "Sinister Footwear" (a portion of which had already been arranged for the rock band, and released, on *You Are What You Is*), was to receive its world premiere with the Berkeley Symphony Orchestra and the Oakland Ballet Company in the spring of 1984. Another composition, "The Perfect Stranger," was commissioned by French composer Pierre Boulez to be performed in Paris on January 8, with his Ensemble InterContemporain.

This was a major coup for Zappa because it was another link to his adolescent fascination with 20th-century classical music. "I bought my first Boulez album when I was in the twelfth grade: a Columbia recording of *Le Marteau sans maître* (*The Hammer Without a Master*) conducted by Robert Craft," Zappa recalled. Zappa would also attend Boulez's concert with the New York Philharmonic at the Lincoln Center in 1986. The first part of the program featured works by Debussy and Stravinsky, but after the intermission, Boulez started to conduct one of his more subdued pieces. The audience became restless, and some even started to leave the hall — and not quietly. "I would have enjoyed the opportunity to grab a microphone and scream, 'Sit down, assholes! This is one of *the Real Guys!*'" Zappa said in his memoir. Zappa may not have realized that, in his moment of outrage, he was unconsciously summoning an episode that took place in this same city over fifty years earlier.

On the night of January 10, 1931, when Nicolas Slonimsky first conducted Charles Ives' "Three Places in New England," along with Carl Ruggles' "Men and Mountains," at New York's Town Hall, something similar to Zappa's experience at the Lincoln Center took place. Ives described that evening, oddly enough, in the third person: "At this concert he [Ives] sat quietly through the 'boos' and jeers at his own music — but when that wonderful orchestral work 'Men and Mountains' of Carl R was played, a sound of disapproving hiss was heard near him. Ives jumped up and shouted: 'You g-ddarn, sissy-eared mollycoddle — when you hear strong masculine music like this, stand up and use your ears like a man — and don't "flibby" faint over backwards.'" So said another one of "the Real Guys."

6

In Pierre Boulez, Frank Zappa found a contemporary figure to match his philosophical outlook on music. Although not the absurdist that Zappa was, Boulez still had a personality that could be considered rather odd. "Boulez is, to use one of Thomas Nordegg's favorite phrases, *'serious as cancer,'* but he can be funny too," Zappa wrote. "He reminds me a little of the character that Herbert Lom plays in the *Pink Panther* movies. He doesn't have the 'psychotic wink,' but he has some of

THE MEEK SHALL INHERIT NOTHING

that nervous quality about him, as if he might — given the proper excuse — start laughing uncontrollably."

However, there are some in the musical establishment who don't feel so tenderly toward Boulez. Andrew Clark, in the *Financial Times*, wrote of Boulez, "far from the standard-bearer of the musical future, he is already part of its past." Joan Peyser, in her book *To Boulez and Beyond: Music in Europe Since The Rite of Spring*, paints a tragic portrait of Boulez — filled with suicide pacts and celibacy. For his part, Boulez has little time for the popular neoromanticism of composers like Philip Glass, John Adams, or Arvo Pärt. "Very facile," he told Philip Anson of the *Globe and Mail* in March 2000, "easily heard and easily forgotten." Yet if he was once (like Zappa in the '60s) an angry young man who fought at the forefront of the postwar contemporary music scene, "a professional shit-disturber" (as Anson described him) advocating "radical new means of producing and consuming culture," Boulez is today (at seventy-six) very much a part of the musical establishment. Looking back on his tempestuous career, Boulez once remarked, "I sought to convey what I thought musical life should be."

That journey started in 1942 when Boulez joined the Paris Music Conservatory to study composition with the creative French composer Olivier Messiaen, who integrated a wide range of genres — from Gregorian chants to Oriental rhythms — into his music. But after he graduated in 1945, Boulez took lessons from René Leibowitz, who introduced him to serial music (eventually leading Boulez to champion Webern). Boulez developed the habit of deposing as many musical giants as he'd endorse, including Schoenberg, Stockhausen, and even his mentors, Messiaen and Leibowitz. As a composer, Boulez attempted to synthesize the rhythmic dynamics of Stravinsky and Messiaen with the twelve-tone dissonances of Schoenberg and the serialist music of Webern. But unlike Stravinsky, who sought to reinterpret tradition in his neoclassical work, Boulez set out to negate tradition altogether with his own post-Webern form of serialism.

But no matter how much he wanted to break from the past, Boulez's heritage never abandoned him. A score like *Le Marteau sans maître* (1956), which Zappa admired, has one foot in modern serialism and the other in the tonal color of Boulez's French antecedents. By the '50s and '60s, though, Boulez started incorporating electronics into compositions like *Poésie pour pouvoir* (1958). "I was concerned with reconciling opposing elements," Boulez told Joan Peyser in *To Boulez and Beyond*. "I wanted to bring electronic and orchestral sounds together."

Boulez accomplished that by creating L'Institut de recherche et coordination acoustique/musique at the Centre Georges Pompidou in Paris.

The idea grew out of a meeting between the composer and the French president, Georges Pompidou, in 1970, where Boulez had explained his visionary ideas about the future of music. These concepts involved "stripping music of its accumulated dirt and [giving] it the structure it has lacked since the Renaissance." The institute opened in 1977, with Italian composer Luciano Berio as head of the electro-acoustic department, while Yugoslav composer Vinko Globokar researched the potentialities of voices and instruments. Another modern French composer, Jean-Claude Risset, took control of the computer section.

In 1980, however, Boulez laid everyone off and brought in a younger, more savvy crew, which made the technology easier to operate for visiting composers. The next year, the Italian computer expert Giuseppe di Giugno invented the 4X, a digital signal processor capable of 200 million operations per second. Like Zappa, Boulez was trying to create his own laboratory, his own dangerous kitchen with a menu that would invite the audience to partake in the possibilities of technology and music. Yet, as technically driven as both composers were, Boulez drew from a different muse than Zappa. "Boulez writes complex rhythms, but they are mathematically derived, while the rhythms I have are derived from speech patterns," Zappa explained to *The Guardian*. "They should have the same sort of flow that a conversation would have, but when you notate that in terms of rhythmic values, sometimes it looks extremely terrifying on paper." Within a year, they would discover their common ground on *The Perfect Stranger: Boulez Conducts Zappa*.

In January 1983, Zappa spent four and a half days rehearsing with the London Symphony Orchestra at the Hammersmith Odeon. This engagement followed numerous failed attempts to have his orchestral music performed with other orchestras around the world. It also turned into an awful waste of money. In 1976, Zappa had been approached by a rock promoter to do a concert with the Vienna Symphony. For three years, funding was raised from the city, Austrian radio, and Austrian television. The concert was set for July 1979, but just as Austrian television was about to put up its $300,000, it was discovered that they hadn't got the proper authority. Zappa had his manager comb the continent to replace the $300,000, but to no avail. The concert was cancelled. When his expenses were totaled, Zappa had spent close to $125,000 to hear absolutely no music performed.

In 1980 the head of the Holland Festival visited Zappa in his Amsterdam hotel and requested a performance of his orchestral music with the Hague Residentie

THE MEEK SHALL INHERIT NOTHING

Orchestra. Zappa asked for a guarantee of three weeks' rehearsal time, and insisted that someone finance the venture — after the Vienna debacle, he wasn't interested in spending any more of his own money. But although the Holland Festival put up $500,000, and the Dutch government paid the salaries of the musicians in the orchestra, Zappa was saddled with the cost of the recording equipment, the engineer, plus additional payments for the recording sessions for the album. CBS Records got involved to record the concert to take care of that expense, and a road crew was paid for to handle the equipment.

The Ahoy Hall, which could seat 8,000 patrons, was the setting. But since it was an indoor bicycle-racing arena the rest of the year, special equipment had to be installed to improve the acoustics. To pay for the rehearsal and performance salaries, plus travel expenses, Zappa booked a four-month rock tour, but when a couple of musicians in the band secretly tried to get their salaries raised, Zappa cancelled the tour. A week later, however, Zappa got a letter from the Residentie Orchestra saying they had hired a lawyer to negotiate their royalties from the record album.

It utterly baffled Zappa that a composer would pay royalties to the musicians in an orchestra for simply performing his music. He was so incensed that a composer could be held to ransom by "a greedy bunch of mechanics" that he refused to have them ever play his music. "It was determined shortly thereafter that the cost of going through all of this intercontinental frolic had brought my 'serious music involvement' to about $250,000 and I still hadn't heard a note of it," Zappa told *Musician* in 1981. "There you have it, folks . . . two orchestral stupidities: a conceptual double concerto for inaudible instruments on two continents, perfectly performed by some of the most exceptional musicians of our time."

Which brings us to England during the 1983 winter of Zappa's discontent. Originally, he had asked for the BBC Orchestra, who he had worked with at the Royal Albert Hall in 1968. But they were booked for five years. So he recruited the London Symphony Orchestra. To seat the 107-piece ensemble, they settled for Twickenham Studios, normally a film studio, where they occupied a soundstage saddled with bad acoustics. Zappa wanted this to be the first multitrack digital recording of a symphony orchestra, so it was important that it sounded first-rate. Before they could start, Zappa had to satisfy the union regulations for rehearsals — a concert was held at the Barbican Hall on January 11. This was followed by three days of recording new works — "Bob in Dacron," "Sad Jane," and "Mo 'n' Herb's Vacation." They also performed new versions of "Pedro's Dowry" and an orchestral version of "Envelopes," from *Ship Arriving Too Late to Save a Drowning Witch*. "Bogus Pomp" was an expanded version of themes from *200 Motels* that had also appeared, in a shorter form, on *Orchestral Favorites*. "Strictly Genteel" was the same instrumental arrangement of the finale from *200 Motels* and was also featured on *Orchestral Favorites*.

The conductor for the sessions was Kent Nagano, who began his career by conducting the Berkeley Symphony Orchestra. Nagano had always been interested in Zappa, but assumed that the sardonic music of the Mothers was all that he did. "I remember being very young and seeing Frank on *Johnny Carson* conducting the Mothers of Invention," Nagano recalled. "His attire and appearance left quite an impression on me. But I wasn't really that familiar with him as a musician until around 1967 when some older friends introduced me to his music." Years later, Nagano found out about Boulez's interest in Zappa's music. Since Nagano had conducted many works of 20th-century music, he wanted to see some of Zappa's scores. "Frank was right there right next to me," Nagano told Don Menn, remembering the rehearsals. "He demonstrated that he had impeccable ears and absolute command of the scores.... I include Frank in the category of composers who are keenly in tune with their own work, how it's being rehearsed, how it's developing, and who can participate and help correct the wrong notes, make suggestions, and change phrasing on the spot in ways that might be easier or more musical to play."

Zappa also had a fond recollection of their meeting. "Some friends of his brought him to the show and he came backstage afterwards," Zappa told Miles in 1983. "I said, 'Yeah, sure I write music, want to see some scores?' and he said, 'Yeah,' so I sent them to him and he flipped out.... That guy is a world-class conductor and the orchestra really appreciated him."

But it's a shame the orchestra didn't appreciate the music a little more. "On the last day of the last session for [*London Symphony Orchestra, Vol. 1*], I was trying to record a piece called 'Strictly Genteel,'" Zappa recalled. "Union rules specified a short break every hour, and during the last hour of the session, the entire trumpet section left the Twickenham Studio grounds and invaded a pub across the street, arriving back to work fifteen minutes late." In a recording studio that charges by the hour, the break lasted an eternity. When the trumpet section returned, they were hammered.

Since the orchestra wouldn't do any overtime, Zappa had to record "Strictly Genteel" in the brief studio time remaining — errors and all. "They made so many mistakes, and played so badly on that piece, that it required forty edits (within

THE MEEK SHALL INHERIT NOTHING

seven minutes of music) to try and cover them," Zappa remarked. "We used every mixing trick in the book to hide the out-of-tune notes." It would take another four years before new digital equipment would enable Zappa to finally remix and release "Strictly Genteel."

But David Ocker, who played solo clarinet and would write the liner notes for the *Francesco Zappa* album, sometimes thought Zappa failed to acknowledge the difficulties from the musicians' perspective. "Frank hadn't the foggiest notion of what it was like to show up at a session, take out your instrument, have someone slam a sheet of music in front of you, and be expected to cut it," Ocker explained, "then be told to do it differently by some composer or conductor or other, and still not develop a bad attitude." Ocker believed Zappa saw the orchestra as a "big rock band," or a "big synthesizer" that just needed its knobs twirled.

Only a selection of these recordings would be included on *London Symphony Orchestra, Vol. I*: the beautifully melancholic "Sad Jane," the cartoon splendor of "Pedro's Dowry," the colorful vamping textures of "Envelopes," and the majestically abstract "Mo 'n Herb's Vacation," with its Varèsian percussion and David Ocker's intermittent clarinet solos that helped provide a modern texture.

Zappa had described the performances of these pieces as "high-class 'demos' of what actually resides in the scores." Indeed the record lacks the rhythmic swagger of *Orchestral Favorites*, but *London Symphony Orchestra, Vol. I* is still a pristine recording with splendid moments. Sections of "Sad Jane" are every bit as wistful as "Watermelon in Easter Hay." Although "Pedro's Dowry" is nowhere near as loose (or funny) as on *Orchestral Favorites*, it does have an inspired solo by first violin Ashley Arbuckle during its disco section. Yet there is a formality to the album that runs counter to Zappa's loose yet complex constructs. Besides the unavoidable errors, the performances lack the personality of putting on the lampshade. *London Symphony Orchestra, Vol. I* would be released on June 9, 1983. While it didn't make the *Billboard* classical chart, Zappa received fifteen other commissions because of the record.

On February 9, 1983, Zappa got involved with another tribute to Edgard Varèse, this time at the San Francisco War Memorial Opera House. It was the one-hundredth anniversary of Varèse's birth, and Zappa conducted the San Francisco Contemporary Chamber Musicians performing *Intégrales* and *Ionisation*, as well as some compositions by Webern.

In October, Zappa sued Warner Brothers for damages, charging that the company provided misleading statements and thwarted his legal right to audit their accounts. Zappa asked for $2.4 million in damages, $600,000 in royalties due his music firms, and $1 million in exemplary and punitive damages. It was the beginning of his effort to win back the rights to his master recordings. Once he did, he planned to re-release them — but not in the form many fans remembered them. "We're remixing everything," Zappa announced in *Guitar Player*. "I don't know whether we'll be able to pull it off in time because there's an awful lot of work to be done to meet the deadline, but I'm hoping by Mother's Day to have five boxes with seven albums in each of them, covering the entire catalog. And we'll divide them up so that the first box is like all the early Mothers stuff plus one extra disc of material from that era that's never been released before. And the same goes for the rest of the boxes; each will have one disc of things that were done during that time that never got released."

This series would be called *The Old Masters Box*, and Volume One was released in April 1985. It would include *Freak Out!*, *Absolutely Free*, *We're Only in It for the Money*, *Lumpy Gravy*, *Cruising With Ruben & the Jets*, and a *Mystery Disc* that featured material dating back to the Studio Z days, early Mothers' rehearsal, and live recordings, plus the singles "Big Leg Emma" and "Why Don'tcha Do Me Right?" What annoyed many Zappa purists was his stripping the bass and drum parts from the masters of *We're Only in It for the Money* and *Cruising With Ruben & the Jets*, and replacing them with Barrow's bass and Wackerman's drums. Zappa claimed that the tapes were in poor shape.

"In the case of the first four albums, the condition of the analog tapes was so dreadful you couldn't believe it," Zappa told Steve Birchall in *Digital Audio*. "On the two-track original mixes, the oxide had fallen off the tape and you could see through it. It was stored badly; the stuff was rancid. In some instances we had to go back to the original eight-track masters or four-track masters or whatever we could find. Some of them weren't available. One of the eight-track masters for 'Stuff Up the Cracks' from the *Ruben & the Jets* album is gone and no one knows where it is. All we could do was to re-equalize the two-track mix for that song. *Freak Out!* is re-EQed from the two-track mix, as is *Absolutely Free*. But *We're Only in It for the Money* is remixed from the original masters with brand-new digitally recorded drums and digitally recorded bass added. We took off the original mono drum set and put on classy drums and all that. We did the same thing on *Ruben & the Jets*. On *Lumpy Gravy*, we used a combination of the original two-track masters plus newly overdubbed material."

Yet there were still qualms about these newly refurbished discs. Barrow was ambivalent about the task. "On the one hand, as a musician, I'm always happy to be employed and doing sessions is always fun," he told *T'Mershi Duween*. "But on the other hand, I did try to talk Frank out of it the best I could." Part of Zappa's desire to do this was his need for the sound and performance to be up to the new digital technology he was employing. For those who lamented the old recordings, he simply considered them fetishists. Zappa felt no need to be nostalgic for the past.

But some of the musicians who played on those original sessions begged to differ. "When I sat down and listened to the CD, I got sick in the pit of my stomach," Bunk Gardner remarked. "It wasn't so much sterilized, but the music was from one era and you could tell the rhythm section was from the 1980s. It didn't make sense at all to me. And the thing that blew my mind was — didn't Frank hear that?" Of course, he did. That's why it's also possible that his resentment of the old Mothers provoked his decision to remake the tracks.

Early in 1982, some of the ex-Mothers, including Jimmy Carl Black and Don Preston, put together a group called the Grandmothers and released an album called *Looking Up Granny's Dress*, which was released on Rhino Records. Not only did they perform Zappa's material without compensating or getting permission from the maestro, they also included his unreleased original version of "Deseri" from Studio Z in 1962. Black, Preston, and Gardner also sued Zappa in a $13 million lawsuit for royalties they felt should have been received for their contributions to the '60s albums on MGM/Verve and Bizarre. United Press International reported the claim on January 24, 1985. At that time, the three petitioners encouraged other ex-Mothers to join them. Ray Collins, Art Tripp, and even Zappa's old friend Motorhead Sherwood jumped into the fray. The amount was amended to $16.4 million. Since they felt owed their outstanding royalties, the ex-Mothers had no regrets about playing old Mothers' material.

Zappa, however, saw something more devious at work. "If they want to appeal to the writing public at large, it's easier to get more coverage if you call me an asshole than it is if you say I'm a nice guy," Zappa wrote in *Frank Zappa: In His Own Words*. "But the fact of the matter is, what they're doing isn't particularly defensible from an artistic standpoint, because it's a rip-off. They're not paying me for the use of my compositions that they're performing onstage, they're using my name and the work that I've done in order to earn income for themselves, and then they present me with the total ingratitude of treating me like an asshole in their performance."

Zappa's decision to re-record and remix his music was another way of treating his early compositions as music not chained to the moment of its creation. He didn't wish his records to become prized objects for listeners who developed a romantic attachment to them. If music was to exist purely for its own sake, it wasn't to be the wallpaper for some fan's lifestyle. By retooling his records for the digital age, Zappa perfected the sound while laying waste the audience's sentimental demands.

One December evening in 1982, Zappa observed a familiar figure at his front door. "I get a lot of weird calls, and someone suddenly called up saying, 'This is Bob Dylan, and I want to play you my new songs,'" Zappa told Robin Denselow of *The Guardian*. "Now, I've never met him and I don't know his voice, but I looked at the video screen to see who was at the gate, and there, in the freezing cold, was a figure with no coat and an open shirt. I sent someone down to check to make sure it was not a Charles Manson, but it was him." Zappa brought Dylan to the studio and sat him at a piano. Dylan played eleven songs that he proposed for a new album he hoped Zappa would produce. Zappa was impressed by the tunes and was eager to do the album. His suggestions, though, were — as far as Dylan was concerned — somewhere out in left field. "I said he should subcontract out the songs to Giorgio Moroder . . . he should do a complete synthesizer track and Dylan should play guitar and harmonica over the top."

Zappa's suggestions, when considered, were more provocative than preposterous. He saw the possibility of Dylan again taking leave of his latest persona — which, at that time, was a born-again Christian troubadour. Zappa must have imagined the reaction the public would have to hearing Dylan's trademark acoustic guitar and harmonica over a throbbing synthesizer bed — especially one created by disco maven Giorgio Moroder, who had provided the percolating drone for Blondie's sexy "Call Me" and Donna Summer's quivering hit "I Feel Love!"

When Bob Dylan had gone electric back in the '60s, he broke free from the shackles of the movement that pigeonholed him as a protest singer. Zappa had been stunned by Dylan's radical departure. "Dylan's 'Subterranean Homesick Blues' was a monster record," Zappa told author Michael Gray. "I heard the thing and I was jumping all over the car. And when I heard the one after that, 'Like a Rolling Stone,' I wanted to quit the music business because I felt that if this wins, and it does what it's supposed to do, I don't need to do anything." But Zappa also parodied Dylan's struggle to find his individual voice in a pop construct that had

THE MEEK SHALL INHERIT NOTHING

been created around him. In "Debra Kadabra," for instance, Captain Beefheart reduced some lines from "Mr. Tambourine Man" ("Cast your dancing spell my way/I promise to go under it") to the hypnotic sway of a grade-Z science-fiction film. In "Flakes," singer Adrian Belew diminished the indelible power of Dylan's protest songs to mere complaints about bureaucratic incompetence.

In one of Zappa's last interviews for *Playboy*, he described a complete shift from his initial reactions to Dylan's music. "As for Dylan, *Highway 61 Revisited* was really good," Zappa explained. "Then we got *Blonde on Blonde* and it started to sound like cowboy music, and you know what I think of cowboy music." (Zappa was no doubt confusing that urban blues record with Dylan's country ballads on *Nashville Skyline*.) The collaboration, however, never came to fruition. Conflicting schedules, plus (according to Dylan) Zappa asking for too much money for the project and wanting members from his own band to be on the sessions, put the brakes on their efforts. Dylan's songs found a home on *Infidels*, produced by Mark Knopfler of Dire Straits. Despite its title, *Infidels* was more secular than Dylan's previous records — and Moroder's synthesizers were nowhere to be heard.

By 1984, synthesizers weren't far from Zappa's thoughts. He discovered a new technology called the synclavier, a keyboard instrument that combined the sampling capabilities of a synthesizer with the software of a computer. It allowed the composer to program a score and hear the machine play it back note for note. Biographer Neil Slaven is perceptive in determining how Zappa's music would be affected by the synclavier. "From now on, [Zappa] would be able to work in a medium that was not available to his musical antecedents; he could create his own compositional language, exploring tonal rhythmic theories that were inconceivable at the time of Varèse's death," Slaven explains. "The older man had been excited by the possibilities of electronic sound, an alien universe which he strived to embrace. But the embryonic resources at his disposal could provide no more than the crudest of wave forms with few inherent musical qualities. The synclavier, even in its basic form, let Frank's imagination take flight in an infinity of directions."

It indeed was the machine's numerous capabilities that excited Zappa. "The synclavier allows the composer not only to have his piece performed with precision, but to *style* the performance as well — he can be his own conductor, controlling the dynamics or any other performance parameters," Zappa wrote. "He can bring his idea to the audience in pure form, allowing them to hear *the music*, rather than the ego problems of a group of players who don't give a shit about *the composition*." With the synclavier, Zappa had also solved one of the great musical problems encountered by Conlon Nancarrow, one of his antecedents. Born in 1912, Nancarrow was an American-born Mexican innovator in modern music who perforated notes on player piano rolls as a way to mark unusual rhythms and notes. Once fed back into the piano player, the rolls demonstrated what Nicolas Slonimsky once called "[a] method of composition [that gave] him total freedom in conjuring up the most complex contrapuntal, harmonic, and rhythmic combinations that no human pianist or number of human pianists could possibly perform." A single bar sometimes contained a few dozen notes that Nancarrow had to painstakingly stamp into the roll.

The synclavier allowed Zappa to compose music set apart from the ego of the performer, which he saw as one of the core failings of popular music. The purely technical utopianism offered by the synclavier did have one fault for Zappa — it didn't allow for *any* human interaction. That meant that the element of chance — something John Cage had introduced into the musical puzzle years earlier — was nonexistent, which limited the wide range of Zappa's musical interests. Zappa knew that the machine could "play ostinatos — cheerfully — until it's blue in the face (except it never gets blue in the face)." He also realized, though, that "machines don't decide to say things like *'We're Beatrice'* in precisely the 'wrong' place in the middle of a song, and make people laugh."

Zappa tried to find a way to integrate the human element with the wonders of the machine. For the moment, it was an either/or problem. "Subtracting the bullshit and mistakes, if I had to choose between live musicians or La Machine," Zappa wrote in his memoirs in 1989, "I must admit, from time to time I'm *almost* tempted to opt for the 'human element.'"

When he teamed up with Pierre Boulez for the recording of *The Perfect Stranger: Boulez Conducts Zappa* in January 1984, Zappa found a way to combine both the human and machine worlds. Boulez was willing to take the kinds of risks required to solve pertinent issues. "[I] was attracted by the energy and spontaneity of some pop artists," Boulez told the *Sunday Times Magazine* in 1985. "They are not afraid to experiment. With scores like Zappa's, I have the opportunity of breaking down musical ghettos in a dignified way." *The Perfect Stranger* was a large step for both men in integrating those languishing musical ghettos. The album contains three pieces featuring Boulez's Ensemble InterContemporain and four synclavier compositions under Zappa's direction.

"The Perfect Stranger" opens shrewdly with the simulated sound of a doorbell, while the strings invite us to enter the composition. Zappa, in the album notes,

THE MEEK SHALL INHERIT NOTHING

indicates that the piece is about "a door-to-door salesman, accompanied by his faithful gypsy-mutant industrial vacuum cleaner [who] cavorts licentiously with a slovenly housewife." The vacuum cleaner ties the piece to Cal Schenkel's interior artwork for *Chunga's Revenge*, which shows this happily lewd machine dancing with free abandon around a gypsy campfire. Ensemble InterContemporain perform Zappa's music with both great humor and musical adroitness, in sharp contrast to the London Symphony Orchestra, whose performances were impersonal by comparison.

"Naval Aviation in Art?" — which had a sparse texture on *Orchestral Favorites* — shows more the influence of Boulez on this version. Rather than stretching out the musical tension, Boulez builds methodically on the multiple chords. "The Girl in the Magnesium Dress" is the first synclavier composition released on record. Nancarrow's influence is clear in just how the steady stream of notes sound like water falling on sheet metal. To create the song's more colorful qualities, Zappa used a synthesized Fender Rhodes and vibes.

"Dupree's Paradise," performed by Ensemble InterContemporain, recasts a piece performed by the 1973 rock band. Zappa describes the song as being "about a bar on Avalon Boulevard in Watts at 6:00 a.m. on a Sunday in 1964, during the early morning jam session. For about seven minutes, the customers (winos, musicians, degenerates, and policemen) do the things that set them apart from the rest of society." In this version, it's a little hard to hear the deliberately disheveled jazz arrangements that gave the original (on *You Can't Do That on Stage Anymore, Vol. 2*) such distinction. Yet "Dupree's Paradise" is still stunningly brisk and graced with a shipshape arrangement that the Ensemble bring to life.

"Love Story" is a brief synclavier composition that attempts to capture the image of "an elderly Republican couple attempting sex while break-dancing." The disjointed bubbling sounds resemble Peter Wolf's synthesizer solo from "Sy Borg" (*Joe's Garage*) being blown to tiny pieces. "Outside Now, Again" is the guitar solo from "Outside Now" (again, *Joe's Garage*) transcribed for the synclavier. As in the original song, the melodic theme is used as a continuous drone, while the notes from the guitar solo are played on the keyboard overtop. The effect is minimalist, and less mournful than the original. This may be why Zappa describes the piece as being about a cast in a soup line waiting for "pitiful sustenance" handed out by "people dressed to look like grant-givers from the National Endowment for the Arts." He calls the piece "perfectly suited to minimalist choreography."

"Jonestown" is an eerie masterpiece of dread that has the power to unnerve a listener. The song commemorates the horrific mass suicide by the 913 followers of the People's Temple and their crazed minister, Jim Jones, in the jungles of Guyana in 1978. Neil Slaven writes, "'Jonestown' establishes a bleak aural landscape of tremulous sustained chords that imply paranoia. Percussion effects cut through the stereo but the principal elements are raw, gouging metallic sounds that increase during the middle section of the seven-minute piece, accompanied by siren-like ascending notes. The effect is otherworldly and threatening, maintaining an absence of hope that underscores the tragedy of the real event and Frank's own opinion of the perniciousness of all forms of religion."

Zappa described "Jonestown" as "a boring, ugly dance evoking the essential nature of all religions. A person pretending to be a messenger from God bangs on the side of the communal beverage tub with the skull of a former child, silently mouthing the words, 'Come and get it!'" That eerie metallic clatter, combined with chime-like percussion, could today just as easily evoke the mass suicide of the Heaven's Gate cult — who died dreaming of an afterlife in space.

The cover for *The Perfect Stranger*, by American realist painter Donald Roller Wilson, features a dog named Patricia in a high chair alongside bottles of Heinz ketchup, baby's milk, and a Budweiser. The title of the painting, though, like most of Wilson's work, is nearly endless:

> PATRICIA'S LATE-NIGHT COMPLIMENTARY SNACK AT MONTE'S
> AND RICHARD YOAKUM'S BOULEVARD HOUSTON TOWNHOUSE
> WHERE (THE NIGHT BEFORE) DON HAD GONE UP IN SMOKE.
>
> PATRICIA'S THICK GREEN LENSES FILTERED OUT THE SHADES OF
> RED REFLECTED FROM THE HEINZ-SIGHT OF HER BOTTLE —
> (THAT BRAND OF KETCHUP WE ALL LOVE SO WELL)
>
> BUT MRS. JENKINS' GLASS LENSES WERE A ROSY RED AND WHEN
> SHE SHOOK THE CONTENTS OF THAT BOTTLE — (THAT KIND OF
> KETCHUP WE ALL LOVE SO WELL)
>
> SHE DIDN'T THINK TO SHIELD HER EYES TO NULLIFY THE RED
> AND THE HOT BRIGHT LIGHT HAD LEFT HER BLIND; BUDWEISER
> (THAT TYPE OF BEER WE ALL LOVE SO WELL)

THE MEEK SHALL INHERIT NOTHING

> SO, WHILE PATRICIA WATCHED THAT NIGHT, HER FRIEND WENT UP IN SMOKE LIKE DON HAD DONE, HER FLAMES LEAPED HIGHER AND HIGHER (PAT FEARING THAT JENKINS SURELY WENT TO HELL)
>
> BUT PATRICIA WAITED YEARS AND YEARS TO SEE IF SHE'D COME BACK SHE WAITED BY THE TABLE WITH HER BOTTLE (ENGAGED AND FAITHFUL IN HER SENTINEL)

Wilson evokes images that could easily fit into some of Zappa's songs or one of Beefheart's song-poems. Borrowing some of the anthropomorphic qualities of Cassius Marcellus Coolidge's "Poker Dogs," Wilson adds a touch of the ridiculous so crystalline that his paintings have the surreal sophistication of waking dreams.

Like Zappa, Wilson synthesized numerous aesthetic streams — in his case, photo-realism, narrative, and history painting — to create his own original vision. "Wilson shares something with all of them," writes art critic Ralph T. Coe, "the precise painting, the dreaminess, the moral tales . . . mixing them together with such intensity and control, humor, and terror, that while we can identify individual parts, we can't make them make sense in combination as a whole." Wilson had once commented that he was "interested in helping the average man get out from where he is and get over to the other side." This sentiment was no doubt appealing to Zappa, who had been doing the same in music for twenty years. Wilson's work would appear on the cover of two more Zappa recordings in the next year.

The Perfect Stranger reached No. 7 on the Billboard Classical Album Charts, and the title track landed Zappa his third Grammy nomination for Best New Classical Composition.

7

Zappa never realized his dream of developing a Broadway play on the life of Lenny Bruce, but he probably couldn't have written the original cast production of *Thing-Fish* without him. One of the key elements of *Thing-Fish* is linked to a popular Bruce routine. What appeared to be, at first, a stinging satire of the Broadway stage became a savage assault on political and sexual attitudes during the Reagan years. The AIDS epidemic, which was killing homosexuals and Haitians in large numbers, was another key component of this insurgent satire. The simple idea behind *Thing-Fish* was that somebody has manufactured a disease called AIDS, for use as a weapon, and they start testing it on convicts. When the tests backfire, mutants are created.

Within a few years of the outbreak of AIDS, it was recognized as a sexually transmitted disease, but Surgeon-General Everett Koop linked the disease to tainted blood from green monkeys in Africa. "If this is supposed to be a sexually transmittable disease," Zappa remarked to talk-show host Joan Rivers in 1986, "then who is plooking the monkeys?"

The AIDS epidemic had arrived just when fundamentalist Christianity had found legitimacy through the Republican Party. The fundamentalists perceived this horrifying crisis as part of God's plan to punish the wicked. Aware of the LSD experiments conducted by the U.S. government on civilians during the '50s and '60s, Zappa had his own theory about the origins of AIDS. "A few years ago, genetic engineering became a huge stock market issue," Zappa said in 1987. "It was suddenly possible to mutate bacteria and produce super-specific germs which would affect only certain ethnic groups. You then have a really cheap cost-effective way of putting your enemies' lights out without damaging real estate." Zappa figured that if this capability was put into the hands of fundamentalists, Armageddon would become a self-fulfilling prophecy. "After all, fundamentalists believe that sex is a sin, especially the way that gay guys do it. . . . Especially after the rhetoric flying around when AIDS was first 'discovered.' Religious leaders like Pat Robertson and Jerry Falwell were gleefully claiming that it was divine retribution from God — it gets rid of gays, prostitutes, and intravenous drug users."

The other key group to suffer were blacks. *Thing-Fish* tells the story of a white yuppie couple named Harry and Rhonda who, attending a Broadway play, discover that the actors are made up of a group of Mammy Nuns, led by a character named Thing-Fish. They were former prisoners at San Quentin and part of a biological experiment that had gone awry. An Evil Prince (who sometimes worked as a theater critic) spent most of his time in a secret government laboratory where he created a "secret potion" to rid the world of "highly rhythmic individuals and sissy-boys." As he sings in "The Evil Prince":

Only the boring and bland will survive
Only the lamest of lameness will thrive
Take it or leave it, you won't be alive
If you are overtly CREATIVE!

THE MEEK SHALL INHERIT NOTHING

While gays and Haitians were "dropping like flies," thanks to his invention, the prisoners tested in San Quentin survived because the potion was mixed in with their mashed potatoes. But that was no blessing — they turned into ugly creatures in Aunt Jemima clothes, with heads like potatoes, lips like ducks', and sprouting handkerchiefs (just like the ones Louis Armstrong used to mop up his sweat). The Mammy Nuns, named after the famous minstrel tune sung by Al Jolson, had huge hands fitted with Jolson-style white gloves. When they lifted their skirts, the Mammy Nuns revealed "customized lawn jockeys with the outstretched lantern-bearing arm positioned between their legs." But instead of a lantern, they possessed a "shower-head plumbing fixture" used to piss through after they were rendered incontinent.

Thing-Fish (Ike Willis) spoke in what Zappa called a "pseudo-negrocious" dialect inspired by the character Kingfish from *Amos 'n' Andy*. Harry and Rhonda are attending the opening night of this Broadway play hoping that a show "with colored folks in it would guarantee GOOD, SOLID, MUSICAL ENTERTAINMENT." But they end up being drawn into the Mammy Nuns' version of stagecraft, which reveals the couple's innermost fantasies and perversions, aberrations that are masked by their white blandness.

Thing-Fish turns the origins of minstrelsy on its head. It is a stunning, fearless attack on racism and the homogenization of American culture in the '80s. Oddly enough, *Thing-Fish* was also Zappa's most reviled work — even by some of his staunchest fans.

According to Ben Watson, Zappa was summarizing key ideologies like religion, politics, and race that have always been used by the Church, or authoritarian governments, to keep citizens both ignorant and subservient. "However, instead of producing an ideal resolution of those conflicts by proposing a series of liberal taboos," Watson writes, "Zappa proposes the use of all those taboos by the underdog, not just a return, but a *revenge* of the repressed." *Thing-Fish* is essentially a further development of the themes first explored earlier in the decade with *You Are What You Is*. Not only does the story grow from the racial myths propagated in that album's title song, the song itself is featured in this musical along with two other numbers, "Mudd Club" and "The Meek Shall Inherit Nothing," from that same album.

Zappa also recycled a collection of rearranged and retitled songs for *Thing-Fish*, including the backing tracks from "The Torture Never Stops" and "Ms. Pinky" from *Zoot Allures*, "The Blue Light" from *Tinsel Town Rebellion*, and "No

Not Now" from *Ship Arriving Too Late to Save a Drowning Witch*. It was Zappa's plan to include a vast selection of songs — new and old — as a means to reinterpret his work through the purview of this musical. He even reintroduced characters from the past: Quentin Robert DeNameland, the philosopher from "The Adventures of Greggery Peccary," is now a televangelist, and Potato-Headed Bobby from "San Ber'dino" and "Advance Romance" is one of the Mammy Nuns.

The new songs include "The Mammy Nuns" — where Thing-Fish introduces his minstrel troupe while they urinate on Harry and Rhonda (Thing-Fish, in one spirited moment, asks, "Didja get any onya?") — and "He's So Gay," featuring Harry as a young boy. This song is done as a mock Village People disco vamp, concluding with a quote from Culture Club's "Do You Really Want to Hurt Me?" The adolescent Harry seeks to become gay not as an expression of his inner desires, but (like Bobby Brown) as an act of sadomasochistic submission:

> *Maybe he wants a little spanking*
> *Maybe he'll eat a little chain*
> *Maybe his lover should be thanking him*
> *For the way he makes it sprinkle*
> *Into drops of* GOLDEN RAIN.

Once again, Zappa was attacked by pressure groups — this time gay rights organizations, for his gratuitous attacks on their sexuality. "I'm not antigay," Zappa told *Playboy* in 1993. "When Ross Perot announced he was running for president, I wanted him to choose Barney Frank as a vice-presidential candidate. He is one of the most impressive guys in Congress. He is a great model for young gay men." What Zappa is satirizing in "He's So Gay" is how both gay and straight people submit to degradation as a means to conform. Despite the widespread belief that North American society was undergoing a sexual revolution designed to free the individual, Zappa begged to differ.

"The Crab-Grass Baby" is a song about the progeny of an inflatable doll ("Artificial Rhonda") and Quentin Robert DeNameland. With its computer-generated voice, the Crab-Grass Baby recites a litany of stock phrases from Zappa records — from Motorhead Sherwood's discussion of cars on *Lumpy Gravy* to Moon Unit's Valley-speak on "Valley Girl." The baby's disembodied voice was the very first synclavier experiment Zappa had attempted. "The background vocals are a repeated vocal chant with this computer voice singing over it," Zappa told

THE MEEK SHALL INHERIT NOTHING

Keyboard in 1987. "The computer voice is done with a little card that fits into an IBM computer, and the stereo background vocals were our first attempt at stereo sampling using the mono system."

"The White Boy Troubles" is an ensemble track whose form resembles the Coasters' 1954 hit "Down in Mexico," while "Brown Moses" is a gospel number featuring Johnny "Guitar" Watson in the title role. Brown Moses comes to the Crab-Grass Baby's rescue until his own weaknesses force him to offer up the baby as collateral for a bottle of wine or gin. "I love 'Brown Moses,'" Zappa told author Ben Watson. "It's a great song to sing, it's a fun song to sing. Actually, I'm a pretty decent composer of Negro spirituals." Indeed he is — even if "Brown Moses" is the only one he ever composed. The harmonies between Ike Willis, Ray White, Napoleon Murphy Brock, and Zappa add beautiful support to Watson's robust vocal.

"Wistful Wit a Fist-Full" is a twisted Broadway number done up in a mock Al Jolson impersonation where the Evil Prince — after ingesting some chitlins — sings like Harry and talks like the Thing-Fish:

> *I gets clammy, sayin'* MAMMY
> *I gets chills up my spine!*
> *I gets wistful,*
> *Wit a fistful*
> *Of ve-NE-she-um bline!*

In "Briefcase Boogie," Rhonda is reduced to wearing a dildo and fucking her briefcase in anger because Harry got it on with a Mammy Nun. She later confronts Harry with a view of male and female relations not yet dreamed about on Broadway:

> *While* YOU *became* LAWYERS *and* ACCOUNTANTS, *and read* PLAYBOY *and bought a pipe,* WE PLANNED *and* DREAMED *and* FUCKED OUR BRIEFCASES *while you weren't looking! Yes,* HARRY! *That's right! And we've actually been able to* REPRODUCE OURSELVES FOR YEARS THAT WAY . . . FOR *YEARS,* HARRY, *but* YOU NEVER KNEW! *Did you? You worm . . . You played* GOLF! *You watched* FOOTBALL! *You drank* BEER! *We* EVOLVED! *We only look like* WANDAS *and* RHONDAS! *We are* SUPURB,

HARRY! We are perfect in EVERY WAY! And you? What are you? You are the all-American cocksucker . . . jizzing all over your leather cocksucker costume after beating the snot out of yourself with a rubber MAMMY! I simply can't respect you, HARRY! You are NO GOOD.

Thing-Fish is a compendium of Zappa's most explicit attacks on political and sexual hypocrisy in American culture collected together in one huge volley. When it was released in November 1984, many weren't sure they wanted to come near it.

Not surprisingly (given the subject matter), the first bit of publicity for *Thing-Fish* came courtesy of Larry Flynt's *Hustler* magazine. "Frank was a genius, a rebel," Flynt told Connie Bruck in the *New Yorker* in 1999. "And Frank and I in all our conversations had a very honest dialogue. We were never really out of sync politically or socially." They had, in fact, much in common. Not only were they both strong supporters of the First Amendment, they had both fought for it before Congress or in court. Flynt had political aspirations to run for president that were cut short by a would-be assassin's bullet in 1984, the same year he and Zappa met.

"Whether you agree with his editorial policies, his sense of humor or his sexual attitudes (even I do not score 100 per cent in all those categories), we ought to stop and think for a moment about what has been done to this guy in the name of AMERICAN JUSTICE," Zappa wrote in *Hustler* in April 1984. The magazine carried a twenty-one-page color photo spread of an excerpt from the *Thing-Fish* story, with Thing-Fish and the Mammy Nuns decorated in prosthetic rubber masks. The feature displayed porn actress Annie Ample in the coveted role of Rhonda. She wrote about the photo shoot in her autobiography:

[Zappa] picked me out of the Faces book that most performers are in if they have an agent. I was perfect to play a part in what was going to be his first big musical stage production. Before I went to L.A., Frank and I spent hours on the phone talking. In fact, he auditioned me on the phone, and when we talked he always wanted me in character. I was supposed to be a domineering housewife with a horrible, high-pitched voice. "Harry, yer a worm," I repeated over and over again when we were talking.

THE MEEK SHALL INHERIT NOTHING

> I went to Zappa's studio, which is in his basement and is technically as good as any around. He showed me how he does the recording and the mixing right there. Then I met his wife and children. They all are terrific people. Zappa doesn't drink or do drugs. He proves that you can be in show business and have it all together.
>
> Zappa decided that he first wanted me to do publicity for his new album, *Thing-Fish*. In it, he had a song about a rubber doll. He'd heard about Slutty Suzy and Sluts Are Us in my act, and thought that Suzy and I would fit right into his plans. As part of the promotion, he was producing a celebrity layout for *Hustler*. That was fine with me as long as I didn't have to do any acrobatic shots. It took three of the wildest days of photography I'd ever gone through. I was paid $2,000 a day. The magazine got twenty-one pages out of it. As usual, I was underpaid given the results.
>
> My hair was white and ratted out about a foot around my head. I wore crazy-looking glasses, which had boxes with nude legs hanging out of them. They put a scar on my chest, and naturally I stripped through the pages of the magazine. I started out in a Santa Claus outfit and went slowly down to a pencil and a briefcase.
>
> The set, like Zappa, was bizarre. They must have spent thousands of dollars on it. There was a house with phony snow and dozens of pink flamingos in front of it. In the background, there was a huge poster of Pat Boone with his penis hanging out.

Zappa's assault on conformity and homogeneity in American culture didn't stop with *Thing-Fish* — he hit the lecture circuit. In April 1984, Zappa was the keynote speaker at the 19th Festival Conference of the American Society of University Composers held at Ohio State University in Columbus. What he said to the group was hardly reassuring, kind, or compassionate.

Zappa began by saying he wasn't interested in their organization. He then cautioned everyone present: "Before I go on, let me warn you that I *talk dirty*, and that I will say things you will neither enjoy nor agree with. You shouldn't feel threatened, though, because I am *a mere buffoon*, and you are all *Serious American Composers.*"

He proceeded to describe himself as a composer who didn't like teachers, schools, or "most of the things you believe in — and if that weren't bad enough, I earn a living by playing the *electric guitar.*" Zappa then proceeded to give his "speech." It began with a question that was central to Zappa's career in music. "Why do people continue to compose music, and even pretend to teach others how to do it, when they already know the answer? Nobody gives a fuck."

As smug and cynical as that might sound, Zappa was actually onto something much larger. Nobody giving a fuck was part of what perplexed many of the 19th- and 20th-century composers who preceded Zappa. He spoke with CNN's Sandy Freeman in October 1981 about economic support for artistic freedom. Zappa described the problem to Freeman succinctly: "When we talk about artistic freedom in this country, we sometimes lose sight of the fact that freedom is often dependent on adequate financing. If you have an idea for an invention, for instance, you need the tools and machinery to build it; you may have the freedom to think it up, but you don't have the financial freedom to think it up." Although he went on to castigate unions in America, which he felt had a deeply negative impact on the quality of the arts, Zappa's point was still too significant to ignore or dismiss.

He once told CBC journalist Vicki Gabereau that American culture had turned fraudulent based on the way it treated the arts. "First of all, it's always begging," he said. "There's always a committee raising money for the arts, which is humiliating because the arts is supposed to be the best of what a society has to offer. And you have all these little foundations trying to raise money to keep this alive and that alive." What irked Zappa even more was that the artist who spends years perfecting his craft will make less money than the guy who puts the chairs on the concert stage. "Do you know who really earns that money?" Zappa asked Gabereau. "The union guy who pulls the string that makes the curtain go up. In New York City, Local One, which is the local that provides labor for Broadway, the Met, and Carnegie Hall, those guys will make up to four times what any one musician will make in the orchestra. If nobody cares, and if the values of the society are such that the guy who moves the chair should earn four times the amount of money than the guy who plays the violin, then we should just let it die. It's over."

Zappa had become a composer because he wanted to raise the stakes on questions of value, to test the limits of democracy. He tempered the concept of freedom

THE MEEK SHALL INHERIT NOTHING

of expression with a willingness to incorporate whatever style or subject best fit his imagination. This meant that in the embrace of total freedom came an open challenge to those who created hierarchies of value. Since in Zappa's world, everything was open game for a rock 'n' roll song, an orchestral composition, a satirical observation, or a barbed criticism, his art threatened to expose these hierarchies as just another means of imposing power over others.

Zappa demanded that a free society not censor what it didn't like, or outlaw what it didn't understand, because a truly free society didn't have to fear such challenges to its foundations. A literate and educated society should debate, confront, and question uncomfortable ideas and concepts. But that won't happen if popular taste is dictated, Zappa said in his speech, by "Debbie," the thirteen-year-old daughter of "Average, God-fearing American white folk." For "Debbie" only preferred "short songs with lyrics about boy-girl relationships, sung by persons of indeterminate sex, wearing S&M clothing, and because there is *large money* involved, the major record companies . . . have all but shut down their classical divisions, seldom recording *new music*."

As Zappa brought the discussion closer to home for these aspiring artists, he focused on the role of the composer. "A composer's job involves *the decoration of fragments of time*. Without music to decorate it, time is just a bunch of boring *production deadlines* or dates by which *bills must be paid*. Living composers are entitled to proper compensation for the use of their works. Dead guys don't collect — one reason *their* music is chosen for performance." Zappa explained why the music of these wannabe composers was unlikely to be heard. "By performing pieces that the orchestra members have hacked their way through since conservatory days, the rehearsal costs are minimized — players go into jukebox mode, and spew off *'the classics'* with ease — and the expensive conductor, unencumbered by a score with *'problems'* in it, gets to thrash around in mock ecstasy for the benefit of the committee ladies (who wish he didn't have any pants on)."

Zappa buried some of his more important comments at the end in sarcasm. He suggested his audience give up and change the name of their organization from "ASUC to WE-SUCK." But he did have one final commendable remark. "If the current level of ignorance and illiteracy persists, in about two or three hundred years a *merchandising nostalgia* for *this era* will occur — and guess what music they'll play!"

Zappa took his point even farther: if something resembling "Debbie" was the yardstick for quality back in the age of Haydn, Mozart, and Beethoven, who's to say those icons of artistic genius are the true representatives of the best of that era's musical culture? Zappa told Bob Marshall:

> All the music that people regard as great masterpieces today were written for the amusement of kings, churches, or dictators — that's who was paying the rent. If the man who wrote the music happened to be working in a style that was appealing to the person who was paying for it at the time, he had a hit, he had a job, and he stayed alive. If he didn't, he could lose his fingers, he could lose his head, he could be exiled or he'd starve to death. There was very little in between. All you have to do is look at a book called *Groves Dictionary of Music and Musicians*, and you can see that throughout the ages there have been guys who had hits, and guys who didn't have hits. And it's not necessarily connected to the quality of what they wrote. It's connected to how well they pleased the patron that was paying the freight — and it's the same thing today. So, all the norms, the acceptable norms of classical music, are really the taste norms of the church, the king, or the dictator that has been paying for it down through the ages. It was not the taste of the people. People never got to decide.

To prove his point, while speaking at San Francisco's Palace of Fine Arts on May 20 in the "Speaking of Music" series, Zappa played a few of the synclavier numbers off *The Perfect Stranger*. Then he surprised everyone by playing some excerpts from an obscure 18th-century cellist from Milan named Francesco Zappa. It was Gail and their son Ahmet who had discovered *Groves Dictionary of Music and Musicians* and, through that, Zappa's 18th-century namesake. "She was at a library with Ahmet and came across this book and looked to see if I was in it," Zappa told Vicki Gabereau on CBC Radio. "I wasn't but Francesco was." After the music scores were provided by the music library at the University of California at Berkeley, David Ocker programmed them into the synclavier. The scores were all string trios, except for one piano piece. "They're real fun to listen to because they're real happy," Zappa remarked. "They don't sound anything like the music that I write. . . . As with most of the music from that period, you know how it's going to resolve at the end. It's freeze-dried."

THE MEEK SHALL INHERIT NOTHING

What Zappa found particularly interesting about his predecessor was that some of the harmonic devices Francesco used weren't common in the pre-Romantic era in which he composed. Francesco might have been a little ahead of his time, which would explain why he wasn't so popular. "After [David Ocker] typed in *Op. 1* and we listened to it, I thought, 'Hey, that's a nice tune. I wonder what the rest of it sounds like?' Zappa told *Keyboard*. "He spent about a month typing in a huge amount of these string trios.... They sounded nice, so I thought, 'Why not make an album out of it?'" *Francesco Zappa* was released in November 1984.

By the time he addressed the American Society of University Composers, Zappa was getting fed up with his latest foray into the classical world. For one thing, the minimalist school of Philip Glass, John Adams, and Michael Nyman, where less meant more, was becoming part of a popular alternative trend in modern orchestral music. Zappa believed the appeal of minimalism had its roots more in economics than aesthetics. "One of my pet theories is that the leading cause of minimalism is reduced budgets for rehearsal and reduced budgets for ensemble size," Zappa told *Telos* magazine. "If a guy wants to write something and he knows that there are only a couple of minutes available for rehearsal, there is no way that he is going to write some massive thing for an orchestra.... How can a person be concerned about atonality versus tonality when the real question is how do you get anything played?"

Zappa also believed the minimalist aesthetic was fitting for the decade. "Minimalism, I think, is a perfect form of music to express the spiritual condition of the '80s," he said. "[It] sees itself as a form of music which includes eclectic, popular elements recognizable by an audience as a necessary response to the abstractness of modernism. Consequently, the music is more approachable." If that was true, minimalism could also allow the composer to rationalize the malaise in his own imagination when it came to creating the piece. "It's the only way in which a composer can function in contemporary American life at all, that is to do this shallow, empty, repetitive, disposable stuff, and then verify it... by saying that is the way the society is, and we poor composers can only reflect the society the way it is. There is a certain truth to that, but then on the other hand, why the fuck bother to listen to it?"

Biographer Ben Watson echoes Zappa's sentiments, adding that minimalism's bridging of the culture gap between the classical and pop worlds was only an illusion. "[It] merely provided the soundtrack to a lifestyle elevated 'above' popular culture," Watson writes. "Zappa understands rock as an *experience* in the context of social existence. His extensions of the form recognize that fact. Rather than gratifying the wish to transcend society, his aesthetic is one of sociological materialism: social limits are played out in the processes of the music itself."

Zappa's frustration with the modern classical world reached its nadir during the three nights of concerts to honor the ASUC convention. "The first night, they played 'Naval Aviation in Art?' which is a piece about two and a half minutes long," Zappa told Steve Birchall of *Digital Audio*. "It's really not a very hard piece — passable performance on that." But the next afternoon, the Pro Musica Chamber Orchestra tried to play "The Black Page" and, according to Zappa, "murdered it." On the third night, the Columbus Symphony was scheduled to do the American premiere of "The Perfect Stranger," but Zappa noticed at the rehearsals that the harp player couldn't nail one section of the score. Zappa asked the conductor to leave her out. At the same time, he saw that one of the other participating composers, Nancy Chance, had a score with harp parts. The same harpist couldn't play the piece — but she was left in. "The union in Columbus threatens to shut everybody down if you mess with their harp player," Zappa told Burchall. "This woman has lifetime tenure in the orchestra. You can't even pay her to stay home. There are other competent harpists in town, but the union refuses to let the orchestra hire anybody other than this woman."

For Zappa, the union rules defeated both the composer and the audience: "I stopped touring two years ago and spent the last two years in Modern Music Land — and I'm leaving."

8

Joining Zappa in his return to rock touring in 1984 were Ray White and Ike Willis on rhythm guitars and vocals; Bobby Martin on sax, keyboards, and vocals; Scott Thunes on bass; and Chad Wackerman on drums. And for the first time, with no marimba percussionist, Zappa enlisted Alan Zavod, an additional keyboard player. Zavod was a film composer and a veteran of Jean-Luc Ponty's band. Napoleon Murphy Brock also joined up, but he was cut two months into the tour for using drugs. Zappa told a TV interviewer in Santa Barbara that "chemical alteration is not something that mixes well with precision performance."

While Frank was on tour, Gail decided to consolidate their Barking Pumpkin holdings. It started with the firing of manager Bennett Glotzer and all the other employees. "We'd gotten into a situation where we were really subsidizing Frank's manager," Gail told Don Menn in *Zappa!* "He owed us a lot of money, and so in order to keep the business going, we were taking care of all his outstanding debts, and I was getting very agitated with that. . . . I took over the business, and the first thing I did was fire everybody that worked for us. The lawyers, accountants — I just said, 'That's it, I don't want any help from any of those people,' and went out and found replacement parts."

By 1985, Gail took over the family business. She used a $12,000 bank loan to buy two computers, compiled a mailing list, and prepared a questionnaire to quiz fans about their needs and desires — and a Barking Pumpkin T-shirt was offered for sale. She made the money back almost immediately and set up a new company that Frank called Barfko-Swill. Then, with her sister and one of Frank's production people, she starting stuffing those envelopes full of T-shirts. Despite the problems with censorship and record companies, Zappa always knew — and appreciated — the support of his wife in his vast endeavors. "I'm lucky that I've got a wife who likes that I [compose music] and will take care of the mundane stuff while I'm doing it," Zappa told John Winokur. "Without help, I'd be in deep trouble."

Zappa prepared a new rock album to be released in October called — aptly enough in light of his recent circumstances — *Them or Us*. He originally had an American distribution deal with MCA Records for both *Them or Us* and *Thing-Fish*, while EMI handled the United Kingdom. But a woman in MCA's quality control department was offended by both projects when she heard the test pressings. MCA pulled out of the deal, and EMI took over worldwide distribution rights. Them or us, indeed.

"The Closer You Are," which kicks off this two-album set, is a pure, unadulterated doo-wop cover of the 1956 classic by the Channels. Although the Channels' version never became a hit, it made an indelible imprint on Zappa. When Zappa was DJ for a day on a BBC Radio One disc show in February 1982, he played the song between "Straight Lines" by New Musik and *Hyperprism* by Varèse.

No doubt "The Closer You Are" appealed to Zappa because the Channels' fifteen-year-old lead singer, Earl Lewis, composed the song in reverse construction to doo-wop norms. Instead of beginning the tune with a single lead vocal supported by the group harmony, Lewis inverted the order. On "The Closer You Are" (as on their recordings "Altar of Love," "That's My Desire," and "The Gleam in Your Eye"), the Channels start with a five-part harmony, giving the number a startling immediacy. Zappa recreates that effect in his version. The song's shimmering quality is highlighted by the digital recording, and the close-miking effect brings Ray White, Ike Willis, Bobby Martin, and Zappa right up in the mix. The band performs the track with a striking reverence. Zappa doesn't so much pay tribute by copying the Channels, he instead enhances the original by giving the song a more modern setting to display its sheer beauty.

"In France" is a hilarious anthropological tour of French culture as seen through the eyes of a befuddled American. Like "The White Boy Troubles," the song loosely borrows its structure from the Coasters' 1954 hit "Down in Mexico," and it features a comically exasperated Johnny "Guitar" Watson on lead vocals:

The girls is all salty
The boys is all sweet
The food ain't too shabby
An' they piss in the street
In France.

The song is straight-ahead blues, and Zappa has fun springing puns on the listener. One in particular makes a glancing reference to former Fleetwood Mac guitarist Peter Green:

They got diseases
Like you never seen
Got a mystery blow job
Turn your peter green
In France.

"In France" is based on a true story of a band member who (after being orally serviced) found a green fudge substance oozing out of his organ. Not everyone who heard the song was amused (especially some French fans), but Zappa — as always — remained undaunted. "It was fair commentary on what Frenchness means to a person who is not French and has to be subjected to Frenchness," Zappa told a journalist during promotional interviews for *Them or Us*. "It is not a put-down of the French. It is the facts."

One of those facts centered on the famous toilets that must be used standing up. "I was able to ascertain from some interviews I did in France that the toilet that we're speaking of in the song is referred to in France as the 'Turkish Toilet,'" Zappa

THE MEEK SHALL INHERIT NOTHING

said. "So, if it's a Turkish toilet, then what's it doing in France? 'Cause that's all I know from French toilets is the thing with the bombsight and the two footprints where you pull the chain and if you're lucky it doesn't climb up to your ankles when the stuff comes up out of the hole."

"Ya Hozna" opens with the same repeated guitar riff that begins *Thing-Fish*. We're then treated to a series of operatic voices (Frank, Moon Unit, George Duke, and Napoleon Murphy Brock) singing various phrases backwards. "Ya Hozna" is an ambitious effort that combines recorded material from a number of years. Duke's vocal recitations go back to the mid-'70s when he sang "Sofa"; Moon Unit's are selections from "Valley Girl"; and Zappa quotes himself from "Lonely Little Girl," on *We're Only in It for the Money*. This energetically complex tune mocks the TV evangelists and Moral Majority folks who claimed that heavy metal records contained specially encoded satanic messages. By having Steve Vai's concluding guitar solo *appear* backwards, Zappa makes the point that no words — or music — played backwards will send you to the Lake of Fire.

"Sharleena" is yet another version of this lovely R&B number, only this time arranged in reggae time. It features the shredding sounds of Vai's guitar, plus a guest solo from budding guitarist Dweezil Zappa. Despite the pretty arrangement, "Sharleena" lacks the poignancy the song had on *Chunga's Revenge*. Flo & Eddie (and Sugarcane Harris in the first version of the song) got inside the yearnings of the tune. On *Them or Us*, "Sharleena" is stripped of the emotional core that linked it to the R&B tradition. It also has a patchwork quality that Dweezil alluded to in an interview at the time. "That version was really Frank taking bits of four solos and editing them, so it wasn't even something that was played," Dweezil told *Guitar Player*. "It had no continuity. I mean — I could never repeat it."

"Sinister Footwear II" is the second movement from the ballet originally scored for orchestra (the third movement — also arranged for the rock combo — was featured on *You Are What You Is*). Kent Nagano had already premiered the entire ballet with the Berkeley Symphony at the Zellerbach Auditorium in June 1984. While a stunning example of Zappa's brilliant tinker-toy classicism, "Sinister Footwear II" features a grungier guitar tone — the notes here are driven deep into the ground, buried in feedback, and with much whammy-bar shrieking.

"Truck Driver Divorce," which begins as another country song, borrows some of its narrative from "No Not Now" (more "string beans to Utah") and "Harder Than Your Husband." The song soon veers from its folksy opening with a wailing guitar solo. This shift shocks abruptly, just as the honking horns did in the second half of "Toads of the Short Forest" on *Weasels Ripped My Flesh*. The concluding guitar solo is taken from a live performance of the solo from "Zoot Allures," recorded in New York in 1981.

"Stevie's Spanking" is yet more folklore from the road, depicting some bizarre behavior involving Vai and a groupie named Laurel Fishman. "In 1981, on one of Steve Vai's early tours, we were playing at Notre Dame University, and Laurel Fishman showed up," Zappa explained. "By some twist of fate, Steve wound up with Laurel in his motel room. They engaged in a variety of practices involving a hairbrush, and Steve drooling on his own dork while she jerked him off." While pretty normal for a rock star on the road, their activities didn't stop with the drooling. Besides getting a spanking with the hairbrush, according to Zappa, Vai also penetrated her with "parts of guitars, assorted vegetables, and the drummer's umbrella":

Then she did exclaim:
"There's another game
That we can play with this device,
And then a banana!"

It was slightly green
Vapors in between
Rising up to fill the room
And cook the banana.

As sung by Bobby Martin, the song resembles an oddball cheerleader's cry that — if not for the lyrics — wouldn't be out of place at a football game.

"Baby, Take Your Teeth Out" is a small classic, sung by Ike Willis, that strips away romantic pretension. Inspired by Charlie Mingus' "Passions of a Man," the tune is peppered by some light percussion by Ed Mann. Apparently, Zappa made up the song — in a matter of minutes — during the 1982 tour:

Baby, take your teeth out
I will recline
Baby, take your teeth out
I will recline
There ain't nothin' left to talk about.

THE MEEK SHALL INHERIT NOTHING

Zappa follows this enjoyably ridiculous song about being "gummed" with the sublime "Marque-son's Chicken" (named for Marque Coy, his live-monitor producer since 1981, who used to place a chicken on the microphone stand). "My idea of a good time is a really simple-minded song followed by something that is out to lunch," Zappa told *Guitar Player* in 1983, "and then back to simplicity again, and then out to lunch again. That's the way the world really is: it's not totally complex, and it's not totally simple. It's a combination of both."

The notion of a complex world is the subject of "The Planet of My Dreams," a song intended for his science-fiction musical, *Hunchentoot*. The basic track was recorded in the '70s, and Bob Harris sings it in his high falsetto, accompanied by Duke's parlor piano. Harris praises an Earth that bulges at the seams, as Zappa contrasts the "glory of our sciences" with the planet's "muffled screams":

> And though it often seems
> From television beams
> That ignorance is rampant there
> And Governmental Goons don't care
> I know that I shall not despair
> And CHEAT like ALL THE REST
> I'll just keep on
> With what I do the best!

"Be in My Video" is Zappa's shot at MTV culture and how video distorts our intimate relationship with music. In the song, done as an R&B doo-wop number, Zappa fires barbs at the videos of Peter Gabriel ("I will rent a cage for you/With mi-j-i-nits dressed in white") and David Bowie ("Let's dance the blues/Under the megawatt moonlight"), even though both those artists worked imaginatively within the form. Zappa can't resist taking a shot at Carl Sagan's *Cosmos* TV series, either ("With its billions & billions & billions . . ."), not to mention presenting some of the worst excesses of rock video narratives:

> You can show your legs
> While you're getting in the car, then
> I will look repulsive
> While I mangle my guitar.

"Them or Us" is, like "Rat Tomago," a guitar solo from an already existing track, in this case a 1982 performance of "The Black Page." "Frogs With Dirty Little Lips" features lyrics from Zappa's younger son. "My son Ahmet walked around the house one day singing a song that he made up called 'Frogs With Dirty Little Lips,'" Zappa told Miles in 1982. "The words would change every day, and I'd always try to get him to sing it . . . but he lost interest in it, so while I was in Detroit I had fifteen minutes before the sound check — got out a pen and finished that song." Zappa sings this surreal march in an insinuating voice that is so close-miked it gives him an ominous presence:

> Frogs with dirty little lips
> Dirty little warts on their fingertips
> Dirty 'n green
> Tiny 'n mean
> Floppin' around
> By the edge of the stream.

"Whippin' Post" finally delivers that Allman Brothers' classic the fan in Finland requested over a decade earlier. Sung with a gospel fervor by Bobby Martin, the track has an urgent propulsion that perfectly matches the original. "I like 'Whippin' Post,'" Zappa remarked in 1982. "In fact, I think [the Allman Brothers] even premiered it when we were working together at this pop festival at the baseball stadium in Atlanta years and years ago. It was the first time I heard this song and I liked it then." "Whippin' Post" is a she-done-me-wrong blues similar to Zappa's own "Bamboozled by Love." While often featured as an energetic concert closer, it also fittingly concludes the album.

Them or Us is a diverse bag of goodies — highlighted by agile interplay between drummer Chad Wackerman and bassists Scott Thunes and Arthur Barrow — that cobbles together loose tracks from different sessions over the years. By now, Zappa was so proficient in the studio that you couldn't hear those years separating the tracks. He prepared it for a Christmas release.

While talking to a German journalist in 1984, Zappa asked whether he was familiar with the Unified Field Theory. The scribe said he wasn't, so Zappa explained: "Well . . . in physics . . . the Unified Field Theory explains the interrelationship between how gravity works and atomic energy . . . they're looking for one equation that

THE MEEK SHALL INHERIT NOTHING

explains it all and makes it work." In fact, Zappa was planning to publish a book on the topic — sort of. Originally titled *Christmas in New Jersey*, it was designed as a screenplay. "When we talked to a U.S. publisher, they were concerned that it *look* like a book," Zappa told the journalist. "And so they have taken a position that people won't read it because it doesn't say, 'The leaves fell off the tree,' and 'It's five o'clock,' and it's all in paragraphs." Zappa changed the title to *Them or Us (The Book)* and published it through Barfko-Swill. The book employed Zappa's own Unified Field Theory to integrate his albums into a single composition. "[It] will hold together 'Billy the Mountain,' 'The Adventures of Greggery Peccary,' *Joe's Garage, Them or Us, Francesco Zappa*, and *Thing-Fish* . . . [and] it shows you how they work together to make one long, really complicated story," Zappa explained. Besides commemorating his vast body of work that year, Zappa was also planning a series of commemorative concerts.

The 1984 tour, billed as the Twentieth Anniversary Tour, was (with the exception of Napoleon Murphy Brock's abrupt dismissal) very successful. Covering the U.S., Europe, and Canada, the tour was long — it began in Los Angeles in July, and ended there in December. Many of the shows were recorded on Zappa's new twenty-four-track digital equipment, and the quality of the performances was so stellar that Zappa released about sixty-five tracks on albums over the next few years. One concert, at the Pier in New York on August 26, formed the basis for a Zappa concert video titled *Does Humor Belong in Music?* In his memoir, Zappa put forward his ideas about the role of humor: "I've developed a 'formula' for what these timbres *mean* (to me, at least), so that when I create an arrangement — if I have access to the right instrumental resources — I can put sounds together that tell *more than the story in the lyrics*, especially to American listeners, raised on these subliminal clichés, shaping their audio reality from the cradle to the elevator." Much of that can be seen in the footage from the Pier.

Does Humor Belong in Music? is a concert video crossed with a documentary. Not only do we get the Zappa performance, we're also treated to a collection of interview clips featuring Zappa speaking on topics ranging from Ronald Reagan ("If he asks you into a car, offers you candy, or asks you to fight in Nicaragua, tell him no") to smoking ("To me, a cigarette is *food*. This may be a baffling concept to the people in San Francisco who have this theory that they will *live forever* if they stamp out tobacco smoke"). The concert opens with Zappa disappointing one fan by telling him, "We're not playing 'Greggery Peccary.'"

One constant of the 1984 band was that it was driven by its vocal talents.

Because of the wide contrast in voices — including Willis, White, Martin, and Zappa — they could do more R&B-oriented material. The group also had a strong keyboard section, with Zavod providing a percussive flavor to Martin's more mellifluous playing. Chad Wackerman used an electronic drum kit that gave the group a bionic sound, something common in much '80s rock, only Zappa used this particular timbre as part of his satiric strategy.

The band first launches into the instrumental "Zoot Allures," where Bobby Martin adds a nice melodic French horn accompaniment to Zappa's stabbing guitar lines. "There are some nice close-ups of his picking hand [in this concert]," Dweezil told *Guitar Player*. "[Frank] was holding the pick flush against the meat of both his thumb and his forefinger as though he was picking out whiskers — pluck, pluck, pluck. It's a neat-looking technique, and it makes the sound pop out. It's an aggressive, very masculine sound, for want of a better term. Every note has a lot of power." "Tinsel Town Rebellion" also has a much more powerful presence here than on the original album. It's embellished with hilarious references to Barry Manilow ("I Write the Songs"), Devo ("Whip It"), the Scorpions ("Rock You Like a Hurricane" transformed into "Rock You Like a Nincompoop"), and Culture Club ("I'll Tumble for Ya").

The band rips through "The Dangerous Kitchen" and offers an exuberant performance of "I'm So Gay," which features bassist Scott Thunes in a wig and Zappa tossing in an odd quote about "mining the harbor." This throwaway remark alludes to a news story that broke in April 1984 — CIA agents had mined the harbors of Nicaragua as part of a strategy to overthrow the left-wing Sandinista government of Daniel Ortega. Zappa's incongruous insertion creates a bizarre contrast with the subject of the song. The salacious image of "golden rain" suddenly melds into an insidious rain of bombs.

After a fine medley of "Bobby Brown Goes Down," "Keep It Greasy," and "Honey, Don't You Want a Man Like Me?" (where Helen Reddy is replaced by Twisted Sister as Betty's favorite group, while Betty's deranged suitor now describes her as a "Republican" instead of a "cunt"), Zappa does a speedy Devo-rendition of "Dinah-Moe Humm" that strips the funkiness right out of the song. He follows that with a faithful version of "Cosmik Debris," "Be in My Video" (with another mention of "mining the harbor"), "Dancin' Fool," and a showstopping rendition of "Whippin' Post."

Does Humor Belong in Music?, which would be released by MPI Video in 1986, featured no laser shows, smoke bombs, or overdubs. Zappa had no interest in the

THE MEEK SHALL INHERIT NOTHING

trappings of rock stardom. One interviewer in the video asks Zappa why, if he's so talented, doesn't he just write some No. 1 singles? He replies, evoking the short-lived superstardom of Michael Jackson, "Who wants to go through life with a small nose and wearing a glove on one hand?"

9

In 1982, a revolutionary technology had begun making a bold impact on the recording industry. Sony Records had inaugurated the compact disc, or CD. When this disc, containing digitally processed information, was placed inside a player, a laser beam would read and then transmit the musical information. The end result was music that sounded far clearer than vinyl, and without the wear and tear of scratches from repeated playing. And whereas the average album could hold forty minutes of music, the CD could handle seventy-five minutes. It would last forever and always sound as new as when you first purchased it. By 1984, album sales were lagging behind audiocassettes, and record companies decided to experiment and simultaneously release LP and CD versions of their latest offerings.

The format took off, despite the higher price of the CD. There were even problems meeting the demand. When record companies started to re-release older material on CD, they often didn't know where to find the original master tapes, so inferior analog recordings or deteriorated tapes were sometimes used during the digital mastering. And the CD picked up every nuance — the dropouts and distortions. Zappa, who had been working in the digital format since 1983, was annoyed by the tics and pops on his own vinyl records. "One of the things I always hated about making records was that no matter what the music sounded like coming through the speakers in the control room," Zappa remarked, "by the time you piled it onto analog tape, you had to live with the buildup of *hiss*."

Zappa had to live with this annoyance longer than he'd hoped. His current distributor, Capitol/EMI, was one of the last labels to jump on the CD bandwagon, and they had little interest in manufacturing Frank Zappa CDs. For Capitol/EMI, compact discs still didn't seem profitable enough, although their subsidiary Angel did put out *The Perfect Stranger* on CD in 1985, and EMI released a recording called *Does Humor Belong in Music?* in the U.K. and Germany in 1986. This disc contained no tracks from the Pier concert videotape, but instead was a gathering of songs from various stops on the 1984 tour. Given the ambivalence shown by Capitol/EMI toward the CD market, Zappa looked for a new home for his catalog.

At that time, a new corporation was starting up that embraced the new technology. Rykodisc, based in Salem, Massachusetts, entered the CD market in 1983, just as the format was starting to get its wings. "I hadn't even heard of them before," Zappa told Jim Bessman of *Billboard*. "Then here's this guy named Don Rose who knew something about my catalog and was interested, and it was like one cottage industry talking to another."

In January 1986, Rose, who was Ryko's president, had approached Zappa about signing with the label. "He was high among the list of appropriate artists for early CD release — and one of my first ideas," Rose explained. "He was a pioneer in digital recording. He had purchased one of the first Sony multitrack digital recording machines, and was one of the first popular artists to commit to digital." It also helped that Zappa had regained control of his entire output from the major labels.

The agreement they reached was for three years and covered a maximum of twenty-four releases. The first batch of Zappa CDs were released in fall 1986. They included a special two-for-one deal of *Over-nite Sensation* doubled with *Apostrophe (')*; *We're Only in It for the Money* doubled with *Lumpy Gravy*; *The Grand Wazoo*; *Thing-Fish*; *Shut Up 'n Play Yer Guitar*; *London Symphony Orchestra*; *Them or Us*; and a new album called *Frank Zappa Meets the Mothers of Prevention*. "It was probably the biggest back-catalog issue by a single artist on CD at the time," Rose told *Billboard*. "Frank insisted that they come out simultaneously for greater impact. We went along with him to find out that he was right."

Rather than just reissuing the discs, Zappa and Ryko added extra tracks. They also put together a promotional disc for radio airplay that contained familiar songs like "Peaches en Regalia," "Cosmik Debris," and "Dinah-Moe Humm." The timing was perfect — Zappa's entire career had been tracing the evolution of recording technology. He had begun using two-track at Studio Z in the early '60s, then four-track equipment, and he paved the way with eight-track, twelve-track, and sixteen-track before he jumped to twenty-four-track digital in the '80s. "This is what I've been waiting for since the day I got into the record business. The chance to present whatever quality of material I do to the consumer in its most listenable format."

Before long, he had the chance to finally restore *Zappa in New York* to his original intent — plus add new material. "I'm putting back what was left out, like 'Punky's Whips,'" Zappa said happily. "When you're dealing with vinyl and eighteen to twenty minutes a side, you sequence to accommodate that side length. But with a

THE MEEK SHALL INHERIT NOTHING

seventy-four-minute CD, you can give a much better illusion of live concert material. So I'm going back and restructuring it."

But just as Zappa was celebrating this newfound freedom, forces were brewing that would threaten to take it all away.

10

In 1984, a precociously gifted pop artist caused a stir in both the rock and R&B charts. Hailing from Minneapolis in the late '70s, the artist once known as Prince started his career as a multitalented guitarist, drummer, and pianist. Looking as androgynous and funky as Little Richard in Jimi Hendrix's duds, Prince wrote music that was sexually charged, playfully lewd, and enthusiastically impudent. In short, he was precisely the tonic the '80s needed. "Prince is bad," Johnny "Guitar" Watson remarked. "It's like seeing Sly [Stone], James Brown, and Jimi Hendrix all at once."

At a time when sex was again becoming a mortal sin, Prince turned it into salvation. His first album, *Dirty Mind* (1980), was a blissfully torrid celebration of eroticism. His band, both racially and sexually integrated, was supercharged, just like Sly & the Family Stone before them. Also like Sly, Prince mixed musical genres, which caused mass confusion at radio stations that couldn't decide whether he was R&B or rock. By the time his third album, *1999*, came out in 1982, however, it didn't seem to matter. The infectiously coy "Little Red Corvette" shot into the American Top 10. Thanks to MTV and the video culture it bred, Prince became the first black crossover artist to help broaden the network's musical palette.

At the height of his success in 1984, Prince made his movie debut in the R-rated *Purple Rain*. James Dean had made his astounding debut in *East of Eden* almost thirty years earlier, playing a misunderstood loner. Prince, calling himself the Kid, followed the same pattern, portraying a moody, struggling artist. *Purple Rain* mythologized his status in the pop world, and one song from its soundtrack generated the type of controversy that captured the attention of Frank Zappa — as well as the attention of Mary Elizabeth Gore, the wife of Tennessee senator Al Gore.

"Darling Nikki" had a reference to a young girl masturbating with a magazine. Gore, who went by her childhood nickname Tipper, had bought the *Purple Rain* soundtrack for her eight-year-old daughter. When the girl pointed out the offending line to her mother, Tipper was horrified. She decided something had to be done to protect children from the insidious influence of rock music. Gore would tell *Rolling Stone* in 1985, "We are not censors. We want a tool from the industry that is peddling this stuff to children, a consumer tool with which parents can make an informed decision on what to buy. What we are talking about is a sick new strain of rock music glorifying everything from forced sex to bondage to rape."

Tipper banded together with the wives of prominent senators to form the Parents' Music Resource Center (PMRC). They immediately formed a list known as the "Filthy Fifteen," a wide selection of targeted songs including "Darling Nikki," Sheena Easton's "Sugar Walls" (written and produced by Prince), Judas Priest's "Eat Me Alive," AC/DC's "Let Me Put My Love Into You," and W.A.S.P.'s "Animal (Fuck Like a Beast)." The list reached absurd levels of musical ignorance when tunes like "I'm on Fire" by Bruce Springsteen, Captain and Tennille's "Do That to Me One More Time," and the Jacksons' "Torture" were added.

The PMRC's first attempt to cajole the record industry occurred on May 31, 1985. They wrote to Stanley Gortikov, president of the Recording Industry Association of America (RIAA), to demand ratings for records similar to those used by the motion picture industry. They suggested Gortikov use typical ratings such as X for "profane or sexually explicit," O for "occult," D/A for "drugs or alcohol," and V for "violent." On August 5, Gortikov wrote them back — he refused to comply, though he left the door open for a sticker advising parents of an album's content.

At the same time as the PMRC was launched, a seemingly unrelated piece of legislation called House Resolution 2911 (H.R. 2911) was before the House. This bill was intended to tax blank cassette tapes so the record industry could recover costs from consumers recording copyrighted music. In other words, the mandate was designed to penalize the purchaser and fill the coffers of the record industry. If Congress could pass the legislation, these music czars would have received close to a quarter billion dollars. Not surprisingly (or even coincidentally), one of the bill's co-sponsors was none other than Senator Al Gore. The PMRC met with Edward Fritts, the president of the National Association of Broadcasters. When Fritts' wife attended a PMRC lecture, Fritts started requesting that record labels supply lyric sheets to radio stations to encourage program directors to choose what they would allow on-air. Zappa was appalled at Fritts' calling for programmers to capitulate to what Zappa referred to as "harpies."

Zappa wrote an open letter to the music industry magazine *Cashbox*, called "Extortion, Pure and Simple." He feared that the record industry, hungry for

THE MEEK SHALL INHERIT NOTHING

profits from H.R. 2911, would overlook this violation of the First Amendment. "What is apparently happening is a case of extortion, pure and simple: THE RIAA MUST TAP-DANCE FOR THESE WASHINGTON WIVES OR THE INDUSTRY'S BILL WILL FEEL THE WRATH OF THEIR FAMOUS HUSBANDS," Zappa wrote. "The PMRC makes no secret of their intentions to use 'special relationships' to force this issue. . . . Extortion is still an illegal act, and this issue goes beyond First Amendment considerations. No person married or related to a governmental official should be permitted to waste the nation's time on ill-conceived housewife hobby projects such as this." Charles Ives, earlier in the century, had railed against the cultivated "ladies" and "lily pads" whom he felt were poisoning the musical culture. Zappa lashed out at the "Washington wives" of the PMRC with a comparable venom:

> The PMRC's case is totally without merit, based on a hodge-podge of fundamentalist frogwash and illogical conclusions. For the elected officials who sit idly by while their wives run rabid with anti-sexual pseudo-Christian legislative fervor, there lurks the potential for the same sort of dumb embarrassment caused by Billy Carter's fascinating exploits . . . but when certain people's opinions have the potential to influence my life and the lives of my children because of their special access to legislative machinery, I think it raises important questions of law. Ronald Reagan came to office with the proclaimed intention of getting the federal government off our backs. The secret agenda seems to be not to remove it, but to force certain people to wear it like a lampshade at a D.C. Tupperware party. *Nobody looks good wearing brown lipstick.*

Zappa didn't mince words, either, with a media he found eager to jump in line to have some of that *brown lipstick* applied: "Shrieking in terror at the thought of someone hearing references to masturbation on a Prince record, [the PMRC] put on their *'guardian of the people'* costumes and the media comes running. It is an unfortunate trend of the '80s that the slightest murmur from a special interest group (especially when it has friends in high places) causes a knee-jerk reaction of appeasement from a wide range of industries that ought to know better."

Perhaps Zappa should have known better than to write a letter to President Ronald Reagan — the very guy who brought legitimacy to the moralist agenda.

After all, on *We're Only in It for the Money*, back in 1968, Zappa predicted the creation of a concentration camp for hippies called Camp Reagan, when Reagan was still governor of California. He must have been aware of Reagan's complicity with Senator Joseph McCarthy's House Un-American Activities Committee in fingering fellow actors he thought were Communist sympathizers. Zappa felt, though, that Reagan's "*personal* views on basic Constitutional issues" were "sincere."

Since the PMRC's hearing before Congress was set for September 19, Zappa wanted the president to speak out against it as unconstitutional. "If you support the PMRC (or the NMRC or any other fundamentalist pressure groups) in their efforts to perpetuate the myth that SEX EQUALS SIN, you will help to institutionalize the neurotic misconception that keeps pornographers in business," Zappa wrote in his appeal to Reagan. "In a nation where deranged pressure groups fight for the removal of sexual education from public schools, and parents know so little about sex that they have to call Dr. Ruth on TV for answers to rudimentary anatomical questions, it would seem infinitely more responsible for these esteemed wives and mothers to demand a full-scale Congressional demystification of the subject."

In August, while waiting for a response from the president, Zappa debated these issues with PMRC representative Kandy Stroud, on the CBS television news program *Nightwatch*. It was on this occasion he witnessed firsthand the double standard of the PMRC, and their true political ambitions. "We're in a room with fifty people in a live debate that they eventually cut down," Zappa told TV host Joan Rivers in 1986. "She had her own children sitting in the audience while she winds up reciting in front of them all the words that she thought should be hidden from them. Afterwards, she wanted a picture taken with me and the children. From that moment, I realized there was something strange going on here."

Not surprisingly, Reagan never answered Zappa's letter. Instead, he made a speech in Crystal City, Virginia, declaring everyone in the rock industry pornographers. The PMRC hearings went on as scheduled. Their proposals were heard by the Senate Commerce, Technology, and Transportation Committee, where five of the members had wives in the PMRC. But a wildly incongruous trio of speakers opposed the PMRC at the hearing: Frank Zappa, Dee Snider of Twisted Sister, and America's sunniest folk artist, John Denver. The media coverage was intense, with thirty video teams and fifty photographers. It no doubt seemed odd that none of the three musicians who gave depositions were even *on* the "Filthy Fifteen" list. As for Prince, the artist who sparked the controversy, he was nowhere in sight. "He

THE MEEK SHALL INHERIT NOTHING

went apeshit and sued some spaghetti company for calling their product 'Prince,'" Zappa wrote. "But [he] remained curiously silent during the record-ratings stuff."

In fact, none of the accused spoke out. Talk-show host Arsenio Hall quizzed Zappa about this a few years later. "In China, we saw a number of kids fighting for democracy, and they don't even know what it is," Zappa replied. "We have democracy here, and when it's threatened we just look around and wait for someone else to do something about it." Perhaps the biggest irony was that Zappa went out on a limb when he wasn't even targeted: "None of the artists who made it onto the list . . . had anything in their lyrics *even close* to the stuff in my catalog, and yet, for some reason, I was never accused of being a 'violator.'"

Zappa arrived in Washington wearing his hair short and dressed in a dark, conservative suit. This obviously wasn't the occasion for Dada stagecraft or elaborate freak-outs. This was a serious issue of social policy that concerned one of the fundamental rights of Americans. And Zappa, unlike the yippies of the late '60s, didn't wish to turn the proceedings into guerrilla theater that would only aid the other camp. When he began his deposition, Zappa immediately referred to the PMRC proposal as "an ill-conceived piece of nonsense which fails to deliver any real benefits to children." He then added, "It's my understanding that, in law, First Amendment issues are decided with a preference for the least restrictive alternative. In this context, the PMRC's demands are the equivalent of treating dandruff by decapitation."

Zappa was quick to point out that offended parents were simply not taking responsibility for their children's musical education. "No one has forced Mrs. Baker or Mrs. Gore to bring Prince or Sheena Easton into their homes. Thanks to the Constitution, they are free to buy other forms of music for their children. Apparently they insist on purchasing the works of contemporary recording artists in order to support a personal illusion of aerobic sophistication . . . the complete list of PMRC demands reads like an instruction manual for some sinister kind of 'toilet training program' to housebreak *all* composers and performers because of the lyrics of a few. Ladies, how dare you?"

If the public's mind was preoccupied with the horrors of "porn rock," Zappa said, then the tape taxation bill could be snuck through Congress. Reaching back into his own past, Zappa raised one of his more salient points: "Children in the 'vulnerable' age bracket have a natural love for music. If, as a parent, you believe they should be exposed to something more uplifting than 'Sugar Walls,' support music appreciation programs in schools. Why haven't you considered *your child's need for consumer information*? Music appreciation costs very little compared to sports expenditures. Your children have a right to know that something besides pop music exists." Zappa zeroed in on the secondary motives at work. "You can't distract people from thinking about an unfair tax by talking about music appreciation. For that you need *sex* . . . and *lots of it*." Zappa concluded, "Bad facts make bad law, and people who write bad laws are, in my opinion, more dangerous than songwriters who celebrate sexuality."

After Zappa spoke, many of the senators addressed him. Al Gore called himself a big fan; he said he used to listen to Zappa's music and found him to be an American original. (Zappa would later ask, "It has to make a guy wonder, you know, what albums was he listening to? Was it *Weasels Ripped My Flesh*, or maybe *Lumpy Gravy*, or what?") Gore said no legislation or regulation was being suggested. But Senator Slade Gorton admonished Al Gore; he called Zappa "boorish" and "insulting" and questioned whether he had any comprehension of the Constitution. Senator Paula Hawkins of Florida was outraged over lyrics that talked of "fire and chains and other objectionable tools of gratification." Meanwhile, Senator Ernest Hollings could only respond by calling rock music "outrageous filth."

Democratic Senator James Exon of Nebraska asked the most pertinent question of the day: "Mr. Chairman, if we're not talking about federal regulation, and we're not talking about federal legislation, what is the reason for these hearings?" It was an appropriate question because no legislation did follow. H.R. 2911 didn't pass through Congress. However, "Parental Advisory" stickers were required on rock albums as a way to classify them. Some civil libertarians didn't mind. Camille Paglia, for instance, said that "a ratings system is merely informational and infringes on no one's right to free speech."

Zappa, however, differed. "Record ratings are frequently compared to film ratings," he told Congress. "Apart from the quantitative difference, there is another that is more important: people who act in films are hired to 'pretend.' No matter how the film is rated, it won't hurt them personally. Since many musicians write and perform their own material and stand by it as their art (whether you like it or not), an imposed rating will stigmatize them as *individuals*." So Zappa devised his own warning sticker that told listeners that his album contained "material which a truly free society would neither fear nor suppress." He further advised that "Barking Pumpkin is pleased to provide stimulating digital audio entertainment for those of you who have outgrown the ordinary." Furthermore, "the language

THE MEEK SHALL INHERIT NOTHING

and concepts contained herein are GUARANTEED NOT TO CAUSE ETERNAL TORMENT IN THE PLACE WHERE THE GUY WITH THE HORNS AND THE POINTED STICK CONDUCTS HIS BUSINESS."

This wonderfully scornful sticker was unveiled on his next album, *Frank Zappa Meets the Mothers of Prevention* (November 1985). Although the album was inspired by the PMRC hearings, the opening track (on the U.S. vinyl release), "We're Turning Again," instead brings us back to the '60s. In what appears to be a rewrite of his anti-hippie harangue "Who Needs the Peace Corps?," "We're Turning Again" is a much more incisive investigation of the past:

> *They walkin' round*
> *With stupid flowers in their hair*
> *Stuff 'em up the guns*
> *And the servants of the law*
> *Who had to push 'em around*
> *And later mowed them down*
> *But they were full of all that shit*
> *That they believed in*
> *So what the fuck?*

While it might seem odd that a song lambasting hippie naïveté leads off an album attacking the PMRC, there is an important link. While the Reagan era was committed to wiping out '60s reform, there were movements afoot that sentimentalized aspects of that divisive decade by treating it romantically and nostalgically. Meanwhile, it was baby-boomer Democrats Al and Tipper Gore — and not Moral Majority Republicans — who led the charge to censor rock 'n' roll records. Zappa points out in "We're Turning Again" that some of the perceived impudence of the '60s generation was counterfeit; it, too, could become repressive and authoritarian.

Although the tone of the song appears self-satisfied, it is a pointed attack on how the pseudo-innocence and passivity of the hippie culture became an abdication of responsibility. Zappa is saying that the hippie belief in the goodness of putting flowers in National Guardsmen's guns avoided some ugly realities — especially since the song refers to Allison Krause, one of the victims of the Kent State shootings in 1970. The day before her death, Allison had put a flower in the barrel of a Guardsman's rifle, saying, "Flowers are better than bullets." When Zappa wrote "Mom & Dad" (which clearly anticipated Kent State) for *We're Only in It for the*

Money, he empathized with the kids because he recognized the injustice against them. Now, as the government was about to pass legislation subjecting musicians and composers to ratings and possible censorship, street protests were a thing of the past. Zappa was confronting during the Congressional hearing some of the same people who years earlier had stormed the barricades.

Although "We're Turning Again" (in the voice of Ike Willis' Thing-Fish) takes unforgiving shots at the rowdy behavior of '60s icons like Jimi Hendrix, Janis Joplin, Jim Morrison, Mama Cass Elliot, and Keith Moon, Zappa is hardly dismissive of them. In the song, he envisions going back in time to undo the tragic circumstances that ended their lives. Despite his caustic comments, he's aware that, compared to the music being heard today, something of true value had indeed been lost:

> *Everybody come back*
> *No one can do it like you used to*
> *If you listen to the radio*
> *And what they play today*
> *You can tell right away:*
> *All those assholes really need you!*

Zappa knew that the formatting of radio had changed not only the content of songs, but also the music. "Radio is consumed like wallpaper is consumed," Zappa told *The Progressive* in 1986. "You don't concentrate on the radio, you turn it on while you're working, you turn it on while you're driving. It's not like the old days when families sat around and looked at it. So the stations are formatted to provide a certain texture and ambience that will be consumed by people who view themselves in a certain way. Are you a yuppie? Well, you're going to listen to a certain texture because that reinforces the viewpoint you want to project to other people of who and what you are. It's the same thing as what you leave on your coffee table for people to discover when they come to your apartment. It's not a musical medium, it's an advertising medium."

"Alien Orifice," an instrumental featuring a polyphonic sampling of the synclavier, resembles the staccato tracks "RDNZL" and "The Black Page." "Yo Cats" parodies the session musicians who place the status of their career before the quality of the music they play. "Well, a 'Yo Cat' is *beyond* being a sight-reading cretin," Zappa told Matt Resnicoff of *Musician*. "A 'Yo guy' is part of this special species

THE MEEK SHALL INHERIT NOTHING

that popped up in Hollywood studios — the A-Team mentality. . . . A handful of guys get all the work. . . . And they do it day in, day out, three sessions a day; they grind it out. And one must ask at the end of the day: 'Was it music? Did they care?'" The song's mock jazz-lounge arrangement features keyboardist Tommy Mars and vocalist Ike Willis, who performs with a perfectly cadenced contempt:

> Get your fiddle, get your bow
> Play some footballs on your hole
> Watch your watch, play a little flat
> Make the session go overtime, that's where it's at.

If "We're Turning Again" was an ambivalent lament for a music that died, "Yo Cats" is a song about dead music . . . period:

> You have made it, you are cool
> You have been to the Berklee School
> You give clinics on the side
> Music has died and no one cried.

"What's New in Baltimore?" begins with a wistful melody that becomes an anthem featuring a rousing guitar solo by Zappa. In later performances, the tune would also have lyrics pertaining to his birthplace — and the location of his next fight against music censorship. "Little Beige Sambo," its title a not-so-subtle attack on the assimilation of the black middle class, is an instrumental scored for the synclavier and built on a breathtaking series of rippling glissandos that draw heavily on Conlon Nancarrow's player-piano experiments.

The album's final track, "Porn Wars," ties the album's themes back to the PMRC hearings. This extended piece draws on taped samples from the hearings that are speeded up, looped, and layered overtop one another, as the percussive sounds of the synclavier provide a bed. Zappa's tape experiments, which he first explored with a Dadaist splendor in the '60s, now anticipated the politically volatile work of dub poetry, hip-hop, and rap.

Using the voices of senators Hollings, Gore, Hawkins, Exon, and Paul Tribble Jr. in a manner that made their grandiose statements sound robotic and dehumanizing, Zappa brought out the chilling implications of their intent. He also deftly parodied the monotony of the endless fascination with the questionable lyrics, repeating loops of phrases like Hawkins' "Fire and chains and other objectionable tools of gratification in some twisted minds." Zappa included excerpts from *Thing-Fish*, plus unreleased dialogue from the piano of *Lumpy Gravy*, to round out his scathing attack. "Porn Wars" deserves a place alongside the 20th-century work of composers such as Steve Reich, who had much earlier worked ingeniously with tape-looped voices and music on *It's Gonna Rain* and *Come Out to Show Them*.

Assuming that European audiences wouldn't understand the references in "Porn Wars," Zappa replaced the track on European pressings of the record with songs that didn't appear on the U.S. release. "I Don't Even Care" is a chugging R&B number, sung by (and co-written with) Johnny "Guitar" Watson, who scats associative lyrics over a repeated melody and the background chanting (by Ray White and Bobby Martin) of "I don't even care." The song has such an angry bite that it's obvious the singer indeed *does* care, which makes the track truer to the punk aesthetic of refusal than most punk songs celebrated for doing so:

> *Listen! Standin' in the bread line*
> *Everybody learnin' lyin'*
> *Ain't nobody doing fine*
> *Let me tell you why*
> *I don't even care.*

"One Man — One Vote," "H.R. 2911," and "Aerobics in Bondage" are additional synclavier compositions that Americans didn't hear until the CD was fully restored by Rykodisc in 1995.

Frank Zappa Meets the Mothers of Prevention is not only an inspired polemic but a much fuller integration of Zappa's rock 'n' roll into the new technical frontier he embarked on with *The Perfect Stranger: Boulez Conducts Zappa*.

While Tipper Gore concentrated her latest campaign on instructing parents in the ways rock videos were becoming more gratuitously violent and demeaning to women, Zappa was getting plenty of media coverage exposing the true intentions of the PMRC. "The people who want to censor do not care about saving your children," Zappa told *Playboy*. "They care about one thing — getting reelected. Let's face it, folks: politicians in the United States are the scum of the earth. We have to go after them individually because they're varmints. The legislation they are passing, piece by piece, converts America into a police state." Much of Zappa's

THE MEEK SHALL INHERIT NOTHING

reasoning came from the fact that children wouldn't even understand the meaning of many of the words. "If a kid doesn't know what a blow job is, you can talk about blow jobs for weeks and he isn't going to be affected in any way about that," Zappa told journalist Bob Marshall. "Unless he knows what you're talking about, how's the lyric going to register? It's the same way if you're using the word *parsec* too many times in a sentence. Unless the person knows what it refers to, where's the harm?"

While Zappa was covering the political front in 1985, he hadn't neglected his artistic pursuits. Back in April, the Kronos Quartet, who had earlier commissioned a work from him, premiered the piece, "None of the Above." The Aspen Wind Quintet also premiered Zappa's "Times Beach" at the Alice Tully Hall in New York's Lincoln Center just days after the Kronos concert. The group's oboe player, Claudia Kuntz, explained that they decided to give Zappa the commission for one very good reason: "We felt that Frank Zappa was the quintessential American composer encompassing a wide range of musical experiences, and we felt that he was a really great musician of our time."

But soon this quintessential American composer was back on the political barricades. On February 14, 1986, his former home state of Maryland was holding a hearing to modify pornography statutes. Delegates Judith Toth and Joseph Owens brought before the Maryland State Senate Judiciary a bill to include records, tapes, and CDs under the modification. The Maryland House of Delegates had already passed the legislation, but the Senate vote to make it Maryland law had yet to take place. The day before the hearing, Zappa met informally with legislators in Annapolis to ask how they voted; if they had voted in favor of the bill, he offered them an opportunity to recant. He would read their confessions into the record the next day.

Toth echoed the same bombast as Tipper and the PMRC. She told the committee, "[We should] stop worrying about [children's] 'civil rights,' [and start] worrying about their *mental health*, and about the *health of our society*."

Zappa begged to differ. "There is no *sound* that you can make with your mouth, or *word* that will come out of your mouth, that is *so powerful* that it will *make you go to hell*," he replied. "You can't point to the statistics concerning '*people doing strange things in the vicinity of rock music*,' because all you've got to do is look around at all the normal kids who listen to it and live with it every day who do not commit suicide; they don't commit murder, and they grow up to be, in some cases, *legislators*."

Owens, the chair of the Judiciary Committee, called rock music "the worst type of child abuse we've got in this state, because it hits all the children. This is *mass child abuse*, and that's what it is. When they throw some of this *slime* at these children, it's abuse." Zappa was mystified. "To say that rock music is 'the worst form of child abuse' and 'mass child abuse' is *sky-high rhetoric*," he retorted. Toth was equally insistent, though, that much of rock was "pornography" and that her bill was "constitutional." Zappa took the bill apart piece by piece, examining (with his spiky, satirical precision) its more insidious aspects. "The bill seeks to keep people from seeing, renting, buying, or listening to material described as depicting 'illicit sex' — and the description of what constitutes 'illicit sex' as per this bill, includes *'human genitals in a state of sexual stimulation or arousal.'* Is that *illicit* sex? Perhaps in Maryland," Zappa said to much laughter.

At one point in the proceedings, Zappa turned one of the bill's more ridiculous components into a brief monologue that resembled one of Lenny Bruce's better broadsides. Zappa cited the bill's rejection of material that showed "nude or partially denuded figures, meaning less than completely and opaquely covered human genitals, pubic region, buttocks, or female breasts below a point immediately about the top of the areola." He then began his rather adroit rebuttal. "Now I *like nipples*. I think they look nice — and if you take off the nipple, which is the characterizing, determining factor, what you've got is a blob of *fat* there," Zappa remarked. The gallery started to crack up. "And I think when you're a baby, probably one of the first things that you get interested in is the *nozzle* right there. You get to have it *right up in your face*. You 'grow up with it,' so to speak — and then you grow up in the state of Maryland, and they won't let you see that brown nozzle anymore."

Although Toth's bill was defeated by the committee, she was determined to "bring the record industry to its knees." But she also failed in that endeavor. "My theory is, one of the reasons why [the record industry hasn't] fought all this labeling and censorship regulation is that anytime the record industry stands up on its hind legs, there's going to be one legislator who's gonna come along and recommend a payola hearing," Zappa told Drew Wheeler of *Billboard*. "And then everybody starts quaking in their boots." Zappa cited how, within a month of the PMRC hearings, Al Gore started his own — very brief — payola hearings.

But censorship isn't necessarily rooted in the introduction of a bill. "Censorship doesn't always work by someone taking a pencil and crossing a line out of a book, or forcing a record off the shelves," Zappa said in an interview with

THE MEEK SHALL INHERIT NOTHING

a Maryland TV station. "I recently offered the Peabody Conservatory my services to teach for a couple of weeks — but they were afraid that if they brought me in to teach, they would *lose funding from the state*, because the people who supported the censorship bill had the power to remove funding from the entire Peabody Conservatory."

The rest of 1986 was taken up with music. Zappa coproduced, with engineer Bob Stone, Dweezil's first album, *Havin' a Bad Day*, in August. And by November, he was preparing *The Old Masters, Box 2*, which included remastered albums beginning with *Uncle Meat* through *Just Another Band From L.A.* Another *Mystery Disc* was included that featured more unreleased material. Besides a generous selection from the Mothers of Invention's Royal Festival Hall concert with the BBC Orchestra in 1968, there were various outtakes, including the studio version of the prescient "Agency Man" (just in time for the Reagan era) and a track from the *Uncle Meat* sessions called "Wedding Dress Song/Handsome Cabin Boy," which was a hybrid of two sea chanteys. There was also a field recording telling the story of Willie the Pimp, plus some other live recordings from the Mothers' last tour.

Meanwhile, Zappa was still hard at work improving the synclavier technology at home. In 1986, he'd purchased a sampling device that enabled him to download sounds of various instruments, which he could then modulate however he chose. These samples, or "patches," could only replicate a few notes from each instrument. "Instead of having a patch that is just a saxophone, for example, you can have a patch that is a few notes of the sax, a few of a clarinet, a few of an oboe ... all different instruments, appearing on different notes, all of them on the keyboard," Zappa told *Keyboard* in 1987. The only instrument he didn't sample was his own guitar — but that was only because he wasn't yet happy with the technology. During the eight months Zappa spent enhancing the synclavier, he came up with his first album to win a Grammy Award.

Jazz From Hell (November 1986) was the first totally instrumental album of Zappa's music since his orchestral work on *The Perfect Stranger* and *London Symphony Orchestra*. "Instrumental music is a coming thing in pop," Zappa once told *The Guardian*, "but for years if you didn't sing a song, you didn't make a record. I'm forced to write words to put on a piece of music in order to make it accessible for an audience. I'm not going to deny anything I've said in my songs, but my main interest is in composing music. If I wanted to be a lyricist, I'd write books." Aside from one track, "St. Etienne," a guitar solo recorded at the Palais des Sports in St. Etienne, France, in May 1982, the album is performed on the synclavier.

"Night School" is a bright percussive piece starting off with eight chords that are sustained while Zappa provides an illustrative piano attack. From the opening composition, it's clear that Zappa improved the synclavier's ability to sample different kinds of sounds. "When I first started with the synclavier, we didn't have a very advanced sampling system," Zappa told *Keyboard*. "We had mono sampling with not a lot of RAM. Then, at great expense, I picked up the rest of the new sampling gear. We were doing stereo samples here in the studio before the synclavier even had stereo sampling. We figured out a way to do it, and it changed a lot of ways that you could write for the instrument."

The next track, "The Beltway Bandits" (named after the notorious Washington think-tank), is propelled by quick keyboard and percussion runs augmented by a contrasting squeaking noise resembling the opening of a rusty door.

"While You Were Art II" is essentially the guitar solo "While You Were Out" (from *Shut Up 'n Play Yer Guitar*), scored for the synclavier. Since the pitches in the melody are sharper and crisper than on the guitar solo, the tune has a more cascading quality. But the track also sparked a small controversy in the modern music community. A group called the Ear Unit commissioned a Zappa piece to be performed at the County Museum in Los Angeles. They specifically requested an arrangement of "While You Were Art II," so Zappa provided them with the score. Immediately, there were problems. "When it came time for them to pick up their parts, I played them the electronic realization on the synclavier so they could have an idea of how it should sound," Zappa said. "They said, 'We can't play this. We don't have enough time to rehearse it, because we're playing Elliott Carter, and that's hard, and we're playing this other thing, and that's hard, and we really don't have time to do this.' So I said, 'Well, you're either going to play it right or you're not going to play it at all.'"

Since the Ear Unit had already announced the piece in their program, they had to play it. So Zappa provided a solution. "The problem was solved in this manner: I said, 'Here's what we'll do — I'll have the computer simulate the sound of all the instruments in your group, and I'll make a digital recording of this piece.' . . . I had the computer print out the parts for each musician. Then I made an analog cassette for each musician of what his part was supposed to sound like. That frees the performer to do what he really wants to do, which is look good onstage. He doesn't have to worry about a single note, because the machine takes care of that. Since there were to have been some other pieces with amplification at the concert, I said, 'Okay, great, you're already going to have wires coming out of your instruments, so just go

THE MEEK SHALL INHERIT NOTHING

out there, push the button on the Sony PCM-F1 cassette, and out comes a perfect performance of the piece. You guys work on your choreography, and bingo, we have the missing link between electronic music and 'performance art.'"

But when it came time to play the cassette, it was in a format they couldn't use. Instead, they substituted one of the analog practice cassettes, which put a wall of hiss out into the audience. "I didn't go to the concert, but a friend of mine did," Zappa remarked. "He said you could hardly make out the music; it was a wall of hiss. Nobody knew that they didn't play a note. Not the man who runs the Monday Evening Concerts, not either of the reviewers for the *Los Angeles Times* or the *Herald Examiner*.... Eventually, a guy from the *Los Angeles Times* editorial department called me up (after the reviewer had said how this group 'played modern music with such vibrance'). He had heard from one of the members of the group what had actually happened, so he was a little embarrassed, and he's probably going to do another article about it. I said, 'Do me a favour. Before you write it, come over to my studio and let me play you a recording of the piece the way it was supposed to sound, so you know what you're talking about.'" The critic didn't bother to show up. "To me that's indicative of the type of attention that goes on in the modern music world," Zappa glumly concluded.

"Jazz From Hell" has many of the polyphonic textures of Zappa's later guitar solos, while "G-Spot Tornado" has some of the jumping exuberance of an Eastern European folk melody that's been run through a coffee percolator. The percussive sounds are brittle, and the voice samples sound like they are gasping for breath. It's a brisk, astonishing piece of music.

"Damp Ankles" is an electronic samba that opens with the sound of a water hose — the title refers to a friend of Zappa's who works in a psychiatric institution. Apparently, the patients showed their deep appreciation of this man's care by licking his ankles. "St. Etienne" is a capacious number that contrasts the constricting sounds of the synclavier with live musicians playing. The interplay between Zappa's guitar, Wackerman's drums, and Thunes' bass provides a similar texture to the other pieces on the album, but the track is more open-ended and intimate. "Massagio Galore" is a galloping finale that contains a few voice-sampled "Hi-ho Silvers" (in all likelihood provided by Ike Willis).

One of the more hideous ironies of the whole PMRC business is that Zappa's *Jazz From Hell* had to carry a new warning sticker — even though it was an instrumental album with no "offensive" words. As Ben Watson points out, it became obvious that the PMRC were "out to X-rate certain artists, not particular records."

Nevertheless, even as the album was awarded a Grammy, Zappa figured that the music industry rewarded him as a ploy to silence him. *Jazz From Hell* may not have contained any words, but Zappa certainly wasn't finished talking.

Throughout much of 1987, Zappa appeared on talk shows, continuing his fight against censorship. He also sent out censorship information packages and press clippings, called Z-Pacs, through Barking Pumpkin. "I've spent up to $70,000 of my own money that I've put into a combination of my travel, printing costs, and phone bills just to keep pressure on the other side," Zappa said. "I've done maybe three hundred talk shows and interviews. And those Z-Pacs are still going out the door. I will continue to do it as long as people call up." As Zappa was making the transition from records to CDs, he also began releasing videos. He created a company called Honker Home Video — named after his huge nose. When Sony had refused to issue Zappa's *Does Humor Belong in Music?* video without a warning sticker, MPI Video stepped in to distribute it. Zappa put together his final cut of *Uncle Meat*, the three-hour version of *Baby Snakes*, and *Video From Hell* — a compilation of clips that were a visual equivalent to a Zappa album — for a June 1987 release.

By September, a new digital editing technology caught up to Zappa. Finally, he was able to release *London Symphony Orchestra, Vol. II*. When *Jazz From Hell* came out, many critics complained that the sound of the album was too "cold," "calculating," and lacking in "the human element." Since Zappa's concerns were more musical than humanistic, he took great umbrage. In the spirit of Varèse, Zappa sought a perfect harmony between technology and musical performance that didn't allow for the sentimental attachments listeners can have to performers. "Rock journalists (especially the British ones) who have complained about the 'coldness,' the 'attempts at perfection,' and missing 'human elements' in *Jazz From Hell* should find *LSO Vol. II* a real treat," Zappa wrote in the liner notes. "It is infested with wrong notes and out-of-tune passages." Despite the advances in editing technology, which allowed Zappa to cover up some of the errors, the treacherous cretins still leaked through.

"Bob in Dacron" is a ballet score that had already been performed by the Berkeley Symphony (with Kent Nagano conducting). Though it has a story, about "an urban scoundrel (Bob) in his quest for mid-life erotic gratification," the piece is atmospheric, and not as pointedly dramatic as some of Zappa's other scores. The composition builds on the same ideas he expressed in songs like "Broken Hearts Are for Assholes" and "Dancin' Fool." When the piece was performed by the Berkeley Symphony, a life-size puppet, playing the bartender, gets so frantic

THE MEEK SHALL INHERIT NOTHING

supplying local yuppies with alcohol that "he literally splits in half, continuing his shift with entrails dangling behind."

"Strictly Genteel," originally the finale for *200 Motels*, was ruined by the drunken trumpeters during the re6cording. Despite Zappa's fifty edits to hide their completely out-of-tune notes, their hideous lack of rhythm still diminishes the work. "Bogus Pomp" (also containing themes from *200 Motels*) fares better because while it's a deliberate parody of romantic film-score themes, it contains some lovely romantic music. The principal violinist plays an exquisite solo that wouldn't sound out of place in one of Ralph Vaughan Williams' pastoral scores. The orchestra sounds more comfortable bringing the pomp to "Bogus Pomp" than they do in any of the other pieces. *London Symphony Orchestra, Vol. II* would be the last orchestral artifact from Frank Zappa for years, but the best was yet to come.

11

After making so many television appearances during the PMRC period, Zappa had developed a deeper interest in the medium. One idea he developed was a late-night talk show for adults. It was to be called *Night School* (the opening theme is the same-titled composition on *Jazz From Hell*) and was targeted for ABC television. Zappa would be the host in Los Angeles, while CBS newsman Daniel Schorr, based in Washington, would be a regular reporter known as Professor of Recent History. He would run raw news footage to illustrate to viewers what other news agencies had deleted and why. Even though Schorr was initially skeptical about the venture, he soon had a change of heart. "Now I had, in my youth, been a part-time music critic for the *New York Times*," Schorr told *Musician*. "I like music but I'm very conservative about it, and actively dislike rock in general. In the course of our first talk, I began asking [Zappa] about music and what relationship he thinks his work has — as politely as I could put it — to the great tradition of music. As we got into talking about it, I realized this man knew an enormous lot about Bach, Mozart, and the classic tradition. It wasn't like he had been born yesterday into the rock world, but had come to rock from a great background of music."

Zappa wanted the previous day's news footage converted into three-minute rock videos that he called "News in Heavy Rotation." He also required a live band — ten musicians and three singers — with the broadcast in stereo. The group would also take part in "a cheesy sitcom segment" called "The Future Family."

Night School was to feature a late-night psychology course that would deal with sexual topics — for the first month their field of study would be "The Human Breast — Why Do Americans Like Them So Much?" And, in a parody of educational television, Zappa would give out degrees. "Degrees will be offered for twenty-five dollars," Zappa wrote in his proposal. "Call the *Night School* credit-card hot line and tell the nice lady you need to graduate in a hurry. By return mail you will receive a framed degree that looks better than a real one. For one hundred dollars you can graduate *cum laude*. Each individual *Night School* course offers a degree, so you might want several for your office. We expect that the completion certificate in THE HUMAN BREAST study course to be a favorite." To the surprise of no one, ABC turned down the show.

Zappa continued to appear on talk shows in 1986, discussing censorship. He turned up on CNN's *Crossfire* with John Lofton, where they spent a half-hour calling each other names. Johnny Carson gave Zappa a ten-minute slot on *The Tonight Show* to talk about censorship; and ABC's nightly news show *Nightline*, with Ted Koppel, had Zappa on for eleven minutes. In Canada, CBC Radio's national phone-in show *Cross-Country Checkup* had Zappa discuss with callers whether rock albums should be censored — oddly enough, several educators called up in favor of censorship. Meanwhile, a couple of police officers, who had patrolled many of the rowdiest rock concerts, didn't see how this music had any significant impact on the behavior of fans.

But it was Zappa's appearance on Fox Television Network's *The Late Show*, with Joan Rivers, in November 1986 that raised the possibility for Zappa to have his own show. When Rivers was fired the following May, Fox was looking for a fill-in host. After trying out various television and film stars, Fox asked Zappa to appear on June 12. He agreed, thinking he could do a serious talk show. He suggested as guests Prince, Wynton Marsalis, and the band Cameo. Although Fox was impressed, none of them were available. Zappa then suggested his synclavier as a guest, but Fox wanted to know what they'd have for visuals while Zappa's machine was noodling away. He came up with the modern dance troupe Pilobolus, who specialized in contortionism and acrobatics, but they were also unavailable.

Zappa then recommended going to a vaudeville agency for jugglers, or possibly a "dog show." Fox felt this would turn their program into something resembling *The Gong Show*. And when Zappa talked about changing the look of the show by using hand-held cameras and wide-angle lenses, used today with fresh abandon on programs like *The Conan O'Brien Show*, Fox nixed that idea as well.

THE MEEK SHALL INHERIT NOTHING

"They seemed to have this deep-seated belief that the show was really correct," Zappa told Deborah Caulfield of the *Los Angeles Times*. "They seemed to think, 'This is what the public wants; it's just an accident the ratings are in the toilet.'"

Zappa finally suggested booking Daniel Schorr of CBS and Gerard Thomas Straub, who had been fired from Pat Robertson's *The 700 Club* and was the author of an exposé on televangelism called *Salvation for Sale*. Fox approved Schorr — but just barely. They were, however, adamantly opposed to Straub. Producer John Scura told Zappa, "People want laughs; they'll be nodding out." Zappa didn't agree: "What I would have brought on was not going to be 'educational'; I perceived it as good entertainment. But they seem to think that anybody who watches late-night television has a brain the size of a microbe."

Fox eventually took a pass on Zappa, opting for a rerun in his place. "It's par for the course," Zappa told the *Los Angeles Times* with a chuckle. "After all, this is Hollywood. And that's television." For Zappa, it wasn't a huge loss, because he was just starting to consider touring for the first time in four years. "I keep [a guitar] sitting next to my chair in the studio," Zappa told *SongTalk*, "and I occasionally pluck around on it, but I'm only barely getting some calluses back." Zappa's last rock 'n' roll tour in 1988 — for all its musical proficiency and brilliance — would be a disaster.

CHAPTER SIX

YOU CAN'T DO THAT ON STAGE ANYMORE
(1988-1993)

> *In the '80s, it was not fashionable to stand up for anything. It was a decade where bending over was the thing you did to get ahead. The way up the ladder was with your mouth attached to the anal orifice of the creature — whatever its denomination — in front of you. It was pushing upward and sucking at the same time as you went up the rungs, with the junk bonds spilling out of your pockets, and your mind reeling from the LSD experience that you had in the '60s. The yuppie lived in a special type of aquarium created for him by the Reagan administration. . . . People wish the good old days of the '80s would come back — when there was still something to steal.*
>
> FRANK ZAPPA, quoted in *Drowning in the News Bath*, by John Winokur

> *In the '60s, we believed in a myth — that music had the power to change people's lives. Today, people believe in a myth — that music is just entertainment.*
>
> STANLEY BOOTH, from the afterword to *The True Adventures of the Rolling Stones*

1

In 1988, the right-wing policies of the Reagan era, coupled with rising fundamentalist Christian factions, dominated the Republican Party and, by extension, cultural and political life in the U.S. Whatever Zappa thought of the counterculture, the passivity toward forces trying to undermine Constitutional freedom he found intolerable. Zappa wanted to go back on the road, but he also wanted to be more politically explicit than on previous tours. He considered setting up voter registration booths at each of the shows.

"The United States is the least-registered industrial country on Earth," Zappa told the journalist Miles in 1990. "Something like a mere 15 per cent of the eligible voters between eighteen and twenty-four cast ballots in the 1984 elections. . . . I don't believe an American has a right to complain about the system if he can vote and doesn't." Zappa defended his reasoning to Jane Pauley of *The Today Show*, a year after the tour: "I think that it's important for people to wake up to the fact that in the United States, politics has turned into something . . . not nice. And you need to introduce to the political process new people who might take it seriously."

Besides, 1988 was an election year, and many thought the Democrats could mount an alternative. "The problem with most of the decisions of the last eight years in the Reagan administration is they're all ideologically based and very seldom have the policy decisions been based on practicality, or far long-range thinking," Zappa told journalist Bob Marshall. "It's just been based on whether or not the rhetoric that appears in the news that day is in phase with conservative ideology, or appeasement to certain interest groups. It's not good politics in the true sense of the word. And another political act that you have to bear in mind is as long as people have the right to vote, the vote should be cast in a situation where the person with the ballot in his hand has access to enough information to make a practical decision. And that's where I come in."

From a purely political standpoint, Zappa wasn't naive about the left or the right, either — especially given his experiences with student radicals in the '60s. He looked clearly at how both sides affected an artist trying to work in complete freedom.

"The environment that is hostile to dreamers is always the environment that is run by right-wing administrations because in order for the right-wing administration to maintain its fiction, it has to be ideologically pure and that ideology does not admit for creativity," Zappa remarked. "There is nothing creative about a right-wing administration. The whole goal of it is to freeze time and to move things backward. So, obviously the people who are most at risk, whenever there is a right-wing administration sitting in place, is anybody who is an intellectual dreamer or creative person in any field. They are at risk because they pose a threat to the administration."

But he saw the left as no more friendly to creative minds. "I don't think that the left wing is anything to invest in," Zappa said. "The difference here is that the

YOU CAN'T DO THAT ON STAGE ANYMORE

left has often employed artists and creative people in order to further their goals. For the right-wing administration, the artists and dreamers are a threat to their way of life. And for the left-wing guys, the artists and dreamers are propaganda. So there's a danger coming from both directions. One side would like to snuff you out and the other side would like to co-opt you and usurp you in order to have you do stuff and promote their ideals. So, anybody who's got an imagination has to watch out for both sides. There's only one place where you're safe and that's in the middle."

Zappa saw himself as a practical conservative, distinct from the predatory ideological namesakes who dominated the Republicans in the '80s. "True conservatism is the guy who wants smaller government and lower taxes, and that's me," Zappa said. "And everything else that has been applied to that term has more to do with religious fanaticism and fascist politics, and stuff like that." So, combining some of the tactics of American showbiz pizzazz, Zappa looked at putting together a big-band tour that could, at least in spirit, approach the political theater of Kurt Weill. Rehearsals for the "Broadway the Hard Way" tour began in the fall of 1987.

The initial catalyst for the excursion was a proposed reunion of Zappa with Flo & Eddie. "The idea first came from Flo & Eddie," Zappa explained to *Boston Rock*. "Volman called and said we should go on the road again because we had a lot of fun. I spent $5,000 and rented a rehearsal hall." At first, the band consisted of Tommy Mars, Ike Willis, Bobby Martin, Ray White, Ed Mann, Scott Thunes, and Chad Wackerman. But Mars soon fled, citing difficulties with Thunes. White got summoned to take a phone call — and then never came back.

Flo & Eddie also decided that the times had definitely changed for them since they last sang about Mud Sharks and Bwana Diks. Since that version of the Mothers broke up after Zappa's accident in 1971, Flo & Eddie had cleaned up their image. After doing backup for Bruce Springsteen on his 1981 hit single, "Hungry Heart," they moved on to writing for children's television, plus they had their own radio show in L.A. "We got very, very mainstream, and by the time Frank came back to us and asked us to rejoin the group, we had finally broken all those negative barriers," Flo & Eddie told *Society Pages*. So, although a reunion had been the reason for the tour, they left the group after attending a couple of rehearsals.

Flo & Eddie couldn't be replaced, but with Ray White gone, Zappa needed another guitarist. Another Long Island prodigy, Mike Keneally, fit the bill. Keneally, twenty-seven when he joined the band, had been practicing Zappa songs on his guitar since he was thirteen. It was by chance one day in October 1987, while calling the hotline number for Barfko-Swill, that he heard Zappa was auditioning guitarists for an upcoming tour. Keneally called the studio and told the secretary he knew all the guitar parts to Zappa's songs, and that he also played keyboards and sang. When Keneally got to the audition, it helped that he was so versatile. "The first time I spoke to Frank on the phone he asked me, 'Can you play the middle section of 'Inca Roads' on keyboard?' I said, 'Sure.' Then I had to rush to actually learn it so I wouldn't get caught," Keneally told *The Black Page* in 1989.

In fact, Keneally had been a pianist since he was seven. While playing keyboards in his own band, Drop Control, he decided that picking up a guitar might not be a bad idea. "I decided a good discipline exercise would be to learn all the guitar parts on all the Gentle Giant albums." The turning point for Keneally, though, was Zappa's Halloween show at the Palladium in 1981. "I'd seen Steve [Vai] play with Frank in 1980, but the material in the show was more vocal-oriented," Keneally recalled in *Guitar Player* in 1999. "But the second song in the [Halloween] concert was 'Montana,' and when they got to the 'I'm plucking the old dental floss' section, Steve was super-high in the mix, playing this incredibly complex melody. That melody was not written to be played on the guitar. . . . I heard that and realized for the first time that it was possible to play that kind of stuff on a guitar."

In the final weeks of rehearsals, Zappa added a horn section to augment the band: Zappa alumni Walt Fowler on trumpet and keyboards and Bruce Fowler on trombone; Paul Carmen on alto sax; Albert Wing on tenor sax; and Kurt McGettrick on baritone sax. Through most of the '80s, Zappa had contented himself with synthesized horn sounds, but with a five-man reed section he could perform more complex horn arrangements. He also brought his synclavier along for the tour to play back samples he had of the PMRC hearings and TV evangelists.

The tour looked promising, but there had been ominous signs from the moment Mars left on account of Thunes. Thunes had become the clonemeister, a role once held by Arthur Barrow, but his rugged workouts with the group didn't go down well with many of the members. Thunes worked the band for ten-hour shifts five days a week, over a four-month period. By the time the group hit the road on February 2, 1988, they might have been musically fit, but emotionally they were fit to be tied. Yet, despite the internal struggles, the band was a glorious unit to behold. The tour also offered a range of Zappa material no other group had ever

YOU CAN'T DO THAT ON STAGE ANYMORE

been able to replicate onstage. "All those little effects and things coming in, that's the way it was on the live show," Zappa told *Guitarist* in 1993. "We had three stations generating samples; there was Ed Mann, who had this whole vocabulary of dog barks and bubbles and weird shit. Then there was Chad Wackerman, who had all these strange percussion things hooked up to a big rig, and then there was the synclavier, which I could play when I wasn't playing the guitar." The 1988 ensemble emerged as a sophisticated touring outfit that merged Kurt Weill's political awareness with the musical antics of Spike Jones.

The tour also featured some memorable guests and events. At the February 10 show in Washington, Daniel Schorr turned up to sing "Danny Boy"; in Chicago, Sting joined the group to sing a song by the Police, "Murder by Numbers," that evangelist Jimmy Swaggart said was written by Satan. "I'd never met him before and ran into him at the hotel," Zappa explained to Chicago's WBAI Radio. "So I invited him to the show because he had a day off. He came down and watched the first part of the show from the audience. Then, during the intermission, he came backstage and I asked him if he wanted to come out onstage and do something with us. At first, he said no, he didn't think that there was a way to do it. And I told him that there was no way that he could lose because this band will always make you look good." At the Nassau Coliseum, in late March, Zappa included the L.I. Ballet Company, an ad hoc collection of fans and freaks who wore aprons and danced while the band played "Packard Goose" from *Joe's Garage*. All the while, Zappa was registering voters in every city while performing original songs that would make up the bulk of a new live album.

Broadway the Hard Way, released in October 1988, is a politically charged collection of songs that take on a variety of relevant sacred cows of the '80s: Elvis ("Elvis Has Just Left the Building"), Michael Jackson ("Why Don't You Like Me?"), Wall Street ("Planet of the Baritone Women"), Jesse Jackson ("Rhymin' Man"), the Christian Right ("Jesus Thinks You're a Jerk"), and the Republican Party ("Dickie's Such an Asshole," "When the Lie's So Big").

Zappa begins "Elvis Has Just Left the Building" by quoting the famous title phrase echoed by PA announcers at Presley's concerts after the final encore. Zappa's tone suggests that rock 'n' roll itself — as we now know it — has left the building. Sung by Mike Keneally, in a voice that resembles country singer Johnny Cash (who began his career at Sun Records in the '50s with Elvis), the tune spells out the sordid details of Elvis' last days at Graceland:

He gave away Cadillacs once in a while
Had sex in his underpants
Yes, he had style!
Bell-bottom jump-suits?
That's them in a pile
But he don't need 'em now
'Cause he's making Jesus smile!

Far from being just a cocky put-down of the King, Zappa's song shows us just how pathetically tragic the pantheon of rock had become by the late '80s. Yet he harbored no particular love for Elvis. "No, the only record of Elvis I ever liked was 'Baby, Let's Play House,'" Zappa told biographer Michael Gray. "I was fantastically offended when he did 'Hound Dog' in '56, because I had the original record by Willie Mae Thornton and I said, 'How can anybody *do* that?' Anybody who bought that Elvis record was missing out because they've obviously never even heard Willie Mae Thornton's."

Although Zappa's purist assessment of Elvis ignores Presley's enormous impact on American music, it grows from Zappa's general contempt for Southern white country and blues. His identification with black music (and Willie Mae Thornton's robust and angry original take on "Hound Dog") is based on the notion of being the outsider in America. In Zappa's mind, Elvis was the outsider who's desperate to be on the inside. Which is why his fate in "Elvis Has Just Left the Building" is somewhat less than charitable.

"Planet of the Baritone Women" is a further attack on yuppie careerism, this time focusing on the female corporate camp. The song is a hilarious polka that includes a wailing cadenza from Robert Martin, and a dig at the Bangles' 1985 hit "Walk Like an Egyptian." Zappa's attitudes, borne out of a conservative Italian-American male perspective, stem from his belief that women who climb the corporate ladder (as did Rhonda in *Thing-Fish*) are asexual creatures:

They sing about wheat
They sing about corn
They sing about places
Where women was born

YOU CAN'T DO THAT ON STAGE ANYMORE

They sing about hate!
They sing about fear!
It seems like they all got
A pretty good ear.

Gail Zappa shares her husband's views on this subject. In an interview with Victoria Balfour for the book *Rock Wives*, Gail explained why she had no desire to go out and get a nine-to-five job. "Frank would have seriously questioned it," she remarked candidly. "And I think there's a real problem today that women feel compelled to have jobs. I think if most women sat down and asked themselves why in hell they want to work — why do they want to wear that suit? Why do they want to carry that briefcase? What the fuck does it mean? I think it means that they're competing with their husbands; they have to have some status in their marriage."

Whether or not one agrees, Gail raises an interesting issue concerning the creation of personal identity. Even if she doesn't account for the many career women who aren't married to men— but are hitched instead to their jobs — there is still a level of conforming to an idea of status that can create a false sense of security. Which may be why, at the end of the song, Zappa quotes from Gounod's *Funeral March of the Marionette*, driving home the point about the desire for uniformity in the corporate world.

If "Planet of the Baritone Women" savages the female careerist, "Any Kind of Pain" empathizes with the female victim of corporate ladder-climbing. Here, she is the '80s model of beauty who was "invented in a grim little office on Madison Ave." Not only is she designed with a perfect set of eyes, perfect lips, and a body that shows that "she gets nothin' to eat," she can "take any kind of pain" from the male species. But unlike the women from "Broken Hearts Are for Assholes" or "The Legend of the Illinois Enema Bandit," she receives a certain empathy from Zappa:

She has moved up now
She's come a long way
They give her bunches of words she can say!
If she's in a bold mood
Confinement loaf sounds good
That's right

She's wrong!
Let's end
Her song.

"Confinement loaf" refers to a bean by-product administered to prisoners who were acting up. It had the effect of making them mellow and passive. At one 1988 concert, Zappa asked, "How long will it be before confinement loaf finds its way into U.S. high schools?" Confinement loaf seems an evil fulfillment of what Zappa satirized a few years earlier in *Thing-Fish*, when the prisoners were fed mashed potatoes with "galoot cologne" that turned them into Mammy Nuns.

"Jesus Thinks You're a Jerk" is a classic piece of Americana that brilliantly takes apart the corrupt world of TV evangelism, naming all of its practitioners while tying it intrinsically to the bedrock of the American experience. Alexis de Tocqueville, in his first volume of *Democracy in America* (1835), had pointed out that religious freedom was meant to mean religious diversity and toleration. He wrote that religion was important to the democratic ideal because it "facilitates the use of free institutions." But in the '80s, President Ronald Reagan created a conjunction between religion and politics that was hardly diverse or free. Christian fundamentalism, which had partially grown out of the racial and religious bigotry of the old South, was now integrated with free-enterprise politics.

In the late '70s, Jim and Tammy Faye Bakker set up their PTL (Praise the Lord) Club, a tax-exempt television ministry in Charlotte, North Carolina. By the mid-'80s, they were bilking funds from American citizens to build Heritage U.S.A., a Christian theme park, as well as to add to their personal coffers. Meanwhile, Rev. Jimmy Swaggart, the cousin of Jerry Lee Lewis, had been broadcasting sermons on radio and television to over 145 countries from Baton Rouge, Louisiana, as well as running a Bible college and a recording studio. But in 1985, he borrowed $2 million from his ministry to build three huge mansions in the wealthiest subdivision of Baton Rouge. Jerry Falwell, in Lynchburg, Virginia, was a well-established minister who also had a popular television show, *Old Time Gospel Hour*, that reached over 1.5 million subscribers each week on the Liberty Broadcasting Network. Falwell lived in an opulent house and flew his own jet — all paid for by his ministry. Then there was Pat Robertson, who was the son of a Democratic U.S. senator, who hosted *The 700 Club* in Virginia Beach, Virginia, on the Christian Broadcasting Network. CBN had over 33 million subscribers by the mid-'80s; it was the largest cable system in America. Robertson lived in a

YOU CAN'T DO THAT ON STAGE ANYMORE

$400,000 home owned by the network, and had use of a country home in Hot Springs, Virginia.

Haynes Johnson, in *Sleepwalking Through History*, explains how these individuals managed to questionably raise such an exorbitant amount of money for personal gain. "The complex fundraising network they employed through the public airwaves," Johnson writes, "was made possible by the permissive, deregulated environment of the '80s." But in 1988, the aspirations of these televangelists started to wane — and Zappa was there to celebrate their defeat. In 1987, Jim Bakker of PTL was embroiled in a sexual scandal. An affair with Jessica Hahn, a church volunteer, led to him paying out $265,000 in hush money taken from ministry fundraising. He had also been linked to homosexual relations with male staff. Swaggart had been caught with a prostitute in a New Orleans hotel, where he'd been performing every kind of sexual act but the deed itself. Robertson decided to run for president, but not as a Democrat like his father. He used his ministry to preach from the pulpit of Reagan. In "Jesus Thinks You're a Jerk," Zappa used some of the same compositional tools that Charles Ives employed, creating a vivid picture of American corruption. He wedded a variety of musical themes from the American past, including "The Old Rugged Cross," Stephen Foster's "Dixie," Franz von Suppé's "Light Cavalry Overture," the *Twilight Zone* theme, and (of course) "Louie Louie."

Zappa had constructed this song from ideas already expressed in "Cosmik Debris," "Dumb All Over," "Heavenly Bank Account," and "The Meek Shall Inherit Nothing," but musically it's more complex and more politically volatile, because he names names. First, he takes on Jim and Tammy Faye, attacking their sexual hypocrisy, which was disguised by their piety:

> There's an ugly little weasel 'bout three-foot-nine
> Face puffed up from cryin' 'n lyin'
> 'Cause her sweet little hubby's
> Suckin' prong part-time
> (In the name of the Lord)
>
> Get a clue, little shrew
> Oh yeah, oh yeah
> Jesus thinks you're a jerk.

Then Pat Robertson's plans get a full airing:

> *Robertson says that he's* The One
> *Oh he sure is*
> *If Armageddon*
> *Is your idea of family fun*
> *An' he's got some planned for you!*

Zappa later ties the Moral Majority's policies to their Ku Klux Klan heritage by borrowing an unforgettable image from Billie Holiday's "Strange Fruit":

> *If you ain't Born Again*
> *They wanna mess you up,*
> *screamin'*
> *"No abortion, no-siree!*
> *"Life's too precious, can't you see!"*
> *(What's that hangin' from the neighbor's tree?)*
> *Why it looks like "colored folks" to me.*

Eric Buxton, a Zappa fan, then takes the stage to outline Pat Robertson's dubious political plans while the band plays the *Twilight Zone* theme behind him. Finally, Zappa defines the old rugged cross as one "that burns on somebody's lawn" and says "it still smells rotten." And with the rising chords of "Louie Louie," Zappa and Ike Willis do their final raised-thumb salute to Jim and Tammy Bakker:

> *Jim and Tammy!*
> *Oh baby!*
> *You gotta go!*
> *You really got to go!*

"Jesus Thinks You're a Jerk" is the darker version of Elvis Presley's "An American Trilogy" (where songwriter Mickey Newbury included "Dixie," "Battle Hymn of the Republic," and "All My Trials"). Rather than nostalgically celebrate the country through a combined history of its songs, Zappa exposes the corruption that those songs continue to hide.

YOU CAN'T DO THAT ON STAGE ANYMORE

"Dickie's Such an Asshole," a revival of the Watergate-era song, links us to the present with "When the Lie's So Big." This scathing indictment of the Republican Party carries the same passionate indignation that Ives showed in *Sneak Thief*, a work he wrote to protest the German kaiser attacking Belgium in August 1914. While Zappa calls Pat Robertson a "dangerous cretin," Ives equated the cowardice of the kaiser with the kitsch of German romanticism. Zappa, like Ives, quotes patriotic American songs while vilifying the ruling party:

When the lies get so big
And the fog gets so thick
And the facts disappear
The Republican Trick
Can be played out again
People, please tell me when
We'll be rid of these men.

The Democratic Party, however, doesn't escape the skewer on *Broadway the Hard Way*. Another evangelical figure, Jesse Jackson, who took a serious run at the Democratic presidential nomination, turned out to be as ethically compromised as his brothers of the cloth. Zappa was skeptical about at least one of Jackson's claims. "An article raised some questions about whether or not Martin Luther King actually died in Jesse's arms," Zappa told *Playboy*. "There were reports that Jackson dipped his hands into King's blood or even used chicken blood and rubbed it on his shirt, which he wore for a few days afterward as he met the media. So I did this song about the idea of communicating through nursery rhymes, as Jackson is prone to do."

"Rhymin' Man" is a country tune — filled with rhymes — that once again features Keneally in the vocal guise of Johnny Cash. While "Jesus Thinks You're a Jerk" adroitly deploys a vast selection of American songs, "Rhymin' Man" uses an arsenal worthy of Spike Jones. While running through Jackson's career, Zappa inserts excerpts from Chopin's *Piano Sonata Opus 35* and the themes from the television shows *Mission Impossible* and *The Untouchables*. The song reaches its peak, though, when recounting Jackson's meeting with Nation of Islam leader Louis Farrakhan, where Jackson described New York as "Hymie-town." Quick musical quotes follow each lyric:

Rhymin' Man made a run for prez
("Happy Days Are Here Again")
Farrakhan made him a clown
("Entry of the Gladiators")
Over there near Hymie-town
("Hava Nagila")
Said he was a diplomat
("Hail to the Chief")
Hobbin' an'-a-nobbin' with Arafat
("Happy Days Are Here Again")
Castro was simpatico
("La Cucuracha")
But the U.S. voters, they said, "No!"

Though "Trouble Every Day," "Dumb All Over," and "Stevie's Spanking" have the rhythmic punch of rap music, "Promiscuous" is Frank Zappa's only recorded rap song. Performed in concert just once, on February 26, 1988, at the Royal Oak Theatre in Troy, Michigan, this song is Zappa's answer to Surgeon-General Everett Koop's explanation for AIDS. "HBO ran something like 'Dr. Koop Answers Your Questions About AIDS,'" Zappa told *Playboy*. "On it, I saw him explain how AIDS got from the green monkey to the human population. He speculated about a native who wanted to eat a green monkey, who skinned it, cut his finger, and some of the green monkey's blood got into his blood. The next thing you know, you have this blood-to-blood transmission of the disease. I mean, this is awfully fucking thin. It's right up there with *Grimm's Fairy Tales*."

The album finishes with a hilarious sketch called "The Untouchables" (complete with Nelson Riddle's television score). While the new "untouchables" scan the mug sheet, they see Reagan's entire cabinet, or "suspects from the '80s." These nefarious figures include John Poindexter ("Get back on Felix the Cat where you belong"), Oliver North ("No more 'Secret Government' for you, buddy!"), Vice-President George Bush ("You're still a wimp — I'm sorry"), and, of course, Ronald Reagan ("You're asleep! Wake up! The country's in a mess!").

When Rykodisc released the CD version of *Broadway the Hard Way*, they added some additional tracks that changed the order of the songs. "Why Don't You Like Me?" was a rewrite of "Tell Me You Love Me," dedicated to the confused life of R&B

YOU CAN'T DO THAT ON STAGE ANYMORE

star Michael Jackson. It makes fun of the hip macho style of Jackson's dancing and singing that attempts to disguise his peculiar form of androgyny:

You take the monkey, I'll take the llama
We'll have a party, get me a Pepsi
Michael is Janet, Janet is Michael —
I'm so confused now —
Who is Diana?

"Bacon Fat" is a '50s R&B track by Andre Williams that Zappa performed with the Mothers during the '60s. Here, he changes the lyrics to reflect his appearance in Washington during the PMRC hearings. "Stolen Moments," the next track, is a faithful cover of the delightful Oliver Nelson instrumental, a sixteen-bar composition that derives from a blues in C minor on his 1961 album, *The Blues and the Abstract Truth*. What may have appealed to Zappa about this album was saxophonist Nelson's strategy in creating it. "The musical ideas determine the form and shape of a musical composition," Nelson wrote in the liner notes. "Classical music of the 19th century and contemporary music of our own 20th century brought about the need for adopting a different perspective in order to create music that was meaningful and vital." This track leads into Sting's "Murder by Numbers," whose arrangement differs from the version by the Police on their *Synchronicity* album (1983). Here it adopts the same blues form as "Stolen Moments" (which Zappa reprises to complete Sting's song).

"Jezebel Boy" is a sloppy new song about male prostitutes, while "Hot Plate Heaven at the Green Hotel," from the 1984 tour, fits in perfectly with the themes on *Broadway the Hard Way*. The song addresses both political parties and their relationship to the poor:

Republicans is fine
If you're a multimillionaire
Democrats is fair
If all you own is what you wear
Neither of 'em's REALLY right
'Cause neither of 'em CARE
'Bout that Hot-Plate Heaven
'Cause they ain't never been there.

"What Kind of Girl" is a new version of "What Kind of Girl Do You Think We Are?" from 1971. This time the song addresses Jimmy Swaggart's scandal, while borrowing musically from the Beatles' "Strawberry Fields Forever" and "I Am the Walrus." The inclusion of the Beatles songs probably had lots to do with Mike Keneally, who had been listening to Beatles records since age four. "Although I don't claim to know offhand every note and chord of every Beatle tune," Keneally told *The Black Page* in 1989, "my knowledge was wide-ranging enough to at least provide a starting point for those new arrangements." During the same tour, Zappa cast Swaggart's plight across three Beatles songs — "Norwegian Wood," "Lucy in the Sky With Diamonds," and "Strawberry Fields Forever" — that made up "The Texas Motel Medley." With completely changed lyrics, the songs became "Norwegian Jim," "Louisiana Hooker With Herpes," and "The Texas Motel."

Broadway the Hard Way is not only a terrifically entertaining and sharply observant album, but, as *We're Only in It for the Money* did for the '60s, it preserves the '80s perfectly. "*Broadway the Hard Way* was very specific," Zappa told Q magazine. "It was about the 1988 election and all the televangelist stuff. But that kind of specific stuff, although it gets stale very quickly in the short term, in the long term it may be an interesting historical document the same way *We're Only in It for the Money* was. Because at that time, in '67 or '68, when we did that, it seemed almost redundant to sing about flower power, because we were right in the middle of [it] — so who would give a fuck? But listen to it today and it's the only album from the period that raises an eyebrow about flower power and what hippies were all about."

With the exception of Donovan's prophetic song, "Season of the Witch," which in 1969 anticipated just how self-destructive hippie culture would prove to be, Zappa was correct. "The types of things that people are afraid of have changed to some degree," Zappa said. "Certain basics remain. Death is a constant. Impotence is a constant. Poverty is a constant. But at certain times in American history, certain things become more important than others. With the growth of the yuppie culture, the fear of impoverishment and people laughing at you is probably more dreadful than death or impotence."

In April 1988, while the group continued their tour through the East Coast, and just before embarking for France, Zappa released his sequel to *Shut Up 'n Play Yer Guitar*. It was a two-CD set on Rykodisc simply called *Guitar*. Just like its predecessor, *Guitar* was made up of guitar solos, this time from performances recorded between 1979 and 1984. While the production is more pristine than the former set,

YOU CAN'T DO THAT ON STAGE ANYMORE

Guitar has no *musique concrète* to separate the tracks. While there are some amazing solos collected here, the whole becomes overwhelming and a touch monotonous. If Zappa's art is about bringing incongruous elements together, *Guitar* is only variations of one element.

"Sexual Harassment in the Workplace," a 1981 solo from a performance of "Stinkfoot," wouldn't be out of place on a Stevie Ray Vaughan album. "In-A-Gadda-Stravinsky" is a hilarious and brilliant melding of the psychedelic anthem "In-A-Gadda-Da-Vida" by Iron Butterfly (played by Scott Thunes on bass) and Zappa's performance of the opening notes of *The Rite of Spring* overtop, from a 1984 take of "Let's Move to Cleveland." The original guitar solo from "Outside Now" in 1979 still has a remarkable beauty. "It Ain't Necessarily the Saint James Infirmary" is a terrific blend of the Joe Primrose classic and Gershwin's "It Ain't Necessarily So," from a 1982 performance of "King Kong." While *Shut Up 'n Play Yer Guitar* featured several solos from "Inca Roads," *Guitar* has seven from "Let's Move to Cleveland." *Guitar* earned Zappa his sixth Grammy nomination for Best Rock Instrumental, and charted at No. 82 in England.

2

Back in 1986, Zappa had started to realize his dream of putting out a large series of recordings based on the live performances from all of his bands. By 1988, CD technology helped it become a reality. *You Can't Do That on Stage Anymore* would turn out to be a twelve-CD set, released over the next few years as six double CDs. "The basic idea of that album is that today in live performance there are very few bands that are actually playing anything," Zappa said in 1986. "They go onstage with a freeze-dried show, and in many cases at least 50 per cent of the show is coming out of a sequencer and lip-synched. Audiences have missed out on the golden age, when people went onstage and took a chance, which was probably the main forte of the bands that I had."

But this wasn't to be a commemorative edition to extol the artistic growth of a performer, like the omnibus live three-CD set *Bruce Springsteen Live/1975-1985* was in 1985. *You Can't Do That on Stage Anymore*, while containing all the conceptual continuity of Zappa's universe, was more an epic study in musical texture. "There's a lot of different kinds of things that you can do when you have a band that is not playing a canned show night after night," Zappa told Ted Templeman of *Music* magazine. "A band that is really playing live onstage and can respond to the moment, improvise on it, and develop it to create an event that happens onstage only once and just for that audience. That is the essence of what you can't do onstage anymore."

While *Bruce Springsteen Live/1975-1985* was an energetic and entertaining three-CD overview of that artist's career, it was also a self-conscious attempt to create a pop mythology out of his working-class origins. It traced a linear story that celebrated Springsteen's becoming a voice for the disenfranchised of America. Zappa's intentions weren't that lofty. In his own live set, Zappa embraced ambivalence, sometimes portraying himself as an ally, sometimes an authoritarian, telling the audience to go fuck themselves, and then cutting loose with a freedom that blew any opposition right out of the water. Zappa documented his various bands in all their glory, but also with their assorted warts. He begins the first volume with Mark Volman of Flo & Eddie telling the band how he almost vomited onstage — and swallowed it so he could continue singing. *You Can't Do That on Stage* is an audacious challenge to the listener, and a statement about live performance. Where Springsteen's set comforts the fans by reinforcing what they already know, Zappa's thrives on surprise. Zappa didn't put the performances in chronological order, as if to outline a personal evolution. Sometimes the band — and the performance itself — changes in mid-track. "You have the feeling that you're at a concert, [but] there's no way you could ever see all these people onstage at the same time," Zappa told William Ruhlmann of *Goldmine*. "But if you've got a fairly decent imagination, you could especially put the earphones on and be at a show that spans, what, twenty-five years, with some of the most amazing musicians that were ever put onto a record and there they are, just performing their little hearts out for you." For those who hadn't yet bought a CD player, Zappa released a two-LP sampler of *You Can't Do That on Stage Anymore* in April 1988. Within a month, *Vol. I* was made available on compact disc.

It's in "The Florida Airport Tape," which begins the first set and dates back to April 1970, that Volman reveals his vomiting episode, offering a typically off-center interpretation of the title *You Can't Do That on Stage Anymore*. What follows is a performance of "Sofa" at the ill-fated Rainbow Theatre concert on December 10, 1971. One of the earliest versions of the song, it contains Zappa's preamble about the creation of the universe. Flo & Eddie, singing in German, give the number a beer-hall polka flavor.

"The Mammy Anthem" is from the performance at Stadio Communale, in Palermo, Sicily, on July 14, 1982, which ended in a riot. This instrumental version

YOU CAN'T DO THAT ON STAGE ANYMORE

of the opening song from *Thing-Fish* is a heavy-metal workout featuring the grungy guitar sound Zappa starting using in the '80s. "You Didn't Try to Call Me" is a quickly paced, straightforward version of Zappa's R&B classic from *Freak Out!* and *Cruising With Ruben & the Jets* performed in July 1980 at Olympia Hall in Munich. It's also one of Zappa's first digital live recordings, laid down when Sony was offering bands in Europe use of its new two-track system. Ike Willis and Zappa handle the vocals with the same veneration they brought to doo-wop songs in the '80s bands.

"Diseases of the Band" opens with the concluding notes to "Wet T-Shirt Nite," where Zappa introduces the 1979 band, most of whom have the flu. As he names each member and what they're suffering from, it's obvious he's sizing them up for groupie interest. Since they were performing at the Odeon Hammersmith in London, they had high-quality twenty-four-track analog equipment. Given the physical state of the musicians, Zappa could only hope to get an optimum performance from them on tape. Fortunately, despite bass player Arthur Barrow performing with a bucket next to him, the group played an outstanding concert.

"Tryin' to Grow a Chin" is sung with great effervescence (and inaccuracy) by Denny Walley in what is probably the most energetic performance of the song. Ed Mann's marimbas provide the kind of cartoon splendor that makes the original versions on *Sheik Yerbouti* or *Läther* sound like demos. Since the song is a satire about teenage angst, Zappa spontaneously inserts a line from Sam the Sham & the Pharaohs' "Woolly Bully."

"Let's Make the Water Turn Black/Harry, You're a Beast/The Orange County Lumber Truck" is an instrumental trilogy from the Mothers of Invention's 1969 tour, recorded in Stratford, Connecticut. Its placement on the disc, right after several tracks from later bands, make the performance and recording sound shoddy. Perhaps this was deliberate. In the liner notes to *You Can't Do That on Stage Anymore*, Zappa writes, "Great care has been taken throughout to ensure the best audio quality, however early selections of historical interest performed by the original Mothers of Invention, though not exactly 'hi-fi,' have been included for the amusement of those fetishists who still believe the only 'good' material was performed by that particular group. Hopefully, comparisons to recordings by the later ensembles will put an end to that peculiar misconception."

Of course, most of the '60s Mothers albums were studio creations (with some live material), whereas the '70s and '80s albums were primarily recorded on the road, by virtuoso musicians operating with better touring and recording equipment. But

Zappa was perhaps acknowledging that his audience was now much younger and not particularly interested in the Mothers of Invention. "Get it out of your mind once and for all that what we do is to be consumed by people who were going to concerts in 1967," Zappa told William Ruhlmann of *Goldmine*. "Very few of those people have an interest in what we're doing now or have an inclination to leave their homes to go to a concert . . . 'cause usually the older you get, the lower your tolerance for having people vomit on your shoes."

"The Groupie Routine," from July 7, 1971, is basically "Do You Like My New Car?" (from the *Fillmore* album) with a few variations thrown in, since it was recorded at the Pauley Pavilion in L.A. The performance is from the same concert that comprised the album *Just Another Band From L.A.* "Ruthie-Ruthie" introduces the 1974 band at a concert in New Jersey. The song, which continues the band folklore theme of "The Groupie Routine," is "Louie Louie" with newly minted lyrics involving an episode in the life of Ruth Underwood. "We used to have this featurette in the show which was like a news flash of what happened the night before on the road, and some of those are real sick," Zappa told Ted Templeman. "Napoleon Murphy Brock started making up the words, based on a true story, about a guy who tried to force his way into Ruth Underwood's hotel room in Pittsburgh, Pennsylvania. She had ordered room service and she was wearing some kind of nightgown and she opened the door to push the tray out and this Xerox salesman-type guy tried to jump in the room, and she kicked him in the nuts. Napoleon sang it onstage the next night." The band then launches into an odd little R&B number, "Babette," which explores the peculiar ways that road manager Marty Perelis revealed his love for the canine species.

"I'm the Slime" and "Big Swifty" jump back a year to 1973, with two unreleased powerhouse performances from the Roxy — the same concert that produced *Roxy & Elsewhere*. "Big Swifty" is highlighted by a jumping George Duke solo on both electric piano and synthesizer, with Ruth Underwood periodically breaking in on the vibes. Zappa takes the piece home with a ripping solo of his own.

"Don't Eat the Yellow Snow" takes us back to the flu-ridden 1979 group performing at the Odeon Hammersmith. It is a lively, accurate representation of the extended oratorio, but with elements of audience participation testing the band's resolve.

"We were playing a matinee, doing 'St. Alfonzo's Pancake Breakfast' and 'Don't Eat the Yellow Snow,' and there was this guy in the audience, completely out of his mind, who wanted to recite poetry," Zappa told David Fricke of *Rolling Stone* in

YOU CAN'T DO THAT ON STAGE ANYMORE

1986. "He came up to the stage and kept interrupting the songs. So we worked him into the set, and the result is very strange — mass-audience poetry reading." Besides the surreal verse (and Zappa looking for help to remove the eager poet), the band builds around this spontaneous happening with drama and humor. At one point, when the deranged bard recites a passage about watering a garden, Denny Walley pipes up, "Oh, you want kindergarten." And Zappa performs a reading of his own in response, quoting — inaccurately — from Dylan Thomas' *Under Milk Wood*. Nevertheless, Zappa makes it sound as perfectly fitting as something from his own catalog. The piece also includes "Rollo," the conclusion of "Don't Eat the Yellow Snow," which was not released on *Apostrophe (')*. "Rollo" continues St. Alfonzo's questionable dealings with his parishioners:

> *Some are dealing*
> *Some are standing*
> *All the money they are handing*
> *To some asshole with a basket*
> *Where it goes, we dare not ask it.*

"Plastic People," which opens the second disc, is from a 1969 performance in the Bronx. Although Zappa describes the crowd as "an audience that probably would have preferred the Vanilla Fudge," they sound amiable toward the band. Zappa jokes and cajoles until he finally begins to lecture the crowd — as was his habit in those days — about music. Before launching into the song, he explains how "Plastic People" grew out of "Louie Louie." He also adds some lyrics about the riots on the Sunset Strip not heard on the original studio track:

> *Three nights and days I walked the streets*
> *This town is filled with plastic creeps*
> *Their shoes are brown to match their suits*
> *They got no balls, they got no roots.*

As the song ends, with Zappa's plea for finding love that doesn't become a product of plasticity, he shifts right into "The Torture Never Stops," a song that kills any romantic illusions. This version, from a 1977 show in Germany, is much longer than the track on *Zoot Allures*. While leaving out the continuous thread of female moaning on the album track, Zappa includes a fragment of the big-band classic

"Chattanooga Choo Choo" that powerfully evokes the gang-rape euphemism "pulling a train."

"Fine Girl" and "Zomby Woof" are both from the 1982 fiasco at the Parco Redecessio in Milan. Despite having to swat swarms of mosquitoes that had come from the lake surrounding the "park," the band performs the tunes with vitality and skill. Since the next track, "Sweet Leilani," was recorded in a ballroom in Stratford, Connecticut, in 1969, it seems fitting that Zappa would include a ballroom favorite. The Mothers begin the song earnestly enough, but ultimately turn it into some dissonant honking. Out of the disintegration, the group launches into a competently performed instrumental version of "Oh No."

A brief field recording from 1970 is up next, with drummer Aynsley Dunbar soliciting a "knob job" from a female fan who then happily agrees to give blow jobs to the entire group. Then the 1984 band tears into "Be in My Video," from the *Does Humor Belong in Music?* videotape. Zappa seems to draw a link between the currency of sex between groups and their fans, and the corporatist hand job the record industry gives rock groups producing videos to promote themselves. Two other numbers from the same concert follow, "The Deathless Horsie" and "The Dangerous Kitchen."

"Dumb All Over," "Heavenly Bank Account," and "Suicide Chump" are part of the Halloween concert at the Palladium that MTV aired in 1981. "Dumb All Over" has all the urgency of a rap record, with Zappa's voice no longer encumbered by the echo effect he used on *You Are What You Is*. "Heavenly Bank Account" and "Suicide Chump" demonstrate just how adept the 1981 band was at duplicating — live onstage — the quick tempo changes of the original studio recording. The concluding songs, "Tell Me You Love Me" and "Sofa #2," are from Genoa, Italy, in 1982. "Tell Me You Love Me" is similar to the live version on *Tinsel Town Rebellion*, but at a lightning pace, with Steve Vai's guitar simulating a chainsaw. Just as *You Can't Do That on Stage Anymore, Vol. 1* began with "Sofa," it ends with an instrumental version that is perhaps the loveliest duet between Zappa and Vai.

You Can't Do That on Stage, Vol. 1 is an astonishing attempt to create a musical identity that's stitched together incongruously from various sources and various times. Yet it's also a sampling of the very real risk of revealing one's true musical chops on the stage.

Just when Zappa was releasing *You Can't Do That on Stage Anymore, Vol. 1*, his 1988 band was vowing not to do *anything* onstage anymore. The group's dislike of Thunes had intensified as the tour progressed. However, Thunes had been a Zappa regular since the early '80s, and Zappa certainly appreciated his contributions. "Scott has a unique personality," he told Matt Resnicoff of *Musician*. "He also has unique musical skills. I like the way he plays and I like him as a person, but other people don't. He has a very difficult personality: he refuses to be cordial. He won't do small talk." Mike Keneally, another of Thunes' supporters, agreed. "He's very abrasive. He's brutal. He's blunt," Keneally told *Society Pages*.

Thunes had a different point of view. "Show me a good band, and I'll tell you why there's tension in that band," he told Thomas Wictor in *Bass Player* in 1997. "And for the people who perform it, music very rarely releases tension; it almost always increases tension. And music does not help you to be a nice person. Why should a musician be a nice person? There's no connection there. Tension increases; we all have our issues, and everybody's human." And nowhere was that more true than on the 1988 tour. "[Frank] put up with a bunch of shit to allow the 1988 tour to work — but he wanted all of the juice with none of the blood," Thunes continued. "All of those albums I played on have blood on every track; there's danger inherent in everything on them. . . . I dig tension in my music, because I know from modern classical music that tension can coexist with normalcy."

According to Zappa, the turmoil began with Ed Mann and Chad Wackerman (both of whom had played with Thunes for years without publicly complaining) leading the charge to get Thunes out of the group. The conflict reached its climax in Europe. "Once in Barcelona," said Thunes, "someone in the band came up to me and screamed, 'Don't you know what a privilege it is to play with Frank? How can you ruin his music?' I play a lot of lines; I pick chunks out of the air, and instead of playing bass, I play Scott Thunes' part in the orchestration. . . . So at that particular moment I got out my headphones and put them on, and I started listening to classical music while this guy's mouth went [flapping lower jaw] *Beh-beh-beh-beh*. It was delicious." It wasn't delicious, though, when the band hit Germany.

On their last German date, the promoter, John Jackson, bought the band a huge inscribed cake to celebrate, but Thunes found that his name had been scratched off. By the time the band got to Italy, the bad blood was starting to affect their performance. Before they left Europe — with ten more weeks of bookings still in the U.S. — Zappa called a meeting. Would they still do the tour if Scott Thunes remained in the band? Except for Keneally, everyone else said they would prefer another bass player. Zappa refused. "I didn't want to fire the bass player," he told *Downbeat* in 1991. "It put me in a position where if I had to replace someone, it meant going back into rehearsal, and rehearsals cost money. We had plenty of offers to do concerts in the U.S. that summer, but they just wouldn't do it with Scott."

Oddly enough, Thunes would have accommodated the unhappy musicians. "When [Zappa] told me that, I said, 'I'll gladly quit.' He said, 'That's not the answer. I like you, and I like what you do — except for all the mistakes you've been making.' Because every night onstage, I was surrounded by daggers and completely lost my concentration. For three months, I was a wreck, and the music suffered because of my mistakes."

Zappa knew that if he dumped Thunes, not only would the rehearsals with a new bassist cost more money, Zappa would also have to find someone able to quickly learn a large and difficult repertoire. In Genoa, Italy, the 1988 tour came to an abrupt end. Zappa paid off the group, losing $400,000 of his own money. As for voter registration in the U.S., it stalled at 11,000 people. "I'd been very happy with that band," Zappa told David Mead of *Guitarist*. "The audiences liked it, too, and the reviewers thought it was great." The final irony was that six months later, many of the mutineers started singing a different tune. "I was hearing, 'Man, we made a mistake. Scott's not such a bad guy,'" Zappa told *Musician*. "And the same people who hated his guts were running into him in restaurants and saying, 'Oh, Scott, I'm *sorry*, I don't know what got *into* me,' this kind of stupid, stupid shit. It was just like little children ganging up on a kid at a boys' school."

With the tour kaput, Zappa concentrated on getting the tracks together for *You Can't Do That on Stage Anymore, Vol. 2 (The Helsinki Concert)*, which featured the 1974 band. Since it was an election year, Zappa also tried to contact the Democratic Party, which was running Michael Dukakis against Republican Vice-President George Bush. Zappa had ideas for political ads, as he explained to Kurt Loder of MTV: "I thought the best way to start reducing the effect of the Republican disinformation campaign was to run a series of spots that called into question who these fucking people think they are. So one of the spots had a guy — obviously a Republican — standing on the lawn in front of a mansion, saying, 'I'm a Republican, and I care about the environment.' He points to his house: 'My environment.'"

Zappa had another ad concept that would feature videotape of Manuel Noriega, the then-dictator of Panama — and former ally of the U.S. — whose country controlled much of the drug trade coming into the United States. In this ad, Noriega is seen telling the people of America that Panama is a small country dependent on drug money. Since they have a good relationship with George Bush, voters shouldn't blow it by electing Dukakis. Across the screen, at the end, is a handwritten scrawl that reads, "Thanks — Manny."

Needless to say, the Democrats didn't entertain any of Zappa's ideas. "I mean, as long as they're gonna play footsy with the Republicans and let the Republicans get away with the type of spin-doctoring that they put on everything that comes out," said Zappa, "they're always gonna chomp it. You gotta go for the fuckin' *balls* with these guys." However, the Libertarian Party was so impressed that they named Zappa as a potential candidate for the 1988 election. Zappa declined, because he saw them as extremists, nothing more than "closet anarchists." As far as he was concerned, if they had their way, there wouldn't be *any* government.

Back in 1969, Zappa had never got the opportunity to publish *The Groupie Papers*, but thanks to Poseidon Press in New York, he now had the chance to write his autobiography. Not that he had always wanted to. In 1984, when CBC Radio host Vicki Gabereau asked him if he would write his memoirs, Zappa was indignant: "I resent those kinds of books. I hope that I'm never in a financial position where I have to resort to that." But apparently he changed his mind. *The Real Frank Zappa Book* came across less as an autobiography than as an opportunity for Zappa to discuss a range of topics including music, marriage, politics, the PMRC, and, of course, schmucks. Zappa also wanted to respond to biographies about him that he felt were full of falsehoods. "In January, before the tour, we're rehearsing, and I had this obligation with Simon and Schuster to do the book and I'd been putting it off," Zappa explained to journalist Bob Marshall. "And while we were rehearsing, we'd rehearse from two in the afternoon until one o'clock in the morning, and from 1 until 6 AM, for three weeks, every night I would sit here with this guy and do taped interviews. And we'd just talk about whatever we wanted to talk about, and then he went away and had it transcribed and changed it from the way I talked into book talk."

That interviewer was Peter Occhiogrosso, who, before working on the Zappa book, was writing a study of famous Catholics. "I was a fan of Frank's early albums, but had lost track of him around the time I was writing the book, and had become more interested in jazz," Occhiogrosso told Zappologist Vladimir Sovetov. "But I was looking for 'unusual' Catholics, both practising Catholics and ex-Catholics, like George Carlin, reporter/novelist Jimmy Breslin, novelists Mary Gordon and Robert Stone.... I had heard that Frank grew up Catholic as an Italian-American (like me).

I thought he might have some funny things to say about religion in general because of his dislike of televanglists. I wasn't disappointed."

Zappa, however, was less than impressed. "When [Occhiogrosso] sent it back, I hated it," Zappa remarked. "So, when I finished the tour, I went in and rewrote it. I just took advantage of what he had collated, but I put it back into my own words. So, it's not like 'as told to.' . . . It really has more to do with the way I write and the way I talk than it would have." The hardcover book was popular enough to be issued in paper the following year.

In January 1989, Honker Video finally released the finished *Uncle Meat* film, along with *The True Story of Frank Zappa's 200 Motels*, which featured outtakes and interviews that laid out the whole wild affair. But the big event of the new year was the opening of Joe's Garage. Marque Coy, who worked the monitor for Zappa at concerts, had used a three-room rehearsal facility that for fifteen years had been an equipment storage room. Now, thanks to Gail Zappa, who had the idea, it would be a working studio that anyone could rent out for recording. "The Zappas didn't know what they were going to call it," Coy told Don Menn in the tribute magazine *Zappa!* "I said, 'Well, you own the name.' They said, 'What do you mean?' I said, 'The line in the song goes: "You can jam at Joe's Garage . . ." Let's call it Joe's Garage.'"

And while bands came to jam and record at Joe's Garage, Zappa continued to edit and mix the tapes from the 1988 tour, and prepare the next volume of *You Can't Do That on Stage Anymore*. It was a strenuous task — especially since Zappa had close to 1,970 takes of 120 songs. "Out of that, somebody has to decide which parts of which song are the best version available from any given city, remember it, tell the engineer to mix this city to match that city, and then glue it together to make the album," Zappa told Joe Morgenstern of the *Los Angeles Times Magazine*. "You don't farm that out to anyone else."

Where *You Can't Do That on Stage Anymore, Vol. 2* concentrated on the 1974 band's concert in Helsinki, *Vol. 3* is dominated by the 1984 touring ensemble. Instead of the great diversity of bands heard on *Vol. 1*, Zappa created diversity within the very performances themselves. Sometimes a song would begin in one location, and the conclusion would come from another city. Occasionally a guitar solo was lifted from one performance and edited into an entirely different show — even when the same band was playing. As clever and fascinating as this process was, it was still disingenuous of Zappa to promote the series as featuring a live band without overdubs. While there were no overdubs, Zappa weeded out the

YOU CAN'T DO THAT ON STAGE ANYMORE

errors in live performance by using portions from other shows. Besides the brilliant conceptual premise behind this series, it was still a construct that didn't reflect the reality of the performance.

You Can't Do That on Stage Anymore, Vol. 3 begins with a reggae arrangement of "Sharleena," from the Universal Amphitheatre in L.A. Dweezil Zappa joined the band for this track. It was only the second time the fifteen-year-old had played onstage with his father, and their duet on the guitar bridge is spotless. "It was the last concert of the 1984 tour," Frank Zappa told *Guitar Player*. "I'd been on the road for six months and had just gotten back to town. Dweezil had been rehearsing away, and since we were working at the Universal Amphitheatre, I knew that he wanted to go onstage. He had played a solo on the album version, so he already knew the song." Dweezil had made his onstage debut with his father at age twelve, when the band played the Hammersmith Odeon in 1982. But this was the first time he and his father played a duet. They also did a rousing version of "Whippin' Post" that same night.

"Frank does not have a stock lick that he'll rely on," Dweezil told *Guitar Player*. "Each time he takes a solo, he's composing a piece that goes along with whatever he feels at that moment, and that's what's so twisted — he doesn't think like a guitar player. He thinks in terms of a whole spectrum — like making air sculpture, as he calls it."

"Bamboozled by Love," "Lucille Has Messed My Mind Up," and "Advance Romance" are from a 1984 Thanksgiving concert in Chicago. While "Lucille" and "Advance Romance" resemble the original versions, "Bamboozled by Love" has lost the blues edge it had on *Tinsel Town Rebellion*. However, Zappa cleverly inserts a guitar quote from the 1983 Yes hit "Owner of a Lonely Heart." Next up are "Bobby Brown Goes Down" and "Keep It Greasy," from a December 1984 concert in Seattle. In "Bobby Brown," Ike Willis inserts a mighty "Hi-ho, Silver" at a key moment. "I still don't know why it happened, but I cracked up every time he did it," Zappa told *Pulse*. "It must have been road fatigue. He'd keep yelling in the most inappropriate places. The whole show was riddled with bad Lone Ranger jokes and me not being able to sing the right words. I enjoyed that night." What Zappa didn't recall was that Willis wasn't randomly quoting Lenny Bruce's "Lone Ranger" routine; he was also aware that the phrase "Hi-ho, Silver" (a euphemism for anal sex) was part of "Jewish Princess" on *Sheik Yerbouti* — the same album that premiered "Bobby Brown." The hilarious moment continues appropriately into "Keep It Greasy," a virtual ad for back-door sex.

"Honey, Don't You Want a Man Like Me?" is from the 1984 concert at the Pier, in New York, and was featured on *Does Humor Belong In Music?* "In France" (minus Johnny "Guitar" Watson), from the same Chicago show as "Bamboozled by Love," has Zappa quoting the robot from the '60s TV series *Lost in Space* — "Danger, Will Robinson, danger!" The next track, "Drowning Witch," is a perfect example of song reconstruction. "The 1984 band never played it correctly during its six-month tour," Zappa wrote in the liner notes. "The 1982 band got close on *one* occasion." To get a near-perfect version, Zappa collated the efforts of both groups — and it took him five or six years to do it.

"Ride My Face to Chicago," a rollicking number from the 1984 Chicago show, takes its title from a bit of graffiti Zappa once spotted in the men's room at the Whisky A Go-Go in 1965. "Carol, You Fool" is a doo-wop reggae arrangement that takes its basic construction from Neil Sedaka's "Oh Carol" ("Oh Carol/I am but a fool/Even though you treat me cruel").

"Chana in de Bushwop," like "Frogs With Dirty Little Lips," comes from one of the Zappa children — when Diva was five, she made up the story that forms the basis of the song. This track was part of the repertoire of the 1984 band, and when keyboardist Alan Zavod did his customary solo, he became frenzied. "[He] would end his solo with this thing that everybody called *'the Volcano,'*" Zappa wrote in *The Real Frank Zappa Book*. "He held the sustain pedal down and churned and smashed away to get a big blur going, and then topped it off at the end with a flourish." During their performance of "Chana" at the Bismark Hotel in Chicago, Zappa jumped on the riser, pushed Zavod away, and improvised his own "amateur volcano solo." Zappa's effort creates a Tinkertoy hysteria that reveals the musicians' inner desperation rather than their musical prowess. "There are a lot of reasons why musicians like to play solos onstage — but the usual reason in rock 'n' roll is to get the Blow Job," Zappa explained. "One way to ensure that you look like the greatest thing going when you play *your big solo* is to make sure that you end your solo by going *up the scale*, then grab that last note and repeat it as fast as you can. The statement is the same on any instrument: 'Oh, I'm squirting now!'"

"Joe's Garage" and "Why Does It Hurt When I Pee?" — also from the 1984 Chicago show — are performed in a mock-Devo bionic style characteristic of Zappa's '80s bands doing older material. What distinguishes "Why Does It Hurt When I Pee?" is an improvised lyric about a girl from Salt Lake City. "Our road manager got a call from a local doctor, urging him to warn everyone about a girl with dark hair, riddled with disease, who had caused severe discomfort to twenty-four members of the touring ensemble that had played in town just before us," Zappa wrote in the liner notes to *Vol. 3*. "Unfortunately, a few of our guys got the message too late."

The second disc breaks from the 1984 ensemble by featuring more material from the 1973 band's Roxy show. "Dickie's Such an Asshole" was performed frequently during the Watergate period. But the song was never put on disc until the 1988 version on *Broadway the Hard Way*. At the end of the song — à la Charles Ives — Zappa provides a sample of "Battle Hymn of the Republic" as he describes the litany of disgrace in the waning days of Richard Nixon's regime. "Hands With a Hammer" is a Terry Bozzio drum solo from 1975 in Osaka, Japan. Since acoustic drum solos are now rare in rock, it's startling to hear Bozzio's lovely, dramatic variations. This track leads into a slow, delicate version of "Zoot Allures" from the same concert. Since the guitar solo didn't survive the recording, Zappa edits in one from a 1982 show.

"Society Pages," "I'm a Beautiful Guy," "Beauty Knows No Pain," and "Charlie's Enormous Mouth" come from the 1981 MTV concert and demonstrate the group's agility in duplicating the difficult edits and tempo shifts from *You Are What You Is*. "Cocaine Decisions" begins with a performance by the 1984 band in Chicago, but quickly shifts to the infamous 1982 Palermo concert, where a tear-gas grenade caused a huge riot. You can hear the initial cracking sound as the band fumbles before climbing back into the tune. Before long, the tear-gas stench has Zappa imploring Italian journalist Massimo Bassoli to calm the crowd. As the army and the police fought the crowd, Zappa and the band attempted to carry on. They lead into "Nig Biz," Zappa's satire about the record industry's condescension toward blacks, the concluding number on the 1982 tour. "King Kong" dates back to the '60s, but survived every touring ensemble. For this long cut — over twenty-four minutes — Zappa put together samples from 1971 and 1982, but from three or four different concerts. It's an ambitious undertaking that contrasts the improvised vocal hijinks of the 1982 group in France indulging in wordplay with the term "blow job," and Tommy Mars singing a portion of "The Massive Improve'lence" from *Thing-Fish* ("I want a nun/I want a nun/I want a burro/In the frosty light") a couple of years before the song's release. Ian Underwood also does one of his brilliant, weaving alto sax solos (performed, as on "Chunga's Revenge," with a wah-wah pedal).

During a 1982 portion of the track, Zappa refers to the poetry reading from "Don't Eat the Yellow Snow," included on *Vol. 1*. Just as he's about to quote Denny

Walley's sarcastic retort to the poet, Zappa splices in Walley's exact remark from 1979. (Walley wasn't in the band in 1982.) With "King Kong," "Drowning Witch," and other tunes on this release, Zappa turns the notion of time and place into simple constructs that recording technology allows him to violate and reassemble. In doing so, he sets out to prove that everything — the past and future — happens at once.

You Can't Do That on Stage Anymore, Vol. 3 concludes with a spirited version of "Cosmik Debris" from the 1984 Seattle show. Willis is heard continuing his Lone Ranger references in a comical thread that loops through the decades.

3

When Frank Zappa and Pierre Boulez came together to do *The Perfect Stranger: Boulez Conducts Zappa* in 1984, it was widely assumed the two men had a falling out because only four of the seven pieces featured Boulez and his Ensemble InterContemporain. But the truth was, only four pieces were commissioned. When Zappa and Boulez met again on May 23, 1989, at Schoenberg Hall at UCLA for a joint lecture, "An Evening With Pierre Boulez and Frank Zappa," those rumors were finally put to rest. The event, presented by the UCLA music department and the Los Angeles Philharmonic Orchestra, was designed as a discussion between the two composers, with David Braxton as emcee and a Q&A period with the audience. At the end of the evening, Zappa was asked what his primary goal was. "That's easy," he replied, "I'm still waiting for an accurate performance."

As *You Can't Do That on Stage Anymore, Vol. 3* was being prepared for release in November 1989, a pro-choice rally was being planned for Rancho Park in Los Angeles on November 12, with similar gatherings the same day across the country. The event attracted over 100,000 people, including actors Richard Dreyfuss and Jane Fonda, and the "Rhymin' Man" himself, Jesse Jackson. Back in 1987, Zappa had spoken out against the fundamentalist extremists who were bombing abortion clinics. "We're seeing the same terrorist techniques in the U.S. as those used by Muslim fanatics in the Mideast — the difference is just a matter of costume."

Zappa addressed the crowd briefly. He took what was seen primarily as an issue affecting women's rights, and expanded it to include fundamental rights affecting all Americans. "When someone is anti-choice, they are anti-American," Zappa told the crowd. "It should be clear from recent events that the enemy that America must face is not the Communists over there, it's those deranged right-wing

YOU CAN'T DO THAT ON STAGE ANYMORE

lunatics right here in America. . . . Get the government out of your bedroom, out of your underpants, and put 'em back to work where they belong!" After an enthusiastic reception, Zappa led the gathering in a spontaneous prayer. "Dear sweet Jesus," he intoned. "Don't listen to those other guys — they are not Christians, they are practising voodoo. Not long ago, they prayed to you and demanded the death of a Supreme Court Justice. What's that got to do with Christianity? Huh? Okay, Jesus, we know you're listening because *we* are the good guys!"

The "recent events" Zappa referred to were the massive political changes unfolding overseas. By 1989, Communism was collapsing in the Soviet Union and the rest of Eastern Europe. As a result of the reformist policies of Mikhail Gorbachev, the authoritarian states were starting to wither (only not for the reasons that Vladimir Lenin had predicted).

After *You Can't Do That on Stage Anymore, Vol. 3* hit the stores, Zappa hit the road, travelling four times to Russia and once to Czechoslovakia. His first trip to the Soviet Union, in February 1989, was due to the efforts of Dennis Berardi, of Kramer Guitars, who told Zappa he might open a branch there. Zappa thought that Berardi was insane since he didn't know anything about Russia, so he decided to make his own field trip and find out for himself. Zappa discovered there was a consumer market of close to 289 million people who needed just about everything. "You give me the most random things and I'll find some way that there is a relationship between them," Zappa told Neil Cohen of *Continental Profiles*. "It's just the way my brain works. From meeting people, hearing what they have to say, [and] picking up statements like, 'God, I wish we had this,' and also knowing who did have it someplace else. You would logically try and see if you could make the people cooperate." That spirit of cooperation turned out to be more difficult than Zappa could have imagined.

The first problem was the Russian ruble. It had become a soft currency that was controlled by the Soviet government and not allowed to fluctuate on the world market. In other words, you couldn't exchange it for deutsche marks *or* dollars. The second obstacle was the new business class in Russia, whose entrepreneurial education came from working the black market. Although Zappa kept trying to set up meetings for Western business interests, they fell apart due to the lack of good business sense by the new Russian capitalists. "There are business terms that don't exist in the Soviet vocabulary, like investment, or capital gains," Zappa bemoaned. "Until there is an increase in knowledge as far as how the deals work, and the idea that Western capital is not a present that comes from heaven and lands on your doorstep and suddenly wonderful things happen. Nobody is going to invest a nickel in there unless they're going to get a profit out of it. And profit is another word they don't understand."

But Zappa was also critical of the Cold War attitudes still being encouraged by right-wing forces in the U.S. "They have a brand-new government in Czechoslovakia. But this is followed by a very right-wing commentary that does everything it can to *foster, bolster, and reupholster* the whole Cold War mentality," Zappa explained. "I wish I had every *Wall Street Journal* article I've read that said, 'Can Gorbachev Hold on to Power?' or 'He's Going Out This Time,' trying to come up with names of guys breathing down his neck. It's like scraping the bottom of the Cold War barrel to create this impression that it's all going to evaporate overnight."

Zappa was also interested in both licensing his recordings for this new market and economic collaboration between the West and the East. To accommodate this, he set up a company which was an international licensing, consulting, and social engineering company called Why Not? "Until the Soviet Union folded, we spent fifty years of Cold War cash convincing Americans that we needed to fight against the Evil Empire," Zappa told *Pulse*. "Hey, I traveled to Russia . . . right when it was on the cusp of glasnost. The place was a fucking disaster area. These people couldn't even deliver milk. The CIA knew that, but why didn't they say the Cold War was for shit and Russia wasn't a threat to us? If we had been working with the Russians to develop what they knew, we all would have been better off. The Russians may not have the money, but they have the brains."

Zappa's business ideas were designed to transcend the deep-seated Cold War attitudes. "My idea with Why Not? was to work with the co-ops of inventors, helping them to license their inventions of industrial processes and equipment design in the West." Zappa knew that traveling in Russia would be no pleasant holiday. "The conditions are grim there," he reported. "It's hard to find something to eat, the transportation is a nightmare, and since there's no Russian phone book, it's nearly impossible to get in touch with people unless they've given you their telephone number beforehand."

In 1990, Financial News Network sponsored a trip by Zappa to both the Soviet Union and Czechoslovakia. With the Soviet bloc crumbling, FNN saw an opportunity to expand into a larger international chain. Since Zappa had already made inroads with his Why Not? venture, he seemed like the perfect person to represent them. FNN covered Zappa's arrival in Moscow on January 15. He was to collect material on video for *Focus*, a three-part special he would host, examining Soviet business opportunities. "There's potential in a lot of different areas in the Soviet Union," Zappa explained in *Frank Zappa — A Visual Documentary by Miles*. "But unfortunately there is still a lot of prejudice among us Americans when it comes to working together with the Russians. . . . It is an enormous market and the competition is not necessarily all that hard in every field."

Zappa's visit was timely — he met up with documentary filmmaker Jacques Cousteau, who had commissioned Zappa to write music for *Outrage at Valdez*, a film he was making about the 1989 *Exxon Valdez* oil-spill disaster. Zappa was becoming an ambassador of goodwill, an active citizen of the world, while testing the foundations of what was called democracy in his own homeland. "I wouldn't be surprised if he could carry it into a larger, global political position, a part of the United Nations or something equally major," ex-Mother Howard Kaylan commented at the time. "I saw his picture the other day in the *Daily News*. He didn't look like a rock star. He looked like a world leader."

On January 20, Zappa arrived in Prague to a reception he could have hardly been prepared for. As his plane touched down at the airport, Zappa saw about 5,000 people waiting. "Never in my twenty-five years in the rock 'n' roll business have I gotten off an airplane and seen anything like it," Zappa recalled at the time. "They were totally unprepared for the situation. . . . When I managed to inch my way through the airport . . . it took about a half an hour to go forty feet from the curb to the bus because of the people piling on top of us." He was aware that he had some fans there, but he figured it had everything to do with being an American. "If I'd been a European artist, the audience wouldn't have liked me," Zappa told Nigel Leigh of the BBC. "The thing that was intriguing to Europeans was that I was an American doing this stuff. It made me stick out like a sore thumb."

A year earlier, this sore thumb had received a visit from Michael Kocab, not only a Czech student fighting against the Communist government, but a composer as well. He wanted one of Zappa's orchestral scores played by the Czech Philharmonic. This was unlikely, as Zappa's music had been banned in Czechoslovakia for years. Yet Kocab's request did indicate that a change was afoot. Kocab was now a member of the Czech parliament and one of the main negotiators between the Czech Politburo, the Politburo in Moscow, and the KGB. Zappa carried in his pocket a number of suggestions aimed at helping Czechoslovakia rebuild its economy — ideas on tourism, cellular phones, and magnetodynamic technology.

By October 1989, Russian troops had left Czechoslovakia. The Velvet Revolution had arrived and the new president was Vaclav Havel, a playwright who had just spent four years in prison. Havel was also a huge fan of Zappa and welcomed his visit. "Frank Zappa was one of the gods of the Czech underground during the '70s and '80s," Havel would write in a *New Yorker* tribute to Zappa. "It was an era of complete isolation. Local rock musicians and audiences were hounded by the police, and for those who refused to be swept aside by persecution — who tried to remain true to a culture of their own — Western rock was far more than just a form of music. At that time, Frank Zappa hung somewhere high up in the heavens, a star as inaccessible as the many others whose influence was felt in the local scene, like the Velvet Underground and Captain Beefheart."

What Zappa didn't realize was that at the same time he arrived in Prague, another American noted figure was leaving. While the television crew awaited Zappa's arrival, they discovered that American ambassador Shirley Temple Black was departing. The journalists, knowing only that both were American cultural icons from Hollywood, could see little difference between them. So it didn't seem odd that a Prague news team would storm the former cutie-pie child actress who once sang "The Good Ship Lollipop" and starred in *Rebecca of Sunnybrook Farm*, to get her opinion on the arrival of the man who had written "Broken Hearts Are for Assholes."

Author Paul Berman writes about this unusual coincidence in his polemical book on the American left, *A Tale of Two Utopias*:

> From an American point of view, this was a bizarre, at any rate a foreign, moment in the Eastern Bloc Revolution. No right-minded American would dream of asking Shirley Temple about Frank Zappa. Americans know that the United States is a divided country, at war with itself since the mid-'60s or earlier, splintered into culture and counterculture, right and left. Or who can say what the divisions are, except that they persist, like a guerrilla war that has festered in the jungle unto the second or third generation? The charming Temple, beloved for "The Good Ship Lollipop" and other entertainments, is not from the same America as the pirate-bearded performer of those classics from 1967 and '68, *Lumpy Gravy* and *We're Only in It for the Money*.

YOU CAN'T DO THAT ON STAGE ANYMORE

Asked about her feelings about Frank Zappa, Shirley Temple Black could only look appalled. She muttered something about Moon Unit, but was otherwise speechless. So were the Czech journalists. "People had no way to account for the United States ambassador's boorish airport behavior," Berman writes, "except to mark her down as a cultural ignoramus who lacked the aplomb to boast to all of Central Europe about one of America's finest sons, the brilliant Zappa, a world figure in the field of popular music."

Zappa, meanwhile, fought through the surging masses and made his way to the Hotel Intercontinental. Afterwards, he received excited fans in an old wine cellar where the Union of Socialist Youth used to meet. Berman describes what Zappa saw:

> Zappa's keenest fans looked like Goths and Vandals in leathers and caveman haircuts. They were hippies from 1968, preserved in amber. They stood up to express their gratitude and reveal their wounds. For the love of pirated Zappa tapes, these people had undergone every kind of official torment. "We're going to beat Frank Zappa out of your heads," the police used to say. And here at last was the real-life Zappa standing before his persecuted fans in his oversize black undertaker's suit, puffing Winstons in the smoky marijuana Communist wine cellar, now answering questions, now grabbing a mike and bursting into song. For them alone! Just for them! The hero himself was shaken by the scene. He felt constrained to remind the ebullient hairy mob that in America, too, in the land of loony fundamentalists and would-be censors, not everything was wonderful. "You've been living with secret police for a long time," he told them, looking grave under the spotlight in the hazy smoke. He searched for the *mot juste*. "It will take Americans a while to realize that we have them, too."

Almost a quarter-century after Zappa had asked the question, Who Are the Brain Police?, he finally confronted the real fruit of totalitarianism. Americans took their democracy for granted, flirting with rock-music censorship and allowing Christian fundamentalism to stage a 20th-century witchhunt. While America denounced Zappa as a perverted freak, here were people who had literally taken beatings to hear what Frank Zappa recorded. He suddenly encountered a hideous irony, something that always lurked somewhere in his compositions — those deprived of freedom learn to understand and value it; those who have it, as in America, fail to embrace it.

After spending time with the many fans who came to see him, Zappa made time for the other purpose for his visit — he went to Hradcany Castle to meet with President Havel. Havel told Zappa he was a huge fan of the early Mothers of Invention recordings, especially *Bongo Fury*. Havel was to visit the U.S. the next month, and he asked Zappa to take part in a state concert to honor him. (Location and schedule changes forced Zappa out of the lineup, but he would play in Czechoslovakia the following year.) "He's really a nice man, and he's also, I would say, a reluctant politician," Zappa said, describing Havel to reporters. "I don't think he wanted the job of president. He was kind of thrust into it, and he would probably be just as happy writing, and having his plays performed and his books published, but he was just the right guy to do the job at that time, and he's got the position."

Zappa felt that Havel's greatest weakness was his lack of experience in economics. "I started to talk to him on behalf of FNN: 'What sort of foreign investment is Czechoslovakia looking for? Why should foreign investors put their money into Czechoslovakia?' These questions, Havel said, should be addressed to his financial ministers." At a small lunch, Zappa met with Havel's wife, Olga, and several prominent members of the government to discuss ways the country could increase its income. Later, Zappa requested the presence of Milan Lukes, the Czech minister of culture. He figured the easiest way to prevent an invasion of McDonalds and Pizza Hut outlays was to involve someone who had a fundamental interest in culture. But many skeptics wondered what Zappa knew about advising a nation on its trade and economic development. "It's just like making a piece of music," Zappa told *The Nation*. "You start with the theme. Then, what's the melody? How do you develop the harmony? What's the rhythm below it? You don't have to know about international financing. You just have to know about composition."

Zappa told *The Nation* that he saw many similarities between Austria and Czechoslovakia. "Look at Austria, which does $10 million a year in tourism. Austria has managed to convert its culture — its concert halls, museums, and architecture — into a consumable commodity and at the same time preserve its heritage. Czechoslovakia, with its musical, theatrical, and artistic legacy, has the potential for the same." Zappa requested of the Czech government that he represent Czechoslovakia in the U.S. on matters of trade, tourism, and culture. A letter was drafted and signed by Deputy Prime Minister Valter Komarek, who wrote:

> Dear Sir: I entrust you with leading negotiations with foreign partners for preparation of preliminary projects, possibly drafts of trade agreements directed to participation of foreign firms. It concerns tourist, agricultural, and other enterprises in Czechoslovakia. I am very obliged to you for the help offered in this respect and I am looking to further cooperation.

While he guested on the television program *Kontakt*, Zappa's new post was announced. He then had his lawyer register him in the U.S. as an agent of a foreign country. "Suddenly it looks like I have a new job," Zappa said hopefully. But before he could perform his first duty of office, he hit a snag. Over lunch, President Havel told Zappa that U.S. Vice-President Dan Quayle was soon coming to visit. "I expressed the opinion that I thought it was unfortunate that a person such as President Havel should have to bear the company of somebody as stupid as Dan Quayle for even a few moments of his life," Zappa told Nigel Leigh. "The next thing I know, Quayle doesn't come. Instead [Secretary of State] James Baker III reroutes his trip to Moscow so that he can come blasting into Prague and literally lay down the law to the Czech government. He says, 'You can either do business with the United States or you can do business with Zappa. What'll it be?'"

So Zappa was demoted to the rank of an unofficial emissary for culture. He returned to the land of McDonalds and Pizza Hut. Journalist Jack Anderson described James Baker's threats as purely political — Baker's wife was Susan Baker of the PMRC. According to Anderson, Baker was "carrying an old grudge" from Zappa's remark that Susan was a "bored housewife." In short, it was payback time for Zappa's testimony before Congress.

On February 26, Zappa hosted his first program for FNN: *Frank Zappa's Wild Wild East*. The show provided a thorough analysis of real estate possibilities in Moscow. Zappa also conducted a phone-in interview about Soviet agriculture with a tractor factory from Carolina, plus a conversation with a group of Eastern European policymakers and entrepreneurs.

But just when this new career was opening up for Zappa, a sudden trip to the hospital ER in the spring of 1990, to complain about intestinal blockage, revealed something far more serious. For now, looking out for the interests of nations far away would have to wait. After battles with record companies, televangelists, and government censors, Zappa was now at war with his own body.

4

"I'd been feeling sick for a number of years," Zappa told *Playboy* in 1993. "But nobody diagnosed it." While Zappa was in the emergency ward, the doctors discovered he had prostate cancer. "[They] found out that it had been there for anywhere from eight to ten years, growing undetected by any of my previous doctors. By the time they found it, it was inoperable." Prostate cancer is a tumor in the gland that releases the fluid that carries semen through the penis; the prostate itself surrounds the neck of the bladder. "When I went into the hospital, the cancer had grown to where I could no longer take a piss," Zappa told David Sheff. "In order for me just to survive, they had to poke a hole in my bladder." For over a year, Zappa had a hose leading from his bladder to a bag tied to his leg.

Doctors started Zappa on twelve bouts of radiation to shrink the tumor. "I went through radiation and that fucked me up pretty good," Zappa recalled. "They were supposed to give me twelve shots of that, but I got to number eleven and I was so sick that I said I couldn't go back. The result of the radiation was that the tumor was shrunken to the point where I could get rid of the bag and could piss again, but there were bad side effects." Zappa started to cancel activities he'd planned. In June, he was to attend the Meeting of the World contemporary music festival in Finland. That same month, Vaclav Havel had invited Zappa to Prague to witness Czechoslovakia's first presidential election. Zappa's cancellations sparked rumors that he was terminally ill. The Zappa family refused comment.

While he battled the disease, Zappa did what he always did — he worked on music. By fall 1990, he started assembling three different CDs: *The Lost Episodes*, unreleased outtakes and early Studio Z material (some of which had already been issued on *Mystery Disc*); *Ahead of Their Time*, the full concert recording of the Mothers of Invention with the BBC Orchestra at Royal Albert Hall in 1968; and a sequel to *Lumpy Gravy* entitled *Civilization Phaze III*. *Ahead of Their Time* was delayed, because the lawsuit by the six former Mothers of Invention players was still before the courts. By February 1991, the issue of unpaid royalties for the

YOU CAN'T DO THAT ON STAGE ANYMORE

MGM/Verve recordings was resolved when Zappa settled out of court. The nature of the settlement was never made public.

In May 1990, while those axes were being buried, *Billboard* published a huge tribute to Zappa in celebration of twenty-five years in the music business. Drew Wheeler did a lengthy interview with him, and the magazine ran ads featuring congratulations. *Playboy* called Zappa "rock's greatest defender of the First Amendment," while John Jackson, who booked the European end of the 1988 tour, wrote: "In 1966, an impressionable nine-year-old heard 'It Can't Happen Here,' by the Mothers of Invention, receive a resounding miss from the panel of judges on BBC's *Juke Box Jury*. Twenty-two years later, he booked the forty-four-date European leg of the Broadway the Hard Way tour seen by some 315,000 customers . . . the impressionable nine-year-old got in for free. Thanks, Frank!"

Billboard also ran a tribute by Rykodisc, who announced the release of newly remastered CDs of *Zoot Allures*, *Sheik Yerbouti*, *Just Another Band From L.A.*, *Weasels Ripped My Flesh*, *Chunga's Revenge*, *Tinsel Town Rebellion*, *You Are What You Is*, and *Fillmore East, June 1971*. But Rykodisc had accidentally destroyed a pressing of *Sheik Yerbouti*, which left "Yo' Mama" ten minutes shorter than its twelve-minutes-plus length.

Zappa, incensed, announced that his involvement with Rykodisc would terminate after the release of the final volume of *You Can't Do That on Stage Anymore*. Zappa asked if Australia's Festival Records was interested in distributing the Barking Pumpkin catalog, but Gail discovered that union conditions would create another crisis. The Zappas decided that all future CDs would come out through their own cottage industry. The first, in April 1991, was the two-CD set of concerts from the ill-fated 1988 tour, appropriately titled *The Best Band You Never Heard in Your Life*, followed in June by *Make a Jazz Noise Here*.

The 1988 touring band may not have indulged in the outrageous antics of the Mothers of Invention from the '60s, the straightforward lewdness of Flo & Eddie, or the funky charm of the mid-'70s ensembles, but it's musical skill surpassed all the groups that came before it. This congregation could play *anything*. Some highlights on *The Best Band You Never Heard in Your Life*: a Doc Severinson–style "Heavy Duty Judy"; a hilarious reggae version of Johnny Cash's "Ring of Fire" (which becomes a metaphor for hemorrhoids); Ravel's *Bolero*, also done in reggae time (with some added mariachi and a brief but appropriate quote from the Knack's "My Sharona"); a stunningly energetic, horn-driven medley of "Florentine Pogen," "Andy," and "Inca Roads" from *One Size Fits All*; a Thing-Fish version of

Jimi Hendrix's "Purple Haze"; some lethal swipes at Jimmy Swaggart in "Lonesome Cowboy Burt," "More Trouble Every Day," and "Penguin in Bondage"; and a peerless cover of Led Zeppelin's "Stairway to Heaven."

What makes "Stairway" such a fascinating choice (besides its obvious metaphor for the fundamentalist Christianity Zappa was lampooning) is that it was a classic already overripe for parody. It's given a lively ska arrangement, and Ike Willis sings with soulful integrity, backed by Zappa's stinging blues guitar and ridiculous Spike Jones sound effects. The contrast between sincerity and absurdity brings a thrilling tension that is both funny and moving in its passion. But when the song reaches its climax, we hear Jimmy Page's soaring guitar solo played — note for note — by the horn section.

Unlike parodists like "Weird Al" Yankovic, who self-consciously trash a song simply by aping its basic elements, Zappa brings to the song a new interpretation that parodies the number while making it something new. As for the reggae arrangements of familiar songs, that was nothing new in the Zappa canon. "Most of the bands I've had since the early 1980s have been doing reggae," Zappa told *Downbeat* in 1991. "It's just that nobody ever wrote about it. There's two things that we've done a lot of: reggaes and waltzes. . . . One thing we were experimenting with on the '88 tour was mariachi rhythm, superimposing mariachi rhythm on top of reggae."

Make a Jazz Noise Here is a mostly instrumental double CD that concentrates on the more complex Zappa orchestrations. It opens simply enough with "Stinkfoot" (given a Jimmy Swaggart interpretation), but is followed by a new, abstract instrumental piece called "When Yuppies Go to Hell." Another recent composition is a guitar solo called "Star Wars Won't Work," named after Ronald Reagan's pet missile-defense system in space. "For those cowboys who think that Star Wars is gonna save us from alien attack," Zappa asked, "does it ever occur to you that Star Wars doesn't kill germs?" The same medley of "Let's Make the Water Turn Black," "Harry, You're a Beast," and "The Orange County Lumber Truck" that the 1969 band played on *You Can't Do That on Stage Anymore, Vol. 1* is given a much tighter performance here.

The 1988 band could shift gears with bold confidence. In "Big Swifty," they seamlessly meld themes from Wagner's *Lohengrin*, the "Habanera" from Bizet's *Carmen*, and Tchaikovsky's *1812 Overture*, while parodying jazz pianist Erroll Garner's penchant for making "jazz noises" as he played. There's a gorgeous big-band arrangement of "Black Napkins," a New Age version of "The Black Page," a glittering interpretation of *Sinister Footwear, 2nd Movement*, and a sparkling version of "Alien Orifice." While *Best Band* has Ravel's *Bolero*, *Make a Jazz Noise Here* is not outdone — it features a spunky performance of the "Royal March" from Stravinsky's *L'Histoire du soldat* and a lyrically appealing interpretation of the theme from Bartok's gorgeous *Piano Concerto #3* (both arranged by Scott Thunes).

Both albums offered ample evidence that Zappa's 1988 tour was tragic simply because this enormously gifted group didn't survive long enough to fulfill its promise. Loaded with the adeptness and individual temperament of a Duke Ellington or Stan Kenton big band, Zappa's group sadly couldn't withstand the internal pressures.

Despite his illness, Zappa was seriously considering running for president in the 1992 election. Having watched Republican administrations wreak havoc on the country for a decade, he figured he could certainly do no worse. "Democracy is one of those things that looks good on paper, but we've come to a crossroads in contemporary America where we really ought to decide: do we want it?" Zappa asked journalist John Winokur. "When you have a preponderance of people in this country who will willingly accept censorship — in fact, ask for it, or demand it in the case of the Gulf War — you've got a problem." Continuing the discussion of the 1991 Gulf War, where America tried to exorcise the lingering horror of the Vietnam War by taking on Iraq's Saddam Hussein, Zappa told Alastair Sutherland of *Music Express*, "Things are getting worse in the United States. The whole mood is on the verge of becoming a police state. For a while, every time you turned on the TV there was a fucking military parade, yellow ribbons, missile launchers, people lining the streets trying to feel good about themselves because we'd killed how many Iraqis — we'll never know the real number. And for what? Saddam Hussein is still in power."

When he talked to Bob Guccione Jr. of *Spin*, Zappa summed up his disgust with the '80s. "The only way you can feel good about the '80s is if you can't feel anything at all," Zappa said. "In a ten-year period, 12 per cent of the homeless are Vietnam vets with nowhere to go, maybe 30 per cent were dumped out of mental institutions when Reagan closed them in the early part of the '80s, and the rest of the people were families that got dispossessed during Reagan's depression during '82–'83, when his economics first took its toll, and other people are making a zillion dollars in the stock market by selling junk bonds and renting puffed air to each other." Zappa had hopes of creating a platform built on integrity. "The idea is to run as a non-partisan candidate and urge other people around the country to not only run but resign from the Democratic and the Republican parties because the Democrats stand for nothing except 'I wish I was a Republican' and the Republicans stand for raw, unbridled evil and greed and ignorance smothered in balloons and ribbons." Although Zappa wanted to do a feasibility study, it would never be completed due to his failing health and the immense work his candidacy would involve. But if "Zappa for President" wasn't in the cards, an end to his woes in Modern Music Land was finally in sight.

Jeffrey Burns, an American pianist who lived in Berlin, visited Zappa that spring with a proposition. He was doing regular premieres of modern piano pieces through Berlin's Akademie der Kuenste, and he asked Zappa to write some piano music that would be performed there under Zappa's supervision. Zappa gave Burns the sheet music for a piano piece — named for Ruth Underwood — called "Ruth Is Sleeping," and told him that many a piano player had given up in despair trying to negotiate its complexity. Burns was game, even if Zappa didn't think he had a prayer. In the meantime, Zappa received another visit, this time from German filmmaker Henning Lohner, who in May 1991 had made a documentary on Zappa for German television. He suggested that the 1992 Frankfurt Festival head, Dr. Dieter Rexroth, solicit Zappa for an orchestral work. At first Zappa thought this would be painstaking, given his woes with similar offers in the past, but there was also interest from Karsten Witt, the director of the Vienna Concert House, and Rexroth's eventual successor, Andreas Molich-Zebhauser, to have Zappa's music performed by this eighteen-piece modern-music orchestra, the Ensemble Modern. Molich-Zebhauser, it turned out, was the general manager and director of the Deutsche Ensemble Academy, an umbrella organization of three orchestras that included the Ensemble Modern.

"My first reaction was that I couldn't believe it," Molich-Zebhauser told Don Menn. "Five years ago, when I learned that Frank was a composer of serious classical music, I told my partners, 'Okay, there's some of these pop stars who try to do this kind of stuff, but I'm quite sure that he is just a beginner.' I was really surprised when I saw the high level of compositions like 'Mo 'n' Herb's Vacation.'" On May 23, 1991, Rexroth, Molich-Zebhauser, and Lohner visited Zappa in L.A. to try to convince him to accept. They told him he was one of only four composers being considered for the festival — the others were John Cage, Alexander Knaifel, and Karlheinz Stockhausen.

"Like many musicians, I was very interested in the music Frank wrote in the past, but there have been only a very few classical performances of his serious

YOU CAN'T DO THAT ON STAGE ANYMORE

music," Molich-Zebhauser said. "This was a start of a very special and new way of composing. Normally in the classical field, a composer gets a commission, sits at his desk for a couple of months writing down notes, delivers a score to an orchestra which rehearses it, and in the last rehearsals the composer comes in and says, 'Oh yes, here you have to change something, and here please a little louder.' The opposite is true with our project."

In July, the Ensemble Modern arrived for two weeks of discussion, with the hope of collaborating. So that Zappa could get a sense of their musical interests and skill, they gave him a couple of CDs that featured their interpretations of the music of Kurt Weill and Helmut Lachenmann, while Zappa shared with them some of his synclavier pieces. Although Zappa was not a huge fan of Weill (despite inheriting a similar proclivity for political theater), he was intrigued by the group's style and ability. In short, he liked their attitude. That month, they worked with Zappa in Joe's Garage, sampling each of their instruments into his new Synclavier 9600, which gave him much better sampling capabilities.

The project the Ensemble Modern and Zappa would work on together would come to be known as *The Yellow Shark*. Given the long history of fish imagery in Zappa's work (enough to rival the poodles), the title seemed fitting. Molich-Zebhauser and Peter Rundel, the conductor of the Ensemble Modern, had spotted a sculpture of a huge, yellow fish above Zappa's basement fireplace. It was a marlin, but Molich-Zebhauser thought it was a shark (assuming perhaps that this was the true Mud Shark). Zappa corrected him and explained that a fan, Mark Beam, had given him the piece in 1988.

Mark Beam was a Zappaphile who had created a whole collection of fish sculptures from papier-mâché, a surfboard, fiberglass, and paint. Gail phoned Beam when the ensemble expressed interest in his shark, and Zappa offered to pay for the name and any "Yellow Shark" merchandise produced for the series of concerts they were planning. Beam agreed. And while the ensemble and Zappa schemed with the aid of a fiberglass "yellow shark," *You Can't Do That on Stage Anymore, Vol. 4* was released.

For the first time in the series, there were no liner notes in the CD booklet, which may have indicated the state of Zappa's health by the time it came out. As well, a number of errors around dates and performances added to the confusion. Yet even with those deficiencies, *Vol. 4* is one of the strongest discs in the series. "Little Rubber Girl," from a Halloween performance at the Palladium in 1978, begins with the opening lines to Zappa's "Go Cry on Somebody Else's Shoulder" from *Freak Out!* But it quickly turns into another variation on the mechanical sex acts examined with much more aplomb in "Ms. Pinky." While Denny Walley mimics a soul singer's pleas — describing the various ways he's going to violate this artificial female — Zappa does an R&B vocal overlay, repeating variations on the title. "Stick Together," performed by the 1984 group, is a peppier version of Zappa's anti-union tune. The '84 band also performs daring new arrangements of "My Guitar Wants to Kill Your Mama" and "Willie the Pimp."

The action then shifts back to the 1973 Roxy shows for "Montana," until, midway through, Zappa abruptly splices back to the 1984 group. They continue with the spiritual "Brown Moses," plus "The Evil Prince," from *Thing-Fish*. Ray White's lead vocal on "The Evil Prince" has a stronger urgency than Napoleon Murphy Brock's in the musical, and Zappa provides a stinging guitar solo. "Approximate," from Italy in 1982, is the early '70s track that blends improvised vocal pitches with contrapuntal rhythms. In this compact version, the group includes a quote from the Bee Gees' "Stayin' Alive" and from a Heinz Ketchup commercial. This giddy, atonal number slides into a pretty 1980 performance of Zappa's doo-wop gem, "Love of My Life," from the Mudd Club.

A short musical excerpt from "Be-Bop Tango" is an appropriate introduction to a 1984 performance of "Let's Move to Cleveland" featuring jazz saxophonist Archie Shepp at the Fine Arts Center Concert Hall in Amherst, Massachusetts. Unlike many modernist jazz performers, Shepp blended rock rhythms, tonalities, as well as jazz swing. His style of playing, seeped in the blues, perfectly suits the drawn-out melody of "Cleveland."

The more abstract "You Call That Music?" from a 1969 Mothers performance at Columbia University, is the kind of atonal absurdism that was already in full bloom on "Didja Get Any Onya?" After the acoustic atonality of the 1969 Mothers, we're thrust into a 1978 performance of "Pound for Brown — Solos," featuring the electronic chicanery of Peter Wolf on mini-Moog and Tommy Mars on electric piano. Once the 1984 group performs "The Black Page" as a quick waltz, the 1988 band makes its first appearance on *You Can't Do That on Stage Anymore*. "Take Me Out to the Ball Game" is the Jack Norworth and Albert Von Tilzer tune traditionally sung at the ballpark during the seventh-inning stretch. Walt Fowler and Ike Willis parody Atlanta broadcasters Skip Carey and Pete Van Wearen, while the group does an outrageous vamp on the tune that evokes some of Spike Jones' ridiculous comic brilliance. "I think 'Take Me Out to the Ball Game' is one of the most outstandingly absurd things ever to appear on an FZ release," remarked

YOU CAN'T DO THAT ON STAGE ANYMORE

guitarist Mike Keneally. By the end, Willis does a wistful rendition of the song accompanied by Fowler's beautifully stated solo trumpet.

"Filthy Habits," the feedback-drenched guitar composition from *Sleep Dirt*, now has the added color of the augmented 1988 horn section. "The Torture Never Stops (Original Version)" is the recording of "Why Doesn't Someone Get Him a Pepsi?" from the 1975 *Bongo Fury* tour that featured Captain Beefheart. It's also the song that Zappa offered Beefheart — in vain — for his *Ice Cream for Crow* album in 1982. Beginning with the riff from Howlin' Wolf's "Smokestack Lightnin'," the band settles into a steady groove lead by Walley's slide guitar. While Zappa brought out the lascivious qualities of the song on *Zoot Allures*, Beefheart's dramatic reading comes right out of the strangely mythic tales rooted in the Delta blues.

"Church Chat," which begins the second disc, is a mock sermon from France in 1982 about the nature of sin — it recounts the various implements Steve Vai employed to penetrate a groupie. Naturally this leads into a staggering version of "Stevie's Spanking," which becomes a heavy-metal extravaganza where Vai and Zappa trade aggressive, electrifying solos. Eventually they join in a lively duet, creating an aural landscape that resembles fire trucks racing to a three-alarm blaze. A plaintive performance of "Outside Now" by the 1984 band follows, leading into a lightning-quick version of "Disco Boy" from 1982.

"Teen-age Wind" (also from 1982) is performed at a brisk pace before settling into a faithful 1984 rendition of "Truck Driver Divorce." The track "Florentine Pogen" begins with an uncredited 1974 performance and concludes with the 1979 band. There's a sharp contrast between the careful interpretation of what was then a new song and the confidently quick tempo of the 1979 group. "Tiny Sick Tears," a performance from the 1969 concert at the Factory, in the Bronx, is a takeoff of the mid-'60s hit "96 Tears," by ? and the Mysterians, and Jim Morrison's oedipal journey in the Doors' classic "The End." Zappa narrates a story of teenage sexual angst that ends with the lad entering the bedroom of his father, who is beating his meat to *Playboy* and saying, "Not now, son. Not now!"

After using the same brief quote from "Be-Bop Tango" that opens "Let's Move to Cleveland," the 1974 ensemble does a number called "Smell My Beard," in which George Duke tells a backstage story of road manager Marty Perellis' libidinous activities with a groupie. Once finished, he apparently invited Duke to "Smell My Beard." "The Booger Man," the R&B number that follows, is devoted to the details of Perellis' conquest. After a crisp performance of "Carolina Hard-Core Ecstasy" from 1984, the Mothers follow with more dissonant sounds (mixed with some of

Bunk Gardner's sex recordings) that appear to upset one fan at the Fillmore East. When Zappa asks what this agitated fellow is saying, he tells Zappa, "You're fucked." "I'm fucked?" Zappa shouts back. "Why, that's the nicest thing that anyone has said to me all day."

Zappa finishes the set with a solid medley of '50s R&B songs played both by the vocally proficient '84 band ("Little Girl of Mine," "The Closer You Are," "Johnny Darling," and "No, No Cherry"), and the equally adept '82 ensemble ("The Man From Utopia," "Mary Lou"). *You Can't Do That on Stage Anymore, Vol. 4*, released in June 1991, is an ambitious undertaking that provides a wide range of musical styles and sheer proficiency.

5

For years, Zappa had been complaining about the bootleg live and studio recordings of his work available on the market. Bootlegs are illegally recorded or obtained, sold without the artist's permission or input. The sound quality is usually questionable and the price exorbitant — with the artist receiving no royalties. According to *Hot Wacks*, a reference book for bootleg collectors, there are over 150 Zappa bootleg albums or CDs available. Zappa outnumbers the Beatles, the Rolling Stones, and Jimi Hendrix.

As an artist who obsessed about sound, Zappa must have found it particularly painful to hear pieces recorded by a cassette machine in the audience. And then there was the money he was losing in the process. "In a twenty-five-year career, I've experienced the phenomenon of vast quantities of boots being recorded, and really bad recordings that pissed me off," Zappa told *Society Pages*. "That's a pretty strong motivation to get back at these guys, and that's where I got the idea to bootleg the boots." In March, he came up with the inspired idea of buying up bootlegged titles, then reissuing them with the pirates' original artwork — only not credited to them. Zappa had Tom Brown, Rhino's expert on his music, pick ten records out of the vast bootleg collection.

Rhino Records entered the deal and announced they were putting out the ten-album box set called *Beat the Boots*. The records and audio cassettes came in a plain cardboard box with a pop-up illustration of the Mothers onstage. The set also came with a T-shirt and a button that depicted a hand holding a hammer and read, "Beat the Boots." The set was released on the Foo-eee label in July 1991. Named after Rhino founder Richard Foo, the label's logo featured a rhino with a

YOU CAN'T DO THAT ON STAGE ANYMORE

clothespin in its nose going, "Foo-eee!" Rhino saw this as an uncommon commercial opportunity. "Frank is in a unique position to do this because he owns his own material and his own masters," said Faith Raphael, the Rhino product manager. "With other artists, whose labels own the rights to their master tapes, it would be a nightmare to collect permissions for a series like this. But Frank wants to make a statement about bootlegging, and he is hoping other artists will do the same."

The final selection of recordings varied in quality. *'Tis the Season to Be Jelly* was the 1967 Stockholm concert during the Mothers of Invention's first European tour. Since this was taken from a radio broadcast, the recording is generally good, providing an accurate picture of the band at that time. Oddly, the excerpt from Stravinsky's *Petrushka* was available only on the U.S. edition of the album, due to copyright restrictions.

The Ark was Zappa's soundboard recording from the Mothers' 1968 Boston concert; the tape had been stolen at the end of the evening. Although unmixed, it is a listenable bootleg with some fine performances of "My Guitar Wants to Kill Your Mama" and "Uncle Meat/King Kong."

Freaks & Motherfu*#@%!, on the other hand, is a terrible specimen from the Flo & Eddie era during a 1971 concert in New York. The only highlight is the opportunity to hear, on an officially released recording, "Holiday in Berlin" with lyrics.

Piquantique, featuring the 1973 band including Jean-Luc Ponty, is one of the more fascinating discs. Since Zappa released little live material from this generally instrumental ensemble, it's great to hear early versions of "RDNZL," "Dupree's Paradise," and "T'Mershi Duween," and the only official release of "Farther Oblivion." The recording is in mono and is a little flat, but the energy of the performances, divided between the icy cold of Stockholm and the summer wind of Sydney, cut through the banality of the sound.

Unmitigated Audacity is a muddy representation of the 1974 band performing in Chicago during the Mothers' tenth-anniversary celebration. Zappa and the group speed through a medley of songs from *Freak Out!* and finish with "Camarillo Brillo," from *Over-nite Sensation*. Zappa improvises a lyric during "Trouble Every Day" where he sings, "I'm about to get sick of listening to this monitor system." It couldn't have been any worse than this source tape.

Saarbrucken 1978 is a two-record set of the '78 band in a reasonably good recording that features "Don't Eat the Yellow Snow" with the coda "Rollo" included.

Any Way the Wind Blows is another double set, this time featuring the 1979 band in Paris. The source tape appears to come from a radio broadcast that is in stereo, but still fuzzy on the high end.

As An Am begins with a radio interview excerpt in which Zappa explains why bootleggers make him mad, then launches into a couple of recordings from Köln during the 1982 tour. "Young & Monde" is an early version of "Let's Move to Cleveland," ending with a vocal by Bobby Martin. There's also an extended performance of "Sharleena" that was further refined on *Them or Us*. The other side has the 1981 band at the Palladium performing "Black Napkins," "The Black Page," and "The Torture Never Stops." *As An Am* is a moderately clear recording of pieces better represented on officially released Zappa live recordings. "I haven't heard them myself, nor do I intend to," Zappa said emphatically in *Society Pages*. "I make no claim that any of the material contained on these records is of any musical value whatsoever. Besides, if you want crap, now you can get fully authorized affordable crap, and maybe put some sleazebag out of business."

In June 1991, Zappa was off to visit Russia once more, adding a return trip to Czechoslovakia as well. Having now absorbed the high esteem in which he was regarded in these countries, he could bask in a mutual celebration of what appeared to be the end of totalitarian rule. The occasion in Czechoslovakia was the final evacuation of Soviet troops from Czech soil on June 24. This event had deep resonance for those who suffered the thaw of the Prague Spring in 1968, when Soviet tanks crushed any hopes for socialism with a human face. That night, Zappa played guitar with Michael Kocab and his band, Prazsky Vyber (the Prague Selection), at the Prague Sports Hall. They performed an improvised reggae number titled "Improvizace v a Dur s Frankem Zappou" ("Improvisation in A Major With Frank Zappa"). Yet, sadly, it was not the same Frank Zappa this loyal audience had heard in their pirate recordings. He hadn't played the guitar since the 1988 tour, and his illness had begun to take its toll on him. The cancer and radiation treatments had turned his trademark moustache and imperial prematurely gray. He had also gained over forty pounds. But Zappa continued the tour through the Eastern bloc regardless. Five days later, he was in Hungary to play guitar with a local group at the Taban. As if to link the Bartok aura he evoked in "Transylvania Boogie" with the dancing mutant gypsy vacuum cleaner on the inside cover of *Chunga's Revenge*, Zappa joined four Hungarian gypsy jazz musicians, as they wound their way through a twenty-minute improvisation called "One of a Kind."

YOU CAN'T DO THAT ON STAGE ANYMORE

Making his way home through France and the U.K., Zappa appeared on BBC Radio 4's *Midweek*, joining the Irish virtuoso folk group the Chieftains. Zappa and the veteran Irish group got on famously — both had a strong regard for musical tradition. "I know one particular tune from India where the first eight bars are almost identical to an old-style song from the west of Ireland," said Paddy Moloney, the leader of the Chieftains. "You can come across various little pieces and you hear it, and you think, 'My God, that's a jig, I know that' — a couple of little bars and you can match them." Zappa and Moloney became kindred spirits during that program, and it's not hard to see why. Like Zappa, Moloney believed music had no boundaries, and value wasn't determined by culture or ruling hierarchies. In fact, Zappa's utopian view that one size fits all was perfectly articulated in Moloney's enthusiastic revelation. But just in case listeners assumed that cultural pollination was due to conservatory-trained musicians stretching their hands in friendship across the ocean, Hayes asked how certain tunes could possibly pop up on opposite sides of the world? Zappa answered with one word: "Sailors." Gales of laughter filled the studio. Zappa told Moloney to call him up the next time the group was in Los Angeles.

In November 1991, *Zappa's Universe*, the Zappa tribute featuring Keneally, Vai, Thunes, Dweezil, Bozzio, the Persuasions, Rockapella, and Joel Thome and the Orchestra of Our Time, took place in New York. There was much legal fallout from this concert. The Verve label, which had been taken over by Polygram Diversified Entertainment, obtained the audio and video rights to the recorded event. But they wanted to release both a two-CD and a video version of *Zappa's Universe*. When they issued only one CD in September 1993, Polygram filed a lawsuit against Zappa, claiming he wasn't acting in good faith. Zappa insisted that he hadn't given consent in the first place for the two-CD set or the videotape. Eventually, they settled out of court. The tape and CD are still available. Vai's performance of "Sofa" won a Grammy Award — even though his guitar solo was done in the studio later and dubbed onto the live track.

The massive success of *Beat the Boots* led to a sequel of sorts. Since the first volume went through three pressings, selling 20,000 units, Rhino put together a second volume, *Beat the Boots 2*, for release in a limited edition in May 1992. The box was much spiffier than the first. It featured an eight-CD set that included a fabulous scrapbook filled with articles, reviews, and rare photos dating back to Zappa's high school days. It also had a red logo pin and a black beret. The selections, however, lack the range of the first volume. But there are some noteworthy inclusions.

Swiss Cheese/Fire!, for instance, was a two-CD recording of the 1971 Montreux concert that ended — literally — in flames. The source tape is in pretty clear stereo and captures the whole event, including Zappa trying calmly to guide people out any exit they can find, while chaos erupts.

Our Man in Nirvana is an average mono recording of the 1968 band playing live in Fullerton, California. What makes it notable is that it's the only officially released recording of Wild Man Fischer with the group. He sings "I'm the Meany" to what sounds like a stunned, silent crowd.

Disconnected Synapses is a rare documentation of the Flo & Eddie band playing (briefly) with Jean-Luc Ponty in Paris in 1970. They do a rousing "King Kong" (a great track that is unfortunately represented on just about all of the discs included here), plus a rare live take of "Penis Dimension."

Zappa's attack on bootleggers was about more than just going after people who had made illegal tapes. "When I was in Russia, I met one young guy who had worked his way through college by getting my LPs from Yugoslavia and making tapes and selling them," Zappa remarked to *Music Express*. "That didn't bother me so much — bringing a musical artifact into an authoritarian society is understandable. But in the free world there are laws that supposedly exist to protect artists. The problem is, nobody enforces them, and the subtext is 'Who needs you guys anyway? Your business and livelihood don't matter.'"

In June 1992, Paddy Moloney kept his promise and notified Zappa that the Chieftains, who were then working on a new album called *The Celtic Harp*, would be in town. Zappa invited the band to the UMRK studios on June 24. The occasion was the bicentenary of a festival held in Belfast in 1792, when Edward Bunting brought together ten of the foremost Irish harp players. That festival was organized by the Belfast Harpers Society, who wanted to preserve a music they feared would become obsolete. Bunting visited each harper, classifying all of the contemporary harp music he could find, and published the music in books well into the 19th century. The Chieftains selected pieces from Bunting's collection as part of *The Celtic Harp*. At the time, Zappa and his recording engineer, Spencer Chrislu, were experimenting with a four-foot diametric hoop filled with microphones that musicians could assemble themselves around. Zappa had the Chieftans record some of *The Celtic Harp* using this invention.

The results were intoxicating, but when the Chieftains started to flag by midnight, Zappa was by no means tired. He was having a great time. At Zappa's insistence, Paddy Moloney convinced the rest of the group to continue. One track

YOU CAN'T DO THAT ON STAGE ANYMORE

Zappa wanted to record was an old *a cappella* song called "The Green Fields of America." Kevin Conneff was set up to sing the song, but he was exhausted and didn't think his voice was up to the task. They tried three takes, but to no avail. Then Zappa and Chrislu set up a mike in the back room of UMRK, thinking the room's natural ambience would hide whatever problems may lay in Conneff's weary voice. Although Conneff was nowhere pleased with his performance (he desperately wanted to record it again), Zappa was overwhelmed with the fourth take — and his instincts were absolutely correct. "The Green Fields of America" is a powerful emigrant song about leaving the impoverishment of one's homeland to find peace and fulfillment in another country. The slight touch of weariness in Conneff's voice adds a tremulous quality, and the high-wire cadences he achieves balances the tune's hope and skepticism. The Chieftains continued the session until two in the morning, recording eight of the twelve pieces for their album.

As the year wore on, Zappa's condition weakened. Although he continued to battle the cancer, he had energy only to compose and finish projects already in process. Next on his plate was the completion of *You Can't Do That on Stage Anymore*. In August 1992, both *Vol. 5* and *Vol. 6* were released simultaneously in a wooden CD container. This brought Zappa's licensing deal with Rykodisc to an end.

On *Vol. 5*, Zappa focused on two groups: the '60s Mothers of Invention and the '82 band. Each group received a separate disc. Considering Zappa's bad feelings about the original Mothers, it's perhaps surprising he'd devote a whole disc to this group. But it was hard to avoid the simple fact that the music this group produced *definitely* could not be done onstage any longer, considering the state of popular culture.

Most of the material dates from the last tour in 1969, but there are also gems from earlier. "The Downtown Talent Scout," from the 1965 concert at the Fillmore West, is about the surveillance men who used to spy on freaks in Hollywood in the early 60s. "We never knew if they were FBI, CIA, DEA, or what," Zappa recalled in the liner notes, "but they'd do stupid stuff like rush into restaurants . . . and take 8mm movies of anybody who looked too weird, then rush out again to a waiting car." Zappa alluded to these undercover characters later in "Plastic People" ("And there's this guy from the CIA/Creeping around Laurel Canyon"), but "The Downtown Talent Scout" is a full-blown account that captures the air of justifiable paranoia that permeated the '60s:

Modern law and justice
Has advanced to such a point
That a jury trial is useless
They simply take you to the joint.

Because after all you look so freaky
How could anyone believe
That what you think and what you feel
Comes close at all to what is real.

After Zappa calls out, "Blow your harmonica, son," Buzz Gardner's trumpet jumps in instead with the opening notes of "Charles Ives" from the Mothers' 1969 concert at Columbia University. Quoting Ives' *The Unanswered Question*, Gardner's horn is soon joined by Lowell George performing a falsetto. This is the genesis of "Didja Get Any Onya?" from the same tour, combined with the vamp from Captain Beefheart's "The Blimp" from *Trout Mask Replica*.

Zappa called the piece "Charles Ives" not only because of the quote from *The Unanswered Question*, but because of Ives' penchant for combining melodies from different sources. On *Weasels Ripped My Flesh*, Zappa followed the bizarre abstractions of "Didja Get Any Onya?" with the straight R&B cover of Little Richard's "Directly From My Heart to You." Zappa here creates the same contrast by following "Charles Ives" with a cover of the '50s R&B tune "Here Lies Love" by the Four Deuces. Sung by George in a voice that sounds startlingly like Johnny "Guitar" Watson, the track was frequently performed by the 1969 group. There is a tentative tone to George's phrasing that gives perfect pause to the lyrics:

Here lies love
In a grave caused by jealousy
Pain was the pallbearer
And on the tombstone
Was written misery.

"Piano/Drum Duet," featuring Ian Underwood on electric piano and Art Tripp on drums, is a short, nicely executed portion from *200 Motels* ("Bogus Pomp") recorded at the Ark in Boston in 1969. "Mozart Ballet — Piano Sonata in B Flat," recorded in 1969 at the Royal Albert Hall, is a hilarious piece of absurdity that suffers from a lack of visuals. While Underwood expertly performs Mozart's *Piano Sonata in B Flat* on the grand piano, the rest of the group is acting out a twisted ballet that undermines the eloquent beauty of Mozart's composition. Noel Redding, the bass player from the Jimi Hendrix Experience who was backstage, decided to join in. "This involved [Redding] being picked up by our roadie [Kanzus J. Kanzus] and [colliding] violently with Motorhead Sherwood," Zappa explained in the liner notes. "Dick Barber, our road manager, made an appearance with a rubber chicken (pre-rigged with its little belly full of brown ale and shaving foam). After announcing his deep feelings about the species, he vocalized a few of his special snorks and strangled it, causing the grotesque stew within to splorch all over the hallowed stage." The tortured sounds of Don Preston playing the chicken overtop of Mozart's melody is a moment of blissful desecration.

"Chocolate Halvah" is an outrageous vocal duet between George and Roy Estrada that calls to mind Cream's "I Feel Free" — done with a slight Middle Eastern flavor. "JCB & Kansas on the Bus" is a bit of audio verité by recording engineer Dick Kunc that captures Jimmy Carl Black and roadie Kanzus in casual conversation. Of course, with a rock band on the road (especially the Mothers), nothing is ever exactly casual, which is why Zappa found so much of the group's offstage commentary fuel for musical material. In this segment, Black offers an off-the-cuff, lonely rendition of Hank Williams' "Lovesick Blues," which crossfades into a lively rendition of Zappa's main title theme and "The Little March" from *Run Home Slow*.

"Right There" is a combined live and studio performance of "Skweezit Skweezit Skweezit" (heard on *Mystery Disc*), featuring Estrada doing his high wheezings over Gardner's taped sexual escapades. "Where Is Johnny Velvet?," "Return of the Hunch-Back Duke," and "Trouble Every Day" are from the 1969 show at the Factory in the Bronx that produced "Tiny Sick Tears" from *Vol. 4*, "Plastic People" from *Vol. 1*, and "Get a Little" from *Weasels Ripped My Flesh*.

"Johnny Velvet" is more friendly banter between Zappa and the crowd, where he tries to coax someone to come up and sing with the band. When one audience member suggests Johnny Velvet, Johnny is nowhere to be found in the crowd. "Return of the Hunch-Back Duke" is the main theme from "The Little House I Used to Live In" played in the same style featured on *Burnt Weeny Sandwich*, and "Trouble Every Day" is a lacklustre performance of one of Zappa's best pieces of agitprop.

"Proto-Minimalism" is another sample (like "You Call That Music?") from Columbia University. A second segment of audio verité features Black on the bus doing a gritty rendition of Bing Crosby's "Pistol Packin' Mama." This is followed by "My Head?" — a brief dialogue from Art Tripp's birthday party. "My Head?" has the group gathering for a photo session where, according to Zappa, they are "attempting to assume some sort of mutant cluster-fuck pose — and enjoying it more than anyone would have suspected." The latent homosexuality of male rock bands (something Zappa examined explicitly in later songs) is in evidence here. Since Zappa also wrote musical pitches that duplicated human speaking patterns, you can hear those musical qualities at work in "My Head?" as the group riffs on a variety of salacious phrases.

"Meow" has Zappa conducting the group through an electronic abstraction at the Whisky A Go-Go in 1968. "Baked-Bean Boogie" is some classic guitar boogie from Zappa at the Ark in Boston, while "Where's Our Equipment?" comes from the same concert in Copenhagen in 1967 that produced "Ian Underwood Whips It Out" on *Uncle Meat*. It's a beautifully moody piece in which Underwood and Gardner create melodic loops around Jimmy Carl Black's and Billy Mundi's rhythms. This track hails from the first tour of Europe, when Zappa was stricken with gastroenteritis. Since the band's equipment was delayed by a snowstorm, they had to use amps borrowed from blues artist John Mayall. The Mothers' music was recorded by a Danish radio journalist holding a microphone up to the monitor speaker.

"F.Z./JCB Drum Duet" is a stunning display of Zappa's percussive talents, as he and Tripp trade solos with Black, who provides the rhythm. "No Waiting for the Peanuts to Dissolve" is a piece of improvisation that sounds like something out of "King Kong." After a bit of audio verité featuring the band playing cards while "waiting for Vanilla Fudge to finish," Zappa introduces a piece of psychedelia from 1969 called "Underground Freak-Out Music." This same track — minus the intro and somewhat longer — appears on *Mystery Disc* as "Black Beauty." It's one of the only Mothers' songs where George gets to demonstrate his abilities on lead guitar, even though it lacks the sinewy tone he established playing slide with Little Feat. However, George perfectly captures the fuzzy ambience of overamplified psychedelic rock.

"German Lunch" features a whole other side of George. This bit of improvised theater, not performed live onstage but at the Criteria Studios in Miami in 1969, has him playing a German border guard (using the same accent as in "Didja Get Any Onya?") interrogating the band. It's an often funny performance with each musician bringing out his personal idiosyncrasies. Motorhead Sherwood whips a table while George asks him what he's doing. "I'm beating a horse to make it go faster," Sherwood explains. "That's not a horse, it's a table," George replies. "What's the difference?" Sherwood answers. The disc ends with an early studio demo of "My Guitar Wants to Kill Your Mama." Although it's interesting to hear the song in an embryonic state, it isn't a live performance — why is it included here?

The second disc in *Vol. 5* is dedicated to the '82 ensemble and culled from shows in Munich, Bolzano, Frankfurt, and Geneva. Besides the stellar musicianship and the pristine arena-rock sound, this group is in striking contrast to the '60s band. No longer a shaggy-dog outfit brazenly shocking audiences, this highly competent band instead found itself shocked by the behavior of the audience. While usually ducking hypodermic syringes flung by drug users, the '82 group rips through stunning versions of "Moggio," "Easy Meat," "RDNZL," and "A Pound for a Brown (on the Bus)."

Other noteworthy tunes include a version of "Advance Romance" that's not remarkably different from the 1984 rendition on *Vol. 3*, but has a different edit of the guitar solo "Jim & Tammy's Upper Room" from *Guitar*. "The Black Page #2" also has the same solo that made up "Which One Is It?" on *Guitar*. And the new song "Shall We Take Ourselves Seriously?" immortalizes German promoter Fritz Rau, who once had a fit when he discovered asparagus was being fed to roadies backstage. Zappa comes close to having a fit himself at the end, on "Geneva Farewell," when he warns the audience that if any more discarded drug paraphernalia gets tossed onstage, the band will leave. When the bombardment doesn't stop, Zappa ends the concert to a chorus of boos.

You Can't Do That on Stage Anymore, Vol. 6 focuses on the subject of sex and the Halloween concerts. Some highlights include "The M.O.I. Anti-Smut Loyalty Oath," from the 1970 show in Florida where the band was threatened by a redneck if they dared expose themselves like Jim Morrison; a rousing 1988 version of "Honey, Don't You Want a Man Like Me?" that benefits from the horn section and sound effects; a terrific performance of "Shove It Right In" from the 1971 Fillmore concert; "Wind Up Workin' in a Gas Station," from 1975, which benefits greatly from Bianca Thornton's powerhouse backup vocals; Zappa and violinist L. Shankar's two wonderful performances during the 1978 Halloween show at the Palladium — a new instrumental ("Thirteen") and an old favorite ("Take Your Clothes Off When You Dance"); "Lisa's Life Story," a funny oratorio featuring soprano Lisa Popeil at the Santa Monica Civic Auditorium concert in 1980; and a blend of two performances of "Lonesome Cowboy Burt" from 1988 and 1971 that Zappa's Sonic Solutions digital editing equipment made possible.

The final track selected to complete this live omnibus is "Strictly Genteel," from a 1981 performance that is both thrilling and moving. At the end, as the crowd cheers, Zappa reminds the audience not to throw things on the stage. He's reminding us that even though outrageous events took place on this hallowed rostrum, there were real live people performing on it.

6

By the fall 1992, Zappa was looking ahead to the Frankfurt Festival, where his orchestral work might be performed under proper circumstances and with the right group. Besides, it didn't look like there were any more rock tours in the cards for him. "You know, if you're my age, that's not a bad age to be a classical composer," the fifty-one-year-old Zappa told *Society Pages*. "But it's a terrible age to be a rock 'n' roll musician." So now he was preparing for a tour different from any he'd ever experienced. The concerts with the Ensemble Modern were set for September 17 to 19 at the Alte Oper in Frankfurt, then to the Berlin Philharmonie on September 22 and 23, and finally Vienna's Konzerthaus on September 26 and 28.

In July, Frank, Gail, and Moon Unit had flown to Frankfurt to rehearse for two weeks with the Ensemble Modern. The older pieces selected included new arrangements of "Uncle Meat" and "Dog Breath Variations," "A Pound for a Brown (on the Bus)," "Be-Bop Tango," "G-Spot Tornado," "None of the Above," "Times Beach," and an expanded version of "Outrage at Valdez." Getting their world premieres were "Amnerika" (not included on *The Yellow Shark*, but on the posthumous release *Everything Is Healing Nicely*), "Beat the Reaper" (also not on *The Yellow Shark*, but on Zappa's final album, *Civilization Phaze III*), "Pentagon Afternoon," "Get Whitey," "Questi Cazzi di Piccione (Those Fucking Pigeons)," "Ruth Is Sleeping," and "N-Lite" (written for the synclavier and later released on *Civilization Phaze III*).

By then, Zappa was talking to reporters with great enthusiasm. The shows would be recorded and videotaped, with German television broadcasting the opening night on a pay-TV channel. The venues were picked to accommodate Zappa's six-channel surround-sound system, which would provide a unique aural experience for an audience not used to such technical means at a classical concert.

YOU CAN'T DO THAT ON STAGE ANYMORE

The Canadian dance troupe La La La Human Steps, made up of three robust males and three buxom females, were added to provide some dynamic choreography to "G-Spot Tornado." Zappa's own involvement was simply to host and be the conductor on the improvised sections of the program.

The concerts were a huge success. The shows in Frankfurt alone drew over 2,400 fans. "You know what normally happens at a modern music concert," Zappa told Rip Rense. "If you have an audience of 500, it's a success. And [here] you're talking about averaging 2,000 seats a night, and massive, lengthy, encore-demanding applause at the end of the shows. Stunned expressions on the faces of the musicians, the concert organizers, the managers, everybody sitting there with their jaws on the floor. And I don't have to stand there and be Mr. Carnival Barker to draw 'em in."

If there was one downside, it was that Zappa was too ill to appear in Berlin and Vienna, and had to return home on September 22. But, as borne out on *The Yellow Shark*, released in October 1993, the Ensemble Modern was the group created to play Zappa's orchestral music.

The disc begins with Zappa entering the stage to introduce the ensemble. Before he does, he sees a sign that asks, "What's the secret word for tonight?" This became a trademark at Zappa concerts — first heard on record during the *Fillmore East* album when Zappa began "The Mud Shark," and on *The Best Band You Never Heard in Your Life* before Zappa begins his reggae cover of Johnny Cash's "Ring of Fire." On this evening, Zappa tells the crowd that the secret word is . . . and the ensemble lets loose with a series of electronic noises. Once Zappa welcomes the group, he quickly takes the high-culture formalism out of the event by telling the audience that if they wish to throw underpants, they're welcome to.

"Dog Breath/Uncle Meat," arranged by Ali Askin, is given a wonderful, full-blown treatment that brings out the vibrancy in the orchestration. "What I like very much about it," conductor Peter Rundel told Rip Rense, "is that when I heard it the first time, it reminded me very much of Stravinsky, with its irregular patterns. Still, the melody is very much Frank Zappa." Rundel also recognized that Zappa's music has "a speaking quality even if there's no words." Some of that speech-like quality can be heard here in "Outrage at Valdez," Zappa's theme music for the 1990 Cousteau Society documentary on the *Exxon Valdez* oil spill. Naturally, the composition has a melancholic quality where the horn section seems to be in quiet mournful conversation with itself.

"Times Beach II," which resembles Varèse's *Offrandes*, is named after the first toxic disaster on American soil, where an entire population was evacuated after a dioxin spill. The piece was originally commissioned by the Aspen Wind Quintet as a composition with five movements, but the Aspen group couldn't play it properly. Initially, the Ensemble Modern could barely approach the abstract quality of the music, either. After several attempts during rehearsal, the group wanted to abandon it, but the program was short so they couldn't. "It had no dynamics," Peter Rundel remembered, "no articulation — just plain notes. Frank sang the phrases for us. Suddenly it became very lively, and the character of the music came out. It was not an abstract kind of music anymore."

"III Revised," one of the movements from the string quartet *None of the Above* (Zappa so named it because it didn't fall into the same "orbit" as most quartet music), has some of Webern's spareness. Zappa converted this movement from a quartet to a quintet so the bass player wouldn't be "sitting around while the other guys were sawing away."

One of the big challenges for Zappa and the ensemble was "The Girl in the Magnesium Dress." Originally played by the synclavier on *The Perfect Stranger: Boulez Conducts Zappa*, it needed to be translated into a score playable by human beings. The polyphonic quality of the piece gave the group fits at first, but they were determined to get it right. The performance on *The Yellow Shark*, featuring the quick and brittle runs of Conlon Nancarrow's player-piano pieces, is orchestrated for piano, mandolin, and percussion. The mathematical construction, very much in the spirit of Boulez, is even more evident here than on *The Perfect Stranger*.

"Be-Bop Tango" is barely recognizable from the rock version on *Roxy & Elsewhere*. "What's new about it, aside from the instrumentation, is a section in the middle where the players sound like jazz musicians doing that jazz talking," Peter Rundle recalled. "Frank told us to imagine we were suddenly sitting in a restaurant, and had to play [corny cocktail lounge] restaurant piano, with people talking and laughing. It's very funny."

The biggest surprise of the program might be "Ruth Is Sleeping." The American pianist Jeffrey Burns, to whom Zappa had originally given the score, had finally recorded a solo version he wanted to present to Zappa. When Zappa heard the recording, he was so impressed that he asked the ensemble to imitate Burns' interpretation. "Ruth Is Sleeping" is named for the naps Ruth Underwood took under her marimba set during rehearsals — while Zappa was giving instructions to the other members of the '73 band. It's the first piece he composed on the synclavier, and its stunning polyphonic textures eliminate the piece's sense of rhythm.

"None of the Above" is another portion from the string quartet, while "Pentagon Afternoon" is a tone poem dedicated to "the dealers in death" sitting around in the Pentagon — it ends with the sound of plastic ray guns blasting. "Questi Cazzi di Piccione (Those Fucking Pigeons)" addresses a very specific subject. "If you've ever been to Venice, well, instead of trees, they have pigeons, and pigeon by-products," Zappa told Rip Rense. "Which is probably one of the reasons why the town is sinking." The piece is performed without a conductor and is distinguished by the sound of the string players knocking on their instruments to simulate the lethal droppings from the sky.

"Food Gathering in Post Industrial America" is a dramatic oratorio with a science-fiction text. The future that Zappa depicts is filled with rats, desperate groups of wild children, and tritium-enriched sewage. As one of two numbers conducted by Zappa, it features the first dramatic recitation by violinist Hilary Sturt. Sturt details the desperate plight of humankind while horn player Catherine Milliken blows into a didgeridoo that is placed in a spittoon full of water with Vermiculite (a humus helper) on top. "It didn't really help the tone," Zappa recalled, "but it looked good for the television cameras that zoomed in on these little brown scummy things floating on top of the water, and this girl earnestly honking into the spittoon with an enormous wooden dork sticking out of her mouth."

"Welcome to the United States" is pure Zappa absurdism. He conducts a reading by keyboardist Hermann Kretzschmar that's based on a Department of Justice immigration form. Given that most of the group is German, Zappa knew that some of the questions asked in this document ("Were you involved, in any way, in any persecutions associated with Nazi Germany and its allies?") would prove uncomfortable to the ensemble — and the audience. Early in the rehearsals, Zappa had assigned a number of musicians to improvise some spoken material, and Kretzschmar chose his library card as a text. It didn't make for compelling drama, but he had the same deep sinister accent that Theodore Bikel possessed in *200 Motels*. So Zappa introduced Kretzschmar to something a little more hardcore — an alternative magazine on genital piercing, *Piercing Fans International Quarterly*. Kretzschmar gave such an inspired reading of some of the letters to the editor that it no doubt landed him the job for "Welcome to the United States." The track's finest moment comes when Kretzschmar asks, "Have you ever been or are you now involved in espionage or sabotage?" and the group answers back musically with a quote from "Louie Louie."

On "A Pound for a Brown (on the Bus)" and "Exercise #4" (from *Uncle Meat*), the ensemble bring out the comic elements in the scores. "Get Whitey" is a brilliantly complex piece originally composed on the piano, in the key of C, where only the white keys are played. To give the work a more chromatic sound, Zappa transposed into another key — but the provocative title (coming after the Rodney King riots) remained. "G-Spot Tornado," the whirlwind synclavier cut from *Jazz From Hell*, was another piece considered impossible for the group to play. "During the '91 rehearsals, I came in one day and a few of the musicians were trying to play that tune," Zappa told Rip Rense. "They really liked it for some reason and asked whether they could have an arrangement of it for the concert." It's a powerhouse performance, conducted by Zappa, driven by aggressive, Varèsian percussive rhythms. The piece has such an exhilarating spirit that the audience can barely contain its enthusiasm at the end.

The Yellow Shark was Zappa's final triumph where he could integrate all the elements of his work into a modern music ensemble that desired to play it correctly. "In the Yellow Shark evening, there were at least three or four musical styles," said Molich-Zebhauser. "[There were] new arrangements of old music of his, some contemporary pieces, some jokes, the electronics, and the jazz element. And the crowning thing for me was how it all fit together; that it's possible to give one evening with four or five different musical styles, and nobody says, 'Oh my God, what's happening now — oh, forget it.' It seems to be [due to] the personality of Frank that this can work." For one brief European tour, this American utopian had the satisfied smile of a scientist who's long-tested experiment had finally achieved positive results.

Zappa had many plans for 1993, but none would come to fruition. The experience with the Ensemble Modern was so fulfilling that there was talk of having them perform some of Zappa's more theatrical material, like "Billy the Mountain" and "Brown Shoes Don't Make It." Bozzio and Vai were also slated to play with the ensemble in a performance of "Mo 'n Herb's Vacation." Given Zappa's frail state, though, the emphasis was on tributes, rather than plans.

The publishers of *Keyboard* and *Guitar Player* collaborated on a whole magazine devoted to Zappa, simply called *Zappa!* It featured a huge interview with Zappa by editor Don Menn, joined by *Simpsons* creator Matt Groening. The issue also had fascinating interviews with Zappa's staff and family, plus Kent Nagano, Nicolas Slonimsky, and Aynsley Dunbar.

YOU CAN'T DO THAT ON STAGE ANYMORE

In October, Zappa had assembled a two-CD audio artifact from the Flo & Eddie days called *Playground Psychotics*, to give listeners an idea of what touring was all about in the early '70s. However, Zappa was very ill when he came to work on this anthropological study of a rock band on the road. Although it has some fascinating field recordings and concert performances from 1971, it lacks the sharp conceptual sense Zappa usually brought to his projects. It's clear he's trying to get inside the personality and dynamic of the band, its insecurities, its humor, its musical proficiency. But most of the time, it goes over ground already explored much better on the *200 Motels* album.

Playground Psychotics has its moments, though: a funny opening scene where a promotions marketer from Zappa's record company wants to get a shot of the group in a garbage truck for a "publicity stunt"; Zappa's superior mix of the Fillmore material featuring John Lennon and Yoko Ono, which has infinitely more presence than the echo chamber that Phil Spector brought to the tapes on John and Yoko's *Sometime in New York City*; an interview with the manager of the Edgewater Inn about the infamous Mud Shark; an expanded version of "Billy the Mountain"; and tape from the rehearsals of *200 Motels*, where Jeff Simmons tells the band why he's bailing from the movie.

On January 8, 1993, Zappa held a soiree in his studio, partly because BBC producer Nigel Leigh was doing a documentary on him for *The Late Show*. This profile featured new interviews with Ruth Underwood, Motorhead Sherwood, Steve Vai, plus Dweezil and Ahmet. But Zappa was not well on this night. Even so, it was a glorious event that he managed to enjoy despite his pain.

On hand were old friends Johnny "Guitar" Watson, Terry Bozzio, and L. Shankar. And the Chieftains, in town because of Grammy nominations, also turned up. Matt Groening brought with him a group called Huun-Huur-tu, a throat-singing ensemble from Tuva in Russia. Some of this footage got into Nigel Leigh's documentary, and viewers caught an amazing jam session. As the Chieftains provided a drone for the Tuvan throat singers to sing over, Bozzio softly played his congas, while Shankar firmly caressed the strings of his electric violin with his bow. Then Watson called up a set of lyrics that included the Negro spiritual "Bringing in the Sheaves." The combination was funny, touching, and exhilarating. As this crosscultural stew filled the room, Zappa sat in a chair, a guitar across his lap, tapping his foot as he puffed smoke from his cigarette with the most pleasurable grin ever caught on film.

In February, Keneally and Thunes set up a sequel (of sorts) to *Zappa's Universe* at Avery Fisher Hall in New York, with far less trouble than the first one. Both musicians played with a chamber orchestra, performing some of Zappa's classical scores. Also that month, the Chieftains again dropped by to pay a visit. After the spirited session they'd had at UMRK for *The Celtic Harp*, they wanted to do more recording for a new album called *The Long Black Veil*, which would feature guest appearances by Sting, the Rolling Stones, Van Morrison, Sinéad O'Connor, Tom Jones, Marianne Faithfull, and others.

Paddy Moloney had just written a song called "Tennessee Mazurka," a sequel to the lovely Redd Stewart/Pee Wee King ballad "Tennessee Waltz." The Chieftains wanted to record Jones singing this song at UMRK, but the day they chose was particularly bad for Zappa. He helped Moloney work through a difficult section of the medley before finally excusing himself. He had to prepare to go to the hospital for a transfusion. Irish journalist Joe Jackson, who was present, wrote about the occasion for the *Irish Times*: "My first impression was that Frank Zappa did indeed look sallow and pale, a condition that was rather cruelly highlighted by the California sunshine burning its way through the window beside his wickerwork chair." Knowing that Jackson was writing about the Chieftains, Zappa offered to give him a quote or two — especially since he'd heard that the Chieftains weren't as highly regarded in their own country as the rock band U2.

A "quote or two" turned into a fifteen-minute interview done in a dark room, with Zappa talking in the hushed whispers of a weakened man summoning up his reserves. "U2 is the most popular, and successful, musical export coming from Ireland today, but there's no comparison between the musical quality of what they do and what the Chieftains do," Zappa told Jackson. "We play together here nearly every time they are in town, and I love the sound these guys make. I love the melodies, the chord changes, and especially the way their music is performed. Each member of the group is expert on his instrument, not just in terms of technique, but in terms of the concept they have of what the final ensemble product is supposed to sound like. That is something you are only going to get with a group that has been together thirty years."

Zappa had also heard someone in the studio mention that U2 referred to themselves as post-modern rockers. "Post-modern rockers, what does that mean? Do they themselves know?" he asked. "And which would you rather have? Mediocre invention or a direct linear descent from Celtic culture, which is what I hear in the music of the Chieftains? And even if you do stumble across excellent innovation, what are you going to do with it, how are you going to appreciate it, if you don't appreciate your own culture? The Chieftains are their own culture, and I hear

YOU CAN'T DO THAT ON STAGE ANYMORE

traces of not only Celtic history but global history in their work, echoing back to the beginning of time. I've noticed that when they play here in my home with ethnic musicians from all over the world."

When Tom Jones arrived, he got "Tennessee Mazurka" on the third take. *The Long Black Veil* came out a short time after Zappa's death. In the liner notes, it was dedicated to the memory of Frank Zappa.

The only projects Zappa wanted to complete with his remaining time were *Civilization Phaze III, The Lost Episodes,* and a compilation of some of his more controversial songs called *Have I Offended Someone? Civilization Phaze III,* however, would be an amazing coda to his career, bringing Zappa's work full circle.

7

"TIME is not like what people THINK it is," Buddy Wilson said in Frank Zappa's fictional *Them or Us (The Book)* in 1984. "It doesn't START OVER HERE and then GO OVER THERE . . . TIME is just one big LUMP OF STUFF . . . EVERYTHING IS HAPPENING ALL THE TIME! I can prove it to you! When you're watching TV on Channel Nine, there's ALWAYS SOMETHING ELSE on Channel Five, right?" Almost ten years later, Zappa finished a project called *Civilization Phaze III* that became proof of Buddy Wilson's observations. It was a powerful swan song that encompassed the entire scope of Frank Zappa's music. *Civilization Phaze III* successfully created the illusion of going back and forth through time — as though the past and present had magically fused.

After all, it was in 1967 that Frank Zappa had first stuffed a pair of U-87 microphones in a piano at the Apostolic Studios in New York. He covered the keyboard in a drape, put a sandbag on the sustain pedal, and invited people to put their head inside and ramble spontaneously about whatever topic Zappa suggested through the studio's talkback system. "Some of this dialogue — after extensive editing — found its way into the *Lumpy Gravy* album," Zappa wrote in the liner notes to *Civilization Phaze III*. "The rest of it sat in my tape vault for decades, waiting for the glorious day when audio science would develop tools which might allow for its resurrection."

Audio science had caught up with Frank Zappa in 1991. What was "a vague plot regarding pigs and ponies" in 1967 was now, in 1991, a world lost in yuppie careerism, religious superstition, and political opportunism. In depicting this new worldview, not only did Zappa rescue unused conversations from 1967, he added a new group of piano people who would — through the magic of digital editing — provide a contrast to their predecessors. These new residents included Moon Unit, actor Michael Rappaport, Zappa's music preparation assistant Ali N. Askin, his computer assistant Todd Yvega, and the entire brass section of the Ensemble Modern.

Civilization Phaze III was the final part of a trilogy that began with *Lumpy Gravy* and *We're Only in It for the Money*. It was designed as an opera pantomime using varied styles of choreography. The plot was developed from a rotation of suggestions and phrases Zappa provided through the talkback. The piano people improvised on those remarks. On *Lumpy Gravy*, the dialogue had been intercut with orchestral music, *musique concrète*, and sound effects. On *Civilization Phaze III*, the music is made up mostly of synclavier textures and some live performances. In continuity with Gary Kellgren's whispering voice on *We're Only in It for the Money* or the Central Scrutinizer's authoritarian presence on *Joe's Garage*, Zappa is a menacing figure hovering above the piano and speaking through "a decrepit-looking megaphone apparatus."

After Spider Barbour (from 1967) announces that we are entering Phaze III, Zappa announces the first theme: "The audience sits inside of a big piano and they listen to it grow." Spider, All-Night John, and Monica the receptionist pick up on the utopian idea in Zappa's remark and comment on its commercial possibilities. Evoking Haight-Ashbury, and even quoting from Wild Man Fischer's signature song, "Merry Go Round," they come to the conclusion that all you have to do, to do your own thing, "is put a motor in yourself."

This bit of dialogue was also in *Lumpy Gravy*, but it wasn't given the same context it has here. Zappa is introducing the key element of '60s utopian thinking: get active, *motorize* yourself. The piano becomes a '60s commune with its inhabitants happily detaching themselves from the world. Their optimism is built on the idea that maybe they can create a better place inside the piano. But on *Civilization Phaze III*, the world finds a way to close right in on them, because the elements of destruction are hidden within their own hopes. As Greil Marcus writes in *Mystery Train*, "America is a dangerous place, and to find community demands as much as any of us can give. But if America is dangerous, its little utopias, asking nothing, promising safety, are usually worse."

The following musical number, "Put a Motor in Yourself," a syncopated dance performed on the synclavier with a Middle Eastern flavor, brings us out of those sparkling hopes for '60s social change, placing us right smack dab into the horribly

YOU CAN'T DO THAT ON STAGE ANYMORE

expedient '90s. Zappa describes the dance performed during this number in his stage instructions: "A yuppie precision drill team dresses for work in motorized uniforms, eventually engaging in a dance routine featuring ladder climbing, ass-kissing, karate chopping, self-hugging, eventually leading to politics and murder."

"Oh-Ummm" introduces the first signs of discontent in their communal life, when Roy Estrada, Louis Cuneo, and Motorhead Sherwood start fighting for space. The musical number "Reagan at Bitburg" evokes an image of Ronald Reagan, once called a fascist during the '60s by counterculture activists, laying a wreath at the gravesite of an ss officer. After the piano dwellers gather for some pseudo-scientific and poetic dialogues, Jesus makes an appearance in the astonishing "N-Lite." This long, foreboding track that concludes Act I is filled with loud percussive trills, sharp piano glissandos, deep belches, and the gurgling sound of a didgeridoo in water.

The title (which stands for "negative light") comes from a computer code referring to two moments in the piece — one that reminded Zappa of the Village People's disco hit "In the Navy" and a sonic cluster called "Thousand Points of Light." The composition, though, a culmination of everything Zappa learned from Varèse, is an evolution from the eerie synclavier piece "Jonestown" and the wonderfully abstract "When Yuppies Go to Hell," from *Make a Jazz Noise Here*. The dance created for "N-Lite" is designed to show the exterior world "crushed by evil science, ecological disaster, political failure, justice denied, and religious stupidity." Since the '60s group takes false refuge in the piano, the world falls into the hands of yuppie careerists, corrupt politicians, and religious zealots. When Jesus arrives, the dancers try to worship him, but when he examines the mess that's been made of the world (thanks to the perversion of his teachings), he jumps into the piano with them.

In Act II, Zappa introduces the new piano dwellers. But first, the original occupants discuss the origins of the universe, raising Zappa's concept, expressed in the '60s, of the Big Note. Monica first asks if the whole universe revolves around one note. Spider tells her, "No, it doesn't revolve around it; that's what it is. It's one note." As the new piano people take over in the '90s, there's more a collision of conflicting notes at work. Ali Askin and Stefan Dohr of the Ensemble Modern both speak in foreign tongues, while Michael Rappaport (who occupies a section of the piano with Moon Unit) talks tough and racist: "This ain't the U.N., man!" There's nothing but discord and division expressed, not the comfort of home. This dissension extends itself to music. While Stefan talks of Mozart, Rappaport fights for rap and hiphop. Zappa contrasts the splintering of the culture between his '60s group and the new ensemble. The music that links these dialogue sessions — especially the otherworldly "Dio Fa" — is both ominous and understated, creating the aura of an absurdly dark chamber drama.

By the end, Spider and John talk about gathering strength for the future by "understanding our own music." John claims, though, that "we don't even understand our own music." Spider, believing that understanding isn't essential, thinks the music will still give them strength. He then delves further into a dilemma that mirrors Zappa's own career quest. "I think our strength comes from our uncertainty," Spider remarks. "If we understood it we'd be bored with it and then we couldn't gather any strength from it." Agreeing, John adds the final words, "Like if we knew about our music, one of us might talk and then that would be the end of that."

The end does come, in the form of "Beat the Reaper," a highly percussive piece that begins with a simple thunderclap and the sound of falling rain. During the staging of this section, the focus shifts from the piano interior to the exterior world. We see the dancers illustrating "the current fetish for life extending or 'youthening' trends, including meditation, bizarre diets, pill and algae consumption, violent aerobics, The Easy Glider, StairSteppers, etc." As the music dissolves into plucked notes and syncopated percussion, it too evaporates into the stormy night.

In the final track, "Waffenspiel," Zappa's last notes give way to the constant noise of everyday life: the sound of a dog barking, distant urban gunfire, traffic, and the slamming of a car door. The bold and troubling music of Frank Zappa has now departed. He leaves us with something more eternal — the sounds of our bold and troubling world.

8

On March 12, the Meridian Arts Ensemble, an American brass quintet, entertained Zappa with a performance of his music at home. They played "Dupree's Paradise," "Big Swifty," "Harry, You're a Beast," and "The Orange County Lumber Truck." Zappa offered critical feedback that helped them polish the pieces so they could be used on their forthcoming *Smart Went Crazy* CD. They would return in November to show how far they had come in learning his music, and they would be among the last to see him alive. Another proposed project was *Dance Me Outside*, a selection of synclavier compositions that were supposed to be included at the Vienna Festival in May 1994, but it wasn't to be.

YOU CAN'T DO THAT ON STAGE ANYMORE

The last labor of love that Zappa completed took him back to his musical roots. In July, he and the Ensemble Modern recorded an album of Edgard Varèse's music. Zappa had always wanted to record Varèse with state-of-the-art equipment and a group with a supple command of Varèse's dynamics. Composer David Raksin and Nicolas Slonimsky were present at the recording sessions, and they were pleased that Varèse was finally getting the performances his music deserved. Varèse himself might have been impressed. Here, a generation later, was the young boy who had called him as a birthday present from his parents, now finding a way to do this unheralded composer justice — just before his own death. As Zappa and the ensemble began to record some of Varèse's greatest compositions, Zappa told the group, "You are all wonderful, technical musicians. But now it's time to put some eyebrows on it." The album, still unreleased, is called *The Rage and the Fury: The Music of Edgard Varèse*.

In the summer, Zappa contributed to a John Cage tribute album called *A Chance Operation*. The piece he selected was Cage's chance piano composition, "4'33," where the pianist sits at the piano and does not move for four minutes and thirty-three seconds. In the accompanying booklet, in which the other contributors — including James Tenney, the Kronos Quartet, Laurie Anderson, Meredith Monk, and Yoko Ono — provided extensive biographies, Zappa wrote two words: American composer. He also did an interview with David Sheff of *Playboy*, where he went into greater detail about his health than he had with any other publication. By the winter, Zappa's condition started to deteriorate. Bedridden, he could no longer go to the studio. Old friends were coming by to pay their last respects.

One of those guests was Ruth Underwood, who hadn't seen Zappa in years. "He invited me to the house and we enjoyed some nice visits with each other," she recalled for *Musician* magazine. "Last June, he called and asked if he could sample some of my stuff. I was shocked because I hadn't touched a pair of mallets since March of '77. I ended up practising for fourteen hours. . . . I spent four days at Frank's house sampling. This really was a miracle for me — that I could be reunited with him and still have something to offer." Though it was clear to Ruth that he was dying and exhausted, she found the inimitable Zappa spirit intact. "He couldn't leap from one place to another the way he used to," she said, "[but] he was still compelling and intimidating and sharp and exacting and wonderful — maybe more than ever."

Other friends came to see him — sometimes just to listen to some of his R&B and blues record collection. He was returning to the music of his roots, the sounds that he had discovered and loved in his youth. Zappa was connecting to the source of pleasure that once took away the stagnation of living in Lancaster. Now this music was taking away the pain of dying.

In the fall of 1993, Ike Willis dropped by. Zappa wanted Ike to take special care in making sure his music wouldn't fade away. "I went down to visit him and had a long talk," Willis told Charles Frick in *The Aquarian*. "He basically said, "Okay, I still give you permission to play whatever you want, make sure it's okay with Gail first. . . . Go for the gusto, Ike, if you can keep it alive, go ahead and do it, 'cause I can't do it anymore.'"

That night, when Willis got home, he received a phone call from Roddie Gilliard, the leader of a Zappa tribute band called the Muffin Men, asking if he'd consider fronting them on their European tour. Willis agreed — the group was faithful to Zappa's arrangements. Partway through the tour, Willis was asked if he could gather some of the other old band members. From that lineup he would form the Band From Utopia, a ten-piece Zappa alumni group. (A live album called *A Tribute to the Music of Frank Zappa* was recorded at the 1994 Jazz Open Festival in Stuttgart, Germany.) They started their own record label, Muffin Records, which released recordings by Jimmy Carl Black's Grandmothers, Tommy Mars' band Western Vacation Feat, and Arthur Barrow.

On Saturday, December 4, 1993, Zappa died at home with his family present. The news was announced the following Monday by the Zappa family. "Composer Frank Zappa left for his final tour just before 6:00 PM on Saturday, December 4, 1993, and was buried Sunday, December 5, 1993, during a private ceremony attended by the family. He was with his wife Gail and four children, Moon, Dweezil, Ahmet and Diva, at home in Los Angeles at the time of his death."

Before he died, Zappa got to see the Republicans swept from power by Bill Clinton's Democrats, Al Gore become vice-president (which meant Tipper would resign from the PMRC), and his music acclaimed and heard freely in countries where it once had been banned. But Greggery Peccary turned out to be right. Time was indeed an affliction. Yet time would also start to finally be in Frank Zappa's favor.

EPILOGUE

BEAT THE REAPER

(1993-2000)

But were I granted time to complete my work, I would not fail to stamp it with the seal of that Time, now so forcibly present in my mind, and in it I would describe men, even at the risk of giving them the appearance of monstrous beings, as occupying in Time, a much greater place than that so sparingly conceded to them in Space, a place indeed extended beyond measure, because, like giants plunged in the years, they touch at once those periods of their lives — separated by so many days — so far apart in time.

MARCEL PROUST, *Remembrance of Things Past*

Some people think
That if they go too far
They'll never get back
To where the rest of them are
I might be crazy
But there's one thing I know
You might be surprised
At what you find when ya go!

FRANK ZAPPA, "A Token of My Extreme," from *Joe's Garage*

Frank Zappa was buried in an unmarked plot at the Pierce Brothers Westwood Memorial Park in L.A. He joined a motley group of entertainers at that final resting place. Roy Orbison, Marilyn Monroe, Buddy Rich, Dean Martin, and the R&B singer Minnie Ripperton are all buried nearby. Within a month of his death, *The Yellow Shark* (released on Barking Pumpkin Records) made its appearance on the Billboard Classical 50. It was the first time a Zappa album had made the classical chart, and it reached No. 6 by Christmas (it would peak at No. 4).

By then, various tributes were being organized. The New Juilliard Ensemble in New York was going to perform "Dupree's Paradise" at their December 16 concert, but they ended up dedicating the whole show to Zappa. In March 1994, the USA Network launched a new cartoon series called *Duckman*, created by the same people behind *The Simpsons*, including Matt Groening. One of the characters, the dim-witted teenager Ajax, was voiced by Dweezil Zappa. In the first episode alone, "I, Duckman," there were copious Zappa quotes. The song "Let's Make the Water Turn Black," Senator Paula Hawkins' soliloquy in Congress about "fire and chains and other tools of gratification," and even Louis the Turkey and his hyena laugh were featured. At the end of the episode, the screen read, "Dedicated with fond memories to Frank Zappa." Future episodes would cover a wide berth of Zappa music, including "Sinister Footwear II," "Help, I'm a Rock," "The Torture Never Stops," and "Friendly Little Finger." *Duckman* also used unreleased versions of "Theme From *Lumpy Gravy*," "Peaches en Regalia," and "T'Mershi Duween" played on the synclavier. The cartoon's music was written by Todd Yvega, Zappa's synclavier programmer.

By the fall of 1994, Zappa's musical legacy still hadn't found a permanent home. Rhino Records was considered after their work on *Beat the Boots*, but the Zappas finally resolved their differences with Rykodisc. Gail told Drew Wheeler of *Billboard* that before Frank died, "he said, 'I want you out of this business. I want you to relax and have a good time.' I very much appreciate that he was so forceful about establishing how he wanted it sold." On October 7, Rykodisc purchased the entire Zappa catalog, which included over sixty albums being held in the Zappa Family Trust, excluding his last official release, *Civilization Phaze III*, which was handled by mail order (Barfko-Swill) and through retail by the British distribution house Music for Nations.

The price of the catalog was never made public, but Ryko did undergo a $44 million corporate restructuring as a result of the purchase. The label took Zappa's final approved masters and reissued all the albums with new remastered recordings and restored cover art from the original albums (where necessary). They split up the two-fer discs they had originally released (*We're Only in It for the Money/Lumpy Gravy* and *Over-nite Sensation/Apostrophe (')*). In the case of *We're Only in It for the Money*, fans were relieved that Zappa had found a two-track master of the original recording to replace the controversial restored and overdubbed version he released in the '80s. (But since the two-track master was one of the censored versions from the '60s, you still need the '80s version to hear what was cut out.)

The deal with Rykodisc also covered various other projects that were still on the table, including *Have I Offended Someone?*, *The Lost Episodes*, *Strictly Commercial: The Best of Frank Zappa*, *Strictly Genteel* (an overview of his classical work), and the long-awaited *Läther*.

Gail Zappa remounted Zappa Records to issue projects not covered by the Rykodisc deal, including *Everything Is Healing Nicely* (a fascinating behind-the-scenes recording of the rehearsals by the Ensemble Modern as they prepared for *The Yellow Shark*) and *Frank Zappa Plays the Music of Frank Zappa* (a collection of Zappa's favorite guitar pieces — both released and unreleased — assembled by Dweezil).

At the end of 1994, Frank Zappa was inducted into the Rock and Roll Hall of Fame after languishing on the ballot for several years. He was joined by the Allman Brothers (imagine hearing them play "Whippin' Post" together), Al Green, Martha Reeves & the Vandellas, Neil Young, Led Zeppelin ("Stairway to Heaven," anyone?), and Janis Joplin. One entry that would no doubt have amused Frank Zappa was the Orioles. This extraordinary vocal group, who performed (arguably) the very first R&B doo-wop song, "It's Too Soon to Know" in 1948, also happened to be from Baltimore. It seemed cruel that the selection committee had delayed his inclusion until after he was dead. But this callous oversight paled next to how they planned the whole affair. "Ten days before the actual ceremony, we still hadn't received invitations," Gail remarked. "The producer said, 'Oh, that's unconscionable! We can give you two free tickets.' Well, there's five of us, of course. He said, 'We can sell you additional tickets at $1,500 apiece, but you can't sit together.'"

The Zappas decided that Moon Unit would go, since she did express interest, and that she would accept the award. But there was another snag a week before the ceremony. Guitarist Eddie Van Halen, more a contemporary (and friend) of Dweezil, was asked to induct Frank Zappa. When he turned down their offer (he said he didn't give out awards), Gail suggested Johnny "Guitar" Watson, but the Hall refused. Gail then suggested the hard-rock ensemble Aerosmith, but they were already inducting Led Zeppelin. "I asked them who chooses these things and was told 'the Board,'" Gail recalled. "I asked if there were any musicians on the board, and more importantly, are there any black musicians. They had to call me back, and they replied, 'Yes, one: Berry Gordy.'"

The Hall finally came up with their own last-ditch solution — and it couldn't have been more ironic. "We've invited Lou Reed to do it," they told Gail. Given the hostilities in the '60s between the Velvet Underground and the Mothers of Invention, one could hardly blame Gail for choking with laughter. The Zappa kids were dead set against it, but Gail spoke to Reed on the phone. "I told him, 'Listen, you said lots of shitty things about Frank.' We discussed it and he finally said, 'If I said anything flip that was meant to be funny, I'm sorry.' Actually, Frank admired him as a songwriter; 'Femme Fatale' and 'All Tomorrow's Parties' were two of Frank's favorites."

A limo took Moon Unit to the show where she found out that they were cutting the film footage of her father because "the show was running long." Worse, during the broadcast there was no Zappa music — even though every other artist was represented by at least one song. "This is a man who went to Capitol Hill for these people," Gail said, stunned at the thoughtlessness.

As for Reed, he spoke admirably, with a great sensitivity tinged with remorse. "It's very rare in life to know someone who affects things, changes them in a positive way," Reed began. "Frank Zappa was such a person, and of the many regrets I have in life, not knowing him better is one of them." Listing Zappa's many accomplishments, Reed went on to make his strongest remarks. "Frank was a force for reason and honesty in a business deficient in those areas. As we reward some with money for the amusement they supply to the cultural masses, I think the induction of Frank Zappa in the Rock and Roll Hall of Fame distinguishes the Hall as well as the inductee." Gail later remarked, "As Lou said, it honored the Hall to induct Frank — and not the other way around."

There were in fact many tributes to Zappa in the coming years that kept his music vital and current — not to mention original. Project/Object (featuring Ike Willis and other Zappa alumni) have been performing Zappa's music live in clubs across North America. Their great enthusiasm and musical adeptness makes the Zappa legacy a force to contend with into this new century. The Persuasions performed a beautifully diverse *a cappella* selection of Zappa songs (including a vocal rendition of the instrumental opening of *Lumpy Gravy*) for their 1999 release, *Frankly A*

Cappella: The Persuasions Sing Zappa.

Various other ensembles, like the Ensemble Ambrosius from Finland (who did a gorgeous album of Zappa music on baroque instruments) and the Ed Palermo Big Band (who recorded an accurate and exciting jazz album of Zappa covers) provided worthy tributes. All of these groups have tried new ways to express the myriad influences that pulsed through Zappa's compositions. But perhaps the most fitting tribute took place on July 22, 1994. Astronomers had somehow found a place for Zappa in the night sky. Besieged by letters and e-mails, a Cambridge, Massachusetts, astronomy organization named an asteroid that orbits between Mars and Jupiter "Zappafrank." With this unique coronation, Zappa finally became part of that expanding universe he once claimed worked — despite our concerted efforts to continually fuck it up. Now, at least symbolically, he was a permanent part of the time continuum.

Frank Zappa came along in a decade when the doors flew open to anyone possessing a concept and an original sound. Yet, like his antecedents, Zappa was also a man out of his time. He listened to the past and then imagined the future by synthesizing the myriad possibilities in every avenue of music. His greatest strength was his ability to lead, never catering to audience expectations of where he should go next, and always defying trends.

Edgard Varèse once said, "An artist is never ahead of his time, but most people are far behind theirs." Which is why when you enter the Dangerous Kitchen of Frank Zappa, you might find your food already prepared before you've even had a chance to study the menu.

DISCOGRAPHY

There is a huge difference between what Frank Zappa originally released on LP and what is now on CD. Since this book deals primarily with the original LPs until the release of the series *You Can't Do That on Stage Anymore*, when CDs became the standard format, here is a list of the current Zappa CD catalog. Rykodisc issued his catalog twice, with significant changes to the album artwork; I have indicated both release dates. The recordings, however, are listed in chronological order.

1 *Freak Out!* (Rykodisc, 1987/1995) — The whole album has been remixed. "Who Are the Brain Police?" is a little longer and segues directly into "Go Cry on Somebody Else's Shoulder."

2 *Absolutely Free* (Rykodisc, 1987/1995) — No significant difference in sound. In the 1995 release, the complete libretto is included. The 1967 single "Big Leg Emma"/"Why Don'tcha Do Me Right?" is included on both releases.

3 *We're Only in It for the Money/Lumpy Gravy* (Rykodisc, 1986) — This CD release was a two-for-one deal and a mixed blessing. *We're Only in It for the Money* is heavily doctored. In the mid-'80s, Zappa erased the original rhythm tracks and replaced them with Chad Wackerman on drums and Arthur Barrow on bass. On the other hand, he restored the censored sections of "Harry, You're a Beast" and "Mother People." *Lumpy Gravy* is presented in its original form.

4   *We're Only in It for the Money* (Rykodisc, 1995) — After protests from fans, Zappa restored the original 1967 version shortly before he died. Since he used an original LP master as his source, he couldn't include the censored portions of "Harry, You're a Beast" and "Mother People."

5   *Lumpy Gravy* (Rykodisc, 1995) — A newly restored master with better sound quality than on the 1986 version. Unfortunately, the opening section of "Oh No" was accidentally dubbed in mono rather than the original stereo.

6   *Cruising With Ruben & the Jets* (Rykodisc, 1985/1995) — As he did with *We're Only in It for the Money*, Zappa stripped the rhythm tracks and overdubbed the drums and bass (again by Chad Wackerman and Arthur Barrow). Unlike *Money*, though, it wasn't restored in its 1995 re-release. Few fans likely complained, due to the album's lack of popularity. The CD version is radically different from the LP — although not for the better. The sublime "Jelly Roll Gum Drop," with the vocals remixed, sounds cacophonous now. "Later That Night" is missing the concluding joke featuring the singer hiding in the closet from his lover's husband. "Fountain of Love" now begins with sound engineer Dick Kunc introducing it. One of the few highlights is the remix of "Stuff Up the Cracks," with Bunk Gardner's sax more prominent. Zappa's concluding (and still stunning) guitar solo also begins earlier than on the LP. Although it's very difficult to find, you'd be best to seek out the original album.

7   *Uncle Meat* (Rykodisc, 1987/1995) — Despite being remixed, *Uncle Meat* still sounds close to the album source. The CD features the restored artwork, including booklet and lyrics. To accommodate these goodies and take full advantage of additional CD timing, Zappa added excerpts from the film, plus the expendable track "Tengo Na Minchia Tanta" to fill out Disc 2.

8   *Hot Rats* (Rykodisc, 1987/1995) — The CD has been completely remixed with material both added and deleted. It's now a completely different album with a new sound. "Peaches en Regalia" is twenty-one seconds shorter. "Willie the Pimp" opens with a different take of the song. Zappa's guitar solo has also been re-edited with one section added and one deleted. "Son of Mr. Green Genes" is not only twenty-nine seconds shorter than on the LP version, Zappa's guitar solo is more buried in the mix. "Little Umbrellas" has a short recorder solo added into the

DISCOGRAPHY

bridge. "The Gumbo Variations" features over four minutes of new material — including the count-in and a longer Ian Underwood sax solo. Only "It Must Be a Camel" appears untouched. The CD has a sonic brightness that the album lacked, but the rearranged pieces tend to be jarring.

9 *Burnt Weeny Sandwich* (Rykodisc, 1995) — The CD is faithful to the original album. The sound is also greatly improved, with the exception of Ian Underwood's piano intro to "Little House I Used to Live In," which features a bad edit.

10 *Weasels Ripped My Flesh* (Rykodisc, 1990/1995) — A few significant alterations are made. "Didja Get Any Onya?" has over three minutes — of the track "Charles Ives" — added to the conclusion. "Directly From My Heart to You" segues directly into a remixed version of "Prelude to the Afternoon of a Sexually Aroused Gas Mask." "My Guitar Wants to Kill Your Mama" fades out sooner than on the album version.

11 *Chunga's Revenge* (Rykodisc, 1990/1995) — Although there are no alterations to the original LP, the remastered sound is far too bright and thin. It lacks the bottom end of the original record.

12 *200 Motels* (Rykodisc/MGM, 1997) — It took Rykodisc years to secure the rights to the soundtrack to Zappa's film, which lay dormant in the vaults of MGM studio, but the wait was worth it. There are no changes to the original mix since Zappa had already died when the CD was released. But Rykodisc added a wonderful booklet on the making of the film, with photos from the shoot, a miniature movie poster, plus an enhanced CD that features the trailer. There are also four radio promotion spots and the single version of "Magic Fingers." A gem.

13 *The Mothers — Fillmore East, June 1971* (Rykodisc, 1989/1995) — The mix is improved. On the original 1989 CD release, Rykodisc incorrectly cued "Willie the Pimp (Part One)" moments before the song actually began. This is corrected in the 1995 reissue. On both editions, however, "Willie the Pimp (Part Two)" has been inexplicably dropped.

14 *Just Another Band From L.A.* (Rykodisc, 1990/1995) — No major alterations.

15 *Waka/Jawaka* (Rykodisc, 1988/1995) — No major alterations.

16 *The Grand Wazoo* (Rykodisc, 1988/1995) — The 1988 release was remixed with very low output. In 1995, the overall sound was improved. The tracks "The Grand Wazoo" and "For Calvin (and His Next Two Hitch-Hikers)" are reversed on the 1995 edition.

17 *Apostrophe (')/Over-nite Sensation* (Rykodisc, 1986) — Another two-for-one deal with *Apostrophe (')* preceding *Over-nite Sensation* — even though the latter was released first. As with *The Grand Wazoo*, the CD was mastered with a low output.

18 *Over-nite Sensation* (Rykodisc, 1995) — Using the same 1986 mix, the sound has been greatly improved.

19 *Apostrophe (')* (Rykodisc, 1995) — The overall sound is better on this edition, and a lyric book has been added.

20 *Roxy & Elsewhere* (Rykodisc, 1995) — The CD was originally issued on Zappa Records in 1992. In 1995, Rykodisc issued the same master with "Cheepnis" completely remixed.

21 *One Size Fits All* (Rykodisc, 1987/1995) — No major alterations. Besides being a great album, *One Size Fits All* is the best-sounding CD in Zappa's catalogue.

22 *Bongo Fury* (Rykodisc, 1989/1995) — No alterations.

23 *Zoot Allures* (Rykodisc, 1990/1995) — There are only a few modifications. "Ms. Pinky" is six seconds shorter than on the LP. "Find Her Finer" is three seconds shorter. Although a new master is used, the CD sound is significantly inferior to that of the LP.

24 *Läther* (Rykodisc, 1996) — Frank Zappa's aborted four-LP set was finally released in a luxurious three-CD box with a few bonus tracks. "Regyptian Strut" is listed as the 1993 mix, but is actually the same version included on the *Sleep Dirt* CD. "Leather Goods" is a tasty guitar solo, combining Led Zeppelin's "Dazed and Confused" and "Whole Lotta Love." A portion of this solo was used in "Duck Duck

DISCOGRAPHY

Goose." "Revenge of the Knick Knack People" is some *musique concrète* originally used in the film *Baby Snakes*. "Time Is Money" is the instrumental version of one of Zappa's songs from his musical *Hunchentoot*.

25 *Zappa in New York* (Rykodisc, 1995) — Zappa remixed the entire CD and added four tracks. Included are the once-censored "Punky's Whips"; a dramatic instrumental version of "Cruising for Burgers"; a longer take of "Titties 'n Beer," including banter with the crowd; "I'm the Slime," with Zappa being challenged by NBC emcee Don Pardo ("No. I'M THE SLIME! I'M THE SLIME!"); a speedy take on "Pound for a Brown"; and a delicate reading of "The Torture Never Stops," with lovely touches on the flute by Lou Marini. On the downside, the final mix lacks the punch of the original album ("Honey, Don't You Want a Man Like Me?" also features a different take from the 2:02 mark onward). If you don't have the original LP, compare the mixes on some of the same tracks used on *Läther*.

26 *Studio Tan* (Rykodisc, 1991/1995) — Because the original LPs *Studio Tan*, *Sleep Dirt*, and *Orchestral Favorites* were released by Warner Brothers without Zappa's permission, the sound and packaging were not up to Zappa's standards. The CD releases, under his control, corrected the problems. *Studio Tan* has been dramatically remixed — for the better. "The Adventures of Greggery Peccary" sounds fuller, for example. Zappa has reversed the tracks "Revised Music for Guitar and Low Budget Orchestra" and "Lemme Take You to the Beach." He also returned the proper spelling to "RDNZL" (on the LP, it was "Redunzel").

27 *Sleep Dirt* (Rykodisc, 1991/1995) — *Sleep Dirt* has been totally remixed. The instrumentals "Spider of Destiny," "Flambay," and "Time Is Money" — all from Zappa's science-fiction musical, *Hunchentoot* — now feature sparkling vocals by Thana Harris (wife of keyboardist Bob Harris). Zappa replaced drummer Chester Thompson's original tracks with overdubs by Chad Wackerman, including Thompson's work on "Regyptian Strut."

28 *Sheik Yerbouti* (Rykodisc, 1990/1995) — In 1986, EMI records in the U.K. released a pristine CD of *Sheik Yerbouti* drawn from the original LP master. The Rykodisc version is from a 1990 digital remaster. The song "I'm So Cute" is shorter than on the original album and CD.

29 *Orchestral Favorites* (Rykodisc, 1991/1995) — Zappa completely re-equalized the album in 1991 (the stereo left/right channels have also been reversed), greatly improving the sound from the original LP.

30 *Joe's Garage Acts I, II & III* (Rykodisc, 1987/1995) — The CD combines the separate album releases into one box set. Complete with a colorful libretto, *Joe's Garage* benefits from a digital remastering. Two songs, however, are retitled on the CD: "Wet T-Shirt" becomes "Fembots in a Wet T-Shirt," while "Toad-O Line" becomes "On the Bus."

31 *Tinsel Town Rebellion* (Rykodisc, 1990/1995) — *Tinseltown Rebellion*, just like *Sheik Yerbouti*, was first issued on CD in 1986 by EMI using the LP master. On the Rykodisc version, there are some deletions. "For the Young Sophisticate" and "Pick Me, I'm Clean" are missing their concluding notes.

32 *Shut Up 'n Play Yer Guitar* (Rykodisc, 1986/1995) — When Rykodisc first issued this three-record set, they crammed it on two CDs. The 1995 release is significantly better. Now collected on three CDs, the discs come in an attractive box with their individual covers. The new master also has a much improved sound.

33 *You Are What You Is* (Rykodisc, 1990/1995) — Frank Zappa's best album of the '80s is the worst-sounding CD in his catalogue. The original EMI CD, from 1986, used the LP master, which had significantly better sound. In the 1990/1995 issue, *You Are What You Is*, with its massive overdubs, sounds so compressed that the mix is claustrophobic. There are also dropouts littered throughout. The guitar solo in "Dumb All Over" has been edited, and "Conehead" ends a few seconds short of the original. It was rumored on the Internet that there was a new, improved CD (supervised after Zappa's death by his engineer Spencer Chrislu), but according to Barfko-Swill, no such jewel exists.

34 *Ship Arriving Too Late to Save a Drowning Witch* (Rykodisc, 1991/1995) — The EMI CD release in 1986 was sold as a two-for-one package with *The Man From Utopia*. The 1991/1995 Rykodisc version comes solo with a new master. The only alteration is to "I Come From Nowhere," which now ends a few seconds earlier than on the original LP.

DISCOGRAPHY

35 *The Man From Utopia* (Rykodisc, 1992/1995) — When EMI coupled *The Man From Utopia* with *Ship Arriving Too Late to Save a Drowning Witch* in 1986, they used the original LP mix and track order. The Rykodisc release is a new restoration. All the songs have been remixed and resequenced. "Cocaine Decisions" and "Sex" are longer here, while "Stick Together" is a few seconds shorter, and Zappa added new drum and bass tracks (by the usual suspects, Chad Wackerman and Arthur Barrow) to "The Dangerous Kitchen" and "The Jazz Discharge Party Hats." "Moggio" is remixed for the third time. The Rykodisc CD features the bonus doo-wop number "Luigi & the Wise Guys."

36 *Baby Snakes* (Rykodisc, 1995) — Barking Pumpkin Records issued the CD soundtrack of the 1977 Halloween concert at New York City's Palladium in 1988 with a digital remix. The Rykodisc release uses a new master from that source.

37 *Boulez Conducts Zappa: The Perfect Stranger* (Rykodisc, 1992/1995) — This was originally issued on CD in the '80s by EMI/Angel. The Rykodisc release has been digitally remixed to improve the overall sound. The tracks "Outside Now, Again" and "Dupree's Paradise" are now in reverse order.

38 *London Symphony Orchestra, Vol. I & II* (Rykodisc, 1995) — In 1987, Rykodisc released a truncated version of *London Symphony Orchestra* on one disc. This 1995 two-disc set collects all the material from both the original albums. Frank Zappa also remixed and remastered the discs before he died, which makes this digital recording sound even richer.

39 *Them or Us* (Rykodisc, 1994/1995) — The 1986 EMI CD release used the original LP master. In 1990, Zappa digitally remixed it. A number of the tracks — including "Truck Driver Divorce," "Planet of My Dreams," and "The Closer You Are" — are a few seconds shorter than on the LP. The title track, however, is thirteen seconds longer.

40 *Thing-Fish* (Rykodisc, 1989/1995) — There are only a few alterations between the two Rykodisc releases. The 1989 version broke the two CDs between "He's So Gay" and "The Massive Improve'lence" instead of at the end of Act One (which concludes with "Artificial Rhonda"). The 1995 reissue corrects the break.

41 *Frank Zappa Meets the Mothers of Prevention* (Rykodisc, 1986/ 1995) — The EMI CD in 1986 partnered this release with *Jazz From Hell*, using the original European version of the album. When Rykodisc issued the CD the same year, they omitted *Jazz From Hell* and included (as bonus tracks) "One Man — One Vote" and "I Don't Even Care" from the European version of the album. On the 1995 reissue, a new master is used. Some tracks are shorter than their 1986 counterparts: "I Don't Even Care" is trimmed by five seconds and "What's New in Baltimore?" by six seconds. "H.R. 2911" is a bonus track.

42 *Francesco Zappa* (Rykodisc, 1995) — In 1992, Barking Pumpkin first issued the CD. Rykodisc's 1995 release uses a new master that greatly enhances the sound, as well as cleaning up some dropouts that had crept into the original CD.

43 *Does Humor Belong in Music?* (Rykodisc, 1995) — The disc was originally released by EMI in Europe in 1986, but this spiffed-up artifact from the 1984 world tour is greatly superior. The digital recording, with new packaging, is completely remixed and remastered ("Let's Move to Cleveland" is a whole minute longer). Highlights include a lightning-quick *a cappella* performance of "WPLJ," "Cock-Suckers Ball" (which Zappa dedicates to "all the Republicans in the audience"), and a blistering take of "Whippin' Post" from the final show in the tour that features Dweezil Zappa on guitar.

44 *Jazz From Hell* (Rykodisc, 1986/1995) — EMI originally included this album as part of a two-for-one package with *Frank Zappa Meets the Mothers of Prevention*. The 1995 reissue uses a master from a 1990 remix of the album.

45 *Broadway the Hard Way* (Rykodisc, 1989/1995) — The first disc from the ill-fated 1988 tour has eight extra tracks added from the LP release. However, the band introductions to "Dickie's Such an Asshole" and "The Untouchables" are missing on the CD.

46 *Guitar* (Rykodisc, 1988/1995) — Originally released as a two-LP set in 1988, this two-CD set collects thirteen extra tracks. Some of the original tunes are even longer on the CD. "Sunrise Redeemer" adds six seconds and "That Ol' G Minor Thing Again" is thirteen seconds longer. The 1995 release uses a new master.

DISCOGRAPHY

47 *The Best Band You Never Heard in Your Life* (Rykodisc, 1995) — The second release from the 1988 tour was originally issued on CD by Barking Pumpkin in 1991. The 1995 reissue by Rykodisc has new cover art by Cal Schenkel. No other major alterations to this digital recording.

48 *Make a Jazz Noise Here* (Rykodisc, 1995) — This collection from Zappa's final rock tour was first issued by Barking Pumpkin in 1991; the 1995 reissue simply uses a new master.

49 *You Can't Do That on Stage Anymore, Vol. 1-6* (Rykodisc, 1995) — This mammoth compendium of Frank Zappa's live output (six double CDs of live material from 1965 to 1988) was released over a five-year period from 1988 to 1993. The 1995 reissues use new master recordings. Otherwise no alterations were made to the originals.

49 *Ahead of Their Time* (Rykodisc, 1995) — This 1968 Mothers of Invention concert from the Royal Festival Hall in London is a wonderful artifact of the kind of Dada absurdism practised by that particular group. First released by Barking Pumpkin in 1993. There are no alterations to the 1995 reissue.

50 *Playground Psychotics* (Rykodisc, 1995) — Collected field and concert recordings from the 1971 Flo & Eddie touring ensemble are gathered haphazardly. *Playground Psychotics* lacks the crispness and shaping of other Zappa projects (no doubt because of illness and other more urgent matters). Nevertheless, there are some gems here. The Fillmore show with John and Yoko has more presence than the version they issued on *Some Time in New York City* (1971). There's also a complete version of "Billy the Mountain" from the Pauley Pavilion. Some of the field recordings provide a vivid picture of what Zappa explored in *200 Motels*.

51 *The Yellow Shark* (Rykodisc, 1995) — A glorious selection of pieces from the Ensemble Modern's 1992 European tour of Zappa's orchestral works. Originally released on CD by Barking Pumpkin in 1993; the 1995 reissue has no alterations.

52 *Civilization Phaze III* (Zappa Records, 1994) — One of a small number of releases not issued by Rykodisc. *Civilization Phaze III*, Zappa's final work, is a masterpiece that further develops the themes in *We're Only in It for the Money* and *Lumpy Gravy* (it's the third album in that trilogy). Although hard to locate, this two-CD set is a culmination of Zappa's *project/object*.

53 *Frank Zappa Plays the Music of Frank Zappa* (Zappa Records, 1996) — Dweezil Zappa has compiled, as a memorial to his father, some of his favorite guitar compositions, including "Zoot Allures," "Black Napkins," and "Watermelon in Easter Hay." Besides demonstrating great taste, Dweezil has found alternate unreleased live versions of those familiar tracks so we can compare. Sometimes we hear the genesis of a composition, as in "Watermelon," or stunning improvisations, as in the epic "Zoot Allures" recorded live in Japan in 1976. Dweezil has also found unreleased jewels, like the self-explanatory "Merely a Blues in A" from Paris, 1974. His liner notes add poignant insights into Frank Zappa's playing. Not available in stores — order through 818 PUMPKIN (1-818-922-7873).

54 *Everything Is Healing Nicely* (Zappa Records, 1999) — A fascinating document that serves as a blueprint for the original 1991 rehearsals with the Ensemble Modern — just before the *Yellow Shark* tour. Highlights include "Roland's Big Event/Strat Vindaloo," a wonderfully atmospheric jam that redefines cross-cultural music, featuring Zappa on guitar and L. Shankar on violin, along with the Ensemble Modern; an outtake of "Amnerika" from the tour; and Herman Kretzschmar's "Master Ringo," where he reads (with professional aplomb) from a genital-piercing magazine. Not available in stores — order through 818 PUMPKIN (1-818-922-7873).

COMPILATIONS

1 *Strictly Commercial: The Best of Frank Zappa* (Rykodisc, 1995) — A predictable but enjoyable collection of Zappa "hits." You'll find here a basic primer of some of his more accessible numbers: "Dancin' Fool," "Montana," "Valley Girl," and "Be in My Video." But there are also some not-so-obvious choices: the ripping "San Ber'dino," "Trouble Every Day," and "Let's Make the Water Turn Black." The tip of the iceberg.

2 *The Lost Episodes* (Rykodisc, 1996) — Once again, Zappa holds a dark mirror to the Beatles. In 1996, the surviving Beatles released their *Anthology* discs, tracing how they became the Fab Four. By issuing outtakes, live unreleased recordings, and

DISCOGRAPHY

demos, the Beatles reaffirmed their own mythology. In *The Lost Episodes*, Frank Zappa goes the Beatles one better. He makes his scrapbook a lively, funny, and irreverent musical journey, stripping away any aspirations of pop stardom and examining the very ingredients of his music. We get to hear his early experiments with Captain Beefheart ("Lost in a Whirlpool," "Tiger Roach"); his melding of the synclavier with spoken texts recorded years earlier ("The Grand Wazoo"); Kenny and Ronnie's booger stories; his early Studio Z demos ("Fountain of Love," "Any Way the Wind Blows"); plus early versions of "Inca Roads" and a stunning twelve-minute rendition of "Sharleena" featuring Sugar Cane Harris on vocal.

3 *Strictly Genteel: A "Classical" Introduction to Frank Zappa* (Rykodisc, 1997) — Those interested in Zappa's orchestral work should find this exciting collection deeply satisfying. The CD draws on material ranging from "Uncle Meat: Main Title" to the *Yellow Shark* recordings. There are some nice surprises, like "Dwarf Nebula Processional March & Dwarf Nebula" from *Weasels Ripped My Flesh* and the gorgeous "Aybe Sea" from *Burnt Weeny Sandwich*. But Zappa's art is best realized when he daringly mixes musical genres.

4 *Have I Offended Someone?* (Rykodisc, 1997) — Collected here are the majority of "offensive" Frank Zappa songs. But the bonus is that many of the tunes are presented in remixed or alternate versions. "Disco Boy" is completely reconstructed; "Goblin Girl," from *You Are What You Is*, is remixed beautifully (it's a shame Zappa didn't get to redo the whole album); live unreleased versions of "Dumb All Over" and "Tinsel Town Rebellion" are essential; plus "Dinah-Moe Humm," where Zappa adds some edited material back into the song. This release also features cover art by Ralph Steadman and a perceptive essay by Ed Sanders of the Fugs.

5 *Mystery Disc* (Rykodisc, 1998) — Rykodisc collects the two *Mystery Disc* volumes that were once included in the *Old Masters* box set of Mothers of Invention records Zappa released in the '80s. A perfect companion to *The Lost Episodes*, *Mystery Disc* gathers old Studio Z material, Zappa's first club performances at the Village Inn, excerpts from "I Was a Teenage Malt Shop," and early Mothers rehearsals. Some of the material, like "Wedding Dress Song/The Handsome Cabin Boy" and the 1968 Festival Hall show, now appear on other discs.

BIBLIOGRAPHY AND SOURCES

The individual source notes for each chapter are listed at www.ecwpress.com.

BOOKS

Ample, Annie. *The Bare Facts: My Life as a Stripper*. (Key Porter Books, 1988).
Arp, Jean. *Arp on Arp: Poems, Essays, Memories*, ed. Ron Feldman (Viking Press, 1972).
Balfour, Victoria. *Rock Wives* (Morrow, 1986).
Ball, Hugo. *Flight Out of Time* (University of California Press, 1996).
Berman, Paul. *A Tale of Two Utopias* (Norton, 1996).
Bloom, Allan. *The Closing of the American Mind* (Simon & Shuster, 1987).
Bruce, Lenny. *How to Talk Dirty and Influence People* (Playboy Press, 1972).
Buckley, Jonathan and Mark Ellingham, eds. *Classical Music on CD: The Rough Guide*. (Penquin, 1996).
Chusid, Irwin. *Songs in the Key of Z*. (a capella, 2000).
Coe, Ralph T., ed. *The Dreams of Donald Roller Wilson* (Hawthorn Books, 1979).
Cohen, John, ed. *The Essential Lenny Bruce* (Ballantine Books, 1967).
Cole, Richard. *Stairway to Heaven: Led Zeppelin Uncensored* (Harper, 1992).
Dallas, Sheila, ed. *Hutchinson Dictionary of Classical Music* (Helicon Publishing, 1994).
Des Barres, Pamela. *I'm With the Band: Confessions of a Groupie* (Jove Books, 1987).
Eksteins, Modris. *Rites of Spring: The Great War and the Birth of the Modern Age* (Lester & Orpen Dennys, 1989).
Goldman, Albert. *The Lives of John Lennon* (William Morrow, 1988).
Gray, Michael. *Mother! The Frank Zappa Story* (Plexus, 1994).
Halberstam, David. Foreword to Jules Witcover's *The Year the Dream Died: Revisiting 1968 in America* (Warner Books, 1997).

Harkleroad, Bill, with Billy James. *Lunar Notes: Zoot Horn Rollo's Captain Beefheart Experience* (SAF Publishing, 2000).
Horsley, Jake. *The Blood Poets: A Cinema of Savagery 1958-1999, Volume One* (Scarecrow Press, 1999).
Ives, Charles. *Essays Before a Sonata, The Majority, and Other Writings*, ed. by Howard Boatwright (W.W. Norton & Company, 1970).
—. *Memos* (Norton, 1949).
James, Billy. *Necessity Is . . . The Early Years of the Mothers of Invention* (SAF Publishing, 2000).
Johnson, Haynes. *Sleepwalking Through History: America in the Reagan Years* (Norton, 1991).
Kael, Pauline. *Reeling* (Little Brown, 1976).
Kaufman, Phil. *Road Mangler Deluxe* (White Boucke Publishing, 1993).
Kofsky, Frank. *The Age of Rock: Sounds of the American Cultural Revolution* (Vintage Books, 1967).
Kostelanetz, Richard, ed. *The Frank Zappa Companion* (Schirmer Books, 1997).
Lennon, Nigey. *Being Frank: My Time With Frank Zappa* (California Classics Book, 1995).
Lindner, Robert. *Must You Conform?* (Grove Press, 1961).
Loder, Kurt, interview with Frank Zappa. *Bat Chain Puller* (St. Martin's Press, 1990).
MacDonald, Ian. *Revolution in the Head: The Beatles' Records and the Sixties* (Pimlico, 1997).
Marcus, Greil. *Mystery Train: Images of America in Rock & Roll Music* (E.P. Dutton, 1975).
—. *Stranded: Rock and Roll for a Desert Island* (Knopf, 1979).
—. *Ranters & Crowd Pleasers: Punk in Pop Music, 1977–92* (Doubleday, 1993). Also titled: *In the Fascist Bathroom*.
—. *Invisible Republic: Bob Dylan's Basement Tapes* (Henry Holt, 1997). Also titled: *The Old, Weird America*.
Marsh, Dave. *Louie, Louie: The History and Mythology of the World's Most Famous Rock & Roll Song* (New York: Hyperion, 1993).
May, Rollo. *Power and Innocence: A Search for the Sources of Violence* (Delta, 1972).
McKeen, William, ed. *Rock & Roll Is Here to Stay* (Norton, 2000).
Miles. *Zappa: A Visual Documentary* (Omnibus Press, 1993).
—. *Frank Zappa: In His Own Words* (Omnibus Press, 1993).
Orledge, Robert. *Satie Remembered* (Faber & Faber, 1995).
Paglia, Camille. *Sex, Art, and American Culture* (Vintage, 1992).
—. *Vamps & Tramps* (Vintage, 1994).
Peyser, Joan. *To Boulez and Beyond: Music in Europe Since The Rite of Spring* (Billboard Books, 1999).
Pollock, Bruce. *When the Music Mattered: Rock in the '60s* (Holt, Rinehart & Winston, 1983).
Rossiter, Frank R. *Charles Ives & His America* (Liveright, 1975).
Russo, Greg. *Cosmik Debris: The Collected History and Improvisations of Frank Zappa*

BIBLIOGRAPHY AND SOURCES

(Revised Edition) (Crossfire, 1999).
Satie, Erik. *A Mammal's Notebook* (Atlas Press, 1996).
Seydor, Paul. *Peckinpah: The Western Films — A Reconsideration* (University of Illinois Press, 1997).
Slaven, Neil. *Electric Don Quixote* (Omnibus Press, 1996).
Slonimsky, Nicolas. "I Enter the Age of Absurdity," *Perfect Pitch* (Oxford University Press, 1988).
—. *The Portable Baker's Biographical Dictionary of Musicians* (Schirmer Books, 1995).
Thoreau, Henry David. *The Journal of Henry D. Thoreau, Vol. 12*, ed. Bradford Torrey and Francis H. Allen (Boston: Houghton Mifflin Company, 1949).
Walley, David. *No Commercial Potential: The Saga of Frank Zappa (Updated Edition)* (Da Capo, 1996).
Watson, Ben. *Frank Zappa's Negative Dialectics of Poodle Play* (St. Martin's Press, 1993).
Wenner, Jann. *Lennon Remembers* (Rolling Stone Press/Verso, 2000).
Werner, Craig. *A Change Is Gonna Come: Music, Race & the Soul of America* (Plume, 1999).
Zappa, Frank. *Them or Us (The Book)* (Barfko-Swill, 1984).
—. *The Real Frank Zappa Book* (Poseidon Press, 1989).

ARTICLES

Aledort, Andy, "Zappa's Universe: An Interview With Steve Vai and Mike Keneally," *Guitar Player*, Feb. 1999.
Alterman, Lorraine, "If You Get a Headache...," *Los Angeles Free Press*, July 15, 1966.
Anson, Philip, "Boulez on Boulez: Not Quite Blowing Up the Opera Houses" *The Globe and Mail*, March 28, 2000.
Amirkhanian, Charles, "Ode to Gravity," *Society Pages* #6.
Arbus, Doon, and Valerie Wilmer, "In Person: The Mothers of Invention," *Cheetah Magazine*, 1969.
Ball, Hugo, "The Dada Manifesto — 1912," *Kontakte*, Series 1, Number 2, Dec. 1976, back cover.
Bangs, Lester, Grand Funk Railroad album review, "Survival," *Rolling Stone*, June 10, 1971.
—, Mothers of Invention album review, *The Mothers — Fillmore East, June 1971*, *Rolling Stone*, Sept. 30, 1971.
Barrow, Arthur. Arthur Barrow Home Page (darkwing.uoregon.edu/`splat/Arthur Barrow.html). Comments on Zappa also included in *A Definitive Tribute to Frank Zappa*, from the publishers of *Keyboard* and *Guitar Player*, June 1994.
Benediktsson, Jon, and Kolbeinn Arnason, conversation with Frank Zappa, *Society Pages*, March, 23, 1992.
Birchall, Steve, "Modern Music Is a Sick Puppy: A Conversation With Frank Zappa," *Digital Audio*, Oct./Nov. 1984.

Bloom, Michael, "Interview With the Composer," *Trouser Press*, Feb. 1980.
Boulez, Pierre, discussing Zappa, *Musician*, Feb. 1994.
Branton, Michael, "Frank Zappa vs. the World," *BAM Magazine*, Oct. 5, 1979.
Bruck, Connie, "Letter From Los Angeles: Life of the Party," *The New Yorker*, Jan. 25, 1999.
Burnett, Bruce, "A Walk Down Memory Lane With Dick Barber," *Society Pages #4*.
Carr, Roy, "Frank Talking," *NME*, Nov. 27, 1971.
—, "Svengali Zappa and a Horrible Freak Called Beefheart," *NME*, Feb. 12, 1972.
Carson, Tom, film review of *Baby Snakes*, "Zapped Again," *Village Voice*, Jan. 7, 1980.
Caulfield, Deborah, "Frank Zappa Zapped By 'Late Show,'" *Los Angeles Times*, June 12, 1987.
Cerio, Steven, "Interview With Cal Schenkel," *Seconds Magazine #32*, 1995.
Chapman, Rob, Frank Zappa in conversation with Les Carter, KPPC Radio, transcribed as "I Was a Teenage MOOSE Freak!," *Mojo*, Dec. 1998.
'Cherry Ripe,' "At Last the Truth Can Be Told, FRANK ZAPPA Has No Underwear," *NME*, April 17, 1976.
Childs, Andy, "Huge Stars Big Hearts and Little Feat: The Exploits of Lowell George," *Zig Zag Magazine*.
Clark, Sue C., "Mother's Lament: 'They Called Us Entertainment,'" *Rolling Stone*, April 27, 1968.
Cohen, Neil, "Das Capitalist," *Continental Profiles*, 1990.
Colaiuta, Vinnie, "Interview With Vinnie Colaiuta," *Modern Drummer Magazine*, Nov. 1982.
Corn, David, "Frank Zappa — Trading Partner," *The Nation*, March 19, 1990.
Courrier, Kevin, interview with Frank Zappa biographer Ben Watson, "The Dangerous Kitchen: Poodle Play and Frank Zappa," *Menz*, May 1996.
Cucurullo, Warren, discussing Zappa, *Musician*, Feb. 1994.
—, *T'Mershi Duween #36*, Feb. 1994.
Davis, Michael, "Little Band We Used to Play In: Keyboard Kapers With Tommy Mars & Peter Wolf," *Keyboard*, June 1980.
—, "Makes a Jazz Noise," *Downbeat Magazine*, July 1991.
de Klert, Co, conversation with Mark Volman and Howard Kaylan, "Happy Together Part Three," *Society Pages #11*.
Diliberto, John & Kimberly Haas, "Frank Zappa on Edgard Varese," *Downbeat Magazine*, Nov. 21, 1981.
Dimartino, Dave, conversation with Arthur Barrow, "The Addams Family," *Mojo*, March 4, 1994.
Doerschuk, Robert L., "The Zappa Legacy," George Duke and Patrick O'Hearn's remarks on Zappa, *NME*, April 1994.
Doerschuk, Robert L., and Jim Aikin, "Jazz From Hell," *Keyboard Magazine*, Feb. 1987.
Dunbar, Aynsley, interview in *Zappa!* tribute issue, *Keyboard* and *Guitar Player*, 1992.
Farren, Mick, "'What Is a Groupie?' asked his Lordship," *New Music Express*, April 26, 1975.
Felton, David, Frank Zappa/Zubin Mehta concert review, "What Zappa Did to Zubin Mehta," *Rolling Stone*, July 9, 1970.

BIBLIOGRAPHY AND SOURCES

Feenstra, Pete, interview with Motorhead Sherwood, *Real Music*, 1994.

Fletcher, Lucille, unpublished article, "A Connecticut Yankee in Music," from the Fletcher file, Ives Collection. Sourced in Frank Rossiter, *Charles Ives & His America* (Liveright, 1975).

Forte, Dan, conversation with Frank Zappa, *Society Pages* #10, May 1982.

—, "The Sin in Synclavier," *Guitar Player*, June 1986.

Fowler, Bruce, tribute to Frank Zappa, *Musician*, Feb. 1994.

Frame, Pete, "Mothers: The Earliest Days of the Just Another Band From L.A.," *Zig Zag*, June 1975.

Frick, Charles, "Saint Zappa, Halloween Idyll," *The Aquarian*, Oct. 25–Nov. 1, 1995.

Fricke, David, "Frank Talk," *Rolling Stone*, Nov. 6, 1986.

Gill, Andy, "Frank's Wild Years," *Q magazine*, Dec. 1989.

Gleason, Ralph J., "Those Mothers Can Play," *San Francisco Chronicle*, On the Town, 1968.

Goldberg, Michael "Only in It for the Money? Frank & Moon Zappa go AM," *Creem*, Nov. 1982.

Goldwasser, Noe, "Zappa's Inferno," *Guitar World*, April 1987.

Green, Richard, "Metamorphosis of Frank Zappa," NME, Dec. 5, 1970.

Griffiths, David, "Frank Zappa of the Mothers of Invention: The Hard Guy Who Doesn't Radiate Love," *Record Mirror*, Sept. 2, 1967.

Groening, Matt, interview in *Zappa!* tribute issue, *Keyboard* and *Guitar Player*, 1992.

Guccione, Jr., Bob, "Signs of the Times," interview with Frank Zappa, *Spin*, July 1991.

Guitar Player, "Absolutely Frank," March 1994.

Havel, Vaclav, "Revolutionary," *The New Yorker*, Dec. 20, 1993.

Hayes, Jimmy, *Musician*, Feb. 1994.

Heineman, Alan, "Caught In the Act," *Downbeat*, May 1, 1969.

Hopkins, Jerry, "Mother's Day Has Finally Come," *Rolling Stone*, Oct. 1969.

—, interview with Frank Zappa, *The Rolling Stone Interviews* (Paperback Library, 1970).

Ironside, Virginia, "Zappa: Your Mother Couldn't Be More Wrong About Him," *Daily Mail*, June 5, 1969.

Jackson, Joe, "An Indefatigable Inventor," *The Irish Times*, Dec. 10, 1993.

James, Billy, "Motorhead Speaks: The 1993 Electric Yak Interview," *T'Mershi Duween* #31, June 1993.

Johnson, Pete, "More Polemics From Pop Satirist," *Los Angeles Times*, March 18, 1968.

Jones, Jonathan, "Plugged In or Hung Up? (Original Draft)," *Eonta*, Vol. 2, No. 2, 1994, (sourced in Ben Watson's *Frank Zappa's Negative Dialectics of Poodle Play*, St. Martin's Press, 1993).

Kart, Larry, "Frank Zappa: The Mother of Us All," *Downbeat*, Oct. 30, 1969.

Kathman, Christopher, "Who Else But Zappa Still Plays for the Ugly People," *Sounds*, Sept. 16, 1979.

Kaylan, Howard, interview, *Zig Zag*, July 1972.

Kempton, Sally, "Zappa and the Mothers: Ugly Can Be Beautiful," *Village Voice*, 1968.

Keneally, Mike, interview, *Black Page* #24, Aug. 1989.

Kershaw, Alex, "Fearless and Still Fighting," *The Guardian Weekend*, May 15, 1993.
Kloet, Co de, "Happy Together Part Three," *Society Pages* #11.
Lawson, Dick, "*Zig Zag* Unzips Frank Zappa at the Royal Albert Hall," *Zig Zag* 3.
Lebrecht, Norman, "Boulez and the Well Tempered 4X," *Sunday Times Magazine*, Feb. 1985.
Le Roux, Alain, "Ponty Interview," *Le Jazz Webzine*, April 22, 1997.
Lopilato, Peter, "Zappa vs. the Bleeding Gums," *Primo Times*, Dec. 1977.
Lyons, Steve, & Batya Friedman, "The All-American Composer," *The Wire*, 1986.
Manoeuvre, Phillipe, "Stones Harpist Located Down Paris Subway," *New Music Express*, Sept. 23, 1978.
Marcus, Greil, "Life and Life Only," *Rolling Stone*, Jan. 22, 1981 (also included in *Ranters & Crowd Pleasers: Punk in Pop Music 1977–1992*).
Marks, Gary, "The Crimson Twang Bar King: An Interview With Adrian Belew," *T'Mershi Duween* #40, Aug. 1994.
Marquez, Sal, tribute to Frank Zappa, *Musician*, Feb. 1994.
Marsh, Dave, "Are You Hung Up?" *Rock & Rap Confidential*, 1993.
Marshall, Bob, Dr. Carolyn Dean, and Gerald Fialka, "Statistical Density" interview with Frank Zappa, *T'Mershi Duween*, No. 18, April 1991.
McDonald, Ian, "Everything You Wanted to Know About the Mothers . . . But Were Afraid to Ask," *NME*, Sept. 2, 1972.
Mead, David, "Unholy Mother — Frank Zappa," *Guitarist Magazine*, June 1993.
—, "Interview With Eric Clapton," *Guitarist Magazine*, June 1994.
Mendelsohn, John, "Mark, Don & Mel 1969–71," *Rolling Stone*, June 22, 1972.
Menn, Don, "The Mother of All Interviews," in *Zappa!* tribute issue, *Keyboard* and *Guitar Player*, 1992.
—, "Marque Coy Patron Saint at Joe's Garage," *Zappa!* tribute issue, *Keyboard* and *Guitar Player*, 1992.
Milkowski, Bill, "Orchestral Maneuvers," *Modern Recording Technology*, Aug. 1994.
Miles, "Any Resemblence Is Purely Conceptual," *NME*, Dec. 4, 1976.
Miller, Jim, review of *Lumpy Gravy*, *Rolling Stone*, June 22, 1968.
Molich-Zebhauser, Andreas, interview in *Zappa!* tribute issue, *Keyboard* and *Guitar Player*, 1992.
Morgenstern, Joe, "Democracy's Pitchman," *Los Angeles Times Magazine*, Oct. 30, 1988.
Mulhern, Tom, "Not Exactly Duane Allman," *Guitar Player*, Feb. 1983.
Murray, Charles Shaar, "Frankly a Freak," *The Observer*, Sept. 3, 1989.
Nagano, Kent, interview in *Zappa!* tribute issue, *Keyboard* and *Guitar Player*, 1992.
Oberman, Ronnie, interview with Frank Zappa, *The Washington Star*, quoted in *Los Angeles Free Press*, Sept. 16, 1966.
O'Brian, Robert, "It Just Might Be Frank," *RockBill*, Nov. 1984.
Orloff, Kathy, "Sound Track," *The Hollywood Reporter*, Jan. 21, 1970.
Oullette, Dan, "A Rare Interview With Pop's Philosopher King," *Pulse*, Aug. 1993.
Palmer, Tony, "Frank Zappa, The Royal Philharmonic and Me. . . ," *The Observer*, March 28, 1971.

BIBLIOGRAPHY AND SOURCES

Park, Neon, "Weasels Ripped My Flesh — The 100 Greatest Album Covers of All Time, Interview With Neon Park," *Rolling Stone*, Nov. 14, 1991.
Peterson, Clark, "He's Only 38 and He Knows How to Nasty," *Relix Magazine*, Nov. 1979.
Predoehl, Eric, "The Richard Berry Story," *The Richard Berry Webpage*, 1999.
Prentis, Simon, "Anything Anywhere Anytime For No Reason At All," *Society Pages*, May 1989.
Rambali, Paul, "Stern Words in Knightsbridge," *NME*, Jan. 28, 1978.
Rathbone, R. Andrew, "Profile: Mike Keneally," *Guitar Player*, Dec. 1990.
Reed, Lou, speech inducting Frank Zappa into the Rock and Roll Hall of Fame, 1994.
Rense, Rip, "Interview With Frank Zappa," *Los Angeles Times*, Oct. 1, 1992.
Resnicoff, Matt, "Poetic Justice: Frank Zappa Puts Us in Our Place," *Musician*, Nov. 1991.
Rideout, Ernie, "The Clonemeister Speaks: Interview With Arthur Barrow," *A Definitive Tribute to Frank Zappa*, from the publishers of Keyboard and Guitar Player, June 1994.
Rosen, Steve, "One Size Fits All," *Guitar Player*, Jan. 1977.
Rotondi, James, "My Guitar Wants to Kill Your Mama: Frank Zappa's Lethal Axe," *Guitar Player*, Oct. 1995.
Ruhlmann, William, "Frank Zappa: Moving On to Phase Three," *Goldmine*, Jan. 27, 1989.
Rushdie, Salman, "Rock 'n' Roll," *Chapter One: The Members' Almanac*, Winter 1999–2000.
Salvo, Patrick William, "Dialogue: Frank Zappa," *COQ*, Feb. 1974.
Salvo, Patrick William, and Barbara Salvo, "Interview With Frank Zappa," *Melody Maker*, Jan. 4, 1974.
Schenkel, Cal, tribute to Frank Zappa, *Musician*, Feb. 1994.
Schneckloth, Tim, "Frank Zappa: Garni Du Jour, Lizard King Poetry and Slime," *Downbeat Magazine*, May 18, 1978.
Schorr, Daniel, tribute to Frank Zappa, *Musician*, Feb. 1994.
Scoppa, Bud, "The Importance of Being Dweezil," *Guitar World*, July 1987.
Semms, Denn, interview with Frank Zappa, *Society Pages* #1, 1989.
Semms, Denn, Eric Buxton, and Rob Semler, "They're Doing the Interview of the Century," *Society Pages* #2.
Semms, Denn, Tom Troccoli, and Cynthia Littlejohn, "Frank Sez Foo-eee to Boots!" *Society Pages* #5.
Sheff, David, interview with Frank Zappa, *Playboy*, April 1993.
Shelton, Robert, "Son of Suzy Creamcheese," *New York Times*, Dec. 25, 1966.
Sherwood, Motorhead, "Motorhead Speaks: The 1993 Electric Yak Interview," *T'Mershi Duween* #31, June 1993.
Shih, Howard, "Terry Bozzio: Portrait of a Drummer as an Artist," *The Rutgers Review*, 1989.
Simels, Steve, interview with Frank Zappa, *Stereo Review*, April 1979.
Slaven, Neil, interview with fan Howard Thompson, *Electric Don Quixote* (Omnibus, 1996).
Smith, Arnold Jay, and Bob Henschen, "Electronic Projections," *Downbeat*, Jan. 13, 1977.
Smith, Jim, "Kicks in the Ear," *NME*, Jan. 26, 1974.

Smucker, Tom, "Disco," *The Rolling Stone Illustrated History of Rock & Roll* (Random House/Rolling Stone Press, 1980).
Snow, Mat, interview with Ian Gillian, "Duh Duh Durh, Duh Duh *Du Durrh*!," *Q*, Dec. 1989.
Sovetov, Vladimir, "Interview With Peter Occhiogrosso." Internet site (sova@kpbank.ru).
Stern, Chip, review of *Zappa in New York*, *Downbeat*, 1977.
Stix, John, "On the Record: Frank Zappa," *Guitar World*, Sept. 1980.
Sullivan, Dan, "Mothers of Invention at the Garrick," *New York Times*, May 25, 1967.
Sutherland, Alastair, "Make a Zappa Noise Here," *Music Express Magazine*, Jan. 1992.
Swenson, John, "America's Weirdest Rock Star Comes Clean," *High Times*, March 1980.
Templeman, Ted, "Frank Zappa's Revenge," *Music*, July 2, 1987.
Underwood, Ruth, tribute to Frank Zappa, *Musician*, Feb. 1994.
Uunofski, Slev, Tom Brown, and Tom Troccoli, "Tink Walks Amok: The Arthur Barrow Interview," *T'Mershi Duween* #28.
Vai, Steve, "Interviewed by Adrian Belew," *Guitar for the Practicing Musician*, Jan. 1994.
Varèse, Edgard, "The International Composer's Guild Manifesto," July 1921.
Volpacchio, Florindo, "The Mother of All Interviews," *Telos Magazine*, Spring 1991.
Wackerman, Chad, tribute to Frank Zappa, *Musician*, Feb. 1994.
Waddy, Stacy, "Chief Mother of Invention," *The Guardian*, Oct. 14, 1968.
"Warren Goes Way Back," interview with Warren Cucurullo, *T'Mershi Duween* #36, Feb. 1994.
Watts, Michael, "One Size Fits Some," *Melody Maker*, July 12, 1975.
Weitzman, Steve, "Zappa and the Captain Cook," *Rolling Stone*, July 3, 1975.
Wheeler, Drew, "Frank Zappa's Crusade: 25 Years and Counting," *Billboard Magazine*, Zappa 25th Anniversary edition, May 19, 1990.
—, "Cucamonga Science & Beyond," *Billboard Magazine*, Zappa 25th Anniversary edition, May 19, 1990.
Wheeler, Tom, "Zappa & Son," *Guitar Player*, Jan. 1987.
Whittington, Stephen, "Serious Immobilities: On the Centenary of Erik Satie's *Vexations*," Internet. Satie Homepage (af.lu.sel~fogwell/intro.html).
Wictor, Thomas, "Scott Thunes: Requiem for a Heavyweight," *Bass Player Magazine*, March 1997.
Wigg, David, and Norman Luck, "'Too Dirty' Pop Group Banned at Albert Hall," *Daily Express*, Feb. 9, 1971.
Wilding, Phil, "Just When You Thought It Was Safe," *Cutting Edge*, Aug. 1993.
Williams, Liza, "Zappa Zaps the Big Lie," *Los Angeles Free Press*, Dec. 30, 1966.
Williams, Richard, Frank Zappa concert review, *Times of London*, 1983.
Winner, Langdon, essay on Captain Beefheart's *Trout Mask Replica*, *Stranded: Rock & Roll for a Desert Island* (ed. by Greil Marcus) (Knopf, 1979).
Winokur, John, "Frank Zappa: Drowning in the News Bath," interview on the Internet.
Woodard, Josef, "Don Preston: Synthesizer From *Apocalypse Now* to Zappa," *Downbeat*, Aug. 1987.

BIBLIOGRAPHY AND SOURCES

Zappa, Dweezil, interview in *Zappa!* tribute issue, *Keyboard* and *Guitar Player*, 1992.
Zappa, Frank, "The Oracle Has It All Psyched Out," *Life Magazine*, June 28, 1968.
—, "The Incredible History of the Mothers," *Hit Parader*, June 1968.
—, "What Ever Happened to the Mothers of Invention?," *Hit Parader*, April 1970.
—, "Edgard Varèse: The Idol of My Youth," *Stereo Review*, June 1971.
—, "Good Guitar Stuff or Stereotypifications," *Guitar Player*, Jan. 1977.
—, "Absolutely Frank," *Guitar Player*, Nov. 1982.
—, "The Frank Zappa Picture Disk Interview," 1984, uncredited.
—, "On Junk Food for the Soul," *New Perspective*, 1987.
Zappa, Gail, "Zappa & the Rock Unrolled Hall of Farce," Video Information-90's, darkwing.edu/~splat/video_info-90s.html.
Zappa, Moon Unit, interview in *Zappa!* tribute issue, *Keyboard* and *Guitar Player*, 1992.
Zappa, Moon Unit, and Dweezil Zappa, "Hot Poop! News & Spooz!" *Society Pages* #8.
Zollo, Paul, "The Song Talk Interview," *Song Talk*, Vol. 4, Issue 1.

RADIO AND TELEVISION

Cavett, Dick, interview with Frank Zappa, *The Dick Cavett Show*, June 12, 1980. Tape courtesy of Scott Courrier.
Courrier, Kevin, interview with Allen Ginsberg, *On the Arts*, CJRT-FM Toronto, Jan. 10, 1982.
—, interview with John Cage, *On the Arts*, CJRT-FM Toronto, April 25, 1982.
Gabereau, Vicki, interview with Frank Zappa, *Variety Tonight*, CBC Radio, 1984.
Gordon, Karen, interview with Frank Zappa, produced by Phil Coulter in 1991, segments aired on *Two New Hours*, hosted by Richard Paul and co-hosted by Kevin Courrier, CBC Radio Canada, Nov. 1993.
Hall, Arsenio, interview with Frank Zappa, *The Arsenio Hall Show*, FOX-TV, Feb. 1, 1989. Tape courtesy of Steve Carmichael.
Karsh, Benji, interview with Frank Zappa, CHUM-FM Toronto, 1976. Tape courtesy of Brad Gordon.
Keele, Tim, interview with Frank Zappa, CFNY-FM Brampton, 1982. Tape courtesy of Tim Keele.
Kennedy, Paul, "20th Century Spring: The Rite of Spring," CBC Radio, *Ideas*, May 26, 2000. Tape courtesy of Dave Field.
Leigh, Nigel, "The Late Show Special" on the life of Frank Zappa, BBC 2, Dec. 17, 1993.
Marsden, Dave, interview with Frank Zappa, CHUM-FM Toronto, 1974. Tape courtesy of Brad Gordon.
Moloney, Paddy, interview on BBC Radio 4, July 3, 1991.
Pauley, Jane, "The Today Show," June 7, 1989.
Perlich, Martin, unattributed radio interview with Frank Zappa included on *Leatherette* bootleg album, 1972.

Porter, David, interview with Ray Collins, "Genesis of a Music," KPFK radio, Aug. 12, 1989.
Rivers, Joan, interview with Frank Zappa, *The Joan Rivers Show*, FOX-TV, Nov. 21, 1986. Tape courtesy of Steve Carmichael.
Rowland, Steve, and Gail Zappa, "Frank Zappa: American Composer," Public Radio International's "Music Masters" series, 1996.
WBAI Radio Chicago, March 4, 1988. Interview with Frank Zappa. Tape courtesy of Scott Courrier.
Weide, Robert B. *Lenny Bruce: Swear To Tell the Truth*. (HBO, 1998).

CD & LP LINER NOTES

Alfonso, Barry, interviews with Captain Beefheart, Denny Walley, and Bill Harkleroad, included in liner notes for CD release *The Dust Blows Forward (An Anthology): Captain Beefheart & His Magic Band* (Rhino, 1999).
Dawson, Jim, interview with Richard Berry, included in liner notes for CD release *Get Out of the Car* (Ace, 1992).
Feather, Leonard, interview with Dick Bock, included in the liner notes for LP release *King Kong: Jean-Luc Ponty Plays the Music of Frank Zappa* (Liberty, 1970).
French, John "Drumbo," interviews with Jerry Handley, Vic Mortensen, and Gary Lucas, "There Ain't No Santa Claus on the Evenin' Stage," included in liner notes for CD box set *Grow Fins: Captain Beefheart & His Magic Band: Rarities [1965-1982]* (Revenant, 1999).
Gehr, Richard, interview with Joel Thome, included in liner notes for CD release *Zappa's Universe* CD (Verve), 1993 release.
Gilliam, Terry, in liner notes for CD release *Strictly Commercial: The Best of Frank Zappa* (Rykodisc, 1995).
Pelzell, Doc, liner notes to *The Best of Louie Louie* (Rhino, 1988).
Pullen, Don, interviews with Mark Farner and Don Brewer of Grand Funk Railroad, originally published in the *Fleet Journal*, Jan. 1999; also included in the liner notes for CD release *Good Singin' Good Playin'* (Hip Records/Universal, 1999).
Rense, Rip, interviews with Frank Zappa, Andreas Molich-Zebhauser, and Peter Rundel, included in liner notes for CD release *The Yellow Shark* (Rykodisc, 1993).
—, interviews with Don Vliet, Frank Zappa, Tommy Mars, and Terry Bozzio, included in liner notes for CD release *The Lost Episodes* (Rykodisc, 1996).
—, interview with Jimmy Hayes of the Persuasions, included in the liner notes for CD release *Frankly A Cappella: The Persuasions Sing Zappa* (Earthbeat Records, 2000).
Sanders, Ed, liner notes for CD release, *Have I Offended Someone?* (Rykodisc, 1997).
Scoppa, Bud, interviews with Rick Harper, Bill Payne, and Martin Kibbee, included in liner notes for CD box set *Hotcakes and Outtakes: 30 Years of Little Feat* (Rhino, 2001).
Slater, Veronica, liner notes for the CD release *American Music for Chamber Orchestra: Barber: Adagio, Ives: Symphony No. 3, etc*, Neville Marriner, Academy of St. Martin-in-

BIBLIOGRAPHY AND SOURCES

the-Fields (Decca, 1987).

Slaven, Neil, interview with Sandy Hurvitz, included in liner notes for CD release *Sandy's Album Is Here at Last!* (Edsel-Demon, 1994).

Stravinsky, Igor, liner notes for CD release *Stravinsky Conducts Stravinsky: Petrushka & Le Sacre du Printemps*, Columbia Symphony Orchestra, conducted by Igor Stravinsky (CBS Records, 1962).

Teitelbaum, Richard, comments on the electronic ensemble Musica Electtronica Viva, included in liner notes for CD box set OHM: *The Early Gurus of Electonic Music* (Ellipsis Arts, 2000).

Thomas, Bryan, interview with Paul Buff, included in liner notes for CD release *Frank Zappa: Cucamonga* (Del-Fi Records, 1997).

Vincent, Johnny, interviews with Ray Topping and Earl King, included in original liner notes for *The Things I Used to Do*, "Guitar" Slim (Ace, 1987). Re-released with original note on Speciality Records CD in 1991.

Vliet, Don, Captain Beefheart, and Ry Cooder quotes from liner notes for CD release *A Carrot Is as Close as a Rabbit Gets to a Diamond* (Virgin Universal, 1993).

Zappa, Frank, liner notes for *London Symphony Orchestra* (Rykodisc, 1983).

—, liner notes for *You Can't Do That on Stage Anymore (Vol. 3)* (Rykodisc, 1989).

—, liner notes for CD release *You Are What You Is* (Rykodisc, 1990).

—, liner notes for CD release *Ship Arriving Too Late to Save a Drowning Witch* (Rykodisc, 1991).

—, "Project/Object" press kit, quoted in the *Beat the Boots! Scrapbook*, included in *Beat the Boots! #2* CD (Rhino, 1992).

—, liner notes for *You Can't Do That on Stage Anymore (Vol. 5)*, (Rykodisc, 1992).

—, "The M.O.I. Anti-Smut Loyalty Oath," liner notes for CD release *You Can't Do That on Stage Anymore (Vol. 6)* (Rykodisc, 1992).

—, liner notes for CD release *Ahead of Their Time* (Barking Pumpkin, 1993).

—, liner notes for CD release *Civilization Phaze Three* (Zappa Records, 1994).

—, liner notes for CD release *Mystery Disc* (Rykodisc, 1998).

INDEX

"Abba Zaba," 181
Abnuceals Emuukha Electric Symphony & Chorus, 119, 284, 330
Absolutely Free, 37, 44, 54, 56, 67, 110–8, 134, 139, 146, 151, 197, 288, 384
Acappella (The Persuasions), 239
AC/DC, 414
Ace, Johnny, 43
Adams, John, 379, 401
Adderley, Cannonball, 232, 244
"Advance Romance," 283, 394, 457, 485
"The Adventures of Greggery Peccary," 57, 243, 245, 247, 272, 310, 312, 394, 409
Aerni, Dave, 60
"Aerobics in Bondage," 422
Aerosmith, 501
Agar, John, 374
"Agency Man," 174, 425
Age of Rock, The (Kofsky), 211
Agren, Morgan, 6
Ahead of Their Time, 173, 468
AIDS epidemic, 391–2, 444
"The Air," 158
Alfonso, Barry, 280
Algren, Nelson, 1
"Alien Orifice," 420, 471
Allen, Steve, 60, 63
Allen, Woody, 76
"All I Want for Christmas (Is My Two Front Teeth)," 161
Allman Brothers Band, The, 271, 408, 501
"All My Trials," 442
"All–Night" John, 130
"All Night Long," 100, 244, 283
All the Girls in the World Beware!!! (Grand Funk Railroad), 294
"All Tomorrow's Parties," 502
"All You Need Is Love," 211, 237
Almost Famous (Crowe), 234

"Altar of Love," 403
Altenhous, Phyllis, 199
Alterman, Lorraine, 100
Altschul, Mike, 244
Alvin & the Chipmunks, 155
"America Drinks and Goes Home," 56, 114, 117, 122, 200
American Bandstand, 263
American Graffiti, 156
American Scholar (Emerson), 54
"An American Trilogy," 12, 442
Ameriques (Varèse), 27
Amirkhanian, Charles, 161
"Amnerika," 486
"Amnesia Vivace," 113
Amos & Andy, 351
Amos & Andy, 357, 360, 393
Ample, Annie, 396
Anderson, Jack, 467
Anderson, Laurie, 497
Andrews Sisters, 162
"Andy," 277, 469
"Angel in My Life," 12
"Animal (Fuck Like a Beast)," 414
Animalism, 100
Animals, The, 89, 100, 124, 140
Annie Hall, 76
"Anniversary Waltz," 56
Another Side of Bob Dylan, 88
Anson, Philip, 379
"Ant Man Bee," 185
"Any Downers," 360
"Any Kind of Pain," 439
"Any Way the Wind Blows," 66, 89, 95, 155, 242
Any Way the Wind Blows, 478
Apocrypha, 56, 202, 299, 367
"Apostrophe," 267
Apostrophe ('), 60, 264–70, 274–5, 304, 315, 318, 412, 451, 501

"Approximate," 309
Arbuckle, Ashley, 383
Arbus, Doon, 124
Arcana (Varèse), 27
"Arch Godliness of Purplefull Magic," 170
Ark, The, 477
Armstrong, Louis, 12, 47, 393
Armstrong, Ralph, 298
Arp, Jean, 126–7
As An Am, 478
Askin, Ali, 487, 494–5
Aspen Wind Quartet, 423, 488
"Aybe Sea," 189, 204, 217, 309
Aykroyd, Dan, 317
Aynsley Dunbar Retaliation, 198, 201, 244

"Babette," 450
"Baby, Let's Play House," 438
"Baby Love," 113
Baby Ray & the Ferns, 60
"Baby Snakes," 325–6, 377
Baby Snakes, 301, 341, 377, 428
"Baby, Take Your Teeth Out," 406
Bacharach, Burt, 114
Bach, Johann Sebastian, 429
"Back Door Man," 307
"Bacon Fat," 46, 445
"Bad Luck Is On Me," 38
"Baked-Bean Boogie," 484
Baker, James, III, 467
Baker, Roy Thomas, 207
Baker's Biographical Dictionary of Musicians, The (Slonimsky), 364
Baker, Susan, 467
Bakker, Jim, 440–2
Bakker, Tammy Faye, 440–2
Balfour, Victoria, 102–3, 439
"Ballad of a Thin Man," 91
Ballard, William, 44
Ball, Hugo, 126–8
"Bamboozled by Love," 317, 354, 408, 457–8
Band From Utopia, 498
Bangles, 438
Bangs, Lester, 235–6, 294
Barbarella, 148
Barber, Dick "the Snorker", 142, 150, 157, 165, 222, 224, 374, 483
Barbour, Spider, 130, 494, 496
Bar-Keys, 377
Barrow, Arthur, 315–16, 318–19, 348, 359, 362, 365, 374, 384, 408, 436, 449, 498
Bartók, Bela, 174, 216, 356, 364, 366, 471, 478
Basehart, Richard, 374
"Basement Music #1," 302
Bassoli, Massimo, 459
Bat Chain Puller (Captain Beefheart), 295–6
Bat Out of Hell (Meat Loaf), 255
"Battle Hymn of the Republic," 442, 459

Beach Boys, The, 41, 76, 116, 119, 266
Beam, Mark, 473
Beat the Boots, 476, 479, 500
Beat the Boots 2, 479
Beatles, The, 26, 74, 77, 97, 100, 102, 118, 133–4, 141, 153, 149, 211, 233, 238, 266, 300, 446, 476
"Beat the Reaper," 486, 496
Beatty, Warren, 88
"Beauty Knows No Pain," 360, 459
"The Be–Bop Tango," 263–4, 308, 474–5, 486, 488
Beck, Jeff, 145
Beefheart, Captain, 181–3, 185, 198, 196, 202, 247, 249, 273, 277, 280–2, 285–6, 295–6, 336, 387, 391, 464, 475, 482. *See also* Vliet, Don
Bee Gees, The, 306, 474
Beethoven, Ludwig van, 52, 143, 399
Before the Beginning, 194
Beggar's Banquet (The Rolling Stones), 94
Be Glad Then America, 51
"Behind the Sun," 46
Beiderbecke, Bix, 45
Being Frank (Lennon), 14, 154, 257
Belcher, Lorraine, 67, 69–70, 190
Belew, Adrian, 300, 313–14, 321–3, 387
Bell, Norma Jean, 285
"The Beltway Bandits," 426
Belushi, John, 298–9, 309
Bement, Dwight, 58
"Be in My Video," 407, 410, 452
Ben–Hur, 225
Bennett, Bruce, 224
Bennett, Earle, 163
Bennett, Max, 195, 201
Benson, George, 376
Berardi, Dennis, 461
"Berceuse" (Stravinsky), 113
Berg, Alban, 30
Bergano, John, 308
Berio, Luciano, 165, 380
Berkman, Harold, 256
Berlin, Irving, 115
Berman, Paul, 465–5
Bernstein, Leonard, 45
Berry, Chuck, 43, 154
Berry, Richard, 40–2, 44, 91
Bessman, Jim, 412
Best Band You Never Heard in Your Life, The, 469, 471, 487
Bickford, Bruce, 301
"The Big Break," 42
"Big Buns," 295
"Big Leg Emma," 120, 308, 384
"Big Leg Emma's," 120
"The Big Squeeze," 150
"The Big Surfer," 61
"Big Swifty," 311, 450, 470, 496
Bikel, Theodore, 84, 221, 225, 230, 489
Bill Haley & the Comets, 46, 266

INDEX

Billings, William, 51
"Billy the Mountain," 232, 239–40, 242, 311, 409, 490–1
Birchall, Steve, 153, 384
Birdbath, Dr. Horatio Q., 162
Bitches Brew, 160
"Black Beauty," 484
The Blackboard Jungle, 45–6, 167, 266
Black, Jimmy Carl, 72, 76, 87, 98, 124, 136, 153, 156, 159, 172, 174, 191–2, 213, 222, 226, 239, 359, 385, 483–4, 498
"Black Napkins," 285–6, 297, 356, 470, 478
Blackouts, The, 46–7, 50, 68, 75, 261
"The Black Page," 7, 308, 313, 349, 408, 420, 470, 474, 478
Black Page, The, 436, 446
"The Black Page #2," 313, 485
Black Sabbath, 228, 293
Black, Shirley Temple, 464–5
Blakely, Paul, 181
Blake, Peter, 143
Blanc, Mel, 162
"Blessed Relief," 248
"The Blimp," 186, 482
Blonde on Blonde, 90, 387
"Bloodshot Rollin' Red," 274
Blood, Sweat & Tears, 75, 102, 160, 299
Bloom, Allan, 53
Bloom, Leopold, 376
"Blowin' in the Wind," 16
Blue Danube (Strauss), 161
Bluejeans & Moonbeams (Captain Beefheart), 273
"The Blue Light," 353, 369, 393
Blues and the Abstract Truth, The (Oliver Nelson), 445
"Bobby Brown Goes Down," 15, 18, 81, 323–4, 410, 457
"Bob in Dacron," 381, 428
Bock, Dick, 195, 200
"Bogus Pomp," 173, 206, 226, 285, 329, 382, 429, 482
Bolero (Ravel), 469, 471
Bongo Fury, 48, 281–6, 349, 466, 475
Bonham, John, 233
Bono, Sonny, 40
"Bony Moronie," 120
"The Booger Man," 475
Boogie Men, 56
Boone, Pat, 165
Booth, Stanley, 433
Bootleg recordings, 476
Boris Godunov, 118, 365
"Born in the USA," 16
Born Under a Bad Sign, 222
Borodin, Alexander, 34
Bostic, Earl, 47
Boston, Mark, 182
Boulez, Pierre, 10, 26, 271, 378, 389, 460, 488
Bourne, Mike, 215
Bowie, David, 313–14, 407
"Bow Tie Daddy," 77, 138, 150
Bozzio, Dale, 6, 333, 348
Bozzio, Terry, 6, 272, 280, 285–6, 297, 300–1, 305–6, 308–10, 312–14, 321–2, 325, 338, 348, 377, 459, 479, 490–1
Brainiac, 281
Brambell, Wilfrid, 223
Branton, Michael, 334
Braxton, David, 460
"Break Time," 59
Brecht, Bertolt, 226
Brecker, Mike, 299
Brecker, Randy, 299
Breslin, Jimmy, 455
Brewer, Don, 293–5, 307
"Briefcase Boogie," 395
"Bringing in the Sheaves," 289–90, 491
Bringing It All Back Home (Bob Dylan), 88
Broadway the Hard Way, 54, 437, 443–6, 459
Brock, Napoleon Murphy, 258–61, 271, 280, 285, 395, 402, 405, 409, 450, 474
"Broken Hearts Are for Assholes," 11, 305–6, 319, 321, 360, 428, 439, 464
Brooks, Richard, 45
Brothers Karamazov, The (Dostoevsky), 332
Brown, Clarence "Gatemouth", 3, 38–9
Brown, James, 143, 328, 413
"Brown Moses," 395, 474
Brown, Norman O., 265
"Brown Shoes Don't Make It," 7, 54, 116–17, 122, 129, 136, 139, 189, 204, 229, 350, 355, 490
Brown, Tom, 476
Bruce, Honey, 80
Bruce, Jack, 267
Bruce, Lenny, 3, 16, 20, 79–81, 84, 91, 99, 105, 110, 133, 138, 171, 208, 213, 324, 391, 424, 457
Bruce Springsteen Live/1975-1985, 447–8
Bruck, Connie, 396
Buckinghams, The, 75
Buckley, Lord, 181
Buckley, Tim, 180, 256
Buff, Allison, 67
Buffalo Springfield, 94, 106, 111, 134
Buff, Paul, 59–61, 63, 66–7, 70, 91, 333, 377
Bullwinkle, 240
Bunting, Edward, 480
Burdon, Eric, 100, 140, 143
Burns, Jeffrey, 472, 488
Burnt Weeny Sandwich, 37, 57, 189, 202, 204–5, 207, 233, 275, 483
Burroughs, William, 317
Burton, Gary, 190
Bush, George, 444, 454–5
Busoni, Ferruccio, 26
Butcher, Pauline, 165
Butler, Anya, 102–3
Butterfield, Paul, 98
Buxton, Eric, 6, 442
"Bwana Dik," 2, 234, 279
Byers, Bill, 244
Byrds, The, 83–4, 134

Cabaret, 19
Cage, John, 26, 63, 130–2, 152, 210, 311, 472, 497
Cage, Nicolas, 368
"Caldonia," 120, 388
Caliptra Melody Four, The, 162
"Call Any Vegetable," 113, 119, 122, 159, 242
"Call on Me," 181
Camarena, Robert "Frog", 244
"Camarillo Brillo," 251, 254, 281
Cameo, 430
"Canard du Jour," 356
Canby, Vincent, 241
"Candy Corn Madness," 104
Canned Heat, 75, 120, 134
"Can't Afford No Shoes," 272, 275
Captain and Tennille, 414
Captain Beefheart and His Magic Band, 31, 68, 121, 181–2, 192, 198, 273, 296
Captain Beefheart vs. the Grunt People, 67, 69, 202
Captain Glasspack and His Magic Mufflers, 73
"The Captain's Fat Theresa Shoes," 176
"Caravan," 56
Carey, Skip, 474
Carey, Tim, 56, 149
Carlin, George, 455
Carlos, Walter (Wendy), 246
Carlton, Larry, 349
Carmen (Bizet), 161, 470
Carmen, Paul, 436
Carnegie, Dale, 79
"Carolina Hard–Core Ecstasy," 281, 475
"Carol, You Fool," 458
Carpenter, Karen, 1
Carpenter, Richard, 1, 2
Carpenters, 1, 2
Carson, Johnny, 430
Carson, Tom, 341
Carter, Billy, 415
Carter, Elliott, 45, 426
Carter, Les, 30, 40, 158
Cascades, The, 273
Cash, Johnny, 359, 437, 443, 469, 487
"Catholic Girls," 327, 330, 333
Caulfield, Deborah, 431
Cavaliere, Andy, 294
Cavett, Dick, 292
The Celtic Harp (The Chieftains), 480, 492
Central Park in the Dark (Ives), 54, 75
Central Scrutinizer, 19, 97, 330, 332, 335, 338, 340, 360–1, 494
Cerio, Steven, 187
Cerveris, Don, 55, 84
Chad & Jeremy, 75
"Chameleon," 311
"Chana in de Bushwop," 458
Chance Operation, A, 497
Chandler, Gene, 112
Chandler, Raymond, 76

Change Is Gonna Come: Music, Race & the Soul of America, A (Werner), 78, 166
"Changes," 104
Channels, The, 3, 403–4
Chaplin, Charlie, 16, 75
Chariots of the Gods (Von Däniken), 274
"Charlena," 244
Charles, Ray, 100
"Charlie's Enormous Mouth," 360, 459
"Chattanooga Choo Choo," 452
"Cheap Thrills," 155
"Cheepnis," 262–3, 271
Cheka, Mark, 84–5, 106
Cher, 40
"Cherry Pie," 62
Cherry Sisters, 103
Chicago, 26, 75, 94
Chicarelli, Joe, 335
Chieftains, 479–81, 491–2
Chinmoy, Sri, 266
"Chloe," 162
Chopin, Henri, 210
Chrislu, Spencer, 480–1
Christiansen, Jill, 10
Christlieb, Don, 201
Christmas in New Jersey, 409
Christopher Bond & the Bond, 256
"The Chrome–Plated Megaphone of Destiny," 141–2
Chrysalis, 130
"Chucha," 189
"Chunga's Revenge," 459
Chunga's Revenge, 27, 174, 207, 216, 218, 220–2, 233, 262, 352, 375, 389, 405, 469, 478
"Church Chat," 475
Church of Scientology, 336
City Hall Fred, 116–17
"City of Tiny Lites," 275, 326, 356
City Slickers, 163
Civilization Phaze III, 468, 486, 493–4, 500
"The Clap," 27, 218
Clapton, Eric, 132, 135, 140, 169
Clark, Andrew, 379
Clarke, H.A., 50
Clear Spot (Captain Beefheart), 273
"Cleetus Awreetus–Awrightus," 247, 274, 325
Clinton, Bill, 498
"Close–miking" technique, 60
"The Closer You Are," 403
Closing of the American Mind, The (Bloom), 53
Clovers, The, 351
Coasters, The, 42, 115, 395, 404
"Cocaine Decisions," 371–2, 459
"Cocktails for Two," 162
Coe, Ralph T., 391
Cohen, Herb, 84–5, 89, 98–9, 104–5, 116, 143, 147, 150, 180, 221–2, 232, 249, 256, 292–3, 295, 312, 331, 340
Cohen, Martin, 292
Cohen, Neil, 461

INDEX

COINTELPRO, spying by, 194
Colaiuta, Vinnie, 314–15, 348, 352, 366
Colbeck, Julien, 152
Coleman, Ornette, 160, 185
Cole, Nat King, 109
Cole, Richard, 233
Collins, James, 319
Collins, Ray, 60–2, 65, 68, 72–3, 76, 87, 93, 102, 107–8, 111–14, 122, 124, 134, 148, 155, 172, 175, 206, 211, 215, 226, 385
Coltrane, John, 88, 109, 166
Coltrane Time, 88
Come Out to Show Them (Steve Reich), 422
Compact disc, advent of, 411
Complete Works of Edgard Varèse, Volume I, 28
Conan O'Brien Show, The, 430
"Concentration Moon," 71
Coneheads, 317
"Confinement loaf," 440
Congdon, Stuart, 30
Conneff, Kevin, 481
Cooder, Ry, 177, 181–2
Coogan, Jackie, 374
Cooke, Sam, 166
Cooley, Spade, 227
Coolidge, Cassius Marcellus, 391
Coolidge, Martha, 368
Conrad & the Hurricanes, 131
Cooper, Alice, 178, 187
Copland, Aaron, 231
Coronado, Dave, 73
Corso, Gregory, 283
Cosby, Bill, 167
"Cosmik Debris," 81, 266–7, 410, 412, 441, 460
Cosmik Debris (Russo), 28, 261
Cosmos, 407
Cotton, Jeff, 182
Counterpoint: Strict and Free (Clarke), 50
Cousteau, Jacques, 463
Cowell, Henry, 131, 364
Coy, Marque, 407, 456
Craft, Robert, 378
Crazy Jerry, 81–2
Crazy World of Arthur Brown, 145
Cream, 144, 169, 222, 267, 294, 483
Creamcheese, Suzy, 90–1, 97, 101, 107, 145, 157
Creation, The (Haydn), 9
Crests, The, 240
"Crew Slut," 333
Crosby, Bing, 162, 484
Crosby, Stills & Nash, 240
Cross, Christopher, 359, 367
Crossfire, 430
Crowe, Cameron, 234
Crows, The, 31–2
"Cruising for Burgers," 30, 158
Cruising With Ruben & the Jets, 37, 104, 133, 153–6, 158, 165, 170, 384, 449

Crum, Simon, 282
Cuber, Ronnie, 299
Cucamonga, 61
"Cucamonga," 283
Cucamonga Era, The, 194–5
Cucurullo, Warren, 316–17, 337, 348, 356, 377
Cukor, George, 313
Culture Club, 394, 410
Cuneo, Louis "the Turkey", 122, 130–1, 208, 495, 500
Curtin, Jane, 317
"Cuttin' In," 38

Dada movement, 126–8
"Daddy, Daddy, Daddy," 228
Daddy's Dyin'...Who's Got the Will?, 359
Dali, Salvador, 160
Daltry, Roger, 19, 281
"Damp Ankles," 427
Dance Me Outside, 496
"Dance of the Just Plain Folks," 226
"Dance of the Rock 'n' Roll Interviewers," 226
"Dancin' Fool," 93, 243, 298, 318, 326–7, 337, 410, 428
D'Angelo, Beverly, 359
"The Dangerous Kitchen," 7, 373, 410, 452
"Danny Boy," 437
"Darling Nikki," 413–14
Dashev, David, 239
David, Hal, 114
Davies, Rick, 142
Davis, Clive, 87
Davis, Miles, 109, 123, 160, 245
Dawe, Tim, 180
"Day by Day," 361
"Day of Decision," 110
Day of the Locust, The (West), 76
"Dead Girls of London," 320
Dean, James, 16, 413
"The Deathless Horsie," 349, 356, 452
Death Valley Days, 353
"Debra Kadabra," 48, 281, 374, 387
Debussy, Claude, 8, 209, 378
"Dedicated to the One I Love," 244
Deep Purple, 205, 242
"Delia's Gone," 245
Democracy in America (Tocqueville), 440
Denselow, Robin, 386
Density 21.5 (Varèse), 29
"Dental Hygiene Dilemma," 227, 231, 261, 293
Denver, John, 416
Des Barres, Pamela, 83, 165, 175–6, 222. *See also* Miller, Pamela
"Deseri," 155, 385
Deserts (Varèse), 28, 357
Devine, Andy, 278
Devo, 366, 410
Diaghilev, Serge, 34–5
Dick Dale & His Del-Tones, 377
"Dickie's Such an Asshole," 263, 437, 443, 459

Diddley, Bo, 181
"Diddy Wah Diddy," 181
"Didya Get Any Onya?," 186, 207–8, 225, 474, 482, 484
DiMartino, Andy, 273
Dimartino, Dave, 319
"Dinah–Moe Humm," 3, 254, 281, 353, 377, 410, 412
"Dinner with Drac," 61
"Dio Fa," 496
"Directly From My Heart to You," 46, 202, 208, 210
Dire Straits, 387
"Dirty Love," 252–3, 255, 262, 269
Dirty Mind (Prince), 413
"Disco Boy," 290–1, 326, 377, 475
Disconnected Synapses, 480
"Diseases of the Band," 449
Disney, Walt, 268
"Dixie," 441–2
Dixon, Willie, 307
Dmochowski, Alex, 244
Dr. Demento, 270
Dr. Ruth, 416
Dr. Zhivago, 87
Does Humor Belong in Music?, 409–11, 428, 452, 458
"Does This Kind of Life Look Interesting to You?," 228
"Dog Breath/Uncle Meat," 487
"Dog Breath, in the Year of the Plague," 30, 158, 241
"Dog Breath Variations," 285, 486
Dolphy, Eric, 205, 210
"Do Me in Once I'll Be Sad, Do Me in Twice & I'll Know Better (Circular Circulation)," 176
Domino, Fats, 43
Don & Dewey, 40, 195
Don Giovanni (Mozart), 9
"Dong Work for Yuda," 299, 338
Donovan, 174, 446
"Don't Bogart That Joint," 108
"Don't Eat the Yellow Snow," 11, 264, 269, 311, 318, 358, 450–1, 459, 477
"Don't You Ever Wash That Thing?," 262, 271
"Don't You Lie to Me," 117
Doobie Brothers, The, 281
Doors, The, 214, 362, 374
"Doreen," 359–60
Dostoevski, Fyodor, 332
"Do That to Me One More Time," 414
Douglas, Alan, 204–5
Downey, Bob, 160
"Down in de Dew," 304
"Down in Mexico," 395, 404
"The Downtown Talent Scout," 481
"Do You Like My New Car?," 235–6, 450
"Do You Really Want to Hurt Me?," 394
"Drafted Again," 362
Dreyfuss, Richard, 460
Drifters, The, 140
Drop Control, 436
"Drowning Witch," 37, 369–70, 458, 460
Dubcek, Alexander, 172

"Duck Duck Goose," 304
Duckman, 500
Dukakis, Michael, 454–5
Duke, George, 201, 213–14, 217–18, 232, 244–5, 247, 250–3, 259–60, 262, 267–8, 271–5, 277, 280, 283, 297, 304, 307, 309, 321, 405, 450, 475
"Duke of Earl," 112, 220
"Duke of Orchestral Prunes," 309
"Duke of Prunes," 56, 112, 200, 206, 285, 309, 329
"The Duke Regains His Chops," 113
"Dumb All Over," 361, 441, 444, 452
"Dummy Up," 261
Dunbar, Aynsley, 199–202, 206, 213–14, 217, 244, 246, 248, 452, 490
Duncan, Cleave, 61–2
"Duodenum," 131, 234
Dupree, Jack, 120
"Dupree's Paradise," 271, 389, 477, 496, 500
Durante, Jimmy, 284
Duran, Tony, 244, 247–8, 267
Dust Blows Forward, The, 280
"The Dust Blows Forward 'n' the Dust Blows Back," 185
"Dust My Broom," 311
"Dwarf Nebula Processional March & Dwarf Nebula," 210
Dylan, Bob, 16–17, 78, 88, 90–1, 102, 124, 207, 322, 341, 386–7

Eagles, 245
"Earth Angel," 61–2, 155
Ear Unit, 426
East of Eden, 413
Easton, Sheena, 414, 417
Eastwood, Clint, 330
Easy Action (Alice Cooper), 178
Easy Chair, 199
"Easy Meat," 351–2, 356, 370, 485
Easy Rider, 108, 361
"Eat Me Alive," 414
"Eat That Question," 247
"Echidna's Arf (of You)," 262, 271
"Eddie, Are You Kidding?," 240
"Edgard Varèse: The Idol of My Youth," 302
1812 Overture (Tchaikovsky), 470
Eisenhower, Dwight, 15
Eksteins, Modris, 36
"Electric Aunt Jemima," 158
Electric Don Quixote (Slaven), 32, 111
"Electricity," 181–2
Electric Kool-Aid Acid Test, The (Kesey), 115
Electric Ladyland (The Jimi Hendrix Experience), 129
Elfman, Danny, 150
Ellington, Duke, 99, 190–1, 471
Elliot, Mama Cass, 420
"El Loco Cha Cha Cha," 43
"Elusive Butterfly," 240
"Elvis Has Just Left the Building," 437–8
Ely, Jack, 41, 43
Emerson, Ralph Waldo, 54
"The End," 475

INDEX

Ensemble InterContemporain, 378, 388–9, 460
Ensemble Modern, 472–3, 486–8, 490, 494, 497, 501
Entry of the Gladiators (Fucik), 114
"Envelopes," 370, 382–3
Eonta (Jones), 65, 352
"Epistrophy," 267
"The Eric Dolphy Memorial Barbecue," 210
Erka, Christine, 165, 175, 178, 197, 249
Ertegun, Ahmet, 270
Essays Before a Sonata (Ives), 50, 322
Estrada, Roy, 72, 76, 87, 124, 131, 153, 172, 174, 189–92, 203–4, 208–9, 213, 285–6, 291, 301, 304, 325, 369, 374, 483, 495
"Europa (Earth's Cry Heaven's Smile)," 349
Evans, Gil, 201
"Evelyn, a Modified Dog," 277, 283, 304
Evening With Wild Man Fischer, An, 171, 176, 183, 186, 249
Everett, Betty, 262
Evers, Medgar, 61, 344
"Everybody Must Get Stoned," 125
"Every Poor Soul Who's Adrift In the Storm," 231
Everything Is Healing Nicely, 486, 501
"The Evil Prince," 474
"Excentrifugal Forz," 267
"Excerpt From The Uncle Frankie Show," 55
"Exercise #4," 490
Exon, James, 418, 421
Exploding Plastic Inevitable, 98
Exxon Valdez oil-spill, 463, 487

Factory, 175
Faithfull, Marianne, 492
Falwell, Jerry, 392, 440
Fanfare for the Common Man (Copland), 231
Fanoga, Larry, 333
"Farmer John," 40
Farner, Mark, 293–5
Farrakhan, Louis, 443
"Farther Oblivion," 263, 477
"Father O'Blivion," 265
Feather Merchants, The, 162
Featherstone, Coy, 271
Feenstra, Pete, 223, 244
Felton, David, 206
"Fembots in a Wet T–Shirt," 334
"Femme Fatale," 502
Feu d'artifice (Stravinsky), 34
"Fifty–Fifty," 252–3
Fillmore East, June 1971, 196, 232–3, 235, 241, 450, 469, 487
"Filthy Fifteen," (songs), 414
"Filthy Habits," 310, 475
"Find Her Finer," 288–9
"Fine Girl," 350–1, 357, 452
Finnegans Wake (Joyce), 270
"Fire," 145
Firebird, The (Stravinsky), 33–5, 113, 262

First Piano Concerto (Bartók), 364
Fischer, Larry "Wild Man," 170–1, 178–9, 187, 249, 253, 295, 480, 494
Fisher, Eddie, 240
Fishman, Laurel, 406
Fisk, Jack, 359
Five Easy Pieces, 149
Five Man Electrical Band, 361
Flaherty, Robert J., 264
Flairs, The, 42
"Flakes," 322, 387
"Flambé," 309
Flamingos, The, 42
Fleetwood Mac, 404
Flight Out of Time (Ball), 126
Flo & Eddie, 207, 213, 216–17, 219, 226, 231, 233, 235, 240–1, 248, 255, 274, 278, 290, 298, 337, 351, 405, 435, 448, 469, 477, 480, 491
"Florentine Pogen," 272, 275–7, 469, 475
"The Florida Airport Tape," 448
"flower power," FZ attack on, 133
"Flower Punk," 140
Flying Burrito Brothers, 245–6
Flynt, Larry, 396
Fonda, Jane, 148, 460
"Food Gathering in Post Industrial America," 489
"Fool Fool Fool," 351
Foo, Richard, 476
"For Calvin (and His Next Two Hitchhikers)," 246–7, 311–12
For Real (Ruben & the Jets), 244
"For What It's Worth," 106, 111
"For the Young Sophisticate," 304–5, 352
Foss, Lukas, 248
Foster, Stephen, 441
"Fountain of Love," 155
Four Deuces, The, 202, 482
"400 Days of the Year," 157
Fowler, Bruce, 250, 254, 259, 262, 272, 280–1, 297–8, 304, 315, 436
Fowler, Tom, 250, 259, 272, 280, 314–15
Fowler, Walt, 259, 298, 436, 474
Fowley, Kim, 98
Foxx, Redd, 236
Frampton Comes Alive!, 321
Frampton, Peter, 321–2, 359
Francesco Zappa, 383, 401, 409
Frank, Barney, 394
Franken, Dave, 28
Franklin, Aretha, 166, 377
Franklin, Carter, 46
Franklin, Johnny, 46–7, 68, 91
Frankly A Cappella: The Persuasions Sing Zappa, 503
Frank Zappa: A Visual Documentary (Miles), 119, 336, 463
Frank Zappa Guitar Book, The (Vai), 349
Frank Zappa: In His Own Words (Miles), 385
Frank Zappa Meets the Mothers of Prevention, 412, 419, 422

Frank Zappa Plays the Music of Frank Zappa, 501
Frank Zappa's Negative Dialectics of Poodle Play (Watson), 16
Frank Zappa's Wild Wild East, 467
Franzoni, Carl, 83, 92, 106
Fraternity of Man, 108
Freak Out! , 78, 87–98, 91, 101, 148, 270, 300, 384, 449, 474, 477
freak scene, in Los Angeles, 76–7, 83, 106
Freaks & Motherfu*#@%!, 477
Freeman, Sandy, 398
French, John, 181, 296
Frick, Charles, 498
Fricke, David, 450
"Friendly Little Finger," 289, 325, 500
Fritts, Edward, 414
"Frogs With Dirty Little Lips," 408, 458
"Frownland," 184
Frunobulax, 262
Fucik, Julius, 114
Fugs, The, 160, 169
"Full Blown," 57
Funeral March of the Marionette (Gounod), 439
Funicello, Annette, 149
Furnier, Vincent, 178
"The Future Family," 429
"F.Z./ JCB Drum Duet," 484

Gabereau, Vicki, 22, 259, 363, 398, 400, 455
Gabor, Zsa Zsa, 374
Gabriel, Peter, 407
Gaillard, Slim, 249
Gallagher, Eileen, 161
"Gangster of Love," 38
Gardner, Bunk, 48, 81, 109–10, 113, 124, 135, 152, 159–60, 170, 173, 189, 192, 287, 385
Gardner, Buzz, 192, 208, 482–4
Garner, Erroll, 470
Garrick Theatre, stage theatrics at, 122
Gary Puckett & the Union Gap, 58
Gas, Sir Frederick, 163
"Gatemouth Boogie," 38
Gates, David, 181
Gaulle, Charles de, 172
Gaynor, Gloria, 291
"Gee," 32
"Gee, I Like Your Pants," 355
Gehr, Richard, 8
"Geneva Farewell," 485
Gentle Giant, 436
Genuine Floppy Preludes (for a Dog) (Satie), 9
George Duke Trio, 201
George, Lowell, 104, 175–6, 189–90, 192, 208, 225, 369, 482–5
"German Lunch," 189, 484
Geronimo Black, 192
Geronimo Black, 192
Gerry & the Pacemakers, 102

"Get a Little," 210, 212, 310, 483
"Get Whitey," 486, 490
Gill, Andy, 44
Gillespie, Dizzy, 12, 109, 201
Gillette, Penn, 6
Gilliam, Terry, 147
Gillian, Ian, 242
Gilliard, Roddie, 498
"Gimme Dat Thing," 337
"Gimme Shelter," 300
Ginsberg, Allen, 194, 317
"The Girl in the Magnesium Dress," 389, 488
Girls Together Outrageously (GTO), 83, 175, 295
Giugno, Giuseppe di, 380
Glass, Philip, 379, 401
"The Gleam in Your Eye," 403
Gleason, Ralph J., 163
Glinka, Mikhail, 34
Globokar, Vinko, 380
"Gloria," 72, 288
"Glory of Love," 155
Glotzner, Bennett, 299, 301, 402
Glover, Roger, 242
"Go Ahead," 328
"Goblin Girl," 359–60
"Go Cry on Somebody Else's Shoulder," 93, 473
"God Bless America," 117, 156
Godspell, 361
Goldberg, Michael, 369
Goldman, Albert, 237–8
Gong Show, The, 430
"The Good Ship Lollypop," 464
Good Singin' Good Playin' (Grand Funk Railroad), 294–5
Goody, Sam, 28
Gorbachev, Mikhail, 461
Gordon, Jim, 267, 275, 304
Gordon, Karen, 30
Gordon, Mary, 455
Gordy, Berry, 502
Gore, Al, 413–14, 418–19, 421, 424, 498
Gore, Mary Elizabeth (Tipper), 413, 417, 419, 422–3, 498
Gortikov, Stanley, 414
Gorton, Slade, 418
Gould, Glenn, 160, 164
Graham, Bill, 99, 232
Grand Funk Railroad, 228, 233–4, 293–4, 331
Grand Inquisitor, 332
Grandmothers, 385, 498
Grand Wazoo, The, 201–2, 244, 246–8, 250, 267, 276, 298, 304, 309, 312, 325, 412
Grapelli, Stephane, 356
Grass Roots, 87
Grateful Dead, 115, 134, 358
Gravestones (Slonimsky), 364
Gray, Michael, 67, 82, 87, 90, 103, 105–6, 138, 148, 154, 206, 220, 296, 386, 438
Grayson, Carl, 162
Great Underground Arts Masked Ball and Orgy

INDEX

(GUAMBO), 103–4
Green, All, 501
Greenaway, Andy, 272
Greenbaum, Norman, 361
"The Green Beret," 110
"Green Dolphin Street," 56
"The Green Fields of America," 481
Green, Peter, 404
Green, Richard, 180
Grey, Joel, 19
Grimm's Fairy Tales, 444
Groening, Matt, 10, 12, 75, 97, 150, 490–1, 500
Groupie Papers, The, 178, 455
"The Groupie Routine," 450
groupies, rock stars and, 94, 169–70, 234
Grow Fins, 184, 199
"Grunion Run," 70
"G–Spot Tornado," 57, 427, 486–7, 490
Guccione, Bob Jr., 471
Guerico, James, 75, 272
Guerin, John, 195, 201
Guevara, Ruben Ladron de, 243
Guitar, 446–7, 485
"Guitar" Slim (Edward Jones), 38–9, 47, 79
"The Gumbo Variations," 197, 310
Guthrie, Woody, 16
Gutowitz, Samuel, 28
Guy, Bob, 61
Gymnopédies (Satie), 75
Gypsy Love, 300

Haas, Jonathan, 6
"Habanera," 470
Haden, Charlie, 377
Hahn, Jessica, 441
"Hair Pie: Bake I," 185
Halberstam, David, 168
Hall, Arsenio, 417
Hammer without a Master, The (Boulez), 378
Hampton, Lionel, 265
Hancock, Herbie, 311
Handel, George Frideric, 52
Handley, Jerry, 48–9, 181
"The Handsome Cabin Boy," 284
"Hands With a Hammer," 459
Hank Ballard & the Midnighters, 42, 60
Happy Days, 156
Happy Jack (The Who), 117
"Happy New Year," 163
"Happy Together," 207, 235
Hard Day's Night, A, 149, 223
"Harder Than Your Husband," 359, 405
Hardin, Tim, 79
"A Hard Rain's a–Gonna Fall," 16
Hare Krishna movement, 276
Harkleroad, Bill, 182–3
Harmony (Piston), 45
Harper, Rick, 104

Harpo, Slim, 40
Harris, Bob (session keyboardist *Fillmore East*), 232
Harris, Bob (keyboardist *You Are What You Is* etc.), 350, 358, 366, 407
Harris, Don "Sugarcane", 40, 195–7, 201–2, 204, 208, 218–19
Harris, Jeff, 49
Harris, Joel Chandler, 268
Harrison, George, 237, 292
Harrison, Wilbert, 46
"Harry, You're a Beast," 81, 138, 470, 496
"Havana Moon," 43
Have I Offended Someone? , 493, 501
Havel, Olga, 466
Havel, Vaclav, 20, 112, 284, 464, 466–8
"Have Your Way," 29
Havin' a Bad Day (Dweezil Zappa), 425
Hawaii Five-O, 369
Hawkins, Paula, 418, 422, 500
Hawthorne, Nathaniel, 54
Haydn, Franz Joseph, 9, 52–3, 399
Hayes, Isaac, 25, 292
Hayes, Jimmy, 239
Head, 149
Headhunter (Herbie Hancock), 311
Heartbeats, The, 62
"Heavenly Bank Account," 7, 362, 441, 452
Heaven's Gate cult, 390
"Heavies," 140
Heavy Business Record, The, 195
"Heavy Duty Judy," 356, 469
Hefner, Hugh, 80
Heidsieck, Bernard, 210
"Hello My Baby," 54
"Help, I'm a Rock," 86–7, 93, 95–6, 98, 140, 174, 500
Hendrix, Jimi, 39, 129, 140, 145, 160, 166, 169, 174, 290, 294, 300, 413, 420, 470, 476
Hennings, Emmy, 126
Henske, Judy, 181
"Here Comes the Sun," 292
"Here Lies Love," 482
Herman, Woody, 164
Herrod, Marion, 232, 280
"He's So Gay," 394
"He Used to Cut the Grass," 349
Heyden, Victor, 182
"Hey, Girl!," 104
"Hey Joe," 232
"Hey Schoolgirl," 143–4
Higgins, Chuck, 37, 100, 155
Highway 61 Revisited (Bob Dylan), 387
Hilburn, Robert, 241
Hill, Dan, 252, 321
Hill, Joe, 307
hippies, vs. freaks, 76
L'Histoire du soldat (Stravinsky), 37, 114, 248, 310, 471
"A Hit for Varèse," 26, 75
Hlavsa, Milan, 112

Hoffa, Jimmy, 80
"Hog Heaven," 356
"Hold the Line," 335
Holiday, Billie, 442
"Holiday in Berlin," 57, 174, 203, 206, 225, 477
Hollings, Ernest, 418, 421
Holst, Gustav, 113
"Honey, Don't You Want a Man Like Me?," 93, 307–8, 313, 410, 458, 485
Hooker, John Lee, 157
Hopkins, Jerry, 101, 103
Hopkinson, Francis, 51
Horsley, Jake, 179
Hoskyns, Barney, 268
Hot Buttered Soul (Isaac Hayes), 254
Hotel Dixie, 195
"Hot Little Mama," 38
"Hot Plate Heaven at the Green Hotel," 445
Hot Rats, 3, 37, 195–6, 198, 202, 216–18, 220, 244–5, 310
Hot Wacks, 476
"Hound Dog," 438
"House of the Rising Sun," 124
Houston Joe, 28–9
"How Can You Mend a Broken Heart?," 306
"How Could I Be Such a Fool?," 89, 100, 102, 155
Howell, Trevor Charles, 243, 248
Howlin' Wolf, 29, 39, 45, 47, 66, 72, 75, 187, 253, 286, 475
"How's Your Bird?," 60–1
How to Talk Dirty and Influence People (Bruce), 79
"How Would You Like to Have a Head Like That?," 200
"H.R. 2911," 422
Hubbard, L. Ron, 240, 336
Huelsenbeck, Richard, 126
Hughes, Jimmy, 68
Humble Pie, 321
Humperdinck, Englebert, 376
Humphrey, Paul, 195, 197
Humphrey, Ralph, 250, 259, 262, 271
Hunchentoot, 243, 247, 309, 407
"Hungry Freaks, Daddy," 77, 83, 91–2, 122
"Hungry Heart," 435
Hunt, Ray, 72–3
Hurvitz, Sandy, 122, 142, 170
Huskey, Ferlin, 282
Hussein, Saddam, 471
Hutcherson, Bobby, 201
Huun–Huur-tu, 491
Huxley, Aldous, 198
Hyperprism (Varèse), 403

"I," 32
"I Ain't Got No Heart," 92, 350, 352
"I Am a Rock," 95
"I Am the Walrus," 141, 446
"I Am Woman," 308
Ian & Sylvia, 104
Ian, Janis, 165–8
"Ian Underwood Whips It Out," 94, 123, 484

"I Can't Be Satisfied," 245
"(I Can't Get No) Satisfaction," 91–2
Ice Cream for Crow, 296, 475
"I Come From Nowhere," 369
"The Idiot Bastard Son," 7, 58, 140, 180, 200–1
"I Don't Even Care," 422
"I Don't Wanna Get Drafted," 347–8, 363
"I Feel Free," 483
"If I Could Only Be Your Love Again," 244
"If Only She Woulda," 362
"Igor's Boogie," 37, 203
"I Have Been in You," 321
"I Keep Forgetting," 262
Ikettes, The, 255
"I'll Tumble for Ya," 410
Il Trovatore, 161
"I'm a Band Leader," 202
"I'm a Beautiful Guy," 360, 459
"I'm a King Bee," 40
"I'm Eighteen," 178
"I'm in You," 321, 359
I'm in You (Peter Frampton), 321
"I'm on Fire," 414
Immobiles 1-4, 206
"I'm Not Satisfied," 94, 155
"Improvisation in A Major With Frank Zappa," 478
"Improvizace v A Dur s Frankem Zappou," 478
"I'm So Cute," 322
"I'm So Gay," 410
"I'm the Meany," 480
"I'm the Slime," 251, 255, 298, 450
I'm With the Band (Des Barres), 83
"In–A–Gadda–Stravinsky," 447
In a Silent Way (Davis), 160
"Inca Roads," 271–2, 274–5, 315, 355, 436, 469
"In Every Dream Home a Heartache," 288
Infidels, 387
"In France," 404, 458
Ingber, Elliot, 76, 108
Ingle, Red, 162–3
Intégrales (Varèse), 29, 206, 357, 383
"Interstellar Overdrive," 198
"In the Dead of the Night," 349
"In the Midnight Hour," 44, 72
"In the Navy," 495
In the Penal Colony (Kafka), 141, 332
Invisible Republic (Marcus), 16
"Invocation and Ritual Dance of the Young Pumpkin," 37, 113, 197
Ionisation (Varèse), 27–30, 218, 357, 364, 383
"I Promise Not to Come in Your Mouth," 313
Iron Butterfly, 447
Ironside, Victoria, 188
I Spy, 167
"It Ain't Me, Babe," 207
"It Ain't Necessarily the Saint James Infirmary," 447
"It Ain't Necessarily So" (Gershwin), 447
"It Can't Happen Here," 91, 96, 100, 180, 469

INDEX

"It Just Might Be a One–Shot Deal," 245, 247
"It Must Be a Camel," 195, 197
It's Gonna Rain (Steve Reich), 422
"It's Too Soon to Know," 501
Ives, Charles, 3, 14, 50–1, 54–5, 75, 79, 91, 110, 113, 117, 154–5, 162, 164, 186, 208, 289, 322, 364, 378, 415, 441, 443, 459, 482
Ives, George, 52–3
"I Want to Hold Your Hand," 243
I Was a Teenage Malt Shop, 67, 114, 209
"I Write the Songs," 410

Jackie & the Starlites, 3, 189, 204, 219
Jackson, Chuck, 262
Jackson, Jesse, 437, 443, 460
Jackson, Joe, 492
Jackson, John, 453, 469
Jackson, Michael, 411, 437, 445
Jacksons, The, 414
Jagger, Bianca, 272
Jagger, Mick, 92
James, Billy, 48, 98–9, 146, 178–9
James, Elmore, 311
James, Emily, 352
James, Etta, 42
"Jam Rag," 238
Janco, Marcel, 126–7
Jazz Advance (Taylor), 88, 96
"The Jazz Discharge Party Hats," 376
"Jazz From Hell," 427
Jazz From Hell, 427–9, 490
"JCB & Kansas on the Bus," 483
Jeff Beck Group, The, 177, 201
Jefferson Airplane, 134, 165, 169
Jefferson Airplane Loves You, 165
"Jelly Roll Gum Drop," 155
"Jennifer Jones," 171
Jessie, Obie, 338
"Jesus Thinks You're a Jerk," 15, 54, 437, 440–3
Jethro Tull, 205
Jewels, The, 11
"Jewish Princess," 81, 327, 333, 457
"Jezebel Boy," 445
"Jim & Tammy's Upper Room," 485
Jimi Hendrix Experience, The, 223, 483
Jobson, Eddie, 297, 307
Joe Perrino & the Mellotones, 56, 114
"Joe's Garage," 458
Joe's Garage, 6, 19, 54, 97, 199, 299, 304, 330–2, 346, 349, 360, 389, 409, 437, 494, 499
Joe's Garage, Act I, 333–6
Joe's Garage, Acts II & III, 336–41, 272
"Joe the Puny Greaser," 68
John Mayall Blues Band, The, 148, 201
Johnny Otis Band, The, 38
Johnson, Haynes, 344–6, 441
Johnson, Lyndon, 111, 143, 168, 194
Johnson, Pete, 100, 141

Jolson, Al, 393, 395
Jones, Chuck, 57
"Jones Crusher," 323, 377
Jones, Davey, 140, 149
Jones, Edward ("Guitar" Slim), 38–9
Jones, Elvin, 109
Jones, Jim, 115, 390
Jones, Jonathan, 65, 352
Jones, Nick, 144
Jones, Spike, 3, 160–3, 203, 266, 437, 443, 470, 474
Jones, Tom, 376, 492–3
"Jonestown," 115, 390, 495
Joplin, Janis, 134, 299, 420, 501
Jordan, Louis, 120, 253
Joyce, James, 270, 376
Judnich, John, 81, 105
Juke Box Jury, 469
"Jumbo, Go Away," 362
"Jupiter, the Bringer of Jollity" (Holst), 113
Just Another Band From L.A., 232, 239–41, 244, 425, 450, 469
"Just Couldn't Wait," 295
"Justine," 40

Kael, Pauline, 80–1
Kafka, Franz, 141, 332
"Kansas City," 46
Kanzus, Kanzus J., 483
Karsh, Benjamin, 297–8
Kart, Larry, 180
Kaufman, Phil, 301, 335
Kaylan, Howard, 207, 213–16, 221, 226, 229–31, 234–6, 248, 463
K.C. & the Sunshine Band, 321
Keele, Tim, 231
"Keep It Greasy," 338, 410, 457
Kellgren, Gary, 129, 135, 143, 332, 494
Kempton, Sally, 85, 131
Keneally, Mike, 6, 435–7, 443, 446, 453, 475, 479, 491
Kennedy, John F., 61, 344
Kennedy, Paul, 35–6
Kennedy, Robert, 165, 168, 344
Kenton, Stan, 45, 109, 471
Kenyon, Michael, 17–18, 306–7
Kesey, Ken, 115
Khomeini, Ayatollah, 330
Kibbee, Martin, 104
King, B.B., 187
King Crimson, 26, 300
King, Earl, 38–9
Kingfish, 360, 393
"King Kong," 122, 159–60, 174, 180, 206, 235, 238, 242, 352, 447, 459–60, 480, 484
King Kong: Jean–Luc Ponty Plays the Music of Frank Zappa, 200–1, 217, 272, 307
King, Martin Luther, Jr., 166, 268, 344, 443
King, Rodney, 78–9, 490
Kingsmen, The, 41, 43

Kingston Trio, The, 68
Kirk, Rahsaan Roland, 187, 190, 195
Kitt, Eartha, 109
Kleinow, "Sneaky Pete," 246
Knack, The, 469
Knaifel, Alexander, 472
Knight, Terry, 293
Knopfler, Mark, 387
Kocab, Michael, 463, 478
Koda, Michael "Cub," 161
Kofsky, Frank, 98, 211
"Koko Joe," 40
Komanoff, Ruth, 123, 160, 195
Komarek, Valter, 467
Kontakt, 467
Kool–Aid, 115
Kooper, Al, 102, 314
Kopetzky, Helmut, 172
Koop, Everett, 392, 444
Koppel, Ted, 430
Krasnow, Bob, 181–2
Krause, Allison, 419
Krause, Stan, 239
Kretzschmar, Hermann, 489
Kronos Quartet, 423, 497
Krystall, Marty, 377
Kubrick, Stanley, 161
Kunc, Dick, 129, 152, 171, 179, 183, 239, 366, 483
Kuntz, Claudia, 423

Labelle, Patti, 271
Laboe, Art, 63, 70, 87
Lachenmann, Helmut, 473
"The Lad Searches the Night For His Newts," 230
Lady Chatterley's Lover (Lawrence), 229
La La La Human Steps, 487
Lamp of Childhood, 109
Lancelotti, Ricky, 253–4, 304
Lantz, Bill, 171
"Later That Night," 155
Late Show, The, 430, 491
"Latex Solar Beef," 234
Läther, 272, 302–13, 320–1, 323, 340, 352, 355, 449
Lawrence, D.H., 229
Lawson, Dick, 184
Lawson, Jerry, 239
Leaves, The, 83, 232
"Leavin' It All Up to You," 40
Led Zeppelin, 233, 296, 304, 470, 501–2
Lee, Arthur, 87
"The Legend of the Golden Arches," 159
"The Legend of the Illinois Enema Bandit," 17–18, 306–7, 356, 439
Leiber and Stoller, 42
Leibowitz, René, 379
Leigh, Nigel, 6, 17, 24–5, 29, 37, 56, 69, 71, 75, 86, 97, 100, 121, 123, 153, 161, 184, 187, 192, 264, 280, 286, 296, 463, 467, 491

Lenin, Vladimir, 461
Lennon, John, 26, 103, 211, 222, 237–8, 263, 343–4, 491
Lennon, Nigey, 14, 19, 154, 226, 257–8
Lennon Remembers (Wenner), 237
Lenny Bruce: The Berkeley Concert, 171, 188
Leopold, Nathan, Jr., 68
Le Roy, René, 29
Lester, Richard, 149
"Let Me Put My Love Into You," 414
"Let's Make the Water Turn Black," 17, 58, 140, 174, 373, 460, 500
"Let's Make the Water Turn Black/Harry, You're a Beast/ The Orange County Lumber Truck," 449
"Let's Move to Cleveland," 447, 464–5, 478
"The Letter," 155
Lettermen, The, 68
"Letters From Jeepers," 61
"A Letter to My Girlfriend," 39
Lewis, Andre, 285
Lewis, Earl, 403
Lewis, Jerry Lee, 440
Lewis, Sinclair, 96
L.I. Ballet Company, 437
Liberatore, Tanino, 372
Lickert, Martin, 223
Lick My Decals Off, Baby (Captain Beefheart), 273
Life for the Tsar, A (Glinka), 34
"Light Cavalry Overture," 441
"Lightnin' Rod Man," 104–5
Lightnin' Rod Man, 105
Lightnin' Slim, 11, 29, 95
"Like a Rolling Stone," 78, 102, 386
Lincoln, Abraham, 53
Lind, Bob, 240
Lindsay, John, 145
"Lisa's Life Story," 485
"Listen to the Music," 281
Liston, Sonny, 149
Liszt, Franz, 9
"Little Beige Sambo," 421
"Little Bitty Pretty One," 350
"Little Deuce Coupe," 116
Little Eva, 294
Little Feat, 104, 190, 192, 245, 484
Littlefield, Larry, 49
"A Little Green Rosetta," 272, 304, 340
"Little Green Scratchy Sweaters & Corduroy Ponce," 230
"Little House I Used to Live In," 202, 204, 233, 329, 483
Little Julian Herrera & the Tigers, 60
"The Little March," 483
"Little Red Corvette," 413
Little, Rich, 43
Little Richard, 46, 66, 104, 165, 202, 208, 413, 482
"Little Rubber Girl," 473
"The Little Shoemaker," 29
"Little Umbrellas," 197, 248, 309
Little Walter, 87
Lives of John Lennon, The (Goldman), 237

INDEX

Lloyd, A.A., 284
"The Loco–Motion," 294
Loder, Kurt, 59, 133, 142, 238, 454
Loeb & Leopold, 68
Loeb, Richard, 68
Lofton, John, 430
Lohengrin (Wagner), 460
Lohner, Henning, 472
Lom, Herbert, 378
London, Julie, 41
London Symphony Orchestra, Vol. I, 350, 382–3, 412, 425
London Symphony Orchestra, Vol. II, 428–9
"Lonely Little Girl," 150, 405
"The Lone Ranger," 324, 457, 460
"Lonesome Cowboy Burt," 239, 279, 470, 486
"Lonesome Electric Turkey," 235
Long Black Veil, The (The Chieftains), 492–3
Looking Up Granny's Dress (The Grandmothers), 385
Loose Connection, 315
Lord, Brian, 61
Lost Episodes, The, 47, 49, 57, 66, 150, 195, 202, 219, 253, 274, 302, 347, 468, 493, 501
Lost in Space, 458
"Lost in a Whirlpool," 49
"Louie Louie," 40–4, 75, 111, 115, 122, 148, 156, 236, 277, 280, 282, 441–2, 451, 489
Louie Louie: The History and Mythology of the World's Most Famous Rock 'n' Roll Song (Marsh), 42
"Louisiana Hooker with Herpes," 446
Love, 83
"Love in Bloom," 161, 163
Love It to Death, 178
"Love Me Do," 102
"Love of My Life," 155, 235, 352, 474
"Love on an Eleven Year Old Level," 177
"Love to Love You Baby," 287, 297
"Lovesick Blues," 483
"Love Story," 389
"Love Street," 374
Lowell George & the Factory, 104–5
LSD, 106–7, 115, 136, 372, 392
Lucas, Gary, 296
Luce, Clare Boothe, 46
"Lucille Has Messed My Mind Up," 38, 335, 457
Lucille Has Messed My Mind Up (Jeff Simmons), 199, 290
"Lucy in the Sky With Diamonds," 446
Luden's Cough Drops commercial, 150
Lugosi, Bela, 61
Lukes, Milan, 466
Lumpy Gravy, 65, 119, 129–32, 135, 141, 150, 152, 157, 159, 164, 209, 211, 234, 277, 303, 384, 394, 412, 418, 422, 464, 468, 493–4, 501–2
Lyles, Wayne, 46
Lynch, David, 58

Mabon, Willie, 43
MacDonald, Ian, 179

Machine Head (Deep Purple), 242
Madeo, Elwood Jr., 30, 47
"Magdalena," 241–2
"Magic Fingers," 230
Maharishi Yogi, 266
Mahavishnu Orchestra, 266, 298
Make a Jazz Noise Here, 469–71, 495
Malcolm X, 344
Malone, Tom, 299
"The Mammy Anthem," 448
"The Mammy Nuns," 394
Mancini, Henry, 370
Man From Utopia, The, 372
"The Man From Utopia Meets Mary Lou," 374
Manilow, Barry, 410
Mann, Ed, 299, 308, 321, 328, 337, 360, 366, 406, 435, 437, 449, 453
Mann, Herbie, 109
Mann, Sally Anne, 103
Manson, Charles, 76, 179, 190, 386
"Man With the Woman Head," 283–4
Manzarek, Ray, 362
Marcus, Greil, 1, 15–17, 42, 110, 193, 282, 344, 494
Marimba, Ed, 192
Marini, Lou, 299
Marlowe, Philip, 76
"Marque–son's Chicken," 407
Marquez, Sal, 244, 246–8, 250, 254, 258
Marsalis, Wynton, 430
Marsden, Dave, 56, 59, 71, 140, 252, 256
Marsh, Dave, 42, 138
Marshall, Bob, 9, 157, 208, 247, 268, 289, 325, 339, 357, 373, 400, 423, 434, 455
Mars, Tommy, 301, 314, 325, 329, 331, 347–8, 366, 370, 421, 435–6, 459, 474, 498
Marteau sans maître, Le (Boulez), 378–9
Martha Reeves & the Vandellas, 501
Martin, Bobby, 366, 402, 404, 406, 408, 410, 422, 435, 438, 478
Martin, Dean, 500
Martinez, Johnny, 244
Marvin and Johnny, 62
Marx Brothers, The, 161
"Mary Lou," 338
Masekela, Hugh, 134
"Massagio Galore," 427
"The Massive Improve'lence," 459
Mayall, John, 40, 197, 484
Mayfield, Jim, 70
McCarthy, Joseph, 84, 416
McCartney, Paul, 143, 223, 237
McCloskey, Stan, 70
McClure, John, 164
McColl, Ewan, 284
McCrae, George, 291
McDowell, Gertie, 376
MC5, 169
McGettrick, Kurt, 436

McGhee, Brownie, 40
McKillop, Keith, 24
McLaughlin, John, 266, 316
McMacken, David B., 256
McNabb, Kenny, 295
McNally, Maureen, 7
Mead, David, 30–1, 454
Meadows, Edwin "Punky," 309, 312
Meat Loaf, 255
"The Meek Shall Inherit Nothing," 7, 318, 360, 393, 441
Mehta, Zubin, 205–6, 239, 274, 285
Melville, Herman, 104
"Memories of El Monte," 61–2, 70, 86, 155–6
Memos (Ives), 53
"Men and Mountains," 378
Mencken, H. L., 343
Mendelsohn, John, 294
Menn, Don, 12, 47, 194, 205, 355, 382, 403, 456, 472, 490
"Meow," 484
Merely Entertaining Mothers of Invention Record, The, 195
Meridian Arts Ensemble, 496
"Merry Go Round," 171, 494
Messiaen, Olivier, 379
Metal Machine Music (Lou Reed), 212
"Metal Man Has Won His Wings," 66, 165
"Mice," 24
Midnighters, The, 61
"Midnight Sun," 265
Miles (journalist), 47, 119, 153, 291, 312, 323, 336, 382, 408, 434, 463
Milhaud, Darius, 8
Miller, Jim, 164
Miller, Pamela, 175. *See also* Des Barres, Pamela
Milliken, Catherine, 489
Mingus, Charles, 264, 268, 406
Minimalism, in classical composing, 401
Minutudes (Slonimsky), 365
Mirandi, Billy, 328
"Misirlou," 377
"Missing Persons," 348
Mission Impossible, 443
"Miss You," 312
"Mr. Green Genes," 159, 197
"Mr. Tambourine Man," 387
Mitchell, Joni, 220
Mix, Tom, 165
Mocatta, Mr. Justice, 279–80
"The Moche Monster Review," 177
"Moggio," 374, 485
"The M.O.I. Anti–Smut Loyalty Oath," 485
Moire, Davey, 286, 307, 316
Molich–Zebhauser, Andreas, 472–3, 490
Moloney, Paddy, 479–80, 492
Molotov Cocktail Party, 179
"Mom & Dad," 137, 419
Mondo Cane, 85
Mondo Hollywood, 85

"Mo 'n' Herb's Vacation," 381, 383, 472
Monkees, The, 149, 293
Monk, Meredith, 192, 497
Monk, Thelonious, 264, 267
Monroe, Marilyn, 500
"Monster Mash," 61
"Montana," 255, 271, 436, 474
Monteux, Pierre, 33
Monty Python's Flying Circus, 147
Moody Blues, 205
Moon, Doug, 49, 181
Moonglows, The, 155
Moon, Keith, 221, 420
"Moonlight in Vermont," 183
Moral Majority, 362, 405, 419, 442
"More Trouble Every Day," 263, 470
Morgan, Freddy, 162
Morgenstern, Joe, 456
Morning Glory, 120
Moroder, Giorgio, 386
Morrison, Jim, 213–14, 420, 475, 485
Morrison, Sterling, 99
Morrison, Van, 288, 320, 492
Morse, Samuel, 311
Mortensen, Vic, 31, 49, 66–8, 91
Moss, Jerry, 181–2
Most Immaculately Hip Aristocrat, A, 181
"Mo's Vacation," 350
Motherfuckers, 179
"Motherly Love," 94, 216
Mothermania, 170, 180
Mothers of Invention, 2, 6, 14, 33, 48, 67–8, 75–6, 78–9
  absurdist stagecraft of, 122, 180
  folklore concerning, 19
  formation of, 74
  Grammy Awards (1968), performance at, 164
  hippie idealism and, 90
  Mitchell, Joni, with 220
  as musical satirists, 118
  obscenity charges against, 278–9
  personal appearances (physical) of, 124
  personnel changes, 108–9
  The Persuasions with, 239
  re–formation of, 1970, 2–3
  The Velvet Underground, rivalry with, 99
  versatility of, 160
"Mother People," 141, 180
Mother! The Frank Zappa Story (Gray), 67
"Motorhead's Midnight Ranch," 230
Moving Targets (Flo & Eddie), 298
"Mozart Ballet — Piano Sonata in B Flat," 482–3
Mozart, Wolfgang Amadeus, 9, 53, 399, 429, 483, 495
"Ms. Pinky," 287–8, 291, 298, 393, 464
"Mudd Club," 350, 360, 393
"The Mud Shark," 17, 233–4, 260, 487
"Muffin Man," 283, 304, 349
Muffin Men, 498
Muller, Martin, 212

INDEX

Mundi, Billy, 109, 124, 152, 170, 206, 484
"Murder by Numbers," 437, 445
Murray, Charles Shaar, 368
Musica Electronica Viva (MEV), 141
"Music for Electric Violin and Low Budget Orchestra," 200–1
"Music for the Queen's Circus," 173
Musique concrète, 131, 135, 140–1, 150, 157, 195, 215, 303–5, 310, 321, 323, 355, 447
Mussorgsky, Modest, 34, 118
Muthers, The, 68
"My Babe," 87
"My Days Have Been So Wondrous Free," 51
"My Guitar Wants to Kill Your Mama," 189, 210, 474, 477, 485
"My Head?" 484
"My Human Gets Me Blues," 199
"My Little Red Book," 114
"My Sharona," 469
"My Starter Won't Work," 29
Mystery Disc, 55–6, 65, 67–8, 89–90, 190, 384, 425, 468, 483–4
"Mystery Roach," 225
Mystery Train: Images of America in Rock 'n' Roll Music (Marcus), 15, 193, 494
"My Time Is Expensive," 38
My Toy Balloon (Slonimsky), 364

Nagano, Kent, 382, 405, 428, 490
Nancarrow, Conlon, 388–9, 421, 488
"The Nancy and Mary Music," 217
Nanook of the North (Flaherty), 264
"Nanook Rubs It," 265, 269
"Nasal Retentive Calliope Music," 140
Nashville Skyline (Bob Dylan), 387
"Naval Aviation in Art?," 285, 304, 329, 389
"Ned Has a Brainstorm," 67
"Ned the Mumbler," 67
Nehoda, Ron, 301
Neidlinger, Buell, 201, 377
Neil, Fred, 100
Neil, Louanne, 290, 308
Nelson, Oliver, 445
"Never on Sunday," 66
Neville–Ferguson, Janet, 246–7
"New Arrival," 38
New Balladeer, 84
"New Brown Clouds," 247
Newbury, Mickey, 442
New England Psalm Singer, The, 51
Newman, Laraine, 317
New Musik, 403
"News in Heavy Rotation," 429
Nico, 98
Nietzsche, Friedrich, 9
"Nig Biz," 372, 459
Night at the Opera, A, 161
Nightingale, Anne, 144

Night of the Iron Sausage, 285, 299
Nightline, 430
"Night School," 426
Night School, 429–30
Nightwatch, 416
Nijinsky, Vaslav, 35
"Nine Types of Industrial Pollution," 157, 203
"96 tears," 475
"Nite Owl," 56, 62
Nixon, Richard, 2, 194, 263, 362, 459
"N–Lite," 486, 495
No Commercial Potential, 158
No Commercial Potential: The Saga of Frank Zappa (Walley), 44
"None of the Above," 423, 486, 488–9
"No Not Now," 393–4, 405
Nordegg, Thomas, 378
Noriega, Manuel, 454
North, Oliver, 444
"Norwegian Jim," 446
"Norwegian Wood," 446
Norworth, Jack, 474
"No Waiting for the Peanuts to Dissolve," 484
"Now You See It – Now You Don't," 352
"A Nun Suit Painted on Some Old Boxes," 230
Nutmegs, 155, 158
Nyman, Michael, 401

Oberg, Mats, 6
Oberman, Ronnie, 82
Objective Truth Orchestra, 300
O'Brian, Robert, 252
Occhiogrosso, Peter, 374, 455–6
Ocean, 361
"The Ocean Is the Ultimate Solution," 310
Ocker, David, 328, 360, 383, 400–1
O'Connor, Sinéad, 492
Octandre (Varèse), 29
Odetta, 84
Offerrall, Lucy, 221
Official Valley Girl Coloring Book, The (Moon Unit Zappa), 368
Offrandes (Varèse), 487
"Oh Carol," 458
O'Hearn, Patrick, 297, 301, 306, 309–11, 313, 321, 325
"Oh Mein Papa," 240
"Oh No," 77, 108, 123, 131, 237, 263, 452
"Oh–Ummm," 495
Oldies But Goodies, 63
Old Masters Box, The, 384
Old Masters, Box 2, The, 425
"The Old Rugged Cross," 441
Old Time Gospel Hour, 440
Omens, The, 49
"One for My Baby," 43
"One Man — One Vote," 422
"One of a Kind," 478
One Side Fits All, 60, 71, 272, 274–8, 284, 295, 469

Ono, Yoko, 26, 237–8, 491, 497
"On the Bus," 334
"On With the Show," 118
"The Oracle Has It All Psyched Out," 45, 132, 165
"Orange Claw Hammer," 185
"The Orange County Lumber Truck," 72, 175, 212, 263, 470, 496
Orange County Lumber Truck, The, 195
Orbison, Roy, 500
Orchestral Favorites, 285, 299, 302, 304, 309, 329, 382–3, 389
Orchids, The, 40
Orioles, The, 501
Orloff, Kathy, 201
Ortega, Daniel, 410
Osmond, Donny, 369
Osmond, Marie, 369
Oswald, Lee Harvey, 143
"The Other Side of This Life," 100
Otis, Johnny, 45, 75, 91, 195
Otis, Shuggie, 195–6
Ouelette, Dan, 45
Our Man in Nirvana, 133, 171, 480
"Outrage at Valdez," 486–7
Outrage at Valdez, 463
"Outside Now," 349, 356, 389, 447, 475
"Outside Now, Again," 389
"Out to Get You," 295
Over–nite Sensation, 60, 250–6, 269, 274, 290, 304, 412, 477, 501
"Overture to a Holiday in Berlin," 203
Owens, Joseph, 423–4
"Owner of a Lonely Heart," 457

"Pachuko Hop," 155
"Packard Goose," 338, 437
Paganini, Niccolo, 9
Page, Jimmy, 470
Paglia, Camille, 372, 418
Palermo, Ed, 503
Palmer, Tony, 222–4
Pandit, Koula, 267
Panter, Gary, 317, 330
"Panty Rap," 352
Papp, Les, 68
Parade (Satie), 9
"Paradise by the Dashboard Light," 255
Paragons, The, 40
Pardo, Don, 298, 307–8
Parents Music Resource Center (PMRC), 414–24, 467, 498
Park, Neon, 212
Parker, Charlie, 26, 109, 264
Pärt, Arvo, 379
Partch, Harry, 63, 163
"Passions of a Man" (Mingus), 406
Pastorious, Jaco, 377
Paulekas, Godot, 83

Paulekas, Szou, 83
Paulekas, Vito, 83
Pauley, Jane, 434
Paul, Les, 196
Paul Revere & the Raiders, 41
Payne, Bill, 190
"Peaches en Regalia," 196, 235, 242, 298, 355, 412, 500
Peck, Gregory, 311
Peckinpah: The Western Films (Seydor), 52
"Pedro's Dowry," 285, 309, 315, 329, 381, 383
"Penguin in Bondage," 259–60, 281, 470
Penguins, The, 40, 61–2
"Penis Dimension," 228–9, 231, 234, 480
"Pentagon Afternoon," 486, 489
Perellis, Marty, 256, 272, 277, 450, 475
Perfect Pitch (Slonimsky), 364
"The Perfect Stranger," 378, 388
Perfect Stranger: Boulez Conducts Zappa, The, 10, 115, 271, 380, 388, 390–1, 400, 411, 422, 425, 460, 488
Perlich, Martin, 95, 215, 236
Permanent Damage (GTO), 176–8, 186, 199
Perot, Ross, 394
Perry, Richard, 181
Persuasions, The, 6, 239, 479, 502
Peskin, Joel, 244
Peter and the Wolf (Prokofiev), 264
Peter Gunn, 370
Peterson, Chris, 245
Peterson, Clark, 339
Petit Wazoo, 250, 285
Petrushka (Stravinsky), 33, 35, 115, 477
Peyser, Joan, 34, 379
Phaedo (Plato), 8, 269
Phaedrus (Plato), 8
Pharaohs, 43
PHI ZAPPA KRAPPA poster, 146, 364
Phlorescent Leech & Eddie, The, 248
Piano Concerto #3 (Bartok), 471
"Piano/Drum Duets," 482
Piano Sonata Opus 35 (Chopin), 443
Picasso, Pablo, 33
Picker, David, 221
Pickett, Bobby "Boris," 61
"Pick Me, I'm Clean," 354
"Piece No. 2 of Visual Music for Jazz Ensemble and 16 mm Visual Projector," 57
Piercing Fans International Quarterly, 489
Pierrot Lunaire (Schoenberg), 230
"Pigs and Repugnant: Absolutely Free," 121
"Pillow Talk," 287
Pilobolus, 430
Pink Floyd, 26
"Pink Napkins," 356
Pink Panther, 378
Pinske, Mark, 370
Pipkins, The, 337
"Pistol Packin' Mama," 484
Piston, Walter, 45

INDEX

"The Planet of My Dreams," 407
"Planet of the Baritone Women," 437–9
Planets, The (Holst), 113
"Plaster–Casters" (penis sculptors), 169–70, 178
"Plastic People," 44, 87, 106, 111–12, 115, 172, 451, 481, 483
Plastic People of the Universe, 112
Plato, 8, 269
Playground Psychotics, 238, 491
Poème Electronique (Varèse), 31
Poésie pour pouvoir (Boulez), 379
Poindexter, John, 444
Poitier, Sidney, 167
"Po–Jama People," 60, 275–6
Police, The, 437, 445
Pomidou, Georges, 380
Pons, Jim, 232, 248
Ponty, Jean–Luc, 195, 197, 200–1, 217, 250, 252, 258, 272, 307, 356, 402, 477, 480
"Poofter's Froth Wyoming Plans Ahead," 282
Popeil, Lisa, 365, 370, 485
Pop, Iggy, 41, 313
"Porn Wars," 422
Porter, David, 62, 93
Porter, Del, 162
"A Pound for a Brown (On the Bus)," 44, 159, 174, 200, 206, 363, 485–6, 490
"Pound for Brown – Solos," 474
Powell, Mel, 206
Praise the Lord (PTL), 440–1
Prazsky Vyber, 478
"Prélude de l'après–midi d'un faune" (Debussy), 209
"Prelude to the Afternoon of a Sexually Aroused Gas Mask," 190, 208–9
Presented by the Jazz Workshop (Duke), 201
Presley, Elvis, 12, 95, 104, 163, 219, 294, 437–8, 442
"Pressing plant overrun," in record sales, 151
Preston, Don, 44, 109, 134, 146, 156–7, 159, 165, 173, 190–2, 199, 204, 206, 242, 244, 246, 248, 259, 303, 315, 385, 483
Pretties for You, 178
Priest, Judas, 414
Primrose, Joe, 447
Prince, 413–17, 430
Procol Harum, 299
"Progress," 230
Project/Object (band), 502
project/object synthesis, as FZ work strategy, 74
"Project X," 158
"Promiscuous," 444
"Proto–Minimalism," 483
Proust, Marcel, 499
"Puff the Magic Dragon," 68
Pulcinella (Stravinsky), 37
Pullen, Don, 294
Pullen, Purves, 163
"Punky's Whips," 308–9, 312, 377, 412
"Purple Haze," 470
"The Purple Lagoon," 298, 309

Purple Rain (Prince), 413
"Put a Motor in Yourself," 494
"Put Your Hand in the Hand," 361
"Pygmy Twylyte," 260, 271, 326

Quayle, Dan, 467
Queen of Outer Space, 374
"Questi Cazzi di Piccione" (Those Fucking Pigeons), 486, 489
? and the Mysterians, 475
"A Quick One While He's Away," 117

Rabin, Dan, 254
"The Radio Is Broken," 374
Rafelson, Bob, 149
Rage Against the Machine, 16
Rage and the Fury: The Music of Edgard Varèse, The, 497
"Rainy Day Women #12 & 35," 124
Raksin, David, 205, 497
Ramblers, The, 30, 47
Rank, J. Arthur, 119
Ranters & Crowd Pleasers: Punk in Pop Music, 1977–92 (Marcus), 1, 282
Ranxerox, 372
Raphael, Faith, 477
Rappaport, Michael, 494–5
Ra, Sun, 88, 187
"Rat Tomago," 323, 408
Ratzer, Carl, 300
Rau, Fritz, 485
Ravel, Maurice Joseph, 469, 471
Raw Comix, 317
"RDNZL," 271–2, 307, 317, 370, 374, 420, 477, 485
"Reagan at Bitburg," 495
Reagan, Ronald, 16, 137, 174, 343–4, 346, 353, 357, 363, 391, 409, 415–16, 419, 425, 433–4, 440–1, 444, 470–1
Real Frank Zappa Book, The (Zappa), 38, 144, 163, 257, 261, 279, 318, 346, 375, 455, 458
Rebecca of Sunnybrook Farm, 464
Rebel Without a Cause, 45
Rebennack, Mac (Dr. John), 98
Redding Noel, 169, 178, 223, 483
Reddy, Helen, 308, 410
Red Nichols' Five Pennies, 162
Reed, Jimmy, 72, 143
Reed, Lou, 98–9, 212, 502
Reed, Phil, 298
"Regyptian Strut," 304
Reich, Steve, 422
Remembrance of Things Past (Proust), 499
Remington Electric Razor commercial, 150
Renaldo and Clara, 341
Rense, Rip, 66, 195, 239, 253, 487, 489–90
Resnicoff, Matt, 12, 313, 356, 420, 453
"Return of the Hunch–Back Duke," 202, 204, 483
"The Return of the Son of Monster Magnet," 97, 142
Return of the Son of Shut Up 'n Play Yer Guitar, 355
"Revised Music for Guitar and Low–Budget

Orchestra," 272, 307
"Revolution 9," 26
Revolution in the Head (MacDonald), 179
Rexroth, Dr. Dieter, 472
Reynolds, Burt, 330
Rhinoceros, 152
Rhoad, Toubo, 239
"Rhymin' Man," 437, 443
"Rhythm of the Rain," 273
Rich and Famous, 313
Richards, Emil, 285
Rich, Buddy, 500
Richter, Hans, 127
Rick Rivera & the Rhythm Rockers, 43
Riddle, Nelson, 444
"Ride Like the Wind," 359, 367
"Ride My Face to Chicago," 458
Rideout, Ernie, 316
Righteous Brothers, 40, 89
"Right There," 189–90, 287, 483
Riley, Terry, 198
Rimbaud, Arthur, 158
Rimsky–Korsakov, Nikolai, 34, 364
"Ring of Fire," 469, 487
"Riot in Cell Block # 9," 42
Ripperton, Minnie, 500
Rise and Fall of the City of Mahogany, The (Weill and Brecht), 226
Risset, Jean–Claude, 380
Rite of Spring, The (Stravinsky), 14, 25, 33, 35, 37, 113, 155, 203, 370, 447
Rites of Spring (Eksteins), 36
"Ritual Dance of the Child Killer," 97, 113
Rivers, Joan, 271, 392, 416, 430
Rizzuto, Phil, 255
"The Road," 94
"Roadhouse Blues," 362
"Road Ladies," 216
Road Mangler Deluxe (Kaufman), 335
Robertson Pat, 392, 431, 440–3
Roberts, Robert "Buffalo", 244
Robins, The, 42
Roches, The, 176
Rock & Rap Confidential (Marsh), 138
"Rock and Roll Woman," 94
Rockapella, 6, 479
"Rock Around the Clock," 46, 266
Rock, "Babyface" George David, 162
Rock, George, 161
Rockwell, George Lincoln, 88
Rock Wives (Balfour), 102, 330, 439
"Rock You Like a Hurricane," 410
"Rock You Like a Nincompoop," 410
Roddy, Joseph, 28
"Rodney," 177
Rod Stewart & the Faces, 236
Rogers, Milt, 66
Rolling Stone Illustrated History of Rock & Roll, The
(Smucker), 290
Rolling Stones, The, 74, 92, 94, 101, 117–18, 177, 345, 476, 492
"Rollo," 318, 451, 477
"Roll With Me, Henry," 42
Ronstadt, Linda, 150, 160, 245
"Room Service," 271
Roosevelt, Eleanor, 80
Rose, Don, 412
Rossiter, Frank, 9, 26, 40, 52
Rotations, The, 140
Roxy & Elsewhere, 47, 259–64, 270–1, 450, 488
"Royal March," 471
royalties, dispute over, 151
Rozsa, Miklos, 225
"Rubber Shirt," 54, 325, 356
Rube, Art, 39
Ruben & the Jets, 243, 247, 267
"Rudy Wants to Buy Yez a Drink," 218–19, 375
Rue, Jackie, 204
Ruggles, Carl, 378
Ruhlmann, William, 59, 63, 269, 448, 450
"Rumble," 377
Rundel, Peter, 473, 487–8
Run Home Slow, 55, 63, 84, 89, 112, 483
Rushdie, Salman, 147–8
Rush, Otis, 120
Russell, "Sweet Joe," 239
Russian folk music, 34
Russo, Greg, 28, 50, 261, 350
Rustic Protrusion, 195
"Ruthie–Ruthie," 450
"Ruth Is Sleeping," 472, 486, 488

Saarbrucken 1978, 477
"Sad Jane," 381, 383
Safe As Milk, 181
Sagan Carl, 407
"St. Alfonzo's Pancake Breakfast," 265, 283, 303, 315, 450
"St. Etienne," 425, 427
St. Nicholas, Nicky, 177
Saints & Sinners, 69
Salvation for Sale (Straub), 431
Samuels, David, 299
Sandy's Album Is Here at Last! (Sandy Hurvitz), 170
Sano, Ruben, 154–5
Salazar, Fred, 46
Salazar, Wally, 46
Sales, Soupy, 88
Sampson, Charles, 32
Sam the Sham & the Pharaohs, 449
"Sam with the Showing Scalp Flat Top," 282
"San Ber' dino," 71, 277, 394
Sanders, Ed, 169
Santana, Carlos, 266, 286, 349
Sgt. Pepper's Lonely Hearts Club Band (The Beatles), 133, 143
Satie, Erik, 8–10, 13, 20, 75, 149, 154, 161, 197

INDEX

"Satin Doll," 164
"Satumaa," 271
Saturday Night Fever, 291
Saturday Night Live, 298, 309, 317–18
Schacher, Mel, 293
Schenkel, Calvin, 142–3, 165, 171, 180, 187, 197, 199, 204, 212, 233, 246, 269, 274, 389
Scherzofantastique (Stravinsky), 34
Schmitt, Florent, 36
Schneckcloth, Tim, 347
Schneider, Bert, 149
Schoenberg, Arnold, 7, 26–7, 30, 33, 114, 230, 301, 379
Schorr, Daniel, 429, 431, 437
Scorpions, The, 410
Screamin' Jay Hawkins, 328
"Scumbag," 238
Scura, John, 431
Searchers, The, 102
"Searchin' for My Baby," 239
"Season of the Witch," 446
"The Second Movement of the Sinister Footwear," 349
Sedaka, Neil, 458
Seeger, Pete, 84
Semens, Jimmy, 186
"Semi–Fraudulent / Direct–From–Hollywood Overture," 225
Sennett, Mack, 247
"Set Up Two Glasses, Joe," 282
700 Club, The, 431, 440
Seven Songs for the Harpsichord (Hopkinson), 51
Several Boogie, 195
Severinson, Doc, 469
"Sex," 375
Sex, Art, and American Culture (Paglia), 372
"Sexual Harassment in the Workplace," 447
Seydor, Paul, 52
"Shake Your Body," 321
Shakti, 316
"Shall We Take Ourselves Seriously?," 485
Sha Na Na, 154
Shankar, Lakshminarayna (Larry), 316, 320, 485, 491
Shankar, Ravi, 134, 345
Shape of Jazz to Come, The (Coleman), 160
Sharif, Omar, 87
"Sharleena," 219–20, 235, 405, 457, 478
Sheff, David, 23, 468, 497
Sheik Yerbouti, 3, 54, 81, 93, 318, 321–30, 335, 377, 449, 457, 469
Shelton, Robert, 118, 121
"She Painted Up Her Face," 228, 279
Shepp, Archie, 198, 474
Sherman, Bobby, 205
Sherman, Kathryn J. (Kay), 55, 66, 91
Sherwood, Euclid James (Motorhead), 33, 46, 49–50, 58–9, 65, 67–8, 70, 108, 123, 131, 159, 165, 191–2, 199, 203, 206, 209–10, 220, 221–2, 244, 333, 385, 394, 483–5, 491, 495
Shields, The, 62

Shih, Howard, 272, 314
"Ship Ahoy," 304
Ship Arriving Too Late to Save a Drowning Witch, 37, 368–72, 382, 394
"The Shoop Shoop Song (It's in His Kiss)," 262
"Short Fat Fannie," 120
"Shove It Right In," 227, 485
Shriveled Embryos (Satie), 9
Shroyer, Ken, 244
Shut Up 'n Play Yer Guitar, 275, 304, 323, 326, 355, 412, 426, 446–7
Shut Up 'n Play Yer Guitar Some More, 355
"Signs," 361
Simels, Steve, 318
Simmons, Jeff, 38, 199, 206, 213–14, 223, 225, 227–9, 232, 246, 259, 261, 290, 293, 335, 491
Simms, Denn, 43, 302
Simon & Garfunkel, 88, 95, 143–4, 160, 220
Simon, Carly, 272
Simone, Nina, 187
Simpsons, The (Groening), 10, 150, 490, 500
Sinatra, Nancy, 143
"Sincerely," 155
"Sinister Footwear," 377
"Sinister Footwear, 2nd Movement," 470
"Sinister Footwear II," 405, 500
"Sixteen Candles," 240
Sketch of a New Aesthetic of Music (Busoni), 26
"Skinny Legs and All," 120
"Skweezit Skweezit Skweezit," 190, 483
Slack, Freddie, 109
Slater, Veronica, 51
Slaven Neil, 32, 49, 74, 76, 111, 122, 133–4, 136, 143, 149, 164, 170, 172, 179, 196, 199, 216, 222, 224, 242, 248, 280, 340, 387, 390
"Sleep Dirt," 320
Sleep Dirt, 243, 299, 302, 320, 330, 475
Sleeping Beauty (Tchaikovsky), 34
"Sleeping in a Jar," 44
"Sleeping in the Ground," 245
Sleepwalking Through History (Johnson), 344, 441
Slick, Grace, 165
"Slippin' and Slidin'," 66
Sloatman, Gail, 102–3, 105–6, 114, 121, 138, 144–5. *See also* Zappa, Gail
Slonimsky, Nicolas, 363–5, 378, 388, 490
Sly & the Family Stone, 413
Smart Went Crazy (Meridian Arts Ensemble), 496
"Smell My Beard," 475
Smith, Bessie, 49
Smith, Howard, 237
Smith, Neal, 178
"Smog Sucker," 253
"Smoke on the Water," 242
"Smokestack Lightnin'," 286, 475
Smothers, John, 299, 301, 319, 338, 372
Smucker, Tom, 290
Sneak Thief (Ives), 443

Snider, Dee, 416
Snouffer, Alex, 31, 49, 66, 181
"Society Pages," 360, 459
"Society's Child," 165–8
Socrate (Satie), 8, 20
Socrates, 8, 20, 269
"Sofa," 242, 278, 313, 337, 405, 448, 479
"Sofa No. 2," 278, 452
Soft Machine, 198
"Soft–Sell Conclusion," 113
Some Girls (The Rolling Stones), 312
"Some Kind of Wonderful," 294
"Someone Cares for Me," 38
"Something to Remember You By," 39
Sometime in New York City, 238, 491
"Sometimes When We Touch," 252
Song of the South, 268
Sonny and Cher, 101
Sonny Terry & Brownie McGhee, 40, 84, 197
Sonny Wilson Band, 60
"Son of Orange County," 263
"Son of Suzy Creamcheese," 115
"Son of Mr. Green Genes," 5, 197
Soots, The, 66
Soul Brothers Six, 294
"Soul Finger," 377
Soul Giants, The, 72–3
"Soul Motion," 195
Sound of Joy (Ra), 88
"The Sound of Silence," 88, 144
"Soup 'n Old Clothes," 356
Soup and Old Clothes, 195
Southern, Terry, 229
Sovetov, Vladimir, 374, 455
"Space Guitar," 38
"Spaceship," 141
Spaniels, The, 31, 40
Spector, Phil, 79, 82, 491
"Speed–Freak Boogie," 157
"Spider of Destiny," 309
Spike Jones and His City Slickers, 161–2
"Spirit in the Sky," 361
Sprechgesang ("speech–song"), 114
Springsteen, Bruce, 16, 18, 414, 435, 448
Spike Jones and His Five Tacks, 162
Spitz, Mark, 274
Spotlight Kid, The (Captain Beefheart), 273
"Stairway to Heaven," 470, 501
Stairway to Heaven: Led Zeppelin Uncensored (Cole), 233
Stalling, Carl, 57, 247, 309
Standells, The, 175
Starr, Ringo, 221, 223, 225
"The Star–Spangled Banner," 117
"Star Wars Won't Work," 470
"Status Back Baby," 67, 114–15
"Stayin' Alive," 474
"Stay With Me," 236

"Steal Away," 68
"Steal Softly Thru Snow," 185
Stein, Gertrude, 21
Stein, Mark, 233
Steppenwolf, 177
Stern, Chip, 307
"Stevie's Spanking," 406, 444, 475
Stewart, Rod, 177
"Stick It Out," 337
"Stick Together," 218, 375, 474
Stills, Steven, 111
Sting, 16, 437, 445, 492
"Stinkfoot," 268, 447
Stix, John, 303
Stockhausen, Karlheinz, 26, 130, 152, 201, 379, 472
"Stock modules," 163, 279
Stokowski, Leopold, 27
"Stolen Moments," 445
Stone, Bob, 425
Stone Poneys, 150
Stone, Robert, 455
Stone, Sly, 166, 413
"The Story of My Life," 38–9
"Straight Lines," 403
"Straight, No Chaser," 264
Stranded: Rock and Roll for a Desert Island (Marcus), 110, 185
"Strange Fruit," 442
Straub, Gerard Thomas, 431
Strauss, Johann, 161
Stravinsky, Igor, 3, 8, 12–14, 25–7, 33, 35–7, 79, 91, 94, 97, 110, 113, 115, 123, 152, 155, 164, 203, 210, 241, 243, 248, 258, 262, 310–11, 356, 370, 378–9, 471, 477, 487
"Strawberry Fields Forever," 446
"Stray Cat Blues," 94
"The Streets of Fontana," 68
"The Streets of Laredo," 68
Strictly Commercial: The Best of Frank Zappa, 501
"Strictly Genteel," 230, 285, 329, 382–3, 429, 486
Strictly Genteel, 501
Strictly Personal, 182
String Jazz, 377
"The String Quartet," 44
Stroud, Kandy, 416
Stuart, Alice, 75
Studies in Black and White (Slonimsky), 364
Studio Tan, 57, 243, 272, 299, 302, 317, 330
"Stuff Up the Cracks," 155, 384
Sturges, Preston, 163
Sturt, Hilary, 489
"Subterranean Homesick Blues," 386
Sugar Blue, 312,
"Sugar Walls," 414, 417
"Suicide Chump," 362, 452
"Suite: Judy Blue Eyes," 240
Sullivan, Dan, 134
Sullivan, Tim, 89
Summer, Donna, 254, 287, 291, 297

INDEX

Supremes, The, 113
"Sure 'Nuff and Yes I Do," 181
Surfaris, The, 333
Survival (Grand Funk Railroad), 294
"Susan," 75
Sutherland, Alastair, 471
Swaggart, Jimmy, 78, 260, 437, 440, 446, 470
Sweetheart, 300
"Sweet Leilani," 452
Swenson, John, 85, 107, 335
Swift, Jonathan, 79
Swingin' Time, 101–2
Swiss Cheese Fire! , 480
"Sy Borg," 389
Sylvia, 287
Symposium (Plato), 8
Synchronicity (The Police), 445
Synclavier technology, 387–8, 400, 425–6, 473

"Take Me Out to the Ball Game," 474
"Take Your Clothes Off When You Dance," 66, 140, 316, 485
Tale of Two Utopias, A (Berman), 464
Tallmer, Jerry, 79
Tamburini, Stefano, 372
Tampa Red, 117
Taylor, Cecil, 88, 201
Taylor, Derek, 77
Taylor, James, 271
Tchaikovsky, Pyotr Ilich, 34, 209, 470
"Tears Began to Fall," 235
Ted Nugent & and the Amboy Dukes, 256
"Teenage Prostitute," 365, 370–1
"Teen–age Wind," 358–9, 367, 475
"Teeny Weeny Bikini," 269
Teitelbaum, Richard, 141
"Tell Me You Love Me," 217, 219, 230, 352, 444, 452
"Telstar," 60
Templeman, Ted, 447, 450
Temptations, The, 99, 207
"Tennessee Mazurka," 492–3
"Tennessee Waltz," 492
Tenney, James, 497
Terry, Sonny, 40
"The Texas Motel," 446
"The Texas Motel Medley," 446
Tex, Joe, 120
"That Old Rugged Cross," 54
"That's All Right Mama," 13
"That's My Desire," 403
Their Satanic Majesties Request (The Rolling Stones), 118
"Theme From *Burnt Weeny Sandwich*," 203
"Theme From *Lumpy Gravy*," 500
"Theme From the 3rd Movement of Sinister Footwear," 360
"Them or Us," 408
Them or Us, 220, 372, 403–9, 412, 478
Them or Us (The Book) , 243, 409, 493

"There Ain't No Santa Claus on the Evening Stage," 296
Thesaurus of Scales and Melodic Patterns (Slonimsky), 364
"They're Coming to Take Me Away," 104
Thing–Fish, 208, 391–7, 403, 405, 409, 412, 422, 438, 440, 449, 459, 474
"The Things That I Used to Do," 39
"Think It Over," 247
Third Symphony (Ives), 289
Third Wave, 201
"Thirteen," 316, 485
Thomas, Bryan, 63, 66
Thomas, Dylan, 451
Thome, Joel, 6–8, 31, 479
Thompson, Chester, 259, 262, 271–2, 277, 304
Thoreau, Henry David, 40, 55
Thornton, Bianca, 297, 485
Thornton, Willie Mae, 45, 438
"Those Fucking Pigeons," 486, 489
"Those Lonely Lonely Nights," 38
"Thousand Points of Light," 495
"Three Hours Past Midnight," 37–8
"Three Places in New England," 378
"III Revised," 488
Thunes, Scott, 6, 314, 365, 402, 408, 410, 427, 435–6, 447, 452–4, 471, 479, 491
"Tiger Roach," 66, 165
"Time Is Money," 320
"Times Beach," 423, 486
"Times Beach II," 487
"The Times They Are a–Changin'," 16–17, 88
"Tink Walks Amok," 374
"Tinsel Town Rebellion," 353, 410, 457
Tinsel Town Rebellion, 3, 196, 304, 350, 353, 355, 393, 452, 469
"Tiny Sick Tears," 475, 483
Tiny Tim, 175
"Tip–Toe Through the Tulips With Me," 175
'Tis the Season To Be Jelly, 148, 477
"Tits and Ass," 229
"Titties 'n Beer," 2, 37, 268, 310, 312, 377
"T'Mershi Duween," 271, 477, 500
Toad–O, 333
"Toad–O Line," 334–5
"Toads of the Short Forest," 67, 209–10, 304, 311, 406
To Boulez and Beyond (Peyser), 34, 379
Tocqueville, Alexis de, 440
Today Show, The, 434
Token of His Extreme, A, 272, 275
"A Token of My Extreme," 336
"To Is a Preposition, Come Is a Verb," 81
Tomita, 246
Tom & Jerry, 143–4
Tommy (The Who), 19, 117
"Tone clusters," 131
Tonight Show, The, 430
Tony Allen & the Champs, 56, 62
Top Score Singers, 230

Tornadoes, The, 60
"Torture," 414
"The Torture Never Stops," 285–7, 297, 323, 338, 393, 451, 475, 478, 500
Tossi, Ernest, 44, 91
Toth, Judith, 423–4
Toto, 333, 335
Touch Me There (Shankar), 320
Townley, Gilly, 130
Townshend, Pete, 145
Transcendentalists, 54
"Transylvania Boogie," 174, 216, 478
Travolta, John, 291
"Treacherous Cretins," 356
Tribble, Paul, Jr., 421
Tribute to the Music of Frank Zappa, A, 498
"Trio and Group Dancers," 264
Tripp, Arthur Dyer III, 152–3, 157, 160, 165, 171, 173, 190, 192, 201, 305, 482, 484
Trois Gymnopédies, Les (Satie), 10
Trottiner, Mark, 122
"Trouble Every Day," 77–8, 89, 95, 100, 251, 268, 444, 477, 483
Trout Mask Replica, 183–7, 249, 273, 295, 482
"Truck Driver Divorce," 405, 475
True Adventures of the Rolling Stones, The (Booth), 433
"True Love, True Love," 140
True Story of Frank Zappa's 200 Motels, The, 456
Truman, Harry, 67
"Tryin' to Grow a Chin," 305–6, 321–2, 358, 449
Tubb, Ernest, 282
Tubes, The, 228
"Tuna Fish Promenade," 226
Turner, Ike, 255
Turner, Tina, 255
Turpin, Ben, 75
Turtles, The, 207, 215–16, 232, 235
Twain, Mark, 75, 79
"Twenty Small Cigars," 200, 217–18, 248, 309
Twilight Zone, 279, 325, 441–2
"Twinkle Tits," 202, 233
Twisted Sister, 410, 416
200 Motels, 19, 97, 123, 165, 173, 200, 205–6, 216, 220–5, 227–8, 231–4, 239, 241, 246, 256, 261, 278, 285, 293, 301, 332, 382, 429, 482, 489, 491
"200 Years Old," 283
2001: A Space Odyssey, 161
Tzara, Tristan, 126–7

Ulysses (Joyce), 376
Unanswered Question, The (Ives), 186, 208, 482
"Uncle Bernie's Farm," 115
Uncle Meat, 44, 94, 104, 122, 133, 152–3, 156–60, 165, 180, 188, 199–200, 222, 225, 246–7, 254, 263, 301, 303, 425, 428, 456, 484, 486, 490
"Uncle Meat/King Kong," 477
"Uncle Meat: The Main Title Theme," 157, 285, 308
"Uncle Remus," 267–8, 304

Unconditionally Guaranteed (Captain Beefheart), 273
"Underground Freak–Out Music," 484
Under Milk Wood (Thomas), 451
Underwood, Ian, 123, 135, 150, 156, 160, 165, 173, 178, 195, 197, 201, 204, 206, 210, 213–14, 217–19, 245, 250, 254, 258, 298, 311, 459, 482–4
Underwood, Ruth, 30, 250, 257–9, 262, 265, 271, 274, 289–90, 299, 304, 307–9, 370, 450, 472, 488, 491, 497
United Field Theory, of FZ's body of work, 408–9
Unmitigated Audacity, 270, 477
"The Untouchables," 444
Untouchables, The, 443
2, 16, 18, 492

Vadim, Roger, 148
Vai, Steve, 6, 186, 300, 314, 348–50, 366, 370, 376, 405–6, 436, 452, 475, 479, 490–1
Valadon, Suzanne, 8
Valentine, Elmer, 86
"Valerie," 189, 204, 219
Vallee, Rudy, 120, 138
"Valley Girl," 3, 367–9, 394, 405
Valley Girl, 368
Van Halen, Eddie, 501
Vanilla Fudge, 180, 233, 451
Van Wearen, Pete, 474
Varèse, Edgard, 3, 6, 8, 12, 14, 25, 27–32, 37, 54, 67, 75–9, 90–1, 97, 110, 121, 130, 152, 155, 158, 218, 225, 301–2, 347, 357, 364, 383, 387, 403, 428, 487, 490, 495, 497, 503
Varèse, Louise, 31, 357
"Variations on the Carlos Santana Secret Chord Progression," 275, 326, 356
Vassoir, Jeannie, 91, 145
Vaughan, Stevie Ray, 447
Velvetones, The, 155
Velvet Underground, The, 98–9, 112, 259, 464, 502
Velvet Underground and Nico, The, 99
Venet, Nick, 119
"Venus in Furs," 259
Verdi, Giuseppe, 9
Verlaine, Paul, 158
Vernon Green & the Medallions, 155
Vestine, Henry, 75, 120
"Veteran's Day Poppy," 183
Video From Hell, 428
"Village of the Sun," 47, 261, 271
Village People, 218, 394, 495
Vincent, Johnny, 38–9
Violin Concerto in D (Slonimsky), 241
Viscounts, The, 72
Vliet, Don, 47–9, 65–8. See also Beefheart, Captain
Vliet, Glenn, 47
Vliet, Sue, 47
Volman, Mark, 207, 213–15, 221, 226, 229–30, 234, 240, 243, 248, 435, 448
Von Däniken, Erik, 274–5
von Suppé, Franz, 441
Von Tilzer, Albert, 474

INDEX

Wackerman, Chad, 366–7, 374, 384, 402, 408, 410, 427, 435, 437, 453
"Waffenspiel," 496
Wagner, Richard, 9, 126, 470
Wailers, The, 41
"Wait a Minute," 321
Waiting for the Sun (Hoskyns), 268
"Waka/Jawaka," 7
Waka/Jawaka, 244–5, 248, 276, 311, 354
Waldman, Frédéric, 29
Walker, Cindy, 282
Walker, Nelcy, 158
"Walkin' the Boogie," 157
"Walk Like an Egyptian," 438
Wallace, Baldwin, 109
Waller, Fats, 253
Walley, David, 44, 77, 85, 100, 124–5, 151, 190, 257
Walley, Denny, 6, 83, 272, 280, 283, 333–4, 362, 449, 451, 459–60, 474–5
"Waltz for Guitar," 47
Wardlaw, Jack, 22
Warfield, Amos, 48
Warhol, Andy, 98
Warren, Rusty, 236
Warts and All, 348
Washington, George, 51
Washington, Jayotis, 239
W.A.S.P., 414
Watergate scandal, 263
"Watermelon in Easter Hay," 340, 383
Waters, Muddy, 75
Watson, Ben, 16, 17, 37, 82, 109, 117, 139, 177, 213, 231, 241, 250, 256, 263–6, 270, 287, 301, 303, 328–9, 337, 340–1, 393, 395, 427
Watson, Johnny "Guitar," 3, 37–8, 91, 199, 277, 395, 404, 413, 422, 458, 482, 491, 501
Watts, Ernie, 201, 247
Watts, Michael, 284
Watts, Mick, 85
Watts race riots, 77–9
"The Watts Riot Song," 77
Wayne, John, 88
"We Are Not Alone," 377
Weasel Music, The, 195
Weasels Ripped My Flesh, 67, 72, 175, 190, 207–13, 225, 237, 3034, 406, 418, 469, 482–3
Weathermen, 179
Weather Report, 272
Weaver, Winstead "Doodles," 162
Webern, Anton, 3, 12–13, 26, 30, 33, 37, 91, 227, 285, 301, 379, 383
"We Can Shoot You," 158
"Wedding Dress Song/Handsome Cabin Boy," 425
Wednesday Morning 3 A.M. (Simon & Garfunkel), 88
Weill, Kurt, 203, 226, 435, 437, 473
Wein, George, 190
Weitzman, Steve, 273

Welch, Chris, 171
"Welcome to the United States," 489
Welk, Lawrence, 97
"Well (Baby, Please Don't Go)," 238
Wenner, Jann, 237
"We're an American Band," 234, 294
We're Only In It for the Money, 2–3, 58, 66, 71, 81, 133–8, 141–2, 144, 149–52, 155, 193, 237, 325, 357–8, 384, 405, 412, 416, 419, 446, 464, 494, 501
"We're Turning Again," 419–21
Werner, Craig, 78, 166
Western Vacation Feat, 498
West, Nathanael, 76
"Wet T–Shirt Nite," 334, 449
"We've Only Just Begun," 2
Wexler, Haskell, 199–200
What Does It All Mean, 195
"What Do You Want From Life?," 228
"What Ever Happened To All the Fun in the World?," 321, 323
"What Kind of Girl," 446
"What Kind of Girl Do You Think We Are?," 234, 446
"What's New in Baltimore?," 421
"What's the Ugliest Part of Your Body?," 138, 141
"What Will This Evening Bring Me This Morning?," 229
Wheeler, Drew, 60, 102, 424, 469, 500
When Jesus Wept, 51
"When the Lie's So Big," 437, 443
"When Yuppies Go to Hell," 470, 495
"Where is Johnny Velvet?," 483
"Where's Our Equipment?," 484
"Which One Is It?," 485
"Which Way Did the Freaks Go?," 171
"While You Were Out," 356, 426
"Whip It," 410
"Whippin' Post," 271, 408, 410, 457, 501
White Album (The Beatles), 26, 233
White, Barry, 41, 254, 292
"The White Boy Troubles," 395, 404
"White Christmas," 115, 162
White, Eric Walter, 34
White, Ray, 297, 299, 306, 348, 356, 359–60, 366, 372, 395, 402, 404, 410, 422, 435, 474
Whitman, Walt, 185
Whittington, Stephen, 8–9
Whizz Kids, The, 256
Who, The, 19, 117, 134, 145, 221
"Who Are the Brain Police," 77, 89, 93, 96, 100, 102
"Whole Lotta Love," 304
"Who Needs the Peace Corps?," 136, 206, 419
"Why Does It Hurt When I Pee?," 335, 458
"Why Doesn't Someone Get Him a Pepsi?," 286, 296, 475
"Why Don'tcha Do Me Right?," 120–1, 384
"Why Don't You Like Me?," 437, 444
Wictor, Thomas, 453
Wild Bill, 82, 288
Wild, Bill, 244
"Wild Love," 328

Wild One, The, 45
Williams, Andre, 46, 445
Williams, Dink, 58
Williams, Hank, 483
Williams, John, 212
Williams, Kenny, 58–9, 140, 373
Williams, Larry, 120
Williams, Liza, 106
Williamson, Sonny Boy, 47
Williams, Ralph Vaughan, 429
Williams, Richard, 11
Williams, Ronnie, 58–9, 140, 373
William Tell Overture (Rossini), 161–2
"Willie and the Hand Jive," 75
"Willie the Pimp," 197, 234, 247, 273, 474
"Willin'," 190, 369
Willis, Ike, 317, 320, 324, 333, 347–8, 354, 356, 393, 395, 402, 404, 406, 410, 420–1, 427, 435, 442, 449, 457, 460, 470, 474–5, 498, 502
Willis, Jim, 69–70
Wilmer, Valerie, 124
Wilson, Buddy, 493
Wilson, Donald Roller, 390–1
Wilson, Tom, 88–9, 95–6, 98, 100, 135, 148, 151, 192
Wilt, Karsten, 472
Wimberly, Terry, 46
"Wind Up Working in a Gas Station," 286, 485
Wing, Albert, 436
Winner, Langdon, 185
Winokur, John, 403, 433, 471
"Wipeout," 333
"Wistful Wit a Fist-Full," 395
"Within You Without You," 134
Wolfman Jack, 253
Wolf, Peter, 300–1, 321, 331, 337, 366, 389, 474
"Woolly Bully," 449
"Wonderful Wino," 199, 289–90
Woods, Paul, 68
Woody, Harris, 100
"Work With Me, Annie," 42, 60
World's Greatest Sinner, The, 56–7, 61–2, 149, 203
"Wouldn't It Be Sad If There Were No Cones?," 176
"Would You Go All the Way," 217, 262
"Would You Like a Snack?," 165
"Wowie Zowie," 94
WPLJ, 202
Wray, Link, 377

"Ya Hozna," 405
Yankovic, "Weird Al," 470
Yellow Shark, The, 473, 486–8, 490, 500–1
Yes, 457
Yester, Jerry, 181
"YMCA," 218
"Yo Cats," 420–1
"Yo' Mama," 314, 328, 352, 469
"You Are My Sunshine," 43
"You Are What You Is," 357, 360

You Are What You Is, 3, 239, 268, 318, 349–50, 357–63, 367, 377, 393, 405, 452, 459, 469
"You Call That Music?," 474, 483
You Can't Do That On Stage Anymore, 81, 179, 263, 271, 296, 316, 336, 371, 389, 447–9, 469–70, 474
  Vol. 1, 448, 452, 456
  Vol. 2, 454, 456
  Vol. 3, 456–8, 460–1
  Vol. 4, 473
  Vol. 5, 481
  Vol. 6, 481, 485
"You Cheated, You Lied," 62
"You Didn't Try to Call Me," 95, 155, 235, 449
"You Give Me Nothing but the Blues," 39
Youmans, James "Bird Legs," 272, 304, 320
Young & Monde, 478
Young, Neil, 501
"You're Probably Wondering Why I'm Here," 95
"You're a Thousand Miles Away," 62
Your Make-Believe Ballroom, 22, 104
"Your Mouth," 245, 354
Yvega, Todd, 494, 500

Zacherle, John, 61
Zamora, Bob, 244
Zappa!, 355, 456, 490
Zappa: A Biography (Colbeck), 152
Zappa, Ahmet Rodan, 270–1, 400, 408, 491, 498
Zappa, Bobby, 22, 50, 142
Zappa, Carl, 22, 261
Zappa, Diva, 6, 330, 458, 498
Zappa, Dweezil, 6–7, 198, 221, 271, 325, 405, 410, 425, 457, 479, 491, 498, 500–1
Zappa, Francesco, 400–1
Zappa, Francis, 17, 21, 50, 70, 256–7
"Zappafrank," (asteroid), 503
Zappa, Frank
  on AIDS epidemic, 392, 444
  ambiguity in work of, 11
  antecedents of, 10
  on artistic freedom, 398
  autocratic nature of, 190
  Beefheart, Captain, and, 181
  bestiality and, 252
  birth of, 21
  Boulez, Pierre, and, 378–9
  burial of, 500
  business difficulties of, 189–90
  cancer of, 5, 7, 20, 467–8
  censorship fight of, 428
  childhood maladies of, 22–3
  on commercialism of radio, 297–8
  commercials by, 150
  on composing rock music, 21
  cosmological beliefs of, 267, 274
  "cowboy music" and, 227
  Dada influence on, 128
  death of, 498

INDEX

Zappa, Frank continued
on disco culture, 290–1, 326
diverse styles of, 3
drug views of, 106–7, 188
drumming style of, 30–1
explosives, fascination with, 22, 25, 32
feminist attacks on, 138
first band of, 30
first marriage of, 56
first musical instrument of, 24
on "flower power," 133
as goodwill ambassador, 463
with Grand Funk Railroad, 293–5
groupies, preoccupation with, 236
Havel, Vaclav, meeting with, 466
hostility to press of, 338–9
image of, 3
jazz and, 264
jobs of, 56
Lennon, John, and, 237–8
Life magazine article by, 165
long–term friendships, lack of, 25
marijuana and, 107
marriage to Gail Sloatman, 145
on minimalist classical composing, 401
monster magazine lovers, courting of, 85–6
moustache of, 75
on musicians, treatment of, 319–20
musical comedy of, 3
on music technology, 346–7
New York, move to, 121
non–conformity of, 44–5
orchestral music performed, 205
paradoxical qualities of, 10–11
personal appearance of, 11
political music of, 16–18, 20
on politics, 434–5
pornography charges against, 69–70
as "practical conservative," 346, 435
Reed, Lou, rivalry with, 98–9
religion and, 23–4
rhythm and blues influence on, 37–40
on rock journalism, 313
Rock and Roll Hall of Fame induction, 500–1
satirical style of, 9
sexual encounters of, 103, 217
sexuality in music of, 19, 117
sexual repression, commentary on, 139
Slonimsky, Nicolas, and, 363–5
smugness of, 95
"stock modules," use of, 163, 279
Stravinsky, Igor, influenced by, 37, 91
synclavier technology and, 387–8
as synthesizer of musical forms, 13
tributes to, 502–3
union views of, 218, 375
United Field Theory, of his work, 408–9
as utopian, 55
voter registration by, 434, 437
weirdness focus of, 82
youth puppet shows of, 22
Zappa, Gail, 53, 148, 165, 198, 217, 223, 239, 256, 274, 287, 330, 348, 355, 374, 400, 403, 439, 456, 469, 473, 486, 498, 500–2. *See also* Sloatman, Gail
Zappa in New York, 37, 93, 299, 302, 307–8, 312–13, 317, 320, 377, 412
Zappa, Moon Unit, 6–7, 148, 165, 221, 271, 368–9, 394, 405, 465, 486, 494–5, 498, 501–2
Zappa, Patrice Joanne (Candy), 22, 24, 62
Zappa, Rosemarie, 22–3
Zappa's Universe, 6–7, 10, 20, 92, 479, 491
Zarubica, Gail, 138
Zarubica, Pamela Lee, 86–7, 94, 102–3, 105–6, 138–9, 145, 148–9, 156, 165
Zavod, Alan, 402, 458
Zearott, Michael, 284, 330
Ziegenhagen, Marc, 6
"Zolar Czakl," 157–8, 247
"Zomby Woof," 243, 253, 452
"Zoot Allures," 304, 310, 406, 410, 459
Zoot Allures, 199, 285–93, 297, 299, 325, 334, 377, 393, 451, 469, 475
Z-Pacs (censorship information packages), 428
Zukovsky, Michele, 206

Photo by David Bidner

KEVIN COURRIER is a writer/broadcaster and film critic at the Canadian Broadcasting Corporation. He worked for eight years as co-host of the interview program *On the Arts* for CJRT-FM in Toronto during the '80s. Courrier has also written about film and popular culture for *Box Office*, *The Globe and Mail,* and *The Toronto Star*. He is the co-author of *Law & Order: The Unofficial Companion*. Courrier also works part-time at the Royal Conservatory of Music.